PROGRAMMING WITH VISUAL C++

CONCEPTS AND PROJECTS

JAMES ALLERT

COURSE TECHNOLOGY
CENGAGE Learning

Australia • Brazil • Japan • Korea • Mexico • Singapore • Spain • United Kingdom • United States

COURSE TECHNOLOGY
CENGAGE Learning™

Programming with Visual C++: Concepts and Projects
by James Allert

Senior Product Manager: Alyssa Pratt

Acquisitions Editor: Amy Jollymore

Development Editor: Ann Shaffer

Content Project Manager: Erin Dowler

Editorial Assistant: Patrick Frank

Marketing Manager: Bryant Chrzan

Print Buyer: Julio Esperas

Cover Designer: Lisa Kuhn, Curio Press, LLC

Compositor: Integra

Art Director: Marissa Falco

Cover Photo: Jupiterimages Corporation

Copyeditor: Mark Goodin

Proofreader: Brandy Lilly

Indexer: Michael Brackney

For product information and technology assistance, contact us at
Cengage Learning Academic Resource Center, 1-800-423-0563
For permission to use material from this text or product, submit all requests online at **www.cengage.com/permissions**
Further permissions questions can be emailed to
permissionrequest@cengage.com

ISBN-13: 978-1-4239-0186-0

ISBN-10: 1-4239-0186-X

Course Technology Cengage Learning
25 Thomson Place
Boston, MA 02210
USA

Or find us on the World Wide Web at: www.course.com.

Cengage Learning products are represented in Canada by Nelson Education, Ltd.

PowerPoint is a registered trademark of the Microsoft Corporation; Pentium is a registered trademark of Intel Corporation; IBM is a registered trademark of International Business Machines Corporation.

Disclaimer
Course Technology Cengage Learning reserves the right to revise this publication and make changes from time to time in its content without notice.

The programs in this book are for instructional purposes only. They have been tested with care, but are not guaranteed for any particular intent beyond educational purposes. The authors and the publisher do not offer any warranties or representations, nor do they accept any liabilities with respect to the programs.

Printed in Canada
1 2 3 4 5 6 7 12 11 10 09 08

TO

My loving, albeit long-suffering wife,

Deb

BRIEF CONTENTS

PREFACE   xviii

1. Introduction   1

2. Reading, Processing, and Displaying Data   73

3. Integral Data   117

4. Selection   163

5. Repetition   219

6. Methods   269

7. Arrays   327

8. Binary Search   369

9. Sorting   417

10. Recursion   459

11. Pointers   511

12. Linked Lists: The Node Class   573

13. Object-Oriented Programming   635

APPENDIX A   Concepts and Features Covered in Each Chapter   681

APPENDIX B   Documentation and Reference Materials   693

APPENDIX C   Common Errors   703

INDEX   715

TABLE OF CONTENTS

Preface   xviii

1 **INTRODUCTION**   1

Object-Oriented Programming   2

Hardware Fundamentals   6

History of Hardware Development   8

Software Fundamentals   11

History of Software Development   17

The Programming Process   19

Types of Errors   21

A Project Development Strategy   22

The Visual Studio IDE   23

Tutorial: "Hello World!" (1 Button Version)   25
   Problem Analysis   25
   Design   25
   Development and Preliminary Testing   26
   Understanding the Code   46

Testing the Completed Program   49

Debugging a Program   50

On Your Own   53

Quick Review   57

Terms to Know   60

Exercises   63

Programming Exercises   69

2 READING, PROCESSING, AND DISPLAYING DATA 73

Solving Problems	74
Data and Data Types	76
Variables	79
Initializing Variables	82
Data Input	84
The `TryParse()` Method	85
Arithmetic Operations	86
Operator Precedence in Arithmetic Expressions	88
Arithmetic Operators and Strings	90
Shorthand Assignment	92
The Math Library	93
Data Output	94
The `ToString()` Method	94
Tutorial: Addition Program	95
Problem Analysis	95
Design	95
Development	97
Testing	103
On Your Own	104
Quick Review	106
Terms to Know	109
Exercises	111
Programming Exercises	114

3 INTEGRAL DATA 117

The Binary Number System	118
Integral Data Types	119
Data Type Conversion	121
Explicit Type Conversion	122
Implicit Type Conversion	122

Integer Arithmetic   124
Integer Division   124
The Mod Operator (%)   126

Tutorial: Binary Conversion Program   127
Problem Analysis   127
Design   130
Development   134
Testing   151

On Your Own   152

Quick Review   153

Terms to Know   155

Exercises   156

Programming Exercises   157

4 SELECTION   **163**

Control Structures   164

Sequential Control Structures   164

Selection Control Structures   166

Relational Operators   167

Using if Statements to Provide a Single Alternative   168

**Using if...else Statements to Provide
Two Alternatives**   171

Logical Operators   172
The not Operator (!)   173
The and Operator (&&)   174
Determining When to Use the and Operator (&&)
  and the or Operator (||)   176
The or Operator (||)   178

Nested Control Structures   180

Multiple Alternative Selection   182

switch Statements   185

Tutorial: Vacation Planner 186

Problem Analysis 186

Design 188

Development 200

On Your Own 207

Quick Review 208

Terms to Know 210

Exercises 211

Projects 214

5 REPETITION 219

User-Controlled Repetition 220

Accumulating a Sum and Counting 225

Instance Variables 226

Repetition Control Structures 229

The **while** Loop 230

do...while Loops 233

The **for** Loop 235

Common Loop Tasks 241

Formula Translation 241

Accumulating a Product 243

Building a String 245

Generating Random Numbers 246

Finding the Largest Value 249

Counting Specific Values 250

Nested Loops 252

Tutorial: Quality Control Production Log 254

Problem Analysis 254

Design 255

Development 257

Testing 259

On Your Own 259

Quick Review 260

Terms to Know 261

Exercises 263

Programming Exercises 265

6 METHODS 269

Methods 270

System-Defined Class Methods 271

The `System::Math` Class Library 272

System-Defined Instance Methods 274

Application Methods 274

Programmer-Defined Methods 276
Methods without Parameters or a Return Type 277
Methods with Value Parameters 281
Methods with Reference Parameters 285
Methods with a Return Value 288

`Graphics` Class Objects and Methods 290

The Use of Constants 294

Tutorial: Planetary Motion 296
Problem Analysis 296
Design 298
Development 302

On Your Own 310

Quick Review 311

Terms to Know 313

Exercises 315

Programming Exercises 319

7   **ARRAYS**   **327**

Arrays   328

Array Declaration and Initialization   329

Using Arrays   330

Arrays and Instance Methods   332
Passing a Single Element into a Method by Value   332
Passing a Single Element into a Method by Reference   333
Passing an Entire Array into a Method   333

Sequential Search   337
Sequential Search Example   337
Searching with a **for** Loop   338
Counting Comparisons   340
The Search Comparison Log   341

Parallel Arrays   342

Multidimensional Arrays   345

Tutorial: Classroom Seating   348
Problem Analysis   348
Design   349
Development   355
Testing   361

On Your Own   361

Quick Review   362

Terms to Know   363

Exercises   363

Programming Exercises   366

8   **BINARY SEARCH**   **369**

Searching a Sorted List   370

Binary Search Algorithm   371

Binary Search Example   378

Search Analysis 380
Direct Lookup 380
Sequential Search 383
Binary Search 384
Determining the Best Approach to Searching 386

Searching for Strings 387
The **array** Class 387
String Operations 391

Tutorial: Video Store Inventory 392
Problem Analysis 392
Design 394
Development 398

Testing 403

On Your Own 404

Quick Review 404

Terms to Know 406

Exercises 406

Programming Exercises 410

9 **SORTING** 417

Exchanging Data Values in an Array 418

Sorting Strategies 422

The Selection Sort 424

**The Selection Sort's Inner Loop:
Locating the Smallest Unsorted Value** 426

The Bubble Sort 428

**The Bubble Sort's Inner Loop:
Exchanging Values in Adjacent Elements** 429

The Insertion Sort 432

**The Insertion Sort's Inner Loop:
Shifting Data Through Reassignment** 438

Comparing Sorting Algorithms 440

Tutorial: Vertical Bar Chart 441
Problem Analysis 441
Design 442
Development 445
Testing 449

On Your Own 449

Quick Review 450

Terms to Know 451

Exercises 451

Programming Exercises 455

10 RECURSION 459

Factorial Numbers 460

Recursion 462

Recursion Versus Iteration 468

Creating Fractal Images 470

Computer-Generated Fractal Images 473
Drawing Lines with **DrawLine()** 473
The Recursive **DrawBranch()** Method 474

Tutorial: Generating a Fractal Image 477
Problem Analysis 477
Design 478
Development 487
Testing 495

Analysis 496

On Your Own 497

Quick Review 499

Terms to Know 500

Exercises 500

Programming Exercises 504

11 POINTERS — 511

Introduction — 512

Basic Pointer Concepts — 513
Memory Cell Addresses — 514
Creating Pointer Variables — 515
Accessing Data Indirectly Through Pointers — 519

Pointers and Methods — 522

Pointer Return Types — 525

Pointers and Arrays — 526

Pointer Arithmetic — 528

Deleting Pointers — 531

Arrays of Pointers — 532

Sorting With Pointers — 534
The **Swap()** Method — 541

Tutorial: Sorting with a Pointer Array — 545
Problem Description — 545
Design — 548
Development — 557
Testing — 562

On Your Own — 563

Quick Review — 563

Terms to Know — 564

Exercises — 565

Programming Exercises — 569

12 LINKED LISTS: THE Node CLASS — 573

The List Data Structure — 574

The Problem with Arrays — 575

Linked Lists   578

  Creating a Linked List   580

  Inserting a Node   580

  Deleting a Node   582

  Efficiency   583

Class Definitions   583

The Node Class   585

  Constructors   587

  Destructors   588

Class Diagrams   589

Class Definition Files   591

  Header Files   591

  Implementation Files   592

Class Definition Files and Client Code   595

Using Node Objects   596

  Instantiating **Node** Objects   597

  Accessing Node Attributes   597

  Accessing **static** Variables   598

Tutorial: Linked List   598

  Problem Description   598

  Design   603

  Development   611

  Testing   621

On Your Own   622

Quick Review   623

Terms to Know   624

Exercises   626

Programming Exercises   629

13 OBJECT-ORIENTED PROGRAMMING — 635

OOP Example — 637

The Frog Class Definition — 638

Instantiation and Use — 639

Initializing Constructors — 640

Data Hiding — 642

Accessor and Mutator Methods — 643

Utility Methods — 645

Complete Frog Class Definition — 646

Client Code — 648

Tutorial: Maze Program — 650

Problem Analysis — 651

Mouse Class Definition — 652

The **Cell** Class Definition — 655

Design — 657

Development — 664

Testing — 671

On Your Own — 671

Quick Review — 672

Terms to Know — 672

Exercises — 673

Programming Exercises — 676

Appendix A — 681

Appendix B — 693

Appendix C — 703

INDEX — 715

PREFACE TO THE FIRST EDITION

```
c:\Users\jallert\Desktop\Preface\Debug\Preface.exe
Hello.

Press any key to continue . . .
```

This is the programmer's friend, the black box console application. As a college student thirty years ago, I learned how to program black boxes like this, and I have been teaching students to do the same ever since. At least that was the case until recently, when I began cutting back.

It is not that black boxes are bad. In fact one could make the point that they are the most efficient way to learn programming. No fancy graphical user interface (GUI) to confuse us. No nonstandard terminology and syntax. Just good, old-fashioned (and I do mean old-fashioned) C++ coding.

Still, the argument that less is more, the minimalist philosophy of computer science education, doesn't seem to fit today. Every computer program people use, from the Internet to the Xbox, is an interactive visual experience with a robust graphics environment. Compared to them, the black box console application is uninspiring at best. These programs look nothing like the programs most of us actually use. "What is the point? Why are we doing this?" I have been asked on more than one occasion. The traditional answer of course is, "We are doing this because GUI programming is too difficult or distracting for beginners. You can learn those skills in future courses."

However, the argument about waiting until the second or third year of programming before learning how to create a user interface is less compelling than it once was. Visual Basic students for example (usually novice, non–computer science majors) routinely create elaborate GUI programs in introductory courses and have done so for years, while

Computer Science I (CS1) students (computer science majors) make black boxes in Java or C++.

This book is built around the philosophy that computer programs should be interesting and fun to develop at the same time that they challenge you to learn new skills. Microsoft Visual C++ 2008 makes the construction of graphical interfaces quick and easy. It opens up the world of Windows applications to students in a way that still allows an introductory course to focus on the core conceptual issues. CS1 can now go GUI.

This book is the outgrowth of several years of experimenting with Visual Studio and Visual C++ in CS1. I thought it would be tricky integrating a GUI approach into the course, but it was not a formidable task. No prior programming experience is assumed. There is some nonstandard Microsoft Visual C++ terminology, but the trade-off is that it greatly expands the programming possibilities and helps create an educational experience that can be more enjoyable for the student and the professor.

How to Use This Book: Suggestions for Students

This book's guided instruction method presents the step-by-step development of a project, and then challenges students to build and enhance it. It presents key concepts in computer science, along with methods for their implementation in each tutorial. I hope you enjoy the projects in this book and find the inspiration to tinker with them or create new projects based on what you learn. Programming should be challenging and fun. Each chapter is organized into the sections listed below. Here are some suggestions about how to best utilize the resources in each chapter.

Concepts

Each chapter starts with a discussion of important concepts and programming commands. These are the fundamental ideas that allow you to advance your programming knowledge and are intended to have broad application. The concepts section is not intended to be an exhaustive reference work, but targets selected concepts that will apply to the chapter's main project. Each project incorporates both general computer science concepts and implementation techniques specific to the Windows platform. The tables in Appendix A show which concepts are covered in each chapter.

Tutorials

The second half of each chapter centers on a tutorial that demonstrates how to construct a program that implements the concepts learned earlier. A consistent project development strategy is used for each project. The tutorials guide you through the process required to complete a project. Students are encouraged to experiment with their project once it is complete, to teach themselves more by venturing into new territory. An effective way to advance learning is to be creative and to explore new possibilities using something you already know.

On Your Own

The On Your Own section is intended to allow you to expand the capabilities of the tutorial, using knowledge you have gained from the chapter to guide you.

Exercises

At the end of each chapter are a series of short exercises that cover both the conceptual foundation of that project and its implementation.

Quick Review

This section lists the major concepts covered in the chapter. It is a great tool to use when studying for an exam or just reviewing your comprehension of what you read.

Terms to Know

The important terms in each chapter appear in boldface in the text. In addition, a complete list of them is provided at the end of the chapter. An expanded glossary accompanies the book and is available online at *www.course.com*.

Programming Exercises

The exercises at the end of the chapters challenge you to build your programming skills. You are encouraged to create at least one project from the end of each chapter. These projects encourage you to build on your knowledge to create new applications without telling you what to do at each step along the way. Creating your own projects and working along with a tutorial helps solidify both the important ideas and your knowledge of the specific Visual C++ instructions used to illustrate them. It is quite satisfying to know that you created a program, from scratch, with minimal assistance.

Chapter Concepts and Projects

Each of the chapters in this text introduces concepts first and then presents a tutorial. Each chapter is described briefly below. After the chapter-by-chapter explanation, you'll find a figure illustrating the various projects students can create in this book.

Chapter 1

Chapter 1 introduces computers and computer programming. Topics include the fundamental components of a computer, hardware and software concepts, and the basics of program compilation. This overview of essential terms is important to understand the explanations in later chapters. The tutorial in Chapter 1 can be completed quickly and easily in one 50-minute lab session.

Chapter 2

Chapter 2 presents a simple programming task involving arithmetic expressions. With the skills acquired from the completion of the tutorial in Chapter 1, students should be able to work on the tutorial in Chapter 2 on their own.

Chapter 3

Chapter 3 centers on integral data and the arithmetic operators integer division (/) and mod (%). The tutorial makes use of material related to both the binary number system as well as integer division (/) and mod (%). The instructor can consider Chapter 3 optional if he or she prefers to move more rapidly into control structures.

Chapter 4

Chapter 4 covers selection structures in detail. The tutorial implements a vacation reservation system similar to those used on many travel Web sites.

Chapter 5

Chapter 5 covers repetition structures. The project for this chapter generates random numbers and processes them in a variety of ways in the context of a manufacturing program. The more end-of-chapter programming exercises a student does in Chapters 4 and 5, the more comfortable the student will be going on to later chapters.

Chapter 6

Chapter 6 introduces the concept of a method. It also introduces graphical programming using the special drawing tools to create the image of planets revolving around a sun.

Chapter 7

Chapter 7 introduces the concept of an array and uses the data structure to construct a color-coded student seating chart that shows the different achievement levels.

Chapter 8

Chapter 8 implements a search program that demonstrates two kinds of search techniques, sequential and binary. The search program is designed to locate movie names in a video store inventory.

Chapter 9

Chapter 9 experiments with various sorting techniques and draws randomly generated data values, in unsorted and sorted order, as a vertical bar chart.

Chapter 10

Chapter 10 explores the topic of recursion. In this chapter, students create a fractal image and then use menu controls to change its look.

Chapter 11

Chapter 11 introduces pointers. An array of pointers is used to sort data in another array without moving data in the second array.

Chapter 12

Chapter 12 draws linked list by requiring the programmer to create the class definition for a node and then use that definition to create `Node` objects and then link them.

Chapter 13

Chapter 13 requires the student to create several class definitions and add a variety of methods to each. In the end, a two-dimensional array is created in which a mouse runs around looking for a piece of cheese. This project can be expanded to direct the mouse to the cheese using walls within the maze.

This Figure shows some of the tutorial programs and programming exercises the student creates in this book.

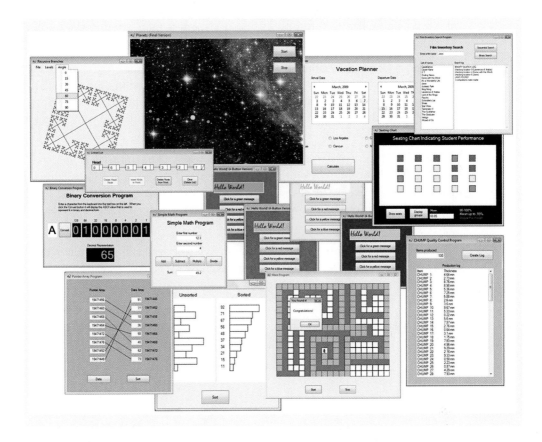

How to Use This Book

Perhaps the most valuable parts of this book are the On Your Own sections at the end of each tutorial and the Programming Exercises at the end of each chapter. These are designed to reinforce the lessons learned during the tutorial and provide the opportunity for original intellectual effort.

The topics in this book necessarily follow in consecutive order with several notable exceptions. Chapter 3 specializes in integral data issues (integer division and mod) as well as binary data representation. These may be too specialized for some tastes, especially for those who wish to get on to control structures as soon as possible. In that case Chapter 3 can be skipped in favor of moving directly into Chapter 4 (selection structures). If possible, the tutorials in Chapter 4 and Chapter 5 (loops) should be supplemented by at least one Programming Exercise project to challenge students to create programs from scratch and to provide extra practice with control structures.

Chapter 6 introduces instance methods and graphics objects. Both are important in later chapters. Chapter 6 is important because it emphasizes the development of instance methods and sets up the use of graphical programming throughout the remainder of the text. The Chapter 6 tutorial is one of the most interesting in the book and a student favorite; it assumes familiarity with both the sine and cosine concepts.

Chapter 7 (arrays), Chapter 8 (binary search), and Chapter 9 (sorting) are topics commonly addressed by CS1 textbooks. Chapter 10 (recursion), however, is a topic often reserved for courses beyond CS1. Like Chapter 6, Chapter 10 is a student favorite, but the topic is challenging. Skipping this chapter will not adversely affect the student's success with Chapters 11, 12, or 13.

Chapter 11 (pointers) is a traditional C++ topic. The tutorial is an academic exercise designed to demonstrate pointer arrays. Chapter 12 is a way of visualizing a linked list. It is not a fully developed abstract data type (common in CS2 courses). The project is used as a transition from pointers to the larger, object-oriented concepts presented in Chapter 13.

Instructors who want to drill down into C++ basics can skip Chapters 3, 10, and even 12, substituting week-long Programming Exercise projects instead. On the other hand, instructors who want to experience a broader range of topics and challenges can follow the book chapter by chapter.

I have found that teaching this material is enjoyable and stimulating. I hope you will too.

FEATURES OF THE BOOK

Over 425 color illustrations and diagrams explain key concepts. Diagrams are often linked to code examples.

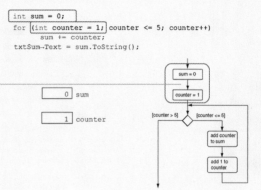

FIGURE 5-13 Initializing sum and counter

Two statements are executed before the condition is checked the first time. One statement initializes the integer variable **sum** to 0. A second statement initializes the **counter** to 1. After initialization the pre-test condition is evaluated as shown in Figure 5-14.

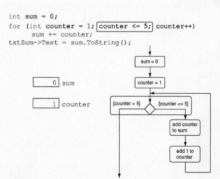

FIGURE 5-14 Pre-test evaluation

The algorithm for a binary search of an array with *n* elements is:

ALGORITHM 8-1: BINARY SEARCH

1. Declare variables (**low** = 0, **high** = *n*-1).
2. While **low** <= **high**:
   - 2.1. Calculate mid (**low** + **high**)/2
   - 2.2. If the target is less than the middle element, set **high** to **mid-1**
   - 2.3. Else if the target is greater than the middle element set **low** to **mid + 1**
   - 2.4. Else (they match) set **low** to **high + 1**

Figure 8-1 illustrates the initial stage of a binary search. Note that the integer array (**arr**) in Figure 8-1 is sorted in ascending order. The integer variable **n** stores the total number of items in the entire list. The integer variable **target** stores the value we are searching for.

You can see from Step 2 in the above algorithm that a **while** loop is the appropriate data structure. The pre-test condition evaluates the relationship between the variables **low** and **high**. The search continues while **low** is less than or equal to **high**.

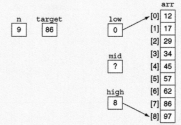

FIGURE 8-1   Initial setting of variables for a binary search for the target value 86

As long as **target** has not been found and portions of the array have still not been searched, the midpoint of the search domain is determined and its value (**mid**) compared to **target**. If they match, the search stops. If **target** does not match **mid**, then the program resets **low** and **high** to define a new search domain, recalculates **mid**, and tries again. This continues until either a match is found or there are no more places to look.

Numbered algorithms and examples are used to show how key concepts are implemented.

Design

As in the project you created in Chapter 6, this project involves the use of **System::Drawing** objects to create a visual representation of data. One difficulty with this project is that the interface shows rows and columns of seats, but the data (student scores) is one-dimensional. This will require a well thought-out design to make sure the results are correct.

INTERFACE SKETCH

The intended final result should resemble the example shown in Figure 7-17. In previous chapters you have drawn images in picture boxes and on **Form1** itself. To create this interface, you will use a container called a **panel** control to display the seating chart. All of the seats will be drawn as colored squares on the panel.

Previews of the interface provide a guide to the construction of the tutorial program

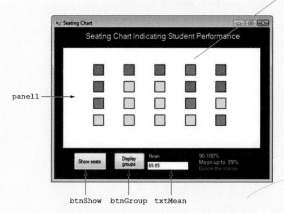

FIGURE 7-17 Color-coded classroom seating chart

The object table for the proposed program is shown in Table 7-1.

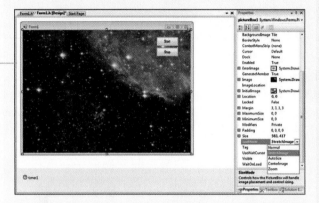

FIGURE 6-24 Setting the picture's SizeMode property to StretchImage.

You should now see the image in **pictureBox1**. This makes a nice beginning for our project.

Setting the Timer The last task in the interface development stage is to set up the Timer control (**timer1**). This is very important. The **timer1**'s **Tick()** event will be activated at regular intervals. Each time the **Tick()** event is activated, your animation will draw the planet in a new location. If you set the **Interval** too high, the animation will be slow. In this case, set the **Interval** property of **timer1** to 10 milliseconds as shown in Figure 6-25. Even if it takes longer than 10 milliseconds to redraw the screen, this is still a good setting because it sets the Timer off in rapid succession. If you need to slow the planet down you can do so later by adjusting the **Interval** property upward.

Screen captures are used to show the student exactly what is required

EXAMPLE 5-15

```
int items;
double thick;

Int32::TryParse(txtItems->Text, items);
for (int i = 0; i<items; i++)
{
    thick = randomNumGen->Next(0,1000)/100.0;
    strLog += "CHUMP   " + i + ":\t" + thick + " mm\r\n";
}
txtLog->Text = strLog;
```

The thickness is a random number from 0 to 999 divided by 100 to produce values with two decimal places. Also notice that **strLog** is built by concatenation using the shorthand operator **+=**. Numeric variables (such as **i** and **thick**) do not have to be explicitly converted to a String using **ToString()** under these circumstances because the string concatenation operators use implicit type conversion on numeric values.

Testing

Run the program several times and scroll the list to make sure the values are all between 0.00 and 99.99. If the first nine values do not align with the rest of the column, you can add another space or two after the word "CHUMP" in the **strLog** assignment statement in the loop to align the values.

ON YOUR OWN

TASK 1. USE ANOTHER LOOP

Modify the program you created in the tutorial to use a **while** loop instead of a **for** loop. It must perform exactly as before.

TASK 2. CALCULATE THE MEAN

Create a new text box on the interface that displays the average chump thickness. Add the necessary variables and processing statements to **btnCreate_Click()** to calculate the mean of the thicknesses.

TASK 3. COUNT UNACCEPTABLE VALUES

In the project description, you learned that chump thicknesses less than 3.00 and greater than 7.00 are a problem. Chumps with a thickness less than 3.00 have higher failure rates, while those above 7.00 indicate a waste of production material. In both cases, the manufacturing equipment may need to be serviced if the rates are too high. Modify your program so that it counts the number of values less than 3.00 and displays this count on the interface. Similarly, count the number of values greater than 7.00 and display that value as well.

The On Your Own section at the end of each tutorial challenges students to demonstrate their understanding of key concepts covered in the tutorial.

QUICK REVIEW

1. User-controlled repetition can simplify problems that require large amounts of data entry.

2. Programs designed to address general solutions will require less maintenance than those designed to solve only one specific problem.

3. A sum is accumulated by the repeated addition of successive values.

4. A counter can be updated by repeated addition of 1 to it.

5. Instance variables have class scope.

6. Instance variables exist as long as your program (an instance of the **Form1** class) is running.

7. Instance variables are declared outside of event handlers.

8. Instance variables retain their contents throughout the program.

9. The values stored in instance variables are accessible from within any event handler.

10. Repetition control structures automate the loop process.

11. Repetition involves repeating the statements contained in a loop body.

12. The loop condition determines whether repetition continues, often by evaluating a loop control variable.

13. The two types of loop conditions are pre-test and post-test.

14. Pre-test loops evaluate a loop condition located at the top of (entrance to) a loop body.

15. Post-test loops evaluate a loop condition located at the bottom of (exit from) a loop body.

16. One pass through the statements in the loop body is known as an iteration.

17. **While** loops are pre-test loops.

18. **While** loops evaluate a conditional expression at the entrance to the loop body to determine whether control passes into it.

19. **While** loops can be counter-controlled but must implement the initialization of the counter outside of the loop and the update within the loop.

20. **Do...while** loops are post-test loops.

21. **Do...while** loops evaluate a conditional expression at the bottom of the loop to determine whether another iteration will be allowed.

22. **Do...while** loops always perform one pass through the loop body.

23. **While** loops do not allow even one iteration if the pre-test evaluates to false the first time it is encountered.

24. The **for** loop is a counter-controlled, pre-test loop.

Quick Review sections at the end of each chapter summarize key points

EXERCISES

Use these choices for the following questions

    a.   **for** loop

    b.   **while** loop

    c.   **do...while** loop

    d.   all of the above

    e.   none of the above

1. ____ Which is a counter-controlled loop?
2. ____ Which is not a pre-test loop?
3. ____ Which is an exit-controlled structure?
4. ____ Which is a selection structure?
5. ____ Which is a repetition structure?

What is the output displayed by each of the following sections of code?

6. _____

```
num = 0;
for( i = -10; i <= 10; i += 7)
    if (i % 2 == 0) num += 1;
txtOut->Text = num.ToString();
```

7. _____

```
num = 0;
for (i = 1; i <= 4; i++)
    num += i;
txtOut->Text = num.ToString();
```

8. _____

```
sum = 0;
for (i = 4; i <= 20; i+= 3) sum += i;
txtOut->Text = sum.ToString();
```

9. Which of these are pre-test loops?

    a.   **for** loop

    b.   **while** loop

    c.   **do...while** loop

    d.   both **for** and **while** loops

    e.   both **while** and **do...while** loops

10. Which of these are post-test loops?

    a.   **for** loop

    b.   **while** loop

    c.   **do...while** loop

    d.   both **for** and **while** loops

    e.   both **while** and **do...while** loops

5

Exercises provide students with short skill and knowledge tests.

Programming Exercises provide additional "on your own" skill building.

20. If double precision variable **num4** is set to 3.0 and integer variable **num5** is set to 4 prior to this method call:

```
num4 = AddNums(num4, num5);
```

What is **num4** set to when the returned value is assigned to it?

a. `3.0`
b. `5.0`
c. `7.0`
d. `15.0`
e. None of the above

PROGRAMMING EXERCISES

6

1. Currency Converter

Write a program that converts an amount of money from U.S. dollars to another currency. The interface is shown in Figure 6-27.

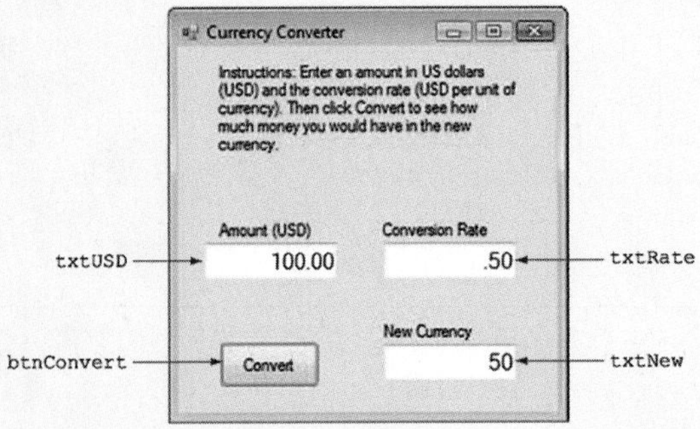

FIGURE 6-27 Currency Converter interface

The user enters an amount of U.S. dollars in **txtUSD** and a conversion rate in **txtRate**. (You can look up the conversion rate for a currency of your choice on the Internet.) When **btnConvert** is clicked, the number of units of new currency is displayed in **txtNew**. For example, you can see in Figure 6-27 that the user entered $100.00 in

The following supplemental materials are available when this book is used in a classroom setting. All instructor teaching tools outlined below are provided to the instructor on a single CD-ROM.

Electronic Instructor's Manual

The Instructor's Manual that accompanies this textbook includes:

- Additional instructional material to assist in class preparation, including suggestions for lecture topics
- Solutions to all the end-of-chapter materials, including the Programming Exercises

ExamView

This textbook is accompanied by ExamView, a powerful testing software package that allows instructors to create and administer printed, computer (LAN-based), and Internet exams. ExamView includes hundreds of questions that correspond to the topics covered in this text, enabling students to generate detailed study guides that include page references for further review. These computer-based and Internet testing components allow students to take exams at their computers, and save the instructor time because each exam is graded automatically.

PowerPoint Presentations

This book comes with Microsoft PowerPoint slides for each chapter. These are included as a teaching aid for classroom presentations, either to make available to students on the network for chapter review or to be printed for classroom distribution. Instructors can add their own slides for additional topics that they introduce to the class.

Distance Learning

Course Technology is proud to offer online content in WebCT and Blackboard to provide the most complete and dynamic learning experience possible. For more information on how to bring distance learning to your course, contact your local Cengage Course Technology sales representative.

Solution Files and Source Code

The solution files for all tutorials and programming exercises are available at *www.course.com*, as well as on the Instructor Resources CD-ROM. The solution files also include the source code for the tutorials and programming exercises.

ACKNOWLEDGMENTS

I want to thank many people for their role in the production of this volume. I received great encouragement from mentors, colleagues, and others at the University of Minnesota, Duluth—especially Steve Holtz and others in the Department of Computer Science. I would like to especially thank the Archibald Bush Foundation for its efforts to promote the study of teaching and learning at the University of Minnesota and to the many faculty members in the Bush group who provided advice, support, and encouragement.

Many thanks to the following reviewers, who provided thorough, precise, and insightful suggestions: Kevan Croteau, Francis Marion University; Brian English, Henderson State University; Catherine Leach, Henderson State University; Heh Miao, Tennessee State University; Katherine Salch, Illinois Central College; Jijun Tang, University of South Carolina; Vitalie Volosin, Troy University; and Emily Wenk, Penn State York. I would like to extend a special thanks to Debbie Sorrentino, Niagara County Community College, and Victor Shtern, Boston University, for their extremely detailed and rigorous critiques of the manuscripts. I have benefited immensely from the work of this fine group of reviewers and endeavored to incorporate much of their wisdom into this book.

I have learned that writing a book is a monumental team effort and would like to thank all of those at Cengage Course Technology who made this book possible. Thanks especially to Amy Jollymore (Acquisitions Editor) for initiating the project and overseeing it and to Alyssa Pratt (Senior Product Manager) for actively coordinating things from the top down. This book would never have been possible without the tireless work of Ann Shaffer, Development Editor, who was always supportive and cheerful. A special thanks to you, Ann. I also gratefully acknowledge the work of Erin Dowler, Content Project Manager, and Tintu Thomas, of Integra, for their many labors in producing this volume. Thanks, also, to Nicole Ashton and John Bosco, whose keen eyes for detail never seemed to miss anything as they tested the code for each chapter. Finally, thanks to Mark Goodin, who served as our able and always helpful copy editor.

This book is dedicated to the people who have helped me the most. First, to my wife Debbie, who patiently waited for me to get through this and never doubted that I would. Second, to my parents, Don and Maxine Allert, for their many years of love and caring. Finally, to my many past and present students, who never stop asking questions and creating interesting new solutions to my perfectly straightforward homework problems.

Thank you all for your contributions and support.

Jim Allert

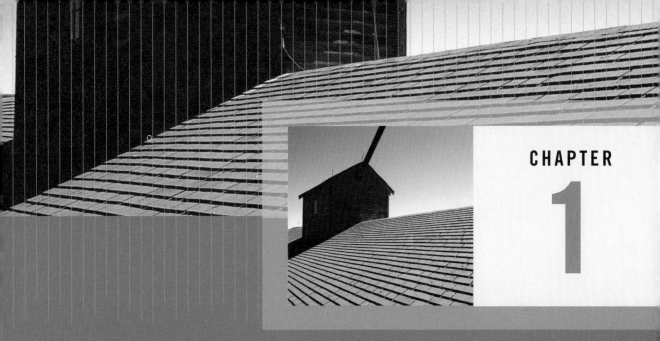

INTRODUCTION

IN THIS CHAPTER, YOU WILL:

- Learn about the fundamental concepts of object-oriented programming
- Explore the fundamental hardware components of a computer
- Learn about the fundamental types of software
- Study important people and events in the history of computer hardware and software development
- Learn about the program compilation process and the project design methodology
- Explore the Visual Studio IDE
- Create your first Microsoft Visual C++ program
- Create and use TextBox and Button controls
- Write and run C++ code that responds to a button click
- Read and interpret error messages

This chapter lays the foundation you need to write your own computer programs. It addresses basic computer science terminology and concepts, as well as the specifics of how to create your first program using Microsoft Visual C++ 2008. Although computer programming may sound like a complicated undertaking, modern tools make it easy for almost anyone to do it. This chapter will introduce you to some of these tools. Very soon, you should be able to take what you have learned here and create fun and useful programs that address your own interests.

Object-Oriented Programming

Visual C++ is a programming language developed by Microsoft for computers running Windows. It is based on the **standard C++** programming language. It also includes a wide assortment of features that allow you to create visual elements with which users can interact.

Visual C++ is one of a group of languages classified as object-oriented. Generally speaking, an **object** is something with identifiable features that you may be able to manipulate. In a computer program, an object could be something you see on the screen, such as a button the user clicks, or it could be something within the program that you don't see on the screen, such as a list of student exam scores used for computing a grade point average. An **object-oriented programming language** is one in which objects are created from a specific list of instructions. These objects can interact with the user or with other objects. Objects usually have a set of **components** consisting of attributes and methods. An **attribute** is a characteristic feature of an object. Often, attributes are data items, such as the size (width and height) of an object. A **method** is an operation the object can perform, such as averaging a group of numbers or changing its width and height.

All objects are constructed from a specific set of instructions, or design specifications. Taken as a whole, the design specifications for an object are called its **class definition**. Class definitions specify the object's attributes and methods. The programs you write in Visual C++ are really just class definitions, from which a rather large object, your program interface, is created. The program **interface** is what you see when your program runs. An interface that contains visual elements for the user to interact with (such as buttons and menus) is called a **graphical user interface (GUI)**. In Visual C++, there is a more general term for the GUI object, however; it is simply called a **form**.

To get a better handle on the concepts related to object-oriented programming, let's consider a more general example. Imagine you want to create a robot. Further, imagine that, after you create the robot, you want to make it possible for other people to make an identical one. You would start by devising a plan that included a rough sketch of the final product. You could also make a list of attributes this robot should possess and the methods (operations) you would expect it to carry out, as shown in Figure 1-1.

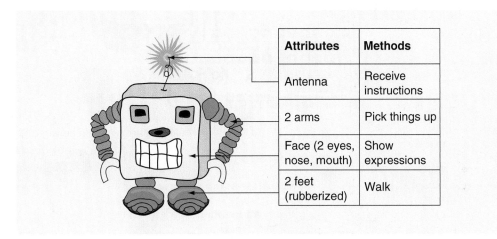

Attributes	Methods
Antenna	Receive instructions
2 arms	Pick things up
Face (2 eyes, nose, mouth)	Show expressions
2 feet (rubberized)	Walk

FIGURE 1-1 Rough sketch of a robot and list of attributes and methods

You could then use the sketch and the list to build the robot. Building the robot is, of course, more complicated than what is described here, but let's assume that you eventually get it to work. To accomplish the second part of your plan—making it possible for other people to build an identical robot—you would need to develop a set of design specifications that list the required parts (for example, a box for the robot's body, rubber treads for the feet, etc.). The design specifications would also have to include illustrations explaining exactly how to put the robot together. Figure 1-2 shows a crude set of design specifications for a robot.

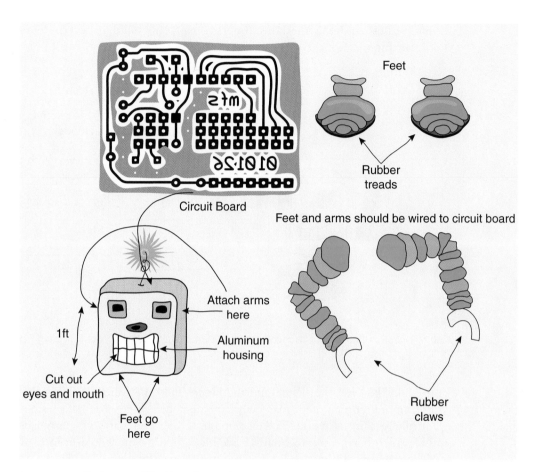

FIGURE 1-2 Design specifications for a robot

The goal of your design specifications would be to allow anyone to create a real, functioning robot object. Assuming people followed your specifications exactly, they would produce a robot that looks and behaves just like your original.

Creating an object-oriented computer program is similar to designing a robot. First, you make a rough sketch of what it will look like on the screen—that is, you sketch the interface. As you design the interface, you must also list the attributes you feel are important, and the methods (operations) you would like the program to perform. Figure 1-3 shows a sample sketch as well as a list of attributes and methods for a program.

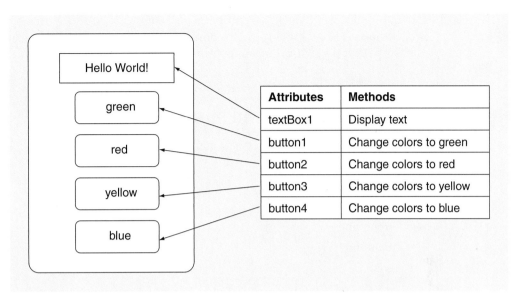

FIGURE 1-3 Program interface and list of attributes and methods (operations)

After you create the sketch and the list of attributes like those shown in Figure 1-3, you need to create the design specifications—or, class definition. A class definition defines the size, location, and functionality of every **control** (such as buttons, textboxes or other visual elements) placed on the form. Among other things, the class definition for a control specifies what that control should do in response to certain events. For example, it specifies what a button should do when the user clicks it. The part of the class definition that tells the control what to do in response to an event is called its **event-handler**.

In Visual C++, as you create the interface for a program, a good part of your class definition is automatically written for you behind the scenes by a program known as the **Windows Forms Designer**. It automatically generates Visual C++ code to define many of the properties of your controls. However, you, the programmer, must write the instructions that go into the event-handlers. You are the one who determines how the program will respond when the user starts interacting with the controls on the form. You need to write the Visual C++ instructions that tell each control what to do.

When your program runs, the controls wait for certain events to occur before respond-ing. An example of a common event is a click on a button. When the user clicks a button, the program responds by running the Visual C++ commands, called Visual C++ **code**, in the button's click event-handler.

In this chapter's tutorial, you will create a simple program. First, you will create the program interface and place commonly used controls (that is, a button and a textbox) on it. You will then write short Visual C++ instructions for the button so that when it is clicked your program will respond by displaying a message in the textbox. Additional tasks provided at the end of the chapter allow you to be more creative by adding instructions to change the color of various aspects of the interface. Before getting to these exercises, however, we should review some basic concepts that explain what a computer is and how it works. A firm grounding in these concepts will allow you to more fully appreciate the programs you create.

Hardware Fundamentals

Most computers have a similar set of components, which are typically grouped into five essential categories:

- input
- output
- processing
- memory
- storage

Input and output are fundamental operations in every computer. You are already familiar with numerous input devices, such as a mouse, keyboard, microphone, scanner, and video camera. Any device with the primary purpose of transmitting data to the internal memory of a computer is classified as an **input device**. Any device with the primary purpose of receiving data from a computer is considered an **output device**. Common output devices include monitors and printers.

Processing is carried out by the **central processing unit (CPU)**. Among other things, the CPU is responsible for logical, numeric, and scheduling tasks. Modern desktop and laptop computers carry out these tasks using microprocessor chips. A modern CPU has a complex structure, but it is possible, to identify elements that all CPUs have in common:

- The **controller** unit is in charge of the transfer of data and instructions to and from memory. It fetches instructions and decodes them so they can be executed.

- The **arithmetic logic unit (ALU)** carries out logical tasks (such as comparisons) and the numerical tasks most often associated with computation.

- Other components include **registers**, which temporarily store data while processing is taking place, and **instruction position indicators**, which keep track of which tasks are up next.

Memory (often called **primary storage**) is responsible for storing data and instructions when a computer is running. A computer's memory utilizes microchips. While these are not part of the CPU, they work in tandem with it. Most computers use a type of memory known as **random access memory (RAM)**, which requires the presence of an electric current to sustain itself. When power is turned off, its contents vanish. For this reason, RAM is often referred to as being "volatile." **Read-only memory (ROM)** is more expensive, but stores information for long periods of time even when the computer is turned off.

Storage devices (often called **secondary storage**) are used to save programs and data cheaply and efficiently outside of the computer's main memory. Storage devices have both input and output capabilities, but their primary purpose is to save information. This includes devices such as magnetic disks (that is, hard and floppy drives), optical disks (such as CDs and DVDs), and flash memory devices (such as USB drives).

NOTE   One type of storage device, flash memory, deserves special consideration. Flash memory is a form of storage that is chip-based, much like RAM, but is not volatile. It stores data for long periods of time without the constant presence of an electric current. Flash memory devices have largely replaced magnetic disks as convenient ways of storing and transporting files. You may find them to be the best method of saving and transporting your projects; however, you will find that it is faster to develop your projects when they are stored on the computer's hard drive.

The relationship between these components is shown in Figure 1–4.

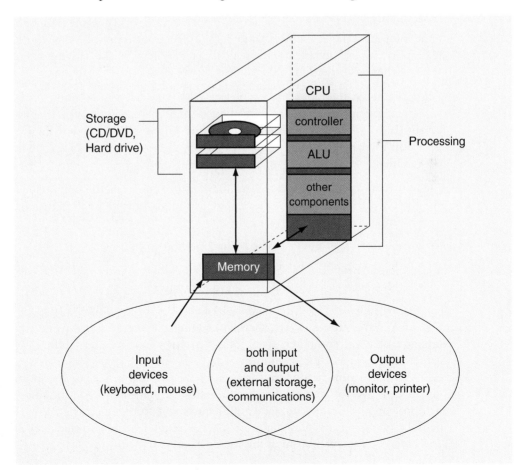

FIGURE 1-4   The fundamental components of a computer

History of Hardware Development

The fundamental components of a computer that we have just discussed evolved from technological advances in a number of fields. Mechanical devices that tabulated numbers or performed tasks in response to instructions have been around for hundreds of years. Among the first programmable machines was a remarkable invention by French weaver Joseph Marie Jacquard. In 1801, he devised an automated loom using sequences of punched cards to regulate the woven patterns. The cards stored instructions, represented as a configuration of holes, and were processed in order as the loom operator controlled and provided power to the device by hand. Punched card technology was adapted to mechanical tabulating devices later in the 1800s and remained popular in computing environments through the late 1900's, as a means of storing both program instructions and data.

The most direct ancestors of the modern computer, however, are the various computing "engines" designed by British mathematician, Charles Babbage, in the 1840s. Often called the "Father of the Computer," Babbage foresaw the day when computing machines that had all five of the components identified in the previous section (that is, input, output, storage, memory, and central processor) could be developed. He developed his own plans for such machines. The technology of the time prevented him from realizing their construction, but his ideas showed remarkable foresight.

Babbage enlisted the aid of Ada Lovelace (also known as the Countess of Lovelace), a mathematician and translator who happened to be the daughter of the English poet, Lord Byron. Babbage benefited from her suggestions on how his Analytical Engine could solve specific mathematical problems. For this reason, she is commonly called the first computer programmer.

These early developments laid the groundwork for the modern computer. However, the computer as we know it was not a realistic possibility until these three crucial advances of the 1900s:

- the invention of electronic binary methods of computing
- the development of machines that were able to store their own programs
- the advent of large-scale electronic circuitry

The first of these advances, the invention of electronic binary methods of computing, was pioneered in the early 1940s by German engineer, Konrad Zuse (inventor of the binary, programmable Z3 computer), and John Vincent Atanasoff and Clifford Berry at Iowa State College in the United States (inventors of the binary, programmable ABC computer). The early **binary computers** represented a real conceptual leap. After all, for human beings who have ten fingers, the most natural method of counting is a base-10 method. Early calculators and tabulating equipment were, therefore, founded on base-10 methods of numeric representation and arithmetic. However, much faster calculation rates could be achieved through the use of **binary arithmetic** (that is, base-2 numbers).

1

At the same time that binary computing devices were being developed, the mathematical underpinnings of computer science were also being established. British mathematician Alan Turing's first, and greatest, contribution came in a paper published in 1936. Titled "On Computable Numbers," this paper proved that any mathematical problem that could be represented by an ordered list of steps could be solved by manipulating simple logical symbols. This conceptual proof has been called a "Turing machine;" it is not a physical device but rather one that exists in the world of formal logic. Turing's paper led to the realization that computers could indeed become universal problem-solving tools.

The next important modern hardware development, machines that were able to store their own programs, followed on the heels of the new binary computing devices. By 1945, mathematician John von Neumann had designed a computer model in which a storage structure, separate from the processing unit, enabled both data and program instructions to be stored in the same place and processed in a series of stages. This process required the fetching and decoding of instructions. This design is the basis for modern electronic computers and is commonly known as **von Neumann architecture**.

It is simply not possible to identify the first computer. Many devices were developed between 1930 to 1950 that might qualify, depending on the definition. Some of these machines were electronic while others were mechanical. Some used binary computing methods while others used decimal methods. Rather than attempting to pinpoint the first computer, it is more helpful to focus on the distinction between early calculators, which performed calculations when manually operated, and early computers, which could be programmed to perform calculations. The actual degree of programmability varied widely among early computing machines. World War II stimulated computing research on both sides of the Atlantic, leading to the development of a host of programmable, electronic machines now famous in the annals of computer science.

One method of making sense of computing from the 1930's until today is to categorize these computers into four separate generations.

The **first generation of computers** was largely defined by the development of sophisticated calculators and electromechanical devices. By the late 1930s and early 1940s, some were programmable and could run on their own until a problem was solved. They included machines such as the Z3 (mentioned earlier) and the Harvard Mark I, produced by IBM using the design of Howard Aiken.

Many of these computers made extensive use of electronic relay circuits and gas-filled switches called **vacuum tubes** to represent numeric states and process data. Two examples of such machines are the ABC computer, mentioned earlier, and the ENIAC, which was designed by researchers John Mauchly and J. Presper Eckert at the University of Pennsylvania. The ENIAC is shown in Figure 1-5.

FIGURE 1-5 The ENIAC (US Army Photo)

The ENIAC and other powerful machines of the 1940's and 50's were notorious for their size, heat, component failure rates, and difficulty to program. Nevertheless, throughout the 1950s, this cumbersome vacuum-tube technology was used in computers of all types.

The **second generation of computers** became possible by the development of transistorized circuitry, which used small, solid-state **transistors** to perform the same switching tasks that older relay circuits and vacuum tubes handled. Transistors proved to be not only smaller, but much faster and more reliable.

Within ten years, further technological advancements led to the development of the **integrated circuit (IC)** and the **third generation of computers**. The IC production process miniaturized transistorized electronic circuitry by layering it onto small wafers of silicon called "chips." These chips could be easily mass-produced. Jack Kilby at Texas Instruments and Robert Noyce at Fairchild Semiconductor in the late 1950s and early 1960s both developed the keys to this generation of computers—semiconductor technology and integrated circuits—independently. However, technologies did not become widely available until the early 1970s.

The **fourth generation of computers** was made possible by the introduction of the very large-scale integration (VLSI) of components onto a single chip. Built on integrated circuit technology, this advance fueled a rapid expansion of the commercial computer industry and led to the desktop, laptop, and handheld computers we use today. Known as a microprocessor, a single chip could now carry out an enormous number of tasks.

1

Microprocessors represent the integration of computing components at a high level with most all essential CPU operations performed on a single chip.

Software Fundamentals

The computer hardware you have just read about cannot do much without computer programs, also known as **software**, to instruct it. Computer programs contain statements that interact with the five fundamental hardware components of a computer. Some statements control input or output operations. Others determine how data are stored and processed. But programs do not just interact with hardware—they may also interact with other programs. There are several different types of software. **System software** includes the operating system (for example, UNIX or Microsoft Windows) and utility programs used to manage files, read from input devices, control output to the screen, and many other functions. System software interfaces directly with hardware components. **Application software** differs from system software in that its purpose is more directly tied to the needs of the user; it uses the resources provided by the operating system (such as processing, memory, input, and output) to perform its tasks. Application software can, in turn, be divided into two types: general- and dedicated-purpose software. Word processors, spreadsheets, databases, e-mail programs, and Web browsers are just a few examples of the wide assortment of **general–purpose software**. **Dedicated–purpose software** is used in industrial, corporate, and research settings to carry out specific tasks, such as controlling a specific manufacturing machine. Dedicated-purpose software tends to be much more expensive than general-purpose software. The various categories of software are illustrated in Figure 1-6.

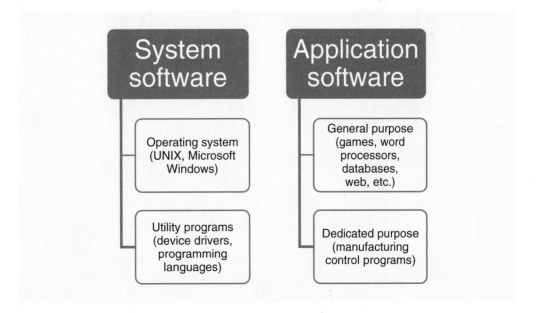

FIGURE 1-6 Types of software

When you turn on your computer, you encounter the first level of software—the operating system (OS). An operating system generally:

- provides a GUI for efficient user access to programs and files
- manages important processes such as the scheduling of critical events
- manages system resources such as the CPU, memory, input, and output

Every computer has an operating system of some kind. Microsoft Windows (in its various manifestations) is the most common OS on personal computers. The most current version at the writing of this text is **Windows Vista**, but the previous version, **Windows XP**, is also common. Macintosh users rely on the OS X operating system, produced by Apple. By contrast, an other widely used operating system, UNIX, began as a product of AT&T Bell Labs in the 1970s and quickly became the dominant operating system on mainframe computers. There are many UNIX-like operating systems that have been developed as the result of voluntary, collaborative efforts by programmers around the world who are willing to share their code for common benefit. This collaborative effort to create software is known as the **Open Source Movement** and its most well-known operating system product is called **Linux**.

Utility software works along with the operating system to accomplish basic tasks. Utility programs typically provide assistance in working with hardware resources. For example, device drivers are commonly used to manage the operation of input and output devices. Other programs, called language compilers, also fall into this category. A **language compiler** is a program that takes the code written by a programmer, constructs the program, and ensures that it runs properly. A language compiler interacts intimately with the operating system. To understand more about operating systems, it is helpful to examine a specific example. The interface of Microsoft Windows Vista, with its Welcome Panel, is shown in Figure 1-7.

FIGURE 1-7 The Microsoft Windows Vista GUI

The Windows Vista interface provides the user with easy access to a wide variety of features related to programs, system information and resources, and hardware settings. The Start button (found in the lower left corner of Figure 1-7) is a control that, when clicked, displays a list, or menu, of recently used programs, as well as other options you can click to gain access to additional applications and utilities as shown in Figure 1-8.

FIGURE 1-8 Start menu in Windows Vista

From the Start menu, the user can access the Control Panel, a utility shown in Figure 1-9.

FIGURE 1-9 The Windows Vista Control Panel

Among other things, the Control Panel provides information on the computer's hardware and operating system, as shown in Figure 1-10.

FIGURE 1-10 Hardware information in the Windows Vista Control Panel

Application software runs "on top of" the operating system software, which, in turn, interfaces with the hardware of the computer as shown in Figure 1-11. The layers of interaction are largely transparent to the user, who only sees the operating system interface or the interface provided by a particular application.

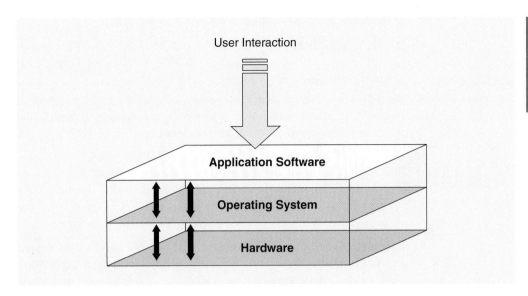

FIGURE 1-11 The hardware/software/user relationship

History of Software Development

Every machine has an underlying configuration of hardware, called its **architecture**, that requires a very specific set of binary instructions (0s and 1s) known as **machine language**. If people could think and solve problems in machine language, then computer programming would be much easier than it is. In fact, however, machine language is alien even to most programmers. In the early days of computing, programming in machine language was the only option but was rapidly replaced by assembly language.

Assembly language consists of a set of short codes, each of which stands for a complex machine code instruction. For example, the assembly language code LD might initiate a machine language instruction to load a value into one of the registers in the CPU. Assembly language programs, although helpful, are still difficult for most programmers to use and are tied to specific computer architectures.

High-level programming languages, which allow people to write programs in code that looks similar to English, came out in the mid-1950s. The first wave included:

- **FORTRAN**, developed by a team headed by John Backus at IBM as a tool for translating formulas. For many years, it was the dominant programming language in the fields of science and engineering.
- **COBOL**, masterminded by Grace Hopper and developed as a programming language tailored to the needs of business users.
- **LISP**, developed by John McCarthy at MIT and used widely for artificial intelligence programming.

In the 1960s, other languages emerged for different purposes:

- **BASIC** was authored by John Kemeny and Thomas Kurtz at Dartmouth for the sole purpose of providing an easy method of entry into the programming world for students.
- **Simula** was developed at the Norwegian Computing Center in Oslo, Norway, for the purpose of simulating the interaction of objects. It was an early object-oriented programming language (from which C++ was ultimately patterned).

The 1970s was an important decade in the computing world, and witnessed the emergence of structured languages. Structured languages made it much easier to write programs that were powerful but still well organized. They did this by providing new statements to organize the logic of the program. These languages included:

- **Pascal**, designed by Swiss computer scientist, Niklaus Wirth. Pascal was an excellent language to use for learning how to program, but was also used for industrial applications, including early versions of the Apple Macintosh operating system. Its strength was that it specified a very strong set of statements (structures) to control programming logic. In Pascal, programs became less confusing to design and develop than in earlier languages.
- **C**, developed by Dennis Ritchie at Bell Laboratories and used to write the UNIX operating system; its structured style and powerful features made it a dominant language. C and UNIX spread together throughout the computer world.
- **Smalltalk**, was developed by an educational research team at the Xerox Palo Alto Research Center (Xerox PARC) headed by Alan Kay. Unusual for its time, Smalltalk was an early object-oriented language.

With only a few exceptions, the computer languages in use through the early 1980s were **procedural languages**. In procedural languages, programs are viewed as a series of tasks (procedures). Data are sent into one procedure (that is, a set of programming statements) after the next until the desired solution to a problem has been achieved. For example, a program might calculate the average of a series of numbers by using one procedure to read them, then another to add them up, another to divide the sum by the correct number, and another to display the result on the screen. Data was sent from one procedure to another, to another.

The development of object-oriented languages was spurred by the need to create programs that simulated complex processes in which objects interact with one another. Examples include programs to model vehicle traffic patterns on city streets, the communication of computers on a network, or the interaction of populations in a specified environment. The hallmark of these programs is that they define how a particular class of objects will look and behave (that is, a class definition) and then allow the programmer to construct as many objects as are required by the simulation.

The standard C++ language, one of the first fully developed object-oriented languages, evolved from the popular C language. C++ was developed by Bjarne Stroustrup, a Norwegian computer scientist working at Bell Laboratories in 1983. Stroustrup originally called it "C with Classes." Since that time, it has become a mainstay of programmers in UNIX operating system environments. It has also been standardized by the International Standards Organization (ISO).

Another object-oriented language, **Java**, was developed by Sun Microsystems, Inc., in the mid-1990s. It shares many characteristics with the Visual C++ programming language of today. Java was originally devised for the purpose of allowing small programs to be transmitted and run over computer networks by devices, such as handheld computers. It is an object-oriented language that employs a unique method, called the **Java Virtual Machine**, which allows it to run on any device that can interpret its special program files, which are known as bytecodes. Java's popularity, due largely to the Java Virtual Machine innovation, quickly made it a dominant language for Internet software development.

Visual C++ was developed by the Microsoft Corporation in the mid-1990s, and continues to be updated by Microsoft. It is an object-oriented programming language that allows programmers to create GUIs for their programs. Visual C++ is one of several languages supported by a larger program development framework, called **Microsoft Visual Studio**. Visual Studio provides a graphical interface, known as an **integrated development environment (IDE)**, that you can use to build object-oriented programs. In the Visual Studio IDE programmers can see the program's interface on the screen as they create it. This greatly aids in program development by simplifying the process of building GUIs. In some respects, programming in Visual C++ is similar to standard C++. However, the GUI component of Visual C++ requires the knowledge of an assortment of classes made available by Microsoft programming libraries. A **programming library** is a collection of class definitions. The programming libraries available in Microsoft Visual C++ contain definitions for such commonly used interface elements as buttons, textboxes, and menus.

This book focuses on the use of Microsoft Visual C++ because of the ease with which it allows you to build a GUI application. This makes it possible to learn and explore all of the fundamental concepts and features of programming languages while producing engaging visual interfaces with little effort.

The Programming Process

Visual C++ is a high-level programming language. High-level languages have the advantage of using a syntax that is similar to English. They include keywords, such as `while`, `if`, and `else`, which are familiar to any English speaker. As a result, a programmer can scan a section of C++ code and quickly get a sense of what the program is supposed to do. (Very few programmers could do the same with machine language code.) Keep in mind, however, that a computer can only process binary instructions. This means that a Visual C++ program (called **source code**) must be translated into machine language instructions (called **object code**) before it will run.

When you are working on a Visual C++ program in Visual Studio, it is easy to run a program by clicking the button labeled "Start Debugging." (Note that programmers often refer to this as the "Debug button" for short.) However, this simple task—clicking a button—makes the process of running a program look much less complicated than it really is. Clicking the Start Debugging button actually launches a program, called a compiler. The **compiler** translates your Visual C++ source code into a binary version that the computer can then run.

As the compiler examines your source code, it may occasionally find something that does not make sense. For example, if you forgot to put a semicolon (**;**) at the end of a C++ command, its absence would confuse the compiler and cause it to stop the compilation process. If compilation ceases prematurely due to such an error, the compiler produces an error message informing the programmer that there is a situation that needs to be fixed before compilation can proceed. The programmer would then have to fix the error and attempt to recompile the source code. Errors in a program are referred to as **bugs**. The cycle of writing source code—attempting to make or compile it, interpreting error reports, and revising the source code until all problems have been solved—is known as debugging a program. The debugging process is depicted in Figure 1-12.

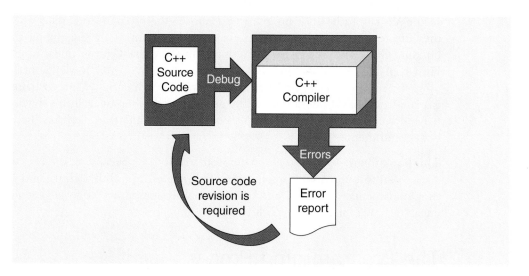

FIGURE 1-12 The debugging process

When the bugs are out, the compilation process continues to completion and the resulting object code file is linked to the system resources it needs, loaded into memory, and begins execution, as shown in Figure 1-13.

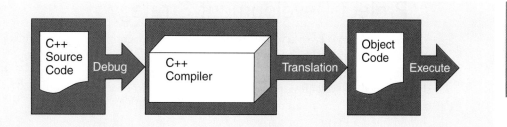

FIGURE 1-13 Successful program compilation

Types of Errors

In the preceding section, you learned that the compiler will fail to run a program if it encounters an error. However, only certain types of errors will cause the compiler to stop running a program. It is possible for a program to contain an error that the compiler does not detect, so that the program runs but produces erroneous results.

In general, programming errors can be divided into three types:

- syntax errors
- logic errors
- runtime errors

The easiest errors to make and fix are **syntax errors**. Syntax errors are often minor typographical errors. The compiler catches these. Some errors may be minor and the compiler will only display a warning message. Other errors (called "fatal errors" are more significant and the compiler will not produce or run the program until they are fixed. Most of the errors in your programs will be syntax errors; fortunately, they are easy to fix—usually by correcting a few characters in a line of code.

The second major type of error, **logic errors**, expose a design flaw hidden in a program. If a program compiles and runs but does not produce the correct result, it is because of a logic error. Usually, logic errors require you to reexamine the way the program was designed.

The third type of error, **runtime errors**, occur while a program is running and usually cause it to stop unexpectedly. The exact nature of a runtime error can vary. Runtime errors usually result from unanticipated data-processing results, unexpected input, or illegal operations relating to the use of memory. Like logic errors, runtime errors may require you to go back and rethink the problem. For example, a user might enter data that result in the program attempting division by zero. Since division by zero is undefined mathematically, asking the computer to perform this operation often results in the immediate termination of a program.

A Project Development Strategy

You are almost ready to try your hand at a simple program. All that remains is to come up with a plan of attack. One of the most important tools a software developer can have is a practical strategy. Programmers in charge of large-scale projects rely on them, and we should, too. A well-designed strategy typically starts by defining a problem, and then explains how to create a computer program that will solve this problem. A good strategy should spell out the steps involved in the following stages: problem analysis, design, development, and testing. The following list summarizes each stage:

- **Problem Analysis:** In this stage, the problem is described in such a way that it is clear exactly what needs to be accomplished.

- **Design:** The goal of this stage is to describe, in detail, a specific solution to the problem. It often begins with a simple sketch of the proposed interface. The solution may include lists of critical information and how they are to be obtained. It also includes a detailed list of instructions describing how this information is used in the solution process.

- **Development:** The development stage takes the design information and produces a computer program from it. The actual program interface is created to allow data to be gathered and results to be displayed. The processing steps from the design stage are translated into specific commands in a programming language.

- **Testing:** When the program is completed according to the design specifications, it is then tested under different scenarios to confirm that it works. If the program fails a test, this could lead to another round of problem analysis, design, and development.

Figure 1-14 illustrates the **project development cycle**. It is shown as a circular process because testing often reveals deficiencies that lead back to problem analysis. Frequently, programs need to be redesigned to accommodate unforeseen or overlooked circumstances or bad assumptions.

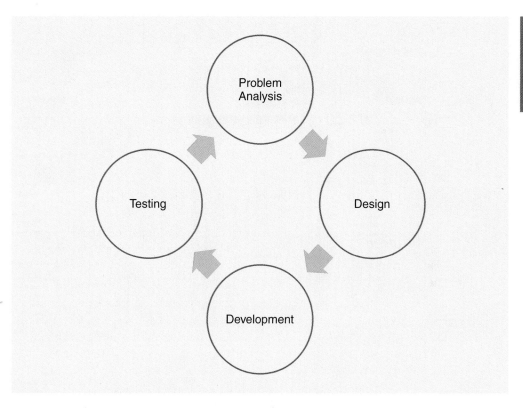

FIGURE 1-14 The project development cycle

The Visual Studio IDE

Soon, you will create your first project in Visual C++. Visual C++ is one of several languages that share a common development environment, called Visual Studio. Visual Studio presents you with a variety of toolbars, menus, and windows. All together, these elements make up the Visual Studio IDE. You will create your applications using tools provided from within the IDE. You can create programs, as well as run, test, and debug them. Figure 1-15 shows some of the tools you will use most often within the IDE.

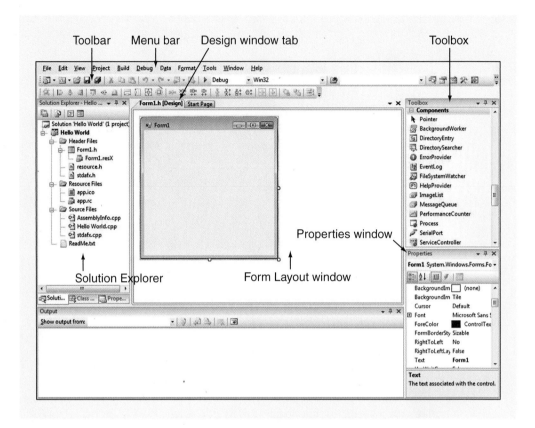

FIGURE 1-15 The Visual Studio Integrated Development Environment (IDE)

At the top of the IDE is a menu bar and a toolbar containing options for performing common tasks, such as saving files, printing them, etc. The Form Layout window, in the center of the IDE, is where you actually build the interface (that is, the form) for your program. You can think of this form (called Form1 by default) as the blank canvas in which you will create your program's interface. Form1 sits within a white tabbed window (the Form Layout window), labeled Form1.h [Design]. The Form1.h [Design] window is the programming space in which you will design your program interface. Throughout this book, we will informally refer to this as the **Design window**.

You can add buttons, textboxes, and many other controls to the form, as well as change its colors and fonts, in order to create the interface you envisioned when you made your preliminary sketch.

The narrow windows to the right of the Design window contain the tools you need to create the interface. Specifically, it contains the Toolbox, which lets you drag controls such as buttons and textboxes onto your form. It also contains the Properties window, which you use to change the size, color, text, and other attributes of the controls that you put on your form.

You will use the Toolbox and the Properties window extensively in each project you create. If one or more of them does not immediately appear, you can select it from the View menu at the top of the IDE. In Figure 1-15, both the Toolbox and the Properties window are located on the right-hand side of the screen; however, their positions are flexible. You can move any window within the IDE by dragging its title bar (that is, the blue area at the top of the window). These windows can be combined together in tabbed fashion or left separate, as you wish. As you work on through the tutorial that follows, experiment until you find the configuration that is most comfortable for you.

Tutorial: "Hello World!" (1 Button Version)

We will use the project development strategy discussed earlier in this chapter as we create the Hello World program. Thus, we'll start by analyzing the problem.

Problem Analysis

The first stage, problem analysis, will be easy for most of the short projects found in this text. However, in the real world, where problems are often very complex, the problem- analysis stage is more involved. The earlier the problem's complexities are sorted out, the better. During the problem-analysis stage, you need to identify what you need to do and what tools you'll need to accomplish the task. If the problem requires data, you should figure out how your program will get and process that data. The goal of the problem-analysis stage is to make sure that you understand the problem. One way to test your awareness of the problem is to try to explain it to someone else. You do not have to know how to solve every detail of the problem at this stage. If portions of the problem are unclear, this is the time to clarify them. In the next stage, you will consider how to address the solution details.

In this tutorial, you will create a program containing a single button and a single textbox. When you click the button, the words "Hello World!" will appear in the textbox. Further enhancements will allow you to change the colors of the foreground and back-ground of the textbox as well as the background color of the form.

Design

We have identified a number of important features of our program, as well as the most important operations it must perform. This is the key to all problem analysis: knowing what objects are required and how they will behave. In this section, you will begin to come to terms with the specifics of the problem by sketching the final product, identifying specific controls needed, and specifying what operations they will carry out.

We have already identified two important controls you will need: a button and a textbox. The button, when you click it, causes "Hello World!" to be displayed in the textbox. In object-oriented programming, the clicking of a button is called a **click event**. Take a moment to draw a rough sketch of this interface (known as a form). The result might look similar to that shown in Figure 1-16.

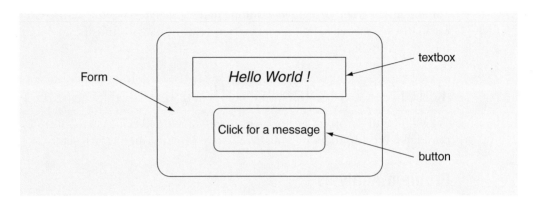

FIGURE 1-16   Interface sketch

Next, consider what tasks need to be accomplished when the button detects that a click event has occurred. Based on the problem description, there is only one task: place the characters "Hello World!" into the textbox.

Development and Preliminary Testing

Having come up with a design sketch and a description of how the program should work, we can now begin creating it. In the first step, creating the interface, we refer to the design sketch. In the second section, writing code, we refer to the list of tasks that the button's click event-handler must execute. Fortunately, there is only one task, so the coding portion of this project will be easy.

CREATE THE INTERFACE

We're ready to start creating the interface, based on the sketch in Figure 1-16.

To begin, start Microsoft Visual C++ 2008 Express Edition and create a new project. Figure 1-17 illustrates how to create a new project from the File menu.

Select the Project menu item

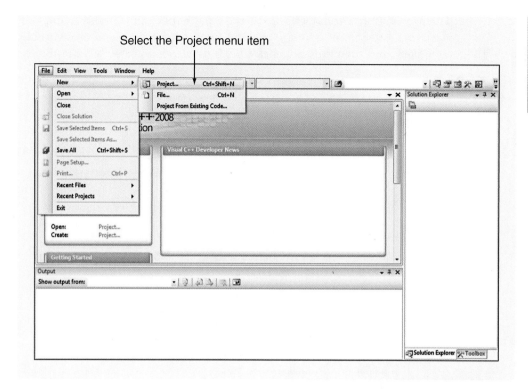

FIGURE 1-17   Creating a new Visual C++ project

Microsoft Visual Studio supports many different kinds of projects. You will create your Visual C++ program using Microsoft's Common Language Runtime (CLR) protocols. Choose to create a CLR project and then select Windows Forms Application as shown in Figure 1-18. It is important to make sure that Windows Forms Application is selected, otherwise you will create an entirely different kind of project and have to delete it and start over. It is also very important to save the new project to a location you can remember. By default, projects are saved to the `Documents\Visual Studio 2008\Projects` folder. You may want to save them to the Desktop instead so that the project is easier to find.

The process is shown in Figure 1-18 as a series of five steps. In this example, the project is saved to the Desktop, which is a useful storage location if you are working in a shared computer lab. When finished, click OK. It usually takes a few seconds for your project to be created.

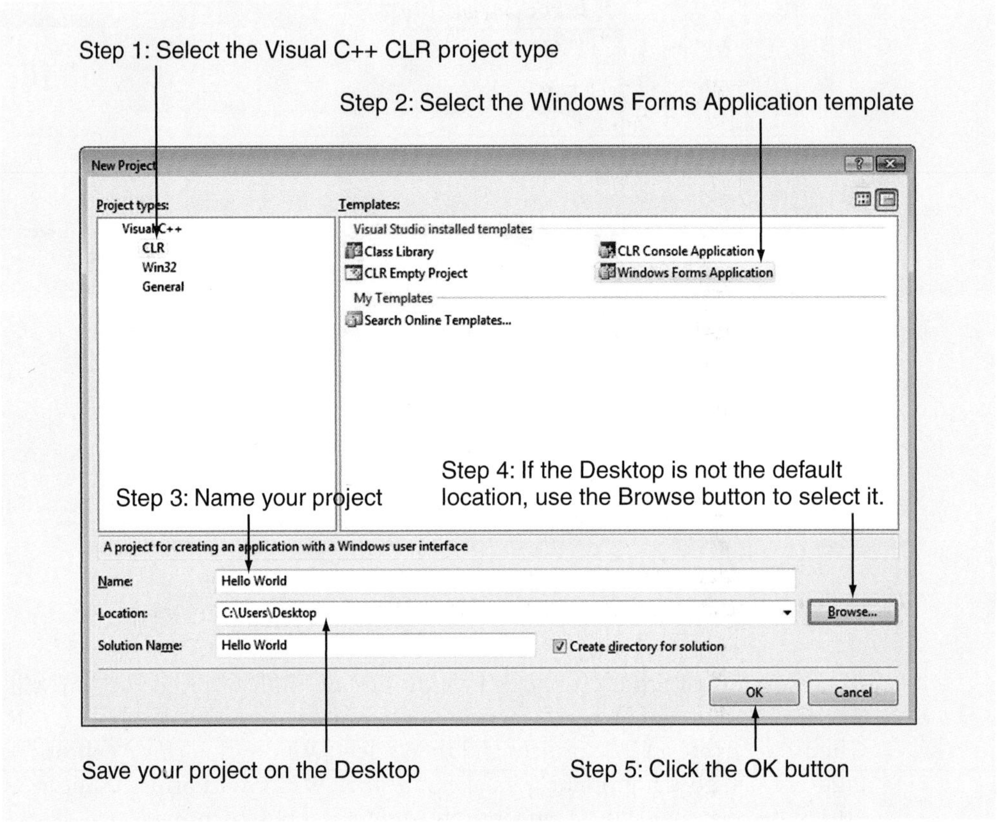

Step 1: Select the Visual C++ CLR project type

Step 2: Select the Windows Forms Application template

New Project			? ✕
Project types:	**Templates:**		⊞ ▤
Visual C++	Visual Studio installed templates		
CLR	📘 Class Library	📄 CLR Console Application	
Win32	📄 CLR Empty Project	📄 Windows Forms Application	
General	My Templates		
	🔍 Search Online Templates...		

Step 3: Name your project

Step 4: If the Desktop is not the default location, use the Browse button to select it.

A project for creating an application with a Windows user interface

Name:	Hello World	
Location:	C:\Users\Desktop	▾ Browse...
Solution Name:	Hello World	☑ Create directory for solution

	OK	Cancel

Save your project on the Desktop

Step 5: Click the OK button

FIGURE 1-18 Establishing project type, name, and save location

After you click the OK button in the New Project dialog box, the Microsoft Visual Studio IDE opens. The various windows, toolbars, and menus that make up the IDE are easily moved, and as a result, it is difficult to predict exactly what your screen will look like. In this book the IDE is set up so that following three windows are docked together at the right side of the screen:

- the Solution Explorer
- the Properties window, and
- the Toolbox

You can see these windows in Figure 1-19.

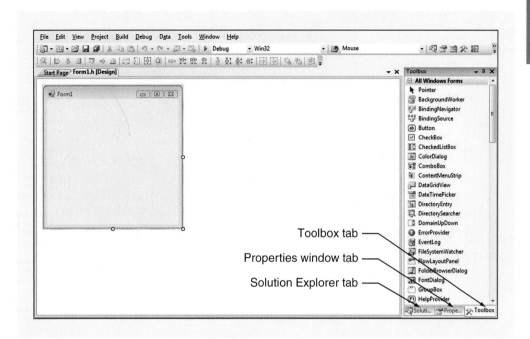

FIGURE 1-19 Three windows open in IDE

Your screen may not resemble Figure 1-19 exactly when you first start up Visual C++. Remove windows you do not need by clicking on the Close box in the upper right-hand corner of that window's title bar.

If the Toolbox does not appear on your screen go to the View menu and click on Toolbox as shown in Figure 1-20. Click on the "Stick pin" icon (also called the Auto-Hide button) to lock it onto your screen.

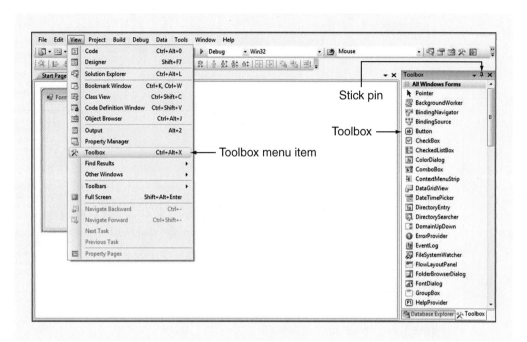

FIGURE 1-20 Opening the Toolbox

Customization of the IDE is almost complete. You just need display the Properties window. To display the Properties window and position it so that it is easy to use in conjunction with the Toolbox, go to the View menu. If there is no Properties Window choice in the dropdown menu list then point to Other Windows, and then click Properties Window, as shown in Figure 1-21.

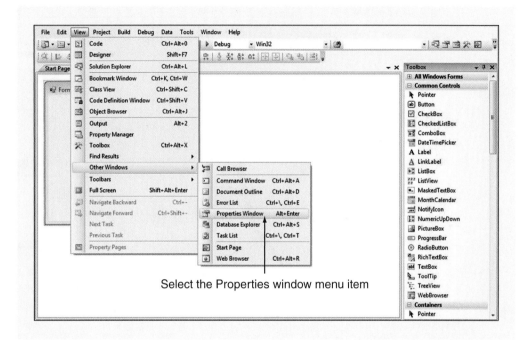

FIGURE 1-21 Selecting of the Properties window

When open, the Properties window shares the right-hand portion of the screen also occupied by the Toolbox, as shown in Figure 1-22.

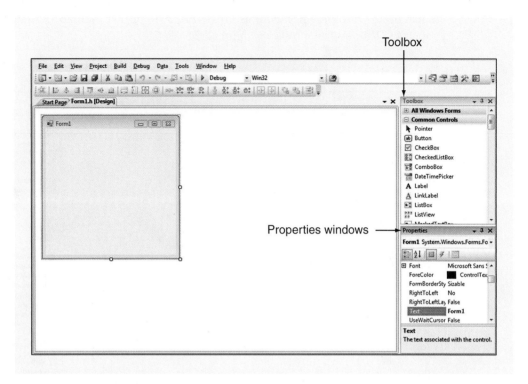

FIGURE 1-22 Toolbox and Properties windows in split window format

It is common for Visual C++ programmers to go back and forth between the Toolbox and the Properties window. Having them close by each other aids in this task. Unfortunately, when both are so short, the amount of vertical scrolling required to locate items in each list can be excessive. To make it possible to work with both more easily, you can reposition the Properties window. By grabbing the Properties window title bar, you can drag the window anywhere on the screen, as shown in Figure 1-23.

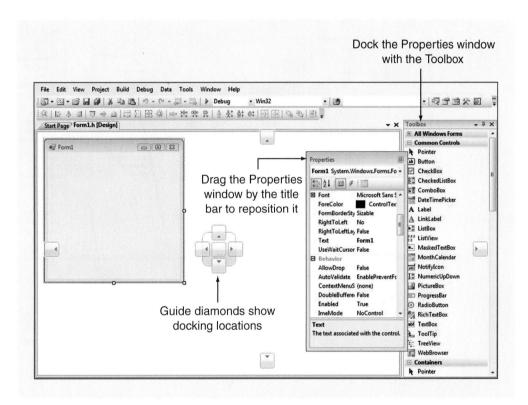

FIGURE 1-23 Repositioning the Properties window by dragging it to a new location

To match the examples in this book, drag the Properties window onto the Toolbox in such a way that the title bar of the Properties window is on top of the title bar of the Toolbox. This docks them together in a tabbed manner, as shown in Figure 1-24. The Solution Explorer window should also be added to the docked windows. Select the Solution Explorer item from the View menu and, when it appears, drag it to the right and dock it with the Toolbox and Properties windows.

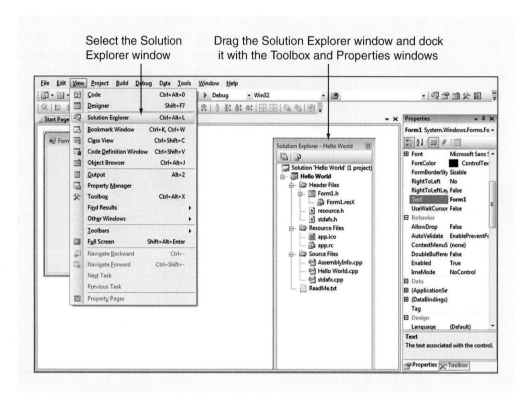

FIGURE 1-24 Docked Toolbox and Properties windows

To move from the Toolbox to the Properties window is now just a matter of selecting the proper tab at the bottom of the window. With this, our customization of the IDE is complete.

THE SOLUTION EXPLORER

The structure of your program is displayed in the **Solution Explorer** window in the tabbed window area at the left of the screen. You can see that the project contains numerous folders and files. These must all be kept together; this is important to remember when saving your project. When you create a Windows Forms Application (the option you chose earlier when creating a new project), a number of folders and files are created by default. As shown in Figure 1-20, your Solution Explorer Window contains header files, resource files, and source files.

Header files contain information that defines the fundamental Visual C++ code your project relies on. You will learn more about what this means later. For now, note that all files in the Header Files folder have an **.h** suffix, identifying them as header files. The most important header file is the **Form1.h** file, which contains the class definition information for the form (that is, your interface). When you write Visual C++ code, you will be writing it inside this file. In this chapter, you don't need to be concerned with the other header files (for example, `resource.h` and `stdafx.h`). We also will not program the resource or source files. For now, keep in mind that all of these files support the way our program (`Form1.h`) works with system resources.

USING THE TOOLBOX

Now, you can use the Toolbox to add two controls to the form: a textbox and a button. The controls in the Toolbox are listed in alphabetical order. You'll have a chance to explore a variety of these controls throughout this book.

To add a textbox to `Form1`, scroll down in the Toolbox until you can see the TextBox item. Double-click the TextBox item. This creates a TextBox (called `textBox1` by default) and places it in the upper left-hand corner of `Form1`, as shown in Figure 1-25. Small white squares, called resizing handles, appear on each end of `textBox1`, indicating that `textBox1` is currently the **selected object** on the form.

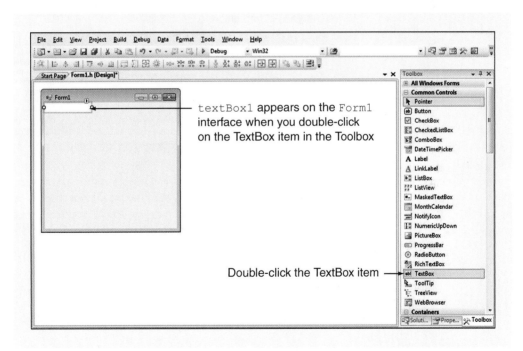

FIGURE 1-25 Using the TextBox item to create textBox1

Position `textBox1` by dragging it to the middle of `Form1`. The exact placement is unimportant.

Next, double-click the Button item in the Toolbox. This creates a Button control on Form1. The Button control, named **button1**, probably overlaps **textBox1;** if so, drag it to a location below **textBox1** as shown in Figure 1-26. Reposition them by dragging them with the mouse to different locations near the center of the form.

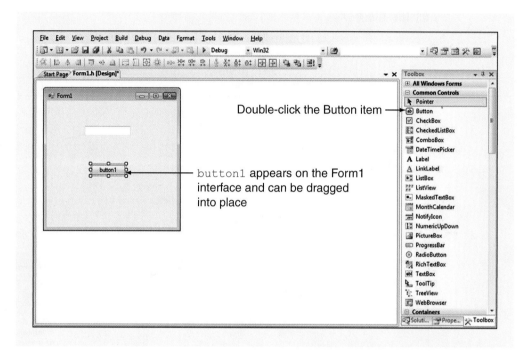

FIGURE 1-26 Creating button1

Notice that **textBox1** is empty and that the text displayed on the button simply says "button1." You will change these properties in the next section. Also, notice that currently the active object on **Form1** is the **button1** you have just added. It is important to keep track of which object on the form is currently active, because the Properties window only displays the properties of the selected object. To make an object active, you click it once.

USING THE PROPERTIES WINDOW

The attributes of a control are known as its **properties**. For instance, the caption text that appears on the button (`button1`) is the button control's `Text` property. To change a control's properties, you use the Properties window. To display the Properties window, click the Properties window tab. If `button1` is the selected object, then the Properties window lists its properties, as shown in Figure 1-27.

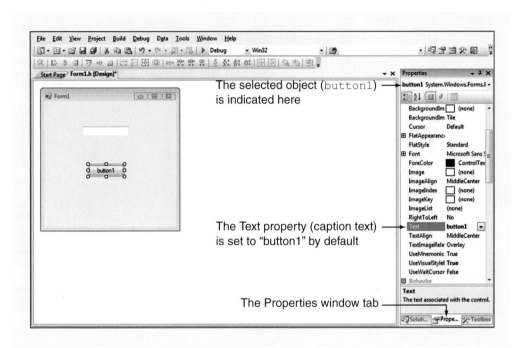

FIGURE 1-27   Locating the Text property of button1 in the Properties window

Every type of control has its own set of properties, although there is some overlap. For instance, all controls have a `Name` property, but only some controls have a `Text` property. The `Text` property for a button specifies the text that appears on the button, and is sometimes referred to as the button's caption. In Figure 1-27, you can see that the `Text` property for the button is set to `button1`. When you create your first button, the default name of the object ("button1") is placed into its `Text` property so that it is displayed.

The Properties window makes it easy to change a setting. Right now, we want to change the **Text** property for the **button1** to something more descriptive. To do this, click in the box to the right of **Text** in the Properties window, delete **button1**, type "Click for a message," and then press the Enter key. Figure 1-28 shows this new **Text** property. You can also see in Figure 1-28 that **button1**, on the form, displays the new caption.

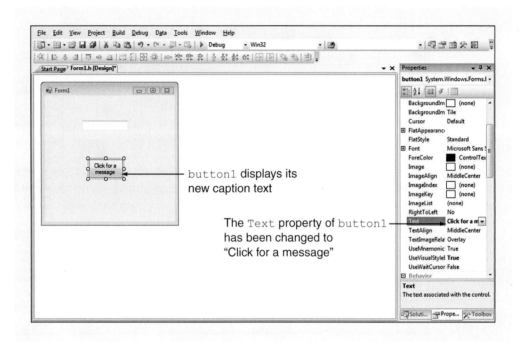

FIGURE 1-28 Changing the Text property of button1

The new caption may not be not fully visible on the button. If you can't see the entire caption, drag the button's resizing handles until the button is large enough to accommodate the text.

In addition to changing the properties of the controls on the form, you can also change the properties of the form itself. Now, let's change the **Text** property of **Form1** to something more descriptive. The **Text** property of a form controls the text you see at the top of the form. As a rule, it is a good idea to display the name of the program at the top of the form, so we'll change the **Text** property for **Form1** to "Hello World!" To do this, make **Form1** the selected object by clicking on it just once anywhere, except on the textbox or button. White resizing-handles appear on the form's border and its properties are displayed in the Properties Window, as shown in Figure 1-29. Change the **Text** property from **Form1** to **Hello World!** Remember to press the Enter key after you type the new property setting. The title displayed in the form's title bar changes from `Form1` to `Hello World!`

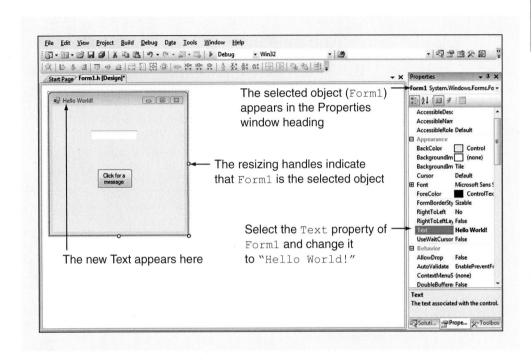

FIGURE 1-29 Changing the `Text` property of `Form1`

NOTE If you accidentally double-click the Form instead of single-clicking to select it, the IDE opens a new window with the tab labelled `Form1.h`. You can return to the Design window by clicking once on the `Form1.h` [Design] tab.

Now, let's take a moment to examine the **Text** property for **textBox1**. Click once on **textBox1** to make it active, and then scroll down in the Properties window until you can see the **Text** property. The **Text** property for a textbox specifies what appears inside the textbox. Currently, **textBox1** is blank, which makes sense because its **Text** property is blank.

You have done a fair amount of work, so it is time to save the project. Click File on the menu bar, and then click Save All. The project is saved to the location you specified earlier (the Desktop), when you first opened Visual Studio. Note that after you initially save a project (as you did when you first started Visual Studio), you should not use the Save As command on the File menu because it could potentially save your **Form1** definition somewhere other than in your project folder. The proper way to save projects is to always save them in the location in which they were created. The Save All command does this. Later, if you want to move the entire project somewhere else (for example, to save it on a USB flash drive), you can do so by exiting Visual Studio and then dragging the entire project folder to the location you want to save it.

RUNNING THE PROGRAM

You have finished creating the interface, and you have saved it. Although you have not written any Visual C++ code, it is tempting to see what happens when the program runs as it is. To do this, click the Start Debugging button on the Visual Studio toolbar. As shown in Figure 1-30, the Start Debugging button is the button with the green triangle, and not the box next to it that says "Debug."

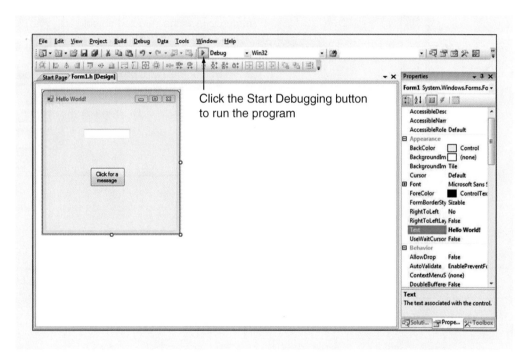

FIGURE 1-30 The Start Debugging button

It will take a few moments for the computer to get the program going. The first time you use Visual C++, you may see a dialog box similar to that shown in Figure 1-31. It indicates that the files in your project do not reflect your latest changes to them ("This project is out of date:") and asks if you would like to "build it." Unless you turn it off, this dialog box will appear whenever you click the Start Debugging button. If you see this dialog box, check the box labeled "Do not show this dialog again." and then click the "Yes" button.

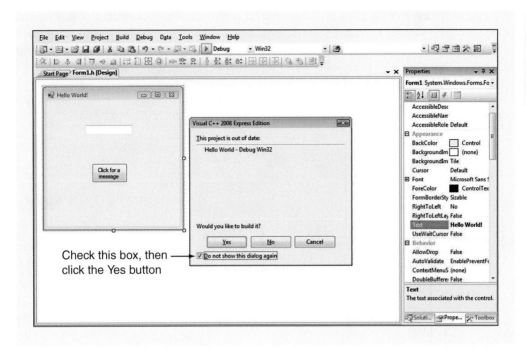

FIGURE 1-31   The "This project is out of date:" dialog box

When the program has compiled, it runs—that is, it **executes**. The interface appears on the screen, on top of the IDE, as shown in Figure 1-32. If you click the "Click for a message" button, nothing happens because we have not yet told the button what to do when it is clicked. That part comes next.

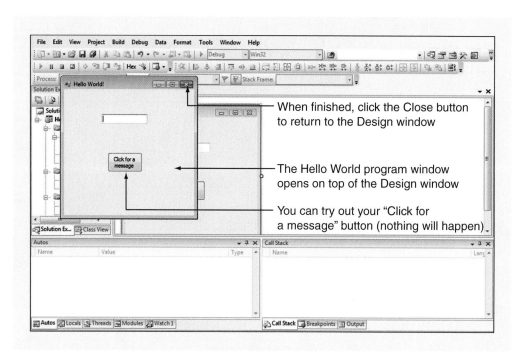

When finished, click the Close button to return to the Design window

The Hello World program window opens on top of the Design window

You can try out your "Click for a message" button (nothing will happen)

FIGURE 1-32 An executing program layered over the IDE

Close the running program by clicking the red Close button in the upper right corner. When the program has closed, you find yourself back in the IDE.

CODING AN EVENT HANDLER

Our next job is to make the button respond to a click event. To make the button functional, we need to write lines of Visual C++ code that will execute when the user clicks the button. Recall that the code that tells a control how to respond to an event is called an event-handler. To start creating the event-handler, double-click `button1` on the form. This takes us from the design window to the **Code Editor** window—called the **Code window** for short. Here we see a behind-the-scenes view of the code that underlies the form. This code is shown in Figure 1-33. Notice that the Code window tab is labeled "Form1.h," whereas the tab for the design window is labeled "Form1.h [Design]." You will need to go back and forth between the Code and Design windows often as you develop projects.

Code window tab   Design window tab

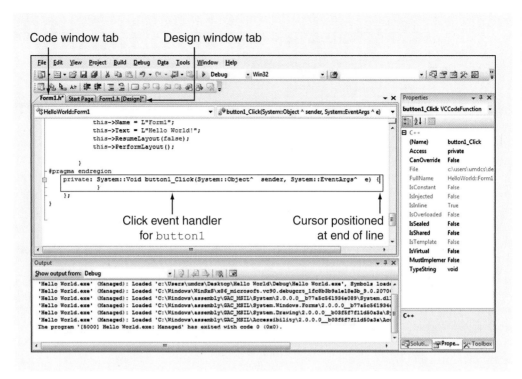

FIGURE 1-33 The Code window

The Code window looks intimidating but you will soon master it. The official name of the click event-handler for button1 is button1_Click. You can see this name in the code in Figure 1-33. Again, at this point, you are not expected to understand the code you see in the code window. But it is a good idea to scan it for things that look familiar. Close the Output window at the bottom of the screen.

The code you see in the code window underlies your program. As you become a more accomplished programmer, you will learn how to interpret all of the code in this window. But for now, you only need to concern yourself with the part of code that allows you to give specific instructions to button1.

Notice that the insertion point for the cursor in Figure 1-33 is positioned at the far right of a long line of code. This is actually at the spot just inside the button's click event-handler. To move the cursor to the start of a new line so that you can type a Visual C++ command, hit the Enter key. Figure 1-34 shows the repositioned cursor.

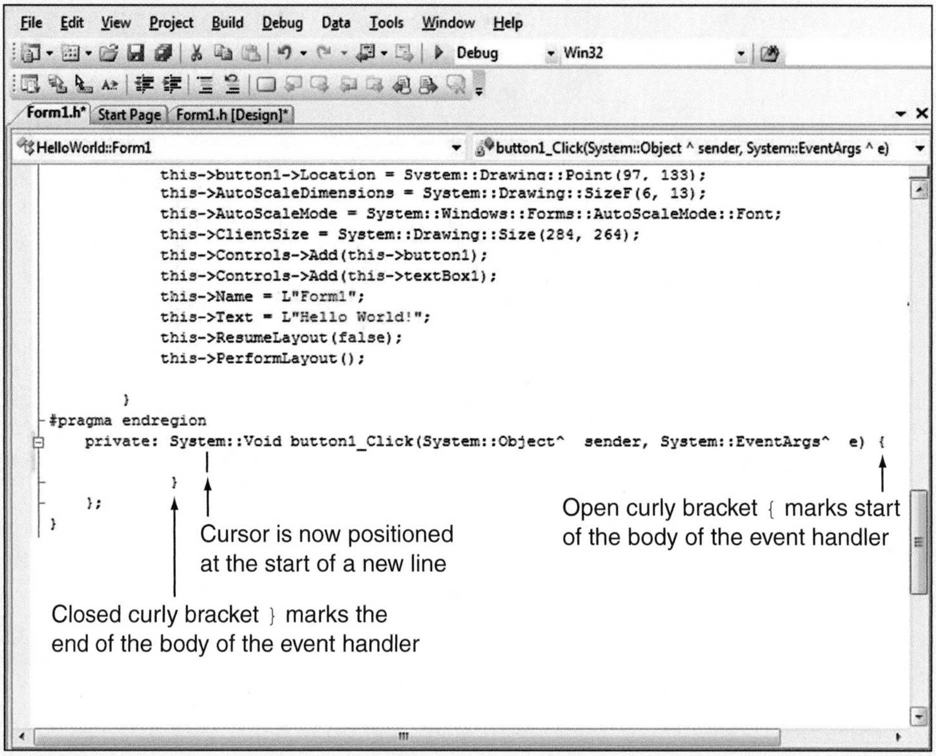

FIGURE 1-34 Code view positioning within the button1_Click event-handler

Event-handlers start with a header line that formally defines them, followed by a pair of curly brackets { } which is intended to enclose all of the Visual C++ commands within them. We will ignore the header line, and instead focus on the location of the { } characters. All of the Visual C++ commands you type for this event-handler must be located inside of them or the program will run incorrectly, or might not run at all. The event-handler code begins after the open curly bracket { and ends before the closed curly bracket }.

At this point, the cursor is positioned inside the click event handler for **button1**. You are ready to type the C++ code that tells the button how to respond to a click. You now need to write code that changes the **Text** property of the textbox to **Hello World!** With the cursor positioned as shown in Figure 1-34, type the line of C++ code shown in Example 1-1.

EXAMPLE 1-1

```
textBox1->Text = "Hello World!";
```

As you type, Visual Studio's IntelliSense™ feature recognizes that **textBox1** is an object belonging to your program and that **->** means you are trying to point to a specific property belonging to that object. The **Statement Completion Dropdown Box** lists items belonging to **textBox1** and allows you to choose. **IntelliSense** is a Microsoft feature built into the IDE that monitors what you are doing and anticipates what you need. It is designed to automate the process of completing a command. If it notices a mistake or recognizes that you might benefit by seeing some information, then it will bring this to your attention. Figure 1-35 shows some of the properties for **textBox1** displayed by IntelliSense, with the list scrolled down so you can see the **Text** property.

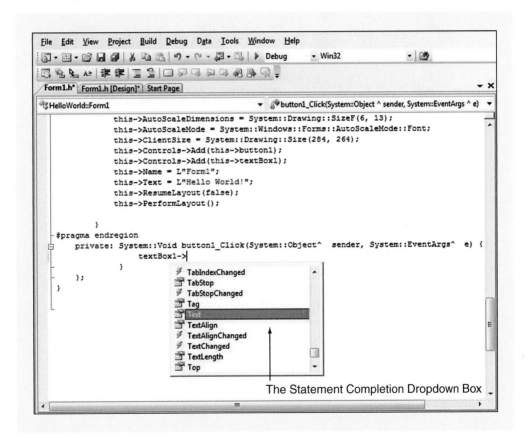

FIGURE 1-35 The Statement Completion Dropdown Box for textBox1

Some programmers prefer to select the property they want from this alphabetized list instead of typing it out.

Your `button1_Click` event–handler should now contain your `"Hello World!"` command, and look exactly like that shown in Example 1-1 and located in the `button1_Click()` event handler as shown in Figure 1-36. Explanations of the code in Figure 1-36 are discussed in following sections. Refer back to Figure 1-36, as necessary.

FIGURE 1-36 Completed `button1_Click` event-handler code

It is time to save your project again. Click File on the menu bar, and then click Save All. Recall that choosing the Save All command keeps your entire project together in one folder. (Do *not* click Save As.)

Understanding the Code

Programming necessarily involves learning a new set of rules that govern what you can and cannot write. Although some of the Visual C++ code we have entered looks like

English, it is quite different from English, especially if you scroll up into the Windows Form-Designer Code section of the Code window.

WINDOWS FORM DESIGNER CODE

You may have noticed that there are dozens of lines of Visual C++ code in your project already, above the `button1_Click` event-handler (see Figure 1-36). They were generated automatically when you created your Windows Forms project and constructed the interface. Do not worry if you cannot understand the Windows Form Designer Code at this point. We will discuss it in more detail later. It is, however, important that you do not make changes in this code. It was created for a reason, and changes may cause your program to stop working.

KEYWORDS

Although much of the code in your program is colored black, some of the words are shown in blue and others in maroon. Visual Studio applies these colors automatically as you type to help you keep track of the various parts of a C++ statement. There are several categories of terms that can be used in a C++ command and each category has its own color coding. A **keyword** is a term that has a predefined meaning in the C++ language and cannot be used in any other context. They are sometimes called reserved words. Keywords are always colored blue in the IDE. In Figure 1-36, you can see that words such as `private`, `this`, and `false` are keywords. The keyword `this` shows up frequently in Windows Designer Code and is used whenever a form wishes to refer to itself. As you work on the programs in this book, you will become very familiar with many Visual C++ key words. A list of standard C++ and Microsoft Visual C++ keywords is given in Appendix B.

Text that appears in a color other than blue represents terms that may vary at the programmer's discretion. The names of various items placed on the form by the programmer, such as `textBox1`, fall into this category. They are not fundamental terms that apply to all programs like keywords are. Most of the code you type will appear in black in the IDE. You will also see maroon used for text, such as on the `Hello World!` message you typed earlier. A collection of characters, such as the `Hello World!` message, is known as a **text string**. You'll learn more about text strings later in this chapter, as well as throughout this book.

CONTROL NAMES AND PROPERTIES

So far, you have created the interface, `Form1`, as well as the `button1` and `textBox1` controls. Earlier, we discovered that each of these controls had a `Text` property that could be directly edited in the Properties window. In Visual C++ code,

```
textBox1->Text
```

is used to identify the `Text` property belonging to the `textBox1` object. The characters `->`, which collectively are called the **pointer membership operator**, are used to indicate (that is, point to) a property belonging to an object. The pointer membership operator can be used to point to any of a object's properties. For example, textboxes have a background color property, called `BackColor`. To point to this property with the pointer membership operator, you type the code shown in Example 1-2.

EXAMPLE 1-2

```
textBox1->BackColor
```

Similarly, to point to the background color property of `Form1`, you would type the code shown in Example 1-3.

EXAMPLE 1-3

```
this->BackColor
```

The keyword `this` is used when you refer to an object (in this case, `Form1`) within its own class definition.

STRINGS AND DELIMITERS

As mentioned earlier, a **text string** is a collection of characters and is often referred to as simply a **string**. When including a string in a program, it is important to indicate exactly what is to be included in the string and what is not. A **delimiter** is a character used to define the limits of an item. Quotation marks, often called double-quotes, are the delimiters used for text strings. In the string `"Hello World!"` the delimiters clearly indicate that the first character is the capital `H` and the last is the exclamation point. Everything between the delimiters is considered to be the string of text that belongs together, including spaces.

THE ASSIGNMENT OPERATOR (=)

The = symbol is called an **assignment operator**. It does not mean "equal to," as in standard algebraic equations; rather, in the context of a Visual C++ command, it refers to an operation that makes a change to an item. In the code you created for your Hello World program (Example 1-1), the `Text` property of `textBox1` is assigned the string of characters `"Hello World!"`.

When your program runs, this instruction will make the message "Hello World!" appear in `textBox1` on the interface. The statement works by assigning the item to the right of the assignment operator (=) to the item on the left of it. In this case, it assigns the text string `"Hello World!"` to the `Text` property of the `textBox1` object, as shown in Figure 1-37.

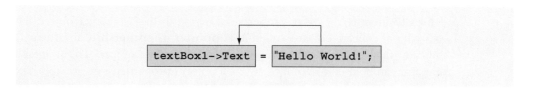

FIGURE 1-37 Assignment of a string to the Text property of textBox1

As a result, the message **"Hello World!"** (without the delimiters) appears in `textBox1` on the interface.

SEMICOLONS

Most C++ statements end with a semicolon (`;`). In C++, semicolons are very important; your code will not execute properly if you omit a semicolon by mistake. The compiler uses semicolons to determine when an instruction is finished. Without them, it will run one line into the next, assuming they are both part of the same command, and be unable to make sense of the result.

Testing the Completed Program

The time has now come to test your completed program and see if it works. Click the Start Debugging button. (Remember to click the green arrow button, and not the button that contains the "Debug" label.) As before, it takes a moment or so before the interface appears on top of the IDE. If everything has gone well, you should be able to click the button to display "Hello World!" in `textBox1`, as shown in Figure 1-38. If the program doesnot run as you expect, you may have made a small mistake typing the command in the code window. Recovering from errors such as this is the topic of the next section.

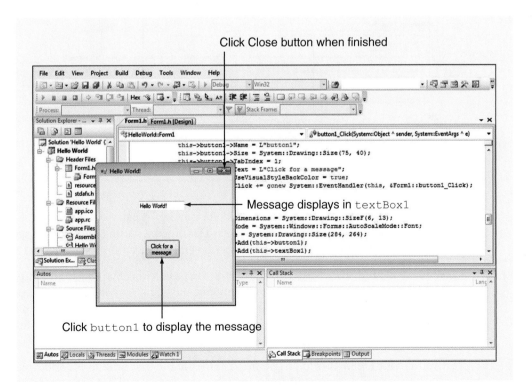

FIGURE 1-38 Hello World program after you click the Start Debugging button

Debugging a Program

What if you make a mistake? If a problem is detected in the debugging process, then you will see a dialog box such as that shown in Figure 1-39. Check the "Do not show this dialog again" checkbox and then click "No" to go back to the code window so that you can locate the error and fix it.

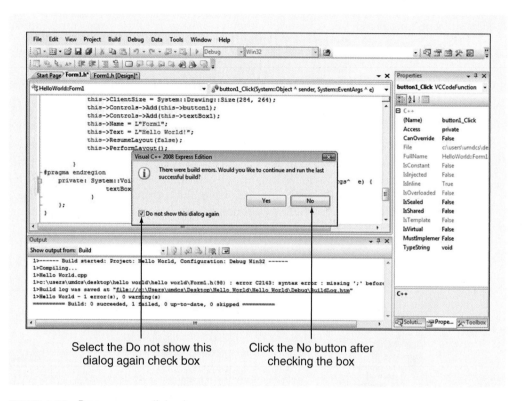

Select the Do not show this
dialog again check box

Click the No button after
checking the box

FIGURE 1-39 Program error dialog box

The most common mistakes are misspellings, missing or extra characters or mismatched sets of delimiters, parentheses, or curly brackets. The mistake causing the error in Figure 1-39 was simply the failure to put a semicolon (;) at the end of the command after **"Hello World!"**

When you find the error, correct it and then click the Start Debugging button again. Your program should run. If an error is detected again, go back to the code and examine it once more. The process of writing code, encountering errors when you attempt to compile it, and having to revise the code is a normal sequence of events in the life of a computer programmer. It is rare that a program works the first time you run it.

Even if your Hello World program ran correctly the first time, it is good to know how to handle mistakes, so we will make an intentional one and see what happens. Switch to code view and remove the semicolon (;) from the end of the statement assigning

"Hello World!" to `textBox1->Text` so that your code now looks like that shown in Figure 1-40. This creates a **fatal error** (that is, an error serious enough to stop your program from running).

After introducing the intentional error, run your program. It will fail to execute and you should see an error message similar to that shown in Figure 1-40.

The IDE provides lots of information to assist you in debugging a program. The Output window records what happens in the debugging process. When errors are encountered, information about them is displayed automatically in the Output window that will help you determine what the problem is. Figure 1-40 shows the Output window for the error caused by the omission of the semicolon.

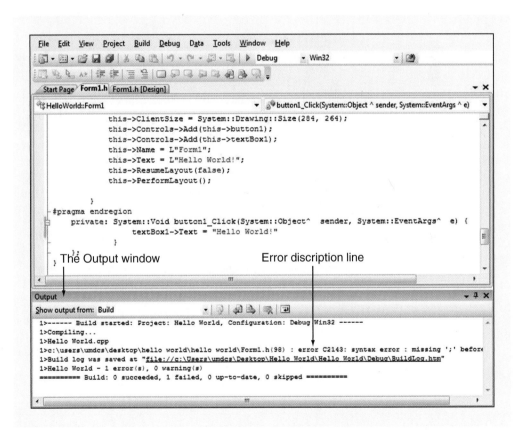

FIGURE 1-40 Locating error descriptions in the Output window

Error descriptions are sometimes difficult to interpret. This one indicates that error C2143 has occurred and that it seems to involve a **"missing ';' before '}'"**. You already know that a semicolon is missing because you were the one who deleted it. So, the error message correctly identified what the problem was. In addition, the error message can even tell you where the problem has been detected. To see this information, double-click on the error description line. The error line becomes highlighted and the code window repositions itself to show the line at which the debugger detected the error, as shown in Figure 1-41. The erroneous line (that is, the line that is missing the semicolon) is indicated by a small error bar on the left side of the screen. Notice that the line at which the error was detected is not always the line that needs to be fixed; however, it is usually close to it. In this case, the semicolon was not found on the line we entered, which was then not detected by the compiler until the line below it. Nevertheless, the Output window has provided valuable assistance to us in resolving the problem.

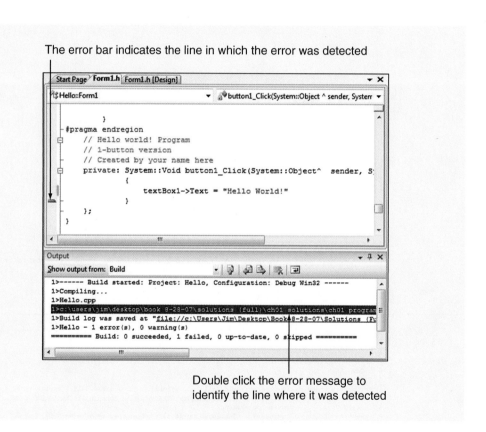

FIGURE 1-41 Locating the line at which the error was detected

Now that you have completed your first small program, you should save it again. The following section challenges you to take the knowledge you have gained and see if you can modify your program to behave in more interesting ways.

1

ON YOUR OWN

Now that you have the basics down, it is time to explore new territory. As you work, keep in mind that if you accidentally close a window, you can use the View menu to get it back again. This includes the Code, Toolbox, and Properties windows.

TASK 1: CHANGE THE TEXTBOX FONT

The Font property of textBox1 controls the size and appearance of the message that is displayed in that textbox. Go to the Font property (in the Properties window) and change the font to something you like. To do this, you will have to click on the ellipsis (...), shown in Figure 1-42, to launch the Microsoft Font Dialog Box.

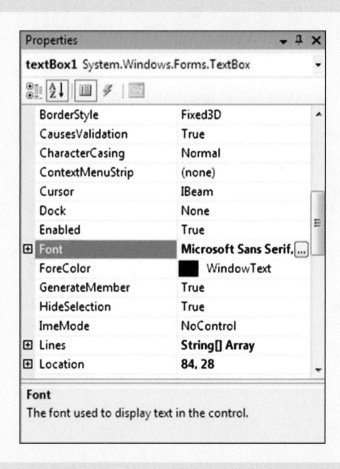

FIGURE 1-42 Properties window view showing the Font property of textBox1

Figure 1-43 shows how to select the font, font style, and size from the font dialog box.

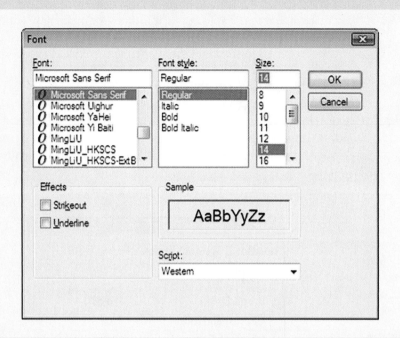

FIGURE 1-43 The font dialog box

Run your program to see how it looks. Depending on the font and size you have chosen, you may need to resize `textBox1` to be able to view all of the text. Remember to save your program after every revision.

TASK 2: ADD MORE BUTTONS

Next, add three more buttons to `Form1`. They will be named `button2`, `button3`, and `button4` by default. To add the buttons, use the Toolbox as before, double-clicking on the Button item in the control list.

TASK 3: CREATE CLICK EVENT-HANDLERS FOR THE NEW BUTTONS

Create click event-handlers for each of your buttons by double-clicking on them in the design window. Type the same code you inserted into `button1`'s click event-handler into each of the other click event-handlers. They should all display the same thing (`"Hello World!"`).

1

Next, change the message so that:

- `button1` displays "Hello green world!"
- `button2` displays "Hello red world!"
- `button3` displays "Hello yellow world!"
- `button4` displays "Hello blue world!"

When you click your buttons, each one should display a different message. Later on, you will change the colors of the messages when they are displayed in the textbox, to make them green, red, yellow, or blue.

TASK 4: CHANGE THE TEXT PROPERTIES OF EACH BUTTON

Change the `Text` properties of the buttons to indicate the colors they will produce. `Button1` should say "Click for a Green Message," `button2` "Click for a Red Message," and so on.

TASK 5: CHANGE THE TEXTBOX FOREGROUND AND BACKGROUND COLORS

Finally, add code that changes the color of the text displayed in the textbox. For example, in Figure 1-44, the text is displayed in red.

FIGURE 1-44 Red colored text displayed in `textBox1`

Every textbox has a property called `ForeColor` that determines what color the foreground of that textbox is set to. To change the `ForeColor` of `textBox1` to red you would enter the command shown in Example 1-4.

```
textBox1->ForeColor = Color::Red;
```

Figure 1-45 shows how the Intellisense property of Visual Studio can even list the colors for you as you type.

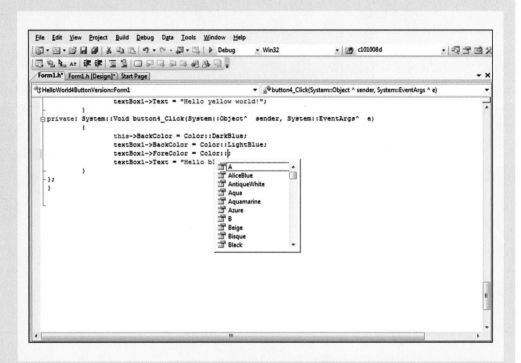

FIGURE 1-45 Color values shown by Intellisense™

You can also change other color-related properties, such as:

```
textBox1->BackColor
```

in the same manner.

TASK 6: CHANGE THE BACKGROUND COLOR OF THE FORM

We have seen how the foreground and background color property of a textbox can be altered. The form itself has a `BackColor` property that can be altered as well. Use the keyword `this` to refer to `Form1` as shown in Example 1-3.

1

Experiment with these to come up with a result you like. A complete list of colors is given in Appendix B. Figure 1-46 shows one version of the completed four-button program.

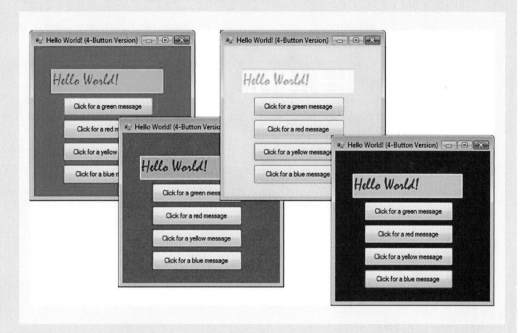

FIGURE 1-46 The four-button version completed

QUICK REVIEW

1. Visual C++ is an object-oriented programming language.

2. Class definitions specify how objects should be constructed.

3. Objects have properties (attributes) and methods (operations).

4. Buttons have click event handler methods.

5. The fundamental components of a computer are input, output, processing, memory, and storage devices.

6. The central processing unit (CPU) carries out the computational tasks associated with computers.

7. The CPU is composed of an arithmetic logic unit (ALU), controller, and other components.

8. The ALU performs comparisons and number crunching.

9. The controller fetches and decodes instructions from memory.

10. Memory is often called primary storage.

11. There are two types of memory: random access memory (RAM) and read-only memory (ROM).

12. RAM memory works directly with the CPU.

13. Secondary storage devices store data and programs when the computer is turned off.

14. Charles Babbage is often called the "Father of the Computer." He created designs of computers in the 1840s.

15. Ada Lovelace assisted Babbage and is sometimes called the "first computer programmer."

16. The first generation of computer hardware is characterized by the development of electronic, binary computers which often relied on vacuum tube technology.

17. The second generation is characterized by machines that could store their own programs and relied largely on transistorized circuits.

18. The third generation is characterized by the use and development of the first integrated circuits.

19. The fourth generation is characterized by large-scale circuitry and the development of microprocessors.

20. There are two main types of software: system and application.

21. System software communicates directly with hardware and often uses utility programs, such as device drivers, to do this.

22. Application software runs on top of the operating system.

23. The two types of application software are general and dedicated purpose.

24. Software development began with machine language.

25. Machine language is difficult to code and understand.

26. Assembly language simplified coding by using short symbols to stand for machine language instructions.

27. High-level languages look similar to English.

28. Examples of high-level languages include FORTRAN, COBOL, LISP, BASIC, Simula, Pascal, C, Smalltalk, standard C++, Java, and Visual C++.

29. Programs written in a high-level language are called source code.

30. Compilers translate source code into object code.

31. The programming process involves a cycle of coding, compiling, and debugging.

32. There are three types of errors: syntax, logic, and runtime.

33. Syntax errors are caught by the compiler and usually result from misspellings, or misplaced or missing characters.

34. Logic errors are those that occur when a program compiles and runs but produces an incorrect result.

1

35. Runtime errors are those that occur when the program compiles and runs but stops unexpectedly.

36. Logic and runtime errors often require a rethinking of the algorithm.

37. The project development process involves problem-analysis, design, development, and testing stages.

38. The project development process is cyclical.

39. The problem-analysis stage is where a concise description of the problem's requirements are determined.

40. The first task in the design stage is to sketch the proposed interface and identify its objects.

41. The design stage is also where the steps required to solve the problem are identified.

42. The development stage begins with the construction of the interface in the IDE.

43. The second part of the development stage involves writing code for the event-handlers, such as button-click events.

44. The testing stage is used to insure that a program works correctly and is able to handle a variety of input and processing situations.

45. The Visual Studio integrated development environment (IDE) contains all of the tools needed to code, compile, and debug.

46. The IDE presents a Form Layout window in which the interface is constructed.

47. The Toolbox contains a list of the controls that can be placed on the form.

48. The Properties window contains a list of the properties of a selected object.

49. A new form is called Form1 by default.

50. Forms, textboxes, and buttons each have a Text property that can be changed directly from the Properties window.

51. Properties can also be changed with Visual C++ code.

52. Visual C++ projects are composed of many folders and files that must be kept together in the same project folder.

53. The Solution Explorer lists the contents of the project.

54. Constructing an interface involves going back and forth between the Toolbox and the Properties windows.

55. To create the event-handler for a button, you double-click the button in the design window.

56. The Intellisense feature of Visual Studio assists you in completing statements by providing lists of terms that may be used.

57. Event-handler code must be entered within the area define by its pair of curly brackets { }.

58. C++ commands generally have a semicolon (;) at the end of them.

59. The Windows Forms Designer automatically generates many lines of Visual C++ code as you create your interface.

60. You should not change anything in the Windows Forms Designer section of your code.

61. Keywords are identified in blue and must be used only in specific, predetermined ways.

62. The keyword `this` refers to the object whose class definition you are working with (commonly `Form1`).

63. The pointer membership operator (`->`) is used to indicate the property of a control.

64. Text strings are surrounded with quotation marks (`""`), called delimiters.

65. To run a program, click the Start Debugging button.

66. The Output window records the process and lists errors, along with their descriptions.

67. Double-clicking an error line in the Output window will highlight the location in your code where the error was detected.

68. `BackColor` refers to the background color of a control.

69. `ForeColor` refers to the foreground color of a control.

TERMS TO KNOW

application software
architecture
arithmetic logic unit (ALU)
assembly language
assignment operator
attribute
BASIC
binary arithmetic
binary computers
bugs
C programming language
central processing unit (CPU)
class definition
click event
COBOL programming language
code
Code Editor window

1

code window
compiler
component(s)
control
controller
dedicated-purpose software
delimiter
design stage
design window
development stage
event-handler
execute(s)
fatal error
form
`Form1`
`Form1.h`
FORTRAN programming language
general-purpose software
generation of computers (first, second, third, and fourth)
graphics user interface (GUI)
header files
high-level programming language
input device
integrated circuit (IC)
integrated development environment (IDE)
IntelliSense™
interface
instruction position indicators
Java programming language
Java Virtual Machine
keyword
language
Linux
LISP programming language
logic error(s)
machine language
memory

method
microprocessor(s)
Microsoft Visual Studio
object
object code
object-oriented programming language
Open Source Movement
output device
Pascal programming language
pointer membership operator
primary storage
problem-analysis stage
procedural language(s)
programming library
project development cycle
properties
Properties window
random access memory (RAM)
read-only memory (ROM)
registers
runtime error(s)
secondary storage
selected object
Simula programming language
Smalltalk programming language
software
Solution Explorer
source code
standard C++ programming language
Start Debugging button
Statement Completion Dropdown Box
storage
string
syntax error(s)

system software

testing stage

text string

Toolbox

transistors

vacuum tubes

Visual C++ programming language

von Neumann architecture

Windows Forms Designer

Windows Vista

Windows XP

EXERCISES

1. _____ stores data and instructions while working directly with the CPU.

   a. The hard drive

   b. RAM memory

   c. A CD drive

   d. An optical disk drive

   e. All of the above

2. Which of these is an example of a secondary storage device?

   a. hard drive

   b. RAM memory

   c. keyboard

   d. monitor

   e. CPU

3. Which components are essential parts of the CPU?

   a. ALU and controller

   b. RAM memory and optical storage

   c. optical storage and the controller

   d. ALU and optical disk drives

   e. storage and the ALU

4. The compilation process _____.

    a. turns source code into object code

    b. identifies syntax errors

    c. launches the debugger

    d. is required to produce an executable program

    e. All of the above

5. Which of the following is *not* an operating system?

    a. Windows Vista

    b. Linux

    c. Visual Studio.NET

    d. DOS

    e. All of the above are operating systems.

6. A high-level language is one that is _____.

    a. made by Microsoft Windows

    b. English-like

    c. verbally communicated

    d. intended for supercomputers

    e. not object-oriented

7. The two general categories of software are _____.

    a. system software and general-purpose software

    b. system software and operating system software

    c. general-purpose software and applications software

    d. applications software and system software

    e. application software and utility software

8. Which of the following is the software that supports application software and interfaces with system hardware is?

    a. general-purpose software

    b. the operating system

    c. utility software

    d. dedicated-purpose software

    e. the compiler

9. In the statement `this->BackColor,` what does `this` refer to?

10. Suppose you see this error message in the Output window:

    `"error C2143: syntax error : missing ';' before '}'`

    What did you do wrong, and how can you fix it?

1

11–13. Fill in the spaces in the paragraph below with the names of prominent figures in the history of computer science.

    a.   Alan Turing

    b.   Jacques Jacquard

    c.   Ada Lovelace

    d.   Charles Babbage

    e.   Grace Hopper

Using punched card technology developed by loom maker 11._____, the English inventor and mathematician, 12. _____, developed plans for his Analytical Engine. Assisted by 13. _____, the daughter of Lord Byron, he created a design that was years ahead of its time.

14–16. Fill in the spaces in the paragraph below with the names of prominent figures in the history of computer science.

    a.   Alan Turing

    b.   Konrad Zuse

    c.   Gottfried von Leibnitz

    d.   Blaise Pascal

    e.   John von Neumann

German scientist, 14. _____, pioneered binary computing. The theoretical foundation of modern computer architecture was laid by 15. _____, whose work assisted in the development of the ENIAC, the first modern, electronic computer. His work paralleled the advances made by 16. _____, often called the founder of modern computer science, who also helped lay the foundation for the field of artificial intelligence.

17–20. Fill in the blanks with the letter of the choices provided. Throughout history, computer-like devices have involved various types of technology. Match the devices listed below with the hardware generation they typify.

    a.   first generation

    b.   second generation

    c.   third generation

    d.   fourth generaton

    17.   ____ Vacuum tubes

    18.   ____ Microprocessors

    19.   ____ Transistors

    20.   ____ Semiconductors

21–25. Match the software products listed below with the individuals most responsible for them.

- a. Grace Hopper
- b. Niklaus Wirth
- c. John Backus
- d. Bjarne Stroustrup
- e. Ada Lovelace

21. ___ FORTRAN

22. ___ C++

23. ___ COBOL

24. ___ Analytical Engine instructions

25. ___ Pascal

26. C++ was originally called _____.

- a. g++
- b. Simula
- c. OOP
- d. C with classes
- e. C++ was always called C++.

27. The original author of the C++ programming language is _____.

- a. Charles Babbage
- b. Bjarne Stroustrup
- c. Nikolas Wirth
- d. John Backus
- e. This language never had a single author.

28. The "Father of the Computer," who designed the Analytical and Difference Engines, was _____.

- a. Charles Babbage
- b. Thomas Watson, Sr.
- c. Ada Lovelace
- d. Bjarne Stroustrup
- e. Konrad Zuse

1

29. The person often called the "First Computer Programmer" was _____.

    a. Charles Babbage

    b. Grace Hopper

    c. Ada Lovelace

    d. Bjarne Stroustrup

    e. John von Neumann

30. Which of the following is *not* one of the five fundamental components of a computer?

    a. input devices

    b. output devices

    c. CPU

    d. printer

    e. memory

31. Algorithms are written in _____.

    a. Visual C++

    b. English

    c. pseudocode

    d. source code

    e. object code

32. To change the `Text` property of a control called `textBox1`, use the _____.

    a. Solution Explorer

    b. Properties window

    c. Toolbox

    d. Tool bar

    e. TextBox button

33. Which of these are synonymous?

    a. data and memory

    b. memory and storage

    c. C++ code and source code

    d. pseudocode and source code

    e. source code and object code

Note: For Exercises 34-41, identify each of the components of the Visual Studio.NET IDE, as shown in Figure 1-47, and explain their significance.

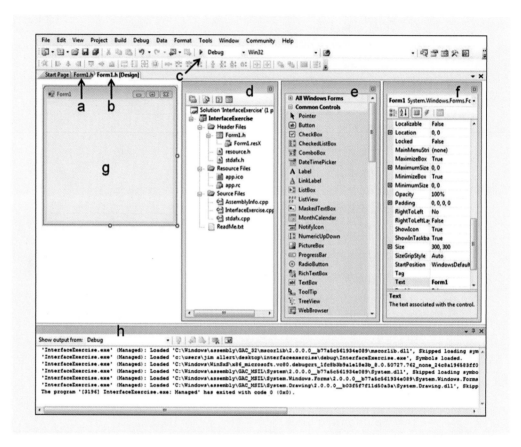

FIGURE 1-47 Identify Visual Studio IDE elements

34. The ToolBox
35. The `Form1` interface
36. The Design window
37. The Properties window
38. The Code window
39. The Output window
40. The Solution Explorer
41. The Start Debugging button

PROGRAMMING EXERCISES

As you work on the following projects, keep in mind that while completing a project as described in this book is rewarding, the real fun starts when you begin to experiment with it on your own. Do not be afraid to try out new ideas. You will probably learn more from your own experimentation and code writing than from the projects presented here. Start with what you know and build up. For example, you could add buttons that you can click to change the font of text displayed on the interface or experiment with different colors.

Do not be afraid of error messages. You will encounter many of them as you develop each project. After you have seen the same ones several times, you will immediately know how to fix them. Learning how to decipher error messages is a valuable skill that you will want to acquire.

1. Create Disaster

One of the most important things you can take away from your first programming experience is the sense that you are in control. You can write the commands, and you can fix the things that go wrong. The biggest source of insecurity for novice programmers is error messages. What do they mean? What caused them? How do I fix them?

This is a good point to start taking control of the error message threat. Open the project you created in this chapter, and double-click on one of the buttons to get into the code window. Now, create an error.

For example, consider the following lines of good, working Visual C++ code:

```
this->BackColor = Color::Green;
textBox1->BackColor = Color::LawnGreen;
textBox1->ForeColor = Color::DarkGreen;
textBox1->Text = "Hello green world!";
```

We know what happens when the (;) is deleted. What happens when other things are missing? In the following steps, you will make one change at a time. After each change, run the program and see if you can understand anything about the error. Once you have worked out the meaning of the error message, restore the code you deleted and create the next error. Since you will already know what caused various errors, reading the error messages will help you learn how to interpret them. It will be very important to know how to read error messages later on, so this is a good time to learn. After you have reviewed an error message, be sure to go back to the code window and correct the error before proceeding on to the next one.

   a. Delete the = operator from the first line, so that it reads:

```
this->BackColor  Color::Green;
```

   b. In the same line, remove the keyword `Color::` (including the two colons) so that the line reads:

```
this->BackColor = Green;
```

   c. Remove the `->BackColor` designator from the identifier `this` so that the line reads:

```
this = Color::Green;
```

   d. Remove the `->` operator so that the line reads:

```
thisBackColor = Color::Green;
```

   e. Remove the quotation marks from around the words "Hello green world!" so that the line reads:

```
textBox1->Text = Hello green world!;
```

You can find complete explanations for these five error messages in Appendix F; but try to figure them out for yourself before you check the Appendix. If you would like to experiment further, feel free to delete anything you want (as long as you remember what you did so you can correct it later).

2. Create Your Own Interface

Sketch the design of an interface, or find a program on the Internet that has a simple interface (for example, textboxes and buttons). From that model, create a new Visual C++ program and drag controls onto it from the Toolbox until you have created an interface that matches your model. You do not have to write the code for this program, just create the interface. Experiment with controls other than textboxes and buttons to see what they produce on your form. Since you are not going to use this program for anything, you should feel free to experiment with a number of the different controls.

3. Online Resources

There are several places you can go on the Internet to locate resources that will be useful to you as you learn Visual C++. The Microsoft Visual C++ Developer Center at: *http://msdn2.microsoft.com/en-us/visualc/default.aspx* is by far the most comprehensive. Whenever you have a question about some aspect of Visual C++ programming, you can usually find the answer, along with valuable examples, on this website.

Start your exploration of this website by locating the important reference library and learning tools. To reach the library, click the Library tab at the top of the screen. To reach the learning tools, click the Learn tab at the top of the screen.

Explore the links you find on these pages and locate the following resource links under the Learn tab:

- Getting Started
- Programming Guide
- Guided Tour
- "How do I . . .?"

Make note of what is available in each section. Print a copy of the "Getting Started" page as a reminder to you of what is available online. Knowing what is available online could save you many hours of frustrating experimentation when you write your own programs.

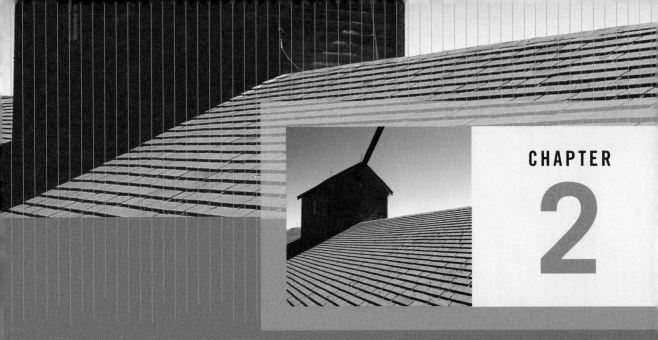

READING, PROCESSING, AND DISPLAYING DATA

IN THIS CHAPTER, YOU WILL:

- Develop algorithms to solve a problems
- Learn about the standard C++ data types
- Declare and initialize variables
- Read data using the `TryParse()` method
- Use the standard C++ arithmetic operators
- Process data using arithmetic expressions
- Abbreviate lines of code using shorthand assignment operators
- Use the `Math::Pow()` and `Math::Sqrt()` methods
- Display output using the `ToString()` method

Solving problems requires a plan. The role of a computer program is to implement that plan. If the original plan is faulty, it does not matter how much you know about a programming language—the program that implements the plan will have the same faults. For this reason, it is important to learn how to solve problems before moving ahead to the specifics of the Visual C++ language. This chapter begins with the general topic of problem solving and then outlines how to proceed from a plan to a programming solution.

Solving Problems

Imagine that as you are walking along a main street, a car pulls up and the driver asks for directions to Pop's Diner. There are several possible ways to respond. Assuming that you want to help the driver and that you know how to get to their desired destination, one method is to provide him or her with a list of instructions based on street signs.

"Keep going until you get to the stop sign on College Street. Take a left on College and follow it along to Woodland Avenue. At the stop sign on Woodland, take a right and continue for about a half mile until you get to 21st Avenue. Take a left on 21st and follow it down to Interstate 35. Go south on the interstate until you reach the exit for Lake Avenue. At Lake, take a left and follow it about five blocks to Pop's Diner."

Another alternative is to use landmarks in addition to street signs:

"Keep going until you get to College Street, then take a left and go until it ends; take a right and continue until you see a small public garden on the right. Turn left at the garden. Keep going until you come to the interstate. If you look to your right, you should see a bridge about two miles away; head there."

Or you might provide directions with far less detail. You could point and say:

"It is about four miles that way. Head down the hill until you get to the lake and follow along the lake shore until you get to the bridge. You will see it."

All of these solutions may be correct, but they may not be equally effective. For example, unless we write down directions, many of us would get lost trying to follow the first solution from memory. At the same time, the last two, without street names, could be confusing. The third solution is easiest to remember, but it would not be surprising if we had to stop and ask somebody else for more detailed instructions once we got closer to our destination.

This example illustrates a fundamental problem in computer science—analyzing a problem and coming up with an effective, verifiable solution that can be implemented as a computer program. If we were giving instructions to a robot instead of the driver of a car, only one of the suggested solutions would probably work—the most detailed one. Landmarks and undetailed descriptions assume too much general background knowledge and would almost certainly be ineffective. The first solution would be the best because the robot could be assumed to have the memory sufficient for the task. It could get to the destination by following the steps in order and doing what it was told.

1. Keep going until you get to the stop sign on College Street.
2. Take a left on College and follow it along to Woodland Avenue.
3. At the stop sign on Woodland, take a right and continue for about a half mile until you get to 21st Avenue.
4. Take a left on 21st and follow it down to Interstate 35.
5. Go south on the interstate until you reach the exit for Lake Avenue.
6. At Lake, take a left and follow it about five blocks to Pop's Diner.

Being able to look at a problem, identify what needs to be done to solve it, and construct an ordered list of steps is an essential computer programming task. We call this ordered list of steps an **algorithm**.

Algorithms are used whenever we design a program segment that carries out a significant action, such as the click event-handler for a button. In the examples above, the algorithm was written in English. This is normally the case, although programmers often shorten the task by abbreviating wherever possible to create an algorithm that looks more like programming language code. This form of writing is called **pseudocode** (false code). Unlike real code written in a programming language, algorithms written in pseudocode are general enough to be understood by almost anyone. From the standpoint of programming languages, they are **language-independent**—that is, they are not tied to any specific programming language. Since they are language-independent, pseudocode algorithms can be handed over to a programmer, who can then decide which programming language to use. In addition, a manager with no programming experience should be able to read a pseudocode algorithm to determine whether it meets his or her requirements.

There may be more than one algorithm for solving a particular problem. Later in the book, we will discuss how to evaluate algorithms to determine which are more efficient at problem solving than others. When designing a program solution, it is usually best to start with a high-level algorithm. A **high-level algorithm** describes the solution process in general terms. Later, as you develop your solution plan, you can add details to each step. The result is called a **low-level algorithm**. Low-level algorithms are excellent guides for programmers because they describe each step very specifically. If done well, low-level algorithms provide pseudocode statements that can be translated into Visual C++ statements almost line by line.

Algorithms usually center on what to do with data. The term **data** refers to the basic information, such as dates, numbers, and names, used by a program. A very simple algorithm that applies to many button click event-handlers looks like this:

ALGORITHM 2-1

1. read the data
2. process the data
3. display the result

In this chapter, you will discover how to translate these simple instructions into Visual C++. The first step is learn about the kinds of data that programs can receive, store, and use.

Data and Data Types

Data includes everything that is entered into your program in one manner or another. For example, a job application program might require you to enter your name, age, grade point average (GPA), and gender (female/male), as shown in Figure 2-1.

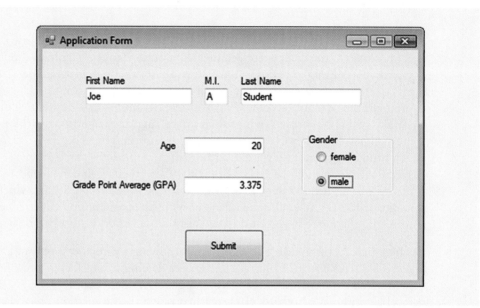

FIGURE 2-1 Application form

Although you often enter data as text, all data are stored in the computer as configurations of **bits** (commonly represented as the binary digits 0 and 1). Think of every binary digit as a switch that is either turned on (1) or off (0). Different configurations of bits stand for different values. A grouping of eight bits is called a **byte**. Figure 2-2 shows one possible configuration of eight bits in one byte.

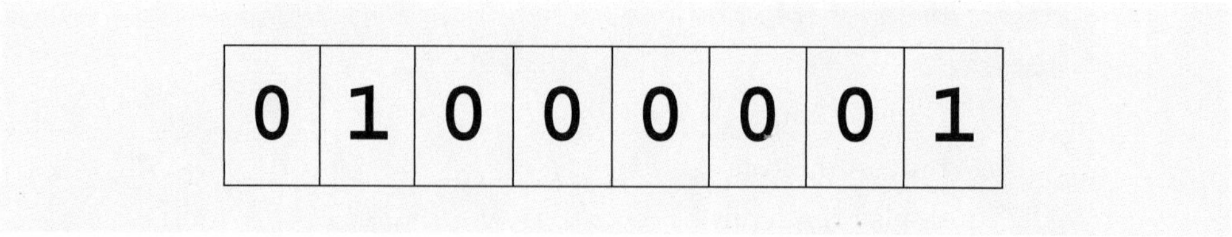

$$0\ 1\ 0\ 0\ 0\ 0\ 0\ 1$$

FIGURE 2-2 One byte (eight bits)

When you create a program, one important task is to indicate what kind of data the program uses. In other words, you need to specify the **data type** for each item of data your program uses. Data types are important because every data item needs to be stored in memory. Memory is allocated in bytes. Some data types require more bytes than others. The compiler generates instructions that allocate memory for the data your program needs, but it must know what type of data it will need to accommodate, so that it sets aside the correct amount of memory and configure it in the proper manner. For example, consider the program represented by the interface in Figure 2-1. It takes only one bit to represent the user's gender (0 = female, 1 = male). Age or GPA, however, may require more than one byte to be represented in binary form. Similarly, a person's name could be a long string of characters requiring many bytes.

The Visual C++ language supports an assortment of data types. In this book, we will only concentrate on a few of them; however, a more complete list is presented in Appendix B. The next few paragraphs discuss some of the most important data types. You will learn the keyword used in C++ code to refer to each data type.

One data type you will use often is the **Boolean data type**. This data type consists only of the values true and false. In C++ code, the keyword **bool** denotes Boolean data. When a user clicks the button in Figure 2-1 to indicate his or her gender, the user is providing Boolean data. The button indicating that the applicant is female has either been clicked or it has not. There are only two options (true or false). Boolean values can be represented by a single bit (1 = true, 0 = false), even though computers usually prefer to allocate at least one full byte for a data type regardless of whether all the bits actually get used.

NOTE The Boolean data type is named after British mathematician George Boole, who developed the mathematics of symbolic logic in the mid-1800s. His work provided an essential foundation for many branches of modern mathematics and computer science. Boolean algebra is also named after him.

Another important data type, the **character data type**, is used for individual characters. In C++ code, the keyword for this data type is **char**. The char data type includes the uppercase and lowercase alphabet (A–Z and a–z), along with punctuation characters (that is, #, %, $, and *) and numerals (0–9). Character data can also be used to represent special characters like tabs, the Enter key, backspace, and many others.

Because computers only process data that can be represented in binary form, the characters you enter from the keyboard are stored as binary numbers. In Windows, the number assignments are specified by a 16-bit (two-byte) international standard, called **Unicode**. In other words, each letter is stored in memory as a series of sixteen 0s and 1s. For example, in the Unicode standard, the uppercase letter A is stored as: 00000000 01000001. The section of Unicode that pertains to English characters is called the **American Standard Code for Information Interchange (ASCII)** and can be found in Appendix B. When char data is used in a C++ command, it is preceded and followed by an apostrophe (sometimes called a single quote). For example, the last letter in the alphabet would appear as follows in C++ code:

'z'

When used in this way, the apostrophes are considered delimiters. As you learned in Chapter 1, a delimiter is a character used to define the limits of an item.

Integer data is used to represent zero, and both positive and negative whole numbers. Integer data do not have a fractional component. For this reason, your age would be considered an integer if it was rounded to the last whole number (for example, 20 years and 3 months would be rounded to 20). In standard C++, there are three different integer data types: **short**, **int**, and **long**. They vary according to the amount of storage space assigned to each. In this text we will often use the **int data type**. Throughout this book, we will refer to the data stored in variables of the int data type as integers. In C++ code, the keyword for the integer data type is int. The compiler allots 32 bits (four bytes) of memory for each integer variable.

A numeric value that is not an integer and requires decimal places (such as a grade point average of 3.245) is called a **real number** and may be represented in one of two ways, depending on the degree of precision required. **Single-precision numbers** require only four bytes (which can represent values as small as 3.4×10^{-38} and as large as 3.4×10^{38}), while **double-precision numbers** require eight bytes and can represent a far larger range of values (1.7×10^{-308} to 1.7×10^{308}). These correspond to the C++ data types, the **float data type** (for single-precision) and the **double data type** (for double-precision). In C++ code, the keyword for the float data type is float and the keyword for the double data type is double.

Data types are either primitive or derived. **Primitive data types** are those that are most fundamental to the C++ language and include Boolean, character, integer, float, and double. Table 2-1 lists the characteristics of the primitive data types mentioned in this chapter.

TABLE 2-1 Commonly Used Primitive Data Types

Data Type	Keyword	Storage Requirement	Range of Values	Description
Boolean	bool	1 byte	0 or 1	Boolean data type. Used to store the values true (1) or false (0).
character	char	1 byte (8 bits)	-127 to 128	Used to represent ASCII character values (Unicode characters require two bytes)

TABLE 2-1 Commonly Used Primitive Data Types (continued)

Data Type	Keyword	Storage Requirement	Range of Values	Description
int	`int`	4 bytes (32 bits)	2,147,183, 648 to 2,147,183, 647	Integer
float	`float`	4 bytes	3.4e -38 to 3.4e 38	Single-precision real numbers
double	`double`	8 bytes	1.7e -308 to 1.7e 308	Double-precision real numbers

Derived data types are constructed from primitive ones. There are a number of derived data types built into the Visual C++ language. Their names are capitalized, by convention, to distinguish them from primitive types. The names of derived types are not C++ keywords.

The derived type you will encounter most often is the **String data type**. The term String (capitalized) should not be confused with the term **string** (lowercase). The capitalized version refers specifically to the Visual C++ String type definition. The term string (lowercase) is a more general term used to describe any collection of text, such as "Hello World!" The String data type consists of a collection of characters (a string of text) along with many other features. Although there is no Visual C++ keyword for the String data type, it will be encountered relatively often in our projects and will be referred to as `String` in Visual C++ code.

Variables

Computer programs use data in a variety of ways. In a typical application, the user fills out several textboxes on the interface and then clicks a button that processes the data and displays the result. This seemingly simple process disguises what may be a long list of complex operations taking place behind the scenes. Data processing typically requires that the information entered into objects on the interface (for example, the `Text` field of a textbox) be read and then converted into a numeric value before it can be processed. This converted data must then be stored in memory so that it can be accessed when needed. The process reverses itself when you wish to display numeric results in a textbox. Results are displayed only after a String has been created to represent them and placed into an output textbox.

A **variable** is a location in the computer's memory, comprised of one or more **memory cells**, used to store data. It is called a variable because its contents may vary. Variables are used to store whatever data your program requires. Creating a variable is referred to as **declaring** it.

Variable declaration is normally one of the first things done in an event-handler because input, processing, and output tasks usually depend on the availability of variables.

A **variable declaration** (the code that declares a variable) does three things:

1. It finds space in the computer's memory that has not been allocated for any other purpose and reserves it.
2. It assigns this memory location a name that you provide.
3. It associates a particular data type with that memory location.

A **variable declaration statement** begins with the data type, followed by the names of the variables you wish to declare. The keywords for data types appear in blue in the Visual Studio IDE. The lines in Example 2-1 declare three variables named `length`, `height`, and `width` using the `int` data type:

EXAMPLE 2-1

```
int length;
int height;
int width;
```

If variables are of the same type, they may also be declared all on one line, as shown in Example 2-2:

EXAMPLE 2-2

```
int length, height, width;
```

The computer keeps track of memory cells by referring to their addresses. A **memory cell address** is a unique number identifying a memory cell. Every memory cell has an address. Every time your program runs, it may allocate different memory cells for your data, depending on what is available.

Fortunately, a programmer does not need to know these memory cell addresses in order to use the computer's memory. Instead, the process works as shown in Figure 2-3. A variable declaration statement such as:

```
int length;
```

establishes the need for enough space in memory to store an integer. The space is allocated from the available memory locations.

In Figure 2-3, there are many available memory locations; the addresses of these memory cells are shown in the right-hand column. Space is set aside for the variable (beginning at address 1345244) and the name `length` is assigned to it. The same process occurs for the declaration of other variables (`height` and `width`). After you write a variable declaration statement, you can refer to the variable in your Visual C++ code simply by its name.

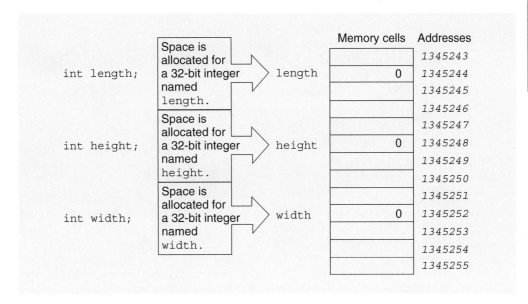

FIGURE 2-3 The declaration process

Example 2-3 shows several examples of variable declarations:

EXAMPLE 2-3

```
bool female;
char middle_initial;
int age;
float average;
double gpa;
```

Variable names should be self-documenting. This means that they should describe the data they contain. Conventional programming uses a single, short word or two. The examples `age`, `middle_initial`, and `gpa` above are appropriate for a person's age, middle initial, and grade point average. No two variables may have the same name.

The following rules apply to variable names:

- They must begin with a letter or an underscore (_) and can only use letters, digits, or underscores (_) in the body of the name.
- They are case sensitive (`height` is not the same as `Height`).
- Spaces cannot be used as separators.

- Each variable name in a program must be unique.
- You cannot use a C++ keyword as a variable name.

Table 2-2 shows examples of invalid variable names.

TABLE 2-2 Invalid Variable Names

Variable Name	Why It Is Invalid
2009GPA	Cannot begin with a digit
first name	Cannot use a space as a separator
total%	Cannot include characters other than letters, numerals, or _ (underscore)
int	Cannot use a keyword as a variable name

You should avoid the temptation of making variable names too long. A name such as theEmployeesFirstName does a good job of describing the data it contains, but will become laborious to type repeatedly in your program. Short variable names, less than three letters, should also be avoided in most circumstances. Short names may be convenient to use when writing code but usually say very little about their purpose. Some examples of valid variable names are shown in Table 2-3.

TABLE 2-3 Valid Variable Names

Variable Name	Correct Usage Rule
GPA2009	Digits must come after the first character
first_name	Underscore notation may be used to separate words
firstName	Pascal notation capitalizes the first letter in a new word (also called camel notation)

Initializing Variables

Initialization refers to the act of putting data into a variable for the first time, after it is declared. By default in Visual C++, all numeric variables are initialized to 0 as part of the declaration process. Non-numeric variables are not initialized by default. Programmers can initialize any variable using assignment statements after it has been declared.

We have seen that assignment statements perform the task to the right of the assignment operator (=) and place the result in the variable to the left of the assignment operator.

As long as the variable on the left is of the same data type as the value on the right, assignment can take place. The result of assigning a value to a variable is shown in Figure 2-4.

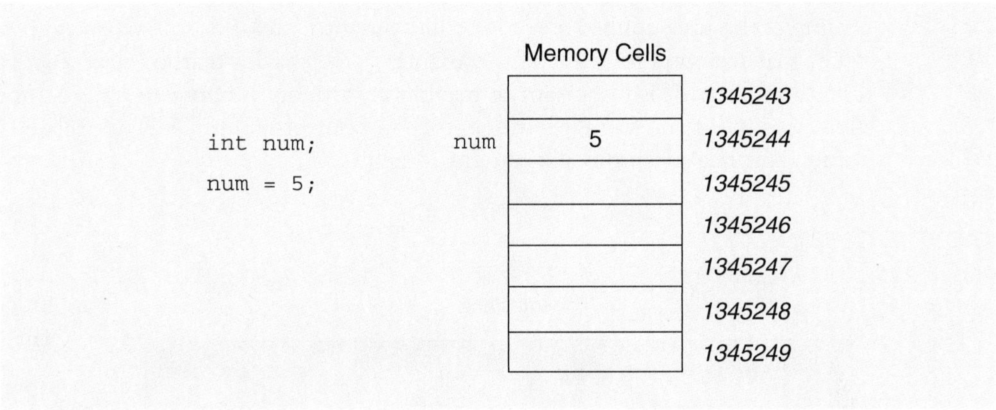

	Memory Cells	
		1345243
num	5	1345244
		1345245
		1345246
		1345247
		1345248
		1345249

```
int num;

num = 5;
```

FIGURE 2-4 The result of assignment

The declarations in Example 2-4 show how a programmer might initialize variables, as they are declared, using an assignment operation.

EXAMPLE 2-4

```
bool female = false;
char middle_initial = 'S';
int age = 20;
float average = 98.6;
double gpa = 3.42;
```

In Example 2-5, two integer variables, num1 and num2, are declared. The default initialization of num1 to 0 takes place automatically, while num2 is explicitly initialized to 5 in the same declaration.

EXAMPLE 2-5

```
int num1, num2  = 5;
```

We have now seen how to declare variables of differing data types and initialize them using assignment statements. In the next section, we turn our attention to the process of getting data from controls on the interface and then assigning it to variables within the program.

Data Input

The process of taking data and storing it in a variable is known as reading data into a variable. Reading data is one of the most common tasks a program performs. For example, the user might enter his or her age into a textbox, at which point the program takes that data and stores it in a variable. Note that, a textbox and a variable are two different things. It is important to be able to distinguish between objects on the interface (like a textbox) and variables in memory in your program. They are related, but not the same. This relationship is illustrated in Figure 2-5.

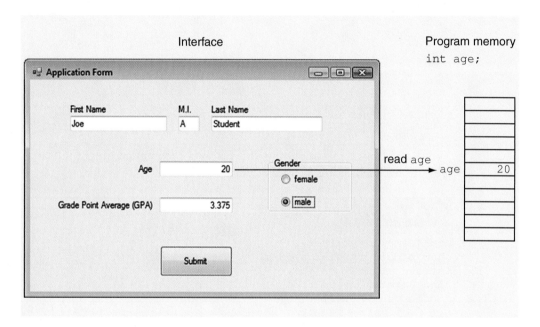

FIGURE 2-5   Reading data from an interface control into a memory variable

Remember that anything a user enters into a textbox is placed in its **Text** property. The **Text** property only accepts character strings. In the interface shown in Figure 2-5, the user has entered an age of 20 into a textbox on the interface. This looks like a number, but, in fact, it is a string of characters. In this case, it is really the string **"20"**. The string **"20"** is not a number at all, in the same way that **"Hello World!"** is not a number.

This underscores a problem with using the textbox control. Because everything entered in a textbox becomes a string, program need a tool to examine strings and determine if they contain only numeric characters, as is the case with the age entered in Figure 2-5. If so, then this tool should also convert the string to a number. In this case, it should convert the string **"20"** to the number 20. In the next section, you learn about how this can be done.

The `TryParse()` Method

The programmer's tool that can convert strings to numbers is the `TryParse()` method, which can be used to read data from a text string by parsing it. **Parsing** is the process by which a program examines a string of text to identify meaningful items. Suppose a textbox in a program interface contains a string of characters entered by the user. `TryParse()` can then examine (parse) the string to see if its contents are meaningful as data of another type, such as an integer. If so, then `TryParse()` can create the new data value and store it in a variable that you designate.

Examine the code shown in Example 2-6. An integer variable called `age` is declared in it. Remember that when an integer is declared, it is automatically initialized to 0 as part of that process. `TryParse()` parses the contents of a string (`textBox1->Text`) and determines if it can be converted to an integer. If it can, then `TryParse()` puts that converted integer value into `age`. If it cannot be successfully parsed, then `age` is not altered and remains 0.

EXAMPLE 2-6

```
int age;
Int32::TryParse(textBox1->Text, age);
```

The second line of this code contains several items that are unfamiliar to you. Take a moment to study it. The structure of this line is important, because you will use it repeatedly as you create Visual C++ applications. `Int32`, at the beginning of the second line, refers to the type of data (a 32-bit integer) you want to obtain from `textBox1->Text` and store in the variable named `age`.

The two colons `::` following `Int32` are called the **scope resolution operator**. **Scope** generally refers to the program unit in which an attribute or method exists. Scope resolution operators are used whenever there is a need to indicate that a method belongs to a particular class. As we shall see, there are many versions of `TryParse()` in the Visual C++ language. In this case, the scope resolution operator helps the compiler resolve any ambiguity by indicating that `TryParse()` belongs to (that is, falls within the scope of) the `Int32` class. We want `TryParse()` to try and parse a string and get a 32-bit integer out of it.

Following the scope resolution operator, we come to the method itself. In C++ code, a method call consists of the name of the method—in this case, `TryParse()`—followed by parentheses containing the information, or **parameters**, the method needs to do its work. The information in the parentheses is known as a **parameter list**. Parameter lists are always enclosed in parentheses, with commas separating the various parameters. `TryParse()` has two parameters. The first is the string to be parsed and the second is the variable into which the result should be put if conversion to an integer is possible. The parameters are shown in Figure 2-6.

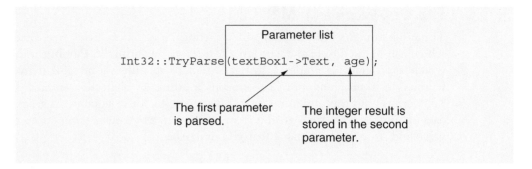

FIGURE 2-6 The `TryParse()` method

C++ provides a `TryParse()` method for every numeric data type. If `textBox1` contained a real number (that is, a float or a double), then `TryParse()` is used in a manner similar to the `Int32` version. In this Example 2-7, `temperature` is declared to be a double and read from the `Text` property of a textbox.

EXAMPLE 2-7

```
double temperature;
Double::TryParse(textBox1->Text, temperature);
```

Now that you are familiar with the primitive data types, and know how to declare variables and initialize them, the next concern is what to do with them. Much of this book will focus on how to process data to solve problems. We will start with one common use of numeric data—performing arithmetic operations.

Arithmetic Operations

An **arithmetic operator** is a symbol that stands for an arithmetic operation. Table 2-4 lists those that are available in the C++ language and provides examples of how they are used. All arithmetic operators are positioned between two items of numeric data, called **operands**. Together an operator and its operands make up a simple **arithmetic expression**.

TABLE 2-4 Arithmetic Operators

Operator	Name	Example
*	Multiplication	`x = 17 * 4;` x is set to 68
/	Division (real)	`x = 17.0 / 4;` x is set to 4.25
/	Division (integer)	`x = 17 / 4;` x is set to 4 (4 goes into 17 4 times, the decimal remainder is dropped). Both operands must be integers.

TABLE 2-4 Arithmetic Operators (continued)

Operator	Name	Example
%	Modulus (Mod)	x = 17 % 4; x is set to 1 (the integer remainder from the division of one integer by another—integer division)
+	Addition	x = 17 + 4; x is set to 21
−	Subtraction	x = 17 − 4; x is set to 13

For example, in the expression below, the operands are the values 4 and 5.

4 + 5

Variables may also be operands as in Example 2-7:

EXAMPLE 2-7

num1 + num2

The result of an arithmetic expression can be assigned to a variable in a complete C++ statement, as shown in Example 2-8:

EXAMPLE 2-8

sum = num1 + num2;

All arithmetic operators require two operands. For this reason, arithmetic operators are considered **binary operators**. Another important fact about arithmetic expressions is that they are always evaluated from left to right. In other words, arithmetic operations are **left to right associative**.

Simple arithmetic operations can sometimes produce code that looks confusing. Take the following example (Example 2-9):

EXAMPLE 2-9

num = num + 1;

The statement makes no sense algebraically; after all, how can a number equal itself + 1? Keep in mind, however, that the = sign is not an equals sign, but an assignment operator. This assignment statement tells the computer to take the value in num, add one to it, and then assign the new result back to the memory cell location to the left of the = operator specified by num. This process is shown in Figure 2-7.

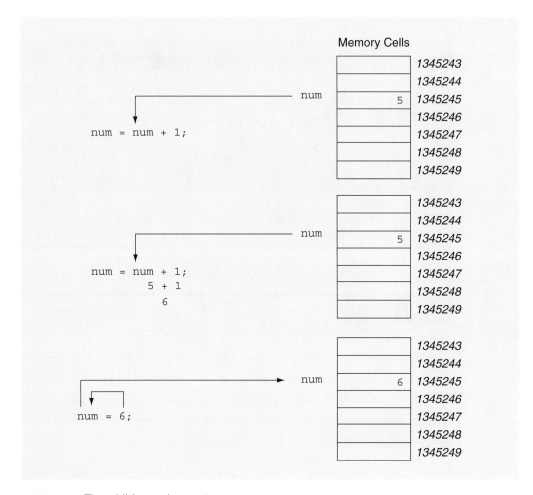

FIGURE 2-7 The addition assignment process

Operator Precedence in Arithmetic Expressions

Operator precedence rules dictate the level of priority an operator has in an expression. In **complex arithmetic expressions** (expressions with multiple operators), the operators with highest precedence are performed first. There are two levels of precedence for arithmetic operators. The **multiplication operator** (*), **division operator** (/), and an operator we shall discuss in more detail in Chapter 3, the **mod operator** (%), occupy the highest level. **Addition** (+) and **subtraction** (-) **operators** are at the lowest level.

Figure 2-8 illustrates the operator precedence in an expression; multiplication goes first in both examples due to its higher precedence level. When the multiplication is completed, the subtraction operation takes place. (Assume that num has been declared to be an integer

2

variable.) An expression tree is used in Figure 2-8 to illustrate this process. An **expression tree** indicates the order of operations with converging diagonal lines indicating the completion of an operation. The converging lines closest to the expression are done first.

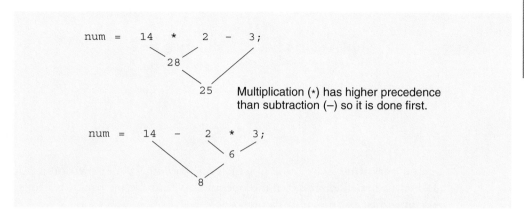

FIGURE 2-8 Expression trees showing order of operations when precedence differs

When operators have the same precedence level, evaluation proceeds from left to right, as shown in Figure 2-9.

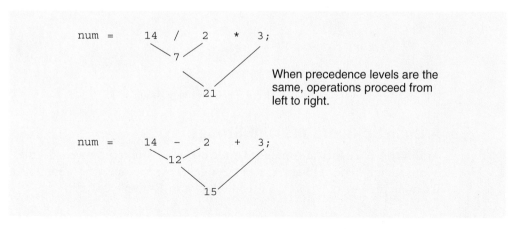

FIGURE 2-9 Expression tree showing left to right associativity when operator precedence is the same

Parentheses can be used to override precedence, however. Operations in parentheses have highest precedence and are always performed before those outside the parentheses, as shown by the examples in Figure 2-10.

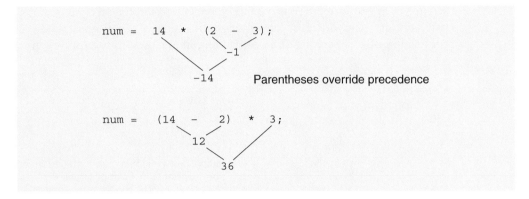

FIGURE 2-10   Expression trees showing the precedence of parenthesized expressions

Nested parentheses are those in which one parenthesized expression is placed inside of another. In nested expressions, the operation within the innermost pair of parentheses is performed first, as shown in Figure 2-11.

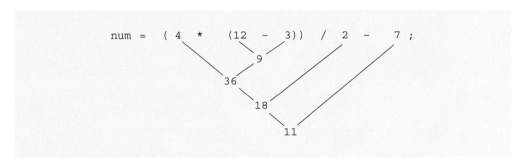

FIGURE 2-11   Expression tree resolving a complex expression

Arithmetic Operators and Strings

Arithmetic operators are intended to work with numeric operands (that is, integers, doubles, and floats). However, it is possible to use the operator (+) with strings as well. Examine the line of Visual C++ code shown in Example 2-10:

EXAMPLE 2-10

```
textBox3->Text = textBox1->Text + textBox2->Text;
```

When two strings serve as operands, the operator (+) takes on a new meaning. In C++, it is common for one operator to stand for different tasks in different circumstances. This is called **operator overloading**. The operator (+) performs addition when its operands are both numeric. However, when both operands are Strings, it takes on a new (overloaded) meaning and joins the two strings together into one. This joining process is carried out by appending the right operand onto the end of the left. This process of joining two strings is called **concatenation** and the overloaded operator (+) is called the **concatenation operator** (+).

To learn more about string concatenation, look at the interface shown in Figure 2-12. The intent of the programmer was to have the user enter integers into **textBox1** and **textBox2**, click the Add button, and see the sum displayed in **textBox3**. The outcome shown was not expected. The sum of the values 12 and 34 is 46, but the result displayed is 1234.

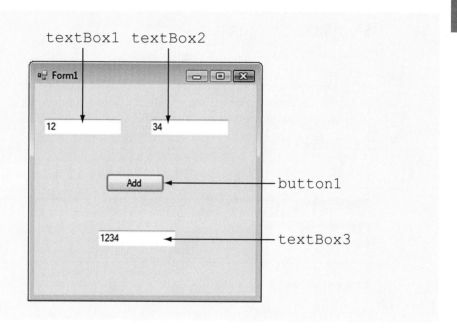

FIGURE 2-12 String concatenation leading to unexpected results in textBox3

This is not the result of some strange mathematical error. Instead, it is the outcome of using the addition operator (+) with strings instead of numbers. The code for the Add button is shown in Example 2-11.

EXAMPLE 2-11

```
private: System::Void button1_Click(System::Object^  sender,
System::EventArgs^  e) {

        textBox3->Text = textBox1->Text + textBox2->Text;
}
```

Notice that the programmer has attempted to add together **textBox1->Text** and **textBox2->Text**. Since the + operator finds itself between operands that are both strings, it concatenates them. The only time that the + operator performs arithmetic addition is when both of its operands are numeric types (for example, **4 + 5**).

This underscores the importance of using `TryParse()` to extract numeric data from strings and store it in numeric variables where arithmetic operations can then be applied. The correct approach would have been for the programmer to declare two integer variables— let's say, `num1` and `num2`. Then, `TryParse()` could be used to store the values from `textBox1->Text` into `num1` and `textBox2->Text` into `num2` as integers. The values in `num1` and `num2` can then be arithmetically added together without difficulty. This is one of the tasks addressed by the Tutorial later in this chapater.

Shorthand Assignment

Some arithmetic operations that involve assignment can be written in a special form that allows you to type them quickly and easily. These abbreviated arithmetic operations are called **shorthand operators**. There is a shorthand operator for each of the standard C++ arithmetic operators. For example, when a value is added to a variable, the shorthand addition assignment operator (+=) may be used. For example:

```
num = num + 1;
```

may be shortened to the statement shown in Example 2-12

EXAMPLE 2-12

```
num += 1;
```

You can use this same shorthand operator with variables and literal values. For example:

```
num1 = num1 + num2;
```

may be shortened to the statement shown in Example 2-13:

EXAMPLE 2-13

```
num1 += num2;
```

There are shorthand assignment operators for all standard arithmetic operations (+=, -=, *=, /=, %=).

In addition, the overloaded operator (+=) is often used with String operands. In such cases, it refers to concatenation, as discussed earlier, and appends the right operand onto the end of the left as shown in Example 2-14

EXAMPLE 2-14

```
textBox1->Text = "Hello ";
textBox1->Text += "World!";
```

Example 2-14 displays the entire phrase "Hello World!" in `textBox1->Text`. The second line of this code uses operator (+=) to concatenate the String `"World!"` onto the String `"Hello "` already stored in `textBox1->Text`.

The Math Library

Arithmetic expressions are often used to represent formulas. However, many common formulas require more than addition, subtraction, multiplication, and division. The **Math library**, part of the `System` namespace, provides a number of common formulas. Among the most useful are the `Math::Pow()` method and the `Math::Sqrt()` method.

For example, consider the Pythagorean formula for calculating the length of the hypotenuse of a right triangle. The sides adjacent to the right angle are called *a* and *b* and the hypotenuse is *c*, as shown in Figure 2-13, along with the formula for calculating the length of side *c*.

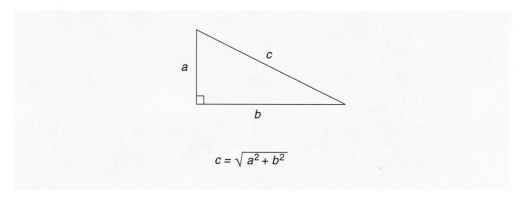

FIGURE 2-13 Sides of a right triangle

The code for this formula uses the `Math::Pow()` method to square the length of sides *a* and *b*, along with `Math::Sqrt()` to calculate the square root.

The `Math::Pow()` method requires two parameters—a value and an exponent. For example, it may be used to find the value 2^3 as shown in Example 2-15.

EXAMPLE 2-15

```
Math::Pow(2,3)
```

The `Math::Sqrt()` method requires only one parameter, real or integer, and produces a result, the square root of the parameter, which is a real number (double). For example, it may be used in the following manner to yield the square root of 45 as shown in Example 2-16.

EXAMPLE 2-16

```
Math::Sqrt(45)
```

The parameters for **Math** methods may be literal values, such as 45, or variables. Example 2-17 below shows a complex arithmetic expression that is the code for the calculation of the length of side *c* using the formula from Figure 2-14.

EXAMPLE 2-17

```
c = Math::Sqrt(Math::Pow(a,2) + Math::Pow(b,2));
```

A list of commonly used Math library methods is provided in Appendix B.

Data Output

Once data processing is complete, the next task is to convey the results back onto the interface. This is generally accomplished by putting them into the **Text** property of a textbox designated to display output. You will recall that to read data from the interface, we took it as a string from the **Text** property of a textbox, converted it to an integer, and stored it in an integer variable. To display an integer, we must reverse the process by converting it to a string and then assigning it to the **Text** property of a textbox. As you will learn in the next section, the **ToString()** method, makes this possible.

The ToString() Method

Converting data to a string is a common task. For this reason, every data type has a built-in method, called **ToString()**, which is designed to handle this conversion. Notice that the parameter list, which must be included when using any method, is empty. Conversion of a variable to a string is accomplished as shown in Example 2-18 for the integer variable **sum**:

EXAMPLE 2-18

```
textBox3->Text = sum.ToString();
```

The **ToString()** method does not change the value stored in **sum**. Instead, it creates a string of numeric characters that look like it. For example, if **sum** contains the integer 46, the **ToString()** method produces the string **"46"**. The string representation can then be displayed in the textbox, as shown in Figure 2-14.

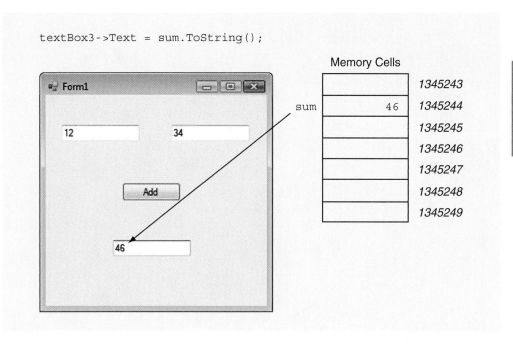

FIGURE 2-14 Displaying a number in a textbox

Tutorial: Addition Program

At this point, you have the programming tools needed to create programs that reads data into variables, process the variables, and display the results. This is an important step forward in the acquisition of programming skills. This tutorial uses the same program design process introduced in Chapter 1 to lead you through the problem analysis, design, development, and testing stages.

Problem Analysis

The task for this tutorial is to construct a simple program to add two numbers and display the result. On the surface, this problem statement seems simple, providing all the information you need to construct the interface and compose an algorithm. However, the problem statement has not specified which kind of numbers to use. Should you use integers, floats, or doubles? The data type of these input values could make a difference and should be decided before you move ahead to the design stage. For the sake of simplicity, we will make all of the data values doubles in this project.

Design

The design stage allows you to determine the specific interface requirements, and the variables that may be required to solve the problem. It also specifies the strategy for the problem's solution and attempts to verify that the strategy is correct before moving ahead to the development stage. You will start with the interface.

INTERFACE

The sketch shown in Figure 2-15 is a rough approximation of what your program will look like. It includes the controls that we identified in the problem-analysis stage.

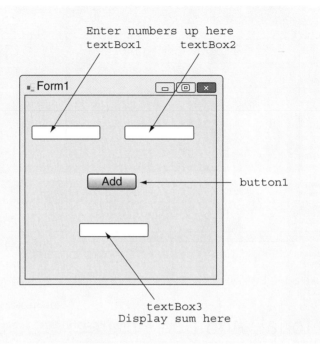

FIGURE 2-15 Addition program interface sketch

Table 2-5 lists each object shown on the interface in Figure 2-15, along with its intended use, and any events for that control that can be foreseen at this time, such as the click event for a button. The Event column is reserved for user interactions, such as clicking a button, which will trigger an event-handler to respond. Thus, the Event column is intentionally left blank for controls that the user will only view or enter data into. Event-handlers are where most of your Visual C++ code writing will take place. For this reason, it is important to identify them early.

TABLE 2-5 Control Table

Usage	Object	Event
Input	textBox1	
	textBox2	
Processing	button1	Click()
Output	textBox3	

DATA TABLE

The interface design tasks provide important clues as to the variables your program will require. For example, it is clear that we need three integer variables—one for the data that comes from textBox1, a second for the data that comes from textBox2, and a third to store the sum of the first two. A **data table** (such as shown in Table 2-6) concisely defines the name, data type, and purpose of each variable. Data tables identify variables that will be used to store information gathered from objects on the interface.

TABLE 2-6 Data Table

Variable Name	Data Type	Purpose
num1	double	Stores the data from textBox1
num2	double	Stores the data from textBox2
sum	double	The sum of num1 and num2

ALGORITHM

Now that you have clearly identified the controls required for the interface and the data required for the processing portion of the program, you can turn your attention to the algorithm for the button's click event. The algorithm is a crucial part of the design stage because it identifies the series of instructions the click event-handler will carry out. The data table in Table 2-6 indicates that three variables are required to solve the problem. For clarity, the algorithm should refer to them. In particular, the first statement in our algorithm should refer to the creation (declaration) of these variables. Thus, the algorithm looks like this:

ALGORITHM 2-2

1. Declare variables (num1, num2, and sum)
2. Read num1
3. Read num2
4. Compute sum
5. Display sum

Development

We have now completed the design portion of this project, and are ready to begin developing the program. As you develop each of the program's components, you can refer back to the interface sketch, data table, and algorithm you created during the design stage. The remainder of this tutorial assumes that you are now familiar with working in the Visual Studio IDE. If necessary, review the Tutorial in Chapter 1 to make sure you understand how to start Visual Studio and add controls to a form.

CREATE THE INTERFACE

Start Visual Studio, as described in Chapter 1, and create a Windows Forms Project named "Addition". Create an interface with three textboxes and one button, similar to the interface sketch in Figure 2-15. In addition, place four Label controls from the Toolbox onto the form, one above each textbox and one at the top of the form, as shown in Figure 2-16.

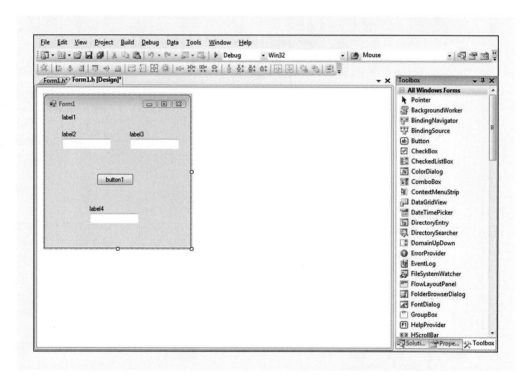

FIGURE 2-16 Interface with label controls

Change the Text properties of each of the interface objects to those shown in Table 2-7.

TABLE 2-7 Text Property Settings

Object	Text Property
Form1	Addition Program
label1	Addition Program
label2	Enter first number

TABLE 2-7 Text Property Settings (continued)

Object	Text Property
`label3`	Enter second number
`label4`	Sum:
`button1`	Add

At this point, the `TextAlign` property of all three textboxes is set to Left (left-justified) by default. This means that anything entered into and displayed by them is aligned at the left side of the textbox. However, in the program you are creating, the textboxes will display numbers, which are generally right-justified (aligned on the right). To change the `TextAlign` property on all three textbox controls to right-justified at once, make `textBox1` the selected object, press and hold the **control key (Ctrl)**, and then select each of the other two textboxes by clicking them once with the mouse. When you are finished, all three textboxes are shown as selected and the Properties window displays the properties they all have in common, as shown in Figure 2-17. At this point you can change the `TextAlign` property for all three controls to right-justified.

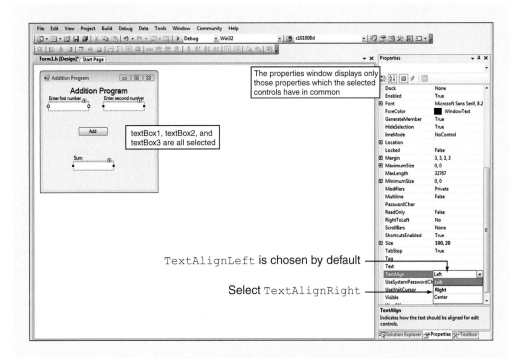

FIGURE 2-17 Multiple control selections and the common Properties window

Next, select `label1` and change its `Font` property so that the size is at least 14. Then, reposition the label so that it is approximately in the center of the top of the form. When your interface design is complete, it should look something like the one shown in Figure 2-18.

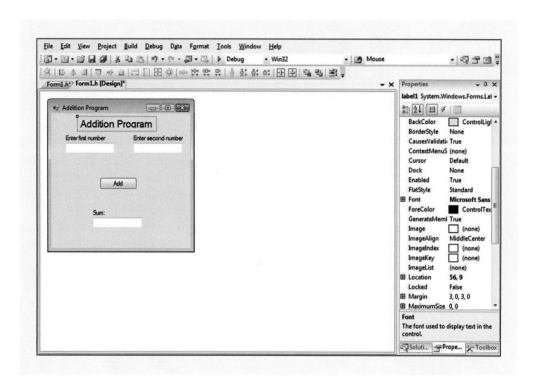

FIGURE 2-18 The `Form1` interface with all textbox and button controls

CODING

The data table identified three variables (`num1`, `num2`, and `sum`) that you will need to declare. It also specifies that they must each have a data type of `double`. Our code must implement each of the steps listed in the algorithm. This means that, first, data is read into `num1` and `num2` from `textBox1->Text` and `textBox2->Text`, respectively, using the `TryParse()` method discussed earlier. The data are then added together and assigned to the variable named `sum`. Finally, a string is created from the value stored in `sum` and displayed in `textBox3->Text`, which displays it on the interface. The correspondence between the algorithm and the code is shown in Figure 2-19.

Algorithm	Visual C++ code
1. Declare variables	`double num1, num2, sum;`
2. Read num1	`Double::TryParse(text1->Text, num1);`
3. Read num2	`Double::TryParse(text2->Text, num2);`
4. Compute sum	`sum = num1 + num2;`
5. Display sum	`textBox3->Text = sum.ToString ();`

FIGURE 2-19 Correspondence between algorithm steps and Visual C++ code

To create the **button1_Click()** event-handler, double-click button1 to go to the Code window and enter the Visual C++ commands shown in Figure 2-19. The result should look like that shown in Figure 2-20, with your Visual C++ code contained within the **button1_Click()** event-handler.

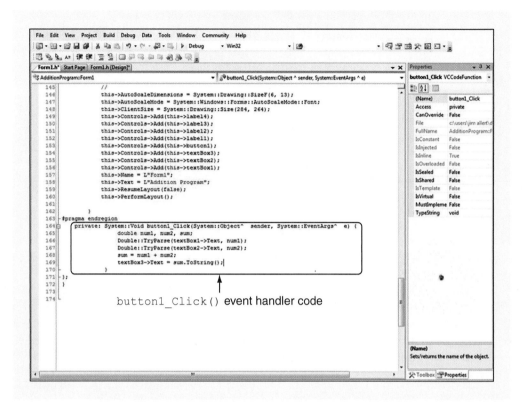

FIGURE 2-20 `button1_Click()` event-handler code

Before you proceed to the testing stage, take a moment to examine the code you have written. If you put this program aside and came back to it in six months or a year, would you know what each of the statements do? Programmers are often faced with the task of revising old programs of their own or even those of other programmers. In both instances, it is important to have some kind of documentation accompanying the code that explains what is going on. Lines of documentation within code are called **comments**. Comments may be placed on a line by themselves or at the end of a finished statement (after the semicolon). They are ignored by the compiler.

There are two ways to comment your code. **Block comments** can run for many lines. They are delimited by the set of characters /* at the beginning and */ at the end. Comment delimiters are identified by the IDE and colored green, along with all of the text between them. **Line comments** begin with the characters // and turn all of the text remaining in a line into a comment. They may be used in a variety of ways: to identify sections of code, provide more information about variables, or explain complex operations.

Add comments to your code, as shown in Figure 2-21.

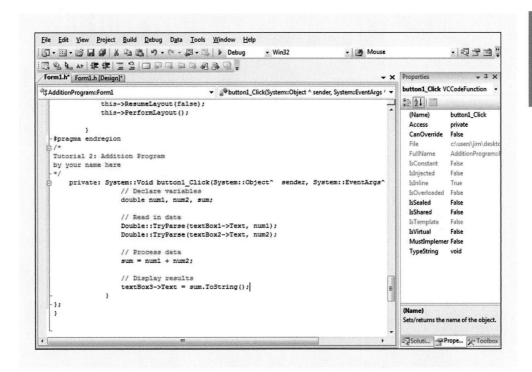

FIGURE 2-21 Commented code

Testing

Run your program. It should work as shown in Figure 2-22. If not, locate the error in the Output window and debug it, as you learned to do in Chapter 1. Make sure your code matches the commented code shown in Figure 2-21 exactly.

FIGURE 2-22 The completed addition program

ON YOUR OWN

You can make a number of modifications to the relatively simple program you have just produced to give it a more user-friendly interface. In the following sections, you will make some useful modifications.

TASK 1: MODIFY THE INTERFACE

Rearrange the controls on the form, resize them, and add more labels to create a more pleasing interface. This is a good time to experiment with the controls and their properties to become more familiar with what you can do. Figure 2-23 shows an improved user interface.

FIGURE 2-23 Improved addition program interface

2

After you are finished, run your program again to make sure that it works. If you make changes to the interface, but find that they do not show up when you run the program, your program did not recompile. This can happen if you make minor interface changes without modifying the underlying C++ code. To force your program to recompile, go to the Build menu and select Build Solution, or Rebuild Solution, and then run the program again, as shown in Figure 2-24.

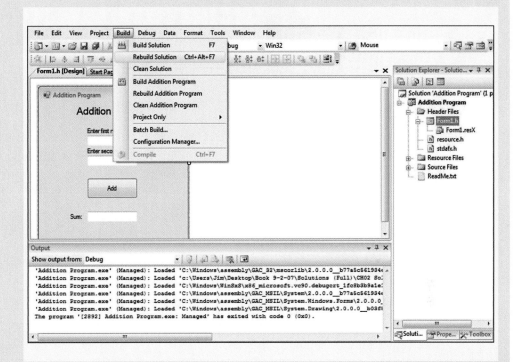

FIGURE 2-24 Rebuilding the project

TASK 2: ADD MORE OPERATIONS (–, *, /)

You have successfully created a program that adds two numbers (using the `double` data type). Now, you can add more buttons to this program to handle other arithmetic operations. Place three more buttons on the form, as shown in Figure 2-25.

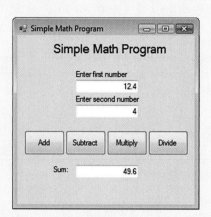

FIGURE 2-25 Multiple button version of program

One of the additional buttons should handle subtraction (–), another multiplication (*), and the final one the **integer division operator (/)**. Create the event-handlers required to perform each arithmetic task. You should avoid dividing by 0, of course, unless you want further experience with the debugger.

QUICK REVIEW

1. An algorithm is an ordered list of steps used to solve a problem.
2. Pseudocode is the abbreviated form of English used to write algorithms.
3. Algorithms are intended to be computer language-independent (not written in C++).
4. High-level algorithms describe a solution in general terms.
5. A high-level solution for many problems has three steps (that is, read data, process data, and display results)
6. Low-level algorithms give detailed problem-solving information.
7. Data is unprocessed information.
8. Data is represented in the computer using binary digits, called bits.
9. A collection of eight bits is called a byte.
10. The primitive C++ data types introduced in this chapter are Boolean, character, integer, float, and double.
11. The keywords for the primitive C++ data types are `bool`, `char`, `int`, `float`, and `double`.

2

12. Boolean data (`bool`) stores the values true and false.

13. Character data (`char`) stores individual characters.

14. Character codes are defined by the Unicode standards.

15. The English character subset of Unicode is called ASCII.

16. Integer data stores positive and negative whole numbers and zero.

17. Real numbers are stored as `float` or `double`.

18. The `double` data type uses twice the amount of memory as a `float`.

19. Derived types are constructed from primitive ones.

20. The Visual C++ language provides a derived type, called `String`.

21. Derived type names are not C++ keywords.

22. The `String` data type is derived from the character data type.

23. A variable is a named location in memory with an associated data type.

24. Variable declarations allocate memory, assign it a name, and associate a data type with it.

25. Variable names should be self-documenting.

26. Variable names must start with a letter or underscore (_).

27. Variable names may not include spaces or punctuation marks.

28. The first character in a variable name must be a letter; the remainder of the name can include letters, digits, or underscores.

29. Case matters when variables names are used in C++ code.

30. Initialization refers to the process of assigning a value to a variable for the first time.

31. By default, integers, floats, and doubles are automatically initialized to 0 when declared.

32. Variables may be initialized with assignment statements.

33. The System namespace contains libraries of methods unique to each data type.

34. `Int32` is the name of a library of integer-related methods.

35. Data is read into variables from textboxes using the `TryParse()` method.

36. Parsing examines a string of characters looking for a specified meaningful item (such as a string that would make sense if turned into an integer).

37. Parsing methods, such as `TryParse()`, use parameter lists to specify the data they require.

38. The first parameter in the `TryParse()` method identifies the string to be parsed.

39. The second parameter in the `TryParse()` method identifies the variable to be updated if the parse is successful.

40. If the `TryParse()` method is unable to parse a string, then it does not change the second parameter.

41. There are five arithmetic operators: * (multiplication), / (division), % (mod), + (addition), and − (subtraction).

42. The arithmetic operators are all binary (that is, require two operands).

43. The arithmetic operators are all left to right associative.

44. An overloaded operator is one that performs differently with data of different types.

45. An arithmetic expression consists of an arithmetic operator surrounded by two numeric operands. For example: (num1 + num2, or 4 + 5)

46. If there are more than two arithmetic operators in an expression, they are processed according to their precedence level.

47. Multiplication, division, and mod have precedence over addition and subtraction.

48. If operators in an expression have the same precedence, then they are processed from left to right.

49. Parentheses may be used to override precedence rules.

50. Expression trees may be used to diagram the order of operations in a complex arithmetic expression.

51. Parentheses may be used to group operations in an arithmetic expression.

52. Parentheses may be nested within each other.

53. Operations in parentheses are performed before operations outside of them.

54. If parentheses are nested, then evaluation of the expression starts with the innermost set.

55. Strings may be joined together through a process known as concatenation.

56. The string concatenation operator is +.

57. The addition operator (+) is overloaded to either add numbers or concatenate strings.

58. Shorthand operators simplify arithmetic operations that update a variable.

59. The Math library, within the System namespace, contains methods that perform commonly used mathematical tasks.

60. The `Math::Pow()` method is used to raise a value to a specified power.

61. The `Math::Sqrt()` method is used to find the square root of a number.

62. To display numeric output in the **Text** property of a textbox, the data must be converted to the String data type.

63. The `ToString()` method performs a temporary conversion of numeric data.

64. A control table is used to identify the controls in an interface sketch.

65. A data table is used to identify the variables required by a program.

66. Pseudocode refers to the variables identified in the data table.

67. Text in textboxes is automatically left justified.

68. The `TextAlign` property of a textbox is used to right-justify or center text.

69. To make multiple objects active at one time, select them one at a time while holding down the Ctrl (control) key.

70. When multiple objects are active, only the properties they have in common are shown in the Properties window.

71. There are two styles of comments: block style and line comments.

72. Block comments, which may stretch for many lines, are surrounded by the delimiters `/* ... */`.

73. Line comments must appear on a line of their own, or at the end of a line, and begin with the characters `//`.

TERMS TO KNOW

addition operator (+)
algorithm
American Standard Code for Information Interchange (ASCII)
arithmetic expression
arithmetic operator
binary operator(s)
bit
block comments
`bool`
Boolean data type
byte
`char`
character data type
comments
complex arithmetic expression(s)
concatenation
concatenation operator (+=)
control key (Ctrl)
data
data table
data type
declare
derived data type
division operator (/)

```
double
```
double data type
double-precision numbers
expression tree
```
float
```
float data type
high-level algorithm
initialization
```
int
```
```
Int32
```
int data type
integer data
integer division operator (/)
language-independent
left to right associative
line comments
low-level algorithm
Math library
```
Math::Pow();
```
```
Math::Sqrt();
```
memory cell
memory cell address
mod operator (%)
multiplication operator (*)
nested parentheses
operand(s)
operator overloading
operator precedence
parameter(s)
parameter list
parse(ing)
primitive data types
pseudocode
real number
scope
scope resolution operator (::)

shorthand addition assignment operator (+=)
single-precision numbers
subtraction operator (–)
string
`String`
String data type
`System` **namespace**
`ToString()` **method**
`TryParse()` **method**
Unicode
variable
variable declaration
variable declaration statement

EXERCISES

1. A group of eight bits is called _____.

   a. a word of memory

   b. a pixel

   c. a byte

   d. a character

   e. a bitmap

2. A character variable (`char`) is stored in _____.

   a. 8 bits

   b. 16 bits

   c. 32 bits

   d. 64 bits

   e. none of the above

3. An integer (`int`) is stored in _____.

   a. 8 bits

   b. 16 bits

   c. 32 bits

   d. 64 bits

   e. none of the above

4.   A double precision real number (`double`) is stored in _____.

    a.   8 bits

    b.   16 bits

    c.   32 bits

    d.   64 bits

    e.   none of the above

5.   Which of the following is a valid variable name?

    a.   `16bits`

    b.   `first name`

    c.   `!`

    d.   `wind_chill`

    e.   All of these are valid.

6.   Which of the following is *not* a C++ keyword?

    a.   `int`

    b.   `public`

    c.   `zipCode`

    d.   `class`

    e.   `char`

7.   ASCII code (an English subset of Unicode) represents every keyboard character in _____.

    a.   8 bits

    b.   16 bits

    c.   32 bits

    d.   64 bits

    e.   none of the above

Use the following choices for Questions 8-12.

    a.   `textBox2->Text = result.ToString();`

    b.   `int num;`

    c.   `Int32::TryParse(textBox1->Text, num1);`

    d.   `num = num1 + num2;`

    e.   `Declare num;`

8.   Which of the statements is written in pseudocode?

9.   Which of the statements is a C++ variable declaration?

10. Which is an input statement?

11. Which statement would be used to display output?

12. Which is a C++ assignment statement?

2

13. When a variable is declared _____.

   a. space is allocated in memory for the variable

   b. a data type is associated with that space

   c. a name is associated with that space

   d. all of the above

Refer to the program interface shown in Figure 2-26 for Questions 14 and 15.

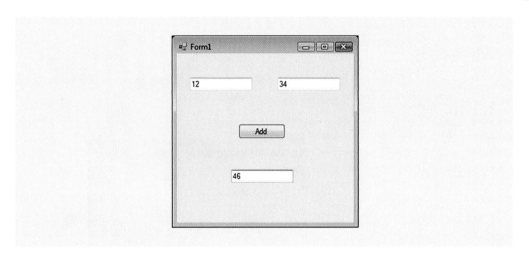

FIGURE 2-26 Form1 program interface

14. To right-justify the text in the textboxes, which property should be changed?

   a. `TextAlign`

   b. `Right-Justify`

   c. `Left-Justify`

   d. `Add`

15. To make all three textboxes active, click each textbox one by one while holding down the _____ key.

   a. Alt

   b. Enter

   c. +

   d. Ctrl

For Questions 16–20, evaluate the expressions by drawing expression trees.

16. 5 + 3 * 6 – 3

17. (5 + 7) / 2 + 6

18. 5 + 3 * (2 – (6 – 3))

19. 24 / 6 / 2

20. 24 / (6 / 2)

PROGRAMMING EXERCISES

1. Hypotenuse Calculator

Create a project with an interface, similar to the one shown in Figure 2-27, that calculates the length of the hypotenuse of a right triangle. The user should enter the length of the two sides (*a* and *b*) adjacent to the right angle.

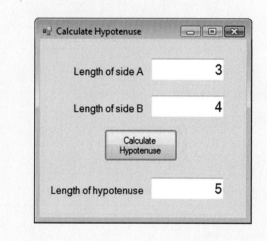

FIGURE 2-27 Hypotenuse program

2. Area Calculator

Create a project, with an interface similar to the one shown in Figure 2-28, that calculates the area of certain geometric shapes. The user should enter the length of the base (b) and height (h). Use the following formulas:

Rectangle: *b * h*

Parallelogram: *b * h*

Triangle: *(b * h) / 2*

Cube: *(b * h) * 6*

Pyramid: $(2 * b * h) + b^2$

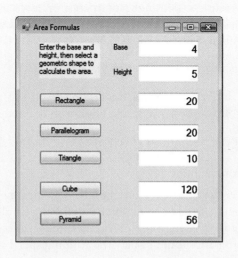

FIGURE 2-28 Area Formulas interface

3. Interest Calculator

Create a project, with an interface similar to the one shown in Figure 2-29, that calculates the value of an investment given the initial principal, annual rate of interest, and term of the investment (in years). Before using the rate value in a calculation, your program should take the rate value entered by the user and convert it to a percentage by dividing it by 100.

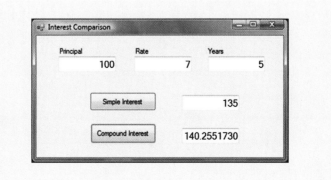

FIGURE 2-29 Interest comparison

The program should allow the user to compare the value of the investment based on both a simple interest calculation and a compound interest calculation. Simple interest means that your investment does not pay interest on anything but the initial principal. In other words, it does not pay interest on previously earned interest. The formula for the simple interest calculation is:

principal with simple interest $=$ *principal * (1 + [years * rate])*

Compound interest calculates interest on both the principal and any interest that has accumulated from previous years. The formula for the compound interest calculation is:

principal with compound interest $=$ *principal * (1 + rate)^{years}*

4. Runners Calculator

Design and create your own program to help a runner calculate speed in miles per hour. The user should be able to enter the number of miles run (for example, a marathon is 26.2 miles) and finishing time in minutes (for example, 221 minutes). In response to this input, the program should display the running speed in minutes per mile (that is, minutes divided by miles).

5. Grade Percentages

A computer science class has exams and assignments totaling 550 points. There are three exams (100 points each) and various projects (adding up to a possible total of 250 points). Grades are assigned based on the student's percentage of total points. Write a program that allows the user to enter his or her three exam scores and the total points received for all projects and calculate their percentage of total points. The program should not display the user's grade, just the percentage of total points.

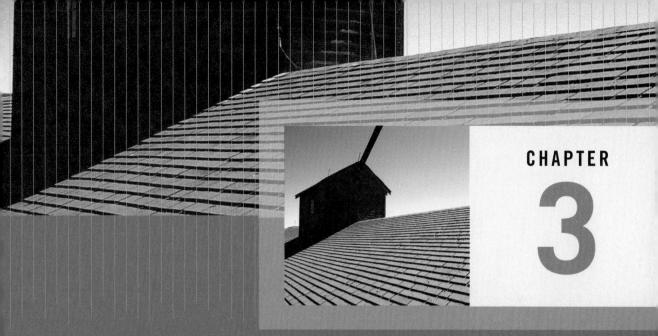

INTEGRAL DATA

IN THIS CHAPTER, YOU WILL:

- Learn about the binary representation of integers
- Discover similarities between integer and character data
- Learn about methods for converting data from one type to another
- Become familiar with integer division and its uses
- Learn to use the mod operator (%)
- Use the mod operator (%) and integer division to convert a character to its binary representation

In Chapter 2, you learned how to declare variables and write code that accepts data from the interface, processes the data, and displays output. You also learned how to write code for simple arithmetic expressions using addition, subtraction, multiplication, and division. The Chapter 2 tutorial focused on real numbers. In this chapter, the focus turns to data types related to integers (that is, integral data types). You will gain a deeper knowledge of the way binary numbers are used to represent data values in a program. You will also examine the strong ties between character and integer data, and use the unique integer arithmetic operators, integer division and mod, to construct the representation of a binary number from an integer.

The Binary Number System

There are ten digits (0–9) in the **decimal number system** (also known as the **base 10 number system**, or simply **base 10**). We are familiar with the use of these digits as place values in decimal numbers. For example, we interpret the number 65 as six groups of ten and five groups of one. Each place represents a power of ten and each place value represents how many there are. Figure 3-1 illustrates this concept.

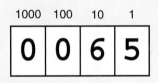

FIGURE 3-1 Decimal (base-10) representation of the number 65

As we have seen, all data is represented in binary form in the computer's memory using only two digits (0 and 1). In the **binary number system** (also known as the **base 2 number system**, or simply **base 2**), each succeeding place increases by a factor of 2, rather than by a factor of 10, as in the base 10 number system. The binary number system and the base 10 number system can each be used to represent the same number, although the number will look quite different in each system. Figure 3-2 shows how the binary number 1000001 (base 2) is interpreted as one group of 64 plus one group of 1 for a total of 65 in base 10.

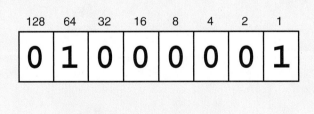

FIGURE 3-2 Binary representation of the decimal integer 65

The number shown in Figure 3-2 is a collection of eight bits, or as we saw in Chapter 2, one byte. The smallest unit of memory to which your computer assigns an address is a single byte; thus, eight-bit numbers are very important. Eight-bit bytes are the building blocks of all data types. Boolean data (represented in C++ code by the keyword `bool`) are stored in one eight-bit byte, even though only one bit is required to represent the value (1 = `true`, 0 = `false`). Standard ASCII character data (represented in C++ code by the keyword `char`) are stored in a single byte, although the extended set of characters (Unicode) requires two or more bytes. Visual C++ data types each have an assigned size designated in bytes. Integer data are stored in either a group of two bytes (`short`) or four bytes (`int` and `long`). Real numbers are stored in either four bytes (`float`) or eight bytes (`double`).

You might be surprised by the range of integers that eight bits can accommodate. If all eight bits are set to 1, the resulting configuration (11111111) corresponds to the decimal number 255 (128 + 64 + 32 + 16 + 8 + 4 + 2 + 1). If all bits are set to 0, the configuration (00000000) corresponds to the number 0. This yields a range of 256 possible values (0–255).

Integral Data Types

We have seen how the decimal integers 0–255 may be represented in binary form in an eight-bit byte. **Integral data types** are those whose binary representations are based on integers. Integral data types include not just the various forms of integers (`short`, `int`, and `long`), but also character (`char`) and Boolean (`bool`) data types. As you know, Boolean data only need to represent two integers (0 and 1), for true or false. Character data can be used to represent any of the standard characters entered from a computer keyboard. However, computers do not really store characters as we know them; they store them as binary numbers. So, as we learned in Chapter 2, each character is assigned an integer value (that is, an ASCII code). For example, the ASCII code for the character 'A' is the decimal number 65, 'B' is 66, 'C' is 67, and so on. The ASCII codes for the most commonly used characters have decimal values 0–127 and are listed in Appendix B.

From the computer's standpoint, a particular configuration of eight bits could be read as a character or an integer, depending on the data type of variable in which it is stored. For example, the first assignment statement shown in Figure 3-3 places the character 'A' into the character variable `myChar`. This means that `myChar` stores the ASCII code of the character 'A', which is the binary number 01000001 (decimal 65). The second assignment statement stores the value 65 in integer variable `num`. This means that `num` also stores the binary number 01000001, although integers are allotted four bytes of storage instead of one for character data.

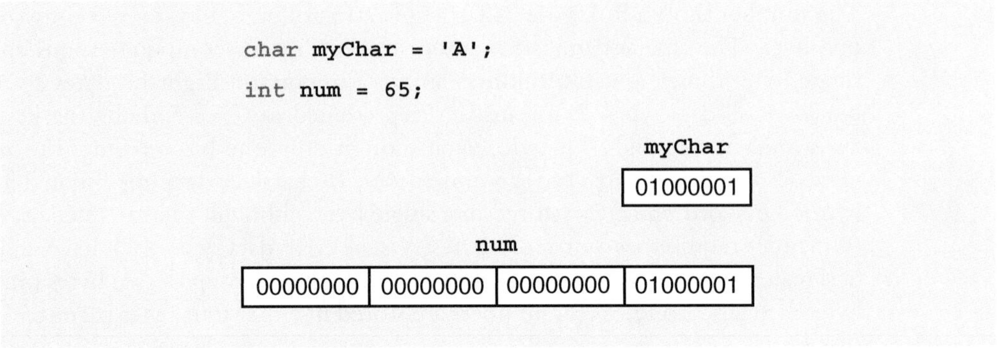

```
char myChar = 'A';

int num = 65;
```

myChar

| 01000001 |

num

| 00000000 | 00000000 | 00000000 | 01000001 |

FIGURE 3-3 Identical bit configurations for `char` and `int` variables

This leads to a very interesting situation. Since character data is a smaller integral data type, it can be used to assign a value to an integer variable. The statements in Example 3-1 are valid C++ code. The character 'A' is assigned to variable `myChar`. The contents of `myChar` are then assigned to integer variable `num`.

EXAMPLE 3-1: ASSIGNING A `char` TO AN `int`

```
char myChar = 'A';
int num = myChar;
```

The result is that the integer variable `num` contains the value 65.

This is because assignment statements simply copy the bits from one variable into another, in a process known as **bitwise copying** as depicted by the arrows in Figure 3-4.

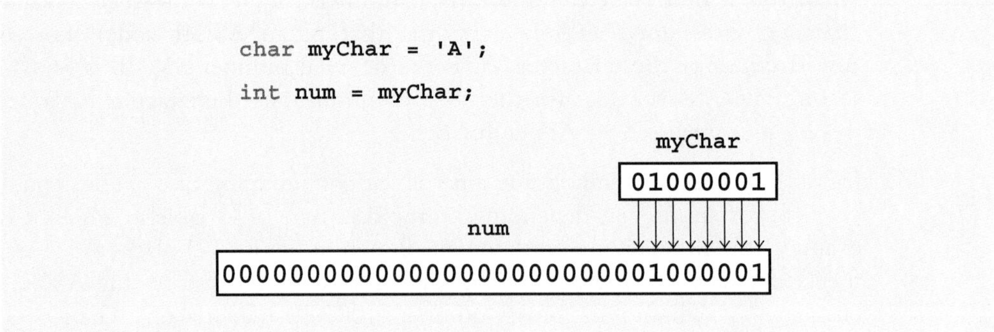

```
char myChar = 'A';

int num = myChar;
```

myChar

| 01000001 |

num

| 00000000000000000000000001000001 |

FIGURE 3-4 Assignment by bitwise copying

We have seen how character data can be assigned to an integer variable. It does not work quite as well the other way around, due to differences in the size (number of bytes) of each data type. Figure 3-5 illustrates this problem. Let us assume that the integer value 321 is assigned to a character variable. The integer is larger than 255 (the largest value that can be represented in ASCII character data using eight bits). It cannot, therefore, be transferred into the character variable using bitwise assignment without data being lost in the process.

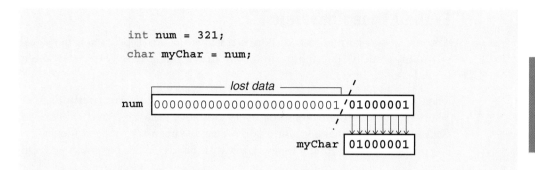

```
int num = 321;
char myChar = num;
```

FIGURE 3-5 Invalid assignment of integer data to a character variable leading to the loss of data

Compilers often warn you of problems like this with a warning message (that is, a **compiler warning**). Compiler warnings will not stop your program from compiling, but indicate that the program may produce incorrect results when it runs.

Data Type Conversion

One of the advantages of having so many data types is that your programs can accommodate a wide variety of values. This makes it possible to solve many types of common problems. However, when different data types interact with one another, incompatibility issues can sometimes arise.

You have already discovered the need to be able to convert values from one data type to another. For example, we have already learned that numeric data must be converted to strings of text before being displayed in a textbox. If this is not done, the compiler will flag the line as a fatal error.

```
int num = 3;
textBox1->Text = num;    // ERROR - Incompatible types
```

The `Text` property of a textbox requires data of the `String` type; no other type will do. Integer data (such as that provided by `num`) is not acceptable. To remedy this situation, the `ToString()` method is used to convert the integer contained in `num` to a `String` for the purpose of displaying it, as shown in Example 3-2.

EXAMPLE 3-2: CONVERTING AN INTEGER TO A String

```
textBox1->Text = num.ToString();   // Compatible types
```

The conversion process does not alter the contents of the variable `num`. Instead, it reads the value stored in `num` and uses it to make a converted value (in this case, a

`String`), which can be processed by the rest of the statement (in this case, assigned to `textBox1->Text`).

Explicit Type Conversion

The use of special methods to convert data from one type to another is called **explicit type conversion**. The most commonly used explicit type conversion method in Visual C++ is `ToString()`.

There are other explicit type conversion methods, called **Convert methods** (see Appendix B). There are `Convert` methods for every primitive data type and the `String` data type. For example, this statement, using `Convert::ToString()`, displays the value stored in `num` in a textbox by converting it to a string of text, just as we did previously in Example 3-2.

```
textBox1->Text = Convert::ToString(num);
```

In the Example 3-3 we have two numeric variables of different data types. The integer variable `intNum` is assigned the value 3. The double-precision variable `dblNum` is then assigned the value stored in `intNum`. The integer in `intNum` is converted to a double, using an explicit `Convert::ToDouble()` method. As a result, `dblNum` will contain the value 3.0 (a double-precision number).

EXAMPLE 3-3: CONVERTING AND int TO A double

```
int intNum = 3;
double dblNum = Convert::ToDouble(intNum);
```

All of the explicit data type conversion examples so far are unique to Visual C++. However, we should also be aware that standard C++ also provides for data type conversion. The data type conversion process used in standard C++ is called **type casting**. Type casting refers to the process of representing one data type as another. Explicit data type casting can be used on all standard C++ primitive data types. Rather than using `Convert` methods, the keyword name of the conversion type is placed in parentheses in front of the variable or value to be converted. In Example 3-4 the value stored in `intNum` is type cast (converted) into a `double` before being assigned to `dblNum`. The result is that `dblNum` contains the double-precision number 3.0.

EXAMPLE 3-4: TYPE CASTING AN int AS A double

```
int intNum = 3;
double dblNum = (double) intNum;
```

Implicit Type Conversion

It would be laborious to have to write explicit conversion statements whenever data types differed in an expression. Thankfully, many conversions from one data type to another take place automatically according to a set of rules that are implicit (built into) in the C++ language. This type of conversion is known as **implicit type conversion**. For example, Example 3-5 produces the same result as example 3-3 without the use of a `Convert()` method. Although the data types of `intNum` and `dblNum` differ, conversion is not a problem. It happens automatically. The variable `dblNum` will end up containing the double-precision number 3.0 because the compiler recognized the data type incompatibility and handled the conversion implicitly.

EXAMPLE 3-5: IMPLICIT TYPE CONVERSION

```
int intNum = 3;
double dblNum = intNum;
```

As long as the original data type (in this case, integer) does not have a larger range of possible values than the data type it is being converted to (in this case, `double`), the conversion process can take place automatically, without any warnings or fatal error messages from the compiler.

The process of converting data to a data type with a larger range of values is called **data type promotion**. It is shown by the arrow on the left-hand side of Figure 3-6 (known as the **data type hierarchy**). In the data type hierarchy, the size of each data type (in bits) is arranged from largest (on top) to smallest (below). The range of values for each data type is also included, so you can see how many values each data type represents. It is safe to convert data from one type to another only if the receiving type has a range of values that equals or exceeds the original.

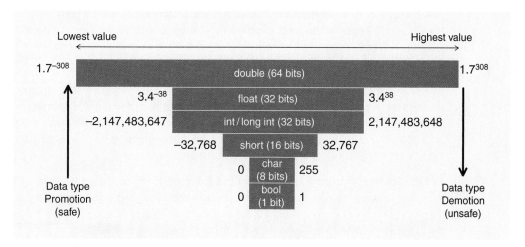

FIGURE 3-6 The data type hierarchy

Data type promotion can be done implicitly because it is not possible for the lower type to represent a value that the higher type cannot. Character data can be promoted to integer or double without difficulty.

The opposite of type promotion, **data type demotion**, is shown by the downward arrow on the right-hand side of Figure 3-6. Data type demotion, which is defined as the process of converting a variable to a data type with a smaller range of values, is inherently unsafe because it may lead to data loss and potentially incorrect results. Figure 3-5, earlier in this chapter, provided an example of such a loss of data.

The complier is always on guard against errors caused by trying to assign a value to a variable with which it is incompatible. Integer operations are especially prone to these situations, especially when division is used. The next section provides several startling examples of how a relatively simple arithmetic task such as division can turn into a data disaster if the programmer is unaware of what is going on.

Integer Arithmetic

In Chapter 2, you learned about arithmetic operators and the process of evaluating arithmetic expressions. For addition, subtraction, and multiplication, arithmetic operations work as you would expect them to. However, integer division (/) and the mod operator (%) are the exception. They are different because they focus on two arithmetic operations that are reserved for integers only. This section provides more detail on how these two integer operations work.

Integer Division

Integer division is the process of dividing one integer by another. The **integer division operator (/)** is the same as the real number division operator (/). The basic rule of integer division is that an integer divided by an integer always yields an integer result; any remainder is truncated. **Truncation** means dropping the fractional remainder, not rounding it.

Let us consider an example. You have just purchased a newspaper at the campus bookstore. The cost was 65 cents. If you give the clerk $1.00, what is the maximum number of quarters you can get back with your change? This is an integer division problem. The total amount of change (35 cents) divided by 25 (the number of cents in a quarter) is 1.4 quarters. Quarters, however, do not come in fractional units. The number of whole times that 25 goes into 35 is 1. Your change will include no more than one quarter. The example illustrates the two types of division: integer and real number division.

Let us look at this from the perspective of C++ code. How can you tell from Example 3-6 whether integer- or real number division is being used? Will `quarters` be set to 1.4 or 1?

EXAMPLE 3-6: DIVISION (AN AMBIGUOUS RESULT)

```
change = 35;
quarters = change / 25;
```

To answer this question, you must know the data types of each variable. If `change` was declared to be a real number (that is, either a `float` or a `double`), then the result of dividing it by 25 will be the value 1.4. However, if change was declared to be an integer, then the result of dividing it by 25 (also an integer) is 1 (integer division). This is because whenever the compiler detects that both the numerator and the denominator of a division process are integers, as in this case, it uses the rules of integer division to perform the operation. The result will be the number of whole times the denominator (25) went into the numerator (35), otherwise known as the **integer quotient**.

We should also consider one other aspect of Example 3-6. What about the data type of the variable quarters? Let us assume that change was declared to be an integer. If quarters had also been declared an integer, then it would be assigned the value 1. If quarters had been declared a double, then it would be assigned the value 1.0, as implicit type conversion would have converted the result of integer division (the integer 1) to the double-precision value 1.0. So, assigning the result of an arithmetic expression to a double-precision variable does not protect against integer division having already truncated data before the assignment took place.

Type conversion helps avoid integer division problems. In Example 3-7, let us assume that the total of 10 integer quiz scores is 478 and is stored in an integer variable called sum. The result assigned to average will be 47.0 not 47.8.

EXAMPLE 3-7: INTEGER DIVISION

```
double average;
int sum = 478;
average = sum / 10;
```

The perils of integer division are evident here. The result was 47.0 (an incorrect average) because both the numerator (sum) and the denominator (10) are integers. The result of the division process will be the integer 47 (10 goes into 478 exactly 47 times with the remainder truncated).

Explicit type conversion is the solution to this problem. It can be used to convert either the numerator or the denominator to a double before the division process takes place. This forces real number division to occur, with the result being the real number 47.8.

The code segment in Example 3-8 illustrates explicit conversion of sum using standard C++ type casting to change the numerator to a double before division takes place.

EXAMPLE 3-8: TYPE CONVERSION OF (int TO double)

```
average = (double) sum / 10;
```

As we shall see, integer division is not all bad. In fact, it has a crucial role to play in solving many arithmetic problems.

The Mod Operator (%)

A complement to the integer division operator (/) is known as the modulus, or **mod operator (%)**. Combined with the mod operator (%), integer division can be a useful tool. As explained in Chapter 2, the mod operator (%) yields the integer remainder from integer division. Figure 3-7 shows the relationship between integer division and the mod operator. Integer division yields the integer quotient, while the mod operation yields the amount left over, as an integer, otherwise known as the **integer remainder**.

Integer quotient   Integer remainder

$$\frac{7}{3} = 2 \text{ remainder } 1$$

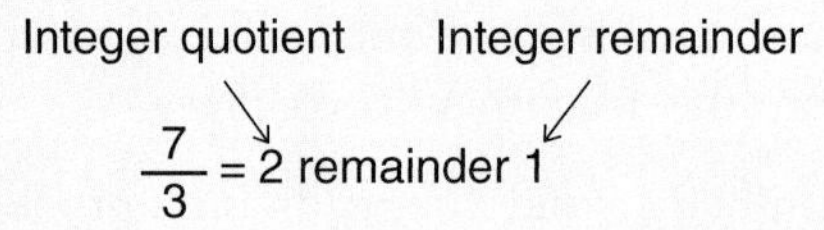

FIGURE 3-7 The relationship between the integer quotient and integer remainder

The expression 7 / 3 is implemented by integer division and yields the integer quotient 2. Using the mod operator, the expression 7 % 3 yields the integer remainder 1. For example, the following statement would assign the value 1 to the variable num:

```
num = 7 % 3;
```

If the denominator goes into the numerator evenly, without a remainder, then the mod operation results in 0 being assigned to num, as shown in this program segment:

```
num = 6 % 3;
```

Let us return to the matter of determining how much change you will receive when purchasing a newspaper, presented at the start of the previous section. You will remember that the cost of the newspaper was 65 cents, for which you paid $1.00. We used integer division to determine the maximum number of quarters that could be returned with your change. You might have been paying special attention to how many quarters you got back because you want to use them to feed a parking meter. The next question, then, is: "After I get my change back and take out the quarters, how much will I have left?" This is answered by the mod operation, as shown in Figure 3-8.

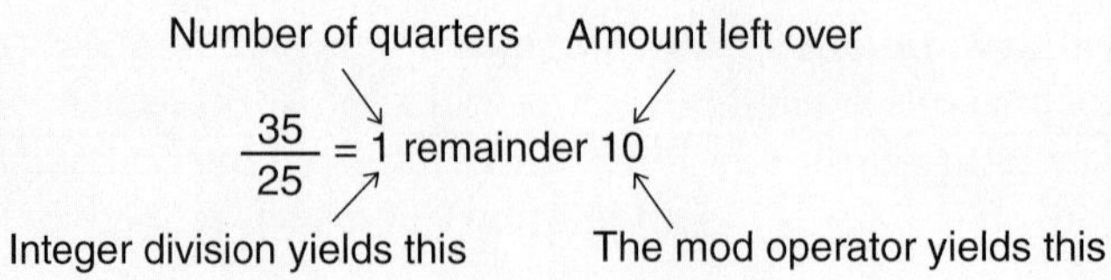

Number of quarters   Amount left over

$$\frac{35}{25} = 1 \text{ remainder } 10$$

Integer division yields this   The mod operator yields this

FIGURE 3-8 Integer division and the mod operator used to calculate change

The remainder from integer division is the specialty of the mod operator (%). In Example 3-9 the mod operator is used to determine the amount left over once quarters have been removed from the change you got back.

3

EXAMPLE 3-9: USING THE MOD OPERATOR (%)

```
int amount;
int change = 35;
amount = change % 25;
```

The denominator 25 goes into the numerator 35 once with 10 left over. The left over remainder (10) is determined by the mod operator (%) and then assigned to the variable amount.

Tutorial: Binary Conversion Program

In this tutorial, you create a program that converts standard ASCII characters into binary numbers. The process involves many of the concepts covered earlier. You will need to use assignment statements that involve both integer division and the mod operator (%), as well as both explicit and implicit type conversion.

Problem Analysis

Construct a project that allows the user to type a keyboard character into a textbox and then see its ASCII code (both in binary and decimal forms) when the Convert button is clicked. The program should look similar to that shown in Figure 3-9.

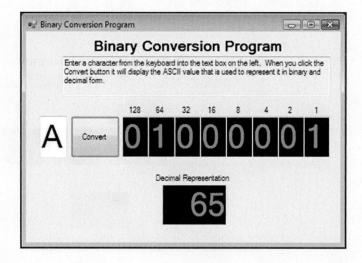

FIGURE 3-9 Binary conversion program

The letter 'A' is represented by the decimal integer 65. To determine the binary version of the decimal 65, integer division and the mod operations are used. Let us take a look at this more closely before we begin. The binary number shown in Figure 3-9 (01000001) is composed of 1 group of 64 and 1 group of 1, for a total of 65. How did the program arrive at this result? Let us look at the process used to determine the left-most binary digit in Figure 3-9. That digit represents the number of groups of 128 that are contained in our number. In other words, how many groups of 128 are there in the integer 65? Using what we know of integer division and the mod operator (%), we discover that 128 goes into 65 zero times with 65 left over, as shown in Figure 3-10.

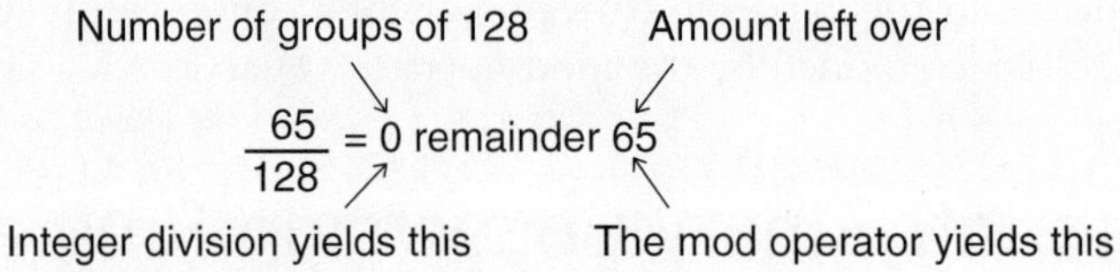

Number of groups of 128   Amount left over

$$\frac{65}{128} = 0 \text{ remainder } 65$$

Integer division yields this   The mod operator yields this

FIGURE 3-10 Integer division and the mod operator for the left-most bit (128)

Integer division tells us that there are 0 groups of 128 in the value 65, and so we assign 0 to the appropriate textbox, as shown in Figure 3-11.

$$\frac{65}{128} = 0 \text{ remainder } 65$$

Integer division yields this result
and puts the result here

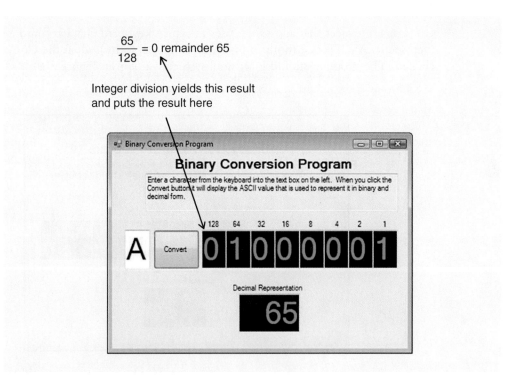

FIGURE 3-11 Displaying the groups of 128

The process continues for the next textbox, the groups of 64, as shown in Figure 3-12. This time, we find that there is exactly one group of 64 in the value 65 and, therefore, assign the value 1 to the appropriate textbox.

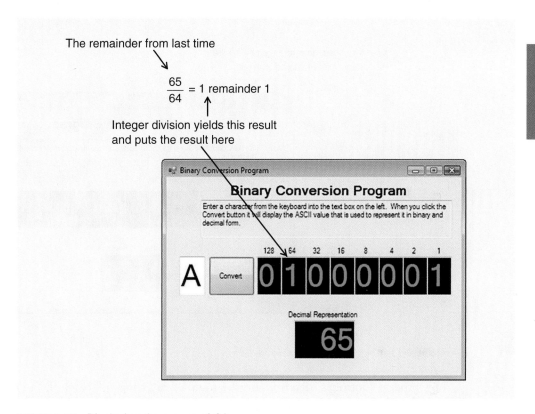

FIGURE 3-12 Displaying the groups of 64

Before proceeding, we need to keep in mind that we are trying to build the binary representation of the decimal 65. By placing a 1 in the second bit from the left, we have just accounted for 64. The remainder (1) is all that is left to account for. Nevertheless, we proceed systematically down the line, looking for groups of 32, then 16, then 8, then 4, then 2, then 1. The next binary digit (groups of 32) is calculated as shown in Figure 3-13.

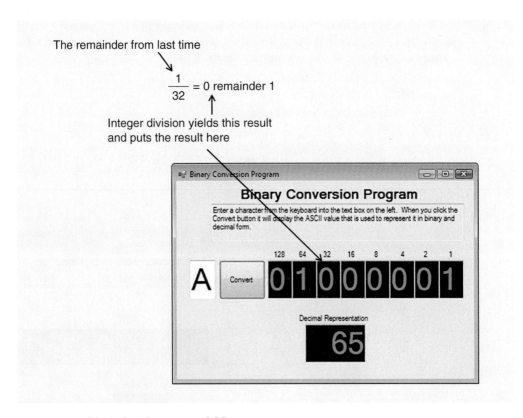

The remainder from last time

$$\frac{1}{32} = 0 \text{ remainder } 1$$

Integer division yields this result
and puts the result here

FIGURE 3-13 Displaying the groups of 32

This process continues, determining the number of groups of 16, 8, 4, 2, and finally 1, until the entire binary sequence has been assigned.

Design

The Design stage of this project is the same as in earlier chapters. First, you must create a rough sketch of the interface, identify the objects and variables required, and write the required algorithms before proceeding to the code development stage. The following sections walk you through these parts of the Design stage.

INTERFACE SKETCH

A preliminary sketch, including labeled controls, is shown in Figure 3-14. Rather than using the default names (for example, `textBox1`, `textBox2`, `button1`, `button2`, `label1`, `label2`, etc.) for your controls, this a good time to adopt the more standard naming conventions used in Visual C++. Controls that play a significant role in your program, such as textboxes and buttons, should have more descriptive names than `textBox1` or `button1`.

The name of a control should start with a three- letter prefix that stands for the control type, followed by a more descriptive name that summarizes the control's purpose. For example, the button in Figure 3-14 is intended to convert a character to binary and decimal form, so the name `btnConvert` is appropriate. Similarly, the user will enter a character into `txtChar` instead of `textBox1`. Its decimal conversion will be displayed in `txtDec` and so on.

We may choose whatever names we want, but the first three letters will always indicate what type of control it is (btn for button, txt for textbox). The interface sketch shown in Figure 3-14 includes a series of textboxes for storing each of the binary digits. The names of the textboxes represent the places in the binary numbering system as shown as `txt128`, `txt64`, `txt32`, and so on. The instructions will be printed in a textbox called `txtInstruct`.

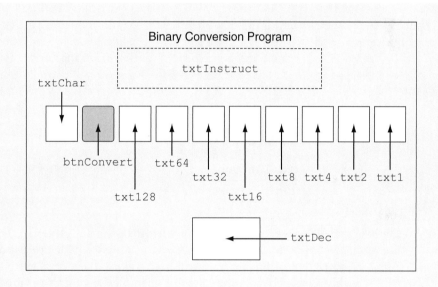

FIGURE 3-14 Preliminary interface sketch

Table 3-1 is a **control table**. It identifies all of the objects used on your program interface to control user interaction. The control table lists how each object will be used in the first column on the left (Usage). The types of usage correspond to the main program tasks discussed in Chapter 2 (for example, data input, processing, and output). Column 2 (Object) identifies the objects associated with each usage category by name. These names are those identified in your interface sketch. The third column (Event) indicates any event-handlers that an object requires. Since the interface provides a button for the user to click, we note that a click event will be required. The fourth column (Description) provides general descriptive information about purpose of the control and any events associated with it.

TABLE 3-1 Control Table Based On Our Interface Sketch

Usage	Object	Event	Description
Input	txtChar		Displays a keyboard character
Processing	btnConvert	Click()	Converts the contents of ASCII txtChar to binary and decimal
Output	txt128		The number of groups of 128
	txt64		The number of groups of 64
	txt32		The number of groups of 32
	txt16		The number of groups of 16
	txt8		The number of groups of 8
	txt4		The number of groups of 4
	txt2		The number of groups of 2
	txt1		The number of groups of 1
	txtDec		Displays the decimal conversion
	txtInstruct		Displays instructions

DATA TABLE

The interface design section focused on what the program's interface will look like. Our attention now turns to designing the way the program will process data. We start by listing the variables that the program will need to keep track of. Table 3-2 lists several that can be readily identified from the initial problem description. Your program will need to read and store the character entered by the user in txtChar. The variable myChar, identified in Table 3-2, will store the character. In addition, the program will need to store the integer number corresponding to the ASCII code of the character stored in myChar. The variable num will perform this task.

TABLE 3-2 Data Table Based On Our Problem Analysis

Variable Name	Data Type	Purpose
myChar	char	Stores the input character from txtChar
num	int	Stores the decimal integer version of myChar

ALGORITHM

Looking back to Table 3-1, all but one of the interface controls are textboxes. The only event-handler we have identified is the click event of btnConvert. Let us start with a preliminary, **high-level algorithm** for that event-handler. A high-level algorithm is one that does not contain much detail. Its purpose is to provide a starting point for problem solving by identifying the main tasks and ordering them, as shown in Algorithm 3-1.

3

ALGORITHM 3-1: HIGH-LEVEL ALGORITHM

1. Declare variables.
2. Read the input data.
3. Process the data.
4. Display the results.

Our goal in algorithm development is to arrive at a solution that is detailed enough to allow a programmer to translate it into code without having to think about the solution strategy.

A detailed algorithm is called a **low-level algorithm**. Low-level algorithms are the result of analyzing what goes on in each step of a high-level algorithm and coming up with an ordered list of subtasks that must be accomplished in that step. The process of analysis and refinement that each step undergoes is called **stepwise development**.

Step 3 of Algorithm 3-1 is where most of the important work gets done. Within this step, your program needs to convert the character from txtChar into an integer (num). The value stored in num can then be displayed in txtDec. Next, determine how many times 128 goes into the value stored in num. When we know this, we can display that value in txt128. We can use the amount left over once the groups of 128 have been removed for the next step, determining how many times 64 goes into it, and display that result in txt64 and so on.

Processing and displaying are woven together here. Step 3 of Algorithm 3-1 may be elaborated as shown in Algorithm 3-2.

ALGORITHM 3-2: PROCESSING A CHARACTER

3. Process the character.
   3.1. Convert the character to a decimal value and store it in num.
   3.2. Display the value stored in num in txtDec.
   3.3. Determine how many times 128 goes into num and display it in txt128.
   3.4. Set num to the amount left over after groups of 128, if any, were removed.

3.5. Determine how many times 64 goes into num and display it in txt64.

3.6. Set num to the amount left over after groups of 64, if any, were removed.

3.7. Determine how many times 32 goes into num and display it in txt32.

3.8. Set num to the amount left over after groups of 32, if any, were removed.

3.9. Determine how many times 16 goes into num and display it in txt16.

3.10. Set num to the amount left over after groups of 16, if any, were removed.

3.11. Determine how many times 8 goes into num and display it in txt8.

3.12. Set num to the amount left over after groups of 8, if any, were removed.

3.13. Determine how many times 4 goes into num and display it in txt4.

3.14. Set num to the amount left over after groups of 4, if any, were removed.

3.15. Determine how many times 2 goes into num and display it in txt2.

3.16. Display the amount left over in txt1 after groups of 2, if any, were removed.

Development

With the interface design finalized, we now turn our attention to its implementation. First, we create the interface, and then we code our algorithm into the event-handler for the Convert button (btnConvert).

CREATE THE INTERFACE

The interface for this project needs more space than previous ones. We need to leave room for a large number of controls. The top of the form will contain a textbox in which the user can enter a character. The corresponding binary representation of its ASCII value is then displayed in eight textboxes, labeled to indicate the value of each digit in binary arithmetic.

To begin, create a new Windows Forms Applications project named "Binary Conversion Program" and resize the form until it is 500 x 350 pixels, as shown in Figure 3-15. Click once on the form to select it, and then locate its **Size property** in the Properties window. The Size property has two values (width and height). Set the Size property to 500 (for width) and 350 (for height).

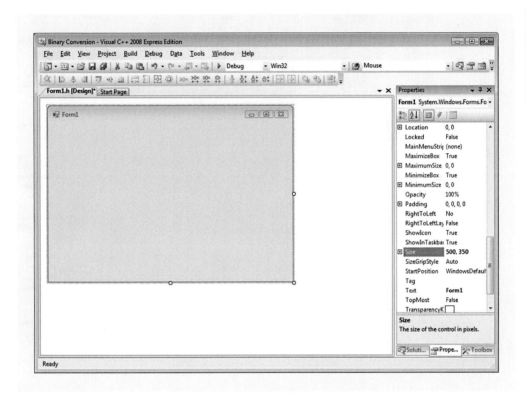

FIGURE 3-15 Form1 size settings set to 500 x 350 pixels

NOTE As you work on creating the interface for your project, you will need to place many controls on the form and reposition them. If you accidentally click twice on the control, the IDE will switch to code view (the code editor window). Do not try to delete any of the code you see in the code editor. To get back to Design view, click the Form1.h[Design] tab at the top of the screen.

Next, you need to place a number of textboxes and labels on the form. Using the Toolbox, create a label and a textbox. Position them approximately as shown in Figure 3-16.

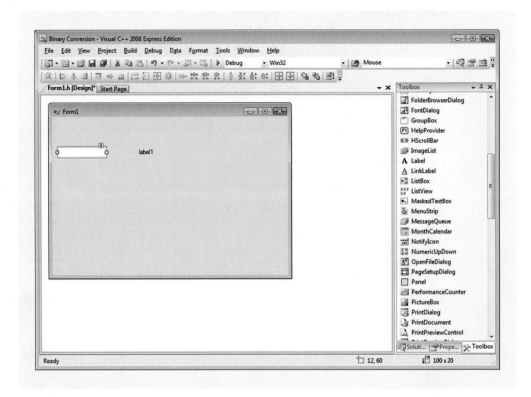

FIGURE 3-16 Placing textboxes and labels onto `Form1`

Make the following changes:

- Change the **Text** property of **Form1** to "Binary Conversion Program".
- Change the **Text** property of **label1** to "Binary Conversion Program" and its **Font** property to Microsoft Sans Serif, Bold, 16.
- Position **label1** so that it is approximately centered, near the top of **Form1**.
- Change the **Font** property of **textBox1** to Microsoft Sans Serif, Bold, 36.
- Change the **Size** property of **textBox1** to 42, 62.

The **Size** property is important. It must be large enough to display any character in the chosen font. If the **Size** is not large enough, your program will work for some characters but, seemingly, not for others.

The resulting interface should look like that shown in Figure 3-17.

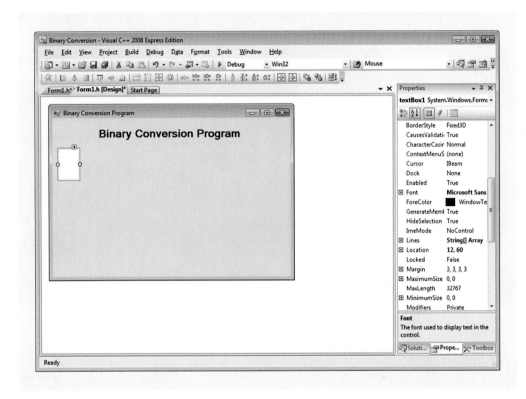

FIGURE 3-17 Binary Conversion Program interface

By default, textboxes can contain up to 32,767 characters. For our purposes, however, we want our textbox to contain only one.

Change the **MaxLength** property of **textBox1** to 1 as shown in Figure 3-18. The **MaxLength property** determines the maximum length of the text string that can be entered into it by the user. Since the intent is to read only one character, this will make sure that no more than one can be entered by the user.

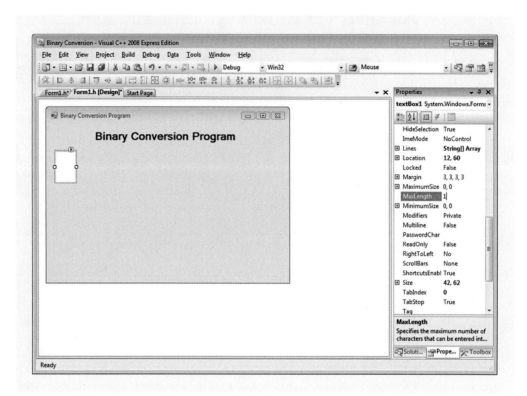

FIGURE 3-18   Changing the MaxLength property to 1

Now, create eight textboxes. Resize them and position them side-by-side in a manner similar to that shown in Figure 3-19.

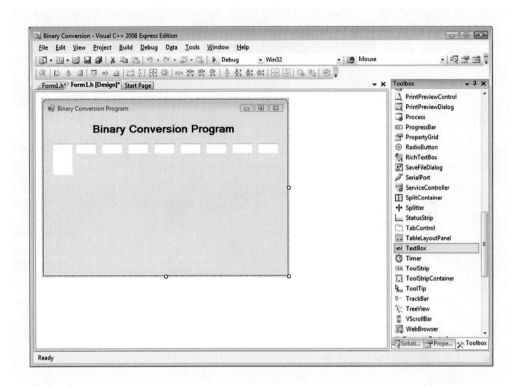

FIGURE 3-19 Placement of eight textboxes on `Form1`

Select all eight textboxes at once by either highlighting the area around them or clicking once on each of them while holding down the Ctrl key. If you choose to use the Ctrl key, it is important that you do not accidentally also select **Form1** as well. When you have finished selecting all eight textboxes, the resizing handles on all eight textboxes will appear as shown in Figure 3-20. The resizing handles on **Form1** should not be present after all eight textboxes have been selected.

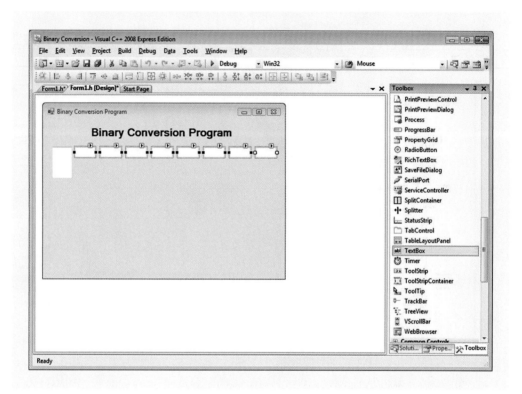

FIGURE 3-20   The selection of all eight textboxes

With all eight textboxes selected, look at the Properties window. It now displays all of the properties that these controls share in common. Any change to a property will affect all eight textboxes.

- Change the **Font** property to Microsoft San Serif, Bold, 36.
- Set the **Size** properties to 42, 62.

When you have finished with these steps, all of your textboxes should be the same size.

NOTE   If you accidentally had **Form1** selected when you made these changes, you will see a dramatic change in your project (**Form1** will shrink down to 42 x 62 pixels). You can go back to the way it was before and work through this step again by clicking Undo under the Edit menu at the top of the screen.

Your textboxes may be somewhat irregularly spaced across the screen. To position them more closely together, you have several options. Select the same eight textboxes again. Then use the **Decrease Horizontal Spacing button** on the toolbar (shown in Figure 3-21) to position them together.

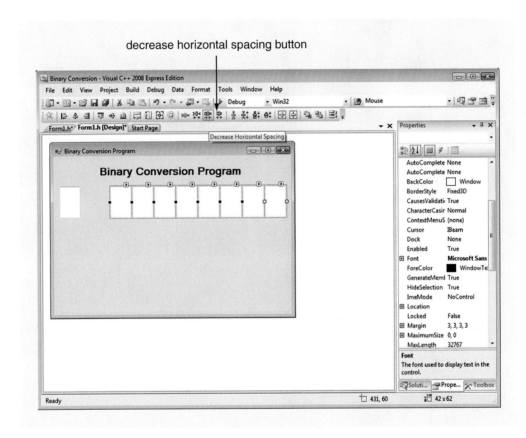

FIGURE 3-21 The toolbar selection to decrease horizontal spacing

Another method of removing horizontal spacing between the textboxes is to select them all and then use the **Format menu**, as shown in Figure 3-22, to remove all of the space between the selected textboxes.

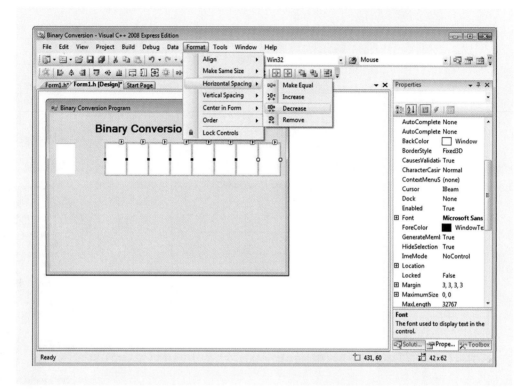

FIGURE 3-22   Removal of horizontal spacing from the Format menu

After removing the horizontal spacing, you are ready to place Label controls above each textbox. Select these from the Toolbox. Change the **Text** property of the labels to the numbers 1, 2, 4, 8, 16, 32, 64, and 128. These numbers represent the various powers of 2 (2^0, 2^1, 2^2, 2^3, 2^4, 2^5, 2^6, 2^7). Arrange the labels similar to those shown selected in Figure 3-23.

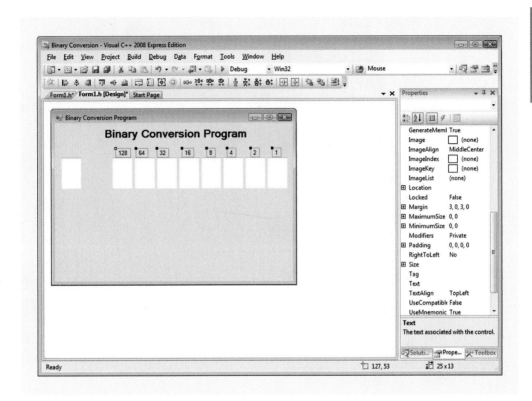

FIGURE 3-23 Arrangement of textbox labels from right to left as increasing powers of 2

Set the following properties of each of the eight textboxes beneath the labels.

- Change the **ReadOnly** property to **True**.
- Set the **BackColor** property to **Black**, or another color you prefer.
- Set the **ForeColor** property to a bright **Lime** green, or another color you prefer.

Figure 3-24 shows the selection of these textboxes. The **ReadOnly textboxes** prevents users from entering data directly into the output boxes. Feel free to experiment with an output color scheme that you think looks best.

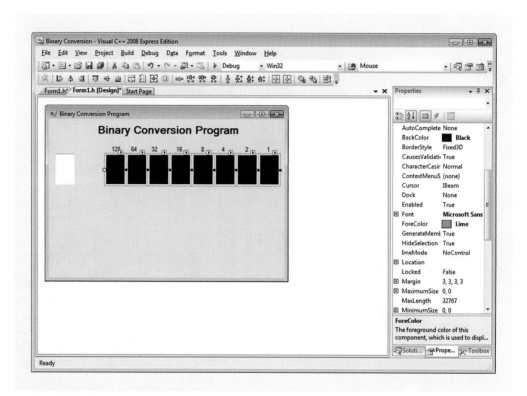

FIGURE 3-24 Setting properties for multiple selected textboxes

Before proceeding further, we need to rename the textboxes. From left to right, change their **Name properties** individually to match the names shown in Figure 3-25. To change the Name property, locate it in the Properties window, enter the name you want, and then hit the Enter key. It may take a few seconds for each renaming task to complete. Don't forget to also change the name of **textbox1**, the first one you created and the furthest one to the left, to **txtChar**. It is easy to accidentally double-click on a textbox while doing this and open the code view window. As noted earlier, if this happens to you, ignore the event-handler you accidentally created do not delete the code, and simply use the **Form1.h[Design]** tab to come back to the design window.

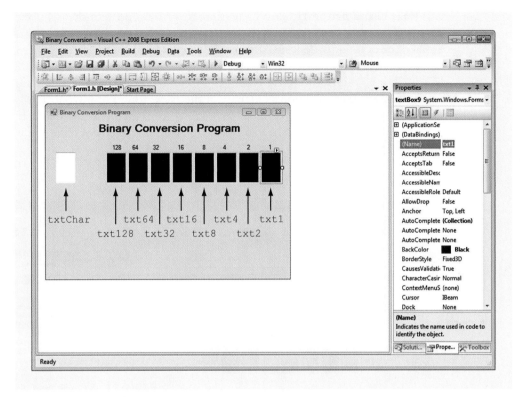

FIGURE 3-25 Textbox names

To complete your interface design, you need to add the following controls to your interface:

- `btnConvert` positioned between `txtChar` and txt128. Set the Text property to "Convert".

- `txtDec`, the `textbox` for your decimal number display. Center it in the lower portion of the interface. Change its `BackColor` property to Black and its `ForeColor` to Lime.

- a label for `txtDec`. Positioned immediately above `txtDec` and set its Text property to "Decimal Representation".

- `txtInstruct`, the instructions `textBox`. Position it immediately below the "Binary Conversion Program" label. You may need to move other controls around to create enough space for it.

Set the following properties for `txtInstruct`:

- Set the `Multiline` property to `True`.

- Set its `ReadOnly` property to `True` (so data cannot be entered in it).

- Change its `BackColor` to `Control` if it is not already set to that value.

- Set the `BorderStyle` to `None`.

The **Multiline property** allows a textbox to accommodate more than one line of text. This will be important when you use `txtInstruct` to display the instructions. The `BackColor` setting to `Control` makes the background color of `txtInstruct` identical to that of `Form1`. The **BorderStyle** property controls the appearance of the boundaries of a textbox. Setting it to `None` turns off any visible border around `txtInstruct`. As a result, `txtInstruct` will look like part of the background of `Form1`. This simplifies the interface by reducing the number of distracting visual elements. Reposition the controls on `Form1` when you are finished so that your final interface looks like the one shown in Figure 3-26.

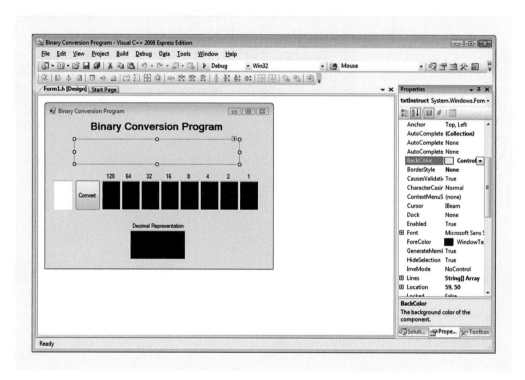

FIGURE 3-26 Changing the `BackColor` property of `txtInstruct` to `Control`

Finally, we should make one additional change to `txtDec`. It will display up to a 3-digit integer, and it should do so in a manner we are familiar with. Numbers are generally displayed right-justified. Text is generally displayed left-justified. The **TextAlign property** allows you to change the justification of text in a textbox. Since the job of `txtDec` is to display a number, its contents should be right-justified.

- Change the `TextAlign` property to `Right`.

A summary of the settings described for the textboxes in this tutorial is given in Table 3–3.

TABLE 3-3 Property Settings for Textboxes

Control	Property	Setting
txtChar	Size	42, 62
	Font	Microsoft San Serif, Bold, 36
	MaxLength	1
txt128, txt64, txt32, txt16, txt8, txt4, txt2, txt1	Size	42, 62
	BackColor	Black
	ForeColor	Lime
	ReadOnly	True
	Font	Microsoft San Serif, Bold, 36
	TextAlign	Right
txtDec	BackColor	Black
	ForeColor	Lime
	ReadOnly	True
	Font	Microsoft San Serif, Bold, 36
txtInstruct	Multiline	True
	BorderStyle	None
	ReadOnly	True
	BackColor	Control

CODING

The next task is to write the Visual C++ code for the event handlers. In Table 3-1 we identified the click event of btnConvert, referred to as btnConvert_Click(), as the place where the data processing will take place. However, there is one other event-handler you may not have been aware of that could come in handy in this project. It is the load event-handler for the form itself. When the program loads and Form1 appears on the screen, the **Form1_Load() event-handler** runs automatically. This event-handler is the perfect location to place assignment statements that make sure the program is properly set up from the start. For example, you may wish to place "0" into all of the binary number textboxes so that this is what the user sees at the start of the program. `Form1_Load()` can be used to initialize controls before the program begins. The `Form1_Load()` event-handler will be an important part of many future tutorials and projects. Future control tables will need to consider this event as well.

CODING THE `Form1_Load()` EVENT HANDLER

To open the `Form1_Load()` event-handler in the code window, make sure you are in the Design window, position the mouse pointer anywhere on the form except on top of any of the textboxes or buttons. Double-click the form itself. This opens the `Form1_Load()` event-handler in the code window. Here, you can initialize textboxes to the characters you want them to display at program startup. In this case, we want to put a space into `txtChar`, zeros into each of the binary digit textboxes, and display the instructions, as shown in Example 3-10.

EXAMPLE 3-10: CODING `Form1_Load()`

```
private: System::Void Form1_Load(System::Object^  sender,
System::EventArgs^  e)
{
    txt1->Text = "0";
    txt2->Text = "0";
    txt4->Text = "0";
    txt8->Text = "0";
    txt16->Text = "0";
    txt32->Text = "0";
    txt64->Text = "0";
    txt128->Text = "0";
    txtChar->Text = " ";   // A single space
    txtInstruct->Text = "Enter a character from the keyboard into the text
box on the left.  When you click the Convert button it will display the
ASCII value that is used to represent it in binary and decimal form.";
}
```

When you have finished the code for `Form1_Load()` as shown, run your program. The eight binary digit textboxes should now each display 0, as shown in Figure 3-27. In addition, `txtChar` is set to highlight only one character and the instructions are displayed in `txtInstruct`.

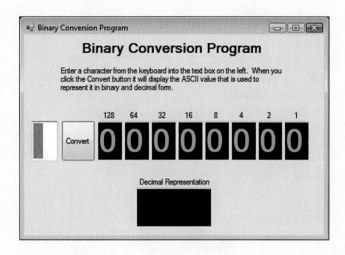

FIGURE 3-27 The initial appearance of `Form1` upon loading

CODING THE CONVERT BUTTON (`btnConvert_Click()`)

Following the algorithm devised earlier for the click event-handler, the first task is to read the character from `txtChar->Text`. To accomplish this, you declare a character variable (`myChar`), as planned back in the data table, and read the contents of `txtChar->Text` into it. It would seem that the following statement should do this; however, it turns out to be an example of data type incompatibility.

```
char myChar = txtChar->Text;  // Incompatible types
```

Variable `myChar` is type `char` and `txtChar->Text` is a string of text. A string of text cannot be demoted to a single character. Fortunately, there is a way to specify that you would like only the first character in a string of text (called character 0) simply by adding "[0]" to the `Text` designator, as shown in Example 3-11.

EXAMPLE 3-11: ASSIGNING THE FIRST CHARACTER

```
char myChar = txtChar->Text[0];  // Assigns first character
```

The first character of `txtChar->Text` is now able to be assigned to `myChar`.

Next, you need to assign the ASCII code for the character in `myChar` to integer variable (`num`). As we saw earlier in this chapter, this process is easy because of the underlying integral nature of both data types. The assignment can be done directly and is shown in Example 3-12.

EXAMPLE 3-12: ASSIGNING A CHARACTER TO AN INTEGER

```
int num = myChar;
```

The value of num is the decimal equivalent of the ASCII character in myChar. If myChar contained the character "A" then num now contains its ASCII code (65). The integer value in num can be immediately displayed on the form as shown in Example 3-13.

EXAMPLE 3-13: DISPLAYING THE BASE-10 INTEGER

```
txtDec->Text = num.ToString();
```

Next, following the steps of the algorithm and using the principles of integer division and mod discussed earlier, divide the value stored in num by 128 (integer division) to determine how many groups of 128 are represented and display this amount in txt128 as shown in Example 3-14.

EXAMPLE 3-14: DISPLAYING GROUPS OF 128

```
txt128->Text = (num / 128).ToString();
```

The amount left over after the groups of 128 have been removed is provided by the mod operator (%) and that remainder should then be reassigned to num as shown in Example 3-15.

EXAMPLE 3-15: REMAINDER AFTER DIVISION BY 128

```
num = num % 128;
```

This process continues down the line with each succeeding place value (64, 32, 16, 8, 4, 2, 1). The code for this process is shown in Example 3-16.

EXAMPLE 3-16: DISPLAYING OTHER PLACE VALUES

```
txt64->Text = (num / 64).ToString();
num = num % 64;
txt32->Text = (num / 32).ToString();
num = num % 32;
txt16->Text = (num / 16).ToString();
num = num % 16;
txt8->Text = (num / 8).ToString();
num = num % 8;
txt4->Text = (num / 4).ToString();
num = num % 4;
txt2->Text = (num / 2).ToString();
txt1->Text = (num % 2).ToString();
```

The process is diagrammed in Figure 3-28. Notice that num starts with the value 65 stored in it. As the program progress through each step, the value in num, shown in its own box, reflects the remainder from the last operation.

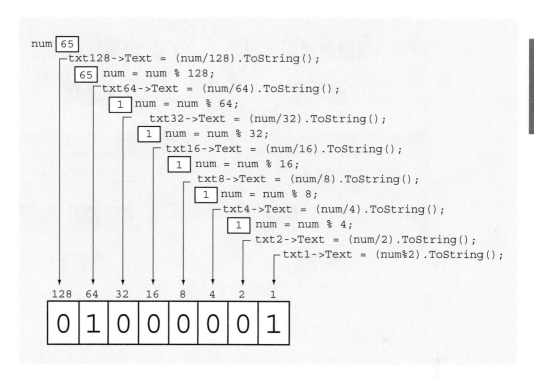

FIGURE 3-28 Construction of the binary representation of the decimal value 65 stored in num

Testing

Try your program with a variety of different characters. You will notice that txtChar cannot contain more than one character, so you will need to backspace, or otherwise delete its current contents before you can enter the next one.

Your project should be able to correctly convert keyboard characters. Demonstrate an upper- and lowercase letter, numeral, and special character, as shown in the examples in Figure 3-29.

FIGURE 3-29 Correct conversion of normal keyboard characters

You can also check the decimal value produced by your program using the ASCII Table in Appendix B.

ON YOUR OWN

1. DEMONSTRATE YOUR UNDERSTANDING

To make sure you have mastered the concepts presented in this chapter, create a diagram similar to that shown in Figure 3-28. Starting with a number other than 65, show what happens to num at each step (shown as boxes next to the code) and by filling in the binary digits as they are calculated. Some values that are especially instructive are 255, 128, and 1.

2. Convert::ToString()

Rewrite your program so that it uses **Convert::ToString** wherever the **ToString()** method was used. It should run just as before.

3. SHORTHAND OPERATORS

Shorthand operators were discussed in Chapter 2. They are used whenever a variable updates itself. Examine your code for situations in which assignment statements are used to update a variable. There are many examples in this program. Change each arithmetic assignment expression to its shorthand version, for example, a statement such as:

```
num = num % 4;
```

can be shortened to:

```
num %= 4;.
```

using the shorthand mod assignment operator (%=).

QUICK REVIEW

1. The decimal (base 10) number system is used to represent numbers with placeholders representing powers of 10.

2. The base 10 number system has 10 digits (0–9).

3. The binary (base 2) number system is used to represent numbers with placeholders representing powers of 2.

4. The base 2 number system has two digits (0 and 1).

5. Any number that can be represented in base 10 can also be represented in base 2, although it will look very different.

6. The smallest unit of addressable memory is a byte (8 bits).

7. Boolean data are represented by a single bit.

8. Character data may be stored in a single byte.

9. Integer data (`int`) is stored in four bytes.

10. Eight bits can represent 256 different values (0–255).

11. Integral data types represent their values by using binary integers.

12. Boolen and character data are integral data types, as of course, are all integers.

13. Characters are assigned integers corresponding to the ASCII specifications.

14. Character data can be assigned directly to an integer variable because it is an integer.

15. The assignment process copies bits one by one from one variable to another.

16. Although characters can be assigned to integers, the reserve is problematic because integers require more bits to be represented than characters.

17. Compilers detect inappropriate assignments between incompatible data types.

18. Data conversion methods help convert data from one type to another.

19. The `ToString()` method is commonly used to convert numeric data to a text string so that it can be displayed in a textbox.

20. Explicit type conversion uses methods such as `ToString()` and the System `Convert` methods to facilitate data type conversion.

21. Conventional C++ uses type casting instead of `Convert` methods to do explicit data conversion.

22. Implicit type conversion automatically promotes data from one type to another.

23. Data type promotion is generally safe and handled implicitly.

24. Data type demotion may lead to a loss of data and may produce a fatal error upon compilation.

25. The data type hierarchy refers to promotion from smaller data types to larger ones.

26. Integer division is not the same as real number division but uses the same operator (/).

27. When division occurs between two integer operands, the result, that is, the integer quotient, is always an integer.

28. Any fractional component from integer division is truncated (that is, dropped).

29. Accidental integer division can be prevented by type-casting the numerator or denominator as a real number.

30. The mod operator (`%`) is used to capture the integer remainder from integer division.

31. The binary number that represents a decimal number can be constructed through a process of integer division and mod.

32. A control table specifies the main control objects used by your program.

33. A data table specifies the variables used by your program.

34. A high-level algorithm is used to provide a general description of the tasks your program must accomplish.

35. A low-level algorithm is a detailed list of instructions.

36. Stepwise refinement is used to transform a high-level algorithm into a low-level one.

37. The number of characters a textbox can contain is controlled by the `MaxLength` property.

38. To select more than one control, hold down the Ctrl key while clicking to select them.

39. The `ReadOnly` property of a textbox can be set to `True` to disallow user interaction.

40. The `Multiline` property of a textbox allows it to contain more than one line.

41. The `Form1_Load()` event-handler executes when your program begins to load into memory and execute.

42. The `Form1_Load()` event-handler can be used to initialize controls.

3

TERMS TO KNOW

base 2 number system (base 2)
base 10 number system (base 10)
binary number system
bitwise copying
`BorderStyle` **property**
compiler warning
control table
`Convert` **methods**
`Convert::ToDouble()`
`Convert::ToString()`
data type hierarchy
data type demotion
data type promotion
decimal number system
Decrease Horizontal Spacing button
explicit type conversion
Format menu
`Form1_Load()` **event-handler**
high-level algorithm
implicit type conversion
integer division
integer division operator (/)
integer quotient
integer remainder
integral data type(s)
low-level algorithm
`MaxLength` **property (textbox)**

Multiline property (textbox)

mod operator (%)

Name property(ies)

ReadOnly property (textbox)

Size property

stepwise development

TextAlign property (textbox)

truncation

type casting

EXERCISES

What is the value of these integer division expressions?

1. 23 / 5
2. 5 / 8
3. 0 / 8

What is the value of these mod (%) expressions?

4. 35 % 7
5. 13 % 13
6. 5 % 8

Translate each of the following integers to its binary (8-bit) representation.

7. 1 5 6
8. 9 3
9. 2 5 5

Translate each of the following binary expressions to decimal (base 10).

10. 0 0 0 0 0 1 1 1
11. 0 1 1 1 0 1 0 0
12. 1 1 0 0 1 1 0 1

Why would the following arithmetic expression be inappropriate?

13. 8 % 0

Which of the following conversions would be considered a data type demotion?:

14. Converting an `int` to a `double`.
15. Converting a `char` to a `double`.
16. Converting an `int` to a `String`.
17. Converting a `char` to an `int`.

18. Converting an `int` to a `char`.

19. Which of the conversions performed above (Questions 14–18) could be done using implicit type conversion?

20. Assuming that the variables `children` and `households` were declared as integers and that `childrenPerHousehold` was declared to be a double, what kind of explicit data type conversion is used in this statement? Why was type conversion necessary?

```
childrenPerHousehold = children / (double) households;
```

PROGRAMMING EXERCISES

1. Demonstrate Integer and Real Number Division

Write a program, with an interface similar to the one shown in Figure 3-30, that demonstrates integer and real number division. The program should allow the user to enter an integer numerator and denominator. When the user clicks the Calculate button, the program should calculate the integer quotient and remainder (using integer division and mod) as well as the result of real number division.

NOTE To produce real number division, you will need to convert either the numerator or the denominator to a real number using `Convert::ToDouble()`.

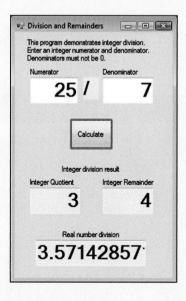

FIGURE 3-30 Integer and real number division program

2. Convert Methods

Create a program with an interface similar to the one shown in Figure 3-31. The user enters a character into the textbox `txtChar`, as in your tutorial, and clicks a Convert button to display the converted result in `txtConvert`. The `BackColor` of `txtConvert` is set to the `BackColor` of the conversion button that was clicked. In this case, the red button (Convert to Integer) was clicked, thus the red `BackColor` of `txtConvert`.

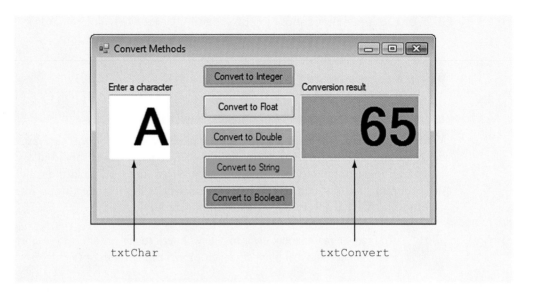

FIGURE 3-31 Conversion program interface

There are five conversions that can take place. Each conversion button implements a different type of conversion. The code for the integer conversion shown in Figure 3-31 is provided in Example 3-17.

EXAMPLE 3-17: CODE FOR `btnToInteger_Click()`

```
private: System::Void btnToInteger_Click(System::Object^  sender,
System::EventArgs^  e) {
    char myChar = txtChar->Text[0];
    int num = Convert::ToInt32(myChar);
    txtConvert->BackColor = Color::LightSalmon;
    txtConvert->Text = num.ToString();
}
```

The four examples (a–d) in Figure 3-32 illustrate the outcome of each of the other conversions.

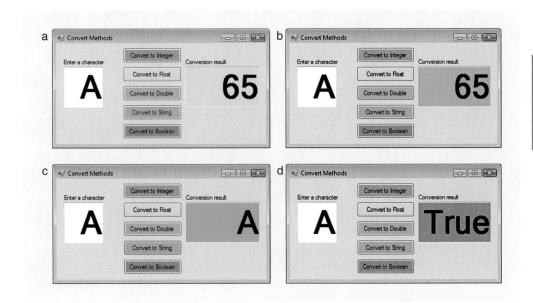

FIGURE 3-32 Conversion results for (a) float, (b) double, (c) String, and (d) Boolean data conversion

`Convert` methods may be used where appropriate for each button. If we assume that the character variable used to store the input character is called `myChar`, then the conversion process for each button proceeds as described below:

- Conversion to an `int`—use `Convert::ToInt32(myChar)`.
- Conversion to a `float`—use `Convert::ToSingle(myChar)`.
- Conversion to a `double`—use `Convert::ToDouble(myChar)`.
- Conversion to a `String`—compare the results you get from these three conversion methods:
  ○ `Convert::ToString(myChar)`
  ○ `myChar.ToString()`
  ○ `Char::ToString(myChar)`
- Conversion to a Boolean value—use `Convert::ToBoolean(myChar)`.

3. Convert Base 10 to Base 2

Create a program with an interface similar to the one shown in Figure 3-33. Converting an integer from base 10 to base 2 can be done using integer division and mod. The base 2 value can then be displayed by changing it to a string as it is assigned to the output textbox.

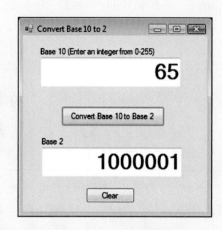

FIGURE 3-33 Program to convert base 10 integers to base 2

Your base 2 number can be constructed as an integer. The lines below declare an integer for the base 10 number and a `long` integer for the base 2 number. This is because the number of places needed to represent a binary value as a base 10 integer is so large.

Examine the code segment below to see how to begin. We start by determining how many times 128 goes into the `base10` number using integer division and then multiplying the result by 10,000,000 to move that value into the proper position for our binary representation. Thus, if the base 10 number was 128, then `base10 / 128` would be 1 and the value stored in `base2` would be 10000000 (the binary equivalent):

```
int base10;
long base2 = 0;
base10 = Convert::ToInt32(txtBase10->Text);
base2 = base10 / 128 * 10000000;
base10 %= 128;
```

The shorthand assignment operator (%=) divides `base10` by 128 and assigns the remainder back into `base10`.

4. Data Type Hierarchy

The interface shown in Figure 3-34 contains five centered buttons corresponding to five different types of data type conversion. The top button (labeled Double) reads an integer, converts it to a double-precision number, and displays the result in the lower left. The next one down, labeled Float, reads an integer, converts it to a single-precision number, and displays it. The next one does nothing more than read the integer and display it (no conversion is necessary). The button labeled Char reads the integer, converts it to data of the char type and displays that. The button at the bottom (Bool) reads the integer, converts it to a Boolean value, and displays that.

Taken together, these buttons represent the data type hierarchy chart. Some conversions represent data type promotion (`float` and `double`) while others represent demotion (`char` and `bool`).

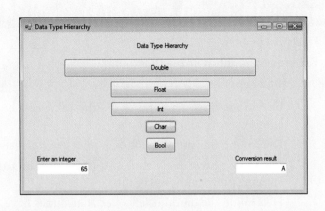

FIGURE 3-34 Program to convert base 10 integers to base 8

Implement this program so that each conversion works appropriately. Note that data type demotion may result in data loss or worse. When converting the integer to a character, for example, integers larger than 255 will yield unexpected results, and very large integers may cause a runtime error terminating the program.

Code for the first button (`btnDouble`) is provided in Example 3-18 to get you started:

EXAMPLE 3-18: CODE FOR `btnDouble_Click()`

```
private: System::Void btnDouble_Click(System::Object^  sender,
System::EventArgs^  e) {
    int intNum;
    double dblNum;
    Int32::TryParse(txtInt->Text, intNum);
    dblNum = Convert::ToDouble(intNum);
    txtConvert->Text = dblNum.ToString();
}
```

Refer to the `Convert` methods used in Programming Exercise 2 for hints on how each conversion may be performed. The conversion to character data is easily done, but converting a character to a text string so that it can be displayed may take you several tries as you experiment with the various character-to-string conversion options.

5. Vending Machine Program

Write a program that calculates the fewest number of coins required to dispense change from a vending machine. Your program should indicate the numbers of quarters, dimes, nickels, and pennies, as shown in Figure 3-35. Dispense up to 99. Create a control table naming each control on the interface and identifying the key events. Create a data table identifying the variables. The key algorithm for this project is shown in Algorithm 3-3.

ALGORITHM 3-3: VENDING MACHINE ALGORITHM

1. Declare variables.

2. Read the amount of change (amount).

3. Process the amount.

    3.1. Determine how many times 25 (the value of a quarter) goes into the amount (store and display this quantity).

    3.2. Determine the amount left over after quarters have been removed.

    3.3. Determine how many times 10 (the value of a dime) goes into the amount (store and display this).

    3.4. Determine the amount left over after dimes have been removed.

    3.5. Determine how many times 5 (the value of a nickel) goes into the amount (store and display this)

    3.6. Determine the amount left over after nickels are removed (this is the number of pennies—store and display it).

    3.7. Add up the sum of the number of quarters, dimes, nickels, and pennies and display it.

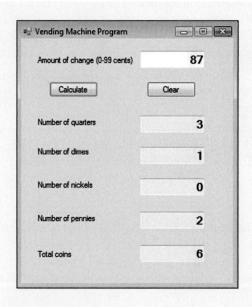

FIGURE 3-35 Vending machine program

The Clear button should assign an empty string to the **Text** field of every textbox, allowing the user to begin again.

SELECTION

IN THIS CHAPTER, YOU WILL:

■ Discover what control structures are and why they are important
■ Learn the difference between sequential control structures
  and selection control structures
■ Compare values using relational operators
■ Use an `if` statement to select single alternative
■ Use an `if...else` statement to select one of two alternatives
■ Develop an understanding of logical operators and their use
  in complex expressions
■ Create nested control structures
■ Become familiar with multiple selection
  and the switch statement

In daily life, you are often faced with situations in which you have to decide on a course of action based on whether something is true. For example, if it is warm tomorrow, you will go to the beach; otherwise, you won't. If you win the lottery, you will buy a mansion; otherwise, you won't. In programming, the ability to write code that can make decisions based on whether something is true or not is a crucial skill. In this chapter, you will learn how to write programs that select between one or more courses of action. You will also see how to combine several decisions into a control structure that selects one course of action out of many.

Control Structures

The fundamental building blocks of all programs are **control structures**. They are the most essential tools in the programmers' toolbox. Control structures are statements that determine the flow of the logical process. There are three major types of control structures: sequential, selection, and repetition. Each control structure has unique features. The control structure categories and features are listed in Figure 4-1.

I. Sequential

    a. Execute each statement in sequential order

    b. No statement is skipped

    c. No statement is repeated

II. Selection

    a. Allow statements to be skipped by providing alternatives

III. Repetition

    a. Allow statements to be repeated

FIGURE 4-1 Outline of control structures

All of the programs you have written so far were governed by sequential control. Selection control structures are covered in this chapter. Repetition control structures are covered in Chapter 5.

Sequential Control Structures

Sequential control structures are characterized by ordered, linear processes. In a sequential control structure, each statement is performed in order. No statement is skipped and no statement is repeated. We have already made use of sequential control structures. For example, the algorithm shown here is sequential

1. Read data.
2. Process data.
3. Display results.

The short Visual C++ program you wrote for your tutorial project in Chapter 2 and the longer program for the tutorial in Chapter 3 were both based on sequential control structures.

As another example, consider a simple program that assigns scores a letter grade based on a numeric point total. The interface for this program, which has two parts, is shown in Figure 4-2. In the first part, a **score** of 75 has been entered and the grade "Pass" is displayed. In the second, a **score** of 25 has been entered, with the same result.

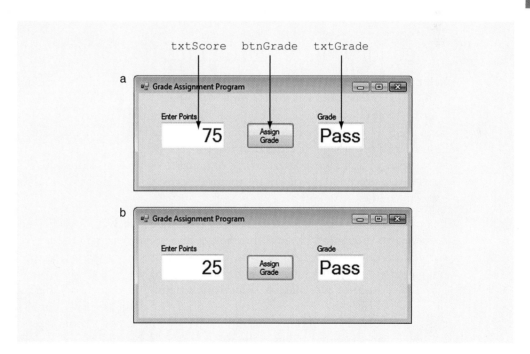

FIGURE 4-2 Grade Assignment Program interface

The code for the click event-handler, **btnGrade_Click()**, is a sequence of three statements as shown in Example 4-1. They are executed in order; none are skipped, and none are repeated.

EXAMPLE 4-1: SEQUENTIAL CONTROL

```
private: System::Void btnGrade_Click(System::Object^  sender,
System::EventArgs^  e)
{
   int score;
   Int32::TryParse(txtScore->Text, score);
   txtGrade->Text = "Pass";
}
```

This unfinished version of the program is quite charitable when it comes to grades, however. Everyone passes, regardless of the **score**. This is because, although the program reads **score**, it doesn't evaluate it, or make any decisions about it. No statement is used to differentiate passing from failing marks. To add this kind of functionality to the program, you would have to add a selection control structure, as explained in the following section.

Selection Control Structures

Selection control structures are instructions used to provide alternative courses of action, such as pass and fail. In Example 4-1, there is a clear need to select some scores (passing scores) from others (failing scores). A common method of selection involves comparing two values, such as a score and a cutoff value. For example, the value 60 might be used as a cutoff value for the decision process. Scores less than 60 (failing scores) are treated one way and scores greater than or equal to 60 (passing scores) are treated another way. The key to building selection structures begins with an understanding of how values are compared.

Examine the diagrams in Figure 4-3. They illustrate two ways in which scores may be processed to distinguish passing from failing marks. The diagram on the left indicates a **single alternative selection** process, in which scores below 60 are ignored, while the rest are reported as passing by displaying a message to that effect. The diagram on the left indicates a **double alternative selection** structure, in which a different message is displayed in either case. For scores less than 60, the message is "Fail". For all other scores, the message is "Pass". Notice that in each case the decision point, represented as a diamond shape, is crucial. This is the point at which a Boolean expression is evaluated.

A **Boolean expression** is an expression that can be evaluated as either true or false and is used by control structures to determine which instructions to execute next. For example, given an exam score, the expression "score is greater than or equal to 60" is either true or false. Expressions such as this are often used as the conditions to decide whether specific actions should be taken. This is illustrated in the paths of a flow diagram. Path selection is based on the evaluation of the Boolean expression. Only one path can be selected.

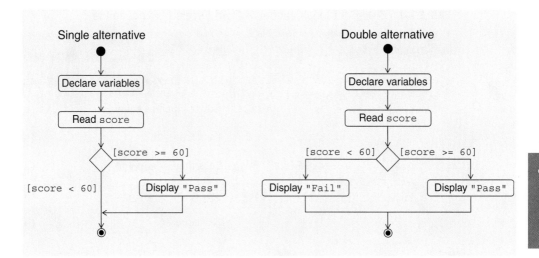

FIGURE 4-3 Flow diagrams for single- and double alternative selection structures

Relational Operators

Selection usually depends on comparison, which, in turn, depends on relational operators. **Relational operators** tell the compiler to examine the relationship between two values. You are probably already familiar with some relational operators, such as the **less than operator (<)**. For example, you know that the expression score < 60 can be read as "score is less than 60." Figure 4-3 also illustrates the **greater than or equal to operator (>=)**. The expression score >= 60 is read as "score is greater than or equal to 60."

Table 4-1 lists all the C++ relational operators grouped into two categories according to their precedence. The **equal to operator (==)** and **not equal to operator (!=)** have lower precedence than other relational operators.

TABLE 4-1 C++ Relational Operators: Two Levels of Precedence

Precedence	Operator	Name	Example
1	>	Greater than	(a > b)
	>=	Greater than or equal to	(a >+ b)
	<	Less than	(a < b)
	<=	Less than or equal to	(a <= b)
2	==	Equal to	(a == b)
	!=	Not equal to	(a != b)

Conditional expressions, in which relational operators are used, evaluate to either `true` or `false`. For example, an expression such as `(score < 60)` evaluates to `false` when the assignment value of the variable `score` is 75 and `true` when the `score` is 25. All relational operators are **binary operators** (they require two operands) and are **left-to-right associative** (are evaluated from left to right).

NOTE An easy error to make, and a very hard one to find since the compiler will not catch it, occurs when the programmer confuses the relational operator == (equal to) with the assignment operator = (assign to). The expression (num1 == num2) is read as "the value stored in num1 is equal to the value stored in num2", and its outcome is either `true` or `false`. The similar looking expression (num1 = num2) is read as "assign the value stored in num2 to num1". Its outcome is the destruction of the value stored in num1 and its replacement by the value stored in num2. As you can see, these two expressions mean very different things and may behave in very different ways. To avoid confusion, the assignment operator (=) should not be used within a Boolean expression.

Using `if` Statements to Provide a Single Alternative

In order to make decisions, we often have to evaluate one or more factors. For example, if you get tickets, you will go to the concert this weekend. If you do not get tickets, you must find something else to do. Computer programs must also be able to select from alternative courses of action, depending on the situations they encounter. This is why the control structures that handle these situations are called selection structures. They select a task, or set of tasks, to perform only after evaluating a condition to see what is appropriate.

In C++, the primary selection structure is the **if statement**. The `if` statement is used to evaluate a single condition, and perform a specific action if that condition turns out to be true. The first half of the example described earlier provides a real-life version of an `if` statement: "If I get concert tickets, I will go to the concert." Later in this chapter, you will learn about another type of selection statement, the **if...else statement**, which allows you to select from two possible actions (for example, going to the concert or finding something else to do), based on whether or not a condition is true (for example, whether you get tickets).

All `if` statements begin with the keyword `if`, followed by the Boolean expression (in parentheses) and then the C++ statement to be performed if the condition evaluates to true, as shown:

```
if  ( Boolean expression ) statement;
```

Returning to our earlier example of the grading program (Figure 4-1), how could we modify this program so that only scores of 60 or above allow "Pass" to be displayed? The Visual C++ code for a `btnGrade_Click()` event-handler, shown in Example 4-2, is a modification of the code originally presented in Example 4-1. It contains an `if` statement at the bottom. In this statement, the left operand, `score`, is compared to the right operand, 60 (the pass/fail cutoff value). The result of the comparison is either `true` (the value in `score` is greater than or equal to 60) or `false` (`score` is less than 60). If the expression evaluates to `true`, then `"Pass"` is displayed in `txtGrade->Text`. If the expression evaluates to `false`, then no action is taken.

EXAMPLE 4-2: USE OF THE `if` STATEMENT

```
private: System::Void btnGrade_Click(System::Object^  sender,
System::EventArgs^  e)
{
   int score;
   Int32::TryParse(txtScore->Text, score);
   if (score >= 60) txtGrade->Text = "Pass";
}
```

To indicate that you want to include multiple statements in an alternative, you must enclose the multiple statements in curly brackets { }, as shown in the general form here:

```
if  ( conditional expression )
{
   statement1;
   statement2;
   statement3;
}
```

In the `btnGrade_Click()` event-handler code shown in Example 4-3, "Pass" is placed into `txtGrade->Text` and the background color of that textbox is turned green if `score` is greater than or equal to 60. As in the previous example, there is no prescribed course of action for a `score` less than 60. The `if` statement provides tasks only for situations where the Boolean expression (`score >= 60`) evaluates to `true`.

EXAMPLE 4-3: USING A MULTIPLE TASK `if` STATEMENT

```
private: System::Void btnGrade_Click(System::Object^  sender,
System::EventArgs^  e)
{
    int score;
    Int32::TryParse(txtScore->Text, score);
    if (score >= 60)
    {
        txtGrade->Text = "Pass";
        txtGrade->BackColor = Color::Green;
    }
}
```

The result is shown in Figure 4-4, which consists of two parts. In Figure 4-4a, a score of 60 or greater (in this case, 75) results in the word "Pass" being displayed on a green background. In Figure 4-4b, a score of less than 60 (in this case, 25) results in no action; that is, nothing is displayed in the textbox.

FIGURE 4-4 Processing passing scores with an `if` statement

Using `if...else` Statements to Provide Two Alternatives

As you have seen, the `if` statement allows you to create a program that can evaluate a condition and then perform an action if that condition is `true`. To provide an additional course of action, which the program performs only when the condition turns out to be `false`, you use an `if...else` statement. In real life, the `if...else` statement is equivalent to the example we examined earlier: "If you get concert tickets, you will go to the concert. Otherwise (else), you will find something else to do." An `if...else` statement is also referred to as a **double alternative `if` statement** because it provides two possible alternatives.

The general form of the `if...else` statement begins with the keyword `if` followed by a condition, in parentheses. The next line contains the task that should be performed if the condition evaluates to `true`. Next, the keyword `else` indicates that a second alternative is provided. The statement in the `else` clause is executed only if the original condition evaluates to `false`. The general form is shown here:

```
if   ( conditional expression )
    statements to be performed if the expression is true
else
    statements to be performed if the expression is false
```

In the case of our grade assignment program, we want to be able to display the outcome of each `score` in terms of a passing or failing grade. If the `score` is greater than or equal to (>=) 60, then the value of the expression is `true` and the first alternative is executed ("Pass"). If the `score` is less than 60, the value of the expression is `false` and the second alternative is executed ("Fail"). If an alternative consists of multiple statements, you need to enclose them in curly brackets { }. In Example 4-4, two tasks are associated with each alternative:

EXAMPLE 4-4: USING THE `if...else` STATEMENT

```cpp
private: System::Void btnGrade_Click(System::Object^ sender,
System::EventArgs^ e)
{
  int score;
    Int32::TryParse(txtScore->Text, score);
    if (score >= 60)
    {
        txtGrade->Text = "Pass";
        txtGrade->BackColor = Color::Green;
    }
```

```
    else
    {
        txtGrade->Text = "Fail";
        txtGrade->BackColor = Color::Red;
    }
}
```

This program performs as shown in Figure 4-5. Figure 4-5a shows the grade outcome when the **score** is greater than or equal to 60, and Figure 4-5b shows the outcome when the **score** is less than 60. The colored backgrounds help accentuate the result.

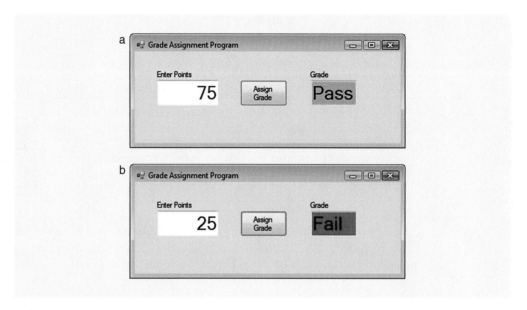

FIGURE 4-5 Multiple alternative, multiple task versions of the grading program

Logical Operators

The decision to attend a concert if you can get tickets is easy to make, unless there are complications. Let us assume that the concert is out of town and will require you to be gone all weekend. What if you have an exam Monday morning? You may not wish to go to the concert if it means flunking your exam. In that case, you may need to consider two factors in making a decision. The decision may be described in a variety of ways, each of which will be examined in the sections that follow:

1. "If it is true that I have an exam, then I will *not* try to get tickets."
2. "If it is *not* true that I have an exam, then I will try to get tickets."

3. "If there is no exam *and* I can get tickets, then I will go to the concert."

4. "If I have an exam, *or*, if I cannot get concert tickets, then I will stay home and miss the concert."

Notice that the italicized words "or," "and," and "not" are crucial here. These three terms exist in computer programming languages as well. They are called **logical operators**. Logical operators are used whenever the components of a decision are statements that are either true or false, such as: "I have an exam on Monday" or "I cannot get any concert tickets."

The following sections introduce the following logical operators: the **not operator (!)**, the **and operator (&&)**, and the **or operator (||)**.

The not Operator (!)

Let us consider the first two formulations of the concert problem from the previous section:

1. "If it is true that I have an exam, then I will *not* try to get tickets."

2. "If it is *not* true that I have an exam, then I will try to get tickets."

In the first version, we can identify a condition ("It is true that I have an exam") and a task ("I will *not* try to get tickets"). The second version is similar, but the word *not* has been moved from the task to the condition. The second version has the condition ("It is *not* true that I have an exam") and a task ("I will try to get tickets").

These are two versions of the same selection statement. The second associates the word *not* with the condition rather than the task. When programmers translate algorithms, it is common to encounter conditions with a *not* in them. The not operator (!) allows you to translate the logic directly into C++ code.

The not operator (!) can also be used to negate Boolean values. In other words, it changes `true` to `false` and `false` to `true`. Consider the `if` statement shown earlier in Example 4-2. It displayed the word `"Pass"` if the `score` was greater than or equal to 60. We could state the negative version of the condition by using the not operator (!) so that it only reports on failing scores, as shown in Example 4-5.

EXAMPLE 4-5: USE OF THE not (!) OPERATOR

```
private: System::Void btnGrade_Click(System::Object^ sender,
System::EventArgs^ e)
{
    int score;
    Int32::TryParse(txtScore->Text, score);
    if (!(score >= 60)) txtGrade->Text = "Fail";
}
```

Remember that the only way the statement

```
txtGrade->Text = "Fail";
```

can be executed is if the entire condition (!(score >= 60)) evaluates to true.

The if statement in Example 4-4 is read as follows: "If it is *not* true that score is greater than or equal to 60, then display 'Fail.'" The condition (it is *not* true that the score is greater than or equal to 60) has two parts. First, determine whether (score >= 60) is true or false. Second, use the not operator (!) to reverse the outcome.

If the innermost expression evaluates to true, as it will for all passing scores, then the not operator (!) negates, or reverses, this and the final evaluation becomes false, avoiding the "Fail" message. If the score is 75, then the value of (score >= 60) is true, but the value of the entire expression is changed to false. This is a good thing, too. A score of 75 would otherwise have produced the word "Fail" written in textGrade->Text.

If the score was 25, then the value of (score >= 60) is false and the not operator (!) reverses it to true (appropriately producing the message "Fail"). Table 4-2 illustrates the result of applying the not operator (!) to Boolean expressions.

TABLE 4-2 Evaluation Table for the not Operator (!) Using the Expression (!(score >= 60))

Score	Operand (score >= 60)	Result after Using not Operator (!) !(score >= 60)
75	true	false
25	false	true

The and Operator (&&)

Consider an improved version of the exam grading program, whose interface is shown in Figure 4-6. The interface for this version tests scores as they are entered to determine whether they are valid. Valid scores are those within the range of 0–100. If the score falls within that range, a message box appears with the message "Valid score." A **MessageBox** is a small window that displays on the screen and remains open until the user clicks the OK button. After the user clicks the OK button in the MessageBox, the program continues.

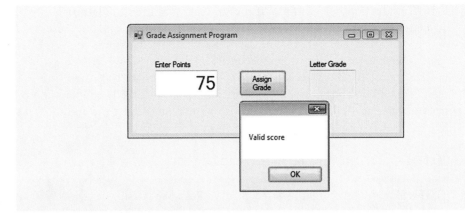

FIGURE 4-6 Grade Assignment Program

The `if...else` statement shown in Example 4-5 illustrates how the and operator (`&&`) is used in conjunction with two relational comparisons to produce the `MessageBox` output.

The general form of MessageBox syntax is shown here:

```
MessageBox::Show("your message here");
```

The programmer specifies the message that should be shown by placing it in the parentheses `()` after the **`MessageBox::Show()`** method name. As long as the message is a text string, it can be displayed in the `MessageBox` when the program runs.

Look at the code in Example 4-6. From the standpoint of the and operator (`&&`), there are two operands. The left operand is the result of evaluating the expression (`score >= 0`) and its right operand is the result of evaluating the expression (`score <= 100`). If it is true that (`score >= 0`) and (`score <= 100`), then "Valid score" is displayed; otherwise, "Invalid score" is displayed.

EXAMPLE 4-6: MESSAGEBOX WITH `if...else` STATEMENT

```
private: System::Void btnAssign_Click(System::Object^  sender,
System::EventArgs^  e) {
   int score;
   Int32::TryParse(textBox1->Text, score);
   if ((score >= 0) && (score <= 100))
      MessageBox::Show("Valid score");
   else
      MessageBox::Show("Invalid score");
}
```

Let's consider another example. If the score is 75, then the left operand (score >= 0) evaluates to true and so does the right operand (score <= 100). An evaluation of the entire condition depends on the Boolean value of the operands. If both the left and right operands are true, then the entire expression, resolved using the and operator (&&), is true. If the score is less than 0 or greater than 100, then one or more of the operands will be false and the entire expression, resolved using the and operator (&&), becomes false. Table 4-3 illustrates how the expression ((score >= 0) && (score <= 100)) from Example 4-5 is resolved.

TABLE 4-3 Evaluation Table for the Expression ((score >= 0) && (score <= 100))

Left Operand (score >= 0)	Right Operand (score <= 100)	Result after Using the and Operator (&&) ((score >= 0) && (score <= 100))
true	true	true
true	false	false
false	true	false
false	false	false

Determining When to Use the and Operator (&&) and the or Operator (||)

The and operator (&&) is an important tool that can be used to filter out many errors (such as invalid exam scores) before they occur. However, there are times when other tools are more appropriate. Consider the Simple Calculator program, whose interface is shown in Figure 4-7.

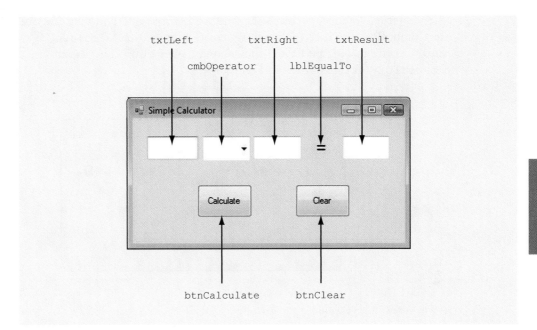

FIGURE 4-7 Simple Calculator program interface

The textboxes `txtLeft` and `txtRight` are intended for integer data entry and `txtResult` is for the output. The user specifies an operation by picking one from a list provided by the `cmbOperator` **ComboBox control**, as shown in Figure 4-8. When the user clicks the ComboBox, a drop-down list of items appears; the user clicks an item to select it. In this case, the items are arithmetic operators (`+,-,*,/,%`). Figure 4-8 shows the selection of the addition operator (+) from the ComboBox list.

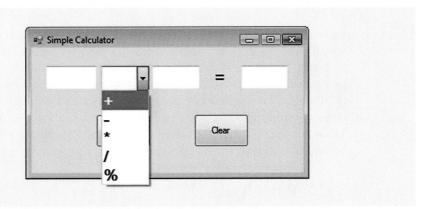

FIGURE 4-8 Selection of the addition operator (+) item from `cmbOperator`

After entering integers in `txtLeft` and `txtRight` and choosing an operation from the ComboBox, the user clicks the Calculate button (`btnCalculate`). The click event reads the data and performs the chosen operation. The result is displayed in `txtResult->Text`, as shown in Figure 4-9.

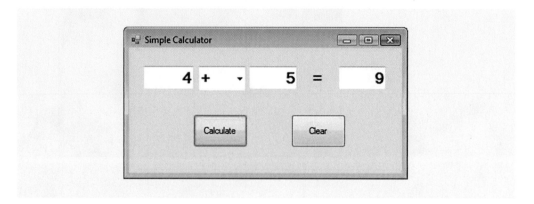

FIGURE 4-9 Simple Calculator program in action

If you were creating this program, it would be important to make sure you had entered data into both operands before attempting to calculate the result. If you left either of them (or both) empty, then the data reading and calculation tasks must not proceed.

Does the following use of the and operator (`&&`) adequately screen out all of the possible ways that operand data might be missing?

```
if ((txtLeft->Text == "") && (txtRight->Text == ""))
    MessageBox::Show("Empty operands");
```

The answer is no. It screens out some, but not all. Consider a situation where the user completely failed to provide data (both `txtLeft` and `txtRight` are left blank). If both textboxes are empty, then, from Table 4-4, both operands evaluate to `true`, and the overall evaluation is `true`. So far, so good; this results in the error message being displayed. However, if data are provided for one operand while the other is left blank, the evaluation result will be `false` (use Table 4-4 to confirm this) and the message will not display. This is a problem, because an error condition should be detected when either of the operand textboxes is left empty, not just when both of them are. The and operator (`&&`) is not the right tool for this job. However, this situation can be easily addressed with the logical operator, the or operator (`| |`), as you will see in the following section.

The or Operator (| |)

The or operator (`| |`) is represented by two adjacent vertical bars (`| |`), sometimes called "pipes". There are no spaces between the `|` characters. Like the and operator (`&&`), the or operator (`| |`) is binary and left-to-right associative.

NOTE The vertical bar | character is found above the same key as the backslash (\), on the right-hand side of the keyboard.

The fundamental difference between the evaluation tables for && and || are these:

- The only way that an && expression evaluates to true is if both operands are true.
- The only way that an || expression evaluates to false is if both operands are false.

This makes the or operator (||) a much better tool for screening out data entry errors, such as in the empty textbox situation discussed in the previous section. Figure 4-10 provides an example of the kind of error message we wish to display when data are missing from either or both operands.

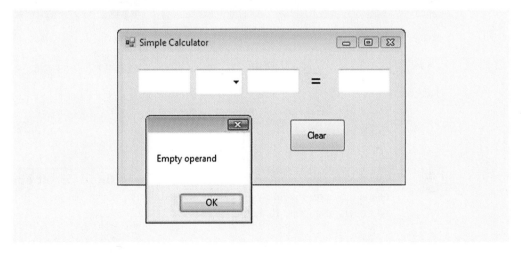

FIGURE 4-10 `MessageBox` output when one or both operands are missing

Example 4-7 uses the or operator (||) to achieve this result.

EXAMPLE 4-7: USING THE OR OPERATOR (||)

```
int num1, num2;
if ((txtLeft->Text == "") || (txtRight->Text == ""))
    MessageBox::Show("Empty operand");
else
{    // Read operands
    Int32::TryParse(txtLeft->Text, num1);
    Int32::TryParse(txtRight->Text, num2);

}
```

Notice that there are three situations in which the error message box is displayed. The Boolean expression in the `if` statement will evaluate to `true` if:

- Both textboxes are empty.
- The left textbox is empty and the right is not.
- The left textbox is not empty but the right is.

These situations correspond to the first three lines in the or operator (||) evaluation table (Table 4-4).

TABLE 4-4 Evaluation Table for the or Operator (||) Using the Expression
`((txtLeft->Text == "") || (txtRight->Text == ""))`

Left Operand (txtLeft->Text == "")	Right Operand (txtRight->Text == "")	Result after Using the or Operator (||) ((txtLeft->Text == "") || (txtRight->Text == ""))
true	true	true
true	false	true
false	true	true
false	false	false

NOTE Both the or operator (||) and the and operator (&&) are **short-circuit operators**. This means that after the left operand is evaluated, it may not be necessary to evaluate the right operand in order to determine the final result.

In Chapter 2, we learned about operator precedence rules. You will remember that precedence refers to the priority level of an operator. At the time, we only had arithmetic and assignment operators to consider, but the previous sections in this chapter on relational and logical operators gives us many more to keep in mind. When writing complex expressions, refer to the operator precedence table in Appendix B for a list of operators with which we are familiar and their order of precedence. Remember that when writing complex conditions, parentheses can be used to control the order of evaluation.

Nested Control Structures

Nesting is a programming technique in which you place one control structure inside of another. Just as you can nest one kitchen bowl inside of another, you can **nest** control structures. For example, consider the Simple Calculator program example used to illustrate the and (&&) and or (||) operators in Figures 4-7 through 4-10. We saw how these operators can be used to screen out error conditions as they occur. In the context of an `if...else` statement, we saw how one alternative handles invalid data (usually by producing an error message) while the other handles valid data (usually by calculating the result). However, that discussion only considered errors that might be introduced when the user fails to fill in the textboxes with the integer operands. You also need to filter out other kinds of errors. For example, what if the user provided numbers for the left and right operands, but failed to select an operator from the ComboBox? Figure 4-11 uses a flow diagram to illustrate the problem and the solution, which involves nested selection control structures.

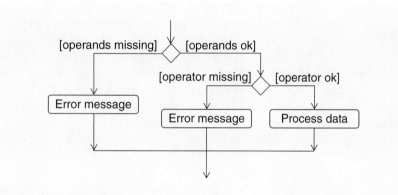

FIGURE 4-11   Nested selection structures

The first decision point evaluates the operands to make sure both have been entered. If not, an error message is produced. Even if the operands are present, we can't process the data until the program has checked the ComboBox to make sure that an operator has been selected. If an operator has been selected, then the program can read and process data. If an operator has not been selected, then an error message is produced and no processing takes place.

The Visual C++ code for this nested structure is shown in Example 4-8.

EXAMPLE 4-8: NESTED `if...else` STATEMENTS

```
int num1, num2;
if ((txtLeft->Text == "") || (txtRight->Text == ""))
    MessageBox::Show("Empty operand");
else
{   // Nested structures
    if (cmbOperator->SelectedIndex == -1)
        MessageBox::Show("Missing operator");
    else
```

```
{  // Process the data

    Int32::TryParse(txtLeft->Text, num1);
    Int32::TryParse(txtRight->Text, num2);
    ...
}
}
```

In Example 4-8, an `if...else` statement is entirely nested within one alternative of another `if...else` statement. The conditional expression of the inner structure compares two values, the **SelectedIndex property** of the ComboBox and the number -1.

To understand how the `SelectedIndex` property works, you need to know that each item in a ComboBox list is automatically assigned an **index value**. Index values are integers that indicate the position of an item in a list. The first actual item in the list has the index value 0, the second has the index value 1, and so on. If the user fails to select any operators from `cmbOperator`, then the blank item at the top of the list is displayed. This has the index value -1, as shown in Figure 4-12. Therefore, checking to see if the user left the operator choice empty amounts to checking to see if the index value (`SelectedIndex`) of the item displayed by `cmbOperator` is -1.

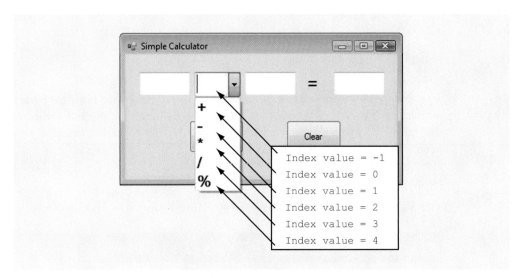

FIGURE 4-12 Index values for `cmbOperator` items

Multiple Alternative Selection

Now, let us examine situations in which more than one alternative path must be available to the program. Take the example of student exam grades presented earlier. This time, let us assume that we wish to assign letter grades according to the scheme presented in Figure 4-13.

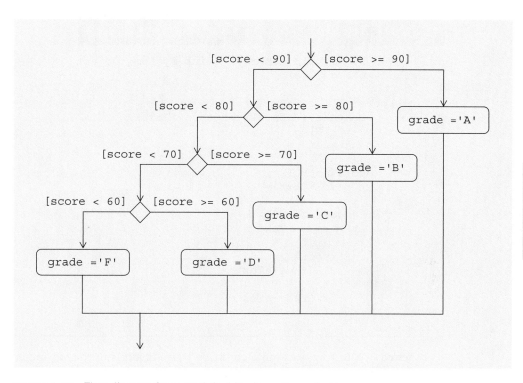

FIGURE 4-13 Flow diagram for nested double alternative selection

In this scenario, scores of 90 or above are assigned the grade "A," 80–89 a "B," 70–79 a "C," 60–69 a "D," and below 60 is an "F." Only one grade is assigned to each score, so the options are mutually exclusive. Only one path will be followed through this control structure.

What about when more than two alternatives are required? There are several ways to achieve this end. One method is to use **nested double alternative `if` statements**. Examine the code segment shown in Example 4-9 and compare it to Figure 4-13. Notice that it uses nested double alternative `if` statements to implement multiple alternative paths. The indenting is used to indicate which statements are nested inside of others. Take a moment to make sure you can follow the logic of this structure. For example, if the score is 95, then the first Boolean expression (`score >= 90`) evaluates to `true`. This means the grade "A" is displayed. All other `if` statements and their tasks are nested within the second (`false`) alternative for that Boolean expression, and so they are skipped.

Similarly, a score of 85 would produce the following effect. First, the expression (`score >= 90`) is evaluated. It is `false`; therefore, control passes to the structure's second alternative. Here, we find another condition: (`score >= 80`). This evaluates to `true`, the true task is performed ("B" is displayed), and all others are skipped because they are nested within that `if` statement's `false` alternative.

EXAMPLE 4-9: NESTED `if...else` STATEMENTS

```
private: System::Void btnGrade_Click(System::Object^  sender,
System::EventArgs^  e)
{
   int score;
   score = Convert::ToInt32(txtScore->Text);
   if (score >= 90)
      txtGrade->Text = "A";
   else
      if (score >= 80)
         txtGrade->Text = "B";
      else
         if (score >= 70)
            txtGrade->Text = "C";
         else
            if (score >= 60)
               txtGrade->Text = "D";
            else
               txtGrade->Text = "F";
}
```

This nested structure appears quite complex. It can be difficult to read and edit. To make the code easier to work with, it's better to use the condensed form of the **multiple alternative `if` statement** to clearly delineate the alternatives in a concise manner, as shown in Example 4-10. This form is preferred over the longer nested double alternative version and operates the same way. In it, each alternative is clearly indicated by an `if`, `else if`, or `else` clause without nesting. This is sometimes known as an **`if...else if...else` statement**. Only one alternative is chosen based on whichever Boolean expression first evaluates to `true`.

EXAMPLE 4-10: `if...else if` STATEMENTS

```
//   MULTIPLE ALTERNATIVE IF
if (score >= 90)
   txtGrade->Text = "A";
else if (score >= 80)
   txtGrade->Text = "B";
else if (score >= 70)
   txtGrade->Text = "C";
else if (score >= 60)
   txtGrade->Text = "D";
else
   txtGrade->Text = "F";
```

The multiple alternative **if** statement is most useful when you have a number of value ranges to deal with. In this case, the first alternative deals with all scores >= 90, the second with the range of values from 80 through 89, and so on.

When faced with a multiple alternative situation involving individual values (as opposed to ranges of values), there is one other selection tool that is specially adapted to handle that situation, known as the **switch statement**.

switch Statements

4

Instead of assigning grades for exam scores running from 0 through 100, assume that you are faced with the problem of assigning grades to scores on a 5-point quiz. One solution is to create a multiple alternative **if** statement. However, you could also use a **switch** statement, which allows you to specify an integral variable, or expression, and then specify actions for each possible value. Each value is known as a **case**. A **switch** statement begins with the keyword **switch**, followed by an integral variable name or expression in parentheses. Next, comes an opening curly brace, {, followed by the various cases, as indicated in the syntax diagram. Syntax features that are optional are enclosed in square brackets [ ].

```
switch (integral variable or expression)
{
case integral value 1: statements; [break;]
case integral value 2: statements; [break;]
   .
   .
   .
case integral value n: statements; [break;]
[default: statements;]
}
```

Cases are indicated by the keyword **case**, followed by the integral value it applies to. Each case is labeled by a unique integral value. The cases may be listed in any order. A colon (**:**) is used to identify the starting point of the **case**. The programmer can put as many statements as necessary into each **case**. When finished, the **break** statement is used to indicate that the case is over and the entire **switch** statement should be exited. An optional default case is used to handle any integral values that were not processed by other cases.

For example, the program segment in Example 4-11 displays a letter grade to correspond to quiz scores from 0 to 5. The first case applies only when the variable **quiz** contains the value 5. In that case, the letter grade "A" is displayed in the textbox. The last part of the first **case statement** is the keyword **break**. This tells the compiler to break out of the control structure—that is, to skip all remaining statements and exit the structure at the bottom. Notice that the fourth **case** statement is not associated with any task and has no **break** statement. This means that control passes to the next case and the statements there are processed.

Finally, notice that a closing curly brace (}) indicates the end of the list of cases in the **switch** statement.

EXAMPLE 4-11: USING A switch STATEMENT

```
switch (quiz)
{
    case 5: txtGrade->Text = "A"; break;
    case 4: txtGrade->Text = "B"; break;
    case 3: txtGrade->Text = "C"; break;
    case 2: txtGrade->Text = "D"; break;
    case 1:
    case 0: txtGrade->Text = "F";
}
```

Many of the cases in Example 4-11, but not all, use a **break statement**. Unlike multiple alternative **if** statements, the alternatives in a **switch** statement are not mutually exclusive. More than one may be executed if **break** statements are omitted.

Tutorial: Vacation Planner

As in earlier chapters, you will now use the concepts you have learned to develop a software application. The application you'll work on in this tutorial makes use of several new controls, including ComboBoxes, GroupBoxes, MonthlyCalendars, and RadioButtons.

Problem Analysis

You have been hired by the manager of the university travel office to help manage the office's vacation reservation system. She asks you to create a vacation planner program that students, staff, and faculty can use to check on hotel prices for selected destination areas. Your program should let the user select his or her vacation destination, number of rooms required, and length of stay. The program should then compute the overall cost of the package. Different locations have different prices per night for hotels as indicated in Table 4-5.

TABLE 4-5 Destination Hotel Prices (Per Room Per Night)

Destination	Nightly Room Rate ($)
Orlando	109.00
Las Vegas	119.00
Los Angeles	119.00
Cancun	129.00
Colorado	129.00
New York	129.00
Hawaii	129.00
Seattle	129.00

In addition, there are discounts for those purchasing more than one room, as shown in Table 4-6.

TABLE 4-6 Multiple Room Discounts (Per Room Per Night)

Rooms	Discount ($)
1	0
2	5
3	6
4	10
5	11
6	11

In other words, if the user wants to reserve four rooms for one night, he or she gets $10 off of the bill for each room (a $40 savings). If he or she wants to reserve four rooms for two nights, the discount is $20 off of the total bill for each room (an $80 savings).

Finally, the program should be set up so that when it loads, by default, the input controls have already been initialized. Specifically, the number of rooms is automatically set to 1 (since most users will only want one room), and the first destination (Orlando) is automatically selected. The user may change any or all of these initialized settings.

Design

The design stage proceeds from problem analysis to an interface sketch, object and data tables, algorithms for key processes, and their testing 1and verification.

INTERFACE SKETCH

The manager of the university travel office wants you to create the interface shown in Figure 4-14. Each control in Figure 4-14 is labeled. Notice the assortment of new controls in this project.

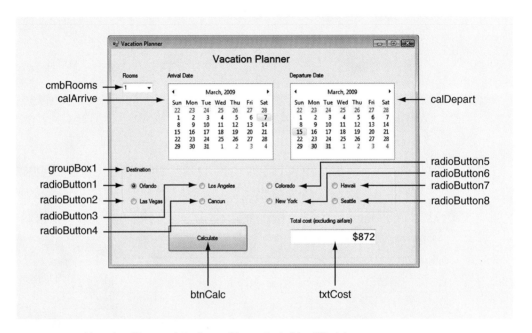

FIGURE 4-14 Vacation Planner interface with controls identified by name

The interface is designed to allow the user to indicate the number of rooms by selecting an option in the ComboBox cmbRooms, the arrival date by clicking a day in calArrive, and the departure date by clicking a day in calDepart. The user selects a destination from the eight choices (radioButton1 − radioButton8) in the Destination GroupBox. When these tasks have been accomplished, the user clicks on btnCalc and the total cost appears in txtCost. The required initialization of the rooms, date, and destination should happen as the project (Form1) loads in the **Form1_Load() event**.

The controls on the interface are listed and described in Table 4-7.

TABLE 4-7 Control Table for the Vacation Planner Program

Usage	Object	Event	Description
Initialization	Form1	Load()	Initializes controls
	cmbRooms		Number of rooms required
	calArrive		Arrival date
	calDepart		Departure date
	groupBox1		Groups destination radiobuttons together
	radioButton1		Destination 1 (Orlando)
Input	radioButton2		Destination 2 (Las Vegas)
	radioButton3		Destination 3 (Los Angeles)
	radioButton4		Destination 4 (Cancun)
	radioButton5		Destination 5 (Colorado)
	radioButton6		Destination 6 (New York)
	radioButton7		Destination 7 (Hawaii)
	radioButton8		Destination 8 (Seattle)
Processing	btnCalc	Click()	Calculate the total cost
Output	txtCost		Displays the total cost

4

DATA TABLE

From the problem description and our knowledge of the interface, we should be able to come up with a rough list of the required variables. The number of rooms is an integer and will be read from cmbRooms. The number of nights is also an integer and is obtained by subtracting the arrival and departure dates (more on this later). The nightly cost of the room, as well as the nightly room discount and total cost, should all be doubles since they are presumably in dollars and cents and are, therefore, real numbers. A Boolean variable can be used to indicate whether a problem was encountered with input data. Table 4-8 contains a list of the variables used in this project.

The arrival and departure dates deserve special attention. In the interface, **monthCalendar controls** are used to provide this information. In the development stage of this project, we shall see how to write statements in C++ code to read the selected date from a month-Calendar control. The date a monthCalendar object provides us comes in the form of an object of the **DateTime data type**. DateTime is not a standard C++ data type. It is a class definition unique to Microsoft Visual Studio and its Visual C++ programming language. A table of DateTime class members is given in Appendix B. For our purposes, however, it is possible to subtract two DateTime objects and get the number of days between them, as an integer. This conveniently calculates the length of the stay, which we store in an integer variable (nights).

TABLE 4-8 Data Table for the Vacation Planner Program

Variable Name	Data Type	Purpose
rooms	int	Number of rooms required (from cmbRooms)
nights	int	Number of nights (from calendar input)
cost	float	Nightly room cost
discount	float	Nightly room discount
total	float	Total cost of all rooms for all nights
arrive	DateTime	Date of arrival
depart	DateTime	Date of departure
ok	bool	Indicates whether the data entered is valid

ALGORITHMS

Table 4-7 identified two event-handlers (`Form1_Load()`, and `btnCalc_Click()`) that need to be coded. The following sections provide the algorithms for each of these event-handlers.

Algorithm for `Form1_Load()` The `Form1 Load()` event algorithm is trivial. It consists of a sequential control structure in which a series of assignment statements are executed to store values into control properties, something like this:

ALGORITHM 4-1

1. Set `cmbRooms` to the first `Item` (1 room).
2. Assign vacation location names ("Orlando," "Las Vegas," etc.) to each radioButton's `Text` property.
3. Check the first radioButton (this turns it on and all other radioButtons off).

Remember that you do not necessarily have to know how to carry out a task in Visual C++ code to write a pseudocode description for it. So, do not be concerned if you do not know how to write the code for any of the steps in this algorithm. Identifying the tasks is the goal of this stage of program development, not writing C++ code.

The Algorithm for btnCalc_Click()   The real work in this program is accomplished in the btnCalc_Click(). As in Chapter 3, let us start with a high–level algorithm and use a process of stepwise refinement to arrive at a detailed solution. The high–level algorithm is:

1. Declare variables.
2. Read the input data.
3. Process the data.

Our data table (Table 4-8) identifies the variables that must be declared in step 1, so our stepwise refinement can focus on the other two steps.

Step 2 is where the input tasks should be addressed. These include reading the number of rooms as well as the arrival and departure dates and the room cost. Note that the room cost varies, depending on the destination the user chooses. If she chooses Orlando (radioButton1), the cost is $109.00. If she chooses Las Vegas or Los Angeles (radioButton2 or radioButton3), the cost is $119.00. If she chooses any other destination, the cost is $129.00. Step 2 can, therefore, be refined as shown in the flowchart and pseudocode in Figure 4–15.

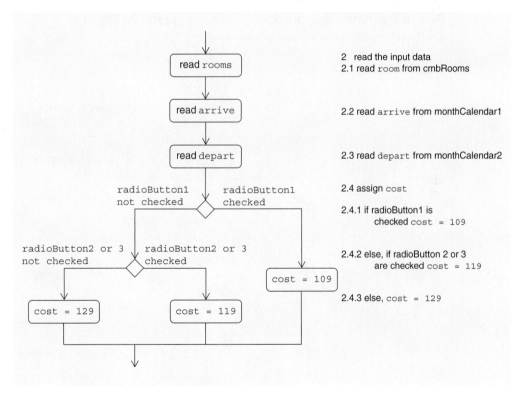

FIGURE 4-15   Flow diagram and pseudocode for step 2

We have refined step 2.4 into three subtasks (2.4.1, 2.4.2, and 2.4.3) representing three separate alternatives. Only one will be executed. Looking ahead to the code that might be required to implement these statements, a multiple alternative if statement should work. In Example 4–12 notice that the second alternative (which wraps across two lines) uses the logical operator || to determine whether either destination had been checked.

EXAMPLE 4-12: DETERMINING ROOM COST

```
if (radioButton1->Checked == true)
   cost = 109.00;
else if ((radioButton2->Checked == true) ||
   (radioButton3->Checked == true))
   cost = 119.00;
else
   cost = 129.00;
```

Next, consider step 3 of the high-level algorithm (processing the data that has been read). This step assumes that data have been read into the variables `rooms`, `arrive`, `depart`, and `cost`. The purpose of this section is to perform the necessary calculations. We need to approach these tasks with caution. Before any calculations are performed, the program should examine the data values to determine whether they are valid. If any are not, then we have a Boolean variable (`ok`) that will store the value `false` (to indicate that further data processing should not proceed). Figure 4-16 shows a flowchart for these steps along with the pseudocode.

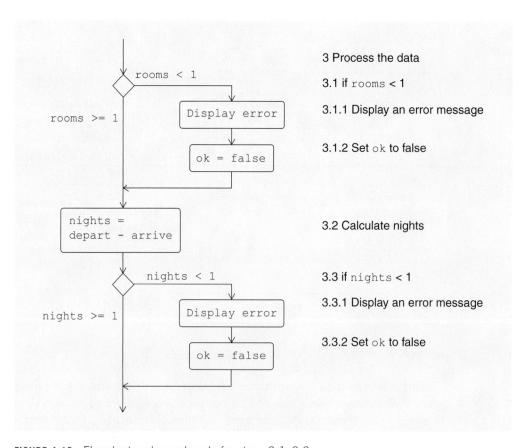

FIGURE 4-16 Flowchart and pseudocode for steps 3.1–3.3

Steps 3.1 and 3.3 require **single alternative selection** structures with multiple tasks. If we look ahead again to the C++ code for step 3.1, we can see how the structure looks when implemented, as shown in Example 4-13.

EXAMPLE 4-13: PROCESSING INVALID rooms DATA

```
if (rooms <= 0)
{
    MessageBox::Show("You must indicate how many rooms.");
    ok = false;
}
```

After steps 3.1, 3.2, and 3.3, the next task is to calculate the total cost. Remember that steps 3.1 and 3.3 looked at data that had been entered and assigned the value `false` to the Boolean variable (`ok`) if there was a problem. If `ok` is set to `false`, processing should stop. On the other hand, if `ok` is set to `true`, then processing can proceed. Thus, step 3.4 needs to evaluate `ok` and determine whether processing should continue. The flowchart and pseudocode for step 3.4 are shown in Figure 4-17.

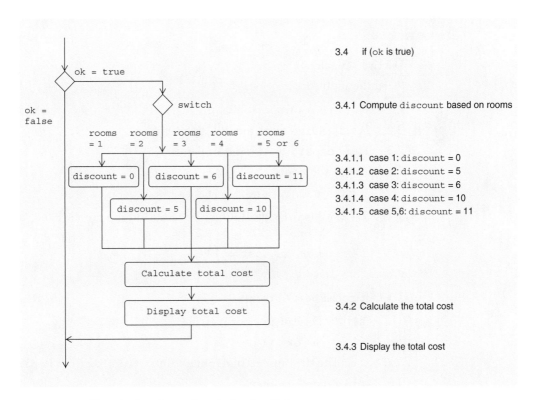

FIGURE 4-17 Flowchart and pseudocode for step 3.4

The most difficult part of this set of steps is 3.4.1, computing the discount. Remember that, according to the rules established in the project description, the discount depends on how many rooms the user requires. The discount information provided earlier in Table 4-6 can be represented as a series of cases in a multiple alternative selection structure. A switch statement would do nicely. Example 4-14 implements this selection structure:

EXAMPLE 4-14: A switch STATEMENT FOR rooms

```
switch (rooms)
{
    case 1: discount = 0; break;
    case 2: discount = 5; break;
    case 3: discount = 6; break;
    case 4: discount = 10; break;
    case 5: case 6: discount = 11;
}
```

Here is our complete, final algorithm:

ALGORITHM 4-2

1. Declare variables.
2. Read the input data.
   2.1. Read rooms from cmbRooms.
   2.2. Read arrive from monthCalendar1.
   2.3. Read depart from monthCalendar2.
   2.4. Assign the cost.
      2.4.1. If radioButton1 is checked, cost = 109.
      2.4.2. Else, if radioButton2 or radioButton3 are checked, then cost = 119.
      2.4.3. Else, the cost = 129.
3. Process the data.
   3.1. If rooms <= 0, then:
      3.1.1. Display an error message.
      3.1.2. Set ok to false.
   3.2. Calculate the number of nights (subtract arrive from depart).
   3.3. If nights < 1, then:
      3.3.1. Display an error message.
      3.3.2. Set ok to false.

3.4. `if (ok is true)`

    3.4.1.   `switch` to the case indicated by `rooms`

        3.4.1.1.   case 1: `discount` $= 0$

        3.4.1.2.   case 2: `discount` $= 5$

        3.4.1.3.   case 3: `discount` $= 6$

        3.4.1.4.   case 4: `discount` $= 10$

        3.4.1.5.   cases 5 and 6: `discount` $= 11$

    3.4.2.   Calculate the `total cost`: `rooms` x `nights` x (`cost − discount`).

    3.4.3.   Display the `total cost`.

4

The algorithm has three major steps corresponding to the tasks of declaring variables, reading input data, and processing the input data. Step 1 contains everything related to variable declaration, step 2 contains all the tasks related to reading data, and step 3 contains all the tasks related to processing data. But will it work?

As our algorithms get longer and more complex, it will be important to verify that their solutions actually work before jumping ahead to the development stage. Identifying deficiencies in the design stage and addressing them then is far more efficient and productive than having to go back and redesign a program after you have typed all the C++ code.

It is possible to test an algorithm before coding it to determine whether it is correct. First, we need to come up with a testing strategy and then walk through the steps of the algorithm, verifying that it passes each test.

TEST STRATEGY

The projects you created in previous chapters were short enough that there was no need to test them systematically before moving from the design to development stages. Longer algorithms such as the one we have just completed, however, require testing. Testing, in turn, requires a test strategy.

We know the variables (from the data table in Table 4-8) and, thanks to our algorithm, we have a good idea of the solution process. The test strategy starts with an identification of the categories of valid and invalid data values our variables might be assigned as the algorithm proceeds from task to task.

First, consider invalid data. Although we can restrict input for some variables to minimize the chance of invalid data entry, we cannot always prevent invalid values. Invalid input possibilities apply to the number of `rooms` and `nights`. A request for less than one room, or less than one night, will be considered invalid.

The cost of the room can be more successfully controlled to block out invalid data. For example, we have provided a series of radiobuttons to indicate destination. As we shall see, it is not going to be possible for the user to click more than one button at a time. Similarly, it will not be possible for the user to leave them all empty. One, and no more than one, will always be selected.

Table 4-9 displays the variables with potential for invalid input. Table 4-9 also identifies the range of valid and invalid values, and provides an example of each. The examples are important because we can use them to test both the algorithm and the finished program.

TABLE 4-9 Valid and Invalid Data

Variable	Valid Values	Invalid Values
rooms	>= 1, example: 2	< 1, example: 0
nights	>= 1, example: 2	< 1, example: 0

To test Algorithm 4-2 each valid and invalid data situation must be examined. A **test scenario** is a set of values that addresses a specific concern. Table 4-10 provides details for test scenarios related to each of the four categories of valid and invalid data identified in Table 4-9.

TABLE 4-10 Scenario 1: rooms and nights Are Both Valid

rooms	arrive	depart	nights	Test Scenarios
2	5/13/09	5/17/09	4	#1 valid data
0	5/13/09	5/17/09	4	#2 rooms is invalid
2	5/13/09	5/10/09	-3	#3 nights is invalid
0	5/13/09	5/10/09	-3	#4 both rooms and nights are invalid

ALGORITHM VERIFICATION

To verify that Algorithm 4-2 correctly screens out invalid data, we need to perform a **structured walk-through**. A structured walk-through records what happens at each input and processing step to verify that is it correct. In a way, it is like a role-playing game in which you get to take on the role of the computer and act out what it does as it runs a program. In this case, we will test the Algorithm 4-2 once for each test scenario. We can only move onto the development stage if the algorithm passes all the scenario tests.

To test an algorithm, we start by constructing a **trace table**. A trace table shows the value of each variable after each step of the algorithm. Algorithm steps are recorded in the left-hand column and the variables are listed across the top. For example, Table 4-11 shows a blank trace table for the first few steps of the algorithm.

TABLE 4-11 Empty Trace Table Showing Variables Across the Top and Algorithm 4-2 Steps Down the Side

Step	rooms	arrive	depart	nights	cost	discount	total	ok
1								
2								
2.1								
2.2								
2.3								
2.4								
...								

In the Step column of Table 4-11, you record the next step of the algorithm. If that step assigns a new value to a variable, then we make sure to record that change in the column for that variable. Let us walk through just the first two steps of the algorithm using the data from test scenario 1 (shown in Table 4-10). Refer to the final version of our algorithm for the step numbers and a description of each step.

Step 1 declares the variables. We already know that numeric variables are initialized to 0 when they are declared, so we can record 0 under the columns for **rooms**, **nights**, and **cost**. An **undefined variable** is one that has not been automatically initialized and includes all non-numeric data types. A question mark (?) indicates that a value is undefined. The first step in the algorithm (variable initialization) is shown in Table 4-12.

TABLE 4-12 Trace Table Setup

Step	rooms	arrive	depart	nights	cost	discount	total	ok
1	0	?	?	0	0.00	0.00	0.00	?

Step 2 is where data input takes place. The subtasks 2.1, 2.2, and 2.3 read data into **rooms**, **arrive**, and **depart**. Step 2.4 assigns a value to **cost** based on one of three alternatives. In this case, assume that **radioButton1** is checked so that the **cost** will be $109.00 (step 2.4.1). Using the data values provided by test scenario 1 (from Table 4-10) and assuming that **radioButton1** is checked (destination Orlando), Table 4-13 traces the data from test scenario 1 through steps 1 and 2.

TABLE 4-13 Trace of Test Scenario 1 through Algorithm 4-2 Steps 1 and 2

Step	rooms	arrive	depart	nights	cost	discount	total	ok
1	0	?	?	?	?	0.00	0.00	?
2								
2.1	2							
2.2		5/13/09						
2.3			5/17/09					
2.4								
2.4.1					109.00			

Data entries such as that shown in Table 4–13 are usually straightforward. We will not need to trace them for the other test scenarios. Its importance lies in the outcome. Notice that in this test scenario, data values are stored in all variables except ok, which remains undefined.

Step 3 assumes that data have been entered in step 2. It screens the data for errors and processes them if none are found. Notice that step 3.1 examines rooms to see if the value is invalid. It is not, so steps 3.1.1 and 3.1.2 (the sub-tasks of step 3.1) can be skipped. Similarly, after nights are calculated in step 3.2, step 3.3 examines nights to see if the data is invalid. It is not, so steps 3.3.1 and 3.3.2 (the sub-tasks of step 3.3) can be skipped. Normally, you would not have to trace steps that make no changes to variables.

Step 3.4 checks to see if ok is set to true (meaning that the data are valid). This step reveals a problem, however. Note that ok was never assigned a value! It is neither true nor false—it is undefined. Set 3.4 needs to evaluate it but cannot because ok does not provide a data value it can use. The trace table has exposed a hidden flaw in our program, as shown in Table 4–14.

TABLE 4-14 Trace of Test Scenario 1 through Algorithm 4-2 Step 3

Step	rooms	arrive	depart	nights	cost	discount	total	ok
3	2	5/13/09	5/17/09	0	109.00	0.00	0.00	?
3.1								
3.2				4				
3.3								
3.4								Problem!

Fortunately, this flaw is easily corrected. We will need to go back to step 1 of our algorithm and make sure ok is initialized to true when declared. If invalid data are encountered in steps 3.1.2 or 3.3.2 then ok will be set to false; otherwise, it will be true when the execution process arrives at step 3.4.

If we assume that this problem has been fixed, and that ok contains the value true, then we can continue on with the trace, as shown in Table 4-15. Notice that step 3.4.1 involves multiple alternatives, only one of which (3.4.1.2) is selected; the rest are omitted from the trace table. The final total is calculated in step 3.4.2 by multiplying rooms × nights × cost and subtracting the quantity rooms × discount.

TABLE 4-15 Trace of Test Scenario 1 from Algorithm 4-2 Step 3.4 Onward

Step	rooms	arrive	depart	nights	cost	discount	total	ok
3.4	2	5/13/09	5/17/09	4	109.00	0.00	0.00	true
3.4.1								
3.4.1.2						5.00		
3.4.2							832.00	
3.4.3								

Having assured ourselves that test scenario 1 works as it should, test scenarios 2, 3, and 4 should be tested in the same manner. Recording only those steps in which the contents of a variable changes, and combining all input into one line (step 2), the trace table for test scenario 2 appears as shown in Table 4-16.

TABLE 4-16 Trace of Test Scenario 2 with Algorithm 4-2

Step	rooms	arrive	depart	nights	cost	discount	total	ok
1	0	?	?	0	0	0.00	0.00	true
2		5/13/09	5/17/09		109			
3.1.1								false
3.2				4				
3.4								

When step 4 is reached, the value of ok is false. The click event ends without taking any action. Similar results are achieved for traces of test scenarios 3 and 4.

Development

The design process has yielded a workable solution to our program. As we proceed with the software development tasks, we will refer back to each design step to inform our actions.

CREATE THE INTERFACE

The interface for this application was given in detail in Figure 4-14. Create a new project called Vacation Planner and construct its interface as follows:

From the Properties window, change the following properties of Form1:

- The Size property should be at least a width of 660 and height of 480 pixels.
- The Text property should say "Vacation Planner".

From the ToolBox, place the following controls on the form to create the interface shown in Figure 4-18:

- a ComboBox control, in the upper left
- two MonthCalendar controls across the top third
- a button in the lower third, to the left
- a TextBox in the lower third to the right
- labels, as shown

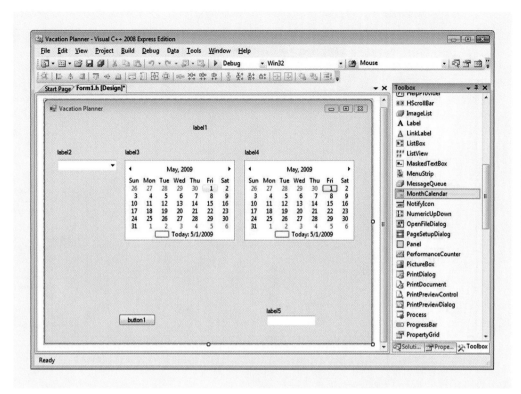

FIGURE 4-18 The initial interface

Next, make sure that `Form1` is selected, and place a **groupbox control** that spans most of the empty space below the calendars. GroupBoxes are containers. They define a bounded area in which a collection of controls (such as RadioButtons) can be placed. It is very important to make sure the GroupBox is the active object before attempting to put other controls inside of it, however. With the GroupBox selected, go back to the ToolBox and create eight radiobuttons to go inside the GroupBox by double-clicking the **radiobutton control** as many times as needed. Each double-click creates a new radiobutton. The radiobuttons will be created on top of one another in `groupBox1`, each one slightly offset, as shown in Figure 4-19.

NOTE   If you did not have the GroupBox selected when the RadioButtons were created they will be placed onto `Form1` instead of in the GroupBox. They cannot be dragged into the GroupBox. In a case like this you should delete them, select the GroupBox, and create them again.

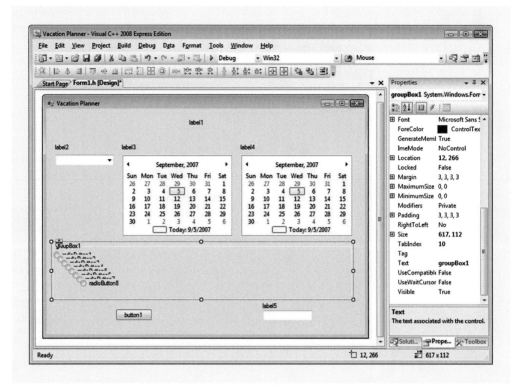

FIGURE 4-19 Selected GroupBox with RadioButtons in their default positions before being moved into position

Complete the interface to match as closely as possible the one shown in Figure 4-20, by doing the following:

- Reposition the RadioButtons within the GroupBox.
- Change the **Text** properties and **Font** (as necessary) of the labels.
- Resize and reposition your controls as needed.
- Rename your controls to match the names given in Figure 4-14.
- Change the **Text** property of the button to **Calculate**.
- Change the **Text** property of **groupBox1** to **Destination**.

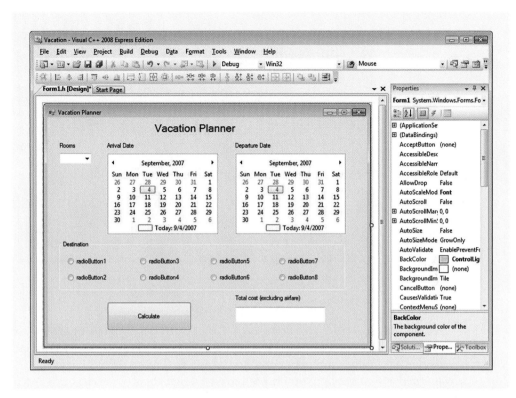

FIGURE 4-20 Final interface

The only interface task remaining is to complete the ComboBox control. As you have learned, ComboBoxes contain lists of items. To create the list, select the ComboBox control and then go to the Properties window and locate the Items property. You will find that the Items property currently says "Collection." Items are a collection of entries that you must create. Click the ellipsis (. . .) to the right of the word "Collection" and the items list pops up. Enter the values 1–6, one per line, as shown in Figure 4–21, and then click OK.

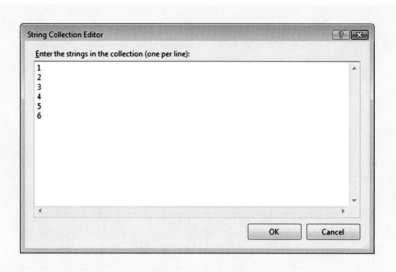

FIGURE 4-21 ComboBox items collection

As we learned earlier, the items in a ComboBox have index numbers associated with them. The first item in the list is assigned an index of 0, the second has an index of 1, and so on. The values for **cmbRooms** are shown in Figure 4–22. These index values were assigned automatically; you do not have to assign them yourself.

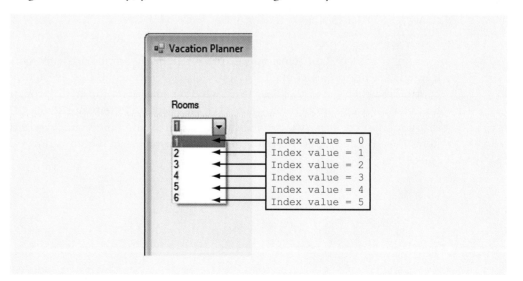

FIGURE 4-22 Index values for cmbRooms items

CODING

Two events were identified in our initial control table, the **Form1_Load()** event and the **btnCalc_Click()** event. First, the **Form1_Load()** event is where control properties can be initialized. The second, the `btnCalc_Click()` event is where we will implement the algorithm we developed earlier.

Coding `Form1_Load()`   Double-clicking on `Form1` in the design window opens up the `Form1_Load()` event-handler. This event-handler executes the commands within it as soon as the program starts, as the form is loading. It is common to use this event-handler as a place to set up default control settings. For example, it would be a good idea to have the number of rooms set to 1 by default, because most users will only want one room. This is a convenience for the user, and also ensures that `cmbRooms` will not accidentally be left empty, leading to another source of error. To set the number of rooms to 1 by default, we can set the `SelectedIndex` value of `cmbRooms` to 0. The command for this is shown in Example 4-15:

EXAMPLE 4-15: USING SELECTEDINDEX

```
cmbRooms->SelectedIndex = 0;
```

We should also initialize the RadioButtons; each one has an assigned destination name, and these can be assigned directly into the **Text** property of each RadioButton. In addition, we should choose one of the RadioButtons as the default by setting its **Checked** property to **true**. When one RadioButton in a GroupBox is checked, all others become unchecked automatically. The complete code for the `Form1_Load()` event is shown in Example 4-16

EXAMPLE 4-16: `Form1_Load()`

```
private: System::Void Form1_Load(System::Object^  sender,
System::EventArgs^  e) {
   cmbRooms->SelectedIndex = 0;
   radioButton1->Text = "Orlando";
   radioButton2->Text = "Las Vegas";
   radioButton3->Text = "Los Angeles";
   radioButton4->Text = "Cancun";
   radioButton5->Text = "Colorado";
   radioButton6->Text = "New York";
   radioButton7->Text = "Hawaii";
   radioButton8->Text = "Seattle";
   radioButton1->Checked = true;
}
```

Coding `btnCalc_Click()`   The code for the calculation process corresponds to the algorithm and incorporates the C++ code examples given when the algorithm was presented. Notice that the Boolean variable `ok` is initialized to **true** at the start to make sure we do not encounter the problem uncovered in our trace.

The date chosen on each calendar (**SelectionStart**) is assigned to the variables **arrive** and **depart**, which are of the DateTime data type. To get the number of nights, simply subtract `arrive` from `depart`, and indicate that the result should be in `Days`. `Days` is an integer. The difference between the arrival and departure dates is the number of nights of accommodation required. The calculation is shown in Example 4-17:

EXAMPLE 4-17: SUBTRACTING DAYS

```
nights = (depart - arrive).Days;
```

Notice that the `if` statement used to screen out valid and invalid data in the processing stage includes a very simple condition:

```
if (ok)
```

Remember that Boolean expressions evaluate to either `true` or `false`. Rather than using a relational expression, such as:

```
if (ok == true)
```

the Boolean variable `ok` already contains the Boolean value that is required. The code in Example 4-18 implements each of the tasks outlined in the algorithm for the Calculate button. The main steps of the algorithm have been turned into comments to make the sequence of events easier to follow.

EXAMPLE 4-18: `btnCalc_Click()`

```
private: System::Void btnCalc_Click(System::Object^  sender,
System::EventArgs^  e) {
// Variable declaration section
    int rooms;
    int nights;
    double cost;
    double discount;
    double total;
    Datetime arrive;
    DateTime depart;
    bool ok = true;

// Read data from input controls
    rooms = Convert::ToInt32(cmbRooms->SelectedItem);

    arrive = calArrive->SelectionStart;
    depart = calDepart->SelectionStart;

    if (radioButton1->Checked == true)
        cost = 109.00;
    else if ((radioButton2->Checked == true) ||
        (radioButton3->Checked == true))
        cost = 119.00;
    else
        cost = 129.00;
```

```
// Check for invalid rooms
   if (rooms <= 0)
   {
      MessageBox::Show("You must indicate how many rooms.");
      ok = false;
   }

// Compute nights
   nights = (depart - arrive).Days;

// Check for invalid nights
   if (nights <= 0)
   {
      MessageBox::Show("You must choose a departure date after
your arrival.");
      ok = false;
   }

// Process valid data
   if (ok)
   {
      switch (rooms)
      {
         case 1: discount = 0; break;
         case 2: discount = 5; break;
         case 3: discount = 6; break;
         case 4: discount = 10; break;
         case 5: case 6: discount = 11;
      }
      total = rooms * nights * (cost - discount);
      txtCost->Text = "$"+ total.ToString();
   }
}
```

4

ON YOUR OWN

TASK 1: TEST SCENARIOS

In the test strategy section of the design stage, four scenarios were created with examples of input data from each. Test your program with each of the four scenarios to verify that it performs as expected.

TASK 2: REWRITE THE SWITCH STATEMENT

Replace the switch statement with a multiple alternative if statement and rerun your program. It should perform as before.

TASK 3: EXTREME NESTING

If you did not use the Boolean variable `ok`, how could you write the program to work correctly? One answer lies in increasing the amount of nesting. For example, examine the indented pseudocode below illustrating nested double alternative `if` statements:

1.1.   if `rooms` is invalid

      1.1.1.   display an error message

1.2.   else

      1.2.1.   if `nights` is invalid

            1.2.1.1.   display an error message

      1.2.2.   else

            1.2.2.1.   process the data.

Rewrite your program so that it uses nested double alternative `if` structures as shown in this pseudocode.

QUICK REVIEW

1. Control structures control the flow of statement execution in your program.

2. The three major types of control structures are: sequential, selection, and repetition.

3. Sequential control structures execute statements in order without skipping or repeating any.

4. Selection structures make it possible to skip statements.

5. Repetition control structures make it possible to repeat statements.

6. Selection structures may provide single, double, or multiple alternatives.

7. Boolean expressions are evaluated to determine whether an alternative is executed.

8. Relational operators are used in Boolean expressions to compare values.

9. The relational operators are: (>, >=, <, <=, ==, !=).

10. Relational operators are binary, left-to-right associative, and have two levels of precedence.

11. Single alternative `if` statements use a Boolean expression to determine whether the alternative is executed.

12. If an alternative requires multiple tasks, they need to be enclosed in { }.

13. A double alternative `if` statement provides two sets of executable statements (one if the condition evaluates to `true` and another if it evaluates to `false`).

14. Logical operators are used to compare Boolean values.

15. The logical operators are the not operator (`!`), the and operator (`&&`), and the or operator (`||`).

16. The not operator (`!`) is a unary operator, while the and operator (`&&`) and the or operator (`||`) are binary.

17. The not operator (`!`) reverses a Boolean value.

18. When the and operator (`&&`) is used, the evaluation result is `true` only if both operands are `true`.

19. When the or operator (`||`) is used, the evaluation result is `false` only when both operands are `false`.

20. Control structures can be nested, that is, placed inside of other control structures.

21. Multiple alternative selection structures can be created from nested double alternative structures.

22. The multiple alternative `if` statement alleviates the nesting problem.

23. Multiple alternative `if` statements are good for situations where ranges of data are being selected.

24. The `if...else if...else` statement implements multiple selection.

25. The `switch` statement is another form of multiple alternative selection.

26. `Switch` statements are good for situations in which individual data values are being selected.

27. The `break` statement allows control to transfer out of the `switch` statement after a case has been processed, much like a multiple alternative `if` statement.

28. If `break` statements are omitted, then control in a `switch` statement passes from one case directly to the next.

29. Index values are used to identify items in a ComboBox using integers.

30. The index value of the first item in a list is 0.

31. The index value of an empty ComboBox is -1.

32. Test strategies identify the variables most likely to contain invalid values.

33. Test scenarios provide sets of valid and invalid data to test a program with.

34. The test scenarios are used to verify the correctness of algorithms.

35. Algorithm verification is done using a structured walk-through with trace tables.

4

TERMS TO KNOW

and operator (&&) Boolean expression

binary operator

`break` statement

`case` statement

ComboBox control

control structure(s)

DateTime data type

double alternative `if` statement

double alternative selection

equal to operator (==)

`Form1_Load()` event

greater than operator (>)

greater than or equal to operator (>=)

GroupBox control

`if` statement

`if...else` statement

`if...else if...else` statement

index value

left-to-right associative

less than operator (<)

less than or equal to operator (<=)

logical operator(s)

MessageBox

`MessageBox::Show()`

MonthCalendar control

multiple alternative `if` statement

multiple alternative selection

nested double alternative `if` statements

nesting

not equal to operator (!=)

not operator (!)

operator precedence

or operator (||)

RadioButton control

relational operator(s)

repetition control structure

SelectedIndex

selection control structure(s)

SelectionStart

sequential control structure(s)

short-circuit operator(s)

single-alternative **if** statements

single alternative selection

structured walk-through

switch statement

test scenario

trace table

unary operator

undefined value

4

EXERCISES

Use the evaluation tables for !, && and || (provided earlier in Tables 4-2, 4-3, and 4-4) to answer Questions 1–7. What is the final evaluation (`true` or `false`) for each Boolean expression?

1. What is the value of the condition ((score >= 0) || (score <= 100)) when `score` is 75?

2. What is the value of the condition in Question 1 when `score` is 150?

3. What is the value of the condition in Question 1 when `score` is –100?

4. What is the value of the condition (!((score >= 0) && (score <= 100))) when `score` is 75?

5. What is the value of the condition in Question 4 when `score` is 150?

6. What is the value of the condition in Question 4 when `score` is –100?

7. What is the value of the condition (!(score > 25) || (score < 100) && (score > 0) when `score` is 50?

8. Multiple selection between three or more alternatives can be implemented in all of the following ways except:

   a. a `switch` statement

   b. a multiple alternative `if` statement

   c. nested double alternative `if` statements

   d. a series of single alternative `if` statements

   e. a double alternative `if` statement

9. A multiple alternative `if` statement allows how many alternatives to be processed?

    a. only one of the alternatives

    b. two alternatives

    c. three alternatives

    d. all of them

10. A `switch` statement would *not* be appropriate for which data type?

    a. char

    b. int

    c. double

    d. All of the above are appropriate.

11. A binary operator _____.

    a. only works on binary numbers.

    b. multiplies its operand by powers of 2.

    c. produces two results.

    d. has two operands.

    e. is left-to-right associative.

12. A(n) _____ is a sequence of operands and operators that reduces to a single value.

    a. function

    b. value

    c. expression

    d. variable

    e. declaration

13. _____ rules are used to determine the order in which operators in an expression are evaluated.

    a. Assignment

    b. Precedence

    c. Evaluation

    d. Side effect

    e. Calculation

14. What is the value of num after this program segment executes?

```
int a = 5;
int b = 6;
int num = 4;

if (a < b)
    num = 1
else if (b > a)
    num = a + b;
else if (a == 5)
    num = a;
else if (a > 0)
    num = b;
else
    num = 0;
```

15. Given the nested if statements below, what is the final value of num?

```
int a = 5;    int b = 6;
num = 4;
if (a < 0)
    if (b > 0)
        num = a + b;
    else
        num = a - b;
```

16. Rewrite the switch statement below using one or more if statements.

```
switch (channel)
{
case 1: txtOut->Text = "ABC"; break;
case 2: txtOut->Text = "CBS"; break;
case 3: txtOut->Text = "MSNBC"; break;
case 4: txtOut->Text = "FOX"; break;
case 5: txtOut->Text = "PBS"; break;
}
```

17. Rewrite the following as a switch statement. Assume that intNum is an integer variable containing a value from 0 to 3 (indicating the current question being answered in a history quiz).

```
if (intNum == 4)
    txtGrade->Text = "A"
else if (intNum == 3)
    txtGrade->Text = "B"
```

```
      else if (intNum == 2)
         txtGrade->Text = "C"
      else if (intNum == 1)
         txtGrade->Text = "D"
      else
         txtGrade->Text = "F"
      end if
```

18. Assume that **quest** is an integer variable containing a question number. Write a **switch** statement that places the last name of a U.S. President into the Text property of textbox **txtOut** according to the following criteria: "Washington" (if **quest** = 0), "Lincoln" (if **quest** = 1), "Jefferson" (if **quest** = 2), or "Roosevelt" (if **quest** = 3).

19. Rewrite your answer to Question 18 using a multiple alternative **if** statement.

20. Rewrite your answer to Question 18 using only properly indented, nested, double alternative **if** statements

Projects

1. Largest Number

Write a program that reads three integers and determines which is the largest. Create an interface for the program similar to the one shown in Figure 4-23. Your program must use nested double alternative **if** statements. You may assume that the data will be entered correctly as integers.

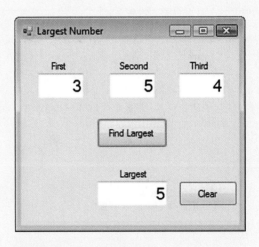

FIGURE 4-23 Interface for program that finds the largest of two integers

2. Parking Problem Solver

Write a program to help a student decide whether it is better to buy a semester parking permit or to pay daily parking fees. In the example below, the user enters the cost of the semester permit, the daily parking cost, and the number of days parking will be required next semester. The program should display a message advising the user to either purchase the permit or pay daily fees. If the user leaves any of the three fields blank, the program should produce an error message. Similarly, if the user enters a negative value or zero, an error message should display. Figure 4-24 shows some possible results. In particular, Figure 4-24a shows the program working correctly with a permit cost of $100.00, daily pass of $2.00, and 51 days of parking required. Figure 4-24b shows a `MessageBox` informing the user that an input item was left blank. Figure 4-24c shows a `MessageBox` that indicates that negative values were entered.

4

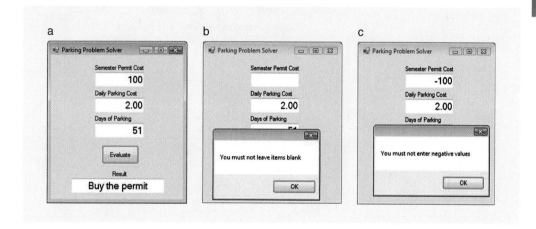

FIGURE 4-24 Outcome results for Parking Problem Solver

3. Integer Calculator

Write the code for the Simple Calculator interface shown earlier in Figures 4-7 through 4-12. Your program should screen out the following errors by popping up an appropriate `MessageBox`.

- Either one or both operands are missing.
- If / or % are chosen as the operator, then the numerator (`txtRight`) must not be 0.

If an error occurs, the form should reset itself after the user has clicked OK in the `MessageBox`. Your program should not perform any computations if an error has occurred.

4. Computer Purchase Program

Write a program with an interface similar to that shown in Figure 4-25. The program should calculate the cost of a computer with the options selected by the user. Use the following pricing information:

Processor: 3GHz ($200), 4GHz ($300)

Memory: 2M ($150), 4M ($250)

Hard drive: 256G ($125), 512G ($200)

Optical drive: CD ($50), CD/DVD ($75), DVD/RW ($100)

Monitor: 17" ($200), 19" ($300), 21" ($400)

FIGURE 4-25 Computer Purchase program

5. Program Design: Game Formulas

Most computer games use formulas to define what happens when a user interacts with the environment. For example, the formula for how much damage your player inflicted on a monster might be something like:

damage = (your strength + your weapon) − monster's protection

Assume that there are 100 possible values for each of the variables on the right side of this formula (from 0 = weak to 99 = strong). You want to write a simple program that allows the user to enter their strength, weapon strength, and monster's protection, and then click a button to find out what the damage will be. If the damage is $<= 0$, then the monster was unaffected by your strike. The higher the damage number, the more damage you inflicted.

Design a complete solution, including an interface sketch, object table, data table, algorithm, table of testing strategy, and tracing examples of good and invalid data, through the algorithm to verify that it is correct. When you are certain your design is correct, create and implement the program.

4

REPETITION

IN THIS CHAPTER, YOU WILL:

- ■ Learn the strengths and weaknesses of user-controlled repetition
- ■ Study the various forms of repetition control structures
- ■ Learn how pre- and post-test loops work
- ■ Use `for` loops, `while` loops, and `do...while` loops
- ■ Generate random numbers
- ■ Learn how the loop process relates to summation, counting, and other common tasks
- ■ Use a loop to construct an extended string of characters

In Chapter 4, you learned that control structures are the fundamental building blocks of all programs. You also learned about three types of control structures: sequential, selection, and repetition. Chapters 1, 2, and 3 featured tutorials that used only sequential control structures. Chapter 4 centered on selection structures. Now, you are ready to explore the third category, repetition structures. Like sequential and selection structures, repetition structures are very important tools. Many of the most basic programming tasks such as summation, counting, processing lists, and building a report with rows and columns of data, center on repetition.

User-Controlled Repetition

The term **user-controlled repetition** refers to the process of repeating a series of interactive tasks, such as entering data into textboxes or clicking a button, to make a program work. For example, suppose a friend who is taking a chemistry class comes to you for help. Your friend is running an experiment that generates five values. She wants you to make a simple program that will perform the following tasks:

- display the five values
- compute the average

One way to solve the problem is to create a data averaging program with an interface similar to the one shown in Figure 5-1.

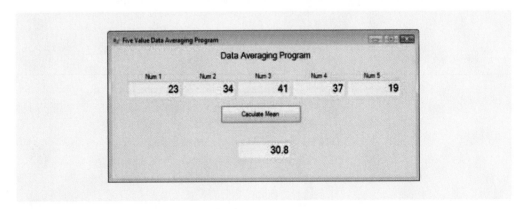

FIGURE 5-1 Data averaging program interface

The data table for this program, shown in Table 5-1, has only seven variables.

TABLE 5-1 Data Table for Data Averaging Program

Variable Name	Data Type	Usage
num1	int	first value
num2	int	second value
num3	int	third value
num4	int	fourth value
num5	int	fifth value
sum	int	sum of all values
mean	double	arithmetic mean

The algorithm for the Calculate button is relatively simple to devise and the Visual C++ code follows naturally from it, as shown in Figure 5-2.

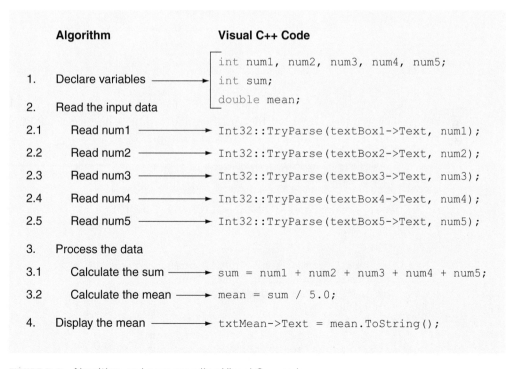

FIGURE 5-2 Algorithm and corresponding Visual C++ code

You can now present a solution to your friend's problem. The program works exactly as you designed.

However, the story is not over. The following week, your friend returns with another request. She now needs to merge the results of three lab groups together. Thus, she needs a new version of your program that will average 15 values.

Consider the changes this requires. You will need ten more textboxes and labels so that the interface looks like the one shown in Figure 5-3.

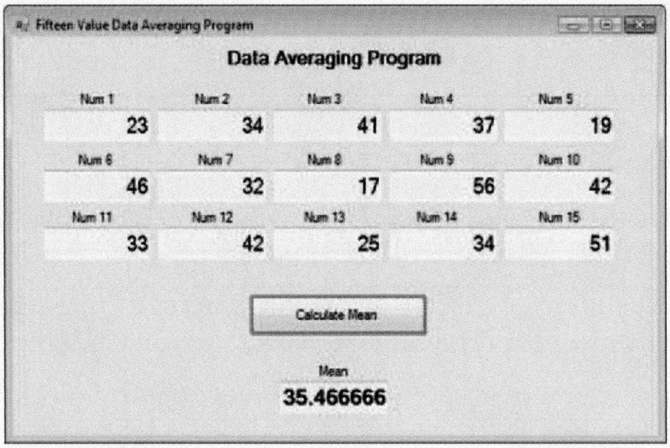

FIGURE 5-3 Fifteen value data averaging program

You also need to create ten additional variables to read data in from the ten additional text boxes. This requires declaring the variables and adding a line for each assignment. The program now is much longer, as shown in Example 5-1.

EXAMPLE 5-1: SUMMATION OF 15 INTEGERS

```
private: System::Void btnMean_Click(System::Object^ sender, System::
EventArgs^ e)
{
        int num1, num2, num3, num4, num5;
        int num6, num7, num8, num9, num10;
        int num11, num12, num13, num14, num15;
        int sum;
        double mean;
        Int32::TryParse(textBox1->Text, num1);
        Int32::TryParse(textBox2->Text, num2);
        Int32::TryParse(textBox3->Text, num3);
        Int32::TryParse(textBox4->Text, num4);
        Int32::TryParse(textBox5->Text, num5);
```

```
        Int32::TryParse(textBox6->Text, num6);
        Int32::TryParse(textBox7->Text, num7);
        Int32::TryParse(textBox8->Text, num8);
        Int32::TryParse(textBox9->Text, num9);
        Int32::TryParse(textBox10->Text, num10);
        Int32::TryParse(textBox11->Text, num11);
        Int32::TryParse(textBox12->Text, num12);
        Int32::TryParse(textBox13->Text, num13);
        Int32::TryParse(textBox14->Text, num14);
        Int32::TryParse(textBox15->Text, num15);
        sum = num1 + num2 + num3 + num4 + num5 +
              num6 + num7 + num8 + num9 + num10 +
              num11 + num12 + num13 + num14 + num15;
        mean = sum / 15.0;
        txtMean->Text = mean.ToString();
}
```

Every time your friend asks you for a change like this, you will have to modify code to suit her needs and then recompile the program. This could become time consuming if she needs many more changes.

Unfortunately, the situation is worse than you suspect. The next week she returns with another request. Her next task is to average all of the results of all of the lab groups in all lab sections of the class. This means averaging 120 numbers!

Do you really want to create a form with 120 text boxes and labels? Do you want to set their properties, and write all that code? Worse, what if these requests continue? Next, she might want a program that averages all of the data for all of the classes for the past three semesters, or some other larger task. What started out as a simple program is on the verge of becoming extremely difficult to manage.

In fact, this is a common programming dilemma. It is easy to underestimate the requirements of a problem and then be caught in a cycle of software revision in which you must respond to one modification after another. The program is always in need of attention and becomes a high-maintenance project.

The solution to the maintenance problem starts with the recognition that the original design was a **single-purpose solution** only. The original design handled only one version of the problem (averaging five numbers). It would have been better to design a **general solution** (averaging any amount of numbers). As a rule, it is usually better to design general solutions. For example, Figure 5-4 shows the interface for a program that can handle any amount of input data.

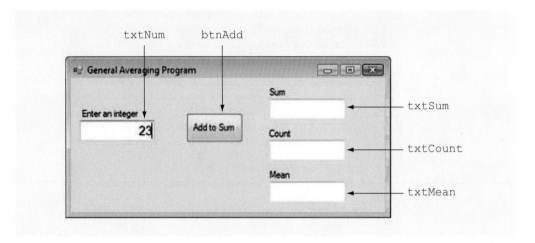

FIGURE 5-4   General averaging program

In this version of the program, the user enters the data items one at a time into `txtNum`, and clicks `btnAdd` after each entry. With each click of `btnAdd`, the number in `txtNum` is added to the `sum`, the `count` increases by one, the `mean` is calculated (`sum / count`), and all three are displayed, as shown in Figure 5-5. Notice that, in addition to displaying the results, `btnAdd` also resets `txtNum` to blank, in preparation for the next number the user wants to enter.

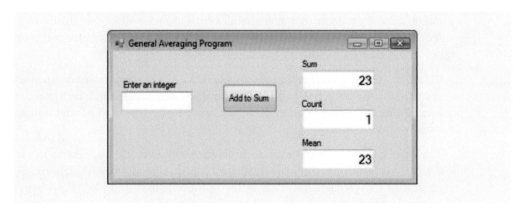

FIGURE 5-5   Result of clicking `btnAdd` after entering the first value

If the user enters the five values, originally shown in Figure 5-1 and clicks `btnAdd` after each entry, the final result will be the one shown in Figure 5-6.

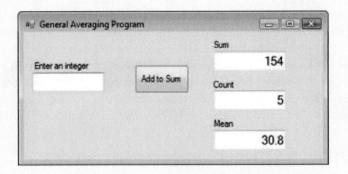

FIGURE 5-6   Results after all five values have been entered

The data table for this version is very economical, requiring only four variables, shown in Table 5-2. This version will handle the summation and processing of 5, 15, 120 or any number of integers.

TABLE 5-2   Data Table for General Averaging Program

Variable Name	Data Type	Usage
count	int	Count of values entered
sum	int	Sum of values entered
num	int	Current value entered
mean	double	Mean of values entered

Accumulating a Sum and Counting

The process of using repetition to add a group of values is called **summation**. The averaging program accumulates the sum of as many integers as the user wants to enter. **Accumulating a sum** is performed by starting out with a variable that will store the result (sum) and initializing it to 0. The program then adds values to sum one at a time. With each addition, sum gets larger. In this program, each time btnAdd is clicked, a number is read from txtNum into num and that value added to the amount stored in sum. In this way, sum increases every time the btnAdd_Click() event takes place.

Counting is also an accumulation process. In the averaging program, count is originally initialized to 0 and increases by one within each btnAdd_Click() event. The value stored in count is incremented with each btnAdd click. Thus count is, in effect, counting the clicks. Because each click reads a value into num, the variable count is really keeping track of how many items of data were read. This will be valuable later on when the program needs count and sum to calculate the mean.

There is a trick to this program, however. To make it work, the variables `sum` and `count` must not be reset to 0 as the program is running. Unfortunately, this will happen if they are declared inside of `btnAdd_Click()` because they would be local variables with respect to that event handler. Local variables are removed from memory when the method to which they belong ends. Local variables are also created from scratch each time an event handler begins execution. For this program you need variables that are more long lasting–that is, you need variables that are created once and are not local to any event handler. Such variables are called instance variables and are the topic of the next section.

Instance Variables

As you will recall from Chapter 2, local variables are variables that are declared inside of a method, such as an event handler. All of the variables used in the Tutorials so far have been local variables. Their scope was confined to the event handler (local scope). A local variable and its contents disappear from memory when its event handler ends.

If you need a variable (and its contents) to continue to exist after an event handler ends, you can create an instance variable instead of a local variable. **Instance variables** exist as long as the program (an instance of `Form1`) is running because they belong to the `Form1` class definition. Another way to say this is that they have **class scope**. This means they exist in memory as long as the program (an object created from the `Form1` class definition) is running. They do not disappear from memory until the entire program ends.

NOTE You will recall from Chapter 1 that the Visual C++ programs created in this book are Windows Forms applications. The Windows Form you create in each project is called `Form1` by default. Your Visual C++ program is really just the definition of how a `Form1` object should look and behave. You add controls to `Form1` to provide its look and event handlers to define how it behaves.

For now, the main thing you need to know about instance variables is that any event handler can use an instance variable at any time and that the instance variable retains its contents even when that event handler ends. This is exactly what is needed for both `sum` and `count`. Their values should increase with every click of `btnAdd`, and remain present from one click event to the next. Later in the Tutorial for this chapter, instance variables will be used to accumulate strings of text and to generate random numbers. Instance variables will play an important role in almost all future projects.

Figure 5-7 indicates the location of instance variable declarations. Notice that they occur immediately after the line:

```
#pragma endregion
```

The `#pragma endregion` statement indicates the end of the region in which the code is automatically produced by the Windows Form Designer as you create a program. You do not normally make any changes in the code in that region as modifications could jeopardize the performance of the program.

Below the #pragma endregion line you are free to write whatever code your program requires. This is where event handlers are automatically placed and where instance variables are declared, as shown in Figure 5-7. Notice that the instance variables sum and count are declared immediately after the Windows Form Designer code section.

FIGURE 5-7 Instance variables, event handlers, and Windows Forms Designer code

Example 5-2 provides a look at the code from Figure 5-7. Note that the code for btnAdd_Click() follows a simple algorithm plan (as illustrated by the comments): declare local variables, read num, process num, display results. Once these tasks have been completed it also resets the txtNum text box on Form1 so that the user may enter the next number. The `Focus()` method seen in the last line of code in Example 5-2 places the insertion point in that text box.

EXAMPLE 5-2: INSTANCE VARIABLE CALCULATING THE MEAN

```
#pragma endregion
// Instance variables
int sum;
int count;
private: System::Void btnAdd_Click(System::Object^  sender,
System::EventArgs^  e)
    {
        // Local variables
        double mean;
        int num;
        // Read num
        Int32::TryParse(txtNum->Text, num);
        // Process num
        sum = sum + num;
        count = count + 1;
        mean = (double) sum / count;
        // Display results
        txtSum->Text = sum.ToString();
        txtCount->Text = count.ToString();
        txtMean->Text = mean.ToString();
        // Reset for next number
        txtNum->Text = "";   // makes the text box blank
        txtNum->Focus();     // puts the cursor in the text box
    }
};
}
```

The `btnAdd_Click()` event handler requires two local variables (`mean` and `num`). It is appropriate that `mean` be declared `double` because it may need to represent a value with decimal places.

The processing section is the key to understanding this program. With each click of `btnAdd`, you can see that processing entails adding the number the user entered (`num`) to `sum` and adding 1 to `count`. In this way, `sum` and `count` get larger as the user enters data and clicks `btnAdd` repeatedly.

Note the statement in which `mean` is calculated:

```
mean = (double) sum / count;
```

This statement requires that either `sum` or `count` be converted to a `double` to avoid integer division. In this case, that conversion is done using conventional C++ typecasting, as discussed in Chapter 3.

Repetition Control Structures

User-controlled repetition works because the user clicks the same button (btnAdd) over and over until all the data items have been read and processed. This kind of repetition is manually controlled. The program in Example 5-1 executed a series of tasks every time the user clicks the button.

Sometimes, however, you want the program to automatically repeat a task, without the user's interaction. For example, if you wanted to use the interface shown in Figure 5-6 to find the sum of 50 numbers you could do it, but it would be a long, boring task, requiring you to enter each number, one at a time, and click btnAdd after each entry. To create a program that would automate the calculations, you need to use a repetition control structure.

Repetition control structures (commonly called **loops**) direct your program to repeat a series of instructions. These instructions are contained within the loop, in a section known as the **loop body**. The loop body may be a single statement ending in a semicolon, or a group of statements enclosed in curly brackets { }. Each repetition of the statement(s) in the loop body is known as an **iteration**.

The number of iterations is controlled by a Boolean expression called a **loop condition**. Recall from the discussion of selection structures in Chapter 4 how Boolean expressions, such as (num > 0), are used to determine which course of action to take. For example, if the Boolean expression evaluates to true, one group of instructions is executed; otherwise another group of instructions is executed. A similar principle applies to loops. If the loop condition is true, then the group of statements in the loop body is executed, and if the expression is false, the loop is over and control passes on to the remainder of the program.

Unlike if statements, the statements in the body of a loop may be executed many times depending on the repeated evaluation of the loop condition. As long as the expression evaluates to true, the loop body tasks are performed. Often, the loop condition focuses on a specific variable, called a **loop control variable**, to determine whether to execute loop body instructions again. The loop condition checks the value of the loop control variable. For example, some loop control variables count the number of iterations. The loop condition may check to make sure the count has not exceeded the maximum number of iterations it will allow.

Loops are often classified according to where the loop condition is placed in relation to the loop body. If the condition comes before the loop body, the loop is called a **pre-test loop**. If the loop condition comes after the loop body it is called a **post-test loop**. Figure 5-8 illustrates the differences between the flow of control represented by pre-test and post-test loops. The flowcharts are read starting from the small black circle and ending at the white circle with the black dot inside it. The diamond shape represents the loop condition. Notice that two paths lead out from the condition depending on the evaluation (true or false). If the evaluation is true, the statements in the loop body are performed. If the evaluation is false, then the loop is over and control transfers on to the next statement after the loop.

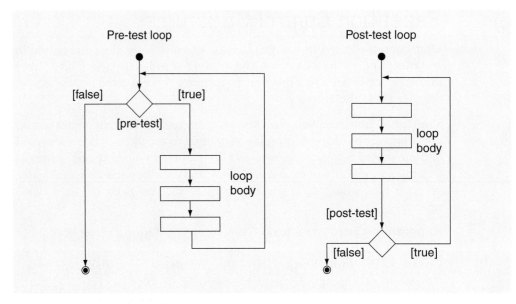

FIGURE 5-8 Flow of control in pre-test and post-test loops

We will examine the repetition process as we look at three specific repetition control statements common in the C++ language: `while` loops, `do...while` loops, and `for` loops.

The `while` Loop

Recall that a user-controlled loop would be a bad choice for a program that was to sum fifty consecutive integers because of the amount of data entry and button clicking required. You can automate the same task using a `while` loop. The **while loop** is a pre-test loop. The loop condition (pre-test) comes before the loop body.

Figure 5-9 is a flow diagram for a `while` loop that adds the sum of the integers from 50 to 99 automatically. It begins by initializing the two key variables `sum` and `num`. The variable `sum` starts out set to 0 and is used to accumulate the sum of all the integers from 50 to 99. The variable `num` will represent each of those integers and serve as the loop control variable. Within the loop body `num` is added to `sum` as the key step in the accumulation process.

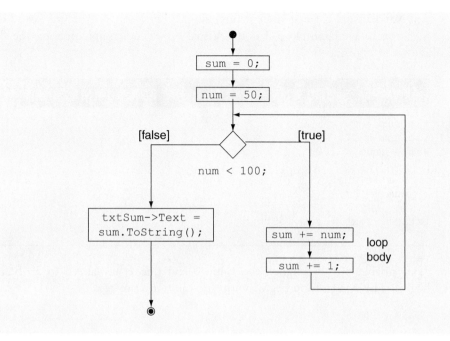

FIGURE 5-9 Flow diagram of a `while` loop used to accumulate the `sum` of integers 50–100

When written in C++ code, the `while` loop begins with the keyword `while` followed by the pre-test condition in parentheses. If the pre-test evaluates to true, the statements in the loop body are performed. When all the tasks in the loop body have been completed, control transfers up to the pre-test condition at the top of the loop and it is evaluated again. If the loop condition is true, then the statements in the loop body are performed again. If the loop condition is false, then the loop is over and control transfers to the next statement after the `while` loop.

The following is the syntax definition of a C++ `while` loop with multiple tasks in the loop body (labeled `task 1 − task n`):

```
while (loop condition)
{
    task 1;
    task 2;
    .
    .
    .
    task n;
}
```

Any valid Visual C++ statement, including other control structures, can be included in the loop body. Example 5-3 is the Visual C++ code implementing the flow diagram shown in Figure 5-9.

EXAMPLE 5-3: USING A `while` LOOP FOR SUMMATION

```
int sum = 0;
int num = 50;
while (num < 100)
{
    sum += num;
    num += 1;
}
txtSum->Text = sum.ToString();
```

The variable `sum` is assigned the value 0 and `num` is initialized to 50 before the loop begins. The `while` loop begins with the following pre-test:

```
while (num < 100)
```

It then evaluates the pre-test condition `(num < 100)` to determine whether the expression is `true` or `false`. In this example, the value stored in `num` is initially set to 50, so the pre-test condition evaluates to `true`. When the condition is true, control is allowed to enter the loop body.

The loop body contains two statements. The first `(sum += num;)` adds the value contained in `num` to that contained in `sum`. The second `(num += 1;)` adds 1 to the value stored in `num`. At this point the statements in the loop body are finished, `sum` is set to 50, and `num` is set to 51.

When the statements in the loop body have been completed, control goes back to the condition at the top of the loop `(num < 100)`. Because `num` is 51, the condition evaluates to `true` and this result transfers control back into the loop body to perform its statements.

This iterative process continues with the value in `num` increasing by one with each iteration until finally the value in `num` becomes greater than 99. When `num` is 100, then evaluation of the loop condition yields `false`. This result transfers control to the next statement after the loop body in which `sum` is displayed in `txtSum->Text`. The loop is now over and the rest of the program can finish.

INCREMENTATION AND DECREMENTATION

Notice that the program shown in Example 5-3 increases `num` by 1 within the loop body. There are three common ways, shown in Example 5-4, to write the code for this task.

EXAMPLE 5-4: THREE WAYS TO INCREMENT A LOOP CONTROL VARIABLE

```
num = num + 1;
num += 1;
num++;
```

The first statement in Example 5-4 is regular assignment, familiar since Chapter 1. The second statement is shorthand assignment using the addition assignment operator (+=) first described in Chapter 2. The third is new and uses the incrementation operator (++). The **incrementation operator (++)** increases the value of an integer variable by 1. There is also a **decrementation operator (--)** used to subtract 1 from the value in a variable.

Incrementation and decrementation operators are common in loop settings, especially in situations where counters are used because counters often need to adjust their value by 1.

There are several versions of each operator depending on where the operator is placed. The **prefix incrementation** and **prefix decrementation** forms place the operator in front of the variable name (++num; or --num;) which has the effect of performing the incrementation or decrementation task immediately when the statement executes. The **postfix incrementation** and **postfix decrementation** operators place the operator behind the variable (num++; or num--;) which delays processing until all other tasks in the statement are finished. For example, the loop in Example 5-3 could have been written quite concisely as shown in Example 5-5 using the postfix incrementation operator to increment num after the summation task (sum += num) had been accomplished.

EXAMPLE 5-5: POSTFIX INCREMENTATION

```
while (num < 100) sum += num++;
```

Note that the while loop in Example 5-5 does not use curly brackets { } to delimit the extent of the loop body. The brackets are only necessary when you have more than one statement within the loop body. Example 5-5 has only one statement within the body of the while loop:

```
sum += num++;
```

Without the brackets, the loop body is assumed to include no more than one statement and the end of the control structure is considered to be the semicolon at the end of the line. The postfix incrementation operator attached to num increments num after adding the value stored in num to sum.

do...while Loops:

The **do...while loop** is similar to the while loop in that it evaluates a loop condition to determine whether control will be allowed to pass on to the statements in the body of the loop. However, rather than using the condition as a pre-test at the top of the loop, the do...while loop uses it as a post-test at the bottom. Figure 5-10 illustrates the flow of control using a do...while loop to solve the summation problem (that is, summing integers from 50–99) discussed in the section on the while loop.

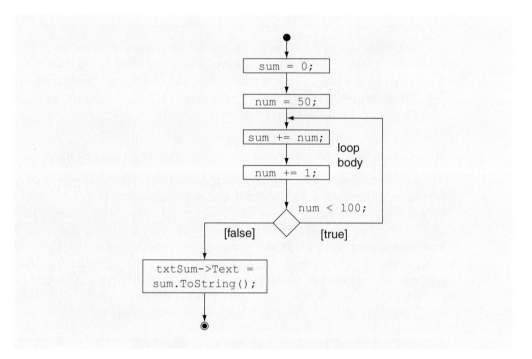

FIGURE 5-10 Flow diagram of a do...while loop used to accumulate the sum of integers 50–100

Notice that the post-test condition is first encountered only after the statements in the body of the loop have been executed one time. This is the primary difference between the while and do...while control structures. The do...while structure always processes statements in the loop body at least once.

The first line of the do...while loop begins with the keyword **do** followed by the loop body. The loop body uses curly brackets { } to enclose any statements that may be in it. When all the tasks in the loop body have been completed the post-test condition is evaluated. If the post-test loop condition is **true** then the statements in the loop body are performed again by transferring control back up to the top of the loop body. If the post-test condition is **false** then control transfers to the next statement after the loop. The following is the syntax of a do...while loop with multiple tasks (task 1 – task n) in the loop body:

```
do
{
    task 1;
    task 2;
    .
    .
    .
    task n;
} while (loop condition);
```

In Example 5-6, the `do...while` loop adds the sum of the integers from 50 to 100. The post-test condition of this `do...while` loop is identical to the pre-test condition of the `while` loop shown in Example 5-3.

EXAMPLE 5-6: USING A `do...while` LOOP FOR SUMMATION

```
int sum = 0;
int num = 50;
do
{
    sum += num;
    num += 1;
} while (num < 100);
txtSum->Text = sum.ToString();
```

When the `do...while` loop begins, it immediately executes the statements in the body of the loop. There is no pre-test. Only after the statements in the body of the loop have executed the first time does the `do...while` loop evaluate the condition (num < 100) to determine whether it is true or false. A post-test evaluation of true sends control back up to the top of the structure (the `do` statement) where the statements in the body of the loop will be executed again.

The `do...while` loop is an appropriate structure for situations in which you know that the first set of data items can be processed without being screened by a test condition. The `while` loop, which always tests data before allowing control to pass into the loop body, is more common.

The `for` Loop

A **for loop** is a pre-test loop that can have its own built-in loop control variable. The syntax for the `for` loop is more complex than `while` or `do...while` because it has features that initialize, test, and update a built-in loop control variable. A common type of loop control variable is a counter. Counters are meant to be updated, usually incremented by 1, with each iteration.

The `for` loop begins with the keyword `for` followed by a set of parentheses in which semicolons divide the statement into three separate clauses: initialization, condition, and update. The **initialization clause** assigns values to variables that the loop requires, such as the loop control variable. It is executed only once, at the start of the loop. The **condition** is the pre-test condition that determines whether the body of the loop may be entered. The **update clause** usually assigns a new value to the loop control variable. The update clause is executed at the end of each iteration, immediately before the loop condition is evaluated. The following is the syntax for a `for` loop with multiple tasks in the loop body:

```
for (initialization; condition; update)
{
    task 1;
    task 2;
    .
    .
    .
    task n;
}
```

The `for` loop shown in Figure 5-11 includes three statements (separated by semicolons) within the parentheses. The loop control variable in this example (`counter`) is assumed to have been declared as an integer prior to the loop.

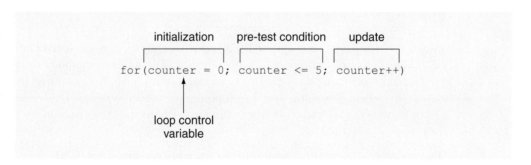

FIGURE 5-11 For loop structure with initialization, pre-test condition and update sections

Now consider a short example of how the `for` loop might be used to add up the values 1, 2, 3, 4, and 5. Figure 5-12 shows the flow diagram for this loop.

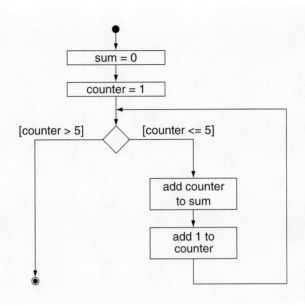

FIGURE 5-12 Flow diagram for a program to add a sum of integers 1 through 5

Because this loop is a pre-test structure, if the statements in the body are to be executed, the entrance condition (the pre-test) must evaluate to **true**. The number of iterations (5) has already been determined before the loop executes. When **counter** is greater than 5, the loop ends and control passes on to whatever statements come next in the program after the loop.

The C++ code for this structure is presented in the code in Example 5-7.

EXAMPLE 5-7: USING A *For* LOOP IN SUMMATION

```
int sum = 0;
for (int counter = 1; counter <= 5; counter++)
    sum += counter;
txtSum->Text = sum.ToString();
```

Figure 5-13 illustrates the first steps in the process of accumulating the **sum**. The highlighted statements in the C++ code match the highlighted steps in the flow diagram beneath it. In addition, the contents of the variables **sum** and **counter** are shown to illustrate how they are affected by these steps.

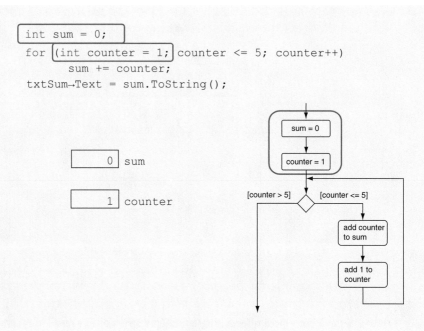

FIGURE 5-13 Initializing sum and counter

Two statements are executed before the condition is checked the first time. One statement initializes the integer variable **sum** to 0. A second statement initializes the **counter** to 1. After initialization the pre-test condition is evaluated as shown in Figure 5-14.

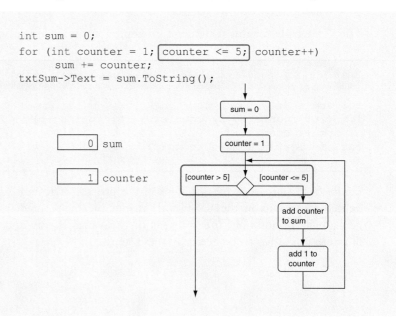

FIGURE 5-14 Pre-test evaluation

Because the pre-test evaluated to **true**, the body of the loop is executed, updating **sum** by adding the value of **counter** to it, as shown in Figure 5-15.

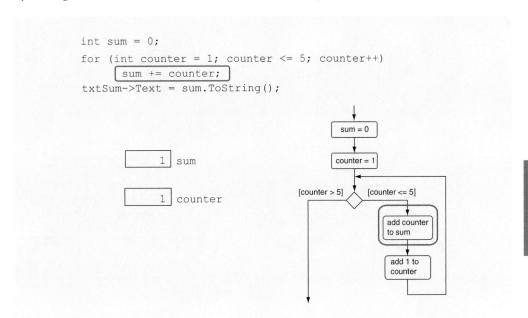

FIGURE 5-15 Accumulating the sum in the loop body

The counter is then incremented before the pre-test is made again, as shown in Figure 5-16.

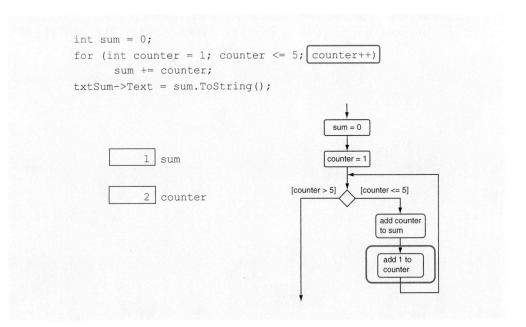

FIGURE 5-16 Updating the counter

The pre-test condition is evaluated again at the top of the loop (Figure 5-17). The decision whether to enter the loop depends on this evalaution. If it evaluates to `true`, then entry is allowed and the body is executed once more.

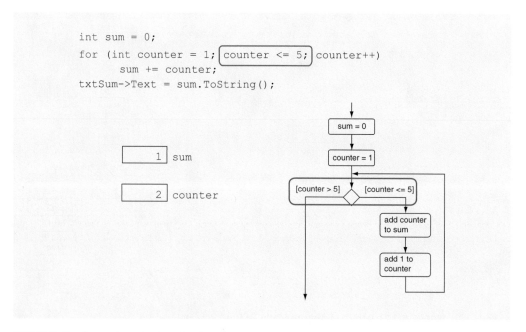

FIGURE 5-17 Second pre-test evaluation

The body of the loop is repeatedly executed until the pre-test evaluates to `false`. At that point control is passed along to the next instruction after the loop (Figure 5-18).

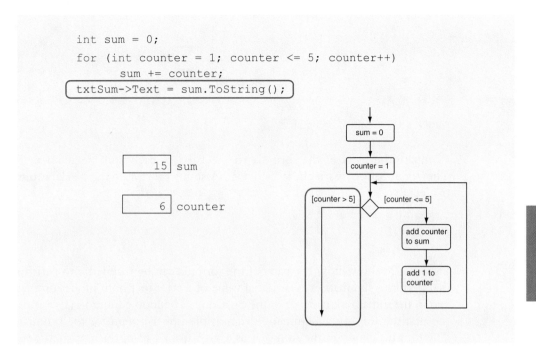

```
int sum = 0;
for (int counter = 1; counter <= 5; counter++)
      sum += counter;
txtSum->Text = sum.ToString();
```

FIGURE 5-18 Execution of the first statement after the loop

Common Loop Tasks

Loops have a wide variety of applications. You have already seen examples of summation and counting. This section explores some of the ways loops may be used to solve other common problems. Many of these examples are incorporated in tutorials and other projects later in this book. The tasks explored in this section include:

- Formula translation
- Accumulating a product
- Building a String
- Generating random numbers
- Finding the largest value
- Counting specific values
- Nested loops

Formula Translation

The formula in Figure 5-19 uses the conventional mathematical notation for summing a range of integers. In particular, the example in Figure 5-19 sums all of the integer values from 1 to n. If n is set to 5, then this formula corresponds to the code presented in Example 5-7 and the extended discussion of **for** loops in the previous section.

$$sum = \sum_{i=1}^{n} i$$

FIGURE 5-19 Summation notation

Compare the parts of the formula to the parts of each code segment in Figure 5-20. The loop control variable is called i. Assume the following declarations have been made:

```
int sum = 0;
int n = 5;
int i;
```

Figure 5-20 shows how the parts of the formula can be mapped into parts of a **for** loop that performs summation. The initial value of i is set to 1 both in the summation formula and in the initialization clause of the **for** loop. The loop condition (i <= n) is signified by the n at the top of the summation sign as the upper bound for the summation process. The formula expresses the sum of i as i goes from 1 to n, this is carried out in the C++ code by the addition assignment of i to sum within the loop body.

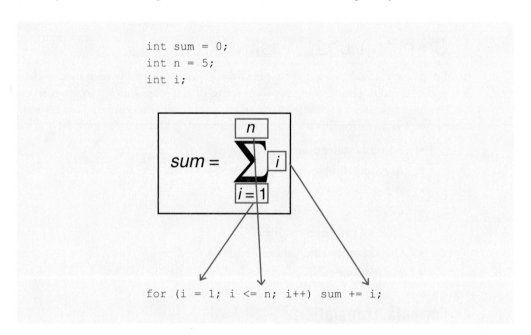

FIGURE 5-20 Summation formula broken into `for` loop format

Similarly, Figure 5-21 shows the correspondance of C++ commands and the key parts of the summation formula when written as a `while` loop.

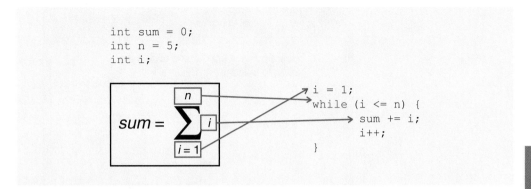

```
int sum = 0;
int n = 5;
int i;
```

$$sum = \sum_{i=1}^{n} i$$

```
i = 1;
while (i <= n) {
    sum += i;
    i++;
}
```

FIGURE 5-21   Summation formula broken into `while` loop format

Accumulating a Product

You can accumulate a product in a manner similar to the way you accumulate a sum, through a repeated series of steps in which the product increases within each iteration. Unlike summation, products are accumulated through repeated multiplication instead of addition. Factorial numbers are great examples of product accumulation. The exclamation mark (!) is used to indicate the factorial function in mathematical notation. We refer to 5! as "5 factorial". A **factorial number** is defined for positive integers in the following manner:

n! is 1 if n is 1

for all other positive integers (n), n! = n x (n-1) x (n-2) x ... 1.

For example, 5! is 5 x 4 x 3 x 2 x 1 = 120.

Figure 5-22 illustrates the factorial program interface.

FIGURE 5-22 Factorial program

The code shown in Example 5-8 is used to read a positive integer (n) and calculate its factorial value (nfact). The program uses an if...else statement to test n, making sure it is a postive integer before using a for loop to multiply successive values of the loop control variable (i) from 1 to n. The shorthand multiplication assignment operator (*=) is used to update variable nfact.

EXAMPLE 5-8: CALCULATING FACTORIAL VALUE

```
private: System::Void btnFact_Click(System::Object^  sender,
System::EventArgs^  e) {
    int n;
    int nfact = 1;
    Int32::TryParse(txtNum->Text, n)
    if (n > 0) {
        for (int i = 1; i <= n; i++)
            nfact *= i;
        txtFact->Text = nfact.ToString();
    }
    else
        MessageBox::Show("Please enter a value > 0");
}
```

Note that `nfact` is initialized to 1. The `for` loop accumulates the product `nfact` through successive multiplication by the loop control variable.

Building a String

Loops can be used to build strings of characters. The code shown in Example 5-9 declares a String variable called `strOut` that is initially set to an empty string (`""`). Because String is a derived type it is declared with the symbol ^, known as the **handle operator**. Think of the handle as pointing to the location in memory where the contents of `strOut` are located.

A `for` loop is used to concatenate a new item with `strOut` during each iteration. The following is the code for the button (`btnConcat`) that concatenates all the integers together into the String variable `strOut`:

EXAMPLE 5-9: CONCATENATING WITH A for LOOP

```
String^ strOut = "";
for (int counter = 0; counter< 10; counter++)
    strOut += counter;
txtOut->Text = strOut;
```

Each pass through the loop appends the loop control variable, `counter` to `strOut`. As `counter` goes from 0 to 9, each of these values is concatenated onto `strOut`. The final output is displayed in the text box `txtOut` in Figure 5-23.

5

FIGURE 5-23 Display of `strOut` built by a `for` loop

You might expect that adding `counter` to `strOut` should mean converting `counter` to the String format first, like this:

```
strOut += counter.ToString();
```

However, the concatenation operator (+) and the shorthand concatenation assignment operator (+=) both do conversion to the String format implicitly. This makes `ToString()` unnecessary.

Generating Random Numbers

Loops are especially good at processing large amounts of data because they can repeat the processing steps on each data value, one at a time, for as many data values as there may be. Although we do not know how to store large quantities of data yet, we can write programs that produce as many random numbers as we need. A **random number** is a number that is selected from a range of values such that each value has the same probability of being chosen. A **random number generator** is a Visual C++ object that produces a random number.

In Visual C++, creating a random number generator object is a two–step process. First, you declare a random number generator variable using the System class definition **Random** as shown:

```
Random^ randomNumGenerator;
```

Notice the use of the handle operator again with this System-defined type. In the second step, the **gcnew** command is used to construct a new **Random** number object, as shown. This is necessary because this object is based on a system-defined class definition.

```
randomNumGenerator = gcnew Random(now.Millisecond);
```

 NOTE   We have not seen **gcnew** before because we have only dealt with variables with simple definitions (primitive types). We can use the **gcnew** command to create many interesting objects using class definitions that already exist in the System namespace. We will learn more about handles and **gcnew** in Chapter 6.

A random number generator must be **seeded**, which means that you need to give it a unique starting point. Seeding a random number generator is accomplished by providing it with a value that is likely to be different each time the program runs. In the preceding code example, this seed value was obtained from a System-defined **Date::Time** variable called **now**, which is set to the current time on the System clock. The number of milliseconds that have elapsed since midnight (**now.Millisecond**) is a good seed value because it will probably be different each time the program runs.

The actual production of the random number occurs when the **Next()** method of the random number generator object is used. In Example 5-10, a random integer from the range 0–99 was specified. The first parameter in the **Next()** method is the lowest value that may be generated (0). The second parameter is the upper bound (100). Random values run from the lowest value up to, but not including, the upper bound.

```
randomNum = randomNumGenerator->Next(0,100);
```

The code for the **btnConcat_Click()** event in Example 5-10 creates **strOut** by concatenating ten random numbers and displays the result.

EXAMPLE 5-10: RANDOM NUMBER GENERATION

```
String^ strOut = "";
int randomNum;   // The random number
DateTime now = DateTime::Now; // The current time (now)
Random^ randomNumGenerator;
randomNumGenerator = gcnew Random(now.Millisecond);

for (int counter = 0; counter < 10; counter++)
{
    randomNum = randomNumGenerator->Next(0,100);
    strOut += randomNum + "   ";
}
txtOut->Text = strOut;
```

In the loop, the random number generator produces one value each time it is called. The loop runs ten times, so ten random numbers are produced. Each number will be within the range specified by the `Next()` method belonging to the random number generator object (0–100). As they are produced, the random numbers along with spaces to separate them (" ") are concatenated onto `strOut`.

The result is displayed in Figure 5-24.

FIGURE 5-24 Random number program

Finding the Largest Value

Building on the random number generator program, examine how to create a program that generates 10 random numbers from 0–100 and determines which is the largest. The interface for this program is shown in Figure 5-25.

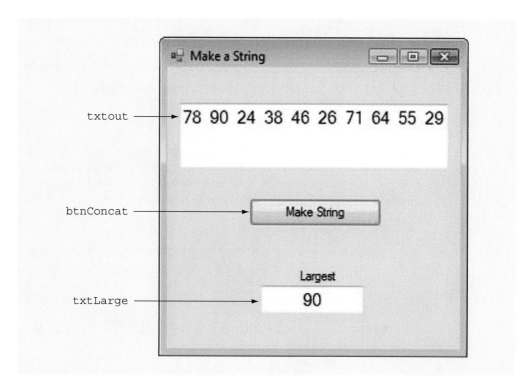

FIGURE 5-25 Finding the largest value

The code for `btnConcat_Click()` is shown in example 5-11. Comments mark those lines that pertain to the commands needed to find the largest value. The variable `large` will store the largest value. Within each loop iteration, an `if` statement is used to compare the random number that has been generated with the value stored in `large` and replace it if the random number is greater. By the end of the loop, `large` will store the greatest random value generated.

EXAMPLE 5-11: FINDING THE LARGEST VALUE

```
int large = 0; // Declare variable to store largest
String^ strOut = "";
int randomNumber;
DateTime now = DateTime::Now;
Random^ randomNumGenerator;
randomNumGenerator = gcnew Random(now.Millisecond);
```

```
for (int counter = 0; counter< 10; counter++)
{
    randomNumber = randomNumGenerator->Next(0,100);
    strOut += randomNumber + "   ";
    // if large < random then replace it with random
    if (large < randomNumber) large = randomNumber;
}
txtOut->Text = strOut;
txtLarge->Text += large; // Display large
```

When the loop ends, `large` is displayed in `txtLarge->Text`.

Counting Specific Values

Another enhancement to the random number generator program is to build a counter into the random number generation process. In this case, you can add an integer variable, called `count`, that keeps track of how many of the random values were larger than 75. The interface for this program is shown in Figure 5-26.

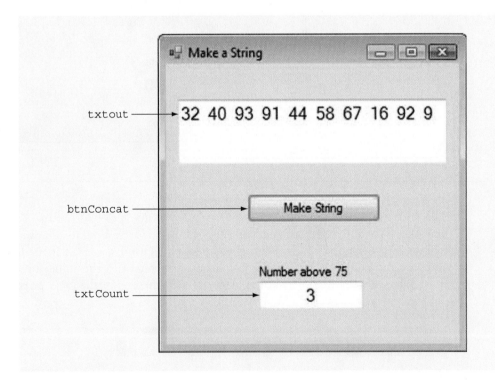

FIGURE 5-26 Counting values greater than 75

The code for `btnConcat_Click()` is shown in Example 5-12. The commented lines highlight the changes necessary to perform this count. Most of the code is substantially the same as that used in the previous two examples, except that an `if` statement is used inside the loop to increment `count` whenever a random number greater than 75 is encountered.

EXAMPLE 5-12: COUNTING VALUES

```
int count = 0; // The count of values > 75
String^ strOut = "";
int randomNumber;
DateTime now = DateTime::Now;

Random^ randomNumGenerator;
randomNumGenerator = gcnew Random(now.Millisecond);

for (int i = 0; i < 10; i++)
{
    randomNumber = randomNumGenerator->Next(0,100);
    strOut += randomNumber + "  ";
    if (randomNumber > 75) count++; // Increment count
}
txtOut->Text = strOut;
txtCount->Text += count; // Display count
```

A `while` loop variation of the `for` loop from Example 5-12 is shown in Example 5-13. This loop counts the number of consecutive random values greater than 75. The loop repeats as long as the random number is greater than 75. Handling situations like this, in which you do not know beforehand how many times the loop body will execute is a strength of the `while` and `do...while` loops.

EXAMPLE 5-13: COUNTING CONSECUTIVE VALUES WITH A while LOOP

```
randomNumber = randomNumGenerator->Next(0,100);
While (randomNumber > 75)
{
    count++;
    randomNumber = randomNumGenerator->Next(0,100);
}
```

Nested Loops

As discussed in Chapter 4, nesting means putting one control structure inside of another. In this example, we examine **nested loops**. The program output is the table shown in Figure 5-27.

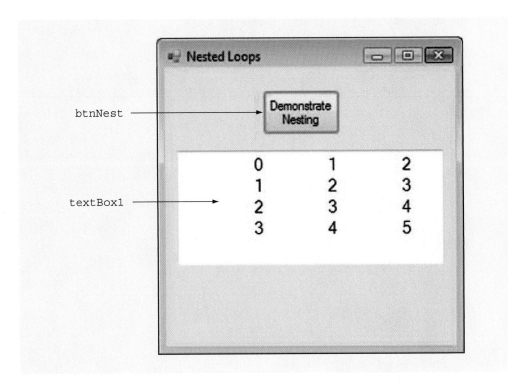

FIGURE 5-27 Nested loop output

The table in Figure 5-27 has four horizontal rows and three vertical columns. It is constructed one row at a time. The code shown in Example 5-13 executes when **btnNest** is clicked. In Example 5-14, the outer loop determines the current row. Nested within it is another loop that determines which of the three columns in that row is the current column. The special characters "\t" produce a tab, and "\r\n" positions the output on the next line.

EXAMPLE 5-14: CREATING A TABLE WITH NESTED LOOPS

```
int row, col;
for (row = 0; row < 4; row++)
{
    for (col = 0; col < 3; col++)
        textBox1->Text += "\t" + (row + col);
    textBox1->Text += "\r\n";
}
```

The process works in the following manner. During the first iteration of the outer loop, `row` is set to 0. Then the inner loop runs three times. The inner loop control variable (`col`) is set to 0 the first time through, then 1 the next time and 2 the last time. During each pass through the inner loop, only one statement is executed. In it, new text is added to `textBox1->Text`. That text consists of a tab character (`\t`) and the quantity (`row + col`). So, when `row` is set to 0 and the columns loop through the values 0, 1, 2, the quantity (`row + col`) is 0 + 0 the first time through the inner loop, 0 + 1 the second and 0 + 2 the third. This produces the top line in the table in Figure 5-27:

0 1 2

When the inner loop finishes, the special character codes (`\r\n`) are added to the text in `textBox1->Text`. These codes direct `textBox1->Text` to start a new line.

Now the outer loop is ready to execute again. In the outer loop, `row` is set to 1. Then the inner loop starts again, adding the `col` values 0, 1, 2 to `row`. The `resulting` output is:

1 2 3

ESCAPE CHARACTER CODES

When creating strings of text you will occasionally need to insert a tab or want the text to go to a new line. Features like these can only be added to a text string by inserting special character designators called **escape character codes**. An **escape character** in C++ is the backslash (`\`) and it gives special meaning to a normal character that follows it. The backslash escape character is not part of the string that will appear. Instead, escape characters provide information to the compiler about how the string should be displayed on the screen.

Common escape character sequences in Visual C++ are `\t`, `\r` and `\n`. The escape character code, `\t` stands for the tab character, `\r` means return to column 1, and `\n` means advance to the next line. In a Windows environment the combination of `\r\n` together tells the compiler to go the first column on the next line (similar to what happens when you hit the Enter key).

 NOTE You may have seen, or even written, standard C++ programs in environments other than Microsoft Windows. Standard C/C++ has strong ties to the Unix operating system. Programmers in that environment use `\n`, instead of `\r\n` to advance to the start of a new line. Otherwise the escape character codes are identical.

Tutorial: Quality Control Production Log

We have now had the opportunity to examine a number of different control structures and explore some smaller programs in which they were used. In this tutorial, you will build on this knowledge by producing a more substantial program that uses loops.

Problem Analysis

The CyberHyperUltraMegaProducts (CHUMP) Corporation, as the name implies, combines small, seemingly unrelated, high-technology components into a new product called a "chump". They produce a large number of chumps each day. Exactly what a chump is and what it does is proprietary information. However, you have been hired to construct a program that will assist in the production quality control process. Your first job is to write a program that monitors the size of the chumps being produced. A specialized machine scans each newly made chump to determine its thickness and will provide this information to your program. Chumps with a thickness less than 3mm are prone to failure. Chumps with a thickness greater than 7mm will work but waste expensive manufacturing material. Your job is to create a program that records the thickness of each chump produced. The interface should allow the user to specify the number of chumps that will be made in a particular production run. Because we don't really have access to a machine that can measure and report on the width of chumps, we will use the random number generator to provide numbers which we will use as thickness measurements. Typical output should look like the output shown in Figure 5-28.

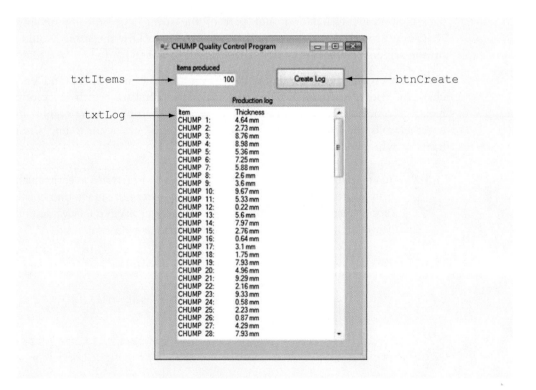

FIGURE 5-28 CHUMP quality control log

One of the keys to this program is envisioning how the chump thickness report log will look. The report log shown in Figure 5-28 is displayed in a multiline text box (make sure its MultiLine property is set to True). Since text boxes can only display strings of text, you will need to store the report in a String variable. For each iteration of the loop that generates a random thickness measurement, your program will add a new line to this String variable. When the loop ends, the contents of the entire String variable are assigned to the text box, producing a two-column report similar to the one shown in Figure 5-28.

Design

The essence of this program is not so much the interface, which is uncomplicated, but the program and variables used to create the report. The central feature of the design process is therefore the algorithm that makes the report. Future projects will require similar report capabilities. Knowing how to create a large string through concatenation is an important practical skill that will test your knowledge of repetition control structures.

INTERFACE

The interface for this program was shown earlier in Figure 5-28. The various controls are identified in the Table 5-3.

TABLE 5-3 Control Table for Chump Quality Control Program

Usage	Object	Event	Description
Initialization	Form1	Load()	Initialize the report String and other variables
Input	txtItems		The number of chumps to be produced
Processing	btnCreate	Click()	Gets chump thicknesses and creates a thickness log
Output	txtLog		Displays the chump thickness log

DATA TABLE

Two types of variables will be used in this program, instance variables and local variables. As you learned earlier in this chapter, instance variables are those that cannot be tied to any event handler because they need to preserve their values as long as the program is running. They must, therefore, have class scope. Local variables are those needed to perform tasks within the btnCreate_Click() event handler.

We have seen that instance variables are those that must retain their values from one event handler call to the next. Variables like the report string in this program are perfect candidates. Instance variables also commonly include variables that are handles (designated by the ^ operator). Handles are associated with objects that often need to be accessible to the code in several different methods. Table 5-4 lists the instance variables for this project that are handles for the System-defined objects String and Random.

TABLE 5-4 Instance Variables

Variable Name	Data Type	Usage
strLog	String^	Chump thickness report log
randomNumGen	Random^	Random number generator

The `Form1_Load()` event handler would be a good place to initialize `strLog` so that it is created with the column headings for the report already in it. We will also let the `Form1_Load()` event handler take care of seeding the random number generator. All it requires is a seed value that comes from the System time (`now`). The random number seed is the only local variable required by `Form1_Load()` so its data table, Table 5-5, is short.

TABLE 5-5 Data Table for `Form1_Load()`

Variable Name	Data Type	Usage
now	Date::Time	The current time

The crucial part of this program is `btnCreate_Click()`. That event handler will need its own set of local variables to perform the operation of building the report. These include a double-precision number that stores the thickness of a chump (`thick`), the number of chumps that the program is simulating production of (`items`), and a loop control variable. These variables are listed in Table 5-6.

TABLE 5-6 Data Table for `btnData_Click()`

Variable Name	Data Type	Usage
thick	double	Chump thickness
items	int	The number of chumps produced
i	int	Loop control variable

ALGORITHM

Two algorithms need to be considered. The first specifies what happens in `Form1_Load()` and the second lists the steps to be accomplished in `btnCreate_Click()`.

Algorithm for `Form1_Load()` The main role of the `Form1_Load()` event handler is to create and initialize instance variables. The following algorithm reflects these tasks.

ALGORITHM 5-1

1. Declare `Date::Time` variable (now)
2. Seed and create `randomNumGen` using variable `now`
3. Create `strLog` and initialize to the first line of the report

---

The algorithm for `Form1_Load()` simply states the required declarations and initialization tasks.

Algorithm for `btnCreate_Click()` The algorithm for `btnCreate_Click()` is the crucial algorithm because it builds the report log. To begin, it needs to read the `items` from `txtItems` so that it knows how many thickness values to randomly generate. Then it executes a loop that repeatedly generates a random thickness value and adds a line to the report. The number of iterations is determined by `items`. When finished, the loop displays the report in `txtLog`. The following algorithm summarizes these steps:

ALGORITHM 5-2

1. Declare variables
2. Read `items` from `txtItems`
3. Do the following for each item
   - 3.1. Generate a random thickness
   - 3.2. Add a line to the report log with that thickness value
4. Display the report log in `txtLog`

This algorithm is straightforward with four steps and two substeps, so we are ready to move on to the development process.

Development

As you consider the development tasks, refer to the algorithms for general directions. The specifics, especially related to generating the random number and creating the report log, are the most challenging part of this tutorial. Examples 5-9 through 5-11 help illustrate the process, so refer to them when necessary.

CREATE THE INTERFACE

The interface was shown earlier in Figure 5-28. Table 5-7 lists the important property settings for the text boxes. Because the report log will be larger than can be displayed in txtLog, even with its Multiline property set to True, its ScrollBars property should be set to Vertical. This allows the user to scroll the report log to view all of its contents.

TABLE 5-7 Property Settings for Interface Text Boxes

Control	Property	Setting
txtItems	TextAlign	Right
txtLog	Multiline	True
	ScrollBars	Vertical

CODING

Instance variables and the use of the Form1_Load() event typically go together. Remember that instance variables that are not primitive types that are often declared using the handle notation (^). Declaring a handle is not the same as constructing the object it is a handle for. The construction of system-defined instance objects often happens in Form1_Load(). The code shown in Example 5-14 shows both instance object handle declarations, outside of the Form1_Load() event handler and the Form1_Load() event handler itself.

EXAMPLE 5-14

```
// Instance variables
Random^ randomNumGen;
String^ strLog;

private: System::Void Form1_Load(System::Object^  sender,
System::EventArgs^  e) {
   DateTime now = DateTime::Now; // Used as seed value
   randomNumGen = gcnew Random(now.Millisecond);
   strLog = gcnew String("Item\t\tThickness\r\n");
   txtLimit->Text = "100";
}
```

Recall the random number generator seeding process from Example 5-10. As for strLog, separate the two headings ("Item" and "Thickness") so that the columns line up below them. This is done by inserting two tab characters (\t\t) into the text string. Similarly, move output to a new line by inserting the newline escape character sequence \r\n.

The btnData_Click() Event Handler Creating the log is a matter of running a loop the designated number of times. The code shown in Example 5-15 implements the algorithm:

EXAMPLE 5-15

```
int items;
double thick;

Int32::TryParse(txtItems->Text, items);
for (int i = 0; i<items; i++)
{
    thick = randomNumGen->Next(0,1000)/100.0;
    strLog += "CHUMP  " + i + ":\t" + thick + " mm\r\n";
}
txtLog->Text = strLog;
```

The thickness is a random number from 0 to 999 divided by 100 to produce values with two decimal places. Also notice that strLog is built by concatenation using the shorthand operator +=. Numeric variables (such as i and thick) do not have to be explicitly converted to a String using ToString() under these circumstances because the string concatenation operators use implicit type conversion on numeric values.

Testing

Run the program several times and scroll the list to make sure the values are all between 0.00 and 99.99. If the first nine values do not align with the rest of the column, you can add another space or two after the word "CHUMP" in the strLog assignment statement in the loop to align the values.

ON YOUR OWN

TASK 1. USE ANOTHER LOOP
Modify the program you created in the tutorial to use a while loop instead of a for loop. It must perform exactly as before.

TASK 2. CALCULATE THE MEAN
Create a new text box on the interface that displays the average chump thickness. Add the necessary variables and processing statements to btnCreate_Click() to calculate the mean of the thicknesses.

TASK 3. COUNT UNACCEPTABLE VALUES
In the project description, you learned that chump thicknesses less than 3.00 and greater than 7.00 are a problem. Chumps with a thickness less than 3.00 have higher failure rates, while those above 7.00 indicate a waste of production material. In both cases, the manufacturing equipment may need to be serviced if the rates are too high. Modify your program so that it counts the number of values less than 3.00 and displays this count on the interface. Similarly, count the number of values greater than 7.00 and display that value as well.

QUICK REVIEW

1. User-controlled repetition can simplify problems that require large amounts of data entry.

2. Programs designed to address general solutions will require less maintenance than those designed to solve only one specific problem.

3. A sum is accumulated by the repeated addition of successive values.

4. A counter can be updated by repeated addition of 1 to it.

5. Instance variables have class scope.

6. Instance variables exist as long as your program (an instance of the `Form1` class) is running.

7. Instance variables are declared outside of event handlers.

8. Instance variables retain their contents throughout the program.

9. The values stored in instance variables are accessible from within any event handler.

10. Repetition control structures automate the loop process.

11. Repetition involves repeating the statements contained in a loop body.

12. The loop condition determines whether repetition continues, often by evaluating a loop control variable.

13. The two types of loop conditions are pre-test and post-test.

14. Pre-test loops evaluate a loop condition located at the top of (entrance to) a loop body.

15. Post-test loops evaluate a loop condition located at the bottom of (exit from) a loop body.

16. One pass through the statements in the loop body is known as an iteration.

17. `While` loops are pre-test loops.

18. `While` loops evaluate a conditional expression at the entrance to the loop body to determine whether control passes into it.

19. `While` loops can be counter-controlled but must implement the initialization of the counter outside of the loop and the update within the loop.

20. `Do...while` loops are post-test loops.

21. `Do...while` loops evaluate a conditional expression at the bottom of the loop to determine whether another iteration will be allowed.

22. `Do...while` loops always perform one pass through the loop body.

23. `While` loops do not allow even one iteration if the pre-test evaluates to false the first time it is encountered.

24. The `for` loop is a counter-controlled, pre-test loop.

25. `For` loops use a parenthesized expression with three clauses: the initializing conditions, pre-test condition, and update condition.

26. Loop control variables are initialized in the first clause of a `for` loop.

27. The initializing clause is done only once, at the start of a loop and then not repeated.

28. The update clause is performed at the end of every iteration before the condition is evaluated.

29. Update conditions often use pre- or post-fix incrementation operators to add 1 to the loop control variable.

30. Update conditions may also use pre- or post-fix decrementation operators to subtract 1 from the loop control variable.

31. Iteration continues in a `for` loop as long as the condition evaluates to `true`.

32. Common processes involving loops include summation, product accumulation, counting, string concatenation, data processing, and determining the largest and/or smallest value.

33. Random numbers are produced by a random number generator object.

34. Random number generator objects need to be "seeded" with a unique starting point.

35. Factorial numbers are an example of accumulation of a product.

36. Nesting refers to a situation in which one loop is entirely contained within the body of another.

37. A table is defined by the number of horizontal rows and vertical columns it contains.

38. Escape characters may be used to insert tabs and new lines into a string.

39. Escape characters have a backslash character in front of them as in `\t` for tab and `\r\n` for new line.

40. String concatenation implicitly converts numeric data to text strings.

TERMS TO KNOW

accumulating a product

class scope

condition

counter-controlled loop

counting

decrementation operator (--)

determinate loop

`do...while loop`

entrance controlled loop
escape character
escape character codes
exit controlled loop
factorial number
`for` loop
`gcnew` command
general solution
handle operator (^)
incrementation
incrementation operator (++)
indeterminate loop
initialization clause
instance variable
iteration
loop
loop body
loop condition
loop control variable
nested loops
post-test loop
postfix decrementation operator (--)
postfix incrementation operator (++)
prefix decrementation operator (--)
prefix incrementation operator (++)
pre-test loop
random number
random number generator
repetition control structure
seeding (a random number generator)
single-purpose solution
summation
update clause
user-controlled repetition
`while` loop

EXERCISES

Use these choices for the following questions

    a.   `for` loop

    b.   `while` loop

    c.   `do...while` loop

    d.   all of the above

    e.   none of the above

1. ___ Which is a counter-controlled loop?

2. ___ Which is not a pre-test loop?

3. ___ Which is an exit-controlled structure?

4. ___ Which is a selection structure?

5. ___ Which is a repetition structure?

What is the output displayed by each of the following sections of code?

6. _____

```
num = 0;
for( i = -10; i <= 10; i += 7)
    if (i % 2 == 0) num += 1;
txtOut->Text = num.ToString();
```

7. _____

```
num = 0;
for (i = 1; i <= 4; i++)
    num += i;
txtOut->Text = num.ToString();
```

8. _____

```
sum = 0;
for (i = 4; i <= 20; i+= 3) sum += i;
txtOut->Text = sum.ToString();
```

9. Which of these are pre-test loops?

    a.   `for` loop

    b.   `while` loop

    c.   `do...while` loop

    d.   both `for` and `while` loops

    e.   both `while` and `do...while` loops

10. Which of these are post-test loops?

    a.   `for` loop

    b.   `while` loop

    c.   `do...while` loop

    d.   both `for` and `while` loops

    e.   both `while` and `do...while` loops

5

11. Which of these was specifically designed for counter-controlled situations?

    a. `for` loop

    b. `while` loop

    c. `do...while` loop

    d. both `for` and `while` loops

    e. both `while` and `do...while` loops

12. Assume that the integer variables named `sum` and `i` have been initialized to 0. Which statement changes final value of `sum` to 15?

    a. `for (; i<=5; i++) sum+= i;`

    b. `while (i<=5) { sum += i; i++ };`

    c. `do { sum += i; i++;} while (i > 5);`

    d. all of the above (a, b, and c)

    e. none of the above

13. Assume an integer variable named `sum` has been initialized to 0. Which statement changes final value of `sum` to 15?

    a. `for (i=5; i>=0; i--) sum = 15;`

    b. `if (sum = 15) i++;`

    c. `if (15) sum = 15;`

    d. all of the above (a, b, and c)

    e. none of the above

14. Which statement produces an infinite loop?

    a. `for (i=5; i<=0; i--) sum += i;`

    b. `if (0) i++;`

    c. `while (0) i++;`

    d. all of the above (a, b, and c)

    e. none of the above

15. Which statement produces an infinite loop? Assume `num` has been initialized to 15.

    a. `for (i=5; i>=0; i++) sum += i;`

    b. `while (num > 0) i++;`

    c. `while (num < 0) i--;`

    d. all of the above (a, b, and c)

    e. none of the above

Use the following choices for questions 16-19:

a. `Random^ randomNumber;`

b. `intx = randomNumber->Next(0,400);`

c. `DateTime now = DateTime::Now;`

d. `randomNumber = gcnew Random( now.Millisecond );`

e. `randomNumber = Random( now.Millisecond );`

16. This statement "seeds" the random number generator.

17. This statement generates a random number.

18. This statement constructs a random number generator.

19. This statement declares a random number variable.

20. What is displayed by the following segment of code?

```
int num;
for (int i = 0; i < 2; i++)
    for (int j = 2; j >= 0; j--) num += i + j;
txtOut->Text = num.ToString();
```

PROGRAMMING EXERCISES

1. Factorial Enhancements

Rewrite the factorial program given in Example 5-8 so that it does not allow the user to enter an integer larger than 10. In addition, convert the `for` loop to a `while` loop.

2. Finding the Smallest Value

Rewrite the program given in Example 5-11 to find the smallest value instead of the largest. Generate random numbers between -50 and 50 instead of 0-100. Hint: You will not be able to use the default initialization of `small` to 0. Instead, initialize it by generating your first random number outside the loop.

3. General Summation Program

Write a general summation program that allows the user to determine where it will begin and end, and what the increment shall be. Create an interface for the program that is similar to the one shown in Figure 5-29.

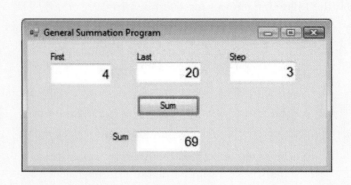

FIGURE 5-29 General summation program

The program you create should sum all the integers from a starting value (`first`) to, and including, the ending value (`last`). The user can also specify an increment (`step`) which may be any integer value. The step value is used to update the loop control variable before each iteration. In the case of the data entered into the interface in Figure 5-29, the result was 4 + 7 + 10 + 13 + 16 + 19, or 69.

Create the program using a `for` loop. Screen `txtStep` to make sure the user has not entered a value that will launch an infinite loop. For example, if the last value is larger than the first, then the step cannot be negative. Similarly, if the last value is smaller than the first, the step cannot be positive. Test the program to make sure it works by using the test data in Table 5-8.

TABLE 5-8 Test Data

Test	first	last	step	total
1	5	8	1	26
2	5	8	2	12
3	5	8	-1	Not allowed
4	8	5	-1	26
5	8	5	-2	14
6	8	5	2	Not allowed

4. Converting `for` Loops to `while` Loops

All `for` loops can be converted to `while` loops. Rewrite Example 5-7 as a `while` loop. When you have succeeded, write a general algorithm that provides a list of instructions that could be used to convert any `for` loop to a `while` loop.

5. Nested Loops

Write a program that produces the pattern of asterisks (*) as shown in Figure 5-30 in a multiline text box. Use nested loops to create the pattern.

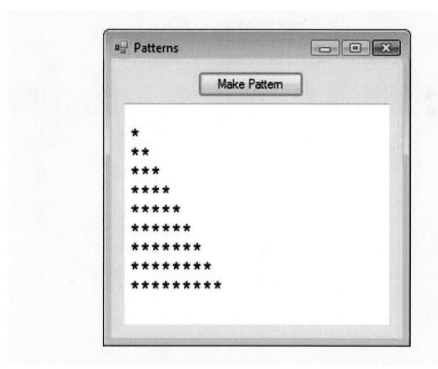

FIGURE 5-30   Asterisk pattern created using nested loops

As an extra challenge, see what other patterns you can produce. Figure 5–31 shows one example.

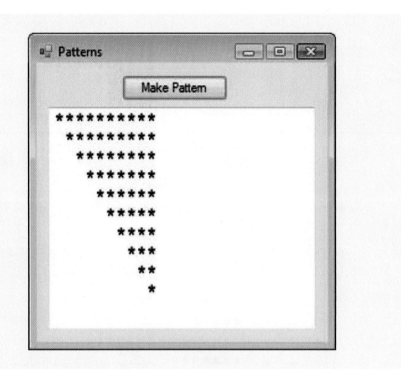

FIGURE 5-31 Asterisk pattern using two nested loops

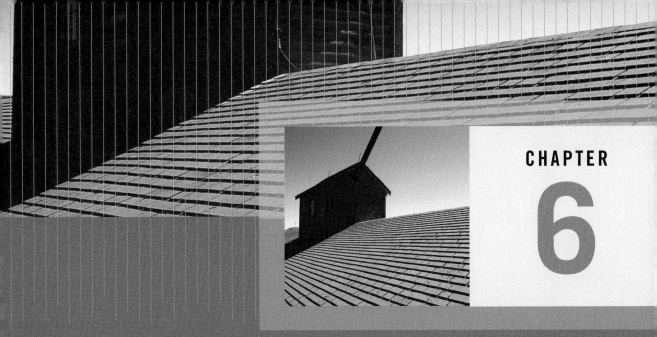

METHODS

IN THIS CHAPTER, YOU WILL:

- ■ Learn how to use system-defined class methods
- ■ Create programmer-defined methods
- ■ Pass data into a method by value
- ■ Pass data into a method by reference
- ■ Use methods with return types
- ■ Explore the use of `System::Drawing` objects and their methods
- ■ Use the `PictureBox` and Timer controls

Chapter 1 introduced the basic tools of visual programming—creating an interface, and writing event handlers. Chapters 2 and 3 explained how to use variables to store data, and how to use elementary Visual C++ statements to process data and display results. In Chapters 4 and 5, the discussion turned to control structures, which are statements that direct how instructions are carried out through selection or repetition. This chapter focuses on how to improve your programming skills by using and writing special-purpose modules of code, called methods. You will create methods to better organize your programs and learn to use objects and methods from the `System` namespace, such as `System::Math` and `System::Drawing`, to create programs with interesting visual effects.

Methods

A **method** is an identifiable, self-contained section of code that performs a specific task, such as calculating the square root of a number or resetting the text boxes on an interface. Methods have many uses and are a common way to add functionality to a program.

There are two types of methods—those belonging to classes (**class methods**) and those belonging to objects (**instance methods**). Many class and instance methods are built into the Visual C++ language and are part of the `System` namespace. These built-in methods are called **system-defined methods**. Your programs so far have made use of a number of these built-in methods. The system-defined methods illustrated in Figure 6-1 are explained in more detail in the sections that follow.

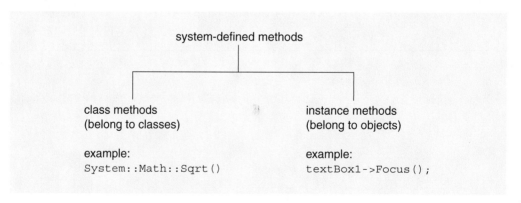

FIGURE 6-1 Types of system-defined methods

This chapter also discusses how you can create methods for your applications (**application instance methods**). Event handlers are one type of an application instance method. Another type of application instance method is called a programmer-defined method, shown in Figure 6-2. **Programmer-defined methods** are instance methods that you can build into the `Form1` class to provide functions and capabilities other than event handling. Programmer-defined methods can add many valuable features to your programs, and they lie at the heart of every project you create. The latter part of the chapter pays special attention to programmer-defined methods.

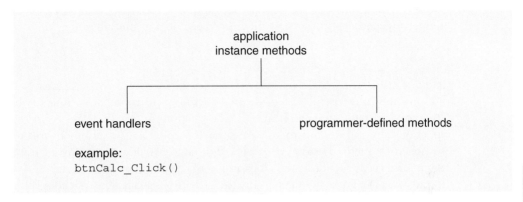

FIGURE 6-2 Application-defined instance methods

System-Defined Class Methods

System-defined class methods are built into the `System` namespace and are ready to be used in your programs as the need arises. You use the scope resolution operator (`::`) to identify the name of a method and the `System` class to which it belongs. The general syntax is:

```
System::Class_name::Method_name()
```

The identifier `System` indicates the namespace the method belongs to. For example, when referring to the method used to calculate a square root (which comes from the `System` class `Math`) you use:

```
System::Math::Sqrt()
```

Use of the identifier `System` is optional, however. If we leave it out, the reference is shortened to:

```
Math::Sqrt()
```

There are a number of methods that exist in classes in the `System` namespace with which you are already familiar. For example, in the following statement:

```
Int32::TryParse(txtNum->Text, num);
```

`TryParse()` is a method belonging to a system-defined class called `Int32` that contains a number of methods that can be used with any 32-bit integer.

Similarly, in this statement:

```
double dblNum = Convert::ToDouble(intNum);
```

`ToDouble()` is a method belonging to the system-defined `Convert` class.

You can think of the `Math`, `Int32`, and `Convert` classes as libraries that contain numerous special-purpose class methods that you can use when needed.

The `System::Math` Class Library

Among the most useful system-defined methods are those belonging to the `Math` class (`System::Math`). `System::Math` is a collection of methods related to mathematical functions. If you wanted to calculate the square root of a number, you could use the square root method **`Math::Sqrt()`**. To raise a value to a power use the method `Math::Pow()`. To find the logarithm of a number you could use the method **`Math::Log()`**. There are many more `Math` methods available. Appendix B lists commonly used `System::Math` methods. A complete list is provided on the Microsoft Developer Network Web site at *http://msdn2.microsoft.com/en-us/library/system.math_methods.aspx*.

Many `Math` methods are used to process data. Data values sent into a method are called **parameters** and are enclosed in parentheses after the method name. For example, when the square root method, **`Math::Sqrt()`**, is used in code it requires one parameter—the value whose square root you want to find. In Example 6-1 the value 16 is sent into the `Sqrt()` method. The method then computes the square root of 16 and assigns the answer to the variable `num`:

EXAMPLE 6-1

```
double num;
num = Math::Sqrt(16);
```

When passing data into methods, you need to be mindful of data types. For example, the `Sqrt()` method can only accept a double precision number as a parameter. Other `Math` methods, such as those dealing with trigonometric functions (sine, cosine, tangent, etc.) are even more specific. The sine of an angle is computed by **`Math::Sin()`**, the cosine by **`Math::Cos()`**, and the tangent by **`Math::Tan()`**. Each requires one double precision parameter, the size of an angle. There are two ways to measure the size of an angle however—in degrees or radians. Most of us are familiar with angles measured in degrees, but C++ `Math` methods require angles to be in radians. To convert an angle from degrees to radians the following formula is used:

$$\text{radians} = \text{degrees} * \pi/180$$

Multiplying the angle measurement in degrees by pi (π) and dividing by 180 yields the angle measurement in radians. The formula for calculating radians is translated into Visual

C++ code as shown using another member of the **System::Math** class, the constant value **Math::PI**. Assume that `angle_radians` is a variable containing the angle measurement in radians and `angle_degrees` is a variable containing the angle measurement in degrees. The conversion from radians to degrees is shown in example 6-2.

EXAMPLE 6-2

```
angle_radians = angle_degrees * Math::PI / 180;
```

Let's look at a brief example. The program shown in Figure 6-3 asks the user to enter an angle (measured in degrees) into **txtDegrees**. When **btnCalc** is clicked, the program computes the angle measurement in radians, displays the result in **txtRad**, and then also computes the sine, cosine, and tangent of that angle, displaying these in **txtSin**, **txtCos**, and **txtTan** respectively.

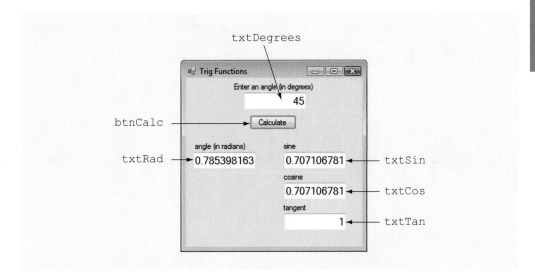

FIGURE 6-3 Program to compute radians, sine, cosine, and tangent of an angle

The code for **btnCalc_Click()** is shown in Example 6-3. The size of the original angle, measured in degrees, is read into the variable **angle_degrees**. The size of the angle measured in radians is then calculated using our formula and stored in the variable **angle_radians**.

EXAMPLE 6-3

```
double angle_degrees, angle_radians;
Double::TryParse(txtDegrees->Text, angle_degrees);
angle_radians = angle_degrees * Math::PI / 180;
txtRad->Text = angle_radians.ToString();
txtSin->Text = Math::Sin(angle_radians).ToString();
txtCos->Text = Math::Cos(angle_radians).ToString();
txtTan->Text = Math::Tan(angle_radians).ToString();
```

Once the variable `angle_radians` has been computed, the rest is trivial because the `Math` methods do all the work. The variable `angle_radians` is displayed and then used as a parameter in calls to `Math::Sin()`, `Math::Cos()`, and `Math::Tan()` to produce and display the sine, cosine, and tangent.

System-Defined Instance Methods

You may recall that every `textBox` object is created from the same system-defined text box class definition. When an object is created from a class definition, it is called an **instance** of that class. For this reason, the methods that belong to any particular `textBox` object are called instance methods. You encountered one of these in Chapter 5 (Example 5-2) in the command

```
textBox1->Focus();
```

which tells the `textBox1` object to execute its built-in method called `Focus()`. This places the cursor in `textBox1`. All `textBox` objects have a `Focus()` method. Notice that this method requires no parameters. This is because it always executes the same set of tasks and does not need any data values.

Another system-defined instance method call used in Chapter 5 occurred in conjunction with the `randomNumGenerator` object (Examples 5-10 and 5-11) and can be seen in the following command:

```
randomNumGenerator->Next(0,100)
```

This statement tells the `randomNumGenerator` object to execute its built-in method called `Next()`, which generates a random number between 0 and 100. The `Next()` method requires two parameters, in this case 0 and 100, because it must know the upper and lower bounds of the random value range.

Application Methods

As you will recall from Chapter 1, `Form1` is really the default name of the large class definition you create when you make a Visual C++ Windows Form application. When you run your program, Visual C++ creates a `Form1` object (your program interface) with all the features and capabilities you designed into it.

Application methods (event handlers and programmer-defined methods) are methods you create as part of your `Form1` class definition. Both of these types require you to write code to define what they do. Programmer-defined methods must be written entirely from scratch, whereas event handlers automatically create part of their code for you.

A **method definition**, specifies how the method will be identified, what its requirements are, and how it works. The **formal definition** of a method consist of a signature line followed by the method body. The **method signature line** (sometimes called a **header line**) contains the following information about the method:

1. **Access mode**—This refers to the extent to which other program units can have access to a method. There are three access modes: `private`, `public`, or `protected`. Most of the methods in this book have an access mode of `private`, which means they can be accessed only by members of the class to which they belong.

2. **Return type**—This refers to the type of data, if any, that the method will send back to the programming unit that called it. Many methods do not return any value and indicate this by using the standard C++ keyword **void** or its Visual C++ counterpart **System::Void** as the return type. Both `void` and `System::Void` mean that the return type is absent.

3. **Name**—This is the **method name**. Method names use the same naming conventions as variables, although to distinguish them from variables, in this text they, are always capitalized.

4. **Parameter list**—This refers to information the method receives from the programming unit that called it. Parameters are discussed later in this chapter in detail.

The **method body** consists of one or more lines of code that are executed when the method runs.

The syntax for a formal method definition is shown here:

```
access_mode: return_type method_name(parameter list)
{
  statement 1;
  statement 2;
  .
  .
  .
  statement n;
}
```

Examine a typical method definition to make sure you can identify each of the components. Figure 6-4 shows the `button1_Click()` event handler for the first button you created back in Chapter 1. Each of the components of the signature line can be identified.

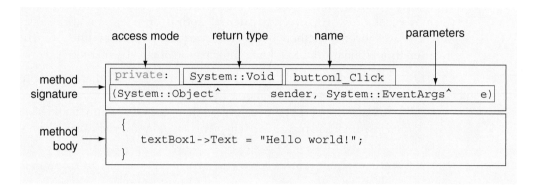

FIGURE 6-4 Method components for `button1_Click()`

The contents of the parameter section of the signature line may be empty, or it may include one or more parameters. Each parameter in a parameter list is separated from the others by a comma. Do not be concerned if you do not understand the parameters in this example. Parameters for event handlers are automatically generated. Later in the chapter, during the discussion of specific examples of programmer-defined methods, you will learn how parameters work. For now, it is sufficient simply to know where to find the parameters in a method signature line.

Programmer-Defined Methods

A programmer-defined method is a method in which both the signature line and body are written by the programmer, unlike event handlers in which the signature line is automatically generated.

There are several reasons why a programmer might want to write a method. First, there are times when a set of tasks is repeated in more than one event handler. This is called **code redundancy**. Programmer-defined methods can help reduce the unnecessary repetition of statements, as you will see in the next section.

A second reason for writing your own methods is to isolate a specific set of related tasks for program-development purposes. Programmers often want to keep statements related to a single task together in one place, where the algorithm and code can be developed without regard to the rest of the program. In large software development projects, a programmer or programming team may be assigned a method with the idea being that when the method is finished it would be inserted into the program.

Methods are also used to simplify an otherwise complicated event handler. For example, a long event handler with numerous control structures and many levels of nesting is difficult to read and debug. By using methods, you can isolate specific tasks, such as reading, processing, or displaying data, and remove that code from the event handler, thus simplifying the event-handler code.

You will see examples of methods created for these purposes as you examine the types of programmer-defined methods listed in Figure 6-5.

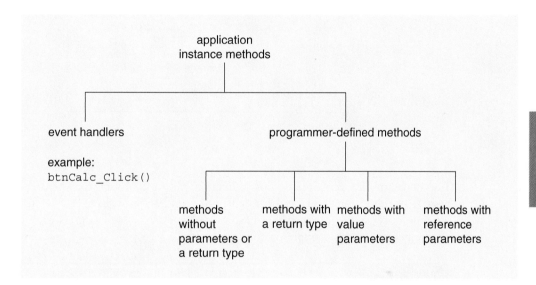

FIGURE 6-5 Application methods, full detail

Methods without Parameters or a Return Type

Examine the program shown in Figure 6-6. The program reads a distance measured in miles and converts it to kilometers when `btnConvert` is clicked. When the user wishes to clear both `txtMiles` and `txtKm` to enter another mileage value, he or she can click `btnClear`.

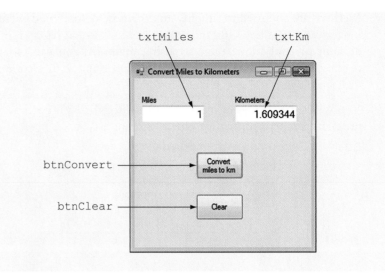

txtMiles   txtKm

FIGURE 6-6 Program to convert miles to kilometers

The code for this program is shown in Example 6-4. Notice that before the program begins, `Form1_Load()` makes sure that both `txtMiles` and `txtKm` are empty by assigning an empty string of text to them. Similarly, `btnClear_Click()` does the same thing. This repetition is an example of code redundancy.

EXAMPLE 6-4

```
private: System::Void Form1_Load(System::Object^
sender, System::EventArgs^ e) {
   txtMiles->Text = "";
   txtKm->Text = "";
}
private: System::Void btnConvert_Click(System::Object^
sender, System::EventArgs^ e) {
   double miles, km;
   Double::TryParse(txtMiles->Text, miles);
   km = 1.609344 * miles;
   txtKm->Text += km;
}
private: System::Void btnClear_Click(System::Object^
sender, System::EventArgs^ e) {
   txtMiles->Text = "";
   txtKm->Text = "";
}
```

In small programs such as this, redundancy is of little concern, but in larger programs the unnecessary duplication of code can make programs larger and more complex than they need to be. You will learn how to address the issue of redundant code in this small example, keeping in mind that the same principles apply to larger programs as well.

Figure 6-7 shows a programmer-defined method whose body contains the tasks that both `Form1_Load()` and `btnClear_Click()` perform. Notice the various parts of this method definition. The access mode is `private`, the return type is `void`, the name is `Reset()`, and there are no parameters.

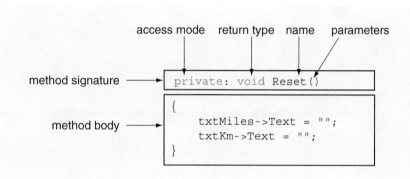

FIGURE 6-7 A method to handle redundant code

This method can be inserted into the program shown in Example 6-1 to reduce redundancy. You recall from Chapter 5 that the code portion of a Visual C++ program is divided into regions. The region in which event handlers are automatically created is at the bottom of the Windows Form Designer code beneath the statement

```
#pragma endregion
```

which marks the end of the region containing automatically generated code.

Figure 6-8 identifies the location of the `Reset()` method definition. It can go anywhere within the programmer code area shown, as long as it is not within an event handler or another method.

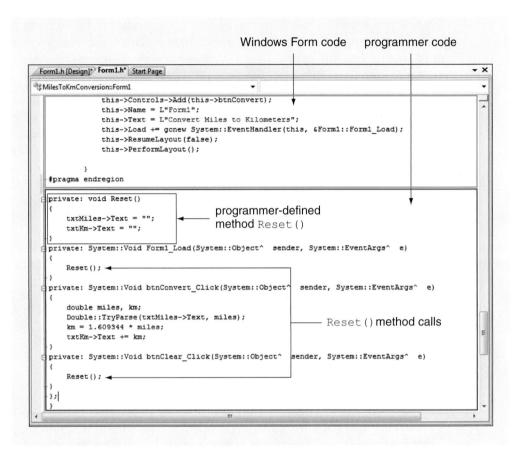

FIGURE 6-8 Location of Reset() method within the programmer code region and Reset() method calls

Methods with a return type of **void** are called by name in the following manner:

```
method_name (argument list);
```

In this case, the **Reset()** method is called twice, once from the **Form1_Load()** event handler and then again from within the **btnClear_Click()** event handler.

When the **Reset()** method is called from an event handler, processing of that event handler ceases and control passes to the **Reset()** method. When the **Reset()** method has finished, control passes back to the event handler that called it to the point immediately after **Reset()** was called.

It is important to distinguish between statements that formally define a method—the method definition—and statements that actually call your methods. The method definition for **Reset()** specifies how the method works. The method call is a command to make it work.

Methods with Value Parameters

When parameters are used with a method, you must consider both the formal definition and how the method will be called. In the formal definition, the signature line specifies the requirements for the parameters. These are called **formal parameters**. Parameter declarations occur in a list separated by commas. The syntax for a formal parameter list is shown here.

```
( data_type parameter_name, data_type parameter_name, ...)
```

In the line that actually calls the method, data is passed into the method through its parameter list. If the parameter list in the method call is not empty, it may contain one or more of the following items:

- A literal value (e.g., 16)
- An expression (e.g., a/2)
- A variable name

These are called **actual arguments**. The syntax for an actual argument list is shown here.

```
(argument1, argument2, ...)
```

The values specified in an actual argument list may be literal values, such as 4 or 5, or they may be specified using variable names to refer to the values stored in them. For example, consider the interface for the program shown in Figure 6-9, which calculates the area of a rectangle. The user enters the width and height into the text boxes txtWidth and txtHeight, and the area is displayed in txtArea. The user clicks btnCalc to perform the calculation.

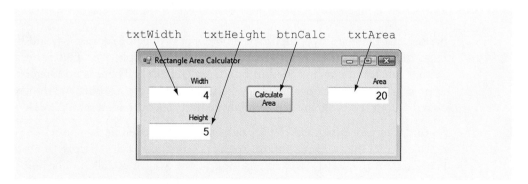

FIGURE 6-9 Rectangle area calculation program

The code for the btnCalc_Click() event handler is short. The version in Example 6-5 contains no programmer-defined methods.

EXAMPLE 6-5

```
private: System::Void btnCalc_Click(System::Object^
sender, System::EventArgs^ e) {
    int width, height, area;
    Int32::TryParse(txtWidth->Text, width);
    Int32::TryParse(txtHeight->Text, height);
    area = width * height;
    txtArea->Text = area.ToString();
}
```

The last two statements in Example 6-5 process the data and display the result. Although the amount of code required to carry out these tasks is small, only two lines, it is frequently the case that data processing and output require many steps. In such a case, a programmer may want to define a method dedicated to the processing and display operations apart from the btnCalc_Click() event handler. Example 6-5 can be modified to demonstrate how such a method, which we shall call ProcessAndDisplay(), would work.

Examine the code for the btnCalc_Click() event handler shown in Example 6-6.

EXAMPLE 6-6

```
private: System::Void btnCalc_Click(System::Object^
sender, System::EventArgs^ e) {
    int width, height;
    Int32::TryParse(txtWidth->Text, width);
    Int32::TryParse(txtHeight->Text, height);
    ProcessAndDisplay(width, height);
}
```

Notice that there are two important differences between Example 6-6 and Example 6-5. First, the variable area is no longer declared in Example 6-6. This is because area is neither calculated nor displayed in btnCalc_Click(). There is no longer any need for its presence in this click event. This is because all of the processing and display tasks occur elsewhere, in the programmer-defined method called ProcessAndDisplay().

Second, the processing and display tasks present in Example 6-5 are gone, having been replaced by the ProcessAndDisplay() method call. Before considering how ProcessAndDisplay() is written, look at the way it is called. The method name is referenced on a line by itself, with the actual arguments width and height in the arguments list. It is necessary that the values stored in width and height be passed into ProcessAndDisplay() because it needs them to calculate area.

Now look at the formal definition for ProcessAndDisplay() seen in Example 6-7. Notice that the formal parameter list declarations create local variables rect_width and rect_height to store the width and height of a rectangle.

EXAMPLE 6-7

```cpp
private: void ProcessAndDisplay(int rect_width, int rect_height)
{
    int area;
    area = rect_width * rect_height;
    txtArea->Text = area.ToString();
}
```

The relationship between the statement calling ProcessAndDisplay() and the formal definition of ProcessAndDisplay() is shown in Figure 6-10.

6

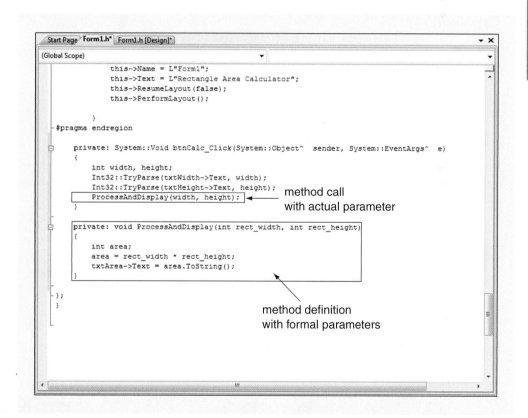

FIGURE 6-10 ProcessAndDisplay() method call and method definition

In Figure 6-9, the user entered 4 into `txtWidth` and 5 into `txtHeight`. The code in Example 6-5 and Example 6-6 stores this as integer data into variables `width` and `height`. The formal parameters for `ProcessAndDisplay()` declare two local variables, `rect_width` and `rect_height`. Figure 6-11 shows the correspondence between the actual parameters (`width` and `height`) and the local variables declared in the formal parameters (`rect_width` and `rect_height`).

The values in the actual arguments are copied into their matching formal parameters when the method is called. This method of data transfer is called **pass-by-value** because the copies of the data values in the actual arguments are passed into the formal parameters, in the method that was called. Formal parameters that receive data using pass-by-value are called **value parameters**.

Pass-by-value is the default method of transferring data in C and C++. Note that if changes are made to the values stored in `rect_width` or `rect_height` in `ProcessAndDisplay()`, these changes would not affect the data stored in `width` and `height` back in `btnCalc_Click()`.

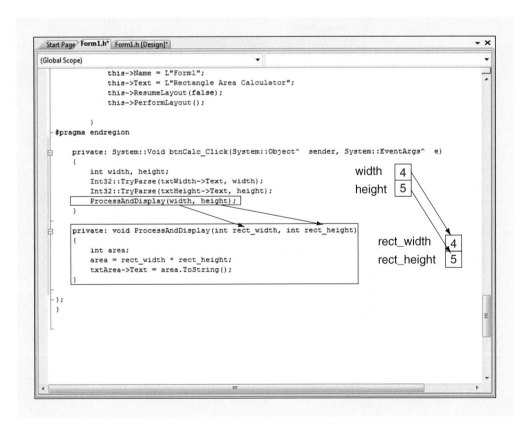

FIGURE 6-11 Pass-by-value correspondence between actual and formal parameters

The important things to remember about the correspondence between the actual parameters in method calls and the formal parameters in method definitions are the following:

- Corresponding actual arguments and formal parameters must have the same data type.

- The number of actual arguments must be the same as the number of formal parameters.

- The data value stored in the first actual argument is always copied into the first formal parameter, the value in the second actual argument always goes into the second formal parameter, and so on.

Notice that once the transfer of values has taken place, the `ProcessAndDisplay()` method has everything it needs to calculate `area` and display it. When `ProcessAndDisplay()` is finished, its local variables are deleted from memory as control returns to `btnCalc_Click()`, the method that called `ProcessAndDisplay()`, to execute any remaining instructions in that method.

Methods with Reference Parameters

We have seen that value parameters may be used to send copies of data values into a method. Value parameters are important because by passing copies of data values into methods they ensure that the original value in the calling program remains intact regardless of what went on in the method that was called. This protects variables from errors that may occur in other methods that use their data.

However, there are times when you want another method to make a change to the value stored in a variable and communicate that change back. For example, you may want to call a method with an uninitialized variable as an actual argument and have that method read a new data value into the variable and return it to you. This can only be done if the called method has the memory cell address of an actual argument. If it does changes can be made to the value stored in the original variable.

A **reference parameter** is a formal parameter name that is an alias for (not a copy of) the actual argument. Reference parameters can be used in methods to access and change values stored in the corresponding actual argument. The **&** symbol is used in the formal parameter declaration to specify that a variable is a reference parameter. **Pass-by-reference** refers to this technique of using reference parameters.

To examine how this works, let us continue with the program calculating the area of a rectangle. The program in Figure 6-11 used a programmer-defined method called `ProcessAndDisplay()` to handle the tasks related to data processing and output. The data input tasks remained in `btnCalc_Click()`. However, these tasks can also be handled in another method. Example 6-8 contains the call to another method named `ReadData()` for the purpose of reading data values into variables `width` and `height` (the actual parameters).

EXAMPLE 6-8

```
private: System::Void btnCalc_Click(System::Object^
sender, System::EventArgs^ e) {
    int width, height;
    ReadData(width, height);
    ProcessAndDisplay(width, height);
}
```

The statements that carry out the reading have been moved into `ReadData()`. Notice how the code for `btnCalc_Click()` is now very concise and readable. The code reads like a high-level algorithm for this operation (declare variables, read data, process and display data) without all the detailed instructions.

The code for `ReadData()` is shown in Example 6-9. Notice the use of the address-of operator (`&`) in the formal parameter declarations.

EXAMPLE 6-9

```
private: void ReadData(int& rect_width, int& rect_height)
{
    Int32::TryParse(txtWidth->Text, rect_width);
    Int32::TryParse(txtHeight->Text, rect_height);
}
```

The formal parameter declaration

```
int& rect_width
```

declares a reference parameter. When data is read into `rect_width` it is actually assigned to the variable `width` (its corresponding actual argument) in `btnCalc_Click()`.

The pass-by-reference process is illustrated in Figure 6-12. Notice that the memory cell address of `width` (342576) is passed to the reference parameter `rect_width`. Similarly, the memory cell address of `height` (588502) is passed to the reference parameter `rect_height`.

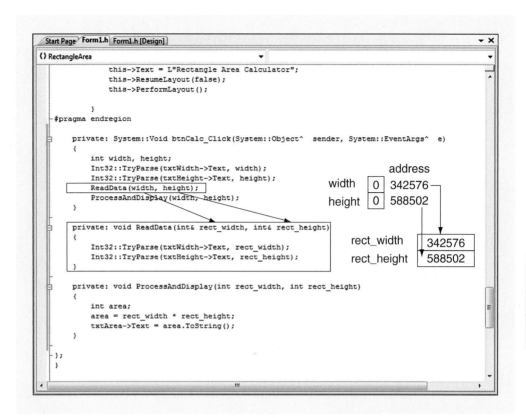

FIGURE 6-12 Pass-by-reference

The statements in the body of method `ReadData()` use the reference parameters (`rect_width` and `rect_height`) to read data directly back into the actual argument variables, as shown in Figure 6-13. The data values (4 for `width` and 5 for `height`) are those originally shown for this application in Figure 6-9.

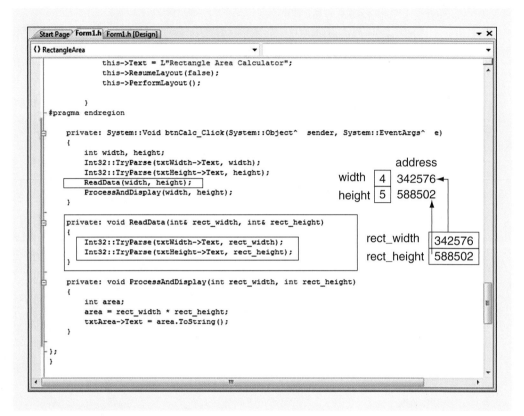

FIGURE 6-13 Updating actual argument variables using reference parameters

Methods with a Return Value

All of the programmer-defined methods used so far have had a `void` return type. Where values needed to be sent back, reference parameters were used. It is common, however, for methods to have **return values** of their own. Any method may have a return value.

Many `System` class methods have return values that may or may not be used. For example, consider `TryParse()`. You have used it in the following manner to read data:

```
Int32::TryParse(textBox1->Text, num);
```

You know that `TryParse()`, in this example, tries to parse `textBox1->Text`, looking for an integer; if it finds one, that value is stored in integer variable `num`. You also know that if `TryParse()` is unable to find an integer in `textBox1->Text` then the value stored in `num` does not change. What is more, `TryParse()` always returns a Boolean value indicating whether the parse attempt was successful. This fact could be used to alert the user to a potential problem, as shown in Example 6-10

EXAMPLE 6-10

```
int num;
bool ok;
ok = Int32::TryParse(txtWidth->Text, num);
if (ok == true)
    MessageBox::Show("Data read successfully");
else
    MessageBox::Show("ERROR reading data");
```

 NOTE Because the variable `ok` contains a Boolean value it can also be used in the conditional expression like this: `if (ok)` without having to be compared to the value `true`.

A similar effect could be achieved with programmer-defined methods. As an example, revisit Figure 6-3 and Example 6-3, the program that calculated the sine, cosine, and tangent of an angle. You remember that the angle was entered in degrees and had to be converted to radians.

A method called `ConvertToRadians()` could be used to do this conversion. When passed the angle measurement in degrees as a value parameter, this method returns the measurement in radians as shown in Example 6-11.

EXAMPLE 6-11

```
double degrees, radians;
Double::TryParse(txtDegrees->Text, degrees);
radians = ConvertToRadians(degrees);
```

The programmer-defined method `ConvertToRadians()` has a return type of `double`. The double precision number it brings back is assigned to `radians`.

The syntax for the **return statement** that brings a value back to the calling program unit is

```
return value;
```

The keyword `return` is followed by a single value, or variable name. For example, the statement

```
return 1;
```

would send back (return) the value 1.

The code for `ConvertToRadians()` is shown in Example 6-12.

EXAMPLE 6-12

```
private: double ConvertToRadians(double angle_degrees)
{
    double angle_radians;
    angle_radians = angle_degrees * Math::PI / 180;
    return angle_radians;
}
```

Graphics Class Objects and Methods

We have now seen a wide variety of method types. The tutorial later in this chapter will allow you to write many different types of programmer-defined methods and use various system-defined class and instance methods. It does this in the context of an application that draws pictures, which is one of the more exciting ways to program in Visual C++. However, before you can create a program that draws pictures, you need to become familiar with some of the tools available in the **System::Drawing** class. These tools make it possible to draw images on the screen.

Figure 6-14 shows the Design view (part a) and the program execution view (part b) of a program that draws a yellow circle. As shown in part a, it contains only two controls: the button **btnDraw** and the picture box **pictureBox1** (which can be used to display images).

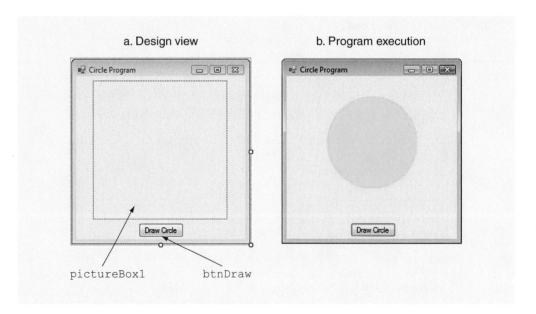

FIGURE 6-14 Circle program—Design view and Program execution view

The idea behind this application is that when the user clicks `btnDraw`, a yellow circle is drawn in `pictureBox1`. To achieve this result, you need to use three tools from the `System::Drawing::Graphics` namespace. A longer list of commonly used `System::Drawing` objects is provided in Appendix B.

Drawing a yellow circle in `pictureBox1` requires three `System::Drawing` objects:

- A `Drawing::Brush` object to fill in the circle with a solid yellow color.
- A `Drawing::Rectangle` object to provide the location and boundaries of the circle.
- A `Drawing::Graphics` object that belongs to `pictureBox1` and uses the `Brush` to draw in the `Rectangle`.

The relationship of these `System::Drawing` objects to one another is analogous to a painter (the `Drawing::Graphics` object) using a paintbrush (the `Drawing::Brush` object) to paint within a designated area (the `Drawing::Rectangle`) on a canvas (`pictureBox1`), as shown in Figure 6-15.

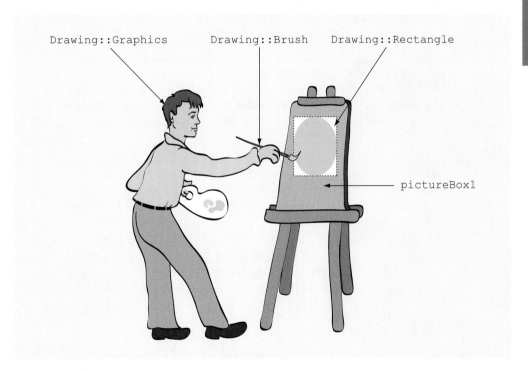

FIGURE 6-15 The relationship of `System::Drawing` objects

Many applications require only one `Drawing::Graphics` object and one `Drawing::Brush` of a designated color. These objects are usually declared as instance objects and initialized in `Form1_Load()`, as you did in similar fashion with the instance objects `strLog` and `randomNumGen` in the Chapter 5 tutorial.

The declarations for the `Drawing::Brush` and `Drawing::Graphics` objects required in this program are shown in Example 6-13.

EXAMPLE 6-13

```
Drawing::Brush^ yellowBrush;
Drawing::Graphics^ g;
```

`Form1_Load()` is used to initialize `yellowBrush` and `g`. Initializing `yellowBrush` so that is becomes a solid yellow color is done by creating a new instance of a `Drawing::SolidBrush` object assigned `Color::Yellow`. `Drawing::Graphics` objects, such as `g`, are constructed using instance methods belonging to system-defined objects, such as `pictureBox1`. The instance method `CreateGraphics()` makes a `Drawing::Graphics` object that belongs to `pictureBox1`. The initialization code for `yellowBrush` and `g` is shown in Example 6-14.

EXAMPLE 6-14

```
yellowBrush = gcnew Drawing::SolidBrush(Color::Yellow);
g = pictureBox1->CreateGraphics();
```

Geometric shapes, such as circles, are drawn by creating a rectangle object (`Drawing::Rectangle`) to define the boundary of the shape and then drawing the shape within it. The `Drawing::Rectangle` object has a location and a size. The location consists of the x- and y-coordinates of the point in its upper-left corner. By default, the x- and y-coordinates of the upper-left corner of `pictureBox1` are (0, 0). The x-coordinate for the rectangle is the number of pixels from the left edge of `pictureBox1`. The y-coordinate is the number of pixels down from the top of `pictureBox1`. The size of the rectangle consists of its width and height, in pixels. For a square, both the width and height are the same.

Figure 6-16 shows a rectangle defined by upper-left corner coordinates x = 38, y = 25 and the width and height each set to 150 pixels.

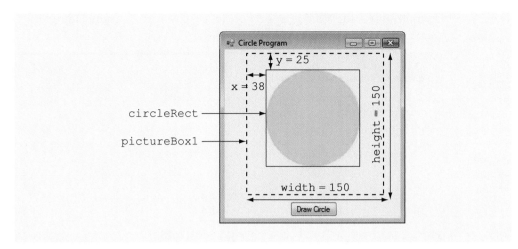

FIGURE 6-16 Defining a rectangle

A `Drawing::Rectangle` object called `circleRect` can be built using the settings shown in Figure 6-16. The syntax for a `Drawing::Rectangle` object declaration statement is shown here. The four critical values (`x`, `y`, `width`, and `height`) are used as parameters to guide the construction process.

```
Drawing::Rectangle rect_name(x,y,width,height);
```

The statement shown in Example 6-15 constructs a `Rectangle` object described in Figure 6-16.

EXAMPLE 6-15

```
Drawing::Rectangle circleRect(38,25,150,150);
```

Once a `Brush` and `Rectangle` object exist, the `Graphics` object can use the `Brush` to draw an object in the `Rectangle`. The command below uses `yellowBrush` to draw an ellipse within the confines of `circleRect`. Because `circleRect` has the same width (150 pixels) as height (150 pixels) the ellipse will too—making it a circle. The `Graphics` object instance method `FillEllipse()` does the work, using the parameters `yellowBrush` and `circleRect` to guide it as shown in Example 6-16.

EXAMPLE 6-16

```
g->FillEllipse(yellowBrush,circleRect);
```

Example 6-17 shows the code for the entire program including instance objects, `Form1_Load()`, and `btnDraw_Click()`.

EXAMPLE 6-17

```
// Instance objects
Drawing::Brush^ yellowBrush;
Drawing::Graphics^ g;

private: System::Void Form1_Load(System::Object^
sender, System::EventArgs^ e) {
   // Initialization
   yellowBrush = gcnew Drawing::SolidBrush(Color::Yellow);
   g = pictureBox1->CreateGraphics();
}

private: System::Void btnDraw_Click(System::Object^
sender, System::EventArgs^ e) {
   // Create Rectangle and draw yellow circle within it
   Drawing::Rectangle circleRect(38,25,150,150);
   g->FillEllipse(yellowBrush,circleRect);
}
```

The Use of Constants

Consider the circle program described in the previous section. When the `Rectangle` object was declared, four parameters (`x`, `y`, `width`, and `height`) were required to initialize it. The values for each of these (`x = 38`, `y = 25`, `width = 150`, and `height = 150`) were used as value parameters in the call to a method that constructed the `Rectangle` object `circleRect`, as shown here:

```
Drawing::Rectangle circleRect(38,25,150,150);
```

Although using literal values in this manner is efficient, it is often more practical to use instance variables instead. If we assume that `x`, `y`, `width`, and `height` were declared as instance variables and initialized in `Form1_Load()` (to 38, 25, 150, and 150, respectively), then they could be used as shown here to produce a `Rectangle` object of the same location and size as before:

```
Drawing::Rectangle circleRect(x,y,width,height);
```

This is preferable because if the program requirements change (say you need a `width` and `height` of 125 instead of 150), changing the lines of code that initialize `width` and `height` will make sure that the correct `width` and `height` values are used everywhere within the program. This is especially important with multiple lines of code that use the same values.

It is generally better to use variables than literal values where you can because it is easier to change one variable assignment than many lines of code with literal values. However, even variables have their weaknesses. As the name *variable* suggests, they allow data value changes. When change occurs by accident, problems arise.

Notice however that in the example above `width` and `height` were always intended to be 150. In this case, rather than making them variables, they might as well be constants. **Constants** are similar to variables in that they represent a named block of memory dedicated to the storage of data values of a designated type. The difference is that the values stored in constants *cannot* be changed while the program is running.

The syntax for declaring a constant is:

```
[static] const data_type const_name;
```

The keyword **const** establishes the value as constants. The optional keyword **static** is used to indicate that only one constant should be created and shared by all objects created from the class. This makes sense for constants because their values are always the same; there is no sense in every object having its own copy. The following statements, placed in the same section of programmer code where instance variables are declared, declare `width` and `height` to be integer constants and then initialize them:

```
static const int width = 150;
static const int height = 150;
```

Example 6-18 shows how both `static` constants (`width` and `height`) and instance variables (`x` and `y`) could be used in the previous program (Example 6-11) to eliminate the use of literal values in the `Rectangle` declaration.

EXAMPLE 6-18

```
// Static constants
static const width = 150;
static const height = 150;
// Instance variables
int x, y;
// Instance objects
Drawing::Brush^ yellowBrush;
Drawing::Graphics^ g;

private: System::Void Form1_Load(System::Object^
sender, System::EventArgs^ e) {
    // Initialization of instance variables
    x = 38;
    y = 25;
    // Initialization of System::Drawing objects
    yellowBrush = gcnew Drawing::SolidBrush(Color::Yellow);
    g = pictureBox1->CreateGraphics();
}
```

6

```
private: System::Void btnDraw_Click(System::Object^
sender, System::EventArgs^ e) {
    // Create Rectangle and draw yellow circle within it
    Drawing::Rectangle circleRect(x,y,width,height);
    g->FillEllipse(yellowBrush,circleRect);
}
```

Notice that when the `Rectangle` object (`circleRect`) is created, only variables and constants are used to define its location and size. The use of static constants will be an important feature of the tutorial in the next section.

Tutorial: Planetary Motion

This tutorial uses the knowledge you have about `System::Drawing` objects to create a short, animated program that illustrates planetary orbits. The first version you create will illustrate the orbit of a single planet, in less than 25 lines of code. The "On Your Own" section then points out areas that can be improved by adding functionality related to the various programmer-defined methods you have studied in this chapter. Several projects at the end of the chapter expand this tutorial further to provide multiple planets in differing orbits with differing speeds, requiring the use of additional programmer-defined methods.

Problem Analysis

This program is designed to simulate planetary motion around a star. You will draw a yellow circle (the sun) and then create a planet that revolves around it on an elliptical path. To simulate the movement of the planet, the program will redraw the planet in a new location along an elliptical path at frequent intervals. If the program redraws the planet fast enough, you will see a smoothly animated planet orbiting a star.

You probably remember something about ellipses from previous geometry courses. An ellipse is a closed curve that is symmetric around the perpendicular intersection of two central axes. Figure 6-17 shows two axes running through a center point (`xcenter`, `ycenter`) of an ellipse. The longest axis is called the major axis, and the shortest is called the minor axis. The distance along the longest axis (in this case, the x axis) from the center to edge is called the semimajor axis (`smajor`). The distance along the shorter axis (in this case, the y axis) from the center to the edge is called the semiminor axis (`sminor`).

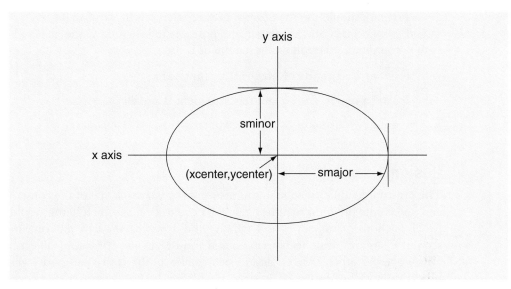

FIGURE 6-17 Basic ellipse concepts

Your goal is to plot the course of a planet as it revolves counter-clockwise in an elliptical orbit around a central star. Starting with an angle of 0 degrees, we will increase the angle by 5 degrees at a time until the angle reaches 360 degrees (so that the planet arrives back at its starting point). At each successive position, a new x and y pair is calculated and the planet is redrawn. This will produce the moving planet effect diagramed in Figure 6-18.

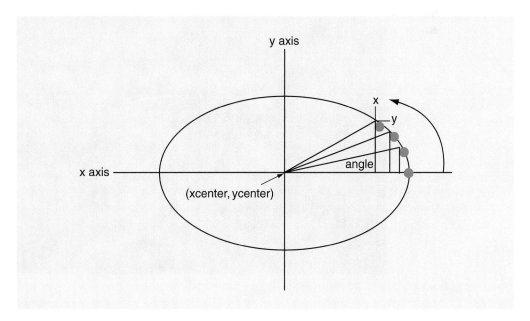

FIGURE 6-18 Planet repositioning

Your program should use the `System::Math` methods for cosine and sine to calculate the x- and y-coordinate of each new planet position and then draw the planet. To calculate a new x-coordinate, the following statement is used:

```
x = xcenter + smajor * Math::Cos(angle);
```

To calculate a new y-coordinate this statement is used:

```
y = ycenter + sminor * Math::Sin(angle);
```

Design

The primary design challenge in this project involves the scope of the constants, variables, and objects the program requires. We will need to decide which items should be available to all methods (class scope) and which should be confined to just one method (local scope). Constants, instance variables, and most `System::Drawing` objects should have class scope. All other variables and objects can be localized to a particular event handler or programmer-defined method.

INTERFACE SKETCH

Figure 6-19 shows a sketch of the program interface. As explained earlier, in this tutorial you will focus on the first step, creating a sun and one revolving planet. Once this is accomplished, you can add more planets in the On Your Own and Programming Exercises sections of this chapter.

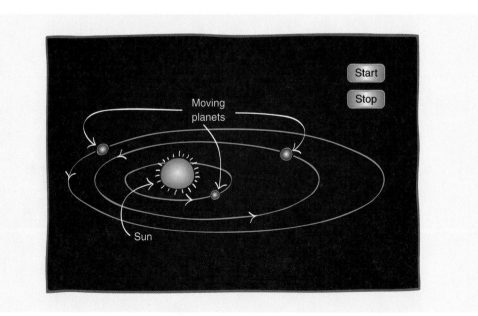

FIGURE 6-19 Preliminary interface sketch of solar system with revolving planets

We will need several controls other than the start and stop buttons shown in the drawing. The heart of the interface is the picture and the animation. This means you will need a `PictureBox` control. A **`PictureBox` control** is used to display images and to create them. You can draw the sun and planets in the picture box on top of whatever image you have chosen to underlie it. Also, because the animated effect requires that new positions for the planets are drawn at regular intervals, you will need a Timer control. A **Timer control** keeps track of time as it goes by and executes a `Tick()` event handler when that time is up. By setting the Timer to recalculate and then redraw the animation every few milliseconds—when its `Tick()` event executes—we can produce a reasonably smooth moving image.

The control table for the proposed program looks like that shown in Table 6-1.

TABLE 6-1 Control Table for the Planet Program (Version 1)

Usage	Object	Event	Description
Initialization	Form1	Load()	
	btnStart	Click()	Starts the Timer
	btnStop	Click()	Stops the Timer
Processing	timer1	Tick()	Calculates new planet positions and redraws them at regular intervals
Output	pictureBox1		Displays the animation

DATA TABLE

Constants and variables are required to make the calculations necessary to move the planet and to draw images in the picture box.

Constants   Values that should not change—that is, constant values—are appropriate for several variables in this program. Most notably, the x- and y-coordinates of the center of the solar system (200, 250). Once defined, the constants `xcenter` and `ycenter`, are used to draw the sun and to calculate every position of the planet. In addition, because you will start with just one planet, the length of its semimajor axis (`smajor` = 150) and semiminor axis (`sminor` = 50) will not change. Table 6-2 lists the constants and their values.

TABLE 6-2   Table of Constants

Variable Name	Data Type	Value	Usage
xcenter	int	200	Center of the ellipse on x axis
ycenter	int	250	Center of the ellipse on y axis
smajor	int	150	Length of semimajor axis (in pixels)
sminor	int	50	Length of semiminor axis (in pixels)

Instance Variables and Drawing Objects   There is only one instance variable in this version of the program, the measurement of the planet angle in degrees (`angle_degrees`). The various `System::Drawing` objects for both the sun and a single planet are shown in Table 6-3. We will use a light blue (`Color::Cyan`) for the planet color.

TABLE 6-3   Instance Variables and Objects

Variable Name	Data/Object Type	Usage
angle_degrees	double	Planet angle (in degrees)
g	Graphics	Graphics object for `pictureBox1`
yellowBrush	Brush	Fills the interior of sun
cyanBrush	Brush	Fills the interior of planet
sunRect	Rectangle	Boundaries for sun
planetRect	Rectangle	Boundaries for planet

Local Variables in the `Tick()` Event Handler   Every time the `Tick()` event handler executes, the planet is drawn in a new location. The various constants and instance variables account for most of what is needed for this to happen, but there are a few loose ends. The x- and y-coordinates of the planet location need to be calculated based on the angle (in radians). These variables are not accounted for elsewhere and therefore are local variables to the `Tick()` method. They are listed in Table 6-4.

TABLE 6-4 Instance Variables and Objects

Variable Name	Data/Object Type	Usage
angle_radians	double	Planet angle (in radians)
x	double	x-coordinate of the planet
y	double	y-coordinate of the planet

ALGORITHM

The crucial algorithm for this project is the one used by the Timer control. We need to decide what happens every time its `Tick()` event executes.

A high-level algorithm for this Timer assumes that we already have an angle and need to calculate a new position for the planet before drawing it. Notice that the last thing this algorithm does is to increase the angle. This ensures that the next time the `Tick()` event executes, the angle is set to a new position as shown in Algorithm 6-1.

ALGORITHM 6-1

1. Declare variables.
2. Refresh the picture box (to remove old images).
3. Draw a sun.
4. Draw a planet.
5. Increase the angle by 5 degrees.

Of these steps, the one requiring the most elaboration is Step 4, in which the x- and y-coordinates are calculated and the planet drawn. The x- and y-coordinates are based on the angle. Because the angle increases by 5 degrees with each click event, it eventually becomes larger than 360 degrees. The code for Step 4 should determine the size of the angle; if it is 360 degrees or larger, it should set the angle back to 0 before converting the angle in degrees to radians, calculating x and y, and drawing the planet. The steps are listed in Algorithm 6-2.

ALGORITHM 6-2

4.1.   If angle >= 360, reset angle to 0.

4.2.   Calculate `angle_radians` from `angle_degrees`.

4.3.   Calculate x.

4.4.   Calculate y.

4.5.   Create the `planetRectangle`.

4.6.   Draw the planet.

Development

This is the first of several versions of the Planets program that you will work on in this chapter. When you create your project, name it "Planets (Version 1)". This is important because we will be referring to the project by name several times in this tutorial and will need to distinguish between versions you will create later in this chapter.

CREATE THE INTERFACE

Begin by constructing a form with a width of 600 pixels and height of 450 pixels as shown in Figure 6-20. Give it the title text "Planets (Version 1)". Next add a picture box, called `pictureBox1`, to the form and resize it to cover all of `Form1` except the borders.

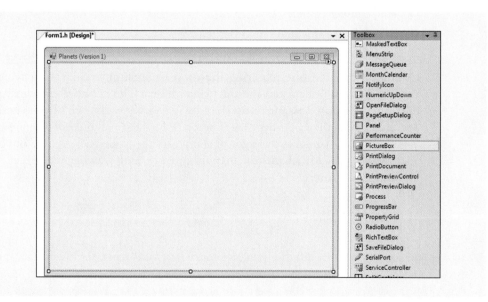

FIGURE 6-20 `Form1` overlaid with `pictureBox1`

Place two buttons on top of **pictureBox1** on the upper right. One is the Start button (**btnStart**), and the second is the Stop button (**btnStop**). Finally, find the Timer control in the Toolbox and double-click it. This places a Timer control (called **timer1**) in the **component tray** beneath your interface, as shown in Figure 6-21. Note that **timer1** will not appear on the interface when the program runs.

After you have added the timer control, save your program and close Visual C++.

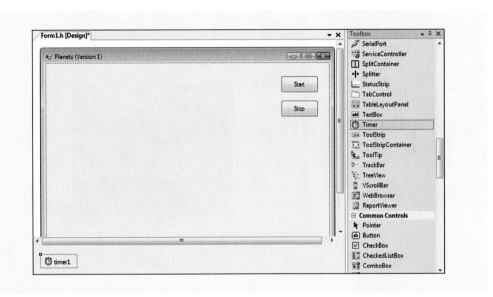

FIGURE 6-21 Timer control

Adding a Background Image This project makes use of a picture box with a background image. Because you are going to draw a sun with a planet in orbit around it, an appropriate background image would be one of the cosmos. A wide assortment of copyright-free images taken by the Hubble space telescope are available on the Web at *http://hubble.nasa.gov/multimedia/astronomy.php*.

The interface shown in this text was created using the image entitled "Extraterrestrial Fireworks" and is credited to the NASA, ESA, and the Hubble Heritage Team (STSci/ AURA; News Release Number: STScI-2006-35). The image shows the remnant of a supernova in the Small Magellanic Cloud galaxy and was downloaded from *http:// hubblesite.org/newscenter/archive/releases/2006/35/image/a/*. Select the medium-sized version of this image and download it to your desktop by right-clicking it and selecting "Save Picture As" from the menu, as shown in Figure 6-22.

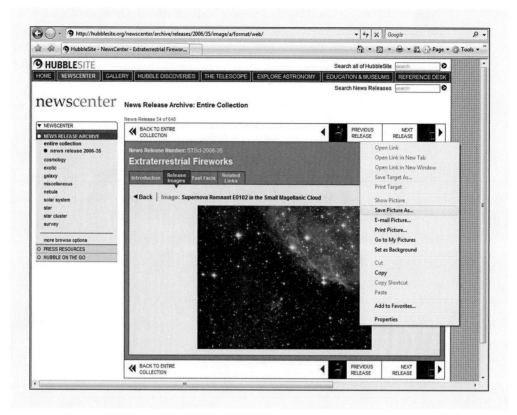

FIGURE 6-22 Saving the image

Use the Save Picture dialog box to save the image as 'web.jpg' to your desktop. This image must be placed within the Planets (Version 1) project folder within your Planets (Version 1) solution folder. It is important that pictures that accompany your project be saved within the project folder.

Now open your project again in Visual C++. You can attach the image file, web.jpg, you just downloaded to `pictureBox1` through its `Image` property in the Properties window. When you click the `Image` property the Open dialog box appears. Browse to the folder you put the image in, select the image, and click Open as shown in Figure 6-23.

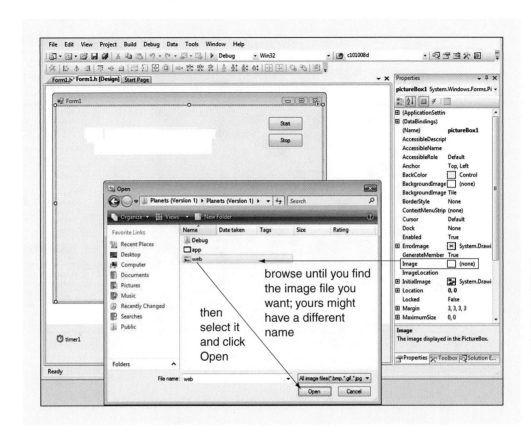

FIGURE 6-23 Opening an image for `pictureBox1`

Once the image is displayed in **pictureBox1**, click on the **SizeMode** property for **pictureBox1** and select **StretchImage** to make the image fit **pictureBox1** as shown in Figure 6-24.

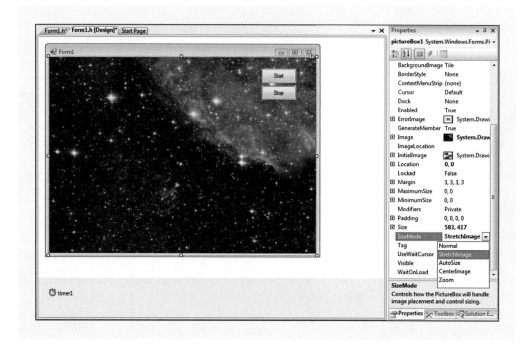

FIGURE 6-24 Setting the picture's `SizeMode` property to `StretchImage`

You should now see the image in **pictureBox1**. This makes a nice beginning for our project.

Setting the Timer The last task in the interface development stage is to set up the Timer control (`timer1`). This is very important. The `timer1`'s `Tick()` event will be activated at regular intervals. Each time the `Tick()` event is activated, your animation will draw the planet in a new location. If you set the `Interval` too high, the animation will be slow. In this case, set the `Interval` property of `timer1` to 10 milliseconds as shown in Figure 6-25. Even if it takes longer than 10 milliseconds to redraw the screen, this is still a good setting because it sets the Timer off in rapid succession. If you need to slow the planet down you can do so later by adjusting the `Interval` property upward.

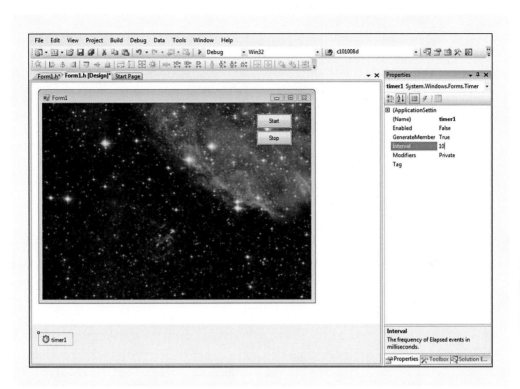

FIGURE 6-25 Setting the `Interval` property of `timer1`

CODING

There is not a large amount of code to write for Version 1 of this program. You need to create the necessary constants, instance variables, and instance objects first and initialize them in `Form1_Load()`, then write the code for several small event handlers. The most important section of code to understand is that which is contained within the `timer1_Tick()` event. Because the Timer will execute many times each second, the instructions in its `Tick()` event handler will be executed repeatedly and are responsible for all of the animation that occurs.

Constants, Instance Variables, and Drawing Objects   The constants, variables, and objects that must be declared at the class level were identified in Tables 6-2 and 6-3. The **static constants**, including the center and axes of the orbit ellipse, are initialized upon declaration. The instance variables and objects are initialized in `Form1_Load()` as shown in Example 6-19.

EXAMPLE 6-19

```
// Static constants
static const int xcenter = 200;
static const int ycenter = 250;
static const int smajor = 150;
static const int sminor = 50;

// Instance variable
double angle_degrees;

// Drawing objects
Drawing::Graphics^ g;
Drawing::Brush^ yellowBrush;    // Yellow for sun
Drawing::Brush^ cyanBrush;      // Cyan for planet
```

The Form1_Load event   In the `Form1_Load()` event the `System::Drawing` objects are constructed as shown in Example 6-20.

EXAMPLE 6-20

```
// Construct drawing objects
g = pictureBox1->CreateGraphics();
yellowBrush = gcnew Drawing::SolidBrush(Color::Yellow);
cyanBrush = gcnew Drawing::SolidBrush(Color::Cyan);
```

The Start button   Whenever `btnStart` is clicked, `angle_degrees` is reset to 0 and `timer1` is turned on (enabled). From that point on, the `timer1_Tick()` event is activated at its designated interval (every 10 milliseconds) as shown in Example 6-21.

EXAMPLE 6-21

```
angle_degrees = 0;
timer1->Enabled = true;
```

The Stop button   The stop button simply stops the Timer by disabling it. This ends the animation as shown in Example 6-22:

EXAMPLE 6-22

```
timer1->Enabled = false;
```

Coding the `timer1_Tick()` event The heart of this program is what happens each time the `timer1_Tick()` event executes. You constructed an algorithm for this event during the design stage, and it can now be implemented. The first step involves the creation of all of the objects needed for drawing, including the x- and y-coordinate position of where the planet should be drawn as shown in Example 6-23.

EXAMPLE 6-23

```
// Declare local variables
int x, y; // x,y coordinates of the planet
double angle_radians; // angle measurement in radians

// Refresh the picture box to remove old images
pictureBox1->Refresh();

// Draw the sun (use a rectangle as a guide)
System::Drawing::Rectangle
sunRect(xcenter,ycenter,16,16);
g->FillEllipse(yellowBrush,sunRect); // draw sun

// Draw the planet
if (angle_degrees >= 360) angle_degrees = 0;
angle_radians = angle_degrees * Math::PI / 180;
// Calculate new x and y
x = xcenter + smajor * Math::Cos(angle_radians);
y = ycenter - sminor * Math::Sin(angle_radians);
// Draw planet
System::Drawing::Rectangle planetRect(x,y,10,10);
g->FillEllipse(cyanBrush,planetRect);

// Increase angle by 5 degrees
angle_degrees += 5;
```

TESTING

Now run the program. You should see a light blue planet orbiting a yellow sun as shown in Figure 6-26.

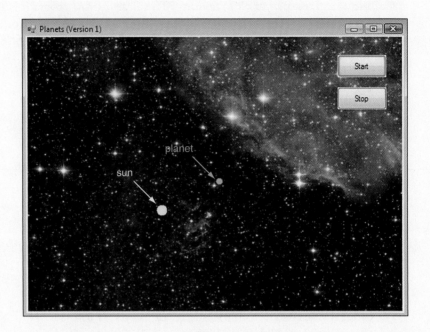

FIGURE 6-26 Final product Planets program (Version 1)

ON YOUR OWN

Now that you have successfully created the orbiting planet program (Version 1) it is time to gain some practical experience with programmer-defined methods. Each of the On Your Own tasks provides the opportunity to modify this program with one or more of your own methods.

TASK 1. INSTANCE METHODS WITH RETURN VALUES (PLANETS VERSION 2)

Earlier in the chapter, we discussed a method called `ConvertToRadians()` that could be used in this program. Modify your program so that the `timer1_Tick()` event handler calls the method like this:

```
angle_radians = ConvertToRadians(angle_degrees);
```

instead of doing the conversion in this line:

```
angle_radians = angle_degrees * Math::PI / 180;
```

TASK 2. INSTANCE METHODS WITH VALUE PARAMETERS (PLANETS VERSION 3)

Create a programmer-defined method that will draw the planet. To do this, replace the following code in `timer1_Tick()`:

```
System::Drawing::Rectangle planetRect(x,y,10,10);
g->FillEllipse(cyanBrush,planetRect);
```

with a call to a programmer-defined method called `DrawPlanet()`. Your `DrawPlanet()` method should have two value parameters, `x` and `y`, and be called in this manner:

```
DrawPlanet(x, y);
```

TASK 3. INSTANCE METHODS WITH REFERENCE PARAMETERS (PLANETS VERSION 4)

Modify the `timer1_Tick()` event handler to call a single method that calculates both `x` and `y`. To do this, replace the lines

```
// Calculate new x and y
x = xcenter + smajor * Math::Cos(angle_radians);
y = ycenter - sminor * Math::Sin(angle_radians);
```

with a call to a programmer-defined method called `SetXY()` that is called in this manner:

```
SetXY(x, y, angle_radians);
```

This method has two reference parameters (`x` and `y`) and one value parameter (`angle_radians`) and uses a pass-by-reference to update `x` and `y`.

6

QUICK REVIEW

1. Methods are identifiable, self-contained program units that can be called upon to perform specific tasks.

2. Some methods are built-in to the `System` namespace (system-defined methods) while others are written in program applications (application methods).

3. There are two kinds of system-defined methods: methods that belong to `System` classes (class methods) and methods that belong to objects (instance methods).

4. System-defined class methods include those within the `System::Math` class.

5. System-defined instance methods are those built into objects such as text boxes and buttons.

6. Application methods are written by the programmer.

7. There are two types of application methods: event handlers (with which you already familiar) and programmer-defined methods.

8. Programmer-defined methods are written entirely by the programmer.

9. Many methods use parameters to acquire data that must be processed.

10. System-defined instance methods are built into system-defined objects, such as text boxes and buttons.

11. Method definitions include a method signature and body.

12. The first line of a method is its signature and contains its access mode, return type, name, and parameter list.

13. If the body of a method is enclosed in a set of curly brackets { }.

14. Programmer-defined methods help reduce code redundancy.

15. Programmer-defined methods are also useful in reducing the complexity of long program segments.

16. Methods are useful because they allow you to isolate the code related to specific tasks.

17. Methods without return values or parameters are used to perform tasks that do not require data to be passed in or sent back.

18. You type programmer-defined methods in the programmer code region immediately after the `#pragma endregion` line and before the closing curly bracket of the `Form1` class definition.

19. Method calls must include parentheses even if there are no parameters.

20. Methods without return types are called using their name on a line by itself.

21. When a method is called, the arguments in the method call are referred to as actual arguments.

22. When a parameter list is used with a method, the parameters in the signature line of the method definition are called formal parameters.

23. Actual and formal parameters must match in terms of data type, size, and number of parameters.

24. The names of actual and formal parameters do not have to match.

25. Pass-by-value is a method of sending data into a method by copying values from the actual parameters to the corresponding formal parameters.

26. Pass-by-value is the default method of transferring data.

27. Pass-by-reference is a method of creating a formal parameter that is an alias for the actual argument.

28. When pass-by-reference is used, the `&` symbol is placed after the data type in the formal parameter declaration.

29. Reference parameters use the reference to acquire and/or change the data stored at that reference location.

30. Reference parameters store the addresses of actual arguments, creating a two-way exchange of data.

31. Methods with return values use a return statement to convey the value back to the programming unit that called them.

32. Return values can be captured by variables in the calling program unit using an assignment statement.

33. The `System::Drawing` namespace contains class definitions for drawing objects.

34. A `Graphics` object is attached to controls, such as picture boxes and forms.

35. A `Brush` object is used to create colored areas.

36. A `Rectangle` object is required to outline the boundaries of ellipses and circles.

37. The `FillEllipse()` method of the `Graphics` object is used to create an ellipse based on a `Rectangle` object and a colored `Brush` object.

38. `Rectangle` objects require the x- and y-coordinates of the upper-left corner along with a width and a height.

39. Constants are similar to variables except their initial value assignments cannot change.

40. Static constants are declared in the programmer code section outside of all event handlers and methods.

41. The keyword `static` in `static constant` means that only one constant is created, and it is shared by all instances of the class.

42. Images may be added to a picture box to give it a picture-based background.

43. PictureBoxes may be "drawn on" by system-defined `Graphics` and `Drawing` objects.

44. The Timer control executes the commands in its `Tick()` event at programmer-defined intervals.

TERMS TO KNOW

access mode

actual argument

address–of operator (&)

application methods

class method

code redundancy

component trayconst

constant

formal argument

formal definition

formal parameter

header line

instance

instance method

`Math::Cos()`

`Math::Log()`

`Math::PI`

`Math::Pow()`

`Math::Sin()`

`Math::Sqrt()`

`Math::Tan()()`

method

method body

method definition

method name

method signature

parameters

parameter list

pass-by-reference

pass-by-value

`PictureBox` **control**

programmer-defined method

reference parameter

return type

return statement

return value

static

`static` **constant**

system-defined method

`System::Math`

`System::Void`

`Tick()` **event**

Timer control

value parameter

`void`

EXERCISES

Questions 1–5 refer to the following programmer-defined method:

```
private: void setxy()
{
    if ((intx > 400) || (intx < 0)) xdir = -xdir;
    if ((inty > 400) || (inty < 0)) ydir = -ydir;
    intx = intx + xincr * xdir;
    inty = inty + yincr * ydir;
}
```

1. The return type specified in the method is _____.

    a. private

    b. void

    c. setxy

    d. intx

    e. None of the above

2. The method's name is _____.

    a. private

    b. void

    c. setxy

    d. intx

    e. None of the above

3. The method's mode of access is _____.

    a. private

    b. void

    c. setxy

    d. intx

    e. None of the above

4. Which of the following is a formal parameter used in the method?

    a. private

    b. void

    c. setxy

    d. intx

    e. None of the above

5. Which of the following is an instance variable used in the method?

    a. `private`

    b. `void`

    c. `setxy`

    d. `intx`

    e. None of the above

6. When a method is called, which of the following do not have to match?

    a. The data types of corresponding actual and formal arguments

    b. The names of corresponding actual and formal arguments

    c. The order of corresponding actual and formal arguments

    d. The number of actual and formal arguments

    e. All of these must match.

7. The default method of passing data into a method is _____.

    a. pass–by–value

    b. pass–by–reference

    c. pass–by–address

    d. pass–by–name

    e. None of the above

8. Which operator is used to indicate that a formal parameter is a reference parameter?

    a. `++`

    b. `+=`

    c. `void`

    d. `&`

9. To ensure that a value will not change, you should declare it as a(n)

    _____.

    a. instance variable

    b. instance method

    c. object

    d. `static const`

    e. None of the above

10. `TryParse()` has a return type of which data type?

    a. `bool`

    b. `int`

    c. `float`

    d. `double`

    e. `char`

The following code for `btnConvert_Click()` converts temperatures from degrees Fahrenheit to degrees Celsius. Refer to it as you answer Questions 11–15.

```
private: System::Void btnConvert_Click(System::Object^
sender, System::EventArgs^ e)
{
    double fahr;
    double celsius;
    fahr = Convert::ToDouble(txtFahr->Text);
    celsius = FahrToCel(fahr);
    txtCel->Text = celsius.ToString();
}
```

11. Which of the following does *not* refer to a method?

   a. `FahrToCel()`

   b. `Convert::ToDouble()`

   c. `ToString()`

   d. `btnConvert_Click()`

   e. `System::Void`

12. Which of the following refers to an event handler?

   a. `FahrToCel()`

   b. `Convert::ToDouble()`

   c. `ToString()`

   d. `btnConvert_Click()`

   e. `System::Void`

13. Which of the following refers to a system-defined instance method belonging to an object?

   a. `FahrToCel()`

   b. `Convert::ToDouble()`

   c. `ToString()`

   d. `btnConvert_Click()`

   e. `System::Void`

14. Which of the following refers to a system-defined class method?

   a. `FahrToCel()`

   b. `Convert::ToDouble()`

   c. `ToString()`

   d. `btnConvert_Click()`

   e. `System::Void`

6

15. Which of the following refers to a programmer-defined method?

    a. `FahrToCel()`

    b. `Convert::ToDouble()`

    c. `ToString()`

    d. `btnConvert_Click()`

    e. `System::Void`

Use this programmer-defined method to answer Questions 16–20.

```
private: double AddNums(double num1, int& num2)
{
    double num3 = num1;
    num1 += num2;
    num2++;
    return num1 + num2 + num3;
}
```

16. Which of the following is a value parameter?

    a. num1

    b. num2

    c. num3

    d. num1 and num2

    e. None of the above

17. Which of the following is a formal parameter?

    a. num1

    b. num2

    c. num3

    d. num1 and num2

    e. None of the above

18. Which of the following is a reference parameter?

    a. num1

    b. num2

    c. num3

    d. num1 and num2

    e. None of the above

19. Which of the following is a valid way to call the method, assuming that integer variable numa is set to 3 and double precision variable numb is set to 6.0?

    a. `numb = AddNums(numb, numa);`

    b. `double numc = AddNums(2.34, numb);`

    c. `numa = AddNums(numb, numa);`

    d. `numb = AddNums(numa, numb);`

    e. None of the above

20. If double precision variable num4 is set to 3.0 and integer variable num5 is set to 4 prior to this method call:

    num4 = AddNums(num4, num5);

    What is num4 set to when the returned value is assigned to it?

    a. 3.0

    b. 5.0

    c. 7.0

    d. 15.0

    e. None of the above

PROGRAMMING EXERCISES

1. Currency Converter

Write a program that converts an amount of money from U.S. dollars to another currency. The interface is shown in Figure 6-27.

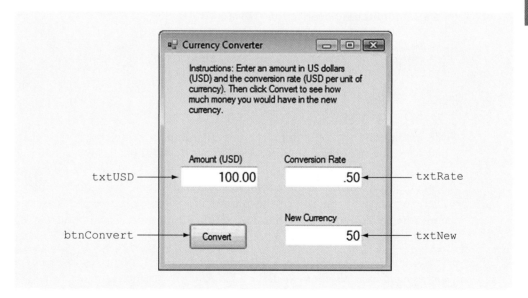

FIGURE 6-27 Currency Converter interface

The user enters an amount of U.S. dollars in txtUSD and a conversion rate in txtRate. (You can look up the conversion rate for a currency of your choice on the Internet.) When btnConvert is clicked, the number of units of new currency is displayed in txtNew. For example, you can see in Figure 6-27 that the user entered $100.00 in txtUSD and a rate of .50 in txtRate. As a result, the new currency calculation shows that you would have 50 monetary units in the new currency.

The code for btnConvert_Click() is shown here:

```
private: System::Void btnConvert_Click(System::Object^
sender, System::EventArgs^ e) {
    double us_dollars, rate, new_money;
    Double::TryParse(txtUSD->Text, us_dollars);
    Double::TryParse(txtRate->Text, rate);
    new_money = us_dollars * rate;
    txtNew->Text = new_money.ToString();
}
```

Rewrite this program so that the variables are declared in btnConvert_Click() as before, but the TryParse() statements execute in a programmer-defined method called ReadData(). In addition, create a method called ConvertIt() that performs the conversion calculation.

When you finish, your program should run just as before, but the code for btnConvert_Click() should look like this:

```
private: System::Void btnConvert_Click(System::Object^
sender, System::EventArgs^ e) {
    double us_dollars, rate, new_money;
    ReadData(us_dollars, rate);
    new_money = ConvertIt(us_dollars, rate);
    txtNew->Text = new_money.ToString();
}
```

2. DPI Calculator

The resolution of a computer monitor is the number of pixels it can display horizontally and vertically. Common monitor resolutions are 1280 pixels horizontally by 1024 pixels vertically, 1280 x 960, 1024 x 768, and 800 x 600. There are many resolution settings depending on whether your monitor has a widescreen or regular format and who the manufacturer is. Your task in this project is to write a program that allows the user to enter the resolution of their monitor and determine how many dots per inch (dpi) the monitor displays. (A dot and a pixel are the same thing.)

For example, a monitor with a resolution of 1280 x 1024 that is 15 inches across and 12 inches high, has a resolution of 1280/15 = 85 pixels per inch horizontally and 1024/12 = 85 pixels per inch vertically. (Normally the vertical and horizontal dimensions are the same.)

Write a program, similar to the one shown in Figure 6-28, that calls a programmer-defined instance method to do the conversion.

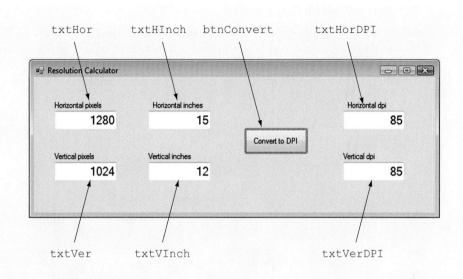

txtHor   txtHInch   btnConvert   txtHorDPI

txtVer   txtVInch   txtVerDPI

6

FIGURE 6-28 DPI Calculator

Your program should read the horizontal and vertical measurements in pixels and inches from the text boxes on the left of the interface. When the user clicks **btnConvert**, the **btnConvert_Click()** event handler should call a programmer-defined method named **FindDPI()** to calculate the horizontal and vertical dpi values and return them to the click event to be displayed. The code for the **btnConvert_Click()** is shown here:

```
private: System::Void btnConvert_Click(System::Object^
sender, System::EventArgs^ e) {
   // number of horizontal and vertical pixels
   double horPixels, verPixels;
   // horizontal and vertical inches
   int hInches, vInches;
   // horizontal and vertical dpi
   int horDPI, verDPI;

   // read in the data
   Double::TryParse(txtHor->Text, horPixels);
   Double::TryParse(txtVer->Text, verPixels);
   Int32::TryParse(txtHInch->Text, hInches);
   Int32::TryParse(txtVInch->Text, vInches);

   // Call FindDPI()
   FindDPI(horPixels, verPixels, hInches, vInches,
   horDPI, verDPI);
   txtHorDPI->Text = horDPI.ToString();
}
```

3. Metric Distance Converter

Construct a program with an interface like the one shown in Figure 6-29. The program allows the user to enter an amount and a metric unit of distance measurement (such as centimeter or kilometer) and then convert the amount to a nonmetric unit (such as inch or mile). Clicking on **btnConvert** displays the conversion.

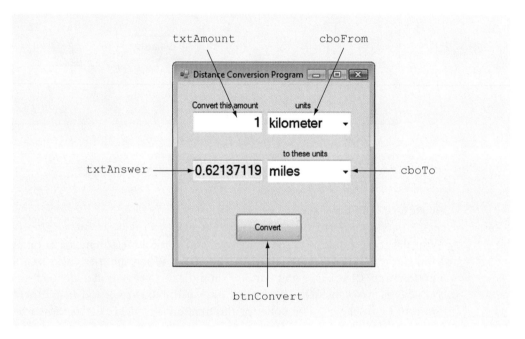

FIGURE 6-29 Distance Conversion Program

In the top combo box the choices should be millimeters, centimeters, meters, and kilometers. In the second combo box the choices should be inches, feet, yards, and miles. Table 6-5 will help you figure out how to do the conversions.

TABLE 6-5 Conversion Equivalents

Unit	Millimeters per Unit
millimeter	1
centimeter	10
meter	1000
kilometer	1000000
inch	25.4

TABLE 6-5   Conversion Equivalents (continued)

Unit	Millimeters per Unit
foot	304.8
yard	914.4
mile	1609344

Write your program so that it successfully implements `ConvertIt()`, a programmer-defined method, in one of three ways:

First, use a programmer-defined method with a return type. The code for `btnConvert_Click()` is shown here:

```
private: System::Void btnConvert_Click(System::Object^
sender, System::EventArgs^ e) {
    double amount, answer;
    Double::TryParse(txtAmount->Text, amount);
    answer = ConvertIt(amount);
    txtAnswer->Text = answer.ToString();
}
```

For the second way, use a programmer-defined method without a return type. In this version nothing is returned. Instead, the answer is displayed in `txtAnswer-Text` from within the `ConvertIt()` method:

```
private: System::Void btnConvert_Click(System::Object^
sender, System::EventArgs^ e) {
    double amount;
    Double::TryParse(txtAmount->Text, amount);
    ConvertIt(amount);
}
```

The third way to implement `ConvertIt()` is to use a programmer-defined method with a reference parameter to return the value.

```
private: System::Void btnConvert_Click(System::Object^
sender, System::EventArgs^ e) {
    double amount, answer;
    Double::TryParse(txtAmount->Text, amount);
    ConvertIt(amount, answer);
    txtAnswer->Text = answer.ToString();
}
```

4.   More Planets

In this project you expand on the planet program you created in the tutorial. To generate more than one planet, all you have to do is call `SetXY()` and `DrawPlanet()` more than once. Each planet should have a different orbit however, so instead of using `smajor` and `sminor`, use literal values as pass-by-value arguments.

To demonstrate, substitute the values for `smajor` (150) and `sminor` (50) in your calls to `SetXY()` and `DrawPlanet()`.

```
SetXY(x, y, angle_radians, 150, 50);
DrawPlanet(x, y, 150, 50);
```

Run the program and verify that it works just as before.

To add more planets, add additional sets of calls to `SetXY()` and `DrawPlanet()` with different values for `smajor` and `sminor`. (*Hint*: Flat elliptical orbits look more convincing. This means that `sminor` should probably not be larger than half of `smajor`.)

Here is an example of a set of calls that create two orbiting planets:

```
SetXY(x, y, angle_radians, 150, 50);
DrawPlanet(x, y, 150, 50);
SetXY(x, y, 200, 75);
DrawPlanet(x, y, angle_radians, 200, 75);
```

You can add as many planets as you like; however, a curious thing happens when you run the program, as shown in Figure 6-30. The planets follow along side-by-side as they orbit the sun.

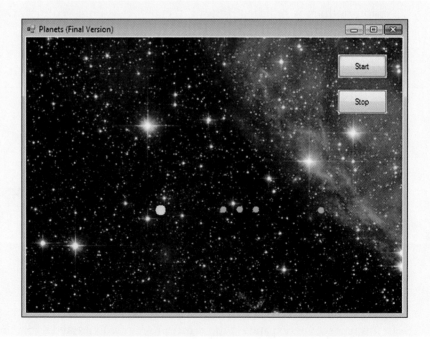

FIGURE 6-30 Multiple planets in different orbits

All planets start at different points on the x axis. Although they are in different orbits, they revolve about the sun in exactly the same length of time, some traveling slower or faster than others. This is because we only have one angle increment value. The program calculates the same number of positions for every planet, so the length of a year (the amount of time it takes for the planet to orbit the star) is the same on all planets. You will fix this problem in Programming Exercise 5.

5. Creating Different Periods of Revolution

To create longer or shorter periods of revolution, you must give each planet its own angle. These should be class instance variables that are initialized to 0 in `Form1_Load()`.

```
double angle1_degrees; // Angle of planet 1
double angle2_degrees; // Angle of planet 2
```

You also need to vary the semimajor and semiminor axis lengths for each planet as shown in the `timer1_Tick` code. The semi-major axis length for planet 1 is 150 and its semi-minor axis length is 50. The semi-major axis length for planet 2 is 200 and the semi-minor length is 75 here.

```
// Draw planet 1
angle_radians = ConvertToRadians(angle1_degrees);
SetXY(x, y, angle_radians, 150, 50);
DrawPlanet(x, y, 1);
// Draw planet 2
angle_radians = ConvertToRadians(angle2_degrees);
SetXY(x, y, angle_radians, 200, 75);
DrawPlanet(x, y, 2);
```

The signature line for `DrawPlanet()`, shown here, includes an integer to indicate which planet is to be drawn:

```
private: void DrawPlanet(int x, int y, int planetNum)
```

This revised program should be more aesthetically pleasing, because the planets have independent orbits of varying year lengths, as shown in Figure 6-31. To make the animation even more convincing, you can change the planet sizes and colors as well.

6

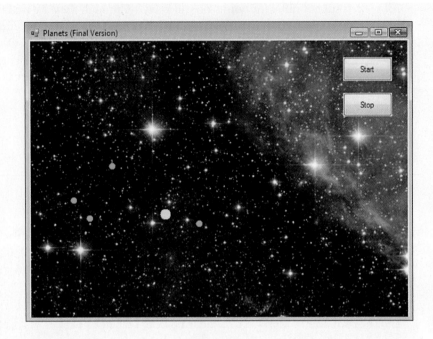

FIGURE 6-31 Multiple planets in orbits with differing angle increments

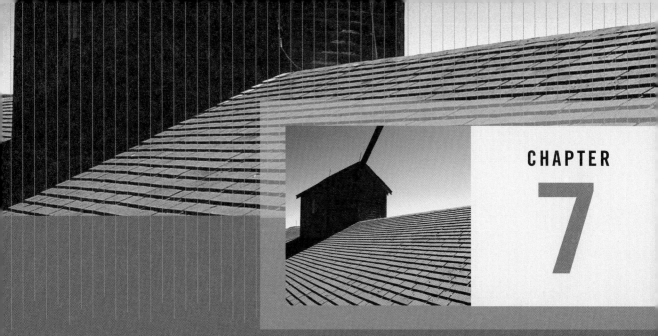

ARRAYS

IN THIS CHAPTER, YOU WILL:

- Learn how to declare and use one-dimensional arrays
- Pass array elements and entire arrays into methods
- Learn how to search for values in an array using the sequential search technique
- Discover how two-dimensional arrays can be used to store and process tables of data
- Gain further experience with nested loops

So far in this book, the need for variables has been minimal. Most of the programs in previous chapters required only a handful of variables. You declared them individually as they were needed. As your programs get larger and more complex, however, they will need to handle larger amounts of data. At that point, individual variable declarations can become cumbersome. To store larger amounts of data, you need to create new forms of data storage such as arrays, the topic of this chapter.

Arrays

A **data structure** is a method of organizing related data values in memory. The simplest and most common data structure is an array. An **array** is a contiguous block of memory cells. In an array, values follow each other in succession and are stored in continuous blocks of memory that are the same size. Each block of memory in an array is called an **array element**. The array's name identifies the entire structure, and **index values** (sometimes called **subscripts**) identify particular elements within that structure. For example, Figure 7-1 illustrates an array named num that stores data values 2, 7, 3, 8, and 6. The first index value in an array is 0, followed by 1, 2, 3 and so on. Thus, in the num array, the data value 2 is stored in the array element whose index value is 0.

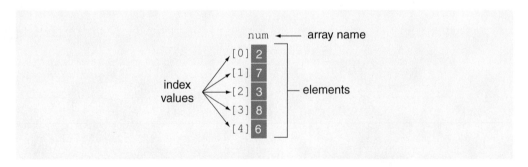

FIGURE 7-1 Array structure

The array shown in Figure 7-1 is considered a one-dimensional array. The term **one-dimensional array** refers to an array that is essentially a list of information. It is possible to create more complicated arrays with two, three, or more dimensions. For now, however, you will focus on one-dimensional arrays; multiple-dimension arrays are discussed later.

Array Declaration and Initialization

Many arrays are declared with a fixed size that cannot be altered while the program is running. This method of declaration is called **static allocation**. Another form of allocation, called **dynamic allocation**, allows the array size to be set at runtime and is also used to create array instance variables. Dynamic allocation will be covered later in this text. This chapter focuses on fixed-size arrays declared within a method or event handler.

There are two ways to declare a fixed-sized array: standard declaration and declaration with a value list. Standard array declaration takes the same format as a variable declaration, except that the array name is followed by one or more pairs of square brackets indicating the array's dimensions and size. For a one-dimensional array, the declaration syntax is:

```
data_type array_name[ n ];
```

The data type of an array may be any of the primitive or derived types available to the program. The array name is constructed using the same rules used for variable names. The number of elements in the array must be an integer and can be designated using a literal value, integer constant, integer variable, or integral expression. For example, the declaration shown in Example 7-1 sets aside space in memory for a one-dimensional array of five integers called num containing five elements (identical to the structure shown in Figure 7-1).

7

EXAMPLE 7-1: ARRAY DECLARATION

```
int num[5];
```

As we saw in Figure 7-1, each element in the array is identified by an index value from 0 to 4. The individual elements in the preceding example are therefore: num[0], num[1], num[2], num[3], and num[4].

NOTE   Keep in mind that array element indices always start with 0. Also, it is important to remember that you can only reference the array elements you have declared. In this example, elements such as num[5] or num[-1] are not part of your array and cannot be accessed. Attempts to do so will cause a runtime error.

To assign data to an array element, you write an assignment statement with the array element to the left of the assignment operator. The lines in Example 7-2 assign data values to each of the five elements of our sample array:

EXAMPLE 7-2: ASSIGNING VALUES TO ARRAY ELEMENTS

```
num[0] = 2;
num[1] = 7;
num[2] = 3;
num[3] = 8;
num[4] = 6;
```

You can also declare an array and assign values to the individual elements using a single statement containing a list of values used to initialize the elements. In this form of declaration, the square brackets are left empty and a value list, enclosed in curly brackets, is used to identify the values that are assigned to elements in the array. The general syntax for this form of initializing declaration for a one-dimensional array is shown here:

```
data_type array_name[] = { value1, value2, ... valuen };
```

The size of the array is automatically set based on the number of values in the list. The first value is stored in the first array element, the second value in the second, and so on. For example, this declaration creates an integer array called num, with five elements. Values are assigned in order (num[0], num[1], etc.) as shown in Example 7-3.

EXAMPLE 7-3: ASSIGNMENT USING A VALUE LIST

```
int num[] = { 2,7,3,8,6 };
```

Using Arrays

Once data has been stored in an array, the program can retrieve the data whenever necessary using a single control structure. For example, to display an array value in a text box, the array name and subscript are used to identify the element as shown in Figure 7-2.

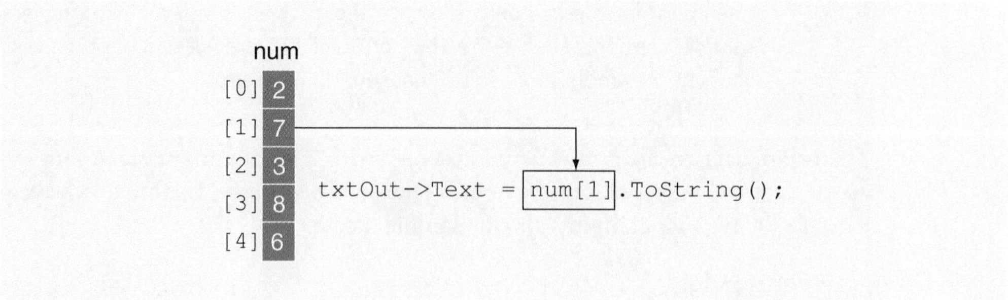

FIGURE 7-2 Accessing an array element

A `for` loop can be used to access each item, in order, using the loop control variable as an index value to identify each element. Example 7-4 shows how a `for` loop can be used to calculate the sum of all values stored in the five elements of `num`.

EXAMPLE 7-4: SUMMATION

```
int sum = 0;
int i;
for ( i = 0; i < 5; i++)
    sum += num[i];
txtSum->Text = sum.ToString();
```

As the value of the loop control variable `i` increases with each iteration, the loop control variable value can be used to access a different element of `num` each time. As a result, a new value is added to the sum in each pass, with the sum accumulating until all of the elements have been added. This process is illustrated in Figure 7-3.

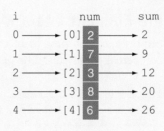

FIGURE 7-3 The summation process using a `for` loop control variable to identify array elements

All of the common loop operations discussed in Chapter 5 (summation, counting, finding the largest value, and so on) can be performed using data from the array. For example, to find the largest value in an array you could assume that the largest value is stored in the first element (`num[0]`) and then proceed to check each of the other elements in turn. Each time a larger value was found, it would replace the previous largest value. Comparisons could then continue until all elements were examined as shown in Example 7-5.

EXAMPLE 7-5: FINDING THE LARGEST VALUE

```
private: System::Void btnLarge_Click(System::Object^ sender,
System::EventArgs^ e) {
 int num[] = { 2, 7, 3, 8, 6 };
 int large = num[0];
 int i;
 for (i=1; i<5; i++)
    if (large < num[i]) large = num[i];
 txtLarge->Text = large.ToString();
}
```

Arrays and Instance Methods

You often need to pass the values stored in individual array elements, or all elements in an array, into instance methods. The following sections explain how to do this.

Passing a Single Element into a Method by Value

To pass the value from only one element of an array into a method, use the array name and element subscript as an actual parameter. The general syntax for this kind of method call is shown here:

```
method_name( array_name[ subscript ]);
```

For example, if num has been declared as an array of five integers, the first element (num[0]) is passed into a programmer-defined instance method called ShowNum() as shown in Example 7-6.

EXAMPLE 7-6: CALLING ShowNum()

```
ShowNum(num[0]);
```

The formal parameter for ShowNum() should be an integer, as shown in Example 7-7, to match the data type of the corresponding actual parameter (num[0]).

EXAMPLE 7-7: ShowNum() METHOD

```
private: void ShowNum( int myNum )
{
 txtNum->Text = myNum.ToString();
}
```

The data value from the actual parameter, num[0], is copied into the formal parameter, myNum, for use in the ShowNum() method.

Passing a Single Element into a Method by Reference

Assume that a programmer-defined instance method called GetNum() exists for the purpose of reading a value from a text box (txtNum) and assigning the value to an array element. The GetNum() method call shown in Example 7-8 uses the first element in the num array (num[0]) as the actual parameter, although any other element in the array could also have been used.

EXAMPLE 7-8: CALLING GetNum()

```
GetNum(num[0]);
```

As you can see, calling a method with an array element as the actual argument is very similar to calling a method with a variable name as the actual argument. The only difference is that with arrays you must specify which element of the array you want by using the subscript.

Now examine GetNum(). GetNum() has one formal parameter called myNum and uses the address-of operator (&) to indicate that myNum is a reference parameter, as shown in Example 7-9.

EXAMPLE 7-9: GetNum() METHOD

```
private: void GetNum( int & myNum )
{
  if (!Int32::TryParse(txtNum->Text, myNum))
    MessageBox::Show("Invalid input");
}
```

In Example 7-9, myNum is used to assign a value to the actual parameter num[0]. The Int32::TryParse() method reads an integer from a text box (txtNum->Text) into myNum. If TryParse() is successful, then the value is stored in the variable (num[0]) referenced by myNum. If TryParse() is not successful, it returns the value false, and the "Invalid Input" message is displayed.

NOTE   Note the use of the logical operator ! (not) in Example 7-9. If TryParse() returns false (meaning that data could not be read into myNum), then the value of the expression (! false) is (true) and the error message is displayed.

Passing an Entire Array into a Method

Arrays, like variables, may be passed as actual parameters into methods that need them. The name of the array serves as the actual parameter and represents the entire array with all of its elements. The syntax for such method calls is:

```
method_name(array_name);
```

Consider the program shown in Figure 7-4. When the user clicks btnMean an array is created, initialized, and the mean is calculated and displayed.

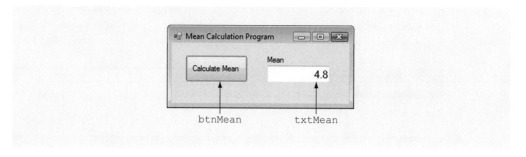

FIGURE 7-4 Mean Calculation Program

The code for btnMean_Click() is shown in Example 7-10. The five element integer array num is declared and then passed into GenerateData() and ComputeMean() as an actual parameter. The programmer-defined instance method GenerateData() initializes the array. Another programmer-defined instance method, ComputeMean(), uses the initialized array to calculate the arithmetic mean.

EXAMPLE 7-10: CODE FOR btnMean()

```
private: System::Void btnMean_Click(System::Object^ sender,
System::EventArgs^ e) {
 int num[5];
 double mean;
 GenerateData(num);
 mean = ComputeMean(num);
 txtMean->Text = mean.ToString();
}
```

 NOTE A common mistake when passing an entire array into a method is to include a subscript. For example, GenerateData(num[5]); might seem like it passes all five elements of num into GenerateData(). However, it only passes in one element: num[5]. The mistake is compounded by the fact that there is no element num[5]. Remember that subscripts in a five element array run from 0 to 4. If you want to pass an entire array into a method do so using only its name, without any square brackets or subscripts in the actual parameter.

Methods such as GenerateData() and ComputeMean(), which receive entire arrays through the parameter list, indicate this by use of a formal parameter name followed by an empty set of square brackets. The syntax for a method signature line with an array as a formal parameter is shown here:

```
access_mode: return_type method_name( data_type array_name[size])
```

For example, the signature line for `GenerateData()` shown in Example 7-11 contains a formal parameter called `numArr[]` that is an array of integers. When a formal parameter is an array, its size may be used to dimension it, or it may be omitted. No dimension size is given in Example 7-11. The size is optional because, unlike single variables, arrays are automatically passed into methods by reference, not by value.

EXAMPLE 7-11: `GenerateData()` SIGNATURE LINE

```
private: void GenerateData(int numArr[])
```

You will recall that pass-by-value makes a copy of the actual argument value and then assigns that copy to the formal parameter. To make pass-by-value copies of arrays, however, would mean duplicating potentially large data structures. For this reason, the default method of passing arrays is by reference. The formal parameter `numArr[]` stores the location in memory of the first element of array `num`. In this way, it points back to the storage allocated for `num` in the calling program unit, as shown in Figure 7-5.

7

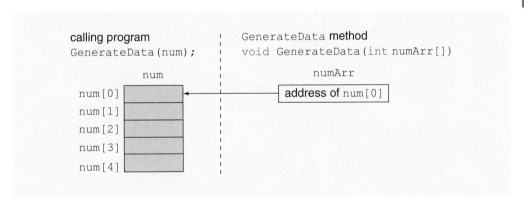

FIGURE 7-5 Formal parameter `numArr[]` stores the address of the first element of the actual parameter array `num`

Every change made to an element referred to using the formal parameter name `numArr` is really made to the corresponding element of array `num` back in the calling program. For example, a statement in `GenerateData()` such as:

```
numArr[2] = 3;
```

assigns the value 3 to array element `num[2]` back in the calling program unit.

The code for GenerateData() shown in Example 7-12 demonstrates how it is used to initialize all of the elements of an array. It assigns five values using separate assignment statements:

EXAMPLE 7-12: GenerateData() METHOD

```
private: void GenerateData(int numArr[])
{
 numArr[0] = 2;
 numArr[1] = 7;
 numArr[2] = 3;
 numArr[3] = 8;
 numArr[4] = 6;
}
```

In effect, whenever an array such as num is passed into a method as an actual parameter there is only one array shared by both the method and the program unit that called it.

It is important to note that GenerateData() has no way of knowing the size of numArr. For this reason it is common to also pass in an integer variable indicating how many elements in numArr are accessible.

Next, refer back to Example 7-10, and consider the way the other programmer-defined method (ComputeMean()) was called with the entire array num as its actual parameter, shown here:

```
mean = ComputeMean(num);
```

The code for ComputeMean() provides another example of how an array may be used in a method. In this case, the values of each element are added together to compute sum and the mean (sum / 5) is returned. Example 7-13 provides the code for ComputeMean().

EXAMPLE 7-13: ComputeMean() METHOD

```
private: double ComputeMean(int item[])
{
 int sum;
 for (i=1; i<5; i++) sum += item[i];
 return (double) sum / 5;
}
```

Notice that the return type of `ComputeMean()` is `double`. To make sure that the calculation of the mean (`sum / 5`) avoided integer division, typecasting was used to change the numerator (`sum`) to a `double` before division took place.

Sequential Search

You have seen how to create arrays, initialize them, and process data stored in them. As mentioned earlier, the main advantage of arrays is their ability to store large amounts of data. With the ability to store large amounts of data comes the need to search through an array to find a specific data value.

Searching an array for a specific item (a **target value**) is a common task, for which loops are ideally suited. You can use loops to perform many different types of searches. This section discusses sequential searching. As the name implies, a **sequential search** looks at items in sequence as it searches for a target value. Usually, a sequential search starts with the first element in the array and searches each successive element until the end of the data structure is reached.

Sequential Search Example

Figure 7-6 shows the interface for a program that allows the user to enter a target value and have the program search an array to see if it is in there. The results of the search are displayed in the multiline text box `txtOut`.

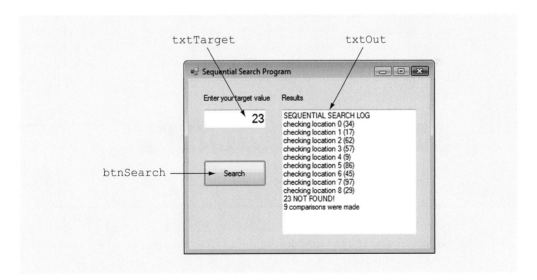

FIGURE 7-6 Sequential Search Program

The sequential search can be used to find a value in an array of any size. Assume that you have an array of integers called `arr` with nine elements. The data is stored in no particular order. The code for `btnSearch_Click()`, which declares the array and reads `target`, is shown in Example 7-14. Notice that once the array `arr` and `target` have been properly initialized, `btnSearch_Click()` calls a programmer-defined method `SeqSearch()` to perform the search operation. Both the array `arr` and `target` are passed into `SeqSearch()` as actual parameters.

EXAMPLE 7-14: CODE FOR `btnSearch_Click()`

```
private: System::Void btnSearch_Click(System::Object^ sender,
System::EventArgs^ e) {
// Declare variables
  int arr[] = { 34, 17, 62, 57, 9, 86, 45, 97, 29 };
  int target;              // the target value

  if (Int32::TryParse(txtTarget->Text, target))
     SeqSearch(arr, target);
  else
     MessageBox::Show("Invalid target. Please try again.");
}
```

Searching with a `for` Loop

A simple and efficient method of searching an array from top to bottom is to use a `for` loop. In Example 7-15, the loop control variable (`i`) is set to 0 initially and used to access array element `[0]`. As the loop control variable increases with each iteration, it is used to check each array element in succession. If the `target` value matches a value in the array then the `break` statement exits from the loop and control passes to the next statement. The code for this loop is shown in Example 7-15.

EXAMPLE 7-15: SEQUENTIAL SEARCH LOOP

```
for (int i=0; i<SIZE; i++)
    if (target == num[i]) break;
```

Notice that there are two ways out of this loop. On the one hand, the loop is over if the target is found and the `break` statement exits the loop. Figure 7-7 illustrates how the loop exits in this manner when searching for the `target` value 57.

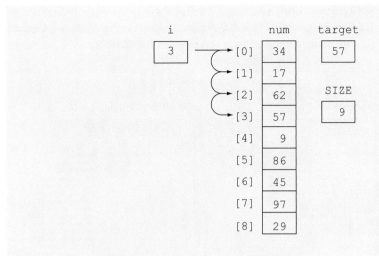

FIGURE 7-7 Sequential search termination when target is found

On the other hand, the loop is over if the conditional expression (i < SIZE) is no longer true. In this case, the loop control variable (i) is no longer less than SIZE, meaning that every element has been examined. Figure 7-8 illustrates how the loop is terminated when the target value (23) cannot be found. Notice that the loop control variable (i) is incremented to 9, which is equal to SIZE, causing the loop to terminate.

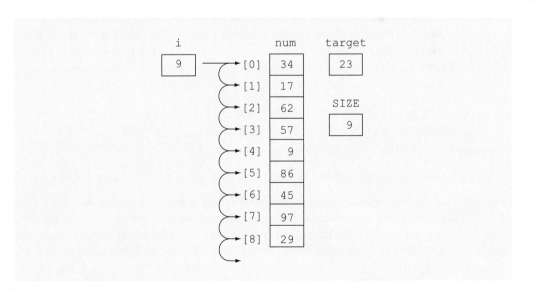

FIGURE 7-8 Sequential search termination when target is not found

Figure 7-9 shows how both successful and unsuccessful sequential searches look when conducted in this program. Figure 7-9a is the successful search (`target` value 57). Figure 7-9b is an unsuccessful search (`target` value 23).

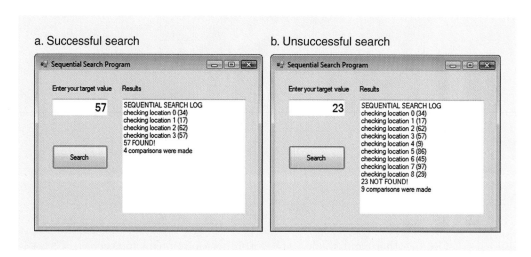

a. Successful search

b. Unsuccessful search

FIGURE 7-9 Successful (left) and unsuccessful (right) search results from a sequential search program

Counting Comparisons

You may have noticed that `txtOut` in Figure 7-6 and Figure 7-9 displays a count of the number of comparisons made. This is a count of the number of times that `target` was compared to a value in an array element. The number of comparisons required before the loop exits can be determined based on what the loop control variable is set to after the loop is over.

Recall that the loop may end for one of two reasons. If the loop exited because every element had been examined, then `i` would contain a value equal to `SIZE`. This is the situation depicted in Figure 7-8. In a nine-element array, `i` would be set to 9 when the loop ended. This is exactly the number of times `target` was compared to an array element, so the number of comparisons is equal to `i` (9 comparisons).

If the loop exited because of the `break` statement, then the number of comparisons is `i + 1`. For example, if `target` matched `num[i]` when `i` was set to 3 then four comparisons would have taken place. This is the situation depicted in Figure 7-7. So if the value in `target` is found the number of elements that `target` was compared to is `i + 1`.

These comparison assignments are coded in a short `if` statement that comes after the loop as shown in Example 7-16:

EXAMPLE 7-16: COMPARISON ASSIGNMENTS

```
if (i < SIZE)
    comparisons = i+1;
else
    comparisons = i;
```

The Search Comparison Log

The code for the `SeqSearch()` method is presented in Example 7-17. In addition to the sequential search loop and the comparison counter, this example also includes a `String` variable called `strLog`. The log keeps track of the comparisons and concatenates the results of each comparison made in the `for` loop, similar to the `strLog` variable you used in Chapter 5.

EXAMPLE 7-17: CODE FOR SeqSearch() METHOD

7

```
private: void SeqSearch(int num[], int target)
{
  int i; // loop control variable
  int comparisons;   // number of target comparisons made
  String^ strLog = "SEQUENTIAL SEARCH LOG " + "\r\n";
  txtOut->Text = ""; // Reset txtOut

  // Sequential search loop
  for (i=0; i<SIZE; i++)
  {
     strLog += "checking location " + i + " (" + num[i] +")\r\n";
     if (target == num[i]) break;
  }

  // Determine reason for loop exit
  if (i < SIZE)
  {
     strLog += target + " FOUND! ";
     comparisons = i+1;
  }
  else
  {
     strLog += target + " NOT FOUND!";
     comparisons = i;
  }

  // Display count of how many target comparisons were made
  strLog += "\r\n" + comparisons + " comparisons were made";
  txtOut->Text = strLog;
}
```

Parallel Arrays

Parallel arrays consist of two or more arrays of the same size containing data that is related. For example, you might have an array called ID that stores the ID numbers of 25 students in a class and another array called **points** that stores the total points of those 25 students. In parallel arrays, corresponding elements are related. **Corresponding elements** of parallel arrays are those with the same index value. For example, the values contained in ID[4] and points[4] belong to the same student.

Let's look at an example. Figure 7-10 shows three arrays, each of the same size. The array labeled **sku** contains the "stock keeping unit," or SKU number of various products. It is common for stores to use SKU numbers to keep track of their inventory. The **sku** array is a list of the SKU numbers of all items currently in stock. The retail cost of these items is stored in the **price** array, and the quantity on hand is contained in the **quant** array.

The arrays named **sku**, **price**, and **quant** are parallel arrays. Not only do they have the same number of elements, but the corresponding elements (the elements with the same indices) are related. For example, sku[2], price[2], and quant[2] pertain to the same product, as indicated in Figure 7-10. The product with a SKU number of 356007 has a retail price of 9.95, and there are currently four on hand.

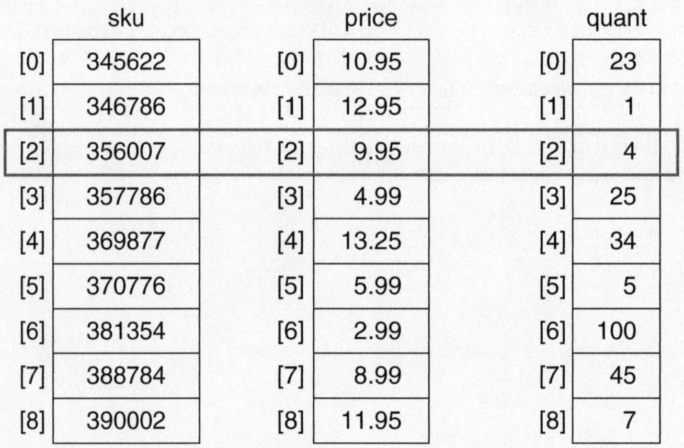

	sku		price		quant
[0]	345622	[0]	10.95	[0]	23
[1]	346786	[1]	12.95	[1]	1
[2]	356007	[2]	9.95	[2]	4
[3]	357786	[3]	4.99	[3]	25
[4]	369877	[4]	13.25	[4]	34
[5]	370776	[5]	5.99	[5]	5
[6]	381354	[6]	2.99	[6]	100
[7]	388784	[7]	8.99	[7]	45
[8]	390002	[8]	11.95	[8]	7

FIGURE 7-10 Parallel arrays for product inventory data (SKU, price, and quantity), with a corresponding element in each array highlighted in red

A common task of most inventory systems is looking up a price or quantity by entering the SKU number. The program shown in Figure 7-11 does exactly that. The user enters a SKU number into **txtSKU**, and the program looks up and displays the price and quantity of that item when **btnSearch** is clicked.

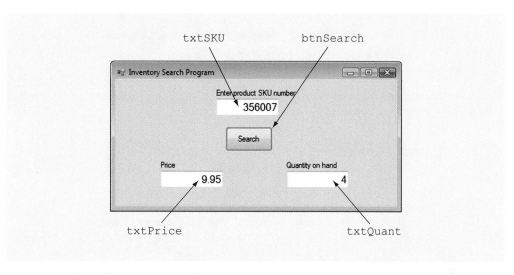

FIGURE 7-11 Inventory program interface

In this program, you can use a sequential search that is similar to the one described in the preceding section. Given an array and a target value, a **for** loop can compare the target (a SKU number) to each value stored in successive elements in the **sku** array. In the sequential search method shown in Example 7-18, the index value (**i**) of the array element that matches the **target** is returned to the calling program unit.

EXAMPLE 7-18: SeqSearch() METHOD RETURNING TARGET LOCATION

```
private: int SeqSearch(int arr[], int target)
{
 int i;
 for (i = 0; i < SIZE; i++)
    if (target == arr[i]) break;
 return i;
}
```

The **SeqSearch()** method is called from **btnSearch_Click()**. The actual arguments of **SeqSearch()** include both the **sku** array and a target (**targetSku**). The value returned from the search is assigned to the variable **index** in this manner:

```
index = SeqSearch(sku, targetSku);
```

The complete code for **btnSearch_Click()**, including the constant declaration and array declarations, is shown in Example 7-19.

EXAMPLE 7-19: CODE FOR btnSearch_Click()

```
// Declare constant (the array size)
static const int SIZE = 9;

private: System::Void btnSearch_Click(System::Object^ sender,
System::EventArgs^ e) {
 // Initialize arrays
 int sku[] = { 345622, 346786, 356007, 357786, 369877, 370776, 381354,
388784, 390002 };
 double price[] = { 10.95, 12.95, 9.95, 4.99, 13.25, 5.99, 2.99, 8.99,
11.95 };
 int quant[] = { 23, 1, 4, 25, 34, 5, 100, 45, 7 };
 int targetSku;   // the target value
 int index; // index location of the target match
 txtPrice->Text = ""; // reset txtPrice
 txtQuant->Text = ""; // reset txtQuant

 if (Int32::TryParse(txtSKU->Text, targetSku))
 { // txtSKU contains an integer
    index = SeqSearch(sku, targetSku);
    if (index < SIZE)
    { // The SKU has been found
       txtPrice->Text = price[index].ToString();
       txtQuant->Text = quant[index].ToString();
    }
    else
       MessageBox::Show("Product SKU not found. Please try again.");
 }
 else
    MessageBox::Show("Product SKU is invalid. Please try again.");
}
```

Notice that nested if...else statements are used to handle situations in which the SKU number can be located and those in which it cannot. The outer if...else statement differentiates between txtSKU entries that are integers and those that are not. The inner if...else statement differentiates between SKU numbers that can be found in the array and those which cannot.

Within the first alternative of the outer if...else statement the sequential search takes place. If the index value that is returned from SeqSearch() is less than SIZE, then the SKU number was found; otherwise, an error message is displayed. Figure 7-12 shows how the program responds when the SKU is invalid (Figure 7-12a) or not found (Figure 7-12b).

a. Invalid SKU

b. SKU not found

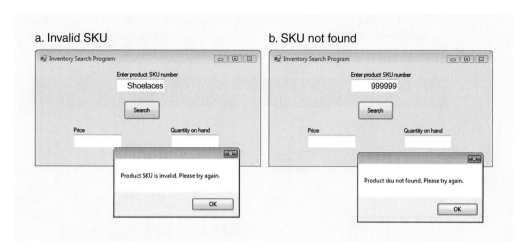

FIGURE 7-12 Program output for invalid SKUs and SKUs that are not found

Multidimensional Arrays

Data comes to us in many ways. One of the most common is as a table or spreadsheet. These are two-dimensional in nature, requiring a row and column designator to identify a specific data value. So far, we have only considered one-dimensional data structures. A one-dimensional array is one in which a single variable (the index value) is all that is required to locate a specific element. **Multidimensional arrays** may be thought of as arrays of arrays and require additional index values to locate elements in each dimension. As the number of array dimensions increase, so does the need for additional identifiers to locate elements. Two-dimensional data structures require two positional locators; three-dimensional arrays require three, and so on.

Conceptually, **two-dimensional arrays** are organized by rows and columns. **Rows** are the horizontal dimension and **columns** are the vertical dimension. Rows and columns are numbered starting at 0. Figure 7-13 illustrates the relationship of rows to columns.

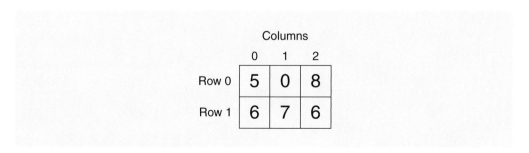

FIGURE 7-13 Row and column designators

To identify a specific element, such as the one storing the value 8 in Figure 7-13, you must specify both the row and column (row 0, column 2). Thus, two-dimensional arrays have two subscripts. The first is the row indicator and the second is the column. In the declaration of a two-dimensional array called `arr2d` (shown in Example 7-20), the array declaration tells us that the array consists of two rows and three columns:

EXAMPLE 7-20: TWO DIMENSIONAL ARRAY DECLARATION

```
const int numRows = 2;
const int numCols = 3;
int arr2d[numRows][numCols] = {{5,0,8},{6,7,6}};
```

In Example 7-20, data is assigned to the elements in **row-major order**. This means that the first group of values (5,0,8) are placed into the elements of the first row (row 0). Similarly, the second group (6,7,6) go into the second row. Data is assigned to consecutive elements in each row, in the order as shown in Figure 7-14.

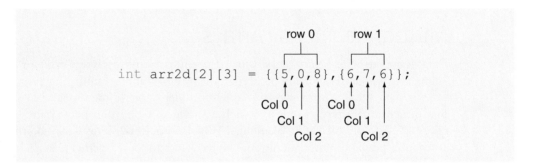

FIGURE 7-14 Two-dimensional array declaration

It should be noted that two-dimensionality is a concept underlying the data structure. Actual storage in memory is always done in a contiguous manner. The declaration above creates the assignment pattern in memory shown in Figure 7-15.

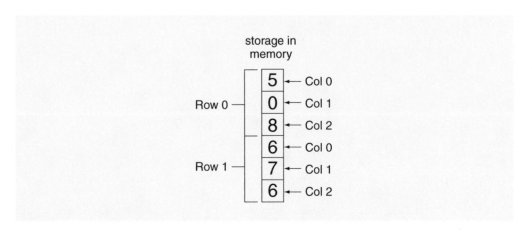

FIGURE 7-15 Storage of two-dimensional data in memory

Consider the interface shown in Figure 7–16. It displays the contents of a two-dimensional data structure.

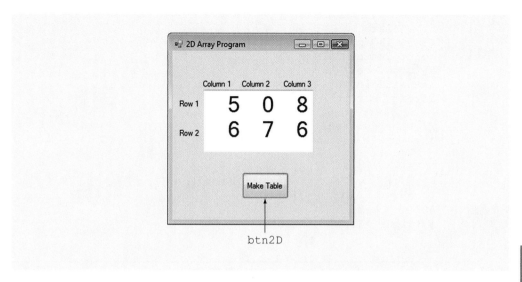

FIGURE 7-16 Displaying two-dimensional data

The data are displayed in the interface by concatenating the `String` representation of the integers in each element of the array. This requires traversing the array. **Array element traversal** is an ordered process in which a loop is used to access each element in an array once, in an orderly manner, such as by row. The loop control variables serve an important function in array element traversal because they indicate the elements that are to be accessed. Among the most common traversal methods is to access the elements in the same order they were originally stored; this is done by accessing the values stored in all columns in row 0, then all columns in row 1, and so on. A `for` loop is used to cycle through the rows. Nested within the `for` loop is another `for` loop that traverses the columns. The complete code for `btn2D_Click()` is shown in Example 7–21.

EXAMPLE 7-21: CODE FOR `btn2D_Click()`

```
private: System::Void btn2D_Click(System::Object^ sender,
System::EventArgs^ e) {
 // Declare variables
 const int numRows = 2;
 const int numCols = 3;
 int row, col;
 int arr2d[numRows][numCols] = {{5,0,8},{6,7,6}};
 String^ strOut = "";

 // Display results
 for (row = 0; row < numRows; row++)
 {
    for (col = 0; col < numCols; col++)
       strOut += " " + (arr2d[row][col]);
    strOut += "\r\n";
 }
 txtTable->Text = strOut;
}
```

The trickiest part of this code segment is following the nested loops. The outer loop control variable **row** is set to 0, then the inner loop runs through all the values of its loop control variable (**col**) before control is passed to the outer loop for its second iteration. In the second iteration, **row** is set to 1 and again the inner loop runs with **col** going from 0 to 2 as before. A trace table is a valuable tool to use at this point to determine whether you can follow the changes to the nested loop control variables. In the following tutorial, you use nested loops and learn to trace them.

Tutorial: Classroom Seating

Is there a relationship between where students sit in a classroom and their grades? You have been assigned a student teaching position at a local secondary school and strongly suspect that there is. Knowing that there is a pattern could help you to focus your attention during lectures and demonstrations. This program explores seating patterns that may be related to course performance by using an array of student scores.

Problem Analysis

To look for such patterns, you want to create a program that draws a seating chart of your classroom. If the user wants, it will also show where people sit and use color coding on the seats to indicate the student's current level of performance. The color-coding scheme is as follows:

- Red—For students who are below the class mean
- Yellow—For students who are at or above the mean but below 90 percent
- Green—For students in the top 10 percent

Design

As in the project you created in Chapter 6, this project involves the use of `System::Drawing` objects to create a visual representation of data. One difficulty with this project is that the interface shows rows and columns of seats, but the data (student scores) is one-dimensional. This will require a well thought-out design to make sure the results are correct.

INTERFACE SKETCH

The intended final result should resemble the example shown in Figure 7-17. In previous chapters you have drawn images in picture boxes and on `Form1` itself. To create this interface, you will use a container called a `panel` control to display the seating chart. All of the seats will be drawn as colored squares on the panel.

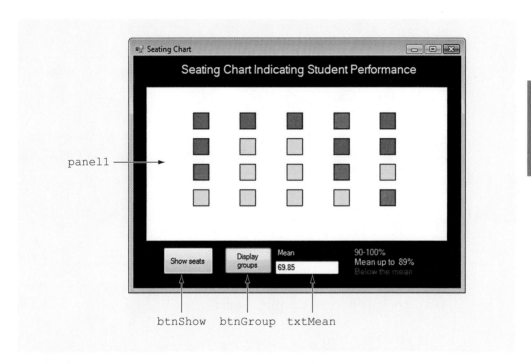

FIGURE 7-17 Color-coded classroom seating chart

The object table for the proposed program is shown in Table 7-1.

TABLE 7-1 Object Event Table for Seating Chart Program

Usage	Object	Event	Description
Initialization	Form1	Load()	Initialize Drawing objects
Processing	btnShow	Click()	Draws seating chart (empty seats)
	btnGroup	Click()	Draws color-coded seat groupings
Output	txtMean		Displays mean score
	panel1		Displays color-coded seats

DATA TABLE

Both constants and variables are required by this program. The number of rows and columns should be represented using class–level constants. There are four rows and five columns. The constants are listed in Table 7-2.

TABLE 7-2 Constants

Constant Name	Data Type	Value
NUMROWS	int	4
NUMCOLS	int	5

According to the problem description, the most important data item in this program is the array of student scores. This needs to be large enough to accommodate up to 20 students. The program has to calculate the sum as well as the mean. We will use local variables to indicate the row and column in the seating chart. These variables are listed in Table 7-3

TABLE 7-3 Data Table

Variable Name	Data Type	Usage
score	double[20]	Array of 20 student scores
row	int	Seat row
col	int	Seat column
sum	double	Sum of all scores
mean	double	Mean score

Variables required for drawing You need to use various `Graphics` objects to draw lines and fill in rectangular areas. These include the mandatory `Graphics` object (`g`) along with `Drawing` objects to draw lines (`blackPen`) and fill in areas (`redBrush`, `yellowBrush`, and `greenBrush`). These are listed in Table 7-4.

TABLE 7-4 Table of Required `Drawing` objects

Variable Name	Data Type	Usage
g	Graphics	Graphics object
blackPen	Pen	Drawing object (used for lines)
redBrush	Brush	Drawing object (used for students below mean)
yellowBrush	Brush	Drawing object (used for students from mean-89%)
greenBrush	Brush	Drawing object (used for students >= 90%)

Algorithm for `btnShow_Click()` First, consider what happens when the user clicks on `btnShow`. The job of this button is to draw the seat configuration, without color coding. The result of clicking `btnShow` is shown in Figure 7-18.

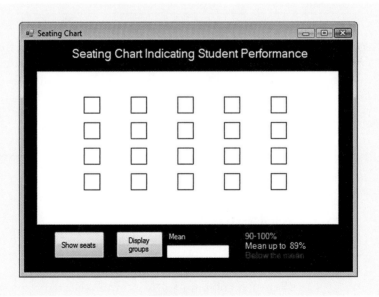

FIGURE 7-18 The seating chart produced by `btnShow`

This button needs to draw the outlines of 20 seats. The seats can be represented by squares (`Rectangle` objects with the same width and height). To begin, you should first refresh the panel to make sure you have a clear area to work with. Next, you begin the process of drawing each `Rectangle` in its appropriate position. You start with the first row (row 0) and go across each of the columns (0–4), drawing rectangles as you go. When the first row is finished, you then do the second row, going across each of is columns (0–4), drawing rectangles as before. This process continues until all of the rows have been finished.

Loops can be used to draw five rectangles in each row, each one positioned further to the right on the panel. The algorithm for these nested loops is shown in Algorithm 7-1. Remember that the logic of the algorithm is reflected in the numbering. Step 2 selects a row, then performs Step 2.1. Because Step 2.1 is a loop, it is repeated for each of the five columns. When all the columns have been processed, control goes back up to Step 2 for the next row and begins the process of executing Step 2.1 again. This means that Step 2 is repeated four times, and within each execution of Step 2, Step 2.1 is repeated five times. This process draws 20 separate rectangles, five at a time in each of four rows.

ALGORITHM 7-1: DRAWING THE SEATING CHART RECTANGLES

1. Refresh the panel.
2. For each row (0–3):

    2.1. For each column (0–4) in the selected row:

        2.1.1. Construct a rectangle.

        2.1.2. Draw the rectangle.

Algorithm for `btnGroup_Click()` The algorithm for `btnGroup` is the heart of this program, even though it is not very long. It must first calculate the mean (you call an instance method for this purpose) and then loop through all of the scores comparing them to the mean to determine the color. Then comes the tricky part—coloring the correct rectangle. The details of that task are addressed later, when we discuss writing the code for this algorithm. An algorithm for the `btnGroup` button is shown in Algorithm 7-2:

ALGORITHM 7-2: COLORING THE SEATS

1. Declare variables (including the array).
2. Calculate mean.
3. Display mean.
4. For each row (0–3):

    4.1. For each column (0–4) within the selected row:

        4.1.1. Determine which score to process.

        4.1.2. Determine the color of that seat based on the score.

        4.1.3. Construct the `Rectangle` object.

        4.1.4. Color the `Rectangle` object.

Take a moment to think about Step 4.1.1—determining which student score to process. You can use the row and column location of a seat to calculate which student is sitting in that seat as follows (the constant NUMCOLS contains the total number of columns in each row):

```
student = (row * NUMCOLS) + col;
```

The formula yields the index value (student) of a value in the score array (score[student]).

Also, notice that Step 4.1.2 has much more going on behind the scenes. This is where a decision structure is needed to determine which color is used for the seat rectangle, based on the score. This will be dealt with in the coding section for this algorithm.

TEST STRATEGY

You will test the algorithm for btnGroup using a much simpler example. Take a class with only six students sitting in two rows and three columns of seats.

The student test score data is: score[] = { 5,12,25,30,40,50};

The mean of these values can be calculated by hand and is $162/6 = 27.0$

We shall assume that the maximum possible score was 50. A score of 45 is 90 percent of 50.

The scores then match up with seats in the manner shown in Figure 7-19. Each of the scores is shown in the scores array on the left. The panel diagram on the right shows the location of each seat along with the score associated with that seat.

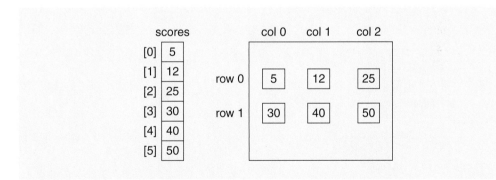

FIGURE 7-19 Correspondence between scores in the array and their Rectangle objects

This represents a typical data configuration. Some scores are above 90 percent, others are below the mean, and the rest are in between.

ALGORITHM VERIFICATION

The trace table (Table 7-5) walks through the steps of the algorithm for the btnGroup() method. Remember that the row count starts at 0 and goes to 1, and the column count starts at 0 and goes to 2. You should slowly read through the trace table to make sure you understand what each step of the algorithm is doing. You might want to make a sketch of Figure 7-19 and color-in the seat squares to show the resulting pattern.

TABLE 7-5 Trace of `btnGroup()` Using the Test Data Set

Algorithm	mean	row	col	student	color	score
Declare variables	0	0	0	0	-	{5,12,25,30,40,50}
2. Calculate mean	27.0					
4. For row = 0		0				
4.1 For col = 0			0			
4.1.1 Determine student (row * 3) + col				0		
4.1.2 Determine color					Red	score[0] = 5
4.1 For next col			1			
4.1.1 Determine student (row * 3) + col				1		
4.1.2 Determine color					Red	score[1] = 12
4.1 For next col			2			
4.1.1 Determine student (row * 3) + col				2		
4.1.2 Determine color					Red	score[2] = 25
4.1 For next col (inner loop done)			3			
4. For next row		1				
4.1 For next col			0			
4.1.1 Determine student (row * 3) + col				3		
4.1.2 Determine color					Yellow	score[3] = 30

TABLE 7-5 Trace of `btnGroup()` Using the Test Data Set (continued)

Algorithm	mean	row	col	student	color	score
4.1 For next col			1			
4.1.1 Determine student (row * 3) + col				4		
4.1.2 Determine color					Yellow	`score[4] = 40`
4.1 For next col			2			
4.1.1 Determine student (row * 3) + col				5		
4.1.2 Determine color					Green	`score[5] = 50`
4.1 For next col (inner loop done)			3			
4. For next row (outer loop done)		2				

If you were coloring a copy of the diagram from Figure 7-19, you should now be looking at a result that looks similar to Figure 7-20.

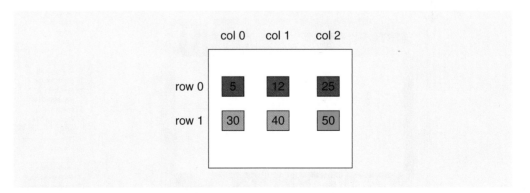

FIGURE 7-20 Result of algorithm test

Development

The design discussion has identified several key algorithms and walked through the one that matches up data values in a one-dimensional array with row and column locations (a two-dimensional graph). Next, we need to figure out exactly how to draw the **Rectangle** objects in the proper position on the panel. That task is explained in the coding section below.

CREATE THE INTERFACE

Begin with **Form1**. The interface for this program consists of **Form1** with an approximate size of 550 x 400. Make the following changes to its appearance. Refer to Figure 7-17 as necessary so that you can see approximately where to place the objects on the form.

- Change the **BackColor** property of **Form1** to black.

- Change its **Text** to "Seating Chart".

- Add the following five labels as shown earlier in Figure 7-17:

    - "Seating Chart Indicating Student Performance"—Use white for the **ForeColor** and choose a font size of at least 16 points.

    - "Mean"—Use white for the **ForeColor**.

    - "90–100%"—Use green for the **ForeColor**.

    - "Mean up to 89%"—Use yellow for the **ForeColor**.

    - "Below the mean"—Use red for the **ForeColor**.

- Add the two buttons (**btnShow** and **btnGroup**) and the text box (**txtMean**).

- Add a **panel** control, with an approximate size of 485 x 240. Set its **BackColor** to white. The **panel** control is located in the Toolbox, shown in Figure 7-21.

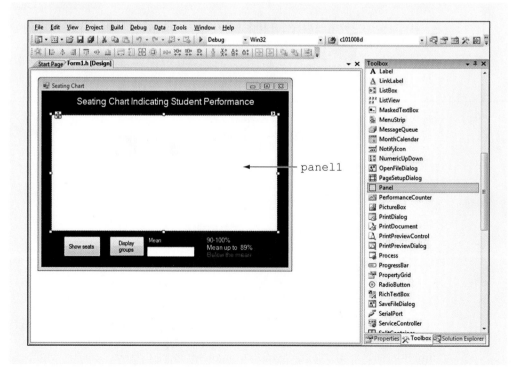

FIGURE 7-21   panel control highlighted in the Containers group in the Toolbox

CODING

The primary coding tasks in this project are to declare and initialize the instance `Drawing` objects, and then implement the event handlers for each button. There is one programmer-defined method that must also be created (to calculate the mean), which is similar to the `ComputeMean()` method shown in Example 7-13.

Constants, Instance Objects, and the `Form1_Load()` Event The various `System::Drawing` objects identified in the first portion of the design stage are declared as instance variables outside of the event handlers, before `Form1_Load()` as shown in Example 7-22.

EXAMPLE 7-22: DECLARING CONSTANTS AND INSTANCE OBJECTS

```
static const int NUMROWS = 4;
static const int NUMCOLS = 5;
Graphics^ g;
Brush^ redBrush;
Brush^ yellowBrush;
Brush^ greenBrush;
Pen^ blackPen;
```

The `Form1_Load()` event is used to construct the `Drawing` objects as shown in Example 7-23. Notice that the `Graphics` object (g) is attached to `panel1`.

EXAMPLE 7-23: CODING THE `Form1_Load()`

```
private: System::Void Form1_Load(System::Object^ sender,
System::EventArgs^ e)
{
 g = panel1->CreateGraphics();
 redBrush = gcnew SolidBrush(Color::Red);
 yellowBrush = gcnew SolidBrush(Color::Yellow);
 greenBrush = gcnew SolidBrush(Color::Green);
 blackPen = gcnew Pen(Color::Black);
}
```

Coding `btnShow_Click()` The main task for this button is to draw 20 rectangles in four rows and five columns in `panel1`. Nested loops control the movement from column to column within each row, and from row to row. However, it is up to you to determine exactly where the rectangles are drawn. You may recall that rectangles are drawn from the upper-left corner. Their constructors need to know the x- and y-coordinates for that point as well as the width and height. In this case, assume that all rectangles used to represent seats have a width and height of 25 pixels.

Consider the horizontal spacing that the rectangles will need. The panel is only 485 pixels wide. A little experimentation shows that 75 pixels is about the right horizontal distance between each one, as shown in Figure 7-22.

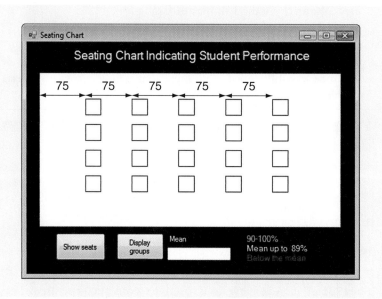

FIGURE 7-22 Horizontal spacing of `Rectangle` objects (75 pixels)

If we start with the x-coordinate set to 75 and then add the quantity `col * 75` to the x-coordinate each time through the inner loop, the result should give us new x-coordinates 75 pixels from one another horizontally.

A similar strategy can be used to calculate where the y-coordinates of the upper-left corner should be. In that case, starting with a y-coordinate of 40 and then adding to it the quantity `row * 40` each time should have the effect of positioning the y-coordinate at a different location for each row, as shown in Figure 7-23.

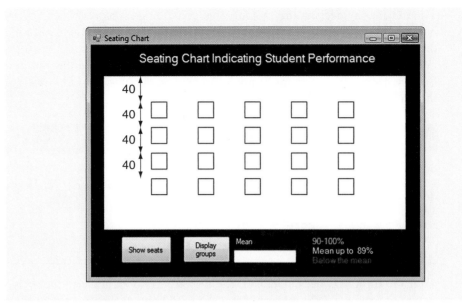

FIGURE 7-23 Vertical spacing of `Rectangle` objects (40 pixels)

The nested loops in Example 7-24 traverse the rows and columns. A `Rectangle` object is constructed based on the row and column designators and the formulas described above. The code for `btnShow` is given in Example 7-24.

EXAMPLE 7-24: CODE FOR `btnShow_Click()`

```
private: System::Void btnShow_Click(System::Object^ sender,
System::EventArgs^ e)
{
 panel1->Refresh();
 for (int row = 0; row < NUMROWS; row++)
 {
    for (int col = 0; col < NUMCOLS; col++)
    {
       Rectangle seat = Rectangle(75 + col * 75,40 + row * 40,25,25);
       g->DrawRectangle(blackPen, seat);
    }
 }
}
```

Coding `btnGroups_Click()` The button that displays the groups of students by coloring in their seat rectangles has many similarities to the algorithm for `btnShow()`. Once it calculates the mean (by calling an instance method), it executes nested loops that check every seat in the class, determines the score of the person sitting there, creates a rectangle in the proper location, and colors it.

The initial array declaration is a long one, containing 20 scores. The only other variables needed are the **mean** and **student**. The **student** variable is used as the index value on the **score** array to match a seat with a student score. Notice that the score array is sent into **CalcMean()**. Passing an array into an instance method like this was discussed earlier (see the discussion preceding Example 7-13). The declarations and initial assignments are shown in Example 7-25.

EXAMPLE 7-25: PASSING ARRAY score INTO CalcMean()

```
double score[20] =
{45,65,11,98,66,56,77,78,56,56,87,71,78,90,78,76,75,72,79,83};
double mean;
int student;
mean = CalcMean(score);
txtMean->Text = mean.ToString();
```

After the mean has been obtained, the nested **for** loops traverse the array elements, as shown in Example 7-26. Notice that within the body of the inner loop, the first task uses **row** and **col** to calculate the array index value of a score (**student**), just as you did with a shorter version of this in the testing and algorithm verification stages of the design section (Table 7-5). Then a **Rectangle** object is constructed based on the row and column location, just as you did in **btnShow()** (Example 7-24).

The multiple-alternative **if** statement examines the score for the student in question and colors the rectangle based on the category the score falls into. When it has finished, it also draws a black outline around it with the **blackPen**.

EXAMPLE 7-26: SELECTION SEAT COLOR

```
for (int row = 0; row < NUMROWS; row++)
{
  for (int col = 0; col < NUMCOLS; col++)
  {
      student = (row*NUMCOLS) + (col);
      Rectangle seat = Rectangle(75 + col * 75,40 + (row * 40),25,25);
      if (score[student] >= 80)
         g->FillRectangle(greenBrush, seat);
      else if (score[student] >= mean)
         g->FillRectangle(yellowBrush, seat);
      else
         g->FillRectangle(redBrush, seat);
      g->DrawRectangle(blackPen, seat);
  }
}
```

Together, Examples 7-25 and 7-26 make up the contents of the `btnGroup_Click()` event handler.

Coding the `CalcMean()` Method The code for this method is similar to that seen in Example 7-13 for `ComputeMean()`. In this case, however, the number of loop iterations is controlled by the local variable `students`, which stores the total number of students in the classroom (calculated by multiplying the number of rows and columns of seats). The code for this method is shown in Example 7-27.

EXAMPLE 7-27: CODE FOR `CalcMean()` METHOD

```
private: double CalcMean(double score[])
{
  double sum = 0; // Sum of all scores
  int students = NUMROWS * NUMCOLS; // The number of students
  for (int i=0; i< students; i++) sum += score[i];
  return sum / students;
}
```

7

Testing

Now run the program. The output should look like that shown in Figure 7-17. Check to make sure that your mean value matches that shown (69.85) and that the seats are correctly colored.

ON YOUR OWN

There are a number of ways that you can enhance the capabilities of this program by analyzing the data stored in the `score` array.

TASK 1: DISPLAY THE HIGHEST SCORE

Modify the tutorial program so that in addition to the text box that displays the mean, you have added a text box that displays the highest score. Write an instance method called `FindLarge()` to do this, and display the result in a text box called `txtLarge`.

TASK 2: DISPLAY A COUNT OF SCORES ABOVE THE MEAN

Further modify the tutorial so that after the mean has been calculated, an instance method named `AboveAverage()` is called that counts the number of scores greater than the mean and displays the result in a text box on the interface.

QUICK REVIEW

1. Data structures organize data in memory.

2. An array is a contiguous block of memory cells.

3. Arrays are composed of individual data containers called elements.

4. Every element has a unique identifying number called an array element index, or subscript.

5. Arrays may either be declared statically or dynamically.

6. Static allocation creates arrays of fixed size that cannot be altered.

7. Dynamic allocation allocates memory for an array at runtime.

8. Array element subscripts start with 0.

9. If there are n elements in an array, the largest subscript is $n-1$.

10. Arrays can be initialized with a value list.

11. For loops work well with arrays because the loop control variable can be used as an array element index value.

12. You can pass an array into a method by putting the array name in the argument list.

13. When passing an array into a method as an actual argument, only the name of the array is used (e.g., num).

14. When passing one element of an array into a method as an actual parameter, the array name along with a specific subscript is required (e.g., num[3]).

15. The term *sequential search* refers to the process of looking for a target value in an array by examining elements in succession.

16. Sequential searches terminate when they find what they are looking for or run out of places to look.

17. A multidimensional array is an array of arrays.

18. Every dimension in an array requires its own index identifier.

19. Two-dimensional arrays are visualized as being laid out in rows and columns.

20. Data displayed in a row runs horizontal.

21. Data displayed in a column runs vertically.

22. Data is assigned to the elements in a two-dimensional array in row-major order. This means that the first data values are assigned to the first row and when that row is full, the second row assignments are made, and so on until all rows are full.

23. Two-dimensionality is a concept underlying a data structure. Actual storage in memory is always done in a contiguous manner, by row.

24. You should use nested loops to traverse the elements of a two-dimensional array.

25. In two-dimensional array traversal, the outer loop selects the row and the inner loop the column within that row.

TERMS TO KNOW

array
array element
array element traversal
column
corresponding elements
data structure
dynamic allocation
index value
multidimensional array
one-dimensional array
parallel array
row
row-major order
sequential search
static allocation
subscript
target value
two-dimensional array

EXERCISES

Questions 1–10 refer to the following array declaration:

```
int num[10] = { 3, 6, 4, 5, 2, 8, 7, 9, 1, 5};
```

1. The number of elements in the array is _____.

   a. 10

   b. 9

   c. 20

   d. n

   e. Cannot be determined

2. The largest array element index value (subscript) is _____.

   a. 10

   b. 9

   c. 5

   d. n

   e. Cannot be determined

3. What value is contained in element num[3]?

   a. 3

   b. 4

   c. 5

   d. 6

   e. Cannot be determined

4. The value 5 appears twice in the array. If 5 was the target value, how would the **for** loop version of the sequential search discussed in this chapter handle this?

   a. It would exit after finding the first match.

   b. It would exit after finding the last match.

   c. It would not exit until both matches had been found.

   d. It would exit when it had run out of places to look.

   e. This would cause an infinite loop.

5. If an integer variable called **student** is set to 7, what is the value of num[student]?

   a. 7

   b. 6

   c. 9

   d. 0

   e. Cannot be determined

6. What would be the proper way to pass num into the method `Calculate()` as an actual parameter?

   a. `Calculate(num[10]);`

   b. `num = Calculate();`

   c. `Calculate(int num[10]);`

   d. `Calculate(num);`

   e. `Calculate(int num[]);`

7. What would be the correct signature line for the method `Calculate()` if its actual parameter was num?

   a.   `private: void Calculate(int num[10])`

   b.   `private: void Calculate(int num[])`

   c.   `private: void Calculate(int num)`

   d.   `private: void Calculate(int & num)`

   e.   None of the above

8. What would be the proper way to pass the value of a single element of num into the method `Calculate()` as an actual parameter?

   a.   `Calculate(num[10]);`

   b.   `Calculate(num[5]);`

   c.   `Calculate(int num[5]);`

   d.   `Calculate(num);`

   e.   `Calculate( [5]);`

9. What is the value of `num[10]`?

   a.   5

   b.   10

   c.   0

   d.   3

   e.   Element `num[10]` is not a legal reference. It is beyond the bounds of the array.

10. How many dimensions does num have?

   a.   10

   b.   2

   c.   1

   d.   0

   e.   Cannot be determined.

For questions 11 through 15, determine if you need to create an array to perform the specified task. Answer "Yes" if an array is necessary and "No" if an array is not necessary. Justify your answer.

11. Read 10 numbers and calculate the mean.

12. Read 10 numbers and display them in a text box.

13. Read 10 numbers and display those above the mean.

14. Read 10 numbers and display them in reverse order.

15. Read 10 numbers and count the number of odd values.

For questions 16–19 refer to Example 7-15 in the text.

16. Rewrite the code shown in Example 7-15 so that it uses a `while` loop instead of a `for` loop.

17. Rewrite the code shown in Example 7-15 so that it starts the search from the last element of the array and goes to the first.

18. Rewrite the code shown in Example 7-15 so that it counts the number of times the target value matched a value stored in the array.

19. Rewrite the code shown in Example 7-15 so that it counts the number of comparisons made until the loop exited.

20. Construct a trace table (Table 7-6) for the nested loop portion of Example 7-21. You may assume that `array2d` has been initialized to `{{5,0,8},{6,7,6}}` and that the constant `numRows` is 2 and the constant `numCols` is 3. The first few lines are provided, you must complete the table beneath them.

TABLE 7-6 Trace Table (unfinished)

Instructions	row	col	strOut
Initial values	0	0	" "
`for (row = 0; row < numRows; row++)`	0		
`for (col = 0; col < numCols; col++)`		0	
`strOut += " " + (arr2d[row][col]);`			" 5"
`for (col = 0; col < numCols; col++)`		1	

PROGRAMMING EXERCISES

1. Direct Search

You are in a bowling league with 20 bowlers. Each bowler wears a unique number on his or her team jersey. The numbers run from 0–19. Write a program that reads a bowler's jersey number and uses it to look up his or her average score in an array of averages called

score. Assume that the average contained in **score[4]** is the average for bowler 4. This is a simple and fast method of finding data in an array without having to perform a sequential search.

2. Random Data

Write a program that creates an array of 100 integers. The program should then generate a random number between 1 and 100 that indicates the number of data values that will be stored in the array. Use a loop to generate the correct amount of random numbers between 1 and 100 as data for the array and then calculate the mean.

3. Parallel Arrays

Create a program that contains the parallel arrays **id** and **score**, as shown here:

```
double score[20] =
{45,65,11,98,66,56,77,78,56,56,87,71,78,90,78,76,75,72,79,83};
int id[20] =
{100,143,132,144,122,127,111,113,120,131,109,101,112,121,115,
105,125,102,116,108};
```

Your program should allow the user to look up the score by entering an ID number into a text box called **txtID** and clicking on a search button called **btnSearch**. If the text entered in **txtID** is not an integer, then display a **MessageBox** with the message "Invalid ID". If the text entered into **txtID** is an integer but cannot be found in the list, display the message "ID not found". Otherwise, if the ID is valid, display the score in a text box named **txtScore**.

4. Row and Column Sums

Modify the two-dimensional array program discussed in this chapter so that it displays the sum of each row in separate text boxes at the end of the row as shown in Figure 7-24.

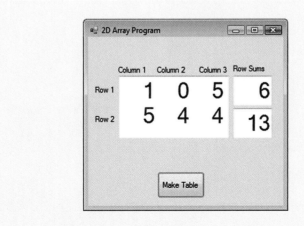

FIGURE 7-24 Two-dimensional array with row sums

To do this you should declare an array of row sums

```
int rowSum[] = {0, 0};
```

and update the appropriate sum within nested loops that traverse the array.

Next, make the modifications necessary to display the column sums as well. Displays the sum of each column in separate textboxes beneath the column as shown in Figure 7-25.

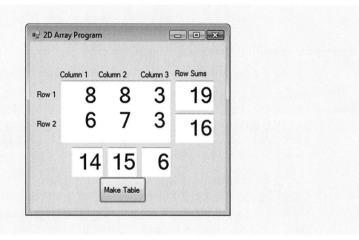

FIGURE 7-25 Two-dimensional array with row and column sums

5. Two-Dimensional Seating and Scores

Modify the final version of your tutorial project so that it uses a two-dimensional array of student scores instead of a one-dimensional array. Your two-dimensional array of scores should have the same number of rows and columns as the arrangement of seats in the classroom. Your program should produce the same results as were obtained from your tutorial program.

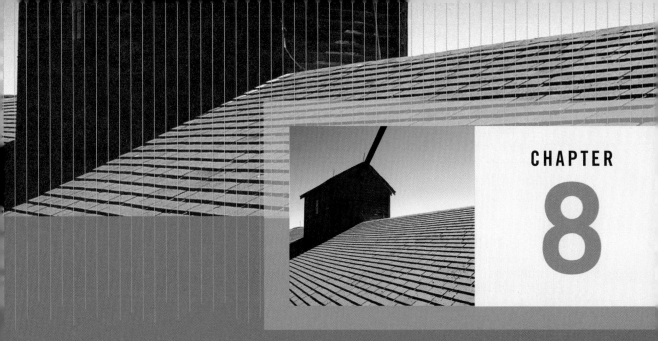

BINARY SEARCH

IN THIS CHAPTER, YOU WILL:

- Learn about the binary search algorithm
- Compare the binary search to other common forms of searching
- Analyze the complexity (big-O) of the binary search
- Create and use arrays of strings
- Compare strings
- Explore uses for the `ListView` control

In Chapter 7, you learned how to use a sequential search to search for a target item in an array. The sequential search is made up of a single loop that accesses successive elements in the array until it either finds what it is looking for or runs out of places to look. Compared to other search techniques, the sequential search is easy to understand and implement. Sequential searches are also the only option for lists in which the data values are stored in an array in no particular order. When searching through data that is ordered (such as an alphabetical list), other search tools are much faster. In this chapter we will study one of these: the binary search.

Searching a Sorted List

Suppose you wanted to look up the phone number of someone whose last name began with the letter *R*. Would you use a sequential search? Remember that a sequential search starts with the first element in the list and searches each element in succession. This would be a poor strategy to use when looking up a name in a telephone directory, because it would mean looking at the first page (the letter A), then the second, then the third, and so on.

It would be far wiser to take advantage of the fact that the names in the telephone directory are arranged alphabetically. Most of us, when looking for a last name beginning with *R*, would simply open the phone book about half way and see where that put us. If the last names on that page began with the letter *N*, you would ignore the first part of the directory (letters A – N) and continue the search in the later portion of the phone book by opening to the middle of the portion with letters O-Z. If, at that point, you found that you had opened to the last names that start with *T*, you would ignore everything from T–Z and open to the middle of the portion of the phone book from O to T. Eventually, this strategy would allow you to find the names beginning with *R*; from there, you could easily complete your search.

The entire list of items to search through is called the **search domain**. Each iteration of the search removes half of the items in the search domain. Thus, when we first pick up the phone book, the search domain consists of the entire phone book. Then we divide the search domain in half and choose which one of the two halves must contain the name we are searching for and ignore the rest. In this way, we have reduced the size of the search domain for the next iteration by half.

You can use a similar technique to search through a list stored in an array. The process of dividing a search domain in half, and then in half again, and so on, until the target value is found, is called a **binary search**. The term *binary* refers to the fact that, in this type of search, you repeatedly divide the search domain into two parts.

The key to the binary search is that the items in the search domain must be ordered. A list, or array, of names that has been arranged in order from lowest to highest

(*A–Z*) is said to be in **ascending order**. The process of putting the list in order is called **sorting**. A phone book is a list of names that have been sorted in ascending order. Imagine a phone book in which all of the names on each page were put there at random. The binary search strategy would no longer work because you could never assume you knew which of two halves of the list a name might be in. A binary search can only find items in a list that has already been sorted. Binary searches will not work on unordered lists. For unsorted arrays, a sequential search is the only alternative.

Binary Search Algorithm

The binary search uses a loop to examine increasingly smaller portions of the array until the target is found or there is nowhere else to look. The key to the binary search algorithm lies in keeping track of three positions:

- Low—The lowest point in the search domain
- Mid—The middle of the search domain
- High—The highest point in the search domain

To understand these concepts, it is helpful to return to the phone book example. The name you want to look up is your target. When you start, you know the first name in the phone book (low) begins with *A*. You know the last name in the phone book (high) begins with *Z*. You then divide the book in half by picking a middle position (mid). The mid position is the one that allows a binary search to zero in on the target value by dividing the search domain in half.

For example, suppose that you have written a binary search to search an array that is sorted in ascending order. You are looking for one particular value (the target). As the program begins it divides the list in half and determines that the mid item is smaller than the target value. That tells the program that it can ignore all the values that are smaller than the mid value. Essentially, it excludes the values below the mid value from future searches. (Recall that the data in the array is arranged in ascending order, so all the data that comes before the mid value is smaller than the mid value.)

The half of the array that the program does not exclude, values above mid, is the search domain for the next iteration. To search it, the program resets low to the lowest position in the new search domain, high to the highest position, and mid to the midpoint between them. The loop then executes again, using this newly defined search domain. In this second iteration, the program evaluates the mid item in the remaining half of the array, and once again decides which half of the remaining data to exclude.

The process continues until the program finds the target value. This is a very fast way to search an array because it discards half the choices in each pass.

8

The algorithm for a binary search of an array with *n* elements is:

ALGORITHM 8-1: BINARY SEARCH

1. Declare variables (`low` = 0, `high` = *n*-1).
2. While `low` <= `high`:

    2.1. Calculate mid (`low` + `high`)`/2`

    2.2. If the target is less than the middle element, set `high` to `mid-1`

    2.3. Else if the target is greater than the middle element set `low` to `mid + 1`

    2.4. Else (they match) set `low` to `high + 1`

Figure 8-1 illustrates the initial stage of a binary search. Note that the integer array (`arr`) in Figure 8-1 is sorted in ascending order. The integer variable n stores the total number of items in the entire list. The integer variable `target` stores the value we are searching for.

You can see from Step 2 in the above algorithm that a `while` loop is the appropriate data structure. The pre-test condition evaluates the relationship between the variables `low` and `high`. The search continues while `low` is less than or equal to `high`.

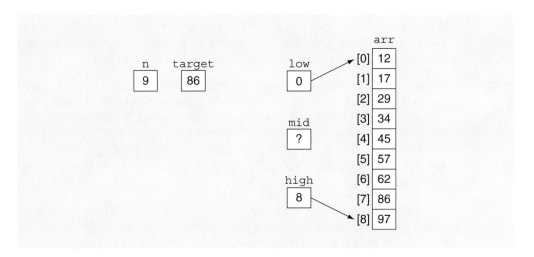

FIGURE 8-1   Initial setting of variables for a binary search for the target value 86

As long as `target` has not been found and portions of the array have still not been searched, the midpoint of the search domain is determined and its value (`mid`) compared to `target`. If they match, the search stops. If `target` does not match `mid`, then the program resets `low` and `high` to define a new search domain, recalculates `mid`, and tries again. This continues until either a match is found or there are no more places to look.

Figures 8-2 through 8-4 illustrate a successful search. In Figure 8-2, the variable `mid` is originally set to 4, calculated as `((low + high) / 2)`.

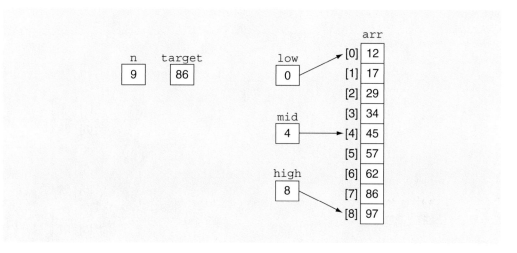

FIGURE 8-2 Initial calculation of `mid`

When the program determines that element [4] does not match `target`, `low` and `high` are reset using the strategy outlined in the algorithm. If `arr[mid]` is less than `target`, then `target` can only be found in array elements with higher subscripts than `mid`. If `arr[mid]` is greater than `target`, then `target` can only be found in array elements with lower subscripts than `mid`. In the first case, `low` is reset to `mid+1`, as shown in Figure 8-3. In the second case, `high` is reset to `mid-1`.

Once `low` and `high` are reset, a new value for `mid` can be calculated. In Figure 8-3 `low` has been set to 5 and `high` remains 8. The new value for `mid` is `(5 + 8)/2 = 6`.

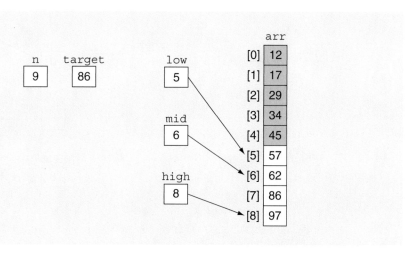

FIGURE 8-3 Resetting low to `mid+1` and recalculation of `mid` for the next pass

8

The process continues as `low` is again set to `mid+1`, as shown in Figure 8-4. This time the target is found in `arr[mid]`. When the target is located the program sets `low` to `high+1` to exit the loop.

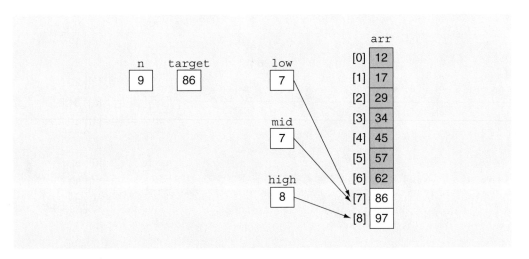

FIGURE 8-4 `target` has been located at element `arr[mid]`

An unsuccessful search is shown in Figures 8-5 through 8-9. Although the process is the same, the search ultimately sets `low` to a value larger than `high` indicating that it has looked in every possible location thus, the loop stops executing. The target value for this search is 38, which is not in the array.

The initial calculation of `mid` is 4 (as shown in Figure 8-5). The program compares `target` to the data stored in `arr[mid]`.

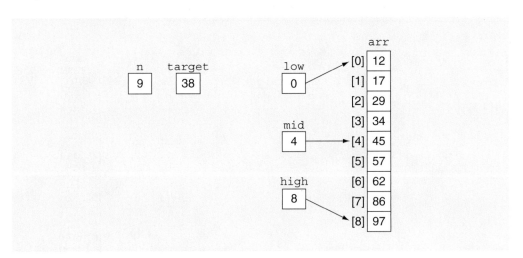

FIGURE 8-5 Initial settings and calculation of `mid` for the binary search, with `target` = 38

Because `target` (38) is less than `arr[4]` (45), there is no need to search the higher elements of the array beyond `mid`. The variable `high` is therefore recalculated to a value that is one less than `mid`. This effectively divides the search domain in half, throwing out half the list. Remaining searches are confined to the elements `arr[0]` through `arr[3]`. A new value for `mid` is calculated (1) and used to access element `arr[1]` and compare it to the `target`, as shown in Figure 8-6.

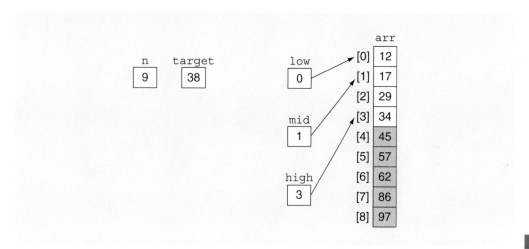

FIGURE 8-6 Recalculation of `mid` for second pass

Because `arr[mid]` does not match `target` and because `target` (38) is greater than `arr[mid]` (that is, 17), further searches can exclude all the elements below `arr[mid]`. Therefore, it resets `low` to `mid+1`. See Figure 8-7. After calculations, `mid` becomes 2. At this point, only two elements remain to be searched, and element `arr[2]` becomes the midpoint of that domain.

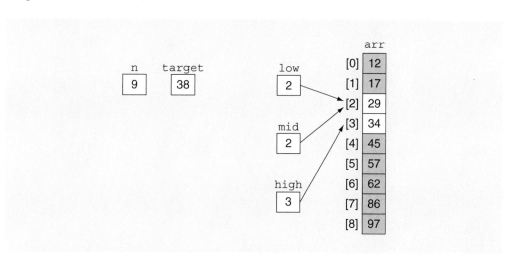

FIGURE 8-7 Resetting `low` and recalculating `mid` in the next pass

When the program discovers that `arr[2]` is less than `target`, it resets `low` (to `mid + 1`) to establish the lower bound for the next search. At this point, `low, mid,` and `high` are set to 3, as shown in Figure 8-8.

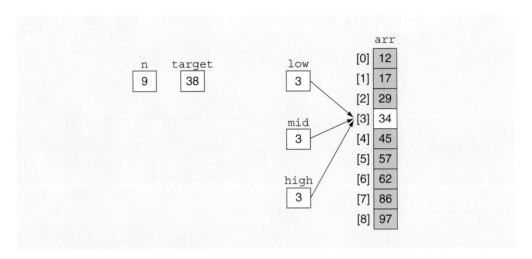

FIGURE 8-8 Final comparison of `arr[mid]` to `target`

When comparison reveals that `arr[3]` is also not equal to `target`, and that `target` is larger than `arr[3]`, the program proceeds as before, adjusting `low` so that it is assigned the value `mid + 1`, as shown in Figure 8-9. At that point, `low` becomes larger than `high`.

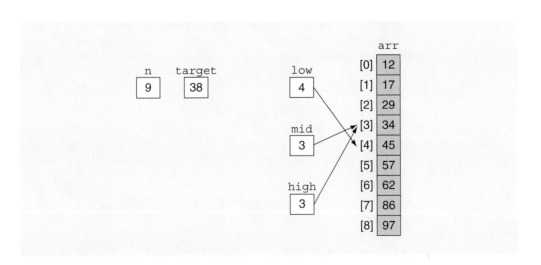

FIGURE 8-9 When low is greater than high the search is over

Refer back to Step 2 of the original algorithm. In Step 2, the `while` loop continues only as long as `low <= high`. The program has now reached a situation in which `low` is greater than `high`. At this point the loop terminates. The search is over, even though no match was found. There are no more places to search for `target`.

The flow diagram in Figure 8-10 illustrates the decision structure of the binary search process we have just examined.

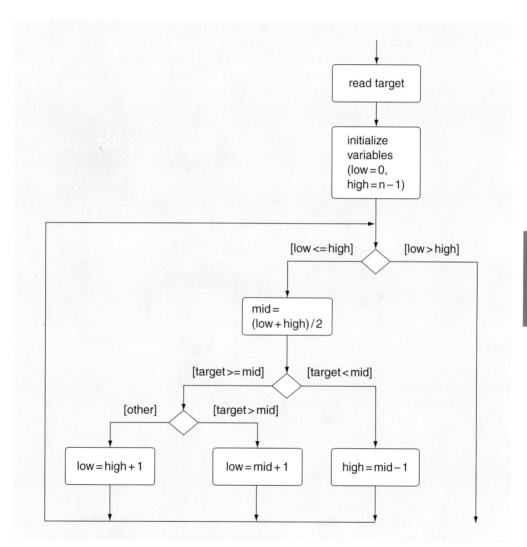

FIGURE 8-10 Flow diagram for the binary search

Notice that the loop terminates when `low` becomes greater than `high`. You have seen in the sequence of figures (Figures 8-5 through 8-9) how `low` can become greater than high in an unsuccessful search. In a successful search low is set to high + 1 when a match has been found. Setting low to high + 1 is a way to intentionally terminate the loop at that point.

Binary Search Example

Let us examine a program that uses a similar binary search. The interface is shown in Figure 8-11. The user enters a target value into txtTarget. When btnSearch is clicked the event handler begins a binary search. The data stored in the search array is shown in txtList. If the search is successful the MessageBox displays "FOUND!". If the search is unsuccessful the MessageBox displays "NOT FOUND!".

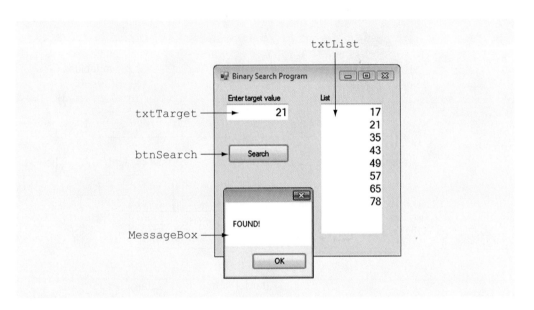

FIGURE 8-11 Binary search program interface

The code for btnSearch_Click() is shown in Example 8-1. It creates and initializes an array (list) of integers in ascending order. The String variable (strList) is used to display the data in the array list. The contents of list are concatenated onto strList using a for loop. After the target value has been read successfully, the program calls the Boolean instance method BinSearch(). The role of BinSearch() is to perform a binary search on the array looking for target. The array list, its size (n), and target are passed into BinSearch(). When BinSearch() finishes, it returns a Boolean value that is used to determine whether to display "FOUND!" or "NOT FOUND!".

EXAMPLE 8-1: btnSearch_Click()

```
private: System::Void btnSearch_Click(System::Object^
sender, System::EventArgs^ e) {
  // Declare variables
  bool found;
  int n = 8;
  int list[] = {17, 21, 35, 43, 49, 57, 65, 78};
  String^ strList = "";

  // Assign list values to strList
  for (int i = 0; i < n; i++) strList += list[i] + "\r\n";

  // Display list
  txtList->Text = strList;

  // Read target
  int target;

  // Process target
  if (Int32::TryParse(txtTarget->Text, target))
  {
   found = BinSearch(list, n, target);
   if (found)
     MessageBox::Show("FOUND! ");
   else
     MessageBox::Show("NOT FOUND!");
  }
  else
   MessageBox::Show("Invalid target - Please enter an integer");
}
```

8

The code within the BinSearch() method is based on our original algorithm (Algorithm 8-1) and is shown in Example 8-2.

EXAMPLE 8-2: BinSearch() METHOD

```
private: bool BinSearch(int list[], int n, int target)
{
  // Declare low, mid and high
  int low = 0, mid, high = n-1;

  // Binary search loop
  while (low <= high)
  {
   // Compute mid
   mid = (low + high) / 2;
```

```
  // Check target against list[mid]
  if (target < list[mid])
    // If target is below list[mid] reset high
    high = mid - 1;
  else if (target > list[mid])
    // If target is above list[mid] reset low
    low = mid + 1;
  else
    // If target is found set low to exit the loop
    low = high + 1;
  }

  // Return true if target found, false if not found
  if (target == list[mid])
   return true;
  else
   return false;
}
```

This version of the binary search program returns the Boolean value `true` if `target` matches a value stored in `list`, and it returns the Boolean value `false` if it does not.

Search Analysis

You have now seen three methods for finding a target in an array:

- Direct lookup (Chapter 7, Programming Exercise 1)
- Sequential search (Chapter 7)
- Binary search

Which of these search techniques is the best depends on the circumstances of your program. Let us review what you know about all three.

Direct Lookup

The direct lookup strategy is the simplest and fastest search technique, but it is only applicable in very specific circumstances. To use it, an array must be set up so that the user enters an integer that can be used as an array element index value.

In case you did not do Programming Exercise 1 in Chapter 7, here is an example: Players on a volleyball team all have different numbers on their uniforms. If the numbers range from 0 to 7, and data for each player is stored in an array in such a way that the data for the player wearing number 0 is stored in element [0], the data for the player wearing number 1 is stored in element [1], and so on, then searching is straightforward.

Examine the program shown in Figure 8-12. It looks up how many assists a volleyball player averages per game. The user enters the uniform number of a volleyball player in `txtUniform` and clicks `btnSearch`. The number of assists per game is displayed in `txtAssists`.

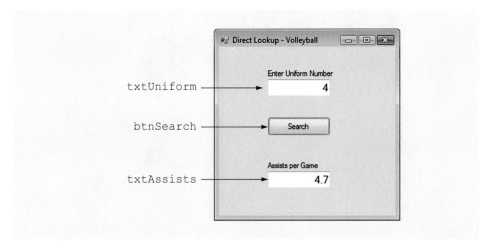

FIGURE 8-12 Direct search example—volleyball assists

The code for `btnSearch` is shown in Example 8-3. Notice that the uniform number is read into the integer variable `num`. Then the assists are located using `num` as the index value on the array (`assists[num]`). The line

```
txtAssists->Text = assists[num].ToString();
```

accesses the element we wish to find in the `assists` array and displays it.

EXAMPLE 8-3: DIRECT LOOKUP

```
private: System::Void btnSearch_Click(System::Object^
sender, System::EventArgs^ e) {
  int num; // A player's uniform number
  double assists[] = {12.3, 14.6, 2.6, 8.6, 4.7, 6.9, 10.1, 5.5};

  if (Int32::TryParse(txtUniform->Text, num))
    txtAssists->Text = assists[num].ToString();
  else
    MessageBox::Show("Invalid uniform number");
}
```

Knowing the uniform number allows this search to directly access the data. This program takes advantage of the fact that uniform numbers share the same range of values as array element indices (0–7), as shown in Figure 8-13. In this example, the user has entered a uniform number (num) of 4, which allows the direct lookup program to go immediately to element (assists[4]) and retrieve the value stored there (4.7).

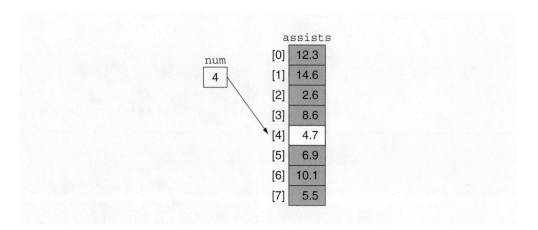

FIGURE 8-13 Direct search using the uniform number (num) to locate an array element

As long as num is one of the array element index values, the data is located immediately. The result is always obtained in one operation, as shown in Figure 8-14 where the number of operations it takes to complete the search is shown on the y-axis and the size of the list on the x-axis.

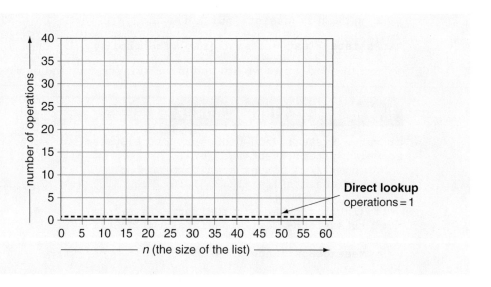

FIGURE 8-14 Plot of the number of operations required vs. size of list for direct lookup

Direct lookup is very fast; it only takes one operation to find the value you are looking for in the list. The important thing to remember is that for direct lookup, it does not even matter how many items are in the list. If there were 100 volleyball players with numbers 0–99 it still only takes one lookup operation to access any player's data.

Direct lookup always takes only one operation to find a value that is in the list. It would be nice if all searching was this fast. However, the unique situation of searching by index value is usually not possible.

Sequential Search

The sequential search, covered in Chapter 7, offers two possible outcomes: the target value is either found in the list or it is not. If you assume that the target value is in the list, what are the best-, average-, and worst-case scenarios for the sequential search? The best-case scenario is that a match is found immediately. In this case, it takes only one comparison to find it, as indicated by Figure 8-15a. The worst-case scenario is that the item is at the bottom of the list, in which case it will take n operations to find it (where n is the number of items in the list), as shown in Figure 8-15c. On average, it will take $n/2$ operations to find the target, as shown in Figure 8-15b.

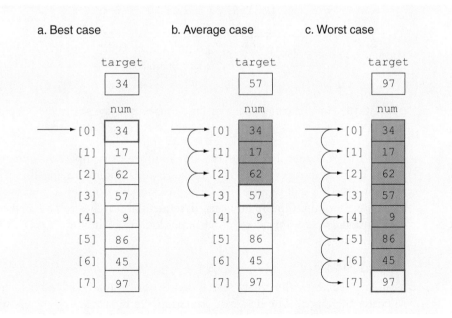

FIGURE 8-15 Best-, average-, and worst-case scenarios for a sequential search

You cannot count on being lucky enough to have all of your sequential searches find what they are looking for on the first comparison. On the contrary, any program written using a sequential search on an unordered list should assume the worst. In fact, if the target value you are searching for is not in the list, the worst-case scenario will always occur before your search realizes that the target value is not there.

Figure 8-16 shows the difference between using direct lookup (where the worst-case scenario is always 1 operation) to the sequential search (where the worst-case scenario for an array of size *n* is always *n* comparison operations).

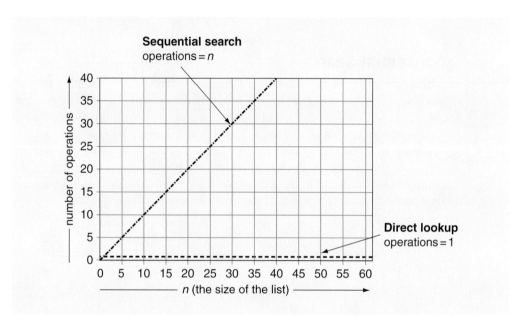

FIGURE 8-16 Plot comparing the worst-case scenarios of the sequential search and direct lookup techniques

Notice that for large lists the maximum number of comparison operations a sequential search could require is as large as the number of items in the list. This means that a sequential search will require more computational resources to find an item in an array, than direct lookup. On the other hand, sequential searches can be used on any list, which is a considerable advantage over the direct lookup technique.

Binary Search

You have seen how the binary search divides the array in half and half and half again until it locates the target. The best-case scenario for a binary search occurs when the target is found on the first pass. This takes only one comparison.

For searches in which the target is in the list, a worst-case scenario would be like that shown in Figure 8-17. In Figure 8-17, `target` had to be compared to `arr[mid]` four times before it was found. The `mid` position was repeatedly recalculated for each divided list. The original array of eight elements was divided three times (into halves of 4 elements, then 2 elements, then 1 element) before the value was found.

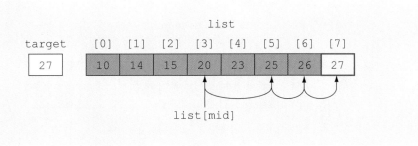

FIGURE 8-17 A worst-case scenario for a binary search, when the target is in the list

Because the binary search divides the list in half each time through the loop, the number of times it can divide an array is determined by the size of the list. An array of 8 items can be divided in half only 3 times (4 items, 2 items, 1 item). An array of 128 elements can be divided in half 7 times. The number of times the list can be divided is the $\log_2$ of n (where n is the size of the list). For a binary search, the worst-case scenario approximates $\log_2 n$. Table 8-1 shows the maximum number of times an array can be divided in half for lists of varying sizes.

TABLE 8-1 Maximum list divisions for various sizes of lists

Size of List (n)	Maximum Number of Divisions ($\log_2 n$)
2	1
4	2
8	3
16	4
32	5
64	6
128	7

You can use the data from Table 8-1 to plot the worst-case scenario for the binary search alongside the other search techniques discussed. The comparative plot is shown in Figure 8-18.

8

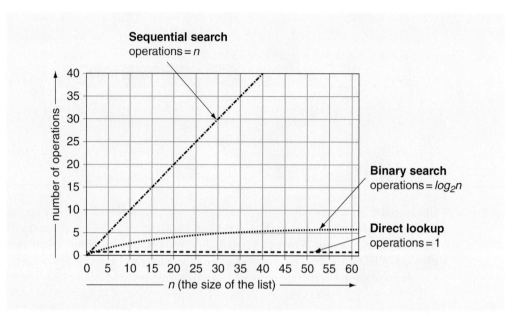

FIGURE 8-18 Plot comparing the worst-case scenarios of direct lookup, sequential search, and binary search

A binary search uses fewer process resources than a sequential search, but it is not as economical as direct lookup.

Determining the Best Approach to Searching

The complexity of a search technique is measured in terms of the amount of system resources it uses to complete a task. Each of the search techniques discussed has its own level of complexity, which can be expressed as an equation. A mathematical equation that specifies the relationship between the number of operations required to complete the search ($f(n)$) and the size of the array of data that must be processed (n) is called a **complexity function**.

For the search methods studied so far, the equations are:

- Direct search—The maximum number of operations is always 1, $f(n) = 1$
- Sequential search—The maximum number of operations is n, $f(n) = n$
- Binary search—The maximum number of operations is $\log_2 n$, $f(n) = \log_2 n$

For example, everything being equal, if an array has 64 elements in it, the worst-case scenario for the number of operations required to find a value in that array is:

- Direct search: $f(64) = 1$, 1 operation
- Sequential search: ($f(64) = 64$), 64 operations
- Binary search: ($f(64) = \log_2 64 = 6$), 6 operations

Computer scientists commonly refer to these complexity functions using a special form of reference called **big-O**. In **big-O notation** the letter O is used to indicate the "order of complexity" of an algorithm and is intended to be an estimate, not the exact number of operations for any particular algorithm. Direct lookup is **O(1)**, meaning that it takes "on the order of 1 operation" to complete. Sequential search is **O(n)**, meaning that it takes "on the order of n operations" to complete. Binary search is **O($\log_2 n$)** meaning that it takes "on the order of $\log_2 n$ operations" to complete. Table 8-2 lists the complexity functions for the search algorithms discussed so far. The form of search you choose to use in any given situation depends on the ordering of the data (the "List Requirements" column of Table 8-2) and the complexity function (big-O) of the algorithm you have selected.

TABLE 8-2 Complexity functions and big-O notation for direct, sequential, and binary searches

Search Technique	Complexity Function	Big-O	List Requirements
Direct lookup	$f(n) = 1$	O(1)	Target must be an array index value
Sequential search	$f(n) = n$	O(n)	None
Binary search	$f(n) = \log_2 n$	O($\log_2 n$)	Array must be sorted

Searching for Strings

The array examples used so far in this book have all centered on arrays of primitive types. However, you often need to search for data stored in arrays of objects such as strings. The tutorial later in this chapter will focus on searching arrays of video titles that are stored as strings. Before you tackle the tutorial, therefore, you should become familiar with the concept of `String` arrays and `String` searching.

The `array` Class

One of the nice features of object-oriented programming languages is that they often provide tools that allow you to quickly create complex data structures by using preestablished definitions. There is a system-defined **array class** that can be used to manage data and objects of any type, such as strings. The general syntax for a declaration that uses an **array** class (referred to by the keyword **array**) is:

```
access_mode: array< data_type >^ array_name;
```

The data type specification can be any primitive data type or a handle to an object derived from other classes. In Example 8-4, the partial declaration refers to an array of strings using the handle notation (**String^**) to denote the data type.

EXAMPLE 8-4: array CLASS (PARTIAL DECLARATION)

```
private: array<String^>
```

Remember, frequently when you refer to a system-defined reference class, you use a handle (^) designator. The handle is a pointer to an object, like a string. An **array** is also an object requiring a handle. The complete declaration of an array of strings, therefore, has two handle references as shown in Example 8-5. In Example 8-5 **nameArr** is the name of the **array** of strings.

EXAMPLE 8-5: ARRAY OF STRINGS (FULL DECLARATION)

```
private: array<String^>^ nameArr;
```

As with the individual **String** variables, you can allocate the memory and assign values using **gcnew**. Example 8-6 shows how an array of 20 strings would be constructed.

EXAMPLE 8-6: ARRAY CONSTRUCTION

```
nameArr = gcnew array<String^>(20);
```

The declaration in Example 8-6 constructs the array, as shown in Figure 8-19. Note that the array elements are empty. Although each element can contain the handle for a **String** none are assigned yet.

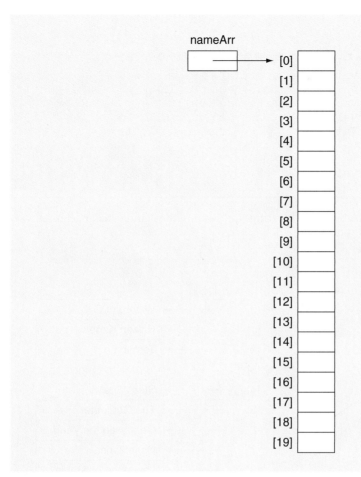

FIGURE 8-19 Construction of `nameArr` as a handle to an `array` of 20 unassigned handles to `strings`

The statements in Example 8-7 construct various strings of video names and assign them to the elements of the array. They are in no particular order. The integers (0–19) refer to the array element the `String` is assigned to. The **SetValue()** method belongs to objects of the `array` class and does the work of assigning a string to the designated element.

EXAMPLE 8-7: USING `array` METHOD `SetValue()`

```
nameArr->SetValue("Wizard of Oz",0);
nameArr->SetValue("Citizen Kane",1);
nameArr->SetValue("Terminator II",2);
nameArr->SetValue("Lord of the Rings",3);
nameArr->SetValue("Star Wars",4);
nameArr->SetValue("The Godfather",5);
nameArr->SetValue("Gone with the Wind",6);
nameArr->SetValue("Casablanca",7);
```

```
nameArr->SetValue("Lawrence of Arabia",8);
nameArr->SetValue("Jaws",9);
nameArr->SetValue("Shrek",10);
nameArr->SetValue("Jurassic Park",11);
nameArr->SetValue("Vertigo",12);
nameArr->SetValue("Schindler's List",13);
nameArr->SetValue("The Graduate",14);
nameArr->SetValue("King Kong",15);
nameArr->SetValue("It's a Wonderful Life",16);
nameArr->SetValue("Finding Nemo",17);
nameArr->SetValue("E.T.",18);
nameArr->SetValue("Psycho",19);
```

Each statement constructs a string and assigns the handle to an element in `nameArr` as shown in Figure 8-20.

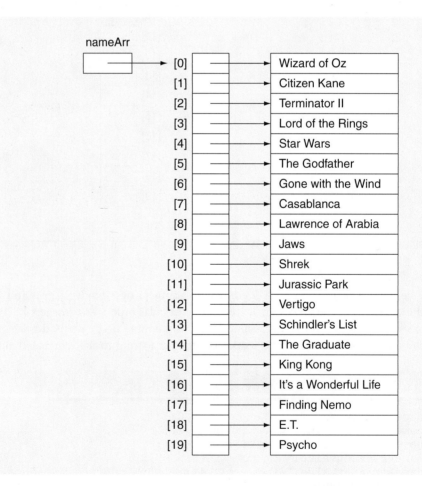

FIGURE 8-20 Construction of the strings assigned to each element of `nameArr`

Once data are stored in `nameArr`, the methods of the `array` class are available to help manage the data. For example, it is common to arrange names or titles (like video names) in ascending order. The **Array::Sort()** method is available within the `Array` namespace and can be called in a variety of manners depending on how you want the sorting to take place. For example,

```
Array::Sort(nameArr);
```

is used to indicate that you want the entire contents of the array sorted in the default manner (which is ascending order).

String Operations

You will be using several `String` operations in this chapter to compare strings. Our previous discussion of the binary search compared an integer target to values in an array of integers. In the tutorial, you will need to be able to compare strings effectively. Unfortunately, comparing strings is not as straightforward as comparing integers. To compare two integers, you simply use the equal-to operator (==), as can be seen in the following `if` statement:

```
if (num1 == num2) MessageBox::Show("The numbers are the same");
```

Rather than using the equal-to operator (==), comparing strings is done through a method called `Compare()` that is built into the `String` class.

Examine the code segment shown in Example 8-8. It uses the `String::Compare()` method to compare two `Strings` (`strTarget` and `nameArr[i]`).

EXAMPLE 8-8: String::Compare() METHOD

```
if (String::Compare(strTarget,nameArr[i])==0)
   found = true;
else
   found = false;
```

The **String::Compare()** method returns one of three values:

- 1, if the first `String` (`strTarget`) is greater than the second (`nameArr[i]`)
- 0, if the two `Strings` are identical
- -1, if the second `String` (`nameArr[i]`) is greater than the first (`strTarget`)

The second new `String` feature introduced in this tutorial is the `String` method `ToUpper()`. When a program uses input from a text box as a target `String` and searches for a match in an array of `Strings`, the problem of case needs to be considered. For example, the user enters the video name *jaws* (all lowercase). Your program should be

8

smart enough to realize that this is a match for the string *Jaws* (beginning with an uppercase letter) but the `String::Compare()` method does not consider them identical. It compares the contents of strings letter by letter using ASCII character codes. If the code is not exactly the same, the strings are not considered to be the same either. To get around this problem, it is common to read the characters entered by the user and convert them all to uppercase using the method **`String::ToUpper()`**, as in Example 8-9.

EXAMPLE 8-9: USE OF `ToUpper()`

```
strTarget = txtTarget->Text->ToUpper();
```

The chain of pointer membership operators (`->`) is easily interpreted if you remember that `->` means that the right operand belongs to the object on the left. The `ToUpper()` method belongs to the `Text` property. The `Text` property belongs to `txtTarget`. The command in Example 8-9 sets `strTarget` to the contents of the `Text` property of `txtTarget` after its contents have been converted to uppercase.

With `strTarget` now converted to uppercase, the comparison operation can take place by comparing `strTarget` to the uppercase version of a video name in the `nameArr` array. Example 8-10 shows how this is accomplished.

EXAMPLE 8-10: USE OF `String::Compare()`

```
if (String::Compare(strTarget,nameArr[i]->ToUpper())==0)
{
  found = true;
}
```

As you can imagine, there are numerous other `String` methods available. A list of common `String` methods is presented in Appendix B.

Tutorial: Video Store Inventory

This project demonstrates the difference between sequential and binary searches by asking you to implement both of them in the same program. The `array` class is used to construct an `array` object containing strings. In addition, a new control, the `ListView` control, is introduced to allow an array of `String` data to be displayed.

Problem Analysis

You have been hired by a local video store to write a program to keep track of rentals and inventory. This is a large task and will take you most of the summer. However, to prepare for it you first want to write a small program that allows the user to search for a film by name. If successful, you may later incorporate this smaller program into your final product. For now, you simply want to demonstrate to yourself that you can do it.

Your program should be able to do the following things:

- Display a list of films on hand.
- Allow the user to enter a name to be searched for.
- Conduct the search using either sequential or binary methods.
- Display the results of the search so that you can see and count the number of comparisons.

When the program runs, it should display a sorted list of film names, allow the user to search for a name, and record the results of the search as it progresses. The results of a sequential search should look like those shown in Figure 8-21.

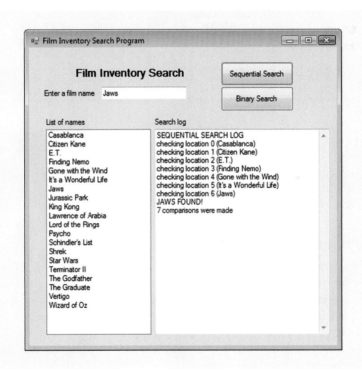

FIGURE 8-21 Sequential search results

The results of a binary search should look like those shown in Figure 8-22.

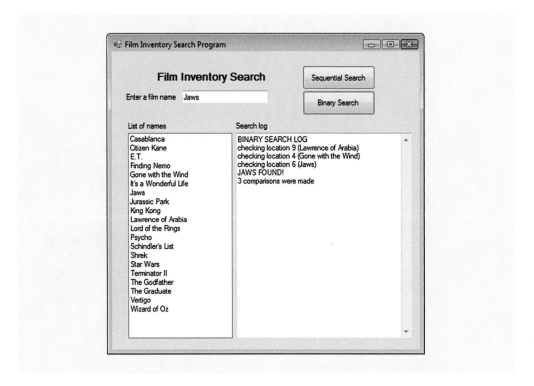

FIGURE 8-22 Binary search results

Design

This program requires you to implement both a sequential and binary search of an array of film names stored as strings. A commonly used object for storing items in a list and displaying them is the **ListView control**. The process of assigning names to a list is referred to as **populating a list**. Your program must populate the ListView control during the Form1_Load() event. A search log displays the result of each and every comparison. A search log is an excellent way to compare the efficiency of the sequential and binary search approaches.

INTERFACE SKETCH

The final interface should look like the example shown in Figure 8-23.

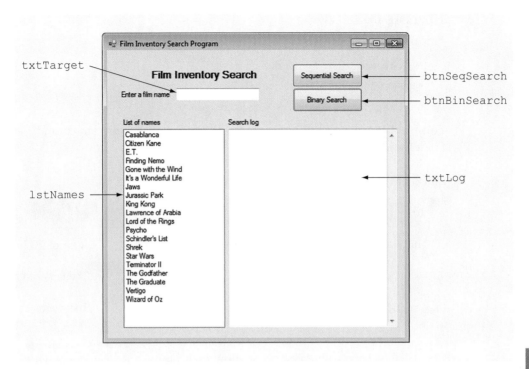

FIGURE 8-23 Film Inventory Search Program

The various objects required by the interface are listed in Table 8-3.

TABLE 8-3 Object event table for Film Inventory Search Program

Usage	Object	Event	Description
Initialization	Form1	Load()	Initialize Drawing objects
Input	txtTarget		Display the film name to be searched for
Processing	btnSeqSearch	Click()	Draws seating chart (empty seats)
	btnBinSearch	Click()	Draws color-coded seat groupings
Output	lstNames		Displays the film names
	txtLog		Results of the search (search log)

8

DATA TABLE

This program centers around three major tasks:

- Creating an array of film names
- Searching for a target name
- Compiling a log as the search progresses

You need instance variables for the array of film names, the target, and the search log. These variables are listed in Table 8-4

TABLE 8-4 Data table—class instance variables

Variable Name	Data Type	Usage
nameArr	String[20]	Array of 20 film names
strTarget	String	The target film name
strLog	String	The search results

You also need a set of variables that allow each button to execute its own type of search. Each button needs its own unique set of local variables, as listed in Table 8-5.

TABLE 8-5 Data table—sequential search

Variable Name	Data Type	Usage
i	int	Loop control variable
found	bool	Indicates whether target has been found

The local variables required for the binary search, in keeping with the algorithm for it discussed earlier, are given in Table 8-6.

TABLE 8-6 Data table—binary search

Variable Name	Data Type	Usage
low	int	Index of lowest element
mid	int	Index of middle element
high	int	Index of highest element
compareResult	int	String comparison result
comparisons	int	Number of comparisons

ALGORITHM FOR btnSeqSearch_Click()

The sequential search button executes a familiar operation. The algorithm for the sequential search is presented here:

ALGORITHM 8-2: SEQUENTIAL SEARCH

1. Declare variables.
2. Read the target film name.
3. Initialize the search log text String "SEQUENTIAL SEARCH".
4. While the target has not been found and there are still places to look:
   - 4.1. Add the next comparison line to the log.
   - 4.2. If the target film name matches a name in the nameArr:
       - 4.2.1. Set found to true.
       - 4.2.2. Exit the loop.
5. Finish the search log:
   - 5.1. If a match was found add "FOUND" and strTarget to the search log.
   - 5.2. Else, add "NOT FOUND" and strTarget to the search log.
6. Display search log in txtLog.

The main job of the program, then, is to search the list until either a matching film name is found or there are no more places to look for one. The program must also concatenate the comparison results to the search log. The search log is initialized before the search loop executes, by creating a string that contains only the title for the search (Step 3). Once the loop begins, the program also concatenates the current comparison (Step 4.1). When the loop is over, the program concatenates the final result onto the String and displays the result in txtLog->Text.

8

ALGORITHM FOR `btnBinSearch_Click()`

The algorithm for `btnBinSearch` (Algorithm 8-3) is similar to Algorithm 8-1 for the binary search, except that it also includes steps for building the search log `String`. The algorithm for `btnBinSearch` also requires a separate variable to count the number of comparisons.

ALGORITHM 8-3: BINARY SEARCH

1. Declare variables (`low` = 0, `high` = n-1, comparisons = 0).
2. Read the target.
3. Initialize the search log text `String` to "BINARY SEARCH".
4. While `low` <= `high`:

    4.1. Increment comparisons.

    4.2. Calculate mid as (`low` + `high`)/2.

    4.3. Add current comparison information to the search log.

    4.4. Compare `strTarget` to `nameArr[mid]`.

    4.5. If `strTarget` is less than `nameArr[mid]` set `high` to `mid-1`.

    4.6. Else if `strTarget` is greater than `nameArr[mid]` set `low` to `mid + 1`.

    4.7. Else (they match) set `low` to `high + 1`.

5. Finish the search log:

    5.1. If a match was found add "FOUND" and `strTarget` to the search log.

    5.2. else, add "NOT FOUND" and `strTarget` to the search log.

6. Display search log in `txtLog`.

This program described in this algorithm searches the list in binary fashion until either a matching film name is found or there are no more places to look for one. The program creates and initializes a search log before the search loop executes by creating the title for the log and storing it as a string (Step 3). Within the search loop, the program concatenates each comparison result (Step 4.3). When the loop is over, the program concatenates the final result onto the search log and displays it in `txtLog->Text`.

Development

The development portion of this project implements a control you have not used before—the `ListView` control, which is used to display lists of items. The `ListView` control's **Items** property is similar to the one used in earlier projects to provide choices for a `ComboBox` control. Although you can assign items through the Properties window, doing so in your C++ code is convenient and allows more programming flexibility. Every `ListView` control has a built-in `Items` collection and each `Items` collection has a method called **Add()** that allows a `ListView Item` to be initialized to a `String`. The

`ListView` control in this project will have its `Items` collection (or list) populated by the names stored in `nameArr`, which must be initialized and sorted first.

CREATE THE INTERFACE

To begin, create a form with dimensions of approximately 500 x 500. Place labels, text boxes, and buttons onto the form as shown in Figure 8-24. The long white rectangle on the left side is the `ListView` control. Make sure you do not accidentally select the `ListBox` control (a common mistake). It is also important to make sure you change the `View` property of the `ListView` control to `List`. The long, white region on the right is a text box with the `Multiline` property set to `true` and a vertical scrollbar.

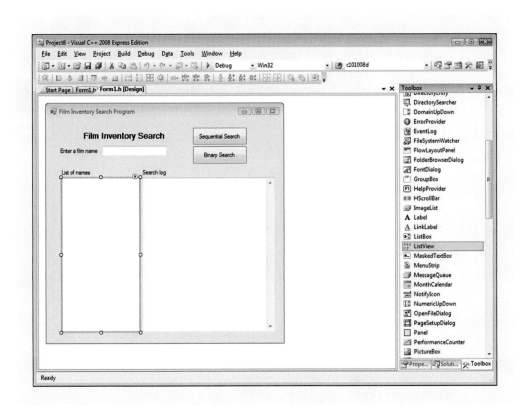

FIGURE 8-24 Interface with `ListView` control selected in the Tool Box

With the elements of the interface now in place, the first order of business is to create the `String` variables and an array of strings to contain film names. Then we must display the array of names in `lstNames`. Finally, we must write code for the sequential and binary search buttons.

CODING

Table 8-4 identified the required instance variables. Notice the syntax of the `array` class declaration. Remember that this declaration only creates space large enough to store a handle, nothing more. The actual data structure (an array of strings) is built in the Form1_Load event.

Instance variables All three of the instance variables identified in Table 8-4 are handles, pointers to reference class objects that have yet to be created. The declarations for these variables looks like this:

```
private: array<String^>^ nameArr;
private: String^ strTarget;
private: String^ strLog;
```

Coding Form1_Load() The array of film names is constructed in the Form1_Load event handler. **Array** objects have a set of built-in methods including one that assigns a string to an indexed location (SetValue). The central data structure (nameArr) is constructed first as an array of 20 String handles. No strings have been assigned to the elements of nameArr yet. The construction of strings and their assignment happens in a series of calls to the SetValue method belonging to nameArr. The first parameter of SetValue is the string to be assigned, and the second parameter is the array element to which it should be assigned. Example 8-11 shows that portion of the Form1_Load() event handler code responsible for initializing nameArr.

EXAMPLE 8-11: Form1_Load()

```
private: System::Void Form1_Load(System::Object^
sender, System::EventArgs^ e) {
  // Construct an array of 20 String handles
  nameArr = gcnew array<String^>(20);
  // Construct Strings and assign them to each array element
  nameArr->SetValue("Wizard of Oz",0);
  nameArr->SetValue("Citizen Kane",1);
  nameArr->SetValue("Terminator II",2);
  nameArr->SetValue("Lord of the Rings",3);
  nameArr->SetValue("Star Wars",4);
  nameArr->SetValue("The Godfather",5);
  nameArr->SetValue("Gone with the Wind",6);
  nameArr->SetValue("Casablanca",7);
  nameArr->SetValue("Lawrence of Arabia",8);
  nameArr->SetValue("Jaws",9);
  nameArr->SetValue("Shrek",10);
  nameArr->SetValue("Jurassic Park",11);
  nameArr->SetValue("Vertigo",12);
  nameArr->SetValue("Schindler's List",13);
  nameArr->SetValue("The Graduate",14);
  nameArr->SetValue("King Kong",15);
  nameArr->SetValue("It's a Wonderful Life",16);
  nameArr->SetValue("Finding Nemo",17);
  nameArr->SetValue("E.T.",18);
  nameArr->SetValue("Psycho",19);
```

After the array of film names has been constructed and initialized and before you put these film names into `lstNames` you should sort them in ascending order using the `Sort()` method that accomodates `array` objects as discussed earlier.

```
// Sort the array
Array::Sort(nameArr);
```

The `ListView` control   All that remains is to use a `for` loop to populate the `Items` of `lstNames`. Each iteration adds another name to `lstNames`. In this case, you want to add the film name (`nameArr[i]`) preceded by text indicating which element the film name is stored in (0–19). The procedure looks like that shown in Example 8-12.

EXAMPLE 8-12: POPULATING A `ListView` CONTROL

```
// Populate lstNames
for (int i=0; i<nameArr->Length; i++)
    lstNames->Items->Add("(" + i +")   " + nameArr[i]);
```

Your last job in `Form1_Load` is to declare and initialize the target and the comparison log.

```
// Construct empty target and comparison log
strTarget = "";
strLog = "";
```

When you have finished writing the code for `Form1_Load()`, save the project and then run it. If the program runs properly, the sorted names in the `nameArr` array should be displayed in the `lstNames` control. At this point, neither of the buttons work because you have yet to write their event handlers; however, `lstNames` should display the sorted list of films.

Coding `btnSeqSearch_Click()`   The sequential search implements the algorithm step by step as shown in Example 8-13. Note the construction of the search log (`strLog`) by concatenation within the loop.

EXAMPLE 8-13: `btnSeqSearch_Click()`

```
private: System::Void
btnSeqSearch_Click(System::Object^ sender,
System::EventArgs^ e) {
  // Declare and initialize variables
  int i;
  bool found = false;
  // Read the target
  strTarget = txtTarget->Text;
  // Initialize strLog
  strLog = "SEQUENTIAL SEARCH LOG " + "\r\n";
```

```
  // Sequential search loop
  for (i = 0; i < nameArr->Length; i++)
  {
    // Add a comparison line to the log
    strLog += "checking location " + i + " (" + nameArr[i] +")\r\n";
    // If the target matches this element in nameArr
    if (String::Compare(strTarget,nameArr[i])==0)
    {
      found = true;
      break;
    }
  }
  // Finish search log
  if (found)
    strLog += strTarget + " FOUND!-";
  else
    strLog += strTarget + " NOT FOUND!";
  // Display search log
  txtLog->Text = strLog + "\r\n" + (i+1) + " comparisons were made";
}
```

Save your program and run it to verify that it works correctly both for targets that are in the list as well as those not in the list.

Coding btnBinSearch_Click()   The code shown in Example 8-14 performs the binary search in accordance with the algorithm devised earlier. The details of the search log concatenation are left up to you to provide in the first Own Your Own task.

EXAMPLE 8-14: btnBinSearch_Click()

```
private: System::Void
btnBinSearch_Click(System::Object^ sender,
System::EventArgs^ e)
{
  // Declare and initialize variables
  int low, high, mid, compareResult;
  int comparisons = 0;
  low = 0;
  high = 19;
  // Read the target
  strTarget = txtTarget->Text;
  // Initialize strLog

  // Binary search
  while (low <= high)
  {
    // Increment the comparison counter
    comparisons++;
```

```
// Calculate mid
mid = (low+high) /2;
// Add a line to str about this comparison

// Compare the target and element nameArr[mid]
compareResult = String::Compare(strTarget, nameArr[mid]);
// Adjust low, or high
if (compareResult < 0) high = mid-1;
else if (compareResult > 0) low = mid + 1;
else low = high + 1;
}
// Finish search log

// Display strLog
txtLog->Text = strLog + "\r\n" + comparisons +
" comparisons were made";
}
```

Testing

Test both types of searches in your program. For the sequential search, verify that your program can:

- Locate an item stored in the first element (best case).
- Locate an item stored in the last element (worst case).
- Locate an item stored in between the first and last element.
- Correctly handle situations in which the target is not in the array.
- Correctly log all sequential search comparisons.

For the binary search, verify that your program can:

- Locate an item stored in the middle element (best case).
- Locate an item that requires four or more comparisons of the list (worst case).
- Locate an item stored above the initial middle element.
- Locate an item stored below the initial middle element.
- Locate an item stored in the first element of the array.
- Locate an item stored in the last element of the array.
- Correctly handle situations in which the target is not in the array.

This is a great program to illustrate the difference between these search methods. Imagine what performance would be like if there were 20,000 names instead of 20.

8

ON YOUR OWN

The program you created in the tutorial would benefit from several enhancements. First, the binary search does not display a search log. Second, the program requires the user to use the exact form of capitalization as `listNames`. Both situations can be improved to offer the user a more informative and flexible experience.

TASK 1: CREATING THE BINARY SEARCH LOG

Write the code necessary to create a search log for the binary search button. Use the code for the sequential search button as a guide in creating this new code.

TASK 2: CASE SENSITIVITY

From the user's standpoint, this program has an unfriendly aspect. When the user enters a target name he or she must type it exactly as it appears in the list, using the correct capitalization. In other words, the program is case sensitive. Modify your program using `ToUpper()` as discussed earlier in the chapter (Examples 8-9 and 8-10) so that it can find the target whether the user types the input in uppercase or lowercase letters or some combination of both.

QUICK REVIEW

1. The part of an array or list that will be searched is called the search domain.
2. A binary search repeatedly divides the search domain in half.
3. The binary search method is similar to looking up a name in a phone book.
4. Binary searches only work on data that are already sorted.
5. Arrays sorted from lowest to highest values are said to be in ascending order.
6. The binary search divides an array in half repeatedly until the target value is located.
7. The binary search always compares the target value to the value stored in the element in the middle of the current search domain.
8. The binary search of an array requires the location of the lowest (`low`), highest (`high`), and middle (`mid`) values in an array.
9. The `mid` is calculated as `(high + low)/2` using integer division.
10. If the target is less than the value stored in `array[mid]`, `high` is reset to `mid – 1`.
11. If the target is greater than the value stored in `array[mid]`, `low` is reset to `mid + 1`.
12. The binary search loop ends when it finds the target or runs out of places to look for it.

13. When `low > high`, the binary search loop will terminate.

14. There are three common search methods used to find a target value in an array: direct lookup, sequential search, and binary search.

15. Direct lookup uses an index value to access the data stored at that location in an array.

16. Direct lookup requires that the value entered by the user be one of the index values in the array.

17. Direct lookup is very fast but often impractical because the target value must match one of the array index values.

18. The sequential search can be used on any array.

19. Sequential searches are generally slower than direct lookup or binary search.

20. Binary searches usually are much faster than sequential searches.

21. Big-O notation is used to indicate the order of complexity of an algorithm.

22. The complexity of a search technique is measured in terms of the amount of system resources it uses to complete a task.

23. The order of complexity (big-O) of direct lookup is O(1).

24. The order of complexity (big-O) of the sequential search is O(n).

25. The order of complexity (big-O) of the binary search is O($\log_2 n$).

26. The system-defined `array` class can be used to make arrays of objects such as `Strings`.

27. The `Array` namespace includes its own `Sort()` method.

28. The `SetValue()` method of the `array` class is used to assign values to its elements.

29. Strings are compared with the `String::Compare()` method.

30. If the first `String` parameter in the `String::Compare()` method is greater than the second, then `String::Compare()` returns 1.

31. If the first `String` parameter in `String::Compare()` is identical to the second, then `String::Compare()` returns 0.

32. If the first `String` parameter in `String::Compare()` is less than the second, then `String::Compare()` returns -1.

33. To convert a `String` to its uppercase equivalent use the built-in `ToUpper()` method.

34. A `ListView` control displays a collection of items.

35. The `ListView` control is populated by adding strings using the `Add()` method.

8

TERMS TO KNOW

Add()
array class
Array::SetValue()
Array::Sort()
ascending order
big-O
big-O notation
binary search
complexity function
Items
ListView control
O(1)
O(*n*)
O(log₂*n*)
populating a list
search domain
sorting
String::Compare()
String::ToUpper()

EXERCISES

1. The most important characteristic of the data structure used by a binary search is that _____.

   a. it must store integers

   b. it must be ordered

   c. it must be randomized

   d. it must store at least 100 values

   e. it must have been initialized to 0

2. To exit the `while` loop of a binary search, the following condition must always be met:

   a. The target must be found.

   b. There must be no more places to look.

   c. `low` must be greater than `high`.

   d. All of the above.

   e. None of the above.

3. If the target value is less than the value stored in `arr[mid]`, then _____.

   a. `low` is set to `mid + 1`

   b. `low` is set to `mid - 1`

   c. `high` is set to `mid + 1`

   d. `high` is set to `mid - 1`

   e. None of the above.

4. When the list is divided in half, `mid` is reset to _____.

   a. `high - low/2`

   b. `(high - mid)/2`

   c. `(high + low)/2`

   d. `high - mid/2`

   e. `mid - low/2`

For questions 5–8, assume that the following code declares the variables required for a 32-element integer array called `arr` that has already been initialized:

```
int low = 0; int high = 31; int mid;
```

5. If used in a search loop, which statement properly assigns values to `mid`?

   a. `mid = low + high/2;`

   b. `mid = (high - low)/2;`

   c. `mid = (high + low)/2;`

   d. `mid = (high - low)/2 - 1;`

   e. `mid = (high - low)/2 + 1;`

6. If used in the search loop, which statement properly reassigns `low`?

   a. `low = mid/2;`

   b. `low = high;`

   c. `low = mid;`

   d. `low = mid + 1;`

   e. `low = mid - 1;`

7. If used in the search loop, which statement properly reassigns `high`?

   a. `high = mid/2;`

   b. `high = low;`

   c. `high = mid;`

   d. `high = mid + 1;`

   e. `high = mid - 1;`

8

8. If `low` is a pointer to `arr[0]` and `high` is a pointer to `arr[31]`, how would `mid` be assigned?

   a. `mid = low + high/2;`

   b. `mid = low + (high - low)/2;`

   c. `mid = (high + low)/2;`

   d. `mid = (high - low)/2 - 1;`

   e. `mid = (high - low)/2 + 1;`

9. Which big-O expression typifies the binary search?

   a. $O(n^2)$

   b. $O(1)$

   c. $O(n \log n)$

   d. $O(\log_2 n)$

   e. $O(n)$

10. Which big-O expression typifies direct lookup?

   a. $O(n^2)$

   b. $O(1)$

   c. $O(n \log n)$

   d. $O(\log_2 n)$

   e. $O(n)$

11. Which big-O expression typifies the sequential search?

   a. $O(n^2)$

   b. $O(1)$

   c. $O(n \log n)$

   d. $O(\log_2 n)$

   e. $O(n)$

12. Which of these search techniques has the highest order of complexity?

   a. Direct lookup

   b. Sequential search

   c. Binary search

13. Which of these search techniques requires a sorted array?

   a. Direct lookup

   b. Sequential search

   c. Binary search

14. Which of these search techniques can be used on any unordered array?

    a. Direct lookup

    b. Sequential search

    c. Binary search

15. Which of the following techniques searches for an array index rather than a value stored in the array?

    a. Direct lookup

    b. Sequential search

    c. Binary search

16. Which of the following expressions would you use to compare the `String` variables `strName1` and `strName2`?

    a. `(strName1 == strName2)`

    b. `(strName1->Text == strName2->Text)`

    c. `(Compare(strName1 == strName2))`

    d. `(String::Compare(strName1 == strName2))`

    e. `(String::Compare(strName1, strName2) == 0)`

17. Which of the following would you use to display the uppercase version of the `String strName` in `txtName->Text`?

    a. `txtName->Text = Upper(strName);`

    b. `txtName->Text = ToUpper(strName);`

    c. `txtName->Text = strName->ToUpper;`

    d. `txtName->Text = strName->ToUpper();`

    e. `txtName->Text = STRNAME;`

18. Which of these declarations would you use for an array of strings named `strArray`?

    a. `private: array<String^> strArray;`

    b. `private: array<String^>^ strArray;`

    c. `private: array<String> strArray;`

    d. `private: array<String>^ strArray;`

    e. `private: array<String> strArray[];`

19. To allocate memory for the `strArray` declared in question 18, which of the following would you use?

    a. `strArray = gcnew array<String^>(20);`

    b. `strArray = gcnew array<String>(20);`

    c. `strArray = gcnew array(20);`

    d. `strArray[20] = gcnew array<String>(20);`

    e. `strArray[20] = array<String>(20);`

8

20. To assign a value to the fourth element of an array of strings named `strArray`, which of the following commands would you use?

   a. `strArray->SetValue("Napoleon Bonaparte",4);`

   b. `strArray->SetValue("Napoleon Bonaparte",3);`

   c. `strArray->SetValue(4,"Napoleon Bonaparte");`

   d. `strArray->SetValue(3) = "Napoleon Bonaparte";`

   e. `strArray[3] = "Napoleon Bonaparte";`

PROGRAMMING EXERCISES

1. Enhancing the Sequential Search

A sequential search can be used on any finite data set. It may be slow but it does the job, and under certain conditions you can speed up such a search considerably. For example, the sequential search you created in the tutorial for this chapter did not take advantage of the fact that the data in `nameArr` was sorted. Consider the situation where the user typed in the film *Lion King* as shown in Figure 8-25.

FIGURE 8-25 Unsuccessful search for *Lion King*

The name *Lion King* is not in the list, and our current program will recognize that, but only after looking at all 20 titles! This is a waste of time in a sorted list. As soon as the program finds *Lord of the Rings* it is clear that all names in the sorted list from that point on are greater than *Lion King* alphabetically, so the program might as well stop searching. The problem is illustrated in Figure 8-26.

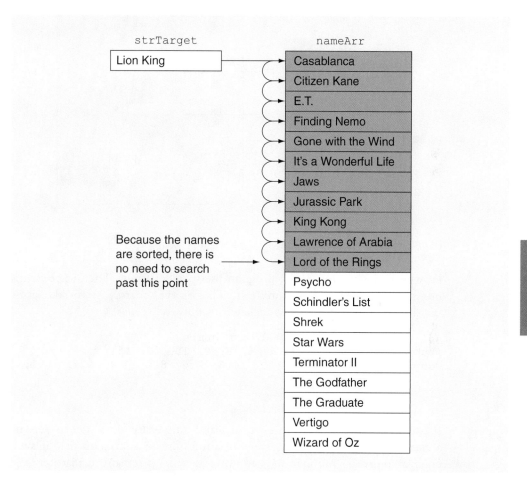

FIGURE 8-26 Sequential search of a sorted list

Rewrite the sequential search method in the tutorial so that the search terminates when it reaches the point where names of films are greater alphabetically than the target you are searching for. Verify that your sequential search works by looking at the number of comparisons in the comparison log.

2. Enhanced Volleyball Program

Figure 8-27 shows a modified version of the volleyball program similar to the one discussed earlier in the section on direct lookup. Using it as a guide, create a version of the uniform number search program that uses a binary search to solve the problem.

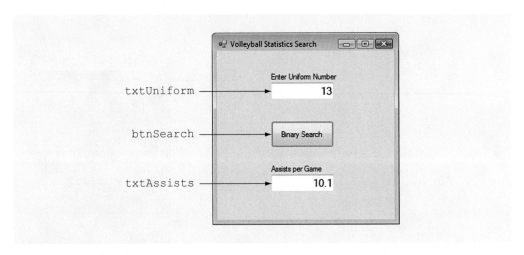

FIGURE 8-27 Binary search version of volleyball program

However, this version of the program uses parallel arrays. The `uniform` array stores the numbers on each player's uniform. The `assists` array stores the assists per game statistics. The following array declarations must be used:

```
int num; // A player's uniform number
double uniform[] = {3, 4, 6, 8, 9, 10, 13, 15};
double assists[] = { 12.3, 14.6, 2.6, 8.6, 4.7, 6.9, 10.1, 5.5};
```

3. Course Data (Class ID Search)

It is common for students to need to search university Web sites to determine whether a class they would like to register for is full. Create a program that allows a student to enter a course ID number and see how many seats remain in that course, as shown in Figure 8-28.

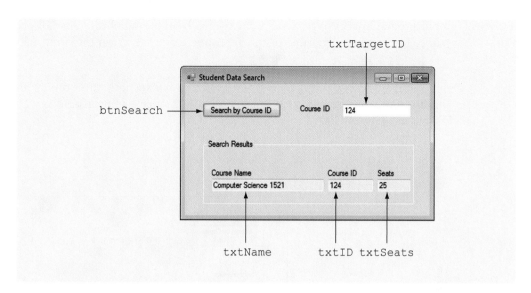

FIGURE 8-28 Course ID number search interface

The data structures for this program consist of three parallel arrays. The data for these arrays is shown in Table 8-7.

TABLE 8-7 Course data

Course Name	Course ID	Seats Available
Computer Sci 1511	123	0
Computer Sci 1521	124	25
Composition 1120	135	14
Math 1296	145	5
Physics 1120	146	0
Biology 1100	149	20
Chemistry 1100	155	17
Anthropology 1210	162	0
Economics 1000	175	12

Your program needs to perform a binary search on the ID number and display the course name, ID, and seats available in the appropriate text boxes on the interface.

4. Course Data (Class Name Search)

This program is similar to Programming Exercise 3, except that this time you will need to modify the binary search so that it searches by course name instead of ID number, as shown in Figure 8-29.

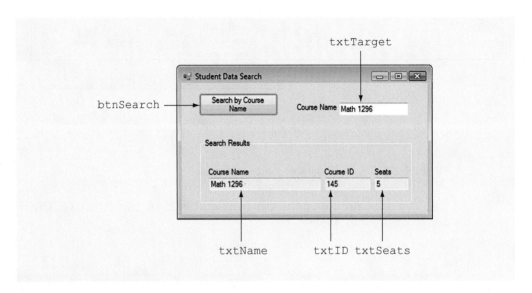

FIGURE 8-29 Course name search interface

5. Searching a ListView Control Directly

The video project you created in the tutorial had two data structures—an array of strings and a ListView control. You used the Sort() method of the array class to put the film names in ascending order. Then the program populated lstNames with the ordered strings from the array. In this project, you will populate the list using a different technique. Within the Form1_Load event, comment out the Sort() method as shown here:

```
// Array::Sort(nameArr);
```

Next, change the Sorting property of lstNames to Ascending as shown in Figure 8-30.

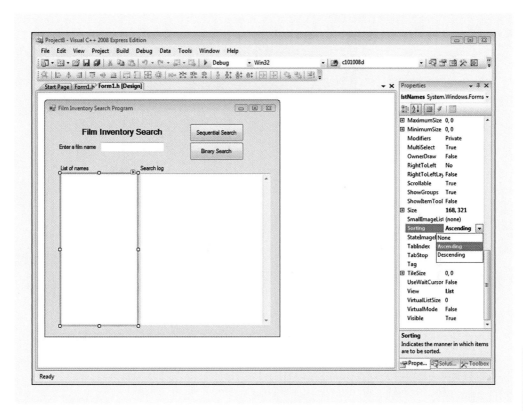

FIGURE 8-30 Changing the `Sorting` property of `lstNames`

When you run the program, the names displayed in **lstNames** should be sorted automatically. Notice, however, that the search routines perform strangely. For example, in Figure 8-31, *Finding Nemo* is the fourth name on the list; however, it took the sequential search 18 comparisons to find this title.

8

FIGURE 8-31 Strange results from a sequential search

Why did this happen? The answer lies in the fact that our search functions are not searching the contents of lstNames. They are searching the array nameArr. In nameArr *Finding Nemo* is the fourth name listed, but in lstNames it is the 18th. Unlike lstNames, nameArr is not sorted. Whether the contents of lstNames are sorted or not makes no difference to the searches because they never look there.

To correct the problem, use lstNames for the search instead of nameArr. The contents of a ListView item can be examined by looking at the Text property of each ListView item instead of elements in nameArr. In other words, the search loop of the sequential search should use:

```
lstNames->Items[i]->Text
```

instead of

```
nameArr[i]
```

Rewrite your program so that it performs sequential and binary searches on lstNames instead of the array nameArr.

SORTING

IN THIS CHAPTER, YOU WILL:

- Create and use a `Swap()` method to exchange data values in arrays
- Use nested loops to sort elements in an array
- Implement a selection sort algorithm
- Learn about the bubble sort technique
- Learn about the insertion sort technique
- Analyze the complexity and efficiency of a sorting algorithm (big-O)

In Chapter 7 you learned about traditional arrays of primitive types and how to use them. In Chapter 8 you learned how to use the system-defined `array` class to create an array of `String` objects. You also learned how to use the binary search to find an item in an array. The binary search technique used in Chapter 8 works only on data that has been sorted (that is, arranged in a particular order). The `Sort()` method that is built into the system-defined `Array` class took care of ordering the data in the arrays we worked with in Chapter 8. Unfortunately, there is no `Sort()` method built into arrays of primitive types.

In this chapter, you examine the algorithms behind various sorting techniques and write your own `Sort()` method for traditional arrays. This will allow you to understand and compare the algorithms and their implementations for the important process of sorting. It also provides the opportunity to use many of the control structures you have learned in previous chapters and become more familiar with nested loops. All of the sorting algorithms discussed in this chapter rely on nested loops to put the data in order.

Exchanging Data Values in an Array

Arrays are either sorted in **ascending order** (lowest to highest) or **descending order** (highest to lowest). For example, the names in a phone book are in ascending order (A-Z). On the other hand, a list of the richest people in the world would usually be arranged in descending order, starting with the wealthiest person first and going down from there.

A central feature of many sorting techniques allows data to be put in their proper order by the reassignment of data values from one array element to another. For example, in Figure 9-1, when the values stored in element `arr[0]` and `arr[7]` are exchanged, then the entire array is sorted in ascending order as shown in the array after the exchange. A data value **exchange** between two memory cells is the process of replacing the value stored in the first with that of the second and also replacing the value in the second with that of the first.

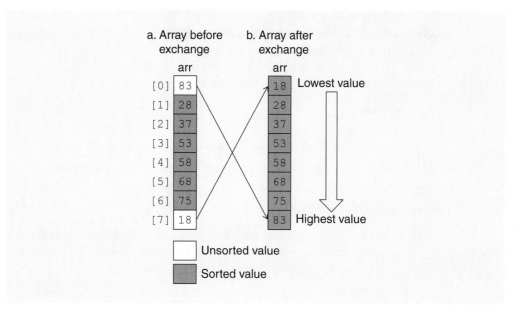

FIGURE 9-1 Exchanging values to create a sorted array

Figure 9-1 depicts an easy example. The exchange of only two values was all that was required to produce a sorted array. Usually many exchanges are required. For this reason, it is common to have an instance method available to exchange values when needed. You shall create one such method, called `Swap()`. The `Swap()` method will be used by several sorting methods developed later in this chapter to exchange values in an array.

The algorithm for the `Swap()` method is short and requires two formal reference parameters (**a** and **b**). The values in **a** and **b** are exchanged in the following manner:

ALGORITHM 9-1: SWAPPING VALUES

1. Declare local integer variable `temp`.
2. Assign the integer stored in `a` to `temp`.
3. Assign the integer stored in `b` to `a`.
4. Assign the integer stored in `temp` to `b`.

The code for the `Swap()` method is shown in Example 9-1. There are two reference parameters (**a** and **b**). As you recall, a reference parameter uses the memory cell address (reference) of the actual argument to access and even change the data value stored in an actual argument. The `Swap()` method exchanges the values stored in the actual arguments. A local variable (`temp`) is used as a temporary storage location for the value in parameter **a**.

EXAMPLE 9-1: THE Swap() METHOD

```
private: void Swap(int& a, int& b)
{
    int temp = a;
    a = b;
    b = temp;
}
```

The `Swap()` method must be called with two actual parameters. For example, the method call statement

```
Swap(arr[7], arr[0]);
```

sends `arr[7]` into the `Swap()` method as the first actual parameter and `arr[0]` into `Swap()` as the second actual parameter. The idea is that the `Swap()` method will exchange the values stored in these two array elements.

Figure 9-2 illustrates the relationship between the actual parameters in the `Swap()` method call and the formal parameters in the `Swap()` defined in the signature line.

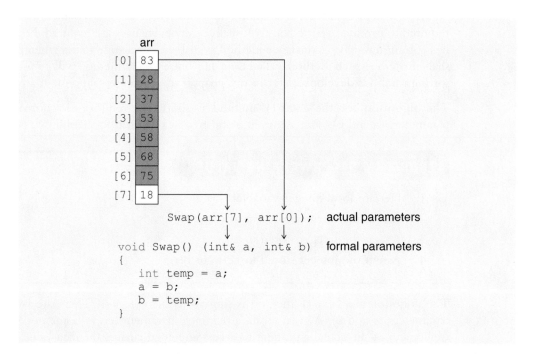

FIGURE 9-2 Calling `Swap()` with array elements as actual parameters

Within the `Swap()` method, the variable `a` contains the address of `arr[7]` and the variable `b` contains the address of `arr[0]`. Figure 9-3 illustrates that the value stored in `arr[7]` can be accessed through the variable `a` and assigned to another variable, such as `temp`, in this manner:

```
int temp = a;
```

Figure 9-3 illustrates the assignment process, highlighted in red.

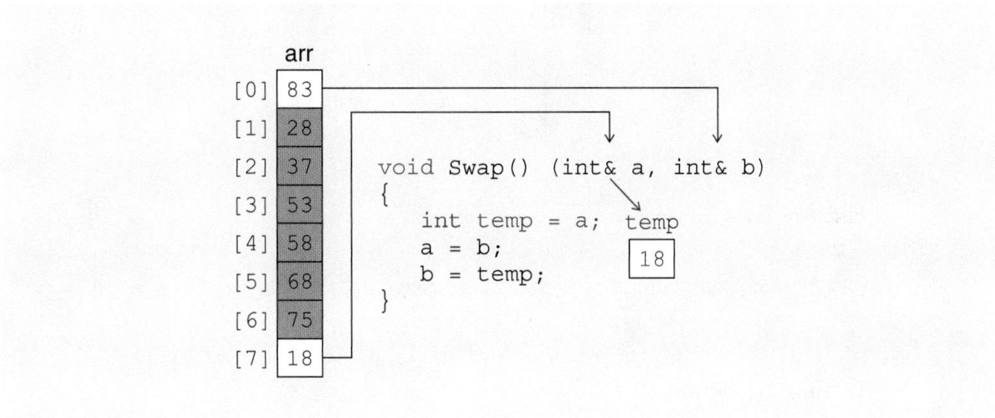

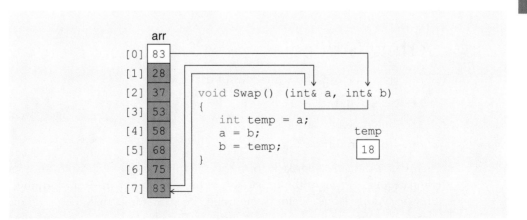

FIGURE 9-3 Assignment of the value stored in `arr[7]` to `temp` using reference parameter a.

With a copy of the data from `arr[7]` now in `temp` the original `arr[7]` value, referenced by `a`, can be replaced with the value from `arr[0]`, referenced by `b`. This completes the first half of the exchange. The step is shown by the statement `a = b;` in Figure 9-4.

9

FIGURE 9-4 Assignment of the value in `arr[0]` to `arr[7]` from within `Swap()`

Finally, the exchange can be completed by assigning the value stored in `temp` to `arr[0]`, referenced through `b`, using the statement `b = temp;` in Figure 9-5.

arr

```
[0] 18
[1] 28
[2] 37      void Swap() (int& a, int& b)
[3] 53      {
[4] 58          int temp = a;
[5] 68          a = b;              temp
              b = temp;            18
[6] 75      }
[7] 83
```

FIGURE 9-5 Completing the exchange by assigning `temp` to `arr[0]`

You will find the `Swap()` method to be an essential tool in implementing the various sorting algorithms that follow.

> **NOTE** It is important that reference parameters be used in any `Swap()` method. If the formal parameter declarations had excluded the address-of operator (`&`), and looked like this: `void Swap(int a, int b)`, then data from `arr[7]` and `arr[0]` would have been passed in by value, not by reference. The `Swap()` method would compile and run but the exchange of the values in `arr[7]` and `arr[0]` would not work. This is because `Swap()` would be working with copies of the data stored in those elements, not the actual array elements themselves.

Sorting Strategies

This chapter discusses three methods of data sorting:

- Selection sort
- Bubble sort
- Insertion sort

Each uses a different approach to the sorting process. This allows us the opportunity to compare different algorithms that solve the same problem—transforming an unsorted array to a sorted one. Before beginning, keep in mind that there are many ways to approach each of these methods of sorting. This chapter explores only a few.

These sorting methods all use nested loops to put the data in order through a process of comparison, data value exchanges, or data value reassignments. The nested loops are critical. Each iteration of the outer loop results in one value from the array being placed in its correct (sorted) position. The role of the inner loop is to do the comparisons or exchanges required to carry out the process.

For example, if there are eight values in an array, the outer loop may make up to eight iterations, depending on the algorithm, placing one value into the correct sorted position each time. The inner loop might determine which value to move and where it should go. The relationship of the inner and outer loops and their tasks is shown in general form in Figure 9-6.

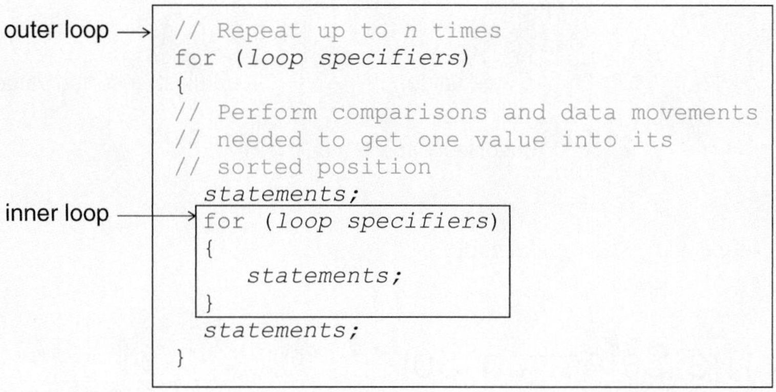

```
outer loop →    // Repeat up to n times
                for (loop specifiers)
                {
                    // Perform comparisons and data movements
                    // needed to get one value into its
                    // sorted position
                    statements;
inner loop →        for (loop specifiers)
                    {
                        statements;
                    }
                    statements;
                }
```

FIGURE 9-6 Nested loops and the sorting process

This means that the sorting process can be viewed as a series of outcomes in which, at the end of each iteration of the outer loop, one unsorted value has been placed in its correct sorted position. For example, Figure 9-7 shows the progression of outcomes in a typical sorting process. The unsorted values are shown in white. Sorted values are shown in yellow.

Notice that the original array (on the far left) contains unsorted values. The same array (on the far right) is completely sorted. The sorted array is the result of a process in which one value is put into its correct position, then another, then another, and so on. Each of the array diagrams in the progression from left to right, represent the outcome of one iteration of the outer loop in which one value was placed into its correct position. In this case, seven repetitions were needed to transform the array from an unsorted state to a sorted one. Each of the eight values was placed into its correct sorted position, one at a time, until there were no more unsorted values.

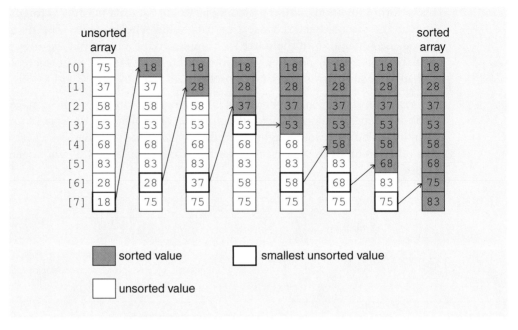

FIGURE 9-7 Sorting sequence

The Selection Sort

Imagine a class of school children lined up against a wall. How would you arrange them in order from shortest to tallest? A very simple method is to scan the group and find the shortest person, select him or her and ask that person to exchange places with the first position in the line. Then you look for the second shortest person, make your selection swap places between that person and the second person in the line. Then you look for the third shortest, make your selection, and swap that person with the person who is third in line and so on. This method of ordering is called the selection sort.

When applied to an array of data values, a **selection sort** is a method of ordering data by repeatedly selecting a value from the unordered portion and exchanging it with another so that the ordered portion expands. Figure 9-8 is an example of a selection sort in which the smallest of the unsorted values is located and exchanged with the first value in the unsorted portion of the array. The progression from an unsorted to a sorted array is characterized by an exchange of values (indicated by the arrows) taking place at the completion of each iteration of the outer loop.

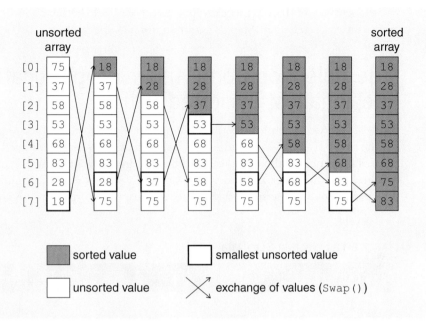

FIGURE 9-8 Selection sort progression

Examine Figure 9-8 closely to ensure you understand its logic. When the smallest value in the unsorted portion of the array is located it is then exchanged with the first value in the unsorted portion of the array.

In an array of *n* elements, the high-level algorithm for a selection sort such as that shown in Figure 9-8 is:

ALGORITHM 9-2: SELECTION SORT

1. For *n* − 1 times, do the following:

   1.1. Locate the smallest value in the unsorted array elements.

   1.2. Exchange the smallest value with the first element in the unsorted portion of the array.

Step 1 of the algorithm repeats the selection and exchange process (Steps 1.1 and 1.2) *n* − 1 times until the array is sorted.

 NOTE Because the purpose of this loop is to exchange one element into its correct position with each iteration, it may seem that this loop should execute *n* times (one iteration for each array element) instead of *n* − 1. However, at the end of the process, when there are only two unsorted values left, swapping them places both in their correct final position. This can be seen in the last exchange on the right in Figure 9-8 (values 75 and 83).

9

The discussion in the next section focuses on Step 1.1. Earlier in this chapter you learned that you can implement Step 1.2 using a `Swap()` method.

The Selection Sort's Inner Loop: Locating the Smallest Unsorted Value

Step 1.1 of Algorithm 9-2 requires the program to find the location of the smallest value in the array. Table 9-1 provides us with a list of the variables needed to accomplish this task. These include the array itself (`data`), a variable containing the number of elements in the array (`n`), outer and inner loop control variables (`i` and `j`), and a variable to store the index value of the smallest value in the unsorted portion of the array (`smallIndex`).

TABLE 9-1   Selection Sort Data Table

Variable	Data Type	Usage
data	int[] array	Data array, values assigned when declared
n	int	The size of the array
i	int	Outer loop control variable
smallIndex	int	Location of the smallest value in the unsorted portion of data
j	int	Inner loop control variable

The algorithm to locate the smallest value in the unsorted portion of an array can now be developed. Its success depends largely on knowing where the unsorted portion of the array begins and ends. As you can see from Figure 9-8, the location of the first element in the unsorted portion is initially the element with an index of 0. The index value of the first unsorted element changes, increasing by one, with each repetition.

The outer loop control variable (`i`) not only counts the number of iterations of the outer loop, it can also be used to indicate where the unsorted portion of the array begins. When `i` is 0 the unsorted portion of the list begins at `data[0]`. When `i` is 1 (after one value has been put into its correct position) the unsorted portion starts at `data[1]`. When `i` is 2 (after a second value has been put into its correct position) the unsorted portion starts at `data[2]`, and so on.

Knowing where the unsorted portion starts greatly simplifies the task of finding the smallest unsorted value. Begin by assuming the smallest value is contained in data[i] (the first unsorted element), and store the value of i in smallIndex. Then a loop is used to compare the value of each unsorted element to the smallest value (data[smallIndex]). Whenever the value stored in an unsorted array element is less than data[smallIndex] its index value is assigned to smallIndex. In this way, the program always keeps track of the location of the smallest value.

The process of finding the smallest value in an unsorted array is shown in Figure 9-9. In part (a) of Figure 9-9, smallIndex has been initially set to 0; assuming that 34, the value in data[0], is the smallest value. The search loop begins at the next unsorted value (data[1]) and continues until it finds a value smaller than 34 (data[smallIndex]). When a smaller value is located, its index value replaces the value stored in smallIndex. In Part a, the value 9 in data[4] is found to be less than the value 34 in data[smallIndex]. In part (b) of Figure 9-9, you see that smallIndex has been changed to 4, the index value of the location in which the smaller value 9 was found. The repetitive process of comparisons continues until all elements have been compared. When finished, the smallest value has been located and the location is stored in smallIndex.

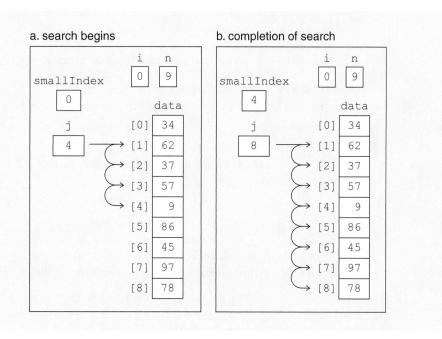

FIGURE 9-9 Locating the smallest value in the unsorted portion of an array

The code for both loops and the entire selection sort process is shown in Example 9-2. The outer loop executes $n - 1$ times. Within the body of the outer loop the three steps in Algorithm 9-3 are executed:

ALGORITHM 9-3: FINDING THE SMALLEST VALUE

1.1. `smallIndex` is assigned the index value of the first element in the unsorted portion of the array.

1.2. A loop, using `j` as its loop control variable, compares the values in each successive unsorted element, replacing `smallIndex` with `j` if `data[j] < data[smallest]`.

1.3. After the loop is finished, the values in the first unsorted element (`data[i]`) and the element storing the smallest value (`data[smallIndex]`) are exchanged.

EXAMPLE 9-2: LOOP TO FIND THE SMALLEST VALUE

```
for (i = 0; i < n-1; i++)
{
// Step 1.1 Find the smallest unsorted value
   // Set location of smallIndex to i
   smallIndex = i;
   // Compare all elements from data[i+1] to data[n-1]
   for (j = i+1; j < n; j++)
      if (data[j] < data[smallIndex]) smallIndex = j;
// Step 1.2 Swap the value in data[smallIndex] with data[i]
   Swap(data[i], data[smallIndex]);
}
```

Notice that the `Swap()` method is called to exchange the first value of the unsorted portion of the array (`data[i]`) with the value stored in the location identified as the smallest (`data[smallIndex]`).

The Bubble Sort

A second type of sort, the **bubble sort**, is a method of sorting data in an array by exchanging data values multiple times in each pass through the outer loop.

Imagine a clear glass into which a cold, carbonated beverage is poured. Initially the liquid froths and bubbles even down near the bottom, but quickly the bubbling action migrates to the top of the glass and eventually the effervescence stops. This phenomenon is similar to what happens during a bubble sort. The movement of bubbles in an effervescing glass is paralleled by the swapping of data values in an array. The bubble sort exchanges data values using a strategy that assigns larger values to their positions at the bottom of the array first and then the exchange process progresses toward the top as it puts smaller values in place.

The bubble sort and selection sort have their similarities. Both use nested loops to accomplish the procedure. In fact, you can use this outer loop for both a bubble sort and a selection sort:

```
for (i = 0; i < n-1; i++)
```

The bubble sort differs from a selection sort in a fundamental way. The selection sort calls the `Swap()` method only once for each outer loop iteration. A bubble sort may call the `Swap()` method numerous times within a single outer loop iteration. The key to the bubble sort is that, within the outer loop, each pair of array elements is examined and are swapped immediately if the value in the first element is greater than the value in the second.

A high-level algorithm for the bubble sort looks like this:

ALGORITHM 9-4: BUBBLE SORT

1. For $n - 1$ times, do the following:

    1.1. Compare the values in each adjacent pair of elements, and swap them if the first is larger than the second.

The Bubble Sort's Inner Loop: Exchanging Values in Adjacent Elements

9

In an array of n elements, there are $n - 1$ adjacent pairs of data values. For example, in an array called `arr`, containing four elements, there are three adjacent pairs of elements: {`arr[0]`, `arr[1]`}, {`arr[1]`, `arr[2]`}, {`arr[2]`, `arr[3]`}. In general, if an array has n elements, it has $n - 1$ adjacent pairs.

Examine Figure 9-10. The arrays shown in this figure have eight elements. This means there are seven adjacent pairs. Now focus on part (a) in Figure 9-10, which shows the array almost sorted. There are only two elements in the unsorted portion of the array, `arr[0]` and `arr[1]`. The inner loop of the bubble sort (Step 1.1 of the high-level algorithm) compares the values in `arr[0]` and `arr[1]`, and if the value stored in `arr[0]` is greater than that stored in `arr[1]` the `Swap()` method is called to exchange them. As a result, this array is now sorted.

Part (b) of Figure 9-10 is only slightly more complicated. In this case, there are three elements in the unsorted portion of the array, `arr[0]`, `arr[1]`, and `arr[2]`. The inner loop of the bubble sort compares the values in each of the pairs of adjacent elements and exchanges them if the first is greater than the second. When it examines the pair {`arr[0]`, `arr[1]`} the result is an exchange as 28 is assigned to `arr[0]` and 37 is assigned to in `arr[1]`. Now the pair {`arr[1]`, `arr[2]`} is compared. Since `arr[1]` now contains 37 and `arr[2]` contains 18 they are exchanged. As a result 18 is assigned to `arr[1]`, and 37 is assigned to `arr[2]`. The net result is that the value 37 was exchanged twice and moved two elements down the array into its sorted position.

Finally, examine part (c) of Figure 9-10. The values in the first pair of unsorted elements {arr[0] , arr[1]} are in their correct position relative to one another (37 is less than 75) and do not have to be exchanged. Similarly, the values in {arr[1], arr[2]} are in their correct position relative to one another (75 is less than 83) and do not have to be exchanged. The same cannot be said for {arr[2], arr[3]}. In this case the value 83 is larger than 37 and is exchanged with it. In fact, the value 83 is so large that it must move again when assigned to the next pair because it is larger than 58, and again when compared to 53, and again when compared to 68, and again when compared to 18. The value 83 is exchanged five times before coming to rest in arr[7] at the bottom.

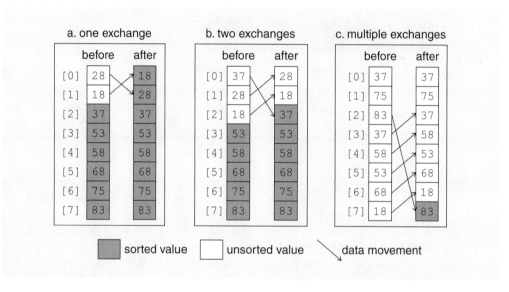

FIGURE 9-10 Bubble sort

The exchange logic of the inner loop of the bubble sort, comparing an element to the one that comes after it in the array and exchanging values if the first is greater than the second, is employed with every adjacent pair of elements in the unsorted portion of the array. This process repeats with each iteration of the outer loop.

Figure 9-11 shows the progression of stages as the outer loop control variable (i) runs from 0 to 7, in a complete bubble sort. Notice that data value exchanges (indicated by the arrows) are much more frequent than in the selection sort (Figure 9-8). Because the logic of the bubble sort is to exchange values in adjacent array elements if the first is larger than the second, the net effect is that the largest element in the unsorted portion of the array is exchanged down the array into its correct sorted position. Each iteration of the outer loop guarantees that the largest unsorted value will be placed into its sorted position. You can see the data exchanges taking place higher and higher in the array, similar to the effervescing bubbles in a glass moving to the top as the glass fills with liquid.

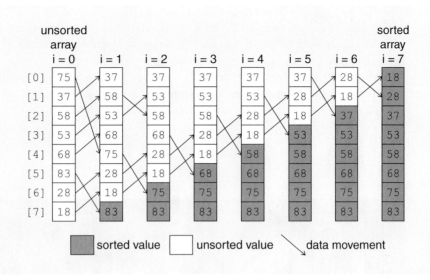

FIGURE 9-11 Bubble sort progression

The code for the bubble sort is quite concise, as shown in Example 9-3. The outer loop executes $n-1$ times, placing at least one value into its sorted position with each iteration. The inner loop compares the values of all adjacent pairs of elements in the unsorted portion of the array and exchanges them if the value in the first element (data[j]) is greater than the value in the element that comes after it (data[j+1]).

EXAMPLE 9-3: BUBBLE SORT CODE

```
//  BUBBLE SORT
// Repeat n-1 times
for (i=0; i < n-1; i++) {
   // inner loop - compares adjacent pairs and swaps
      for (j = 0; j < n-1-i; j++) {
         if (data[j] > data[j+1]) Swap(data[j], data[j+1]);
   } // end inner loop
} // end outer loop
```

It is important for the inner loop to compare only adjacent elements in the unsorted portion of the array. Our algorithm puts the largest values into place at the bottom of the array first and works its way up. Therefore, the first element in the unsorted region is always data[0]. The index location of the last unsorted element changes with each iteration of the outer loop. It is calculated as $n-1-i$ (subtracting the outer loop control variable (i) from $n-1$). This works because i is a count of the number of values that have been placed in their sorted positions.

The Insertion Sort

The selection and bubble sort have common applications, but the sorting strategy that you use most commonly in everyday life may resemble the insertion sort. An **insertion sort** inserts a new value into its correct position by shifting previously sorted values until a vacancy at the correct position opens up.

For example, imagine that you have just been dealt a hand of five cards. From left to right in your hand, you have the jack, 2, ace, king, and 8 of diamonds, in numbered positions 1-5 as shown in Figure 9-12.

FIGURE 9-12 Original hand of cards in numbered positions from left to right

You would like to arrange them in order from lowest (on the left) to highest (on the right). One method is to proceed from left to right in the following manner, looking at one card at a time. Assume the first card (the jack on the far left) is in its proper position. Then remove the second card and insert it into its correct position relative to the first as shown in Figure 9-13. This happens in three steps using a simple insertion sort algorithm:

ALGORITHM 9-5: INSERTING A CARD IN ITS PROPER LOCATION

1. Select the card to be inserted and temporarily remove it from the hand (part (a) of Figure 9-13).
2. Slide all the cards on the left that are greater than the selected card over one position (part [b] of Figure 9-13).
3. Insert the selected card into the vacated spot (part [c] of Figure 9-13).

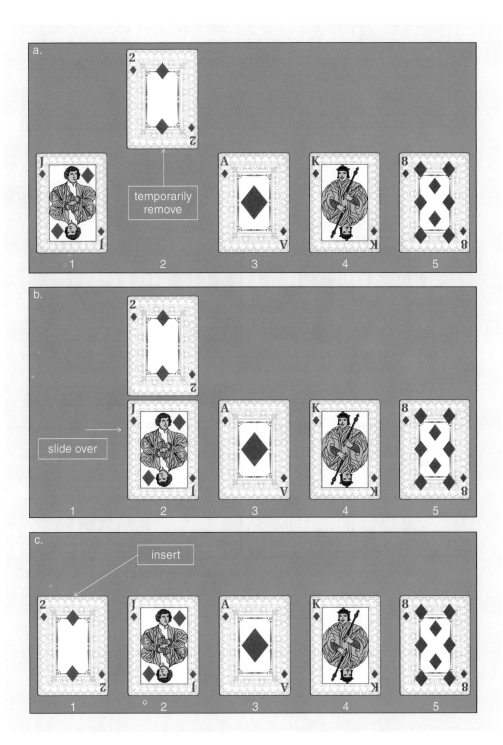

FIGURE 9-13 Selecting and inserting the second card into its correct position

For the next card, the ace (which has the highest denomination of any card in the suit), Algorithm 9-5 is used again, as shown in Figure 9-14. The card is temporarily removed (part [a] of Figure 9-14). This time however, there are no cards of higher denomination, so no cards need to slide over, and the ace is reinserted into the spot it originally occupied (part [b] of Figure 9-14).

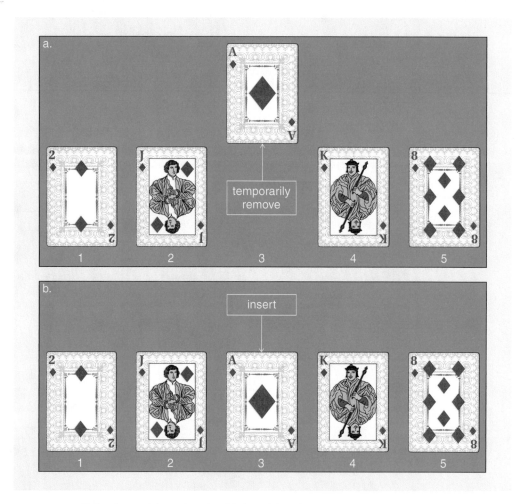

FIGURE 9-14 Selecting and inserting the third card into its correct position

Algorithm 9-5 is applied to the fourth card, the king. It is removed (part [a] of Figure 9-15), cards of higher denomination slide over (part [b] of Figure 9-15), and the king is inserted into the vacated slot (part [c] of Figure 9-15).

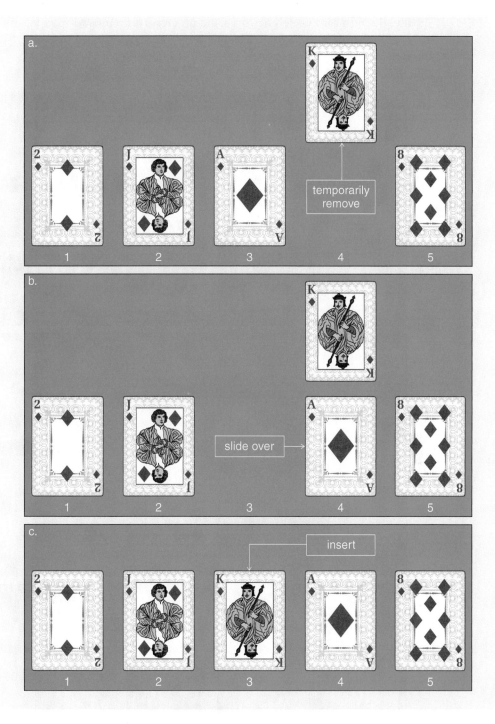

FIGURE 9-15 Selecting and inserting the fourth card into its correct position

Finally, the fifth card undergoes the same process. It is removed (part [a] of Figure 9-16), cards of higher denomination each slide over one spot (part [b] of Figure 9-16), and it is inserted into the spot last vacated (part [c] of Figure 9-16).

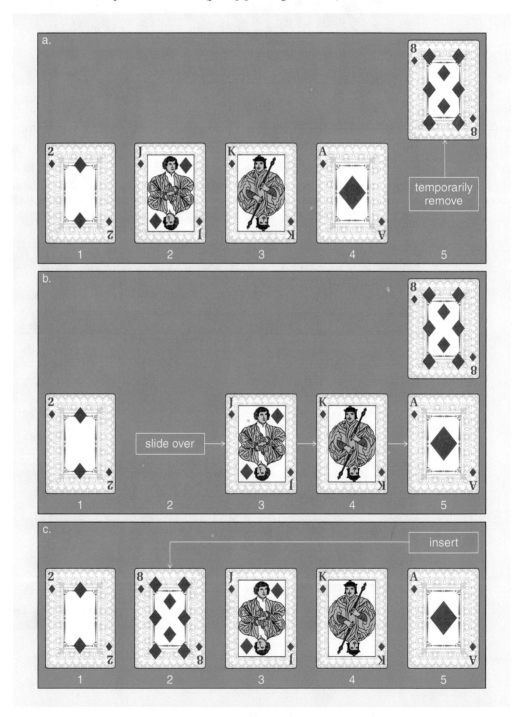

FIGURE 9-16 Selecting and inserting the fifth card into its correct position

The array of cards is now arranged in ascending order from left to right.

The insertion sort is similar to the selection and bubble sorts in several ways. All of them use nested loops to sort data. In fact, the outer loop can be written in a manner that is exactly the same as both the bubble and selection sort:

```
for (i = 0; i < n-1; i++)
```

Each iteration of the outer loop guarantees that the first value in the unsorted portion of the array is placed into its correct position in the sorted portion.

Figure 9-17 illustrates the data movements required to sort an array using the insertion sort technique. The figure shows the progression of stages as the outer loop control variable (i) goes from 0 to 7, in a complete insertion sort. Notice that there are two types of data value movements, just as in the example with the hand of playing cards. The red arrows in Figure 9-17 indicate a shift by reassignment. The value from one element is shifted to the next element in the array. The green arrows indicate the insertion of a value into a vacated array element after the shifting has taken place.

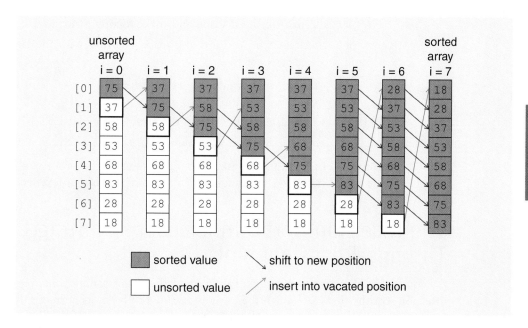

FIGURE 9-17   Ascending order insertion sort

The insertion sort differs from both the selection and bubble sorts in that it does not involve the Swap() method. Instead, data exchanges take place in the manner illustrated by the playing card example. That is, data is exchanged from a temporary location into a position vacated by data that has shifted to a new location.

The key to the insertion sort is that, within the outer loop, one value is selected for insertion into the sorted portion of the array and all sorted values greater than that value are relocated to accommodate its insertion into the correct spot.

Two special variables are required for the insertion sort. One of them, an integer variable called `temp`, temporarily stores the selected unsorted value that you intend to insert. The second, `vacant`, stores the location in the array that is available for insertion. The task of copying a value into `temp` is done immediately before the inner loop. The task of copying the value from `temp` into the vacant array element (`data[vacant]`) is performed immediately after the inner loop. The role of the inner loop is to shift data into position so that the proper element has been vacated and is ready for insertion.

A low-level algorithm for the insertion sort looks like this:

ALGORITHM 9-6: INSERTION SORT

1. For $n - 1$ times, do the following:

    1.1. Select the first unsorted value and make a copy of it (`temp`).

    1.2. For each element in the sorted portion (starting with the largest and moving backwards):

        1.2.1. If the sorted value is > `temp`, then reassign it (shift it to the next position).

    1.3. When finished, copy `temp` into the array element last vacated.

Step 1.2 (the inner loop) and its subtask, Step 1.2.1 describe the process of shifting data into new positions. These tasks are described in more detail in the next section.

The Insertion Sort's Inner Loop: Shifting Data Through Reassignment

As you saw with the playing card example and the data example (Figure 9-17), in an insertion sort the first element in the array is assumed to be in its correct sorted position. Insertion begins with the first element in the unsorted portion of the list. Consider the loop control variable of the outer loop (`i`). When `i` is set to 0 you can assume that element `data[0]` is sorted and that element `data[1]` contains the first unsorted value—the value you want to insert. In general, the first unsorted value is always `data[i+1]`.

The first unsorted value is copied into `temp` as shown in Example 9-4. As a result, you may assume that `data[i+1]` is now vacant and can be reused for other purposes. This is similar to pulling one card out of your hand.

EXAMPLE 9-4: USING A TEMPORARY VARIABLE

```
temp = data[i+1];
```

A vacated array element may still contain a value, but because a copy of that value is now stored in `temp`, the value stored in the original is expendable. In this case, the value from `data[i+1]` is now stored in `temp`, so `data[i+1]` can be reused. The variable `vacant` can be set to `i+1` to indicate which array element is now available for reuse.

Shifting a data value from one array element into the next is accomplished by reassigning a value to a vacated element. If the vacant array element is denoted as `data[vacant]` then the value that is shifted into it comes from the array element immediately below it (`data[vacant-1]`) as shown in Example 9-5.

EXAMPLE 9-5: SHIFTING STORAGE POSITIONS

```
data[vacant] = data[vacant-1];
```

The initialization clause of the inner loop begins by assigning the location of the first unsorted item to `vacant` as in Example 9-6.

EXAMPLE 9-6: ASSIGNING THE VACANT POSITION

9

```
vacant = i+1;
```

The update clause of the inner loop decrements `vacant`. This is important because as one element is shifted up into a vacant element, a new vacancy opens up below.

The process of shifting data into vacant elements continues as long as there are more sorted elements to consider (`vacant > 0`) and the next sorted element is larger than the one to be inserted (`data[vacant - 1] > temp`).

Examine the complete code for the insertion sort, shown in Example 9-7. Notice that the three clauses of the inner loop are spread across three lines. This convention makes them easier to identify on their own, although it works the same as if all three were on one line. With each iteration of the inner loop, another sorted data value is shifted up the array into a vacant element. This makes the array element it came from vacant and available to be assigned a new value. When the loop terminates, the insertion value (`temp`) is assigned to the vacant element.

EXAMPLE 9-7: INSERTION SORT CODE

```
//  INSERTION SORT
int vacant; // position of last vacated element
int temp;   // temporary copy of unsorted value
// outer loop
for (i=0; i < n-1; i++) {
   // inner loop
   temp = data[i+1]; // Copy first unsorted value
   for (vacant = i+1;
   ((vacant > 0) && (data[vacant-1] > temp));
   vacant--)
   {
      data[vacant] = data[vacant-1]; // shift data up
   }  // end inner loop
   data[vacant] = temp; // insert value into vacated element
}  // end outer loop
```

Comparing Sorting Algorithms

You have now examined three different sorting algorithms and their implementation. How can you compare them? Which of these algorithms is the best? One way to answer this question is to determine how complex each algorithm is. In Chapter 8 you used big-O functions to distinguish between the complexity of direct, sequential, and binary searching operations. big-O is a tool that can be applied here as well.

All three of our sorting algorithms use nested loops. In fact, all three use the same outer loop. The number of iterations of the outer loop is $n - 1$ in all cases.

The worst-case scenarios for the inner loops were also the same in all cases: $n - 1$. At worst, the inner loop of the selection sort would have to search $n - 1$ items to find the smallest value. At worst, the inner loop of the bubble sort would have to examine $n - 1$ adjacent pairs of elements. At worst, the inner loop of the insertion sort would have to slide $n - 1$ values into new positions.

Key operations such as comparisons and data movements, if embedded inside of the inner loop of any of these sorting methods could be executed, at worst, $(n - 1)$ $(n - 1)$ or $n^2 - 2n + 1$ times (multiplying the maximum iterations of the outer and inner loops together). Because the dominant term in this expression is n^2, the order of complexity, big-O, of these sorting algorithms is referred to as being $O(n^2)$. From the standpoint of big-O, all three sorting algorithms have the same level of complexity of $O(n^2)$.

However, having the same level of complexity does not mean that each of these sorting techniques are equally efficient. The efficiency of an algorithm is measured by factors such as the speed of task completion and the amount of storage and other computing resources the algorithm requires. Operations such as comparisons and data movements may correlate with speed and serve as indicators of efficiency.

From the standpoint of data movements (exchanging data values or sliding data values down an array by reassigning them), the advantage goes to the selection sort. Unlike the bubble sort and insertion sort, data movements for a selection sort are not located within the inner loop. The worst-case scenario for the selection sort is that it will call the `Swap()` method once for every iteration of the outer loop. The worst-case scenario for the bubble sort could mean calling the `Swap()` method numerous times within the inner loop alone (to say nothing of the inner loop having to repeat itself during each iteration of the outer loop). Similarly, the insertion sort must move data within the inner loop as values slide down the array. In the worst-case scenario for an insertion sort, all of the values in the sorted portion of the array would have to slide one position every time the outer loop executed, making it less efficient than the selection sort.

Tutorial: Vertical Bar Chart

This project provides you with the opportunity to implement one or more sorting algorithms. The interface you create will display the data, both before and after sorting, in the form of a vertical bar chart.

Problem Analysis

In this project you will create a program with an interface that consists of two panels, as shown in Figure 9-18. The panel on the left (`panel1`) displays an array of unsorted data values. The panel on the right (`panel2`) displays the sorted data. Data from an integer array are displayed in both panels as a vertical bar chart, with the data value to the left of the bar that represents it. The length of the bars is the number of pixels indicated by the value. You will sort the data using an ascending order selection sort.

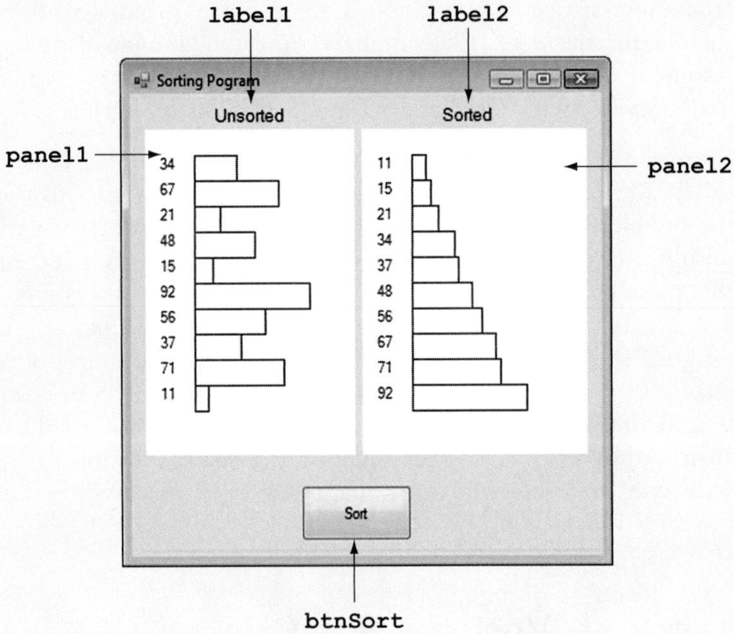

FIGURE 9-18 Unsorted and sorted vertical bar chart data

Design

There is no need for an interface sketch, given the working interface description in Figure 9-18. The main design work for this section focuses on the **Drawing** objects needed to construct the vertical bar chart displays in each panel.

DATA TABLE

This project requires three sets of variables. First, you need the required **Drawing** objects. Second, you need a set of variables for the selection sort code contained in **btnSort_Click()**. Third, you need a set of variables for an instance method called **DrawArray()** that draws the data distribution on the panels. The **btnSort_Click()** event will call **DrawArray()** once to draw the unsorted data in **panel1** and a second time to draw the sorted array in **panel2**.

VARIABLES REQUIRED FOR DRAWING

This program requires two **Graphics** objects (one for each panel). To draw a vertical bar chart, the program must draw **Rectangle** objects at specified locations using the **DrawRectangle()** method of the **Graphics** object. **DrawRectangle()** requires a **Pen** object (**blackPen**). You will also use the **DrawString()** method of the **Graphics** object to display the data values next to the bars in the bar chart. The **DrawString()** method requires a **Brush** object (**blackBrush**) and a **Font** object. You will use the same font shown on the interface in Figure 9-18: 8 point, Arial. Table 9-2 lists the various **Drawing** objects.

TABLE 9-2 Table of Required Drawing Objects

Object Name	Type	Usage
g1	Graphics	Graphics object for panel1
g2	Graphics	Graphics object for panel2
blackPen	Pen	Used to outline rectangles
blackBrush	SolidBrush	Used to draw strings
arial8Font	Font	Used to draw strings

VARIABLES REQUIRED FOR btnSort_Click()

The btnSort_Click() event handler is where the selection sort is implemented. From the examples earlier in the chapter (Table 9-1), you know that you need the variables listed in Table 9-3 to complete the sort operation.

TABLE 9-3 Data Table for btnSort_Click()

Variable	Data Type	Usage
data	int[10] array	Data array, values assigned when declared
n	int	The size of the array
smallIndex	int	Location of the smallest value in the unsorted portion of the array
j	int	Inner loop control variable and location of the current unsorted element
i	int	Outer loop control variable

VARIABLES REQUIRED FOR DrawArray()

The DrawArray() method draws a vertical bar chart on one of the two panels on form1. The signature for DrawArray() is shown in Example 9-8.

9

EXAMPLE 9-8: DrawArray() METHOD SIGNATURE

```
private: void DrawArray(int arr[], int n, int panel)
```

The first formal parameter (arr[]) is an array of integers. The second (n) is the size of that array. The third (panel) is an integer that indicates which panel to draw on (1 = panel1, 2 = panel2).

When first called from btnSort_Click(), DrawArray() needs to know that it must draw on panel1 (unsorted data). This means that the third actual parameter must be the integer 1. For example:

```
DrawArray(data, n, 1);
```

When called the second time from btnSort_Click(), DrawArray() needs to know that it must draw on panel2. This means that the third actual parameter must be the integer 2. For example:

```
DrawArray(data, n, 2);
```

The use of Rectangles and the Drawstring() method requires x- and y-coordinates to locate the point at the upper-left corner of the Drawing object. Rectangles also require a width and height. Variables for DrawArray() are listed in Table 9-4.

TABLE 9-4 Table of Required Drawing Objects

Variable	Data Type	Usage
g	Graphics	Graphics object for drawing on either panel
arr	int[10] array	Data array, values assigned when declared
n	int	The size of the array
panel	int	Which panel to draw on
x	int	The x-coordinate of the upper-left corner
y	int	The y-coordinate of the upper-left corner
height	int	Height of each bar (20 pixels)
width	int	Width of each bar

ALGORITHM FOR DrawArray()

The algorithm for the **DrawArray()** method requires the program to decide which panel to draw on. After this decision has been made, a loop executes, displaying each of the data values and drawing their corresponding bars in the selected panel. The algorithm for the **DrawArray()** method looks like this:

ALGORITHM 9-7: DrawArray()

1. Declare variables.
2. Decide which panel to draw on.

    2.1. If panel = 1 then:

        2.1.1. Refresh panel1.

        2.1.2. Assign panel1's Graphics object to g

    2.2. Else:

        2.2.1. Refresh panel2.

        2.2.2. Assign panel2's Graphics object to g

When drawing the vertical bar chart in a panel, the program starts at a designated x- and y-coordinate and works its way down in the y-axis direction. A loop running *n* times visits each array element and draws a bar representing its data value. If you assign 20 as the width of a bar, then the program can advance down the panel by adding 20 to the y-coordinate each time. This gives each bar a new location directly under the previous one. The algorithm for the drawing loop is shown in Algorithm 9-8.

ALGORITHM 9-8: DRAWING A RECTANGLE

3. For each element in the array from index 0 to *n* − 1:

    3.1. Add 20 to the y-coordinate.

    3.2. Set the width to the array element's data value.

    3.3. Use DrawString() to display the data value on the panel.

    3.4. Construct the Rectangle object.

    3.5. Draw the Rectangle on the panel.

Development

The biggest challenges in this project are found in the sorting algorithm and the task of drawing the bar chart. The following sections discuss the code for all major parts of this project. Pay special attention to the **DrawArray()** method.

CODING

The major coding tasks for this project include the following:

- The `Drawing` object declarations and constructor calls
- The `btnSort_Click()` event handler
- The `Swap()` method—already presented in Example 9-1
- The `DrawArray()` method

Instance variable declarations and `Form1_Load()` The `Drawing` variables were identified in Table 9-4. Their declarations, as well as the constructor calls in `Form1_Load()`, are shown in Example 9-9.

EXAMPLE 9-9: INSTANCE VARIABLES AND `Form1_Load()`

```
// Instance variables
   Pen^ blackPen;
   Graphics^ g1;
   Graphics^ g2;
   Brush^ blackBrush;
   System::Drawing::Font^ arial8Font;

private: System::Void Form1_Load(System::Object^
sender, System::EventArgs^ e) {
   g1 = panel1->CreateGraphics();
   g2 = panel2->CreateGraphics();
   blackPen = gcnew Pen(Color::Black);
   blackBrush = gcnew SolidBrush(Color::Black);
   arial8Font = gcnew System::Drawing::Font("Arial",8);
}
```

This program could have declared all `Drawing` objects in the `DrawArray()` method; however, doing so limits the expansion of this program's capabilities by localizing the `Drawing` objects within the scope of a single method.

Creating the code the `btnSort_Click()` Event Handler The selection sort algorithm is implemented in `btnSort_Click()` using the selection sort strategy developed earlier in the text. The `DrawArray()` method is called twice from this event handler. In response to the first call, the method draws the unsorted data array in `panel1`. The second call occurs after the selection sort is over and the data is sorted; at this point, the method draws the sorted data array in `panel2`.

The variables declared within `btnSort_Click()` include the array (`data[]`), which is assigned its values; the size of the array (n); loop control variables for the outer and inner loops of the selection sort (i and j respectively); and the location of the smallest value (`smallIndex`). The selection sort code from Example 9-2 can be inserted in the middle of `btnSort_Click()` as shown in Example 9-10.

EXAMPLE 9-10: `btnSort_Click()`

```
private: System::Void btnSort_Click(System::Object^
sender, System::EventArgs^ e) {
    int data[] = {34,67,21,48,15,92,56,37,71,11};
    int n = 10; // the size of the array
    int i, j;    // loop control variables
    int smallIndex;  // the index of the smallest value

    DrawArray(data, n, 1); // draw unsorted array in panel1

    // INSERT SELECTION SORT CODE (Example 9-2)

    DrawArray(data, n, 2); // draw sorted array in panel2
}
```

Coding the `DrawArray()` method   The code for the `DrawArray()` method follows the algorithm line for line. In Example 9-11 you see the variable declarations that establish the x- and y-coordinate locations, the height of `Rectangle` objects, and declare the `Graphics` object handle g.

EXAMPLE 9-11: THE `DrawArray()` METHOD

```
// Declare variables
int x = 40;     // x coordinate (40 pixels from the left edge)
int y = 0;      // y coordinate (at the top of the panel)
int height = 20;    // bar height set to 20 pixels
int width;      // the width of the bar
Graphics^ g;
```

Figure 9-19 illustrates the locations of the starting x- and y-coordinates (40, 0) as well as those of the upper-left corner of each bar, used to represent each data value in the array. The x-coordinate does not change throughout the course of the loop. It provides a same horizontal position for each `Rectangle,` ensuring that all of the bars in the vertical bar chart are aligned to the same location on the left side. The height of each rectangle is set to 20 pixels. The width of each rectangle is set to the data value for that array element.

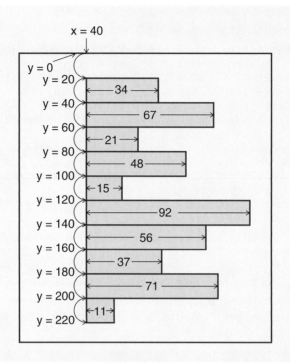

FIGURE 9-19 Vertical bar chart coordinate locations and dimensions

The `Graphics` variable (g) is unassigned (belongs to no object). This allows it to take on the value of one of the other `Graphics` objects (g1 or g2) when the program decides which panel to draw on. See Example 9-12.

EXAMPLE 9-12: ASSIGNING GRAPHICS OBJECTS

```
// Decide which panel to draw on
if (panel == 1)
{
    panel1->Refresh();
    g = g1;
}
else
{
    panel2->Refresh();
    g = g2;
}
```

After the program has selected a panel to draw on, the loop that draws each bar can execute. It adds the bar `height` (20 pixels) to `y` to establish the location of the upper-left corner of the next rectangle. The width of the rectangle is assigned a value from the data array. The data value is then printed (30 pixels to the left of where the bar begins using the `DrawString()` method). Finally the bar (rectangle) is drawn.

EXAMPLE 9-13: DRAWING THE BARS

```
// loop to draw the bars
for (int i = 0; i < n; i++)
{
    y += height;
    width = arr[i];
    g->DrawString(arr[i].ToString(), arial8Font, blackBrush,x-30,y);
    Rectangle bar(x, y, width, height);
    g->DrawRectangle(blackPen, bar);
}
```

Testing

Run your program to test it. The results should match the results shown in Figure 9-18. If the sorting method appears not to be working correctly, check for these three common mistakes:

- Make sure the `Swap()` method uses reference parameters (`&`), not value parameters. If it uses value parameters, no exchanges of data values will take place.
- Make sure the outer loop executes $n - 1$ times.
- Make sure the inner loop begins with `j` set to `i+1` and continues as long as `j` is less than `n`.

9

ON YOUR OWN

This chapter has discussed a number of sorting algorithms, but only implemented one of them, the selection sort. This section provides you with the opportunity to experiment with the other sorting strategies.

TASK 1. BUBBLE SORT BUTTON

Change the **Text** property of `btnSort` to "Selection Sort" and then add a new button with the caption "Bubble Sort". Modify the tutorial project so that, when the new button is clicked, the program sorts the data in ascending order using a bubble sort. Assign your bubble sort data array different values from those in the selection sort's data array.

TASK 2. INSERTION SORT BUTTON

Add a third button labeled "Insertion Sort". Modify the tutorial project so that when this new button is clicked, the program sorts the data in ascending order using an insertion sort. Assign your insertion sort data array different values from those in the selection sort and bubble sort data arrays.

QUICK REVIEW

1. Sorting is the process of arranging data values in order relative to one another.

2. Arrays of primitive types have no built-in sorting method.

3. Data sorted in ascending order is arranged from lowest to highest.

4. Data sorted in descending order is arranged from highest to lowest.

5. An exchange of data values requires that the value from one cell be assigned to a second, while the value in the second cell is assigned to the first.

6. A programmer-defined instance method called `Swap()`, which exchanges values, is commonly used by sorting programs.

7. Exchanging two values in a `Swap()` method requires a temporary variable and three assignment statements.

8. `Swap()` methods require reference parameters.

9. The sorting algorithms covered in this chapter are selection, bubble, and insertion.

10. All three sorting algorithms use nested loops.

11. All three sorting algorithms work with a sorted and unsorted portion of the array.

12. In the course of processing data, the sorted portion grows until it includes every element.

13. After the outer loop executes, one unsorted value is guaranteed to have been correctly placed into its sorted position.

14. The inner loop controls element processing, which differs according to the sorting algorithm.

15. The selection sort selects one item to be put into its proper place for each iteration of the outer loop.

16. The selection sort calls a `Swap()` method once in each iteration of the outer loop.

17. The selection sort requires $n - 1$ iterations of the outer loop.

18. The role of the inner loop in a selection sort discussed in this chapter is to find the location of the smallest unsorted value.

19. The selection sort exchanges the value at the top of the unsorted section with the smallest value in the unsorted portion of the array.

20. The outer loop of a bubble sort makes $n - 1$ iterations.

21. The bubble sort positions the swap method call within the inner loop.

22. The inner loop compares the values of each adjacent pair of array elements and exchanges them according to the ordering principle.

23. The insertion sort does not call a `Swap()` method explicitly, but does exchange data values.

24. The insertion sort algorithm is similar to that used by card players to sort cards in their hand.

25. The outer loop of the insertion sort makes $n - 1$ passes.

26. The inner loop of the insertion sort begins by copying the first data item in the unsorted portion of the list to a temporary memory cell.

27. The inner loop of the insertion sort shifts the sorted data values down the array until it creates an unused, or vacant, element and inserts the value there.

28. The selection, bubble, and insertion sorts each have a big-O of $O(n^2)$.

29. Although their order of complexity may be the same, the efficiency of each type of sort may be very different.

30. Efficiency refers to speed and the use of system resources.

31. The selection sort requires the least amount of data movements and is more efficient in this regard than either the bubble sort or the insertion sort.

TERMS TO KNOW

ascending order
bubble sort
descending order
exchange
insertion sort
$O(n^2)$
selection sort
`Swap()`

EXERCISES

1. How many assignment statements are required to exchange the values stored in two variables?

    a. 2

    b. 3

    c. 4

    d. 5

    e. Cannot be determined

2. The Swap() method requires that the formal parameters be _____.

   a. integers

   b. actual parameters

   c. reference parameters

   d. objects

   e. None of the above

3. Which of the following sorting algorithms calls the Swap() method from the inner loop?

   a. Selection sort

   b. Bubble sort

   c. Insertion sort

   d. All of the above

   e. None of the above

4. Which of the following sorting algorithms calls the Swap() method from the outer loop?

   a. Selection sort

   b. Bubble sort

   c. Insertion sort

   d. All of the above

   e. None of the above

5. Which of the following sorting algorithms shifts data values to create space for the next sorted value?

   a. Selection sort

   b. Bubble sort

   c. Insertion sort

   d. All of the above

   e. None of the above

6. Which sorting method does not call the Swap() method?

   a. Selection sort

   b. Bubble sort

   c. Insertion sort

   d. All of the above

   e. All sorting methods must call a Swap() method

7. Which of the following analogies pertains to the bubble sort?

    a. It resembles effervescing bubbles in a newly poured drink.

    b. Its logic is similar to that used to arrange students in order by height, one student at a time.

    c. It is like arranging playing cards in your hand.

    d. None of the above

8. Which of the following analogies pertains to the insertion sort?

    a. It resembles effervescing bubbles in a newly poured drink.

    b. Its logic is similar to that used to arrange students in order by height, one student at a time.

    c. It is like arranging playing cards in your hand.

    d. None of the above

9. Which of the following analogies pertains to the selection sort?

    a. It resembles effervescing bubbles in a newly poured drink.

    b. Its logic is similar to that used to arrange students in order by height, one student at a time.

    c. It is like arranging playing cards in your hand.

    d. None of the above

10. Which strategy is used by the selection sort discussed in this chapter?

    a. Search an array looking for the smallest value.

    b. Compare the values stored in adjacent array elements, and exchange them if the first is larger than the second.

    c. Select the first value from the unsorted portion of the array, and put it in a vacated array element.

11. Which strategy is used by the bubble sort discussed in this chapter?

    a. Search an array looking for the smallest value.

    b. Compare the values stored in adjacent array elements, and exchange them if the first is larger than the second.

    c. Select the first value from the unsorted portion of the array, and put it in a vacated array element.

12. Which strategy is used by the insertion sort discussed in this chapter?

    a. Search an array looking for the smallest value.

    b. Compare the values stored in adjacent array elements, and exchange them if the first is larger than the second.

    c. Select the first value from the unsorted portion of the array, and put it in a vacated array element.

9

13. Which of the following strategies could a descending order selection sort use?

   a. Search the unsorted portion of the data array for the largest value and exchange it with the first element in the unsorted portion of the array.

   b. Exchange the values in adjacent pairs of array elements only if the first value is smaller than the second.

   c. Shift values in an array only if they are less than the value you want to insert.

14. Which of the following strategies could a descending order insertion sort use?

   a. Search the unsorted portion of the data array for the largest value and exchange it with the first element in the unsorted portion of the array.

   b. Exchange the values in adjacent pairs of array elements only if the first value is smaller than the second.

   c. Shift values in an array only if they are less than the value you want to insert.

15. Which of the following strategies could a descending order bubble sort use?

   a. Search the unsorted portion of the data array for the largest value and exchange it with the first element in the unsorted portion of the array.

   b. Exchange the values in adjacent pairs of array elements only if the first value is smaller than the second.

   c. Shift values in an array only if they are less than the value you want to insert.

16. In the worst-case scenario for a selection sort, the outer loop executes _____.

   a. one time

   b. $n - 1$ times

   c. $n^2 - 2n + 1$ times

   d. n^2 times

17. Which of the following sorting algorithms has an overall complexity of $O(n^2)$?

   a. Selection sort

   b. Bubble sort

   c. Insertion sort

   d. All of the above

   e. None of the above

18. Given an unsorted array, which of these sorting techniques is most likely to sort an array fastest?

   a. Selection sort

   b. Bubble sort

   c. Insertion sort

   d. They will all take the same amount of time.

19. An array contains the following data values {76, 54, 32, 21, 10}. Which of the following is true about the array?

   a. It was produced by a selection sort.

   b. It was produced by an insertion sort.

   c. It is not sorted.

   d. The data are in ascending order.

   e. The data are in descending order.

20. What kind of sort is implemented in the following code? Explain how you know this.

```
void sortit(int a[], int n)

{      for (int i=0; i<n-1; i++)

             for (int j=0; j<n-1; j++)

                    if (a[j] > a[j+1]) swap(a[j], a[j+1]);
}
```

PROGRAMMING EXERCISES

1. **Random Numbers**

   Modify the program you created in the tutorial so that whenever btnSort is clicked it generates an array of 10 random numbers rather than relying on you to assign specific values to your array. After btnSort generates the 10 new random numbers for the array it draws the vertical bar chart of this unsorted, random data in panel1 whenever it is clicked.

2. **Descending Order**

   Modify the project you created in the tutorial so that it sorts the data in descending order instead of ascending order, as shown in Figure 9-20.

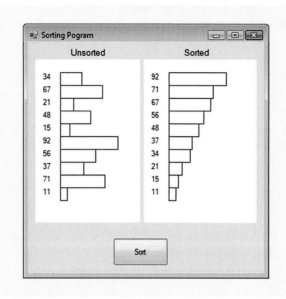

FIGURE 9-20 Descending order selection sort

3. **While Loops**

   While loops can be used to speed up sorting algorithms. For example, one of the biggest problems with a bubble sort constructed of nested for loops is that it mindlessly continues to check all pairs of elements with each iteration of the outer loop even if the list was sorted to begin with. A better version of this sort would notice when the list becomes fully sorted and stop. One method for doing this is to have the algorithm check to see whether any exchanges had to be made in the previous pass through the outer loop. If no exchanges were made, you know that the array has been sorted and the outer loop can be exited.

   Write a program that converts the bubble sort shown in this chapter, changing the outer loop from a for loop to a while loop, so that an early exit is possible when the list becomes sorted.

   You will need to use a Boolean variable to control the outer loop, as in this example:

   ```
   bool sorted = false;
   while (!sorted) {
       // bubble sort statements go here}
   ```

4. **Horizontal Bar Charts—Selection Sort**

   Write a program that produces a horizontal bar chart, like those shown in Figure 9-21. You may initialize an array of twenty integers with values of your own choosing, although they must fall in the range 0 to 13. Include RadioButtons that the user can click in order to select sorting order (ascending or descending) You must use a selection sort for this assignment.

a. program at startup

b. unsorted data

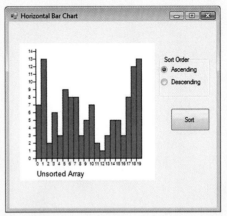

c. ascending order

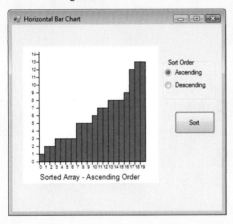

d. descending order

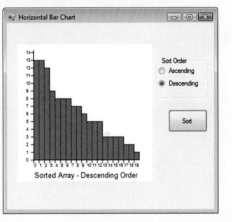

FIGURE 9-21 Horizontal bar chart

When the program begins, the text displayed in the button must be "Start", as shown in Figure 9-21a. Clicking the button displays the unsorted data array as shown in Figure 9-21b and changes the button's **Text** property to "Sort".

From that point on, clicking the button will sort the data in either ascending order (Figure 9-21c) or descending order (Figure 9-21d) and display the data.

5. **Horizontal Bar Charts—Other Sorts**

Implement Programming Exercise 4 using ascending and descending order insertion sorts instead of selection sorts.

RECURSION

IN THIS CHAPTER, YOU WILL:

- Discover how to recognize a recursive problem
- Code a recursive method
- Use recursion to draw fractal images
- Analyze recursion
- Create and code menus

By now you are very familiar with the use of iteration (loops) to solve problems. You have used loops as the framework for both sorting and searching methods. They are of fundamental importance. However, a loop is not the only way to repeat a series of instructions. You can also use recursion, a programming technique in which a method calls itself.

In this chapter you will learn how to use recursion to solve problems that would be very challenging to solve using iteration alone. Along the way, you will see how knowledge of recursive techniques opens up a new world of graphic image production. The chapter begins with a discussion of a simple numeric problem with a recursive solution and ends by applying recursive methods to a program that produces fascinating visual patterns.

Factorial Numbers

As you recall from Chapter 6, factorial numbers are denoted with the exclamation mark (!) symbol.

You will recall that, by definition, 0! is 1. Here are examples of the factorial method used to calculate the factorials of 5, 4, 3, 2, and 1:

$5! = 5 \times 4 \times 3 \times 2 \times 1 = 120$

$4! = 4 \times 3 \times 2 \times 1 = 24$

$3! = 3 \times 2 \times 1 = 6$

$2! = 2 \times 1 = 2$

$1! = 1$

To calculate the factorial of a number you multiply it by each of the successive values smaller than it, down to 1. In general, for any positive integer n,

$n! = n(n-1)(n-2)...1$

Calculating factorial numbers can be done very efficiently using a `for` loop. The steps for calculating 5! are shown in Example 10-1. This example uses the loop control variable (`i`) to provide the values from 5 down to 1. The variable `factorial` starts out set to 1 and then the loop multiplies it by 5, then 4, then 3, then 2, then 1 as the loop control variable (`i`) gets smaller with each iteration. When `i` becomes 0, the loop is over and the calculation of the factorial number `factorial` is finished.

EXAMPLE 10-1: FACTORIAL LOOP

```
int factorial = 1;
for (int i = 5; i > 0; i--)
    factorial *= i;
```

Although loops are efficient ways to calculate factorial numbers, they are not the only way. Notice that 5! is $5 \times 4 \times 3 \times 2 \times 1$, but it is also true that

$$5! = 5 \times 4!$$

as $4! = 4 \times 3 \times 2 \times 1$.

In general, the factorial of any positive integer n is n multiplied by the factorial of $(n-1)$:

$$n! = n \times (n-1)!$$

So, each of the following is also a valid way to express these factorial numbers:

$$5! = 5 \times 4!$$
$$4! = 4 \times 3!$$
$$3! = 3 \times 2!$$
$$2! = 2 \times 1!$$
$$1! = 1$$

This provides us with an interesting new way to solve the problem. Example 10-2 calculates 5! without using a loop. There are five variables (fact1, fact2, fact3, fact4, fact5) that store the factorials of 1, 2, 3, 4, and 5 respectively. You start at the bottom. One factorial is 1 (fact1 = 1;). Two factorial is 2 * 1!. Three factorial is 3 * 2!. Four factorial is 4 * 3!. Finally, five factorial is 5 * 4!.

EXAMPLE 10-2: FACTORIAL SEQUENCE

```
int fact1, fact2, fact3, fact4, fact5;
fact1 = 1;              // 1! = 1
fact2 = 2 * fact1;      // 2! = 2 * 1!
fact3 = 3 * fact2;      // 3! = 3 * 2!
fact4 = 4 * fact3;      // 4! = 4 * 3!
fact5 = 5 * fact4;      // 5! = 5 * 4!
```

What is interesting about this approach is that it starts at the bottom (with 1!) and works its way up to the final answer. At every step, you know the factorial of the previous values and simply multiply that by the current value.

The approach taken in Example 10-2 would not be practical for computing the factorial of a large number because there would be too many steps. For such a situation, the loop is always the better choice as it would not require more instructions than are shown in Example 10-1. However, the value of Example 10-2 is that it illustrates a new way of solving the problem, from the bottom up.

Recursion

Recursion is the process of a method calling itself. This may seem like a strange thing to do, but it is a way to implement the bottom-up approach to a problem similar in some ways to the one you saw in Example 10-2. Let us start with a less mathematical example. Suppose you are looking for a new apartment. You contact a realtor. The realtor knows of a good apartment for you, but will have to contact the landlord to arrange for a viewing. The landlord must contact the current tenant to set up a time. A chain of phone calls is set up that ends with the current tenant, as shown in Figure 10-1.

FIGURE 10-1 Chain of calls to solve apartment problem

When the tenant checks her schedule, she will get back to the landlord. The landlord will get back to the realtor, and finally the realtor will get back to you. A chain of returning calls backtracks through those originally involved until it gets to you, the person who originated the calling sequence, as shown in Figure 10-2 (which must be read from the bottom up).

FIGURE 10-2 Return calls solving the problem (read this figure from the bottom up)

Now consider how these same people could use a similar phone call technique to solve the factorial problem. Because these are all bright people, they should be able to solve the problem of calculating 4! from the bottom up. Assume that each person gets a list of instructions (an algorithm) that looks like this:

ALGORITHM 10-1: FACTORIAL ALGORITHM

1. If you are asked what 1 factorial is, the answer is 1.

2. If you are asked what the factorial of any other positive integer (n) is, you can calculate $n!$ by multiplying n by $(n - 1)!$. However, you will have to call someone who can tell you what $(n - 1)!$ is first. When that person returns your call with the result, you will perform the multiplication to get $n!$ and then get back to the person who called you in the first place to provide your answer.

So if you get a call and are asked what 3! is, you know that 3! is 3 multiplied by 2!. To find out how much 2! is you call someone for that information. When you get the 2! answer, you can multiply that amount by 3 to get 3! and then return the original call.

The calling process is shown in Figure 10-3.

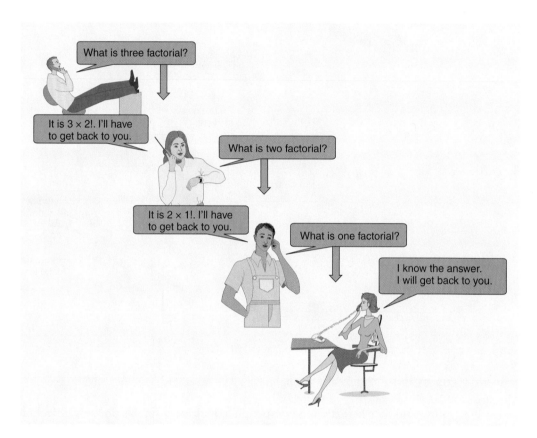

FIGURE 10-3 Chain of calls to solve factorial problem

The last person in the chain has the easy job. One factorial is 1, so she can return the call to the previous caller and tell him. He can use that information to calculate 2! and then return the call to the person that called him, giving his result. She can take that result and multiply it by 3 to get 3! and then return the original call. Now that you know what 3! is, it is a simple matter to multiply that value by 4, arriving at 4!. The return process is shown in Figure 10-4 (which must be read from the bottom up).

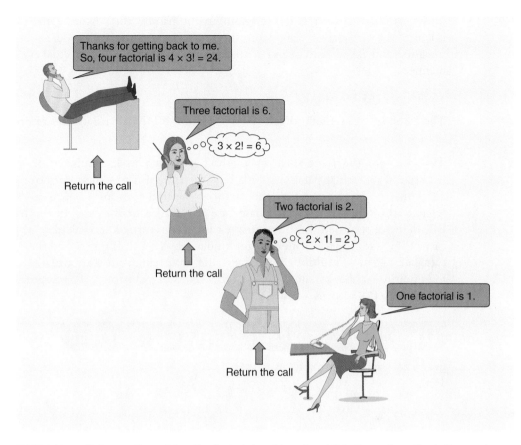

FIGURE 10-4 Return calls, solving the factorial problem (read this figure from the bottom up)

Now take the algorithm you gave each caller and see if it can be turned into a C++ method that can be used to calculate the factorial of any positive integer. The algorithm must handle two situations. The first, called the **base case**, is the situation that applies to the end of the chain of calls. In our example, the base case handles the determination of what 1! is. By definition, 1! is 1.

The second situation, called the **recursive case**, refers to every situation in the chain of calls in which one result cannot be determined until the results are received back from another call. For example, 3! cannot be calculated until 2! has been provided. The process of calling a method that in turn calls another version of that same method is referred to as a **recursive call**. As you have seen, a chain of recursive calls may have to be made until the base case is encountered. (The base case is 1! in the phone call example.) When the base case is encountered, the answer is passed back to the previous call, which allows computation to finish and return to its previous call, and so on until you are back to the original with the answer. This process of returning a chain of method calls is referred to as **recursive backtracking**.

Now, consider how a C++ program might handle this. Assume that you want to calculate the factorial of 4 and store the result in the integer variable `fact4`. You could use a method called `Factorial()` that returns the factorial of its actual argument in this manner:

```
fact4 = Factorial(4);
```

The `Factorial()` method calculates the value of 4! and assigns the returned result to `fact4`.

The code for the `Factorial()` method is shown in Example 10-3. It returns the factorial of its formal parameter (n). For example, if n is 4 then `Factorial()` returns 4!, which is 24. Notice that the factorial method uses an `if...else` statement to separate the two key tasks: the base case and the recursive case. In the base case, if n is 1, then 1 is returned. In the recursive case, n! is returned. To calculate n! the recursive case of the `Factorial()` method multiplies n by (n-1)!. If n is 4 then the recursive case calculates 4! as 4 multiplied by the value returned from `Factorial(3)`. This step temporarily suspends activity in the current version of `Factorial()` until `Factorial(3)` returns a value.

EXAMPLE 10-3: RECURSIVE `Factorial()` METHOD

```
private: int Factorial(int n)
{
    if  (n == 1)
        return 1;              // base case
    else
        return  n * Factorial(n-1);  // recursive case
}
```

Recursive methods call each other to resolve smaller versions of the same problem until the base case is reached, as shown in Figure 10-5. To solve `Factorial(4)` you multiply 4 by `Factorial(3)`. To solve `Factorial(3)` you multiply 3 by `Factorial(2)`. To solve `Factorial(2)` you multiply 2 by `Factorial(1)`.

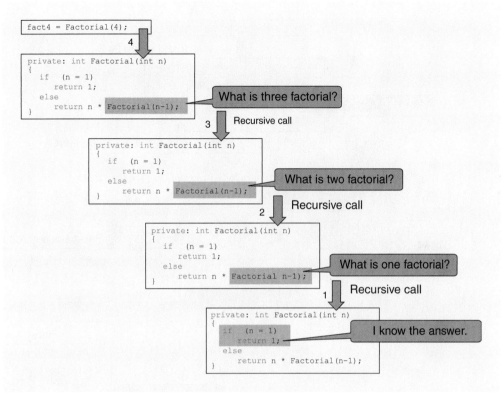

FIGURE 10-5 Chain of recursive calls until factorial base case reached

The base case stops the recursive process by returning 1! (the value 1) to the `Factorial(2)` method that called it. The `Factorial(2)` method can now complete its calculation and return the result to the `Factorial(3)` method that called it. The `Factorial(3)` method can calculate 3! and return the result to the `Factorial(4)` method that called it. The `Factorial(4)` method can calculate 4! and return the result to the statement that called it. The recursive backtracking process continues until a value (24) is returned to the original call

```
fact4 = Factorial(4);
```

as shown in Figure 10-6, which should be read from the bottom up.

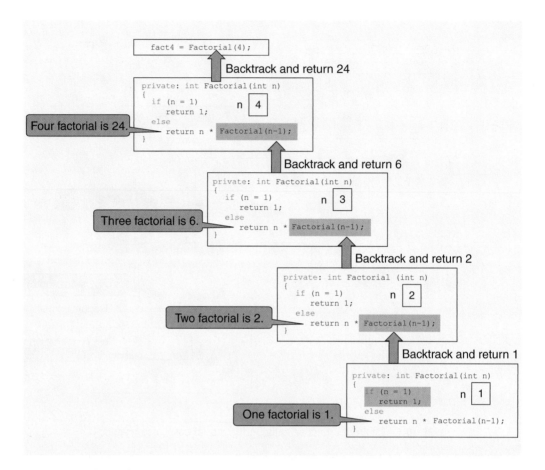

FIGURE 10-6 Recursive backtracking to solve 4! (read this figure from the bottom up)

Recursion Versus Iteration

As you have seen, there are two different ways to use repetition to solve a problem: loops (iterative solutions) and recursion. How do you decide when to use recursion and when to use iteration?

The iterative version (using the `for` loop) has much to offer. Loops are easy to write. In general, recursive solutions are often more difficult to reason through than iterative solutions. For most of us, the recursive process seems alien to our normal way of thinking. The more difficult a program is to design and code, the more difficult it may be to debug and maintain.

The iterative approach is also faster. Iterative code can be executed quickly and directly because, unlike recursion, the program does not have to also manage the memory and processing resources required by repeated method calls.

On the other hand, as we have seen, there is a high degree of correspondence between the definition of factorial (Algorithm 10-1) and the recursive C++ method (Example 10-3). Mathematical definitions, like factorial, that use recursion to define themselves are called **inductive definitions**. There are many mathematical processes with inductive definitions. Recursion is a simple and elegant way of representing them.

Some problems that would require long, complex iterative solutions can be more effectively addressed by short, elegant recursive solutions. For example, consider the problem of drawing fractal images. **Fractal images** are images composed of geometric shapes that repeat the same formula in differing proportions. The word **fractal** refers to the repetition of shapes that sometimes appear as "fractured" images or smaller pieces of a larger shape. The most important method for producing fractals is through recursion. Figure 10-7 is an example of a public domain fractal image available on the Web at http://commons.wikimedia.org/wiki/Image:Mandelpart2.jpg.

In this image you can see shapes built from many smaller versions of similar shapes. The recursive fractal imagery creates a captivating and fanciful landscape.

FIGURE 10-7 Fractal image landscape from *http://commons.wikimedia.org/wiki/Image:Mandelpart2.jpg*

Creating Fractal Images

Although an image such as that shown in Figure 10-7 is beyond the scope of this book, it is possible to create images on a smaller, less complicated scale based on recursive drawing processes. As an illustration of how recursion and fractal images work together, consider the following image creation scenario in which several levels of recursion are used.

We will start by walking through the recursive process as if you were drawing a fractal image by hand. Later, in the tutorial, you will create a computer program that will allow you to select various features and then draw an image for you. To begin the first level of recursion, the initial task involves drawing a line that is 100 pixels long, as shown in Figure 10-8.

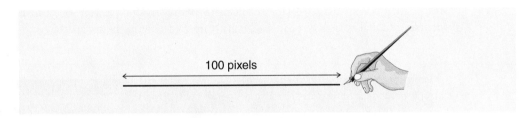

100 pixels

FIGURE 10-8 Level 1—drawing a 100-pixel line

A set of rules determines how each new level of recursive line-drawing proceeds:

- Each new line starts from the end of the previous line.
- Each new line is half the length of the previous line.
- Each new line is drawn at a specified angle relative to the original line.

Now move to a second level of recursion and add more lines (branches) to the original one. Your line drawing method will be used three times, following the rules just established. Each of the three lines is half the length of the original (50 pixels), and each starts at the end point of the original line. The first one runs along the same direction as the original (an angle difference of 0 degrees). The second line runs at a 90-degree difference (+90 clockwise) from the original angle. The third runs at a 90-degree difference (-90 counter-clockwise) from the original angle. The original line (shown in black) and the new lines are shown in Figure 10-9. In effect, you have drawn three branches on the end of the original line.

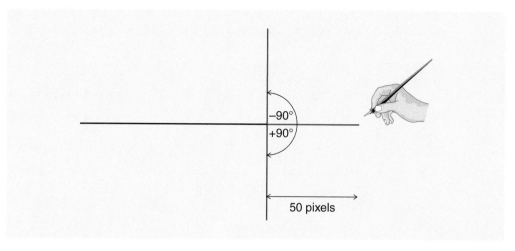

FIGURE 10-9 Level 2—drawing three branches, half as long, from the end point of the original at 0, +90, and -90 degrees

The recursive nature of this problem is about to become apparent because the next level repeats the process for each line branch from the previous level. You drew three lines in level 2, so in level 3 you will have to repeat the process of adding new lines (branches) to the end of each of them. Figure 10-10 illustrates the drawing of three more lines, each 25 pixels in length, at angles of 0, +90, and -90 degrees from the end of one of the previous lines.

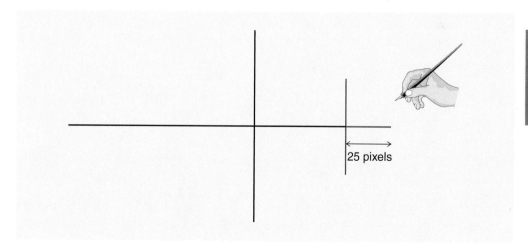

FIGURE 10-10 Level 3—drawing lines for one of the three previous lines

Figure 10-11 illustrates the completion of the tasks at this level. Nine new lines had to be drawn from the end of the three lines drawn at level 2.

FIGURE 10-11 Level 3—completed with branches drawn from the end point of all level-2 lines

The next level, level 4, continues the recursive process by drawing three branches at the end of each of the nine lines drawn in level 3. This will mean the addition of 27 new lines, as shown in Figure 10-12.

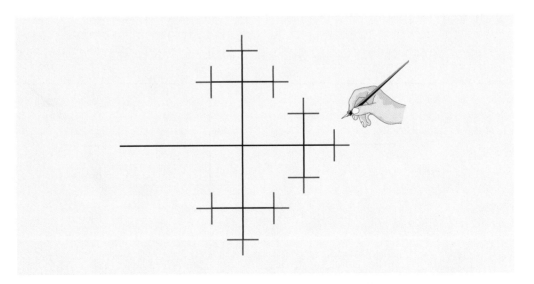

FIGURE 10-12 Level 4—branches added to the end of those created at level 3

Finally, at the fifth level of recursion, three branches are added from the end point of each of the 27 lines created at level 4. This step necessitates drawing 81 new lines as shown in Figure 10-13.

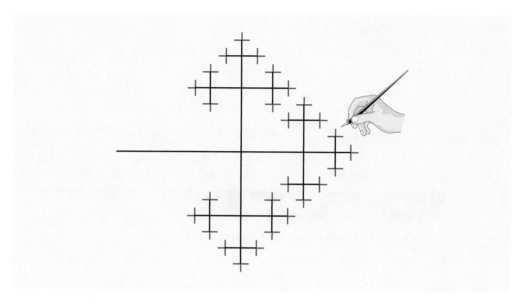

FIGURE 10-13 Level 5—branches added to the end of those created at level 4

The process is recursive. At each level it carries out the same tasks that were carried out at the previous level, only in a smaller version. Of course, the process you started could continue to another level, which would require $3 \times 81 = 243$ lines, and another level ($3 \times 243 = 729$ lines), and so on. At some point you need to stop drawing lines. In this particular case, you decide that level 5 is the stopping point (the base case) and call your drawing complete.

Computer-Generated Fractal Images

The computer can be used to produce an image similar to the one you made in the previous section based on five levels of recursion and a set of rules determining what must happen at each level.

Drawing Lines with `DrawLine()`

You are already familiar with some features of the `System::Graphics` class. In Chapter 6 you used a `Graphics` object and the `FillEllipse()` method to draw a sun and one or more planets revolving around it. In Chapters 7 and 8 you drew rectangles with `DrawRectangle()` and `FillRectangle()`. In this chapter you will use a system-defined class method for drawing lines, called `DrawLine()`. The `DrawLine()` method requires five parameters, as shown below.

```
DrawLine( Pen, x₁, y₁, x₂, y₂)
```

The first parameter is the Pen object with which the line will be drawn. The second and third parameters (x_1, y_1) are the x- and y-coordinates of the starting point of the line. The fourth and fifth parameters (x_2, y_2) are the x- and y-coordinates of the ending point of the line.

Assume that the following integer variables exist in a Visual C++ program and have already been initialized:

- x—The x-coordinate of the start of the line
- y—The y-coordinate of the start of the line
- newX—The x-coordinate of the end of the line
- newY—The y-coordinate of the end of the line
- blackPen—A Drawing::Pen object assigned to Color::Black

Example 10-4 shows how DrawLine() would be used with these particular variables to draw a black line from the point (x, y) to the point (newX, newY).

EXAMPLE 10-4: DRAWING A LINE

```
g->DrawLine(blackPen,x,y,newX,newY);
```

The Recursive DrawBranch() Method

Figure 10-14 shows an image produced with three levels of recursion using the method of drawing by hand discussed earlier. Notice that the branches drawn in each of the level of recursion have a different color. The first level is shown as a black line. The branches added to it (the second level) are green. The branches added in the third level are yellow.

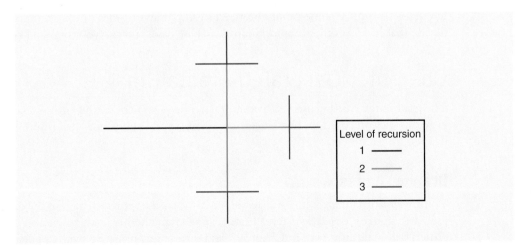

FIGURE 10-14 Three levels of recursion with color used to show which lines are drawn at which level

Now consider a recursive, programmer-defined method called DrawBranch() that uses DrawLine() to draw a line. After the line is drawn, DrawBranch() calls itself recursively three times (to draw three branches off of the end of that line). The process is the same as you did by hand earlier in the chapter. To draw the 13 lines shown in Figure 10-14 `DrawBranch()` must be called 13 times, as shown in Figure 10-15. The recursive calls are colored to correspond to the lines drawn at each level of recursion indicated in Figure 10-14.

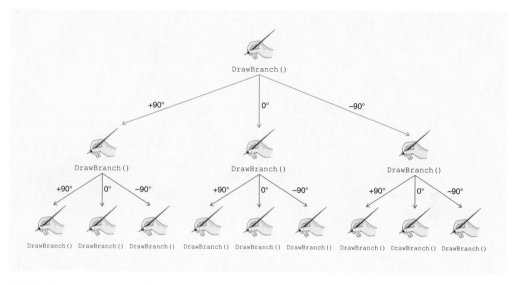

FIGURE 10-15 Recursive calls to `DrawBranch()`

`DrawBranch()` must be given (through parameter passing) the starting point of the line it is to draw, the angle of the line, the length of the line, and the level of recursion it is on. With this information it performs the following tasks:

ALGORITHM EXAMPLE 10-2: `DrawBranch()`

1. Calculate the x-coordinate of the end of the new line (`newX`).
2. Calculate the y-coordinate of the end of the new line (`newY`).
3. Draw a new line from point (`x, y`) to point (`newX, newY`).
4. If the current level of recursion is < maximum level:

    4.1. Call `DrawBranch()` to draw the next branch at the same angle as the current line (0 degrees).

    4.2. Call `DrawBranch()` to draw a branch perpendicular to the current line (+90 degrees).

    4.3. Call `DrawBranch()` to draw a branch perpendicular to the current line (-90 degrees).

The base case is reached when the level of recursion reaches the maximum number of levels (`maxLevels`) chosen by the user. As long as the current level of recursion is less than `maxLevel`, `DrawBranch()` is called three times—each time to draw a branch on the end of the current line, with each branch drawn at a different angle. Figure 10-16 shows the `DrawBranch()` calls at each level.

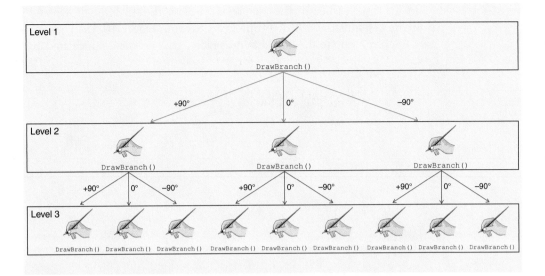

FIGURE 10-16 Levels of recursion for DrawBranch()

DrawBranch() is discussed in more detail as you design and write the code for it in the tutorial. Every call to **DrawBranch()** draws a new line until the maximum level is reached, as shown in Figure 10-17.

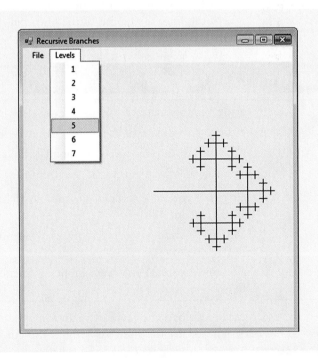

FIGURE 10-17 Computer-generated image using recursive DrawBranch() method

Tutorial: Generating a Fractal Image

The goal of this tutorial is to write a computer program that uses a recursive drawing process to construct the same images created by hand in Figures 10-8 through 10-13 in an automated manner. The On Your Own sections will provide you with additional ways to enhance the images.

Problem Analysis

In this project you will create an interface with menus that allow the user to pick the number of levels of recursion he or she wishes to see. Initially, the result should look very similar to that drawn by hand earlier (Figures 10-9 through 10-13). Compare Figure 10-13 to the image generated by the tutorial program, shown in Figure 10-17. The results look the same because they are made using the same set of rules governing the way recursion is used to draw lines. In the On Your Own section, additional features will be added to increase the patterned effect, as shown in Figure 10-18.

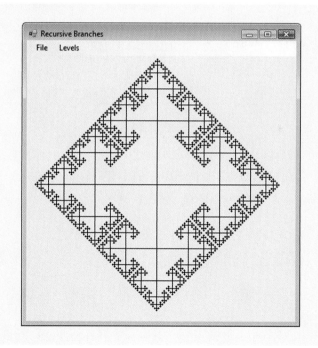

FIGURE 10-18 Four central branches (level = 7)

Design

You need to address two central features of this project in the design stage. First, you need to consider the placement and content of menus on the interface. Second, you need to consider the recursive algorithm that takes the menu options as input and recursively produces the image. Let us start with the interface.

INTERFACE

This program recursively generates the image on the form, so the interface should include ample space for displaying the image. In addition, this program requires a File menu and a Levels menu from which the user can close the program or select the number of levels of recursion desired. The menus and their choices are shown in Figure 10-19. At the top of each menu is an item that serves as the **menu heading**. Menu headings are choices that do not have event handlers that can be activated by clicking on them. Instead, beneath each menu heading are one or more **menu items** that can be activated by clicking on them, as shown in Figure 10-19.

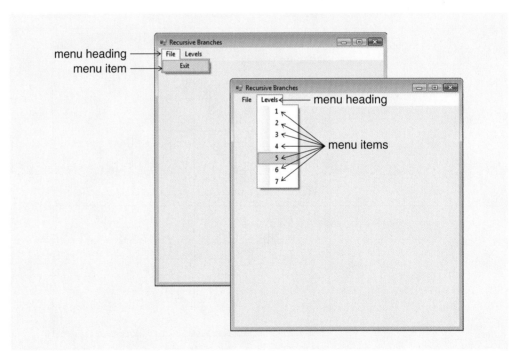

FIGURE 10-19 Menu headings and menu items.

In Visual C++, menus are created using the `MenuStrip` **control**. The items contained within a menu are called `ToolStripMenuItems`. For example, the File menu heading is a control named `fileToolStripMenuItem`, the Exit menu item is a control named `exitToolStripMenuItem`, as shown in Figure 10-20.

FIGURE 10-20 File and Exit menu items and their control names

The Levels menu items and their default control names are shown in Figure 10-21. The purpose of the Levels menu is to allow the user to select the maximum number of levels of recursion in the fractal. The user may choose from 1 to 7 levels.

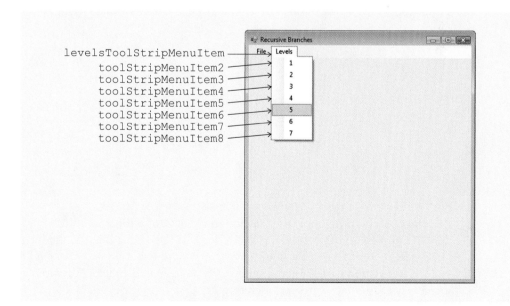

FIGURE 10-21 Levels menu items and their control names

These controls are summarized in Table 10-1. The program will only respond to click events on the menu items below each heading.

TABLE 10-1 Control table

Usage	Object	Event	Description
Initialization	Form1	Load()	Initialize Drawing objects
Processing	fileToolStripMenuItem		File menu heading
	exitToolStripMenuItem	Click()	Close the program
	levelToolStripMenuItem		Levels menu heading
	toolStripMenuItem2	Click()	Process one level of recursion
	toolStripMenuItem3	Click()	Process two levels of recursion
	toolStripMenuItem4	Click()	Process three levels of recursion
	toolStripMenuItem5	Click()	Process four levels of recursion
	toolStripMenuItem6	Click()	Process five levels of recursion
	toolStripMenuItem7	Click()	Process six levels of recursion
	toolStripMenuItem8	Click()	Process seven levels of recursion

DATA TABLE

All aspects of this program center around the selection of the maxLevels for the recursive drawing process and the assigned values for the angle of the line, the line length, and the line's starting point x- and y-coordinates. These must be instance variables because they will be called upon in numerous methods and event handlers. All variables should be integers because they represent discrete values. The instance variables for the program are listed in Table 10-2.

TABLE 10-2 Data table—class instance variables

Variable Name	Data Type	Usage
angle	int	Angle at which the line is drawn (degrees)
length	int	Line length (in pixels)
maxLevels	int	Number of levels of recursion selected
x	int	x-coordinate of branch start (in pixels)
y	int	y-coordinate of branch start (in pixels)

Variables Required for Drawing A minimal number of drawing objects are needed. As in previous projects, you will use a `Graphics` object to draw on `Form1`. In addition, you will use a `blackPen` object to draw the lines (Table 10-3).

TABLE 10-3 Table of required `Graphics` and `Drawing` objects

Object Name	Type	Usage
g	Graphics	Graphics object
blackPen	Pen	Used to draw lines

Variables Required for `DrawBranch()` This program uses the recursive method called `DrawBranch()`. The details about how `DrawBranch()` works are discussed under the Algorithm section later in this chapter. In preparation, Table 10-4 lists the data passed into the `DrawBranch()` method through its arguments.

TABLE 10-4 Data table—`DrawBranch()` formal parameters

Variable Name	Data type	Usage
x	int	x-coordinate of branch start (in pixels)
y	int	y-coordinate of branch start (in pixels)
ang	double	Angle at which the line is to be drawn (degrees)
len	int	Line length (in pixels)
level	int	Level of recursion counter

10

Many of the variables in this data table are similar to the class instance variables from Table 10-2. The values stored in the variables in Table 10-4, however, may change every time `DrawBranch()` is called. For example, the first time `DrawBranch()` is called, the length of the line it must draw (`len`) may be 100 pixels. The next call may set `len` to 50, the next to 25, and so on, until the recursion ends.

The key variable is `level`. It is a counter that increases by 1 with each recursive call. When the program starts, `level` is originally set to 1. Eventually `level` increases to `maxLevels`, signaling that the base case has been reached and that recursion must now cease.

ALGORITHM

There are many event handlers in this program that need to be coded. For example, every menu item has its own click event handler. Fortunately, the algorithms for click event handlers are short. The programmer-defined, recursive method `DrawBranch()`, however, requires some extra attention because of its recursive nature.

Level Menu Item Algorithms The items under the Level menu heading perform in a similar manner. Each time the user selects a Level menu item, the variable assigned to store the selected maximum number of levels of recursion (`maxLevels`) is assigned a unique value and then the `DrawFractal()` method is called to begin the drawing process that produces the selected number of levels of recursion.

For example, when the first Level menu item (`toolStripMenuItem2`) is clicked, its click event carries out the tasks shown in Algorithm 10-3.

ALGORITHM 10-3: `toolStripMenuItem2()`

1. Assign the value 1 to the variable `maxLevels`.
2. Call the method that starts the drawing process (`DrawFractal()`).

Similarly, when the second Level menu item (`toolStripMenuItem3`) is clicked, its click event carries out the tasks shown in Algorithm 10-4.

ALGORITHM 10-4: `toolStripMenuItem3()`

1. Assign the value 2 to the variable `maxLevels`.
2. Call the method that starts the drawing process (`DrawFractal()`).

This sequence of tasks characterizes each Level menu item.

The DrawFractal() Method   The DrawFractal() method refreshes the screen and calls DrawBranch() to begin the recursive drawing process. For the sake of simplicity, in this tutorial you will create a program that draws only one central branch. In the On Your Own section after this tutorial, you can add additional statements to DrawFractal() to construct more branches in the same manner. The DrawFractal() method has a very simple solution, as shown in Algorithm 10-5.

ALGORITHM 10-5: DrawFractal()

1. Refresh the form.
2. Draw a branch.

The DrawBranch() Method   This is the heart of the program. The DrawBranch() method uses data provided by its parameters to draw a single line. The data provided to DrawBranch() through its parameters was provided earlier in Table 10-4.

The algorithm for DrawBranch() was discussed earlier, in the section preceding the tutorial. To draw the line DrawBranch(), you need to calculate the x- and y-coordinates of the end of the new branch (newX and newY) and draw a line from the coordinate (x, y) to (newX, newY). Then, if the current level (level) is greater than 1, DrawBranch() calls itself to draw three other smaller lines that branch off of the current one.

TEST STRATEGY

The most important thing to test in a recursive algorithm is the base case. If it is never reached, then the recursion will be infinite, and the program will eventually fail due to lack of available memory. You have already identified the crucial algorithm statement— Step 4 of DrawBranch()—in which the base case is tested. In the next section you will test to make sure that Step 4 is handled correctly and stops the recursive process.

ALGORITHM VERIFICATION

Recursive methods can be difficult to trace. In the case of fractals, the easiest way to trace the method is to draw the fractal images. Take a simple case and assume that you only want to draw one branch off of the original line. Assume that angle is initially set to 0 (which is a horizontal line), length is 100, and ratio 50. The x-coordinate is 210, and the y-coordinate is 225. If the level is set to 1, then no recursive calls will be made, as shown in Table 10-5.

10

TABLE 10-5 Trace of `DrawBranch()` with 1 level of recursion

Algorithm	maxLevels	x	y	ang	len	level	newX	newY	Comments
Initial settings	1	210	225	0	100	1			
1. Calculate `newX`							310		
2. Calculate `newY`								225	
3. `DrawLine()`									Figure 10-22
4. `level < maxLevels`									False—exit

Table 10-5 demonstrates that when `DrawBranch()` is called with `maxLevels` set to 1, the three branches are not drawn. The result is shown in Figure 10-22.

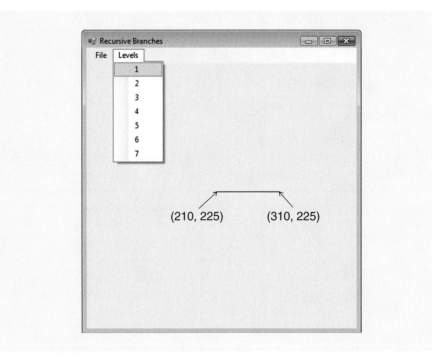

FIGURE 10-22 One branch is drawn when `maxLevels` is set to 1

Next, see what happens when `DrawBranch()` is called with `maxLevels` is set to 2. This starts one set of recursive calls. There are four trace tables in this case because `DrawBranch()` is called initially with `level` set to 1, and this triggers a sequence of three recursive calls to `DrawBranch()`. Table 10-6 illustrates the initial call to `DrawBranch()`.

TABLE 10-6 Initial call to `DrawBranch()` with `maxLevels` set to 2

Algorithm	maxLevels	x	y	ang	len	level	newX	newY	Comments
Initial settings	2	210	225	0	100	1			
1. Calculate **newX**							310		
2. Calculate **newY**								225	
3. DrawLine()									Figure 10-22
4. level < maxLevels									True—begin recursion
4.1 DrawBranch()		310	225	0	50	2			Table 10-7
4.2 DrawBranch()		310	225	90	50	2			Table 10-8
4.3 DrawBranch()		310	225	-90	50	2			Table 10-9

Step 4.1 calls `DrawBranch()` again but with a new set of parameters. Notice that the first two parameters (**x** and **y**) specify the end point of the previous line (310 and 225). This means that this version of `DrawBranch()` starts at that point. In this example, the length is now only 50 pixels. Also, `level` has been increased by 1. The result of the call to Step 4.1 is traced in Table 10-7.

TABLE 10-7 Trace of Step 4.1 recursive call to `DrawBranch()`

Algorithm	maxLevels	x	y	ang	len	level	newX	newY	Comments
Initial settings	2	310	225	0	50	2			
1. Calculate **newX**							360		
2. Calculate **newY**								225	
3. DrawLine()									Figure 10-23
4. level < maxLevels									False—return

Step 4.2 is traced in Table 10-8. The call is the same as that in Step 4.1, except the angle has been changed to 90 degrees off of the original (in a clockwise direction). As a result of this new angle, the **newX** and **newY** positions the new line perpendicular to the original.

TABLE 10-8 Trace of Step 4.2 recursive call to `DrawBranch()`

Algorithm	maxLevels	x	y	ang	len	level	newX	newY	Comments
Parameters	2	310	225	90	50	2			
1. Calculate **newX**							310		
2. Calculate **newY**								275	
3. `DrawLine()`									Figure 10-23
4. **level < maxLevels**									False—return

Step 4.3, traced in Table 10-9, is similar to Step 4.2, except now **angle** is set to –90 degrees, which is perpendicular to the original in the opposite direction of the line drawn in Step 4.2.

TABLE 10-9 Trace of Step 4.3 recursive call to `DrawBranch()`

Algorithm	maxLevels	x	y	ang	len	level	newX	newY	Comments
Parameters	2	310	225	-90	50	2			
1. Calculate **newX**							310		
2. Calculate **newY**								175	
3. `DrawLine()`									Figure 10-23
4. **level < maxLevels**									False—return

The result of all three recursive calls is shown in Figure 10-23. The initial branch is drawn from (210, 225) to (310, 225). The branch resulting from the first recursive call (Step 4.1) runs from (310, 225) to (360, 225). The branch resulting from the second recursive call (Step 4.2) runs from (310, 225) to (310, 275). The branch resulting from the third recursive call runs from (310, 225) to (310, 175).

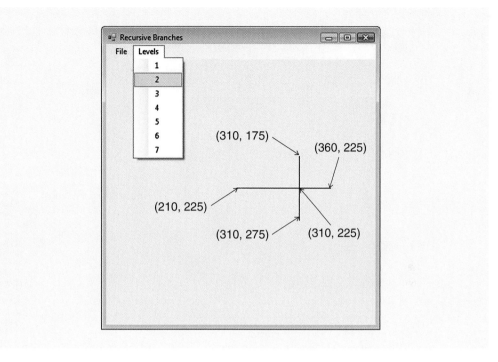

FIGURE 10-23 Level 2 recursion using `DrawBranch()`

In all cases, the base case was activated and recursion stopped when the value in `level` reached the value in `maxLevels`.

Development

Because you have carefully designed this project and tested the algorithms, development should be straightforward. However, you need to code more small items in this project than in previous ones. Each menu item must assign a value to a variable and call `DrawFractal()`. This means writing code for numerous menu item click event handlers. As long as the menu creation and coding go well, however, the rest of the program should follow along easily.

CREATE THE INTERFACE

Create a new project called "Chapter 10 Tutorial". The `Size` property of the form should be set to 450, 475, and its `Text` property set to "Recursive Branches" as shown in Figure 10-24. As you have seen, this project is controlled entirely by menu selections. You can start creating the interface for this project by creating a form and setting its size to 425 by 475. Next, double-click the `MenuStrip` control in the Toolbox. This inserts a menu item control as shown in Figure 10-24.

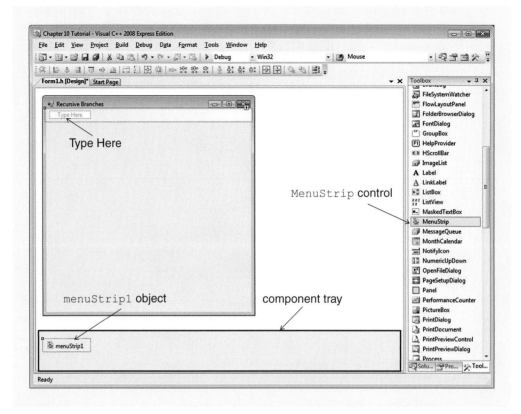

FIGURE 10-24 Selecting the `MenuStrip` control

The control appears in the component tray below the Design window. Also, an empty menu heading appears at the top of the form. The words "Type Here" indicates where to type your first menu heading. Type the word "File" and press the Enter key. You have just created a File menu item that will appear at the top of the interface when the program runs. The cursor is now positioned just below the File menu item in another "Type Here" space. Type the word "Exit" and press the Enter key. A menu item named Exit now appears underneath the File heading as shown in Figure 10-25.

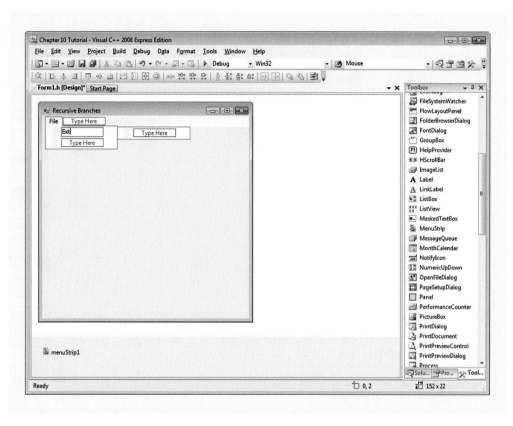

FIGURE 10-25 Creation of the File and Exit menu items

Next, create a menu called "Levels" to the right of the File menu. Then create a list of menu items (1, 2, 3, 4, 5, 6, 7) beneath it as shown in Figure 10-26.

1
0

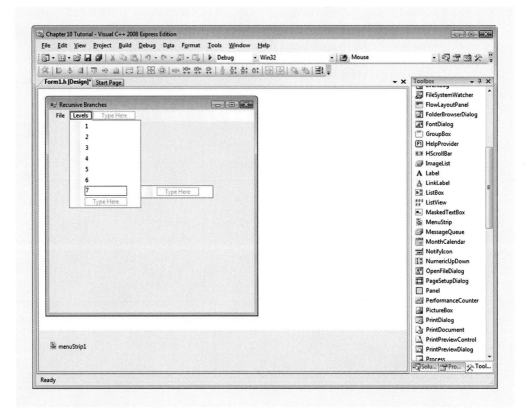

FIGURE 10-26 Creation of the Levels menu heading and menu items choices (1–7)

The interface is now complete, allowing you to move on to the coding stage.

CODING

The coding for this project requires the creation of numerous event handlers for the click events associated with each menu item. The procedure you have used to create event handlers by double-clicking on the object is direct and efficient, but there is another way. The Events button in the Properties window allows you to easily create any of a number of different event handlers for a single object. You will have a chance to use the Events button in this tutorial.

Instance Variables In Table 10-2, you identified the class instance variables required by this program. In Table 10-3, you identified the `Graphics` objects. You start by coding these variables and objects as shown in Example 10-5.

EXAMPLE 10-5: INSTANCE VARIABLES AND OBJECTS

```
// Instance variables
   int maxLevels;  // level of recursion
   int angle;  // angle of the line
   int length; // length of the line
   int x;        // starting x coordiante of the line
   int y;        // starting y coordinate of the line

// Drawing and Graphics objects
   System::Drawing::Graphics^ g;
   System::Drawing::Pen^ blackPen;
```

Coding the Form1_Load Event Handler You initialize the class instance variables and Graphics objects in the Form1_Load event handler as shown in Example 10-6.

EXAMPLE 10-6: THE Form1_Load() EVENT HANDLER

```
private: System::Void Form1_Load(System::Object^  sender,
System::EventArgs^  e) {
// Initialize instance variables
   maxLevels = 3;
   angle = 0;
   length = 100;
   x = 210;
   y = 225;
// Initialize drawing objects
   g = this->CreateGraphics();
   blackPen = gcnew System::Drawing::Pen(Color::Black);
}
```

Coding Menu Click Events The menu items you created were automatically assigned names as they were created (see Figure 10-20 and 10-21). You will create event handlers for each of the menu items except File and Levels (which serve as menu headings only). Under the File menu heading, double-click Exit menu item. This opens the click event handler, exitToolStripMenuItem_Click(). Type the Close() command, which terminates the application as shown in Example 10-7.

EXAMPLE 10-7: THE EXIT MENU ITEM

```
private: System::Void exitToolStripMenuItem_Click(System::Object^
sender, System::EventArgs^  e)
{
   Close();
}
```

Although double-clicking an object is useful when creating event handlers, a technique that is sometimes faster and able to provide a choice of event handler, is to use the Events button in the Properties window (its icon is a lightening bolt). Select one of the menu items under the Levels heading, then go to the Properties window and click the Events button, as shown in Figure 10-27. Notice that you are now able to select the event handler that you would like created. Double-click the click event handler item to create it.

> **NOTE** You can always return to the regular properties display by clicking the Properties button.

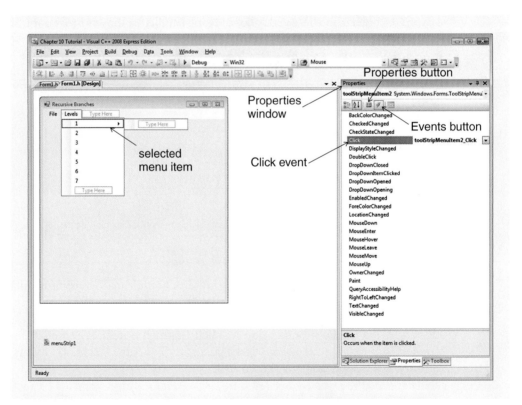

FIGURE 10-27 Events button and event list for the selected menu item

When the Code window appears with the click event handler, enter an assignment statement to set `maxLevels` and a call to the `DrawFractal()` method, as shown in Example 10-8.

EXAMPLE 10-8: MENUITEM FOR LEVEL 1

```
private: System::Void toolStripMenuItem2_Click(System::Object^
sender, System::EventArgs^  e) {
   maxLevels = 1;
   DrawFractal();
}
```

Do the same for each of the other menu items under the Levels heading. Each event handler should assign a value to `maxLevels` and then call the `DrawFractal()` method, which you will write in a moment. The general idea is that every time the user chooses a new level, the `DrawFractal()` method should redraw the image on the screen.

Drawing a Fractal Image—DrawFractal()   The `DrawFractal()` method code implements Algorithm 10-5, which draws only one branch. The `DrawFractal()` method should refresh the image on the form and then call the `DrawBranch()` method, which is responsible for drawing the image on the form.

The method looks like that shown in Example 10-9. Notice that the last actual parameter in the call to `DrawBranch()` is the value 1. This sets the initial level of recursion at 1. It increases with each recursive `DrawBranch()` call until it reaches the same value as that stored in `maxLevels`.

EXAMPLE 10-9: THE DrawFractal() METHOD

```
private: void DrawFractal()
{
   this->Refresh();
   DrawBranch(x,y,angle,length,1);
}
```

Drawing a Branch—DrawBranch()   To draw the line, `DrawBranch()` must be passed the following information through its arguments:

- x—The x-coordinate of the line starting point
- y—The y-coordinate of the line starting point
- ang—The angle of the line (in degrees)
- len—The length of the line
- level—The current level of recursion

The angle (`ang`) is converted to radians, as you remember from Chapter 6, and is used to calculate the end points of the new line (`newX` and `newY`). The newX coordinate is the cosine of the angle multiplied by the line length (`Math::Cos(angle_radians)*len`).

The `newY` coordinate is the sine of the angle multiplied by the line length (`Math::Sin(angle_radians)*len`). The use of `Math::Cos()` and `Math::Sin()` is similar to that used in Chapter 6. The cosine and sine functions serve only to find the correct end point positions, along the designated angle, for the line you want to draw.

Once `newX` and `newY` are calculated, the line from point (`x, y`) to (`newX, newY`) can be drawn using `DrawLine()` in the manner shown in Example 10-10.

EXAMPLE 10-10: THE `DrawLine()` METHOD

```
g->DrawLine(blackPen,x,y,newX,newY);
```

After the line has been drawn, it is time to see if three branches should be added to the end of it. This necessitates checking the level of recursion (`level`). If `level` is less than `maxLevels` then three additional branches are made. If `level` is equal to `maxLevels` it means that you have reached the base case, and the recursive drawing process ends. A typical call to the recursive `DrawBranch()` method resembles the one shown in Example 10-11.

EXAMPLE 10-11: CALLING `DrawBranch()`

```
DrawBranch(newX,newY,ang+90,len/2,level+1);
```

Notice that a recursive call to `DrawBranch()` uses `newX` and `newY` (the end of the current line) as the starting point of the next line. The third parameter, (the angle) may vary. As you saw in the last section, these are the angles of the three branches. The fourth parameter, the length of the branch, is half of the current line length (`len/2`). The fifth parameter is the level of recursion. This parameter adds one to the current level (`level+1`). Adding one to `level` allows it to eventually reach `maxLevels` with each recursive call and eventually stops the recursion by reaching the base case.

The code for the entire `DrawBranch()` method is shown in Example 10-12.

EXAMPLE 10-12: THE `DrawBranch()` METHOD

```
private: void DrawBranch(int x, int y, int ang, int len, int level)
{
    // Convert angle to radians
    double angle_radians = Math::PI* ang/180.0;
    // Determine the endpoints of the line (newX and newY)
    int newX = x + (int) (Math::Cos(angle_radians)*len);
    int newY = y + (int) (Math::Sin(angle_radians)*len);

    // Draw the line
    g->DrawLine(blackPen,x,y,newX,newY);
```

```
// If the level > 1 draw three branches
if (level < maxLevels) {
    // Recursive calls
    DrawBranch(newX,newY,ang,len/2,level+1);
    DrawBranch(newX,newY,ang+90,len/2,level+1);
    DrawBranch(newX,newY,ang-90,len/2,level+1);
}
}
```

Testing

Figure 10-28 shows the image with maxLevels set to 7.

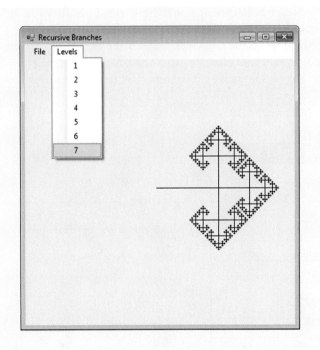

FIGURE 10-28   Seven levels of recursion on a single branch

Congratulations! You have successfully created a fractal image using recursive techniques.

Test your program to make sure that it successfully allows the user to do each of the following:

- Select each of the Level menu items to demonstrate that they work correctly.
- Exit the program successfully from the Exit menu.

Analysis

This is a good project to experiment with by adding new features, as you will do in the On Your Own section and several of the Programming Exercises. You should probably avoid adding too many additional levels, however. Processing time skyrockets with more than 12 or 13 levels. To see why this is, consider your recursive method `DrawBranch()`. When it is called the first time, it draws a single line. From there on, each level of recursion draws three lines onto the end of the previous one.

If you allowed the user to draw more than seven levels, the number of lines, and hence the amount of recursion, increases rapidly. The table in Figure 10-29 indicates where this might lead. At level 16 on this table, over 14 million lines must be drawn! Your computer screen would quickly be unable to elaborate on the diagram beyond level 8 because the program would be calculating, and attempting to draw, line segments smaller than a single pixel. Nevertheless, recursion would continue to calculate and attempt to draw them until all of the levels had been completed, which could take quite a long while. The number of new lines drawn at each level is $3^{maxLevels-1}$. This fits in with the discussion of the complexity measure Big-O in earlier chapters. A recursive process of $O(3^n)$, where n stands for a value such as ($maxLevels - 1$), can be a formidable drain on system resources, as shown in Figure 10-29.

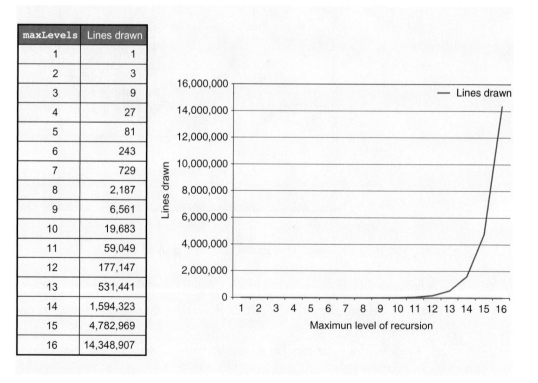

maxLevels	Lines drawn
1	1
2	3
3	9
4	27
5	81
6	243
7	729
8	2,187
9	6,561
10	19,683
11	59,049
12	177,147
13	531,441
14	1,594,323
15	4,782,969
16	14,348,907

FIGURE 10-29 Lines drawn per level of recursion: $O(3^{maxLevels})$

ON YOUR OWN

You are now ready to begin adding new features to demonstrate your understanding of the recursive process. The On Your Own tasks are designed to help you enhance the image, while expanding your knowledge of how the details of the recursive process work.

TASK 1: MORE CENTRAL BRANCHES

The `DrawFractal()` method starts the recursive process by calling `DrawBranch()` once, at an angle of 0 degrees as shown in Figure 10-22. You can create a more complex image by having `DrawFractal()` call `DrawBranch()` several times, each with a different angle.

Modify your `DrawFractal()` method so that it makes four calls to `DrawBranch()`. The first, the one you have already done, establishes the angle at 0 degrees. Your next three calls to `DrawBranch()` should be made using angles of 90, 180, and –90 degrees. For example, to add 90 degrees onto the angle, call `DrawBranch()` like this:

```
DrawBranch(x,y,angle+90,length,1);
```

The result should look like that shown in Figure 10-18.

TASK 2: ADD AN ANGLE MENU

You have seen how to create the Levels menu heading with menu items 1, 2, 3, 4, 5, 6, and 7. Create a menu heading immediately to the right of the Levels heading called Angle. Under the Angle heading, create menu items 0, 15, 30, 45, 60, 75, and 90 as shown in Figure 10-30.

1
0

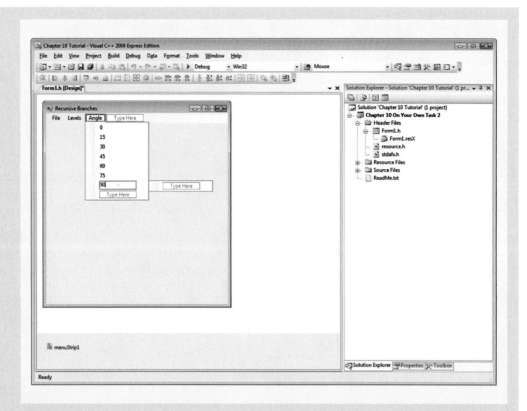

FIGURE 10-30 Adding menu items to control the angle

Create the menu item click event handlers for each of the menu items under the Angle heading. By default, they will probably be named `toolStripMenuItem9` through `toolStripMenuItem15`. For example, the code for `toolStripMenuItem10_Click()` is shown here:

```
private: System::Void toolStripMenuItem10_Click(System::Object^
sender, System::EventArgs^  e) {
   angle = 15;
   DrawFractal();
}
```

Each menu item click event handler assigns a value to the instance variable angle and then calls `DrawFractal()`. Figure 10–31 shows the user selecting 60 degrees under the Angle menu heading. The resulting image, in this case one using seven levels, is tilted 60 degrees (in a clockwise direction) from the original angle setting (0 degrees).

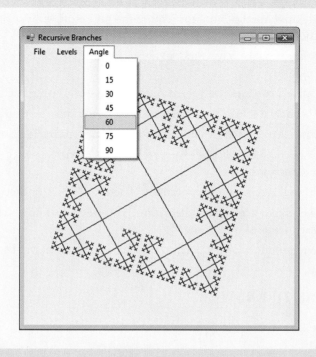

FIGURE 10-31 A seven-level image drawn with an angle selection of 60 degrees.

QUICK REVIEW

1. A factorial number (*n*!) is defined as *n*! = *n* × (*n* − 1)!

2. Factorial numbers can be computed from the bottom up without using a loop.

3. Recursion is an alternative to loops.

4. Recursion is the process of a method calling itself.

5. The factorial problem has a recursive solution.

6. Recursive algorithms define a base case and a recursive case.

7. A base case ends the recursive calling process.

8. In the factorial problem, the base case was reached when 1! was to be computed.

9. After the base case is reached, recursive backtracking begins.

10. The recursive case calls another version of the same method, only with different parameters.

11. Iterative methods are generally faster than recursive ones.

12. Iterative methods do not require the processing power or memory management that recursion does.

13. Programmers often find iterative methods easier to write than recursive ones.

14. Some problems are solved much more easily using recursive techniques.

15. Recursive solutions can elegantly express inductive mathematical functions.

16. Fractal images are examples of a problem best tackled recursively.

17. A fractal image is one composed of geometric shapes of smaller and smaller proportions.

18. Fractal refers to the sometimes "fractured" look of these geometric shapes.

19. To create a recursive algorithm, you need to know what will happen in each level of recursion.

20. Multiple levels of recursion may take place until the base case is reached.

TERMS TO KNOW

base case
fractal
fractal images
inductive definition
menu heading
menu items
`MenuStrip` **control**
recursion
recursive backtracking
recursive call
recursive case

EXERCISES

Use the following recursive method to answer Questions 1–5.

```
private: int addUp(int num[], int i)
{
    if (i == 5)
        return num[i];
    else
        return num[i] + addUp(num, i+1);
}
```

1. Which of the following identifies the base case?

   a. `if (i == 5)`

   b. `return num[i];`

   c. `else`

   d. `return num[i] + addUp(num, i+1);`

   e. `private: int addUp(int num[], int i)`

2. Which of the following lines ends the recursive process?

   a. `if (i == 5)`

   b. `return num[i];`

   c. `else`

   d. `return num[i] + addUp(num, i+1);`

   e. `private: int addUp(int num[], int i)`

3. Which of the following lines defines the data type that the recursive call returns?

   a. `if (i == 5)`

   b. `return num[i];`

   c. `else`

   d. `return num[i] + addUp(num, i+1);`

   e. `private: int addUp(int num[], int i)`

4. Which of the following lines makes a recursive call?

   a. `if (i == 5)`

   b. `return num[i];`

   c. `else`

   d. `return num[i] + addUp(num, i+1);`

   e. `private: int addUp(int num[], int i)`

5. Which of the following lines establishes where the recursive case begins?

   a. `if (i == 5)`

   b. `return num[i];`

   c. `else`

   d. `return num[i] + addUp(num, i+1);`

   e. `private: int addUp(int num[], int i)`

10

6. What happens if a recursive method has no base case?

   a. It launches an infinite series of recursive calls and eventually uses up all available memory.

   b. It does not compile.

   c. It quits after the first call to the method.

   d. It works as expected for all but the base case(s).

   e. It will still work as expected, but not as efficiently.

7. Iteration is usually _____ than recursion.

   a. faster

   b. easier to write

   c. easier to debug

   d. easier to understand

   e. All of the above

8. Recursion should be used when:

   a. A problem is defined in terms of itself

   b. Speed is of the essence

   c. A problem has no formal mathematical definition

   d. System resources are limited

   e. Nested loops are required to solve a problem

9. An example of a problem with a natural recursive solution is:

   a. Reading data into a variable from a text box

   b. Integer division

   c. An if...else decision

   d. Drawing fractal images

   e. Generating random numbers

10. Recursive backtracking begins when:

   a. A recursive method is called

   b. The base case is reached

   c. The recursive case is executed

   d. Something has gone wrong in the recursive process

   e. You run out of memory

11. The cost of recursion is:

     a. Additional processing power
     b. Memory management
     c. Complex debugging
     d. Increased use of system recourses
     e. All of the above

12. Five factorial is:

     a. $5! \times 4!$
     b. $5! \times 4$
     c. $5! \times 4! \times 3! \times 2! \times 1!$
     d. $5 \times 4!$
     e. None of the above

13. The factorial of 1 is:

     a. $0!$
     b. 1
     c. $1 \times 0!$
     d. The base case of the recursive factorial solution
     e. All of the above

14. The big-O of `DrawBranch()` is:

     a. $O(n^2)$
     b. $O(n)$
     c. $O(n^3)$
     d. $O(3^n)$
     e. $O(1)$

15. The big-O of `DrawBranch()` is:

     a. Of a higher order of complexity than the selection sort
     b. Of the same order of complexity as the selection sort
     c. Of a lower order of complexity than the selection sort
     d. Of the same order of complexity as the binary search
     e. Of a lower order of complexity than the sequential search

16. How many times will `DrawBranch()` be called if `maxLevels` is set to 3?

     a. 1
     b. 3
     c. 9
     d. 13
     e. 40

1
0

17. How many lines will be drawn in the third level of recursion of `DrawBranch()`?

    a. 1

    b. 3

    c. 9

    d. 13

    e. 40

18. If a recursive method has no base case, what will happen?

    a. Recursion will end through recursive backtracking.

    b. Recursion will end when the problem is solved.

    c. Recursion will end when the program has used up all available memory.

    d. Recursion will never end.

    e. No recursion will take place.

19. If a recursive method has no recursive case, what will happen?

    a. Recursion will end through recursive backtracking.

    b. Recursion will end when the problem is solved.

    c. Recursion will end when the program has used up all available memory.

    d. Recursion will never end.

    e. No recursion will take place.

20. Which of the methods in the tutorial were recursive?

    a. Only `DrawFractal()`

    b. Only `DrawBranch()`

    c. Both `DrawFractal()` and `DrawBranch()`

    d. All methods

    e. All methods except `DrawBranch()`

PROGRAMMING EXERCISES

1. Factorial Numbers

To demonstrate your understanding of factorials, create a program with an interface similar to the one shown in Figure 10-32. The program should allow the user to enter an integer from 1 to 10. When the user clicks the Factorial button, the program should compute and display the integer's factorial. In addition, the interface should include a recursion log (the multiline text box on the right of the interface) that displays a message indicating when each recursive call was made. It should also indicate when the base case is reached, and it should list all values returned.

FIGURE 10-32 Factorial Numbers interface with Recursion log

2. Shapes and Colors

The fractal tutorial program with its seven levels is interesting, but you can make it more so by revising the program to make the **newX, newY** coordinates the opposite corners of a rectangle. When a **Rectangle** object is defined, it can be used by **DrawBranch()** to display various geometric shapes instead of just lines.

You will recall that **Rectangle** objects are defined by the upper-left corner coordinates (**x, y**), the width and height. You can use the end points of the line (**newX** and **newY**) calculated by **DrawBranch()** to draw rectangles instead of lines. The difference between **x** and **newX** is the width. The difference between **y** and **newY** is the height, as shown in Figure 10-33.

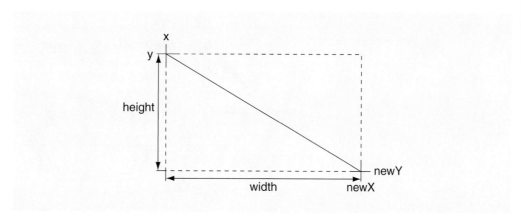

FIGURE 10-33 Using two points to define a rectangle

Positive values are required for width and height parameters. Should either one end up being a negative number (which will occur when `newX` is less than `x` or `newY` is less than `y`), you can use the absolute value method (`Math::Abs`) to make it positive as shown here.

```
myRect(x,y,Math::Abs(newX-x),Math::Abs(newY-y));
```

Now that you have a `Rectangle` object defined, you use it with the `DrawRectangle()`, `FillRectangle()`, `DrawEllipse()`, or `FillEllipse()` methods to create interesting patterns. The `FillRectangle()` and `FillEllipse()` methods require a brush, but this is easily done by creating a `Brush` object within the `DrawBranch()` method and assigning it a color, such as `Color::Red`.

Now, experiment with the program you have created. Figure 10-34 shows three images created with `maxLevels` set to 5. In each image the angle setting is given at the top of the interface example.

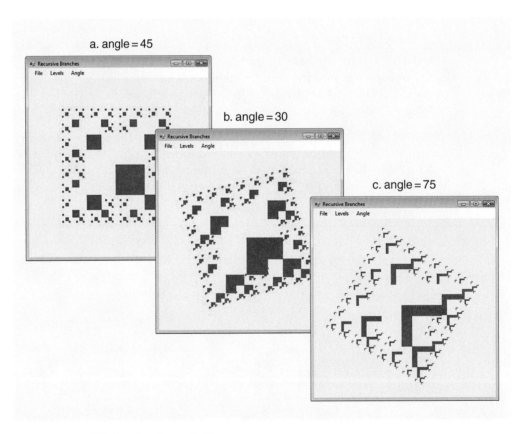

FIGURE 10-34 Filled rectangles and ellipses

Changes in the angle can produce interesting results, or nothing at all. Remember that an angle of 0 or 90 will generate a rectangle with a width or height of 0 (hence no rectangle can be drawn).

Next, make your image display geometric shapes of differing colors. To do this, create a method called NewColor() that randomly selects a color for an object before it is painted on the screen. The signature for NewColor () is:

```
private: System::Drawing::Color NewColor()
```

NewColor() should return a Color that can be used to set the Color property of your brush from within DrawBranch(). Use a switch statement in NewColor() to select the color.

The results of this last change can be dramatic, as shown in Figure 10-35, where both images were produced with angle set to 45 and levels set to 4.

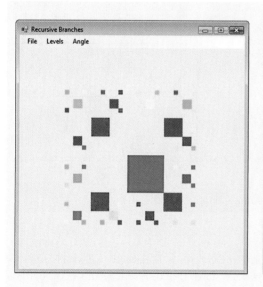
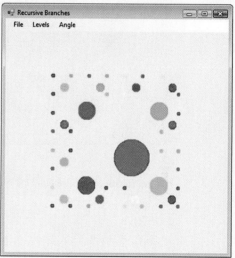

FIGURE 10-35 Randomly colored shapes

3. Additional Menus

Add two additional menus to your tutorial program with the menu headings "Length" and "Ratio".

The menu items under the Length heading are 50 (for 50 pixels), 75 (for 75 pixels), 100 (for 100 pixels), and 150 (for 150 pixels). Your tutorial program is currently set to draw the initial line 100 pixels long. This allows the user to change the initial line length.

The menu items under the Ratio heading are 45 (for 45 percent), 50 (for 50 percent), and 55 (for 55 percent). The ratio determines how much reduction in length occurs at each level of recursion. Your tutorial program is currently set to 50 percent (it divides the line in half at each level of recursion). This allows the user to select different line size reductions. The left image in Figure 10-36 was produced with a line length of 75 and ratio of 50. The right image in Figure 10-36 was produced with a length of 100 and ratio of 45.

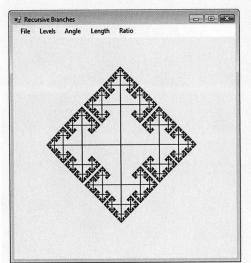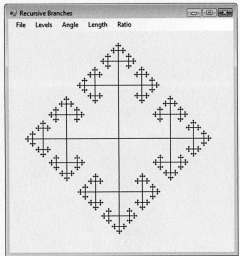

FIGURE 10-36 Images resulting from line length and ratio changes.

4. Trees

This project is based on Programming Exercise 3. Relatively minor changes to the program you created in the tutorial can produce startlingly different results. To begin, add additional levels, up to level 11.

After you have increased the number of levels, add additional Ratio menu items for 60, 65, 70, 75, and 80 percent.

Next, add a menu heading to your project called "Branch Angle". The menu items underneath Branch Angle are 20 (for a branch angle of 20 degrees), 30 (for a branch angle of 30 degrees), and 45 (a branch angle of 45 degrees). When the menu items under the Branch Angle heading are clicked, they should store the designated value in the instance variable `bangle`.

Next, revise the `DrawBranch()` method so that it draws only two branches recursively instead of three, as shown in this code segment. Notice that `bangle` is added to `ang` in the first `DrawBranch()` call and subtracted from `ang` in the second `DrawBranch()` call to change the angle at which the branches are drawn.

```
if (lev < maxLevels) {
    DrawBranch(newX,newY,ang+bangle,len*ratio/100,lev-1);
    DrawBranch(newX,newY,ang-bangle,len*ratio/100,lev-1);
}
```

The user should be able to select the branch angle (`bangle`) from a Branch Angle menu. Figure 10-37 shows an interface with Branch Angle menu items. It also shows the image that results when the user selects 0 for the angle, 50 for the length, 75 for the ratio, 11 for the level, and 20 for the branch angle (`bangle`).

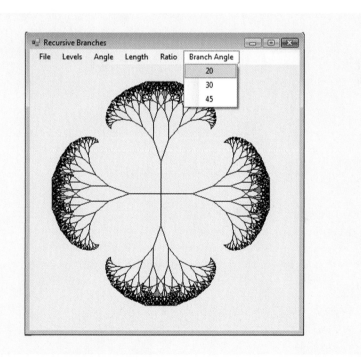

FIGURE 10-37 Tree images generated recursively

Many other images are possible. Figure 10-38 shows a stained glass effect produced by the program when the user selects 0 for the angle, 50 for the length, 70 for the ratio, 11 for the level, and 45 for the branch angle (`bangle`). You can easily produce fractal patterns like this with your program.

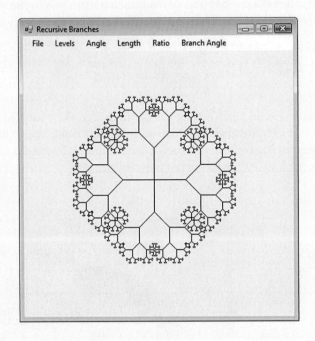

FIGURE 10-38   Recursive stained glass effect

5.   Counting Backwards

To demonstrate your understanding of the recursive process, modify the tutorial program so that it counts down instead of up. The tutorial was designed to start with level = 1 and counting each level of recursion up to maxLevels (the base case). Make the changes necessary to enable it to start by setting the level to maxLevels and then subtract one from level with each recursive call until you reach the value 1 (the base case). Demonstrate that your program works as it did previously. Do not change any menu items.

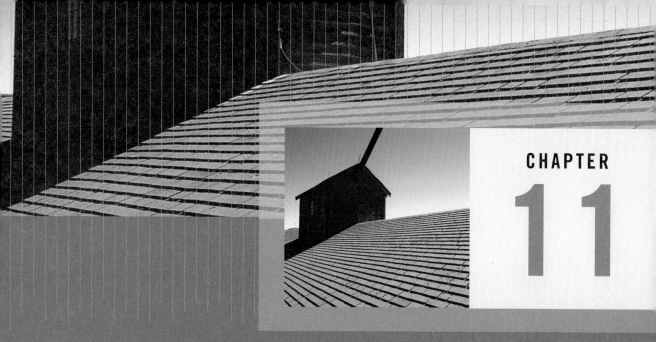

POINTERS

IN THIS CHAPTER, YOU WILL:

- Declare, create, and assign pointers
- Use pointers to indirectly access data in other memory cells
- Experiment with dynamic array allocation
- Use pointer arithmetic to traverse an array
- Use pointer arrays
- Produce sorted lists without moving the data around

Among the most important considerations of any computer program is the way in which it manages memory and processing resources. In previous chapters you learned how to declare, initialize, and use individual variables and arrays. However, you have not spent much time considering how to make the most efficient use of them. In this chapter the discussion turns to ways in which you can improve program efficiency and flexibility by improving the way a program handles data. This will also provide you with a new set of tools to use later on as you create more complex data structures.

Introduction

Assume that one of your college roommates got married last summer, and you had the privilege of attending the ceremony. The wedding was held in a town many miles away, so very few of your mutual college friends could attend. You brought your digital camera and took a lot of great pictures, and now you want to share them with everyone. How will you do this?

There are many options, of which we will consider two common choices. You could e-mail the pictures to all of your friends, or you could put them on a Web page and send everyone the link. E-mailing digital pictures has certain disadvantages. If you send many pictures you could end up bombarding all of your friends' e-mail accounts with large file attachments. People with slow connections would have to wait a long time to download them. Even people with fast connections might find it an inconvenience. Such concerns are always an issue when you pass on information to others by distributing a copy of the information.

Instead of using e-mail, you could use one of the many free Web services that allow you to post your pictures on a Web page. In this arrangement, the images reside in one place—on the Web site. Instead of e-mailing copies of the images to your friends, you e-mail only the Web address. The Web address points to the Web page where the pictures are stored. When one of your friends clicks the link, his or her Web browser displays the pictures.

Of the two options, the least efficient is e-mail. It requires duplication of the images, which in turn requires storage space in everyone's e-mail account. The Web option involves storing the images in only one place.

This example illustrates a common problem in computer science: managing the use of system resources in an efficient manner. Just as it is more efficient to save a large picture file in one location and send out a Web address that others can follow to gain access to it, it is more efficient with many data structures to store them in one location in memory and send out a link (called a pointer) to other methods that may need to access them. To do this requires familiarity with some basic pointer concepts.

Basic Pointer Concepts

As you know, whenever a variable is declared three things happen:

- The variable is given a name.
- The variable is assigned a data type.
- One or more bytes of memory are allocated to store data for that variable.

For example, the declaration

```
int num;
```

on most PCs allocates a block of four bytes of memory to store a 32-bit integer and calls that variable num. This declaration and the allocation of memory cells beginning in the cell with address 1345244 is shown in Figure 11-1.

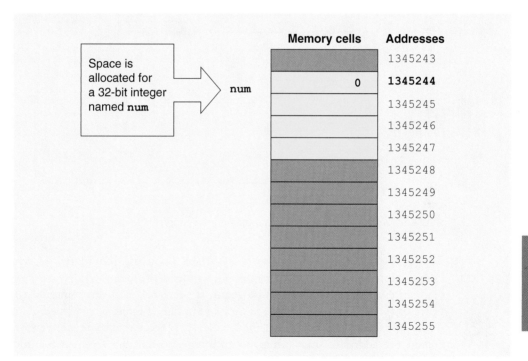

FIGURE 11-1 Association of an allocated memory cell address with the variable num

Every time the program is recompiled and executes, a different block of four bytes may be allocated for num depending upon what is available in RAM at that time. The programmer cannot know in advance which memory cells will be allocated and what their memory cell addresses will be. Because the variable has a name (num), the programmer does not have to know this address. C++ keeps track of which memory cells to access whenever it encounters num in the program code and automatically handles retrieval and assignment tasks related to those memory cells.

Memory Cell Addresses

If you are curious, it is possible to see which memory cell addresses have been chosen for your variables. Figure 11-2 shows the interface for a program in which the code for btnDisplay_Click() declares an integer variable (num) and displays its memory cell address in txtAddress.

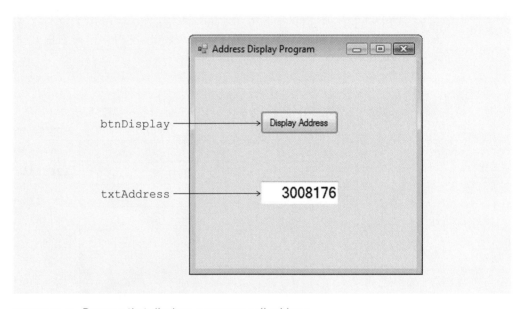

FIGURE 11-2 Program that displays a memory cell address

To get the memory cell address of a variable, you use the address-of operator (&) in conjunction with the variable name. The address-of operator (&) provides the memory cell address of the variable whose name it precedes. You encountered the address-of operator (&) in Chapter 6, where it was used to define reference parameters. Example 11-1 shows the code for btnDisplay_Click(). Notice that type conversion is used to change the address of num (&num) to an integer so that the ToString() method can be used to display it. The use of parentheses is important here. First the address of num is acquired (&num) and then it is converted to an integer (int) before being displayed as a string in txtAddress->Text.

EXAMPLE 11-1: DISPLAYING AN ADDRESS

```
private: System::Void btnDisplay_Click(System::Object^  sender,
System::EventArgs^  e) {
   // This program displays the address
   // assigned to an integer variable
   int num;
   txtAddress->Text = ((int) &num).ToString();
}
```

One of the things that makes programming in a high-level language convenient is that programmers do not need to know the exact memory cell addresses of variables. The programmer can declare a variable and then write code referring to the variable by its name many times without having to know anything about the variable's exact memory cell assignments.

Although there is little reason for the programmer to know the assigned address locations of variables, a C++ program must be able to keep track of them. Every C++ command that refers to a variable must be translated into binary instructions that refer to a specific memory cell address.

Creating Pointer Variables

A **pointer** is a variable that may contain a memory cell address. The term *pointer* is used because memory cell addresses "point to" a location in which data values reside. In Example 11-1, the address of num (&num) could be used as a pointer to num.

Pointer variables are variables that store memory cell addresses. The general syntax for declaring a single pointer variable is

```
data_type* variable_name;
```

Pointer variables are declared using the **pointer data type symbol** (*) in conjunction with a primitive data type. The combination of a primitive type and the * represents a data type called a pointer type. In Example 11-2, a variable called numPtr is declared to be a pointer to an integer (int*). This means that enough memory space is allocated to store a memory cell address. It also means that only an integer can be stored at that address. When multiple pointers are declared on the same line, as in the case of ptr1, ptr2, and ptr3 in Example 11-2, the * symbol adjoins each variable name to indicate that it is a pointer to the data type specified at the start of the line.

EXAMPLE 11-2: DECLARING POINTER VARIABLES

```
int* numPtr;
int *ptr1, *ptr2, *ptr3;
```

The pointer variable `numPtr`, declared in Example 11-2, will contain a pointer when one is assigned to it. Until a valid value of the correct pointer type is assigned, it may be assigned a special system value called a **null pointer** to indicate that it is empty. One way to create a null pointer is to assign a pointer variable the value 0. The Visual C++ keyword `nullptr` (which stands for null pointer) may also be used for this purpose, as seen in Example 11-3. Both the value 0 and `nullptr` are special values that are used to indicate that the pointer is empty.

EXAMPLE 11-3: ASSIGNING THE NULL POINTER

```
int* num1Ptr = 0;  // A null pointer variable
int* num2Ptr = nullptr;  // A null pointer variable
```

Pointers are not integers, they are special pointer types. You cannot assign any literal value other than 0 to a pointer variable.

Assigning actual pointer values to a pointer variable may be done in several ways. Every program has a certain amount of memory available to it for the purpose of dynamic allocation. **Dynamic allocation** means that memory cells are allocated for the program while it is running. The memory resource that supports dynamic allocation is called the **heap**. The `new` operator is used to access the heap, allocate the amount of memory needed by the program, and return the memory cell address of where the newly allocated space begins. The syntax of the `new` operator is

```
new data_type
```

Example 11-4 shows several ways in which `new` may be used. When parentheses are used following the data type, it means that the values in the parentheses are to initialize the newly created variable.

EXAMPLE 11-4: DYNAMIC ALLOCATION USING new

```
int* num1Ptr;  // Declares a pointer variable
// Constructs an integer and assigns its location to num1Ptr
num1Ptr = new int;
int* num2Ptr;  // Declares a pointer variable
// An integer, initialized to 99, and assigned
to num2Ptr
num2Ptr = new int(99);
```

You will use **new** again later in the chapter to construct arrays.

The other way to assign a pointer to a pointer variable is to assign that pointer variable the address of a variable that already exists. In Example 11-5, the address of the integer variable num is assigned to numPtr.

EXAMPLE 11-5: ASSIGNING AN ADDRESS

```
int* numPtr;   // Declares a pointer variable
int num = 5;   // Declares an integer variable and initializes it
numPtr = &num; // Initializes the pointer variable
```

This sets up the relationship shown in Figure 11-3. The C++ declaration and assignment statements are shown on the left side, while the allocation of memory is depicted on the right where the allocated memory cells are shown along with their addresses.

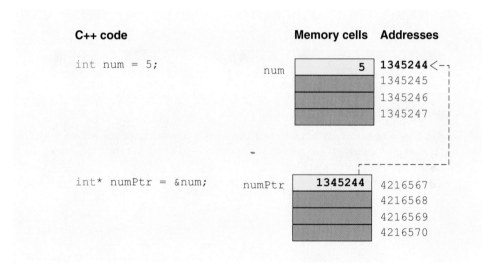

FIGURE 11-3 The variable numPtr stores the address of (pointer to) the variable num

The code for **btnDisplay_Click()** in Figure 11-2 can now be written using the pointer variable **numPtr** to display the address of **num**, as shown in Example 11-6.

EXAMPLE 11-6: DISPLAYING A POINTER

```
private: System::Void btnDisplay_Click(System::Object^  sender,
System::EventArgs^  e) {
// The address of num is assigned to the pointer variable numPtr
// The address of num is then displayed using numPtr
    int num;
    int* numPtr = &num;
    txtAddress->Text = ((int) numPtr).ToString();
}
```

In Example 11-6, the address of num was assigned to numPtr. Every declared variable has an address. Even numPtr must reside in memory somewhere, and that location can also be assigned to another variable. In Example 11-7 a variable has been declared (numPtrPtr) that will contain the address of numPtr. Notice that because it will point to a variable that contains a pointer to an integer, the declaration syntax begins to look strange. The declaration data type specification (int** numPtrPtr) is read as "numPtrPtr is a pointer to a pointer to an integer."

EXAMPLE 11-7: DISPLAYING A POINTER TO A POINTER

```
private: System::Void btnDisplay_Click(System::Object^  sender,
System::EventArgs^  e) {
// The address of num is assigned to the pointer variable numPtr
// The address of numPtr is assigned to the pointer variable numPtrPtr
// The address of numPtr is then displayed using numPtrPtr
    int num;
    int* numPtr = &num;
    int** numPtrPtr = &numPtr;
    txtAddress->Text = ((int) numPtrPtr).ToString();
}
```

This relationship is shown in Figure 11-4. The C++ declarations and assignments are shown on the left and memory cell allocation, along with the address, on the right. If the memory cell assignments in Figure 11-4 were the result of the declarations in Example 11-7, then Example 11-7 would display the integer value 4216567.

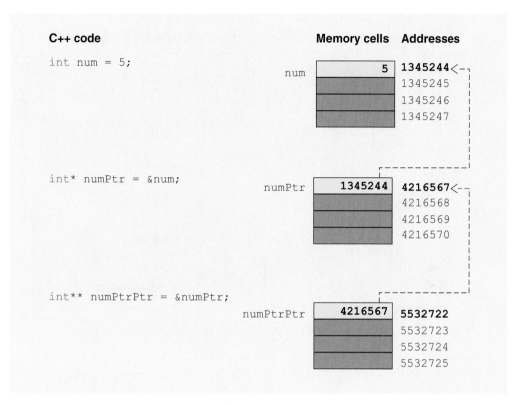

FIGURE 11-4 Variables containing a pointer to an integer (numPtr) and a pointer to a pointer to an integer (numPtrPtr).

Knowing how to declare and use a variable that contains a pointer to another variable that contains a pointer turns out to be a very efficient way of handling data in arrays in some circumstances as we shall see in the tutorial later in this chapter.

Accessing Data Indirectly Through Pointers

You now know how to capture a link to another variable by storing that variable's memory cell address in a pointer variable. Once a pointer variable (like **numPtr**) contains the address of another variable (like **num**) the pointer variable can be used to access the value contained in the variable it points to. This is analogous to the way that a Web address link can be used to access pictures on somebody else's Web site. The address is followed back to its original location, where the information you seek is stored.

The process of using an address to look up information stored elsewhere is called **indirection**. C++ provides an **indirection operator (*)** to allow a pointer to be followed back to the location it points to and access the data stored there. The process of using a pointer to access the contents of the memory cell it points to is called **dereferencing**.

To illustrate how this works, consider the program whose interface is shown in Figure 11-5. The user enters an integer into `txtEnter`. When `btnDisplay` is clicked, the value in `txtEnter->Text` is read into an integer variable called `num`, and the value in `num` is then displayed in `txtNum->Text`.

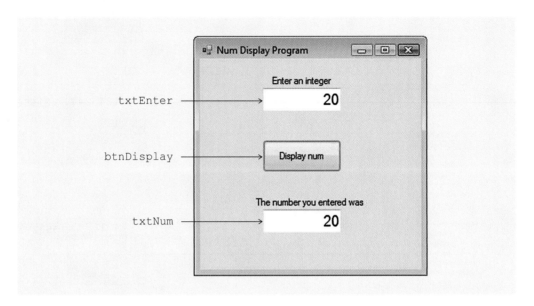

FIGURE 11-5 Displaying the contents of `num` using indirection

The code for `btnDisplay_Click()` is shown in Example 11-8. Notice that `numPtr` was assigned the address of `num`. The indirection operator was then used with `numPtr` to access the data in `num` and display it in `txtNum->Text`.

EXAMPLE 11-8: USING INDIRECTION

```
private: System::Void btnDisplay_Click(System::Object^ sender,
System::EventArgs^ e) {
    int num;
    int* numPtr = &num;

    if (Int32::TryParse(txtEnter->Text, num))
        txtNum->Text = (*numPtr).ToString();
    else
        MessageBox::Show("You failed to enter an integer");
}
```

The program shown in Figure 11-6 displays the value stored in num in three ways:

- On the lower left, txtNum displays the value it obtains from num directly. This is accomplished using num.ToString().

- In the lower middle, txtNumPtr displays the value stored in num by dereferencing numPtr. This is accomplished using the indirection operator in this manner: (*numPtr).ToString().

- At the lower right, txtNumPtrPtr displays the value stored in num using indirection twice (**double indirection**).

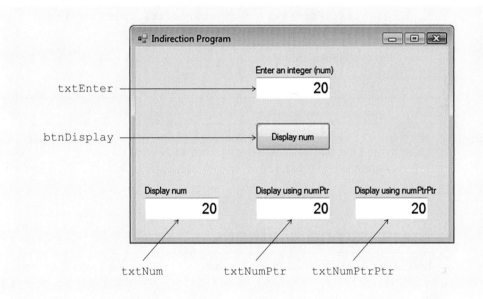

FIGURE 11-6 Displaying a value using indirection

The code for btnDisplay_Click() is shown in Example 11-9. Note the manner in which the indirection operator (*) is used. Each pointer variable is dereferenced the proper number of times to allow it to access the data value stored in num. The variable numPtrPtr uses the indirection operator twice (**), because the dereferencing process must follow the reference in numPtrPtr to numPtr and then on to num. In all cases, however, txtNum, txtNumPtr, and txtNumPtrPtr display the same value—the value stored in num.

EXAMPLE 11-9: USING DOUBLE INDIRECTION

```
private: System::Void btnDisplay_Click(System::Object^  sender,
System::EventArgs^  e) {
    int num;
    int* numPtr = &num;
    int** numPtrPtr = &numPtr;

    if (Int32::TryParse(txtEnter->Text, num))
    {
        txtNum->Text = num.ToString();
        txtNumPtr->Text = (*numPtr).ToString();
        txtNumPtrPtr->Text = (**numPtrPtr).ToString();
    }
    else
        MessageBox::Show("You failed to enter an integer");
}
```

NOTE   It is easy to confuse the pointer data type symbol (*) used in pointer variable declarations with the indirection operator (*) used to dereference a pointer. Their roles complement one another, but represent very different operations.

Pointers and Methods

In Chapter 6, you learned two ways that data can be passed into a method: pass-by-value or pass-by-reference. Parameter passing can also take place using pointers. This technique predates pass-by-reference. However, it is instructive because it shows in more detail how memory cell addresses are used from within a method to access data values stored in variables outside of the method.

To review pass-by-reference, we will use the program interface shown in Figure 11-7, which allows the user to enter data in txtNum1 and txtNum2. After these values are read into program variables num1 and num2 the values stored in those variables are displayed in txtShowNum1 and txtShowNum2.

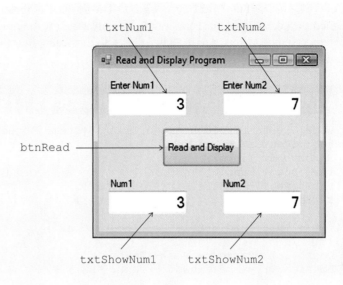

FIGURE 11-7 Program to read and display data

The program segment in Example 11-10 illustrates a situation in which you want to read values into the variables `num1` and `num2` from text boxes `txtNum1` and `txtNum2`, respectively. This is done by calling the `read()` method and passing in `num1` and `num2` by reference.

EXAMPLE 11-10: REFERENCE PARAMETERS

```
private: System::Void btnRead_Click(System::Object^ sender,
System::EventArgs^ e) {
    double num1, num2;
    read(num1, num2);
    txtShowNum1->Text = num1.ToString();
    txtShowNum2->Text = num2.ToString();
}
private: void read(double& n1, double& n2 )
{
    Double::TryParse(txtNum1->Text, n1);
    Double::TryParse(txtNum2->Text, n2);
}
```

Now examine a version of this program written using pointers instead of reference parameters. The code is shown in Example 11-11. This time, the actual arguments are explicitly indicated to be addresses using the address-of operator (`&`). Similarly, the formal parameters are explicitly declared to be pointers to double-precision numbers using a pointer-to-double (`double*`) data type declaration. The actual arguments (`&num1, &num2`) pass the addresses of num1 and num2 into read(). The formal parameters of read(), n1 and n2, are assigned the addresses of num1 and num2. Within read(), the pointer variables n1 and n2 are dereferenced when referred to in TryParse() so that data values may be read into the memory cells they point to.

EXAMPLE 11-11: DEREFERENCING A POINTER ARGUMENT

```
private: System::Void btnRead_Click(System::Object^  sender,
System::EventArgs^  e) {
    double num1, num2;
    read(&num1, &num2);
    txtShowNum1->Text = num1.ToString();
    txtShowNum2->Text = num2.ToString();
}
private: void read(double* n1, double* n2 )
{
    Double::TryParse(txtNum1->Text, *n1);
    Double::TryParse(txtNum2->Text, *n2);
}
```

Figure 11-8 illustrates the relationship between the variables num1 and num2 in btnRead_Click() and n1 and n2 in read(). The addresses of the actual arguments (&num1 and &num2) are passed into read() and assigned to pointer variables n1 and n2, respectively. The pointer variables are then able to assign values to their corresponding arguments through dereferencing. From the diagram, you can assume that the value 3 was read from txtNum1->Text and assigned to num1 by dereferencing n1. Similarly, the value 4 was read from txtNum2->Text and assigned to num2 by dereferencing n2.

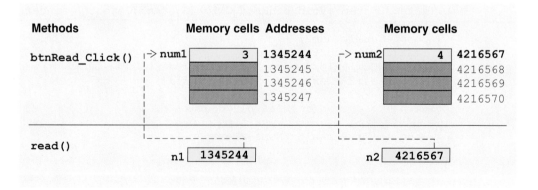

FIGURE 11-8 Passing a pointer (&num) into a method to be stored in pointer variable numPtr

Pointer Return Types

Pointer data types such as `int*` can be used in many ways, just like primitive data types. For example, a method can return a value that is a pointer data type in the same way it might otherwise return an integer, `double`, or some other primitive data type value. Consider the interface shown in Figure 11-9. It allows the user to enter three integers. When the user clicks `btnLarge`, the program displays the largest of the three integers in the text box at the bottom.

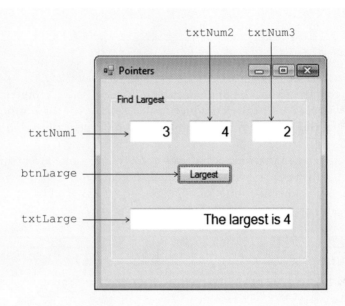

FIGURE 11-9 Interface for program that finds the largest of three integers

The code for `btnLarge_Click()` is shown in Example 11-12. Notice that a pointer variable (`large`) is declared. The `findLarge()` method is called with three actual arguments, the addresses of three integer variables (`&a, &b, &c`), for the purpose of determining which variable holds the largest value. The `findLarge()` method returns a pointer to the variable with the largest value and assigns it to `large`. To display the result, `large` must be dereferenced (`*large`).

11

EXAMPLE 11-12: FINDING THE LARGEST VALUE

```
private: System::Void btnLarge_Click(System::Object^  sender,
System::EventArgs^  e) {
   int a, b, c;
   Int32::TryParse(txtNum1->Text, a);
   Int32::TryParse(txtNum2->Text, b);
   Int32::TryParse(txtNum3->Text, c);
   int* large;
   large = findLarge(&a, &b, &c);  // call findLarge()
   txtLarge->Text = "The largest is " + (*large).ToString();
}
```

Example 11-13 shows the findLarge() method. Notice that the formal arguments (num1, num2, and num3) are all pointer variables. They are passed the addresses of the three integer variables in the actual arguments. A local pointer variable (max) is declared. It will ultimately store a pointer to the variable containing the largest integer value. To begin, max is set to num1, assuming that the largest value is the one that num1 points to. The if statement compares the value stored in the memory cell pointed to by num2 to those pointed to by num3 and max. If the value pointed to by num2 is the largest of those values then max is assigned the address stored in num2. Otherwise, the value pointed to by num3 is compared to the value pointed to by max, and if the value pointed to by num3 is larger, max is assigned the address stored in num3.

EXAMPLE 11-13: CODE FOR findLarge()

```
private: int* findLarge(int *num1, int *num2, int *num3) {
   int *max = num1;
   if ((*num2 > *num3) && (*num2 > *max))
      max = num2;
   else if (*num3 > *max)
      max = num3;
   return max;
}
```

The key to understanding Example 11-13 is to notice when pointers are dereferenced and when they are not. A statement such as max = num3 assigns the contents of a pointer variable (and address) to another pointer variable. On the other hand, expressions such as (*num3 > *max) dereferences both the pointer variable num3 and max so that their contents may be compared to one another.

Pointers and Arrays

Pointers are especially useful when you need to construct arrays. In Chapter 7, you learned how to declare arrays of a fixed size. Using pointer syntax, however, you can declare arrays at runtime through dynamic allocation and size the arrays to fit the requirements of the program. Dynamic allocation is done using the **new** operator, which allocates a designated number of memory cells and returns the address of the first memory cell. The syntax for the **new** operator used to create a one-dimensional array is shown here:

```
new data_type[size];
```

The **new** operator allocates a number of memory cells of the designated data type. A positive integer **size** is used to designate the number of elements. Example 11-14 shows the declaration of a pointer variable **arrPtr**. The **new** operator is then used to allocate memory cells sufficient to store four integers (since each integer takes 4 bytes in a typical Windows environment, a total of 16 bytes are required). The address of the first memory cell in the newly allocated space is returned by **new** and assigned to **arrPtr**.

EXAMPLE 11-14: DYNAMIC ARRAY ALLOCATION

```
int* arrPtr;
arrPtr = new int[4];
```

Figure 11-10 shows the allocation and assignment operations from Example 11-14.

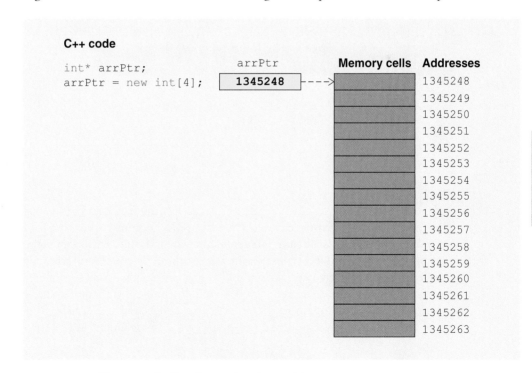

FIGURE 11-10 Memory cell allocation and assignment to arrPtr

In effect, `arrPtr` has now become an array. The pointer variable `arrPtr` contains a pointer to the first memory cell in a block of memory sufficient to store four integers. The new array, accessible through `arrPtr`, can be referenced in the same manner as the fixed-size arrays you are used to, with array element indexing. The first 32-bit integer (spanning four memory cells with addresses 1345248 through 1345251) is designated `arrPtr[0]`, the second integer (spanning memory cells with addresses 1345252 through 1345255) is `arrPtr[1]` and so on, as shown in Figure 11-11.

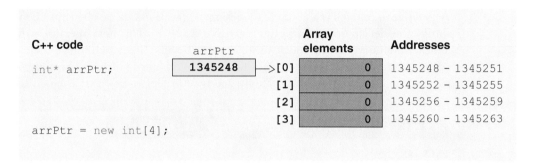

FIGURE 11-11 The `arrPtr` array

The pointer variable `arrPtr` can be referred to as an array using array element indexing, just as any fixed-size array can. Example 11-15 shows how to use a `for` loop to access each of the four elements in the `arrPtr` array and initialize them to 0.

EXAMPLE 11-15: INITIALIZING A DYNAMIC ARRAY

```
int* arrPtr;
arrPtr = new int[4];
for (int i=0; i<4; i++) arrPtr[i] = 0;
```

Pointer Arithmetic

The term **pointer arithmetic** refers to the use of pointers in arithmetic expressions. Most often this entails adding integer values to and subtracting integer values from pointers. This is possible because pointers are numbered memory cell addresses, which behave in some respects like positive integers. Example 11-16 uses pointer arithmetic to initialize the elements of `arrPtr` to 0, just as Example 11-15 did using array element indexing. Notice that a temporary pointer (`temp`) is declared and initialized with the value stored in `arrPtr`. This allows `temp` to point to the first element in the array as the loop begins.

Pointer arithmetic is used in two locations in Example 11-16. The loop continues as long as the precondition (`temp < arrPtr+4`) evaluates to true. Using pointer arithmetic to add 4 to `arrPtr` yields the address of array element `arrPtr[4]`, which is outside of the bounds of the array as the last element in the array is `aryPtr[3]`. The loop is over when `temp` is set to the memory cell address of `arrPtr[4]`.

NOTE   Although the address of `arrPtr[4]` can be calculated, it is beyond the upper bound of the array and is not a memory cell that has been allocated to your program. You should not attempt to utilize an element beyond the upper bounds of an array. Most often, this will cause a runtime error.

The second example of pointer arithmetic occurs when the update clause of the loop (`temp++`) increments `temp` by 1. Because `temp` is a pointer to an integer, incrementing it by 1 causes its value to change to the memory cell location of the next integer, four bytes away. Incrementing `temp` causes `temp` to point to a new element in `arrPtr` prior to each iteration of the loop.

EXAMPLE 11-16: INCREMENTING A POINTER

```
int* arrPtr;
int* temp;
arrPtr = new int[4];
for (temp = arrPtr; temp < arrPtr+4; temp++) *temp = 0;
```

A more complicated example of pointer arithmetic is shown in Example 11-17, where pointer arithmetic is used to perform a binary search on a fixed-size array. Notice that `low`, `mid`, and `high` are all declared to be pointers to integers. The integer array `arr` is searched for a target value by using pointer arithmetic with the memory cell addresses stored in `low`, `mid`, and `high`. Notice that `low` is initially set to the address of the first element in the array: `&(arr[0])`. Similarly, `high` is initially set to the address of the last element in the array `&(arr[7])`. The `while` loop continues to search until `low` becomes greater than `high`. The calculation of `mid` must be done, keeping in mind that `low` and `high` are memory cell addresses, by dividing the difference between `low` and `high` by 2 and then adding the result to the address of the first element (`low`) to get an address that is within the range of valid addresses for the array.

11

EXAMPLE 11-17: BINARY SEARCH USING POINTERS

```
int arr[] = { 9,17,29,34,45,57,62};
int *low, *high, *mid; // Pointer variables
low = &(arr[0]);        // low set to address of arr[0]
high = &(arr[7]);       // high set to address of arr[7]
int target;
Int32::TryParse(txtTarget->Text, target);
while (low <= high)
{
   mid = low + (high - low) /2;
   if (target < *mid) high = mid-1;
   else if (target > *mid) low = mid + 1;
   else low = high + 1;  // Target found
}
if (target == *mid)
   MessageBox::Show( " FOUND! ");
else
   MessageBox::Show( " NOT FOUND! ");
```

Pointer arithmetic is used in every statement in the `while` loop as values are added or subtracted from pointer variables. Figure 11-12 illustrates the binary search process in Example 11-17. Notice that `low`, `mid`, and `high` do not contain array element indices, as they did in Chapter 9. Instead, they contain memory cell addresses that run from 4038824 to 4038848.

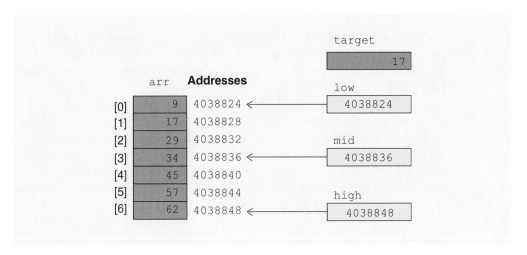

FIGURE 11-12 Binary search using pointers

Deleting Pointers

The biggest problem with pointers is managing their use of memory. If you are not careful, it is possible to create a program that bogs down because it runs out of memory available to it on the heap. You have seen that the `new` operator can be used to dynamically allocate memory on the heap. When there is no longer a need for this memory, it should be deallocated so that it can be used again. If memory is repeatedly allocated but never deallocated, the program could run out of available memory on the heap.

To ensure that memory is managed correctly, the `delete` operator allows you to deallocate memory, returning it to the heap so that it is available for the program later on. The syntax of the `delete` operator is:

```
delete pointer_variable;
```

Example 11-18 shows how the `new` operator is used to allocate space for the pointer variable `ptr`, a pointer to an integer, and when that space is no longer needed the `delete` operator is used to deallocate the memory pointed to by `ptr`, returning it to the heap. The pointer variable (`ptr`) is not deleted, only the memory it pointed to.

EXAMPLE 11-18: DELETING ALLOCATED MEMORY

```
private:  void processData()
{
    int* ptr;
    ptr = new int;
    // The variable ptr is then used
    // When finished the allocated memory is deleted
    delete ptr;
}
```

When the space that was dynamically allocated is an array, a special form of the `delete` operator is used that includes a pair of empty square brackets:

```
delete[] pointer_variable;
```

In Example 11-19, the `delete` operator deallocates the space reserved for the array, making the space in memory available for future use. Remember that the delete operator deallocates the memory pointed to by `num`. It does not delete `num`.

EXAMPLE 11-19: DELETING A DYNAMIC ARRAY

```
private:  void processArray()
{
    double *num;
    num = new double[1000];
// The array pointed to by num is used
// When finished, the allocated memory is deleted
    delete[] num;
}
```

Arrays of Pointers

You have seen how to use **new** to dynamically allocate an array of double-precision numbers. This technique may be used to allocate many different types of arrays. An array of pointers can be constructed in roughly the same manner as an array of doubles or integers. In Example 11-20, you start with an instance variable **ptrArr**, declared to be a pointer to a pointer to an **int**. Space for eight pointers to integer is then allocated for **ptrArr** to point to.

EXAMPLE 11-20: ALLOCATING AN ARRAY OF POINTERS

```
int** ptrArr;
ptrArr = new int*[8];
```

The result is shown in Figure 11-13. The **new** command dynamically allocates space from the heap to store eight pointers to integers. The address of the first memory cell in this newly allocated space (3241231) is returned and assigned to **ptrArr**. Notice that allocating space for pointer variables does not initialize them. None of the eight pointer elements have had pointers assigned to them by our program yet.

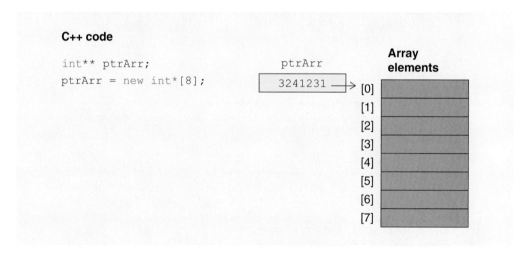

FIGURE 11-13 Pointer array variable declaration and assignment using new

You can initialize the pointer array elements in several ways. A **for** loop can be employed to access each pointer element in sequence, construct an integer object, and assign its address to the corresponding pointer array element. The code for this is shown in Example 11-21. In this example, all newly constructed integers are initialized with the value 0.

EXAMPLE 11-21: DYNAMIC ALLOCATION AND ASSIGNMENT

```
for (i=0; i<8; i++) ptrArr[i] = new int(0);
```

The result is shown in Figure 11-14. Notice that the eight integers allocated by **new** may not necessarily come from adjacent memory cell locations. The pointers to those integers, however, are stored in adjacent locations in an array.

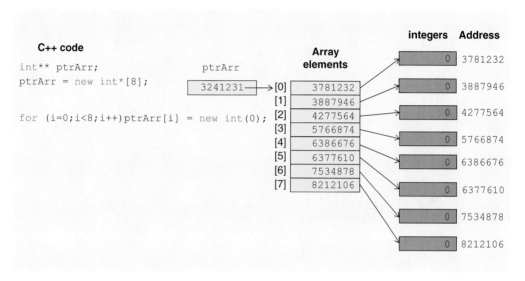

FIGURE 11-14 Initializing the pointer array using new to assign the addresses of dynamically allocated integers

Once each of the elements in the array of pointers has been assigned, the pointers can be used to indirectly access data values stored in the integer locations. The code shown in Example 11-22 shows how the sum of the integers can be accumulated using a **for** loop with a pointer array in which the pointers are dereferenced to access the integer data values.

EXAMPLE 11-22: SUMMATION BY DEREFERENCING POINTERS

```
int sum = 0;
for (int i = 0; i < 8; i++) sum += *ptrArr[i];
textBox1->Text = sum.ToString();
```

Pointer arrays can also be initialized from other arrays as shown in Example 11-23, where the addresses of the elements in the integer array **arrNum** are assigned to the elements of the pointer array **ptrArr**.

EXAMPLE 11-23: INITIALIZING POINTER ARRAY ELEMENTS

```
int arrNum[] = { 91,77,18,36, 55, 40, 62, 73};
for (i=0; i<8; i++) ptrArr[i] = &arrNum[i];
```

The result is that the parallel array **ptrArr** now contains pointers to the elements in **arrNum**, as shown in Figure 11-15.

C++ code

```
int** ptrArr;
ptrArr = new int*[8];


int arrNum[]={91,77,18,36,55,40,62,73}


for (i=0;i<8;i++)ptrArr[i] = &arrNum[i];
```

	ptrArr	Array elements		integers	Addresses
	3241231 → [0]	4038824 → [0]		91	4038824
	[1]	4038828 → [1]		77	4038828
	[2]	4038832 → [2]		18	4038832
	[3]	4038836 → [3]		36	4038836
	[4]	4038840 → [4]		55	4038840
	[5]	4038844 → [5]		40	4038844
	[6]	4038848 → [6]		62	4038848
	[7]	4038852 → [7]		73	4038852

FIGURE 11-15 Array `ptrArr` containing the addresses of corresponding elements in array `arrNum`

Sorting With Pointers

Now let us consider how a larger data structure might use pointers. A **record** of information is a collection of data related to one person or other entity. For example, colleges and universities maintain databases full of student information records. All of the data for a single student might be collected together into a single record of information as shown in Figure 11-16.

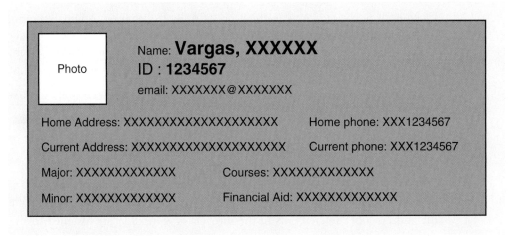

Name: **Vargas, XXXXXX**
ID : **1234567**
email: XXXXXXX@XXXXXXX
Photo

Home Address: XXXXXXXXXXXXXXXXXXXX   Home phone: XXX1234567

Current Address: XXXXXXXXXXXXXXXXXXXXX   Current phone: XXX1234567

Major: XXXXXXXXXXXX   Courses: XXXXXXXXXXXX

Minor: XXXXXXXXXXXX   Financial Aid: XXXXXXXXXXXX

FIGURE 11-16 Student information record

Each record of information contains many items that can be represented by different types of data. For example, the photo might be an image file, the name and addresses may be strings, the ID number might be an integer, and the grade point average a `double`. Although you have not yet learned how to make a data structure of this sort, you can easily imagine what it might look like if it were an array of student records, called `studentData`, as shown in Figure 11-17. Next to each record, the array element subscript of each element and the memory cell address of where the storage of data for that record starts are listed.

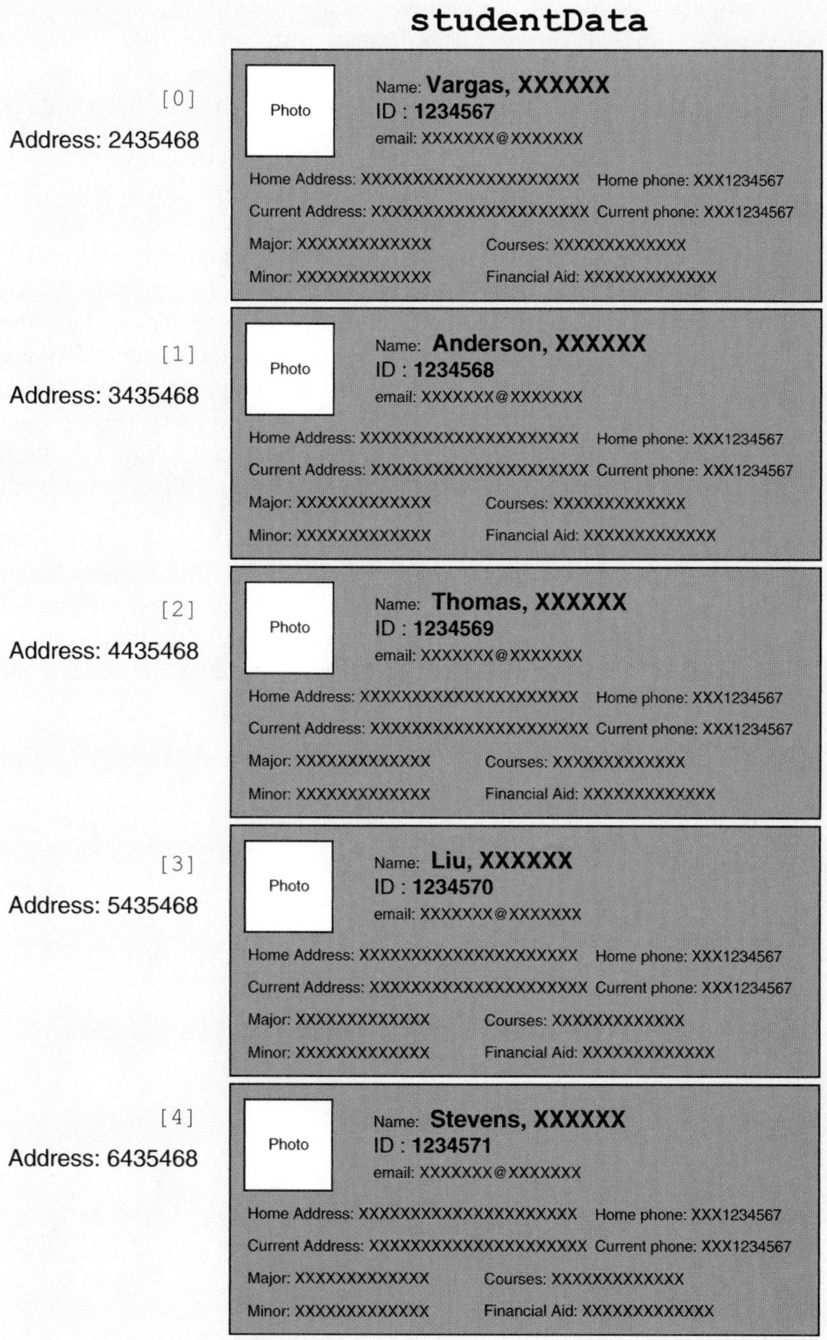

FIGURE 11-17 Array of student records

As students enroll for the first time, they stand in line. One by one they have their picture taken, are assigned an ID number, and are added to the database. Since ID numbers are issued in consecutive order, the database is in order by ID number. Figure 11–17 shows only five elements in the array. The last names are not in alphabetical order because students were added to the database in the order they were standing in the line.

In a real student database there could be tens of thousands of students, accumulated over many years. Each element could take up a considerable amount of storage space. Now, imagine that you wanted to sort this array of student records by name instead of ID number, using one of the sorting techniques discussed earlier in the text. No matter which one you select, the sorting technique would require massive amounts of data movement. Every time one student record was swapped with another, for example, you would need to copy data from one record to another several times. Unlike the simple swap() method you used with integers, the swapping of array elements in this example would take considerable processing resources, and the sorting program would run quite slowly as all of the data was being copied from one location to another in memory every time a swap occurred.

Pointer arrays come to the rescue here. Figure 11–18 shows two arrays. On the right is the student record array. On the left is an array of pointers. Each element in the array of pointers contains the memory cell address of where its corresponding element in the studentData array is stored in memory. By following the pointers from studentPtr[0] down to studentPtr[4] each of the records in the studentData array are accessed in order by ID number.

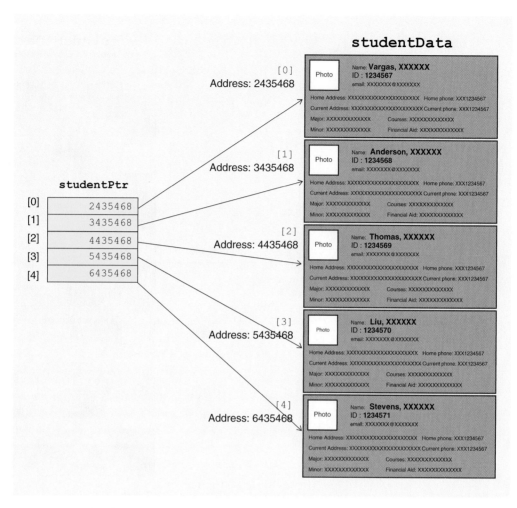

FIGURE 11-18 A pointer array with pointers to corresponding elements in the `studentData` array

Rather than sorting the `studentData` array by swapping its student record elements around, there is another strategy. The data in the `studentData` array can remain where it is. Instead, the pointers in the `studentPtr` array can be swapped. At the end of a typical sort procedure this yields the situation shown in Figure 11-19.

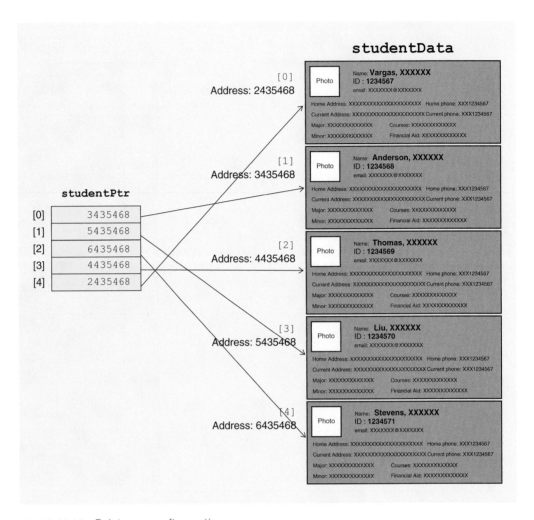

FIGURE 11-19 Pointer array after sorting

Notice that the data in the `studentData` array has not moved or changed in any way. Instead, the pointers in the `studentPtr` array have been exchanged and now point to the records in a new order. By following the pointers from `studentPtr[0]` down to `studentPtr[4]`, each of the records in the `studentData` array are accessed in ascending order by last name (Anderson, Liu, Stevens, Thomas, Vargas). In effect, the information in `studentData` is now accessible in order by last name through the pointer array `studentPtr`, even though the elements in `studentData` remain in the original positions they were first assigned.

The advantages of this technique are realized on data structures such as arrays of student records more so than arrays of primitive data types (which can be easily swapped). However, to gain a practical understanding of how the sorting process works, consider how the strategy of using a pointer array can be employed on a smaller scale, with an array of integers instead of student records.

In Example 11-24, an array of eight integers called `arr` has been declared and dynamically allocated. Similarly, an array of pointers to integers called `ptr` has been declared and dynamically allocated. In addition, the elements of `ptr` have been assigned the memory cell addresses of the corresponding elements in `arr`.

EXAMPLE 11-24: DYNAMIC ALLOCATION OF POINTER ARRAYS

```
// Assign element addresses to ptr
int* arr;
int** ptr;
arr = new int[8];
ptr = new int*[8];
for (i=0; i < 8; i++) ptr[i] = &arr[i];
```

Notice the use of pointer declaration symbol ** twice in the declaration of `ptr`.

`int** ptr;`

This indicates that the data type of `ptr` will store a pointer to a memory cell in which a pointer to an integer resides, as can be seen in Figure 11-20. After the elements of `arr` have been initialized, the relationship of the two arrays (`ptr` and `arr`) is also shown in Figure 11-20. The diagram shows that the location of the first element in `arr` has the address of 59972696, and the location of the first element in `ptr` has the location 31426532.

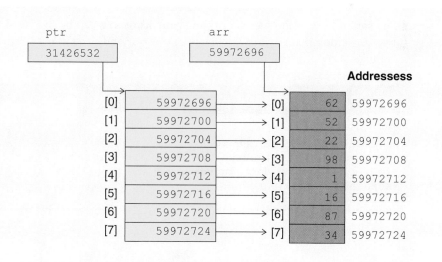

FIGURE 11-20 Pointer array (`ptr`) declaration and assignment to addresses of elements in array `arr`

Now consider how the contents of the pointer array (ptr) can be swapped so that, when finished, they point to the values of the **arr** array in ascending order, as shown in Figure 11-21.

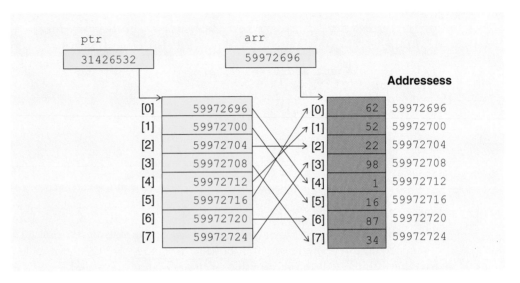

FIGURE 11-21 Pointer array (ptr) assignments to values in data array arr in ascending order

Notice that element **ptr[0]** points to the element with the lowest value in **arr**, **ptr[1]** points to the second lowest value, **ptr[2]** points to the third lowest value, and so on.

The sorted list of values stored in the elements of **arr** can be displayed in a message box by using a loop that traversed the elements in **ptr** and dereferences each pointer as it goes along, as shown in Example 11-25.

EXAMPLE 11-25: PRODUCING A SORTED LIST

```
String^ output = "";
// Create output string with sorted data
for (i=0; i<8; i++) output += (*ptr[i]).ToString() + "\r\n";
// Display sorted data in MessageBox
MessageBox::Show(output);
```

The message box produced by the code shown in Example 11-26 would look like that shown in Figure 11-22.

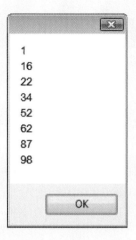

FIGURE 11-22 Message box showing sorted output

To sort the values by reassigning pointers within the `ptr` array, a sort method such as that shown in Example 11-26 could be used. Example 11-26 shows a bubble sort in which the values pointed to by adjacent elements of `ptr` are compared and the pointers are swapped if the first dereferenced value is greater than the second. The inner loop control variable (j) is used to identify a pointer `ptr[j]` and another pointer in the next element (`ptr[j+1]`). The pointers are dereferenced to compare the values stored in them.

EXAMPLE 11-26: SORTING DATA BY SWAPPING POINTERS

```
// Bubble sort the ptr array
for (i=0;  i<7;  i++)
    for (j=0;  j<7-i;  j++)
        if (*ptr[j] > *ptr[j+1])
            swap(&(ptr[j]), &(ptr[j+1]));
```

The key to this sorting technique is the use of a programmer-defined instance method called `swap()` to exchange the pointers stored in two pointer variables.

The `swap()` Method

The `swap()` method shown in Example 11-27 is intriguing because it completely relies on pointers and pointer dereferencing. The actual arguments for the `swap()` method are the addresses of the two adjacent array elements, pointer variables `ptr[j]` and `ptr[j+1]`:

```
swap(&(ptr[j]),  &(ptr[j+1]));
```

For this reason, the formal parameters for **swap()** must be pointers to pointers, as indicated by the use of the **★★** designation in the formal parameter declarations. The code for the **swap()** method is presented in Example 11-27.

EXAMPLE 11-27: swap() METHOD FOR POINTERS

```
private: void swap(int** a, int** b)
{
    int* temp;
    temp = *a;
    *a = *b;
    *b = temp;
}
```

The relationship between the actual arguments and formal parameters is important to understand. Assume that loop control variable j is set to 0. The values pointed to by **ptr[j]** and **ptr[j+1]** are the values 62 and 52 respectively, as shown in Figure 11-23. The addresses of **ptr[0]** and **ptr[1]** are passed into the **swap()** method and assigned to variables **a** and **b**.

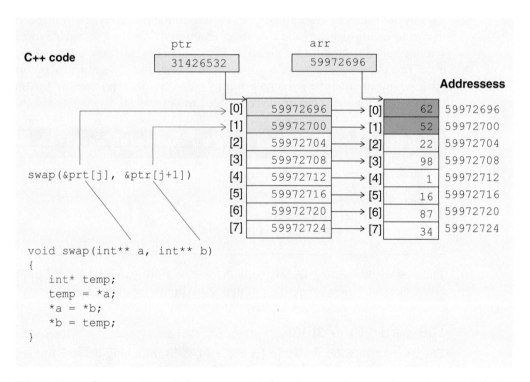

FIGURE 11-23 Correspondence between swap() formal parameters a and b and elements in the pointer array ptr

The `swap()` method then declares a local variable, `temp`, and dereferences variable `a` to assign the pointer value it contains to `temp`. This assignment is shown in Figure 11-24.

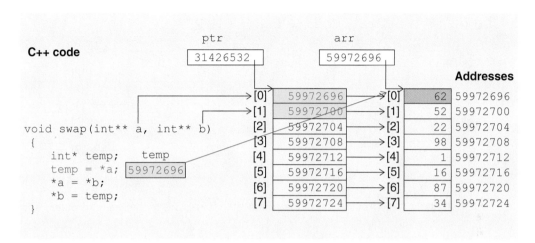

FIGURE 11-24 Assignment of the pointer `ptr[0]` to `temp` using local variable `a`

When variable `b` is dereferenced, the pointer 59972700 is assigned to the location pointed to by variable `a`. This step is colored red in the `swap()` method shown in Figure 11-25.

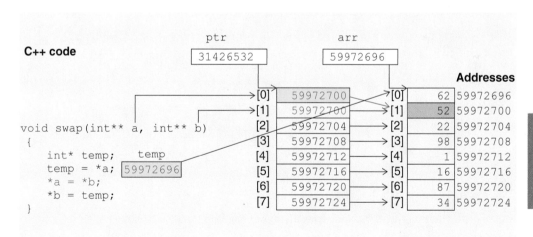

FIGURE 11-25 Dereferencing `b` to store its pointer in the location pointed to by `a`

The final task in the `swap()` method is to assign the contents of `temp` to the location arrived at by dereferencing `b`. The line in `swap()` where this occurs is shown in red in Figure 11-26.

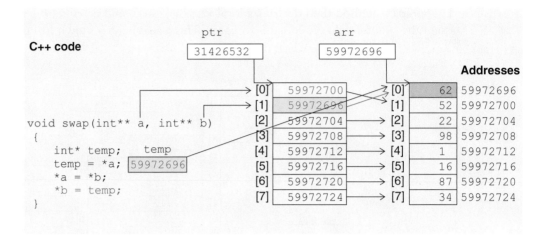

FIGURE 11-26 Assignment of the pointer stored in `temp` to the location pointed to by `b`

As a result, when the **swap()** method is finished, the pointer values in **ptr[0]** and **ptr[1]** have been exchanged. The state of the **ptr** array after calling **swap()** with **ptr[0]** and **ptr[1]** is shown in Figure 11-27.

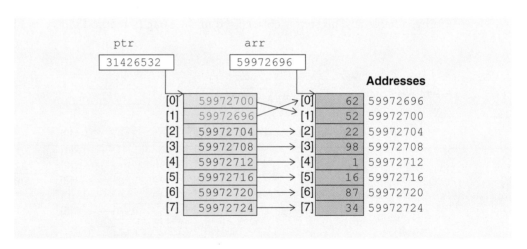

FIGURE 11-27 The `ptr` array after swapping the first two pointers

Note that the data values stored in the first two elements of **arr** have not changed places. However, their pointers, the first two elements of the **ptr** array, have. Further use of this **swap()** method from Example 11-27 in conjunction with the bubble sort method (Example 11-26) would yield the fully sorted pointer array result shown in Figure 11-21. The tutorial will allow you to fully implement this technique.

Tutorial: Sorting with a Pointer Array

This tutorial gives you an opportunity to use the data structures and methods described in the last section. In addition to performing the task of sorting data with a pointer array, the project will display all of the pointer values and data values and then draw connection lines between array elements so that the user can see the connections between the two arrays.

Problem Description

In this project, you create an interface that displays the contents of two arrays, an array of pointers and a data array of integers. Both the pointer array and the data array have eight elements. Text boxes are used to display the values stored in each element of both arrays. A button labeled "Data" allows the user to generate random numbers for the data array. A button labeled "Sort" then sorts the data by swapping values in the pointer array. Figure 11-28 shows the interface you will create for this program.

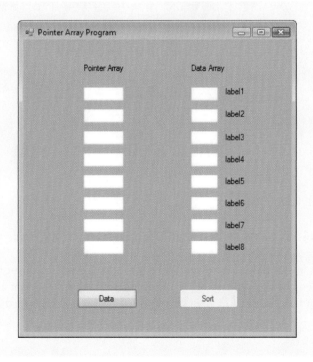

FIGURE 11-28 Tutorial program interface

In the next figure, Figure 11-29, you can see the interface after the user has clicked the Data button. The random integers assigned to each element in the data array are displayed in the eight text boxes under the Data Array heading. The addresses of the elements in which the data are stored are displayed in the eight text boxes to the right of the data array. In addition, the addresses in which the data are stored are also displayed underneath the Pointer Array heading on the interface. Horizontal lines drawn from the pointer array to the data array show the correspondence between the elements in the two data structures.

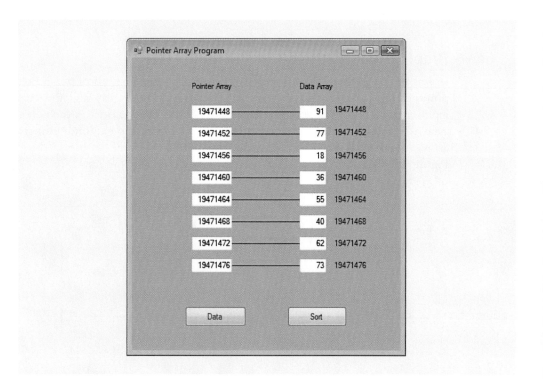

FIGURE 11-29   Initial assignment of pointers to the pointer array

Figure 11-30 shows the interface after the user has clicked the Sort button. The lines between the elements of the two arrays illustrate the fact that, in this program, only the pointers to data are sorted. The data itself remains unsorted. For example, the first element in the pointer array points to the lowest element in the data array, the second pointer to the second lowest, the third pointer to the third lowest, and so on.

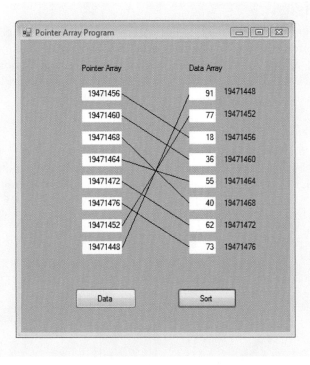

FIGURE 11-30 Result of sorting the data by reassigning pointers in the pointer array

To demonstrate that the data are in their correct order, a message box opens after sorting and displays the data pointed to by the pointers in the pointer array as they are accessed in order from element 0 through element 7. The message box should look something like that shown in Figure 11–31.

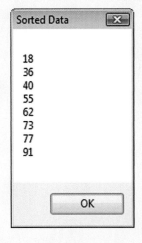

FIGURE 11-31 Message box showing data, in sorted order, as accessed by the pointers

Design

This program is intended to illustrate what happens in the computer's memory as an array of pointers is sorted. The data structures and sorting techniques have been discussed in detail earlier in the text and will require minimal elaboration. After the interface is constructed the chief design tasks center on the algorithms to draw lines correctly between the elements of the two arrays displayed on the interface.

INTERFACE

The interface consists of several sections, each containing multiple controls of the same type. Figure 11-32 shows a section of text boxes for the pointer array and data array, and another in which the labels of the data array are to be displayed.

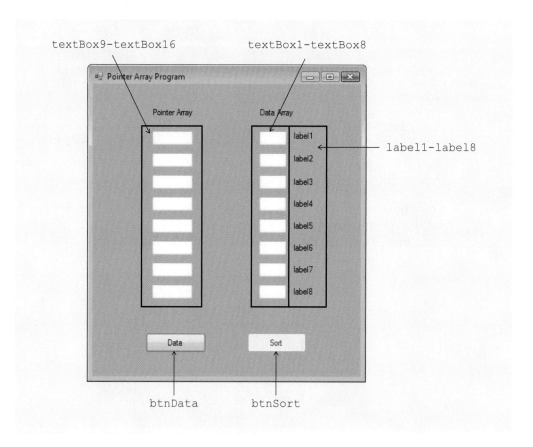

FIGURE 11-32 Interface objects for the Pointer Array program

The various objects included in the interface are listed in Table 11-1.

TABLE 11-1 Control table for indexed array program

Usage	Object	Event	Description
Initialization	Form1	Load()	Initialization
	btnData	Click()	Initialize pointer and data arrays, label addresses and draw lines between corresponding elements
Processing	btnSort	Click()	Sort pointer array, redraw lines between elements to show sorted connection
Output	label1–label8		Display data array element addresses
	textBox1–textBox8		Display the values in the data array
	textBox9–textBox16		Display the values in the pointer array

DATA TABLE

This program centers around two arrays:

- A data array called `arr` containing eight integers
- A pointer array called `ptr` containing pointers to elements of `arr`

The instance variables required are the arrays and various `Drawing` objects. The instance variables are listed in Table 11-2.

TABLE 11-2 Data table—instance variables

Variable Name	Data Type	Usage
arr	int*	Dynamically allocated an array of 8 integers
ptr	int**	Dynamically allocated an array of 8 pointers to integers

The `Drawing` objects required are listed in Table 11-3.

TABLE 11-3 `Drawing` objects

Object	Type	Usage
g	Graphics	`Graphics` object
blackPen	Pen	Used to draw connecting lines

Variables required for `btnData_Click()` The click event for the Data button, `btnData_Click()`, generates random data and stores it in the data array. It also assigns the addresses of the data array elements to the pointer array.

Very few new variables are required here. You need a random number object, several loop control variables, and nothing more. The task of displaying the pointers and drawing lines will be handled by other methods, called `displayPtr()` and `drawLines()`.

Variables required for `btnSort_Click()` The click event for the Sort button, `btnSort_Click()`, uses a bubble sort. It requires no new variables other than the loop control variables. It needs to call the `swap()` method, however. It also requires methods for displaying pointers and drawing lines between the arrays, so it will call `displayPtr()` and `drawLines()`.

Variables required for `drawLines()` The `drawLines()` method draws lines between the pointer and data arrays. It is called by both the `btnData` and `btnSort` click events. The program draws lines from a point adjacent to a pointer text box (`ptrX`, `ptrY`) to a point adjacent to the left side of the data array element text box (`arrX`, `arrY`). Table 11-4 reflects the need for these variables.

TABLE 11-4 Data table—`DrawLines()` method

Variable Name	Data Type	Usage
startY	int	The y location of `textBox1`
ptrX	int	The x location of the right side of `textBox9`
ptrY	int	The y location of the pointer array text box
arrX	int	The x location of the left side of `textBox1`
arrY	int	The y location of the data array text box

ALGORITHMS

The key algorithms in this tutorial are those for each of the buttons and the `drawLines()` algorithm to draw connecting lines between the pointer array elements and the elements of the data array. Because code for the bubble sort and the `swap()` method was presented earlier, algorithms of both procedures can be omitted.

Algorithm for `btnData_Click()`   The click event for the Data button generates random data, assigning it to the data array. It then displays the data array and the addresses of that data. The algorithm also assigns pointers to the pointer array and displays them, while also drawing lines between the two arrays. You do not want the user to click `btnSort` until `btnData` has created the data array and assigned pointers to the pointer array, so you will also add code to `btnData_Click()` that enables `btnSort` only after `btnData_Click()` finishes executing. The algorithm for `btnData_Click()` is shown in Algorithm 11-1.

ALGORITHM 11-1: `btnData_Click()`

1. Declare local variables (and create random number generator).
2. Assign random numbers to data array.
3. Display data array values.
4. Display data array addresses.
5. Assign element addresses to the pointer array.
6. Display the pointer array values.
7. Draw lines connecting the pointer and data array elements.
8. Enable the Sort button.

Algorithm for `btnSort_Click()`   The `btnSort_Click()` event handler sorts the pointer array according to the values in the memory cells they point to. It also displays the sorted pointers, draws the lines between the pointer array elements and data array elements, and displays the sorted data in a message box. Occasionally the message box may appear on top of the form obscuring the display of the lines connecting pointer array elements to data array elements. In situations like this, when the user closes the message box, the connecting lines that it obscured need to be redrawn. The algorithm for `btnSort_Click()` is given in Algorithm 11-2.

1
1

ALGORITHM 11-2: `btnSort_Click()`

1. Declare variables (including the output string).
2. Sort the pointer array.
3. Display sorted pointers in text boxes.
4. Create an output string with sorted data in it.
5. Draw lines connecting the pointer and data array elements.
6. Display the message box with the sorted results.
7. When the message box is closed, redraw the lines.

Algorithm for `drawLines()` The `drawLines()` method is responsible for drawing the lines between pointer array text boxes (`textBox9` through `textBox16`) and data array text boxes (`textBox1` through `textBox8`). You may want to take a minute to review Figures 11-29 and 11-30 and consider how a strategy to draw these lines might be developed.

To write the code for the `drawLines()` method, you need to use the x- and y-coordinates of controls on the interface. Every text box has a `Location` property that includes the x- and y-coordinates (`Location.X` and `Location.Y`) of the upper-left corner of the text box. The x-coordinate is the number of pixels from the left edge of `Form1` to the upper-left corner of the text box. The y-coordinate is the number of pixels from the top of `Form1` to the upper-left corner of the text box. Figure 11-33 illustrates these properties for `textBox9`.

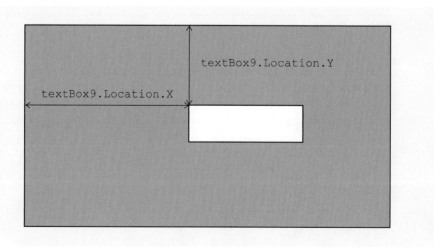

FIGURE 11-33 `textBox9` `Location` property coordinates `X` and `Y`

Similarly, all text boxes have a `Height` and `Width` property, as shown in Figure 11-34. The `Height` is the number of pixels tall, and the `Width` is the number of pixels wide.

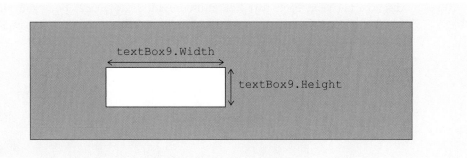

FIGURE 11-34 `textBox Height`, and `Width` properties

Lines are drawn from the pointer array text boxes, such as **textBox9**, starting halfway down the right side. This location is marked as **(ptrX, ptrY)** in Figure 11-35.

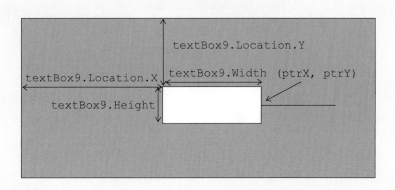

FIGURE 11-35 Location for the starting point (ptrX, ptrY) of a line from a pointer array text box

The x-coordinate (**ptrX**) is the `Location.X` property of the text box plus the width of the text box. The y-coordinate (**ptrY**) is the `Location.Y` property of the text box plus half of the height of the text box. The code for these calculations for **textBox9** is shown in Example 11-28.

EXAMPLE 11-28: INITIALIZING ptrX AND ptrY

```
int ptrX = textBox9->Location.X + textBox9->Width;
int ptrY = textBox9->Location.Y + textBox9->Height/2;
```

There are eight pointer array text boxes. A loop can be used to draw the line from `textBox9`, then the line from `textBox10`, then the line from `textBox11`, and so on through `textBox16`. To move from the location of one text box to the next, the vertical distance between each text box must be added to `ptrY`. For example, if there are 32 pixels between the text boxes, then the y-coordinate of the next line is `ptrY + 32`, as shown in Figure 11-36.

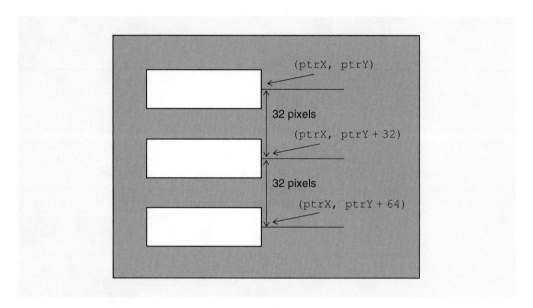

FIGURE 11-36 Repositioning `ptrY` by 32 pixels to find the next line starting point

For each of the text boxes (`textBox9` through `textBox16`) the difference in vertical location is a multiple of the distance between the text boxes. Again assuming that the distance between each text box is 32 pixels, the locations are assigned as shown in Figure 11-37. The yellow highlighted boxes show the calculation of the starting point for each line. The arrows indicate the starting locations.

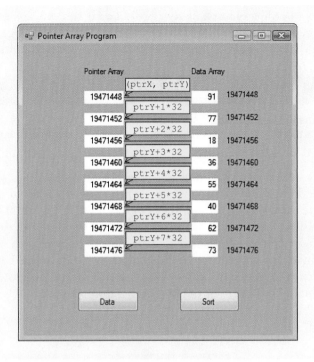

FIGURE 11-37 Calculating vertical locations for the starting line for `textBox9` through `textBox16`

Now that you have determined how to calculate the starting position of each line, turn your attention to calculating the end point. Each line starts at the right side of a pointer array text box and ends at the left side of a data array text box. You use two integer variables (`arrX` and `arrY`) to store the location of the end point of the line in much the same way that you used `ptrX` and `ptrY` to store the locations of the starting point. The end point of the line is located at the left side of the data text boxes (`textBox1` through `textBox8`) as shown in Figure 11–38.

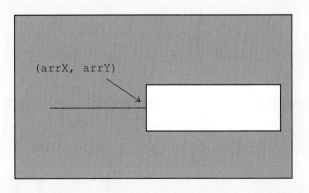

FIGURE 11-38 Location for the ending point (`arrX`, `arrY`) of a line at a data array text box

The x-coordinate, `arrX`, is always the `Location.X` value of the first data array text box (`textBox1`). The y-coordinate of `textBox1`, called `startY`, is `Location.Y` plus half of `textBox1.Height`. Example 11-29 shows how `arrX` and `startY` are calculated.

EXAMPLE 11-29: INITIALIZING arrX AND startY

```
int arrX = textBox1->Location.X;
int startY = textBox1->Location.Y + textBox1->Height/2;
```

To determine the end point of the line, the program uses pointer arithmetic to subtract the address of the first data array element from that stored in the pointer array element. The result is a value from 0 to 7. For example, in Figure 11-39, the memory cell address of the first data array element is 59972696. The address of the first pointer array element, displayed in `textBox9`, is 59972704. Using pointer arithmetic, 59972704 − 59972696 is 8 bytes (two integers). Multiplying 2 by the distance between data array text boxes (32 pixels in this case) provides the information needed to calculate the y-coordinate of the end point (`arrY`) of the line drawn from `textBox9`.

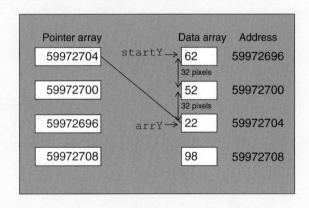

FIGURE 11-39 Calculating `arrY` by a multiple of 32 pixels to find the end point of the next line

The variable `arrY` stores this value and is calculated as shown in Example 11-30.

EXAMPLE 11-30: CALCULATING arrY

```
arrY = startY + ((ptr[0] - &(arr[0])) * 32);
```

The algorithm for this method, shown in Algorithm 11-3, accomplishes the task of drawing all of the lines required to show connections between the pointer and data array text boxes.

ALGORITHM 11-3: DRAWING THE CONNECTING LINES

1. Declare and initialize variables (ptrX, ptrY, arrX, arrY, startY).
2. Refresh the form (to prepare it for drawing).
3. For each of the elements in the ptr array:
   3.1. Calculate arrY.
   3.2. Draw a line from (ptrX, ptrY) to (arrX, arrY).
   3.3. Reposition ptrY (to position it at the next text box).

Development

The most important part of the development process is the relationship between the pointer and data arrays, and between the arrays and their text box representations. Remember that the program does not compare or sort the text boxes on the form. Instead, it compares and sorts the contents of the arrays. The text boxes serve only to display the contents of the arrays before and after the sorting process.

THE INTERFACE

Use Figure 11-32 a guide as you construct the interface. Take care to place the label and text box controls so that the default names match the names in Figure 11-32 exactly. The equal vertical spacing of text boxes is important in this program. Make sure that each of the pointer array text boxes (**textBox9-textBox16**) have the same distance between them. Similarly, make sure that the data array text boxes (**textBox1-textBox8**) have the same distance between them.

CODING

Much of the code for this program has already been presented in this chapter. There are two primary coding tasks: those involving pointers and pointer arithmetic, and those involving drawing the lines connecting pointer array elements with data array elements. The drawing code is not difficult. It involves only one loop. However, in order to understand it, you must have a good command of how pointers are dereferenced.

Instance variable declarations and Form1_Load()   The instance variables and Drawing variables were identified in Tables 11-2 and 11-3. Their declarations, as well as the constructor calls in **Form1_Load()** are shown in Example 11-31. Notice how the pointer variables **arr** and **ptr** become associated with arrays in the **Form1_Load()** event handler when the **new** command is used to dynamically allocate memory assigned to them.

EXAMPLE 11-31: INSTANCE VARIABLES AND `Form1_Load()`

```
int* arr;
int** ptr;
Graphics^ g;
Pen^ blackPen;

private: System::Void Form1_Load(System::Object^  sender,
System::EventArgs^  e) {
    arr = new int[8];
    ptr = new int*[8];
    g = this->CreateGraphics();
    blackPen = gcnew System::Drawing::Pen(Color::Black);
    btnSort->Enabled = false;
}
```

The declaration of `ptr` uses the `**` syntax to indicate that `ptr` can store a pointer to a pointer to an integer. When `ptr` is allocated, an array of eight pointers to integers is created and `ptr` stores the address of the first one. Remember that allocating an array of eight pointers to integers does not initialize the array elements. They need to be assigned actual pointers before they can be used. After `Form1_Load()` is over, `ptr` points to an array that can store eight pointers, even though none are yet assigned to it.

The btnData_Click() event handler The click event handler for the Data button, `btnData_Click()`, creates a random number generator. You used a random number generator for the first time in Chapter 5 when you created the CHUMP project. The click event handler for the Data button uses the random number generator to fill the data array in a loop that visits each element and assigns it a value, as shown in Example 11-32.

EXAMPLE 11-32: RANDOM NUMBER ASSIGNMENT

```
// Declare variables and create random number generator
int i;  // loop control variable
Random^ randomNumber;
DateTime now = DateTime::Now;
randomNumber = gcnew Random( now.Millisecond);

// Assign random numbers to arr
for (i=0; i<8; i++) arr[i] = randomNumber->Next(0,100);
```

Displaying the data array values in the proper text boxes is straightforward, as shown in Example 11-33 for the first and last assignment (you can fill in those in between).

EXAMPLE 11-33: DISPLAYING THE DATA IN arr

```
// Display arr values in textBox1 - textBox8
textBox1->Text = arr[0].ToString();
.
.
.
textBox8->Text = arr[7].ToString();
```

The addresses of each element in arr are assigned to labels on the interface in a similar manner, as shown in Example 11-34 for the first and last assignment, using the technique of type casting the pointer as an integer, discussed previously.

EXAMPLE 11-34: DISPLAYING THE ADDRESSES OF arr

```
// Display arr addresses in label1 - label8
label1->Text = ((int) &arr[0]).ToString();
.
.
.
label8->Text = ((int) &arr[7]).ToString();
```

To assign the addresses of data array arr elements to the corresponding elements in the pointer array ptr, you use a for loop. Example 11-35 shows how this process works using the address of operator (&) to provide the addresses required by the pointer array elements.

EXAMPLE 11-35: INITIALIZING THE ptr ARRAY

```
// Assign element addresses to ptr
for (i=0; i<8; i++) ptr[i] = &arr[i];
```

Three tasks remain for the btnData_Click() event handler:

- Display the ptr array values.
- Draw the lines connecting the two arrays.
- Enable the Sort button so that the user can click it.

The first two are accomplished elsewhere in other methods. The code shown in Example 11-36 calls the displayPtr() and drawLines() methods and then enables the Sort button (btnSort).

EXAMPLE 11-36: DISPLAYING DATA AND DRAWING LINES

```
// Display the pointer array values
displayPtr();
// Draw lines connecting the pointer and data arrays
drawLines();
// Turn on the Sort button
btnSort->Enabled = true;
```

The btnSort_Click() event handler This event handler sorts the pointers in `ptr` in accordance with the order of the values they point to in the data array `arr`. This process, and the use of the bubble sort to perform it, were discussed earlier in the chapter.

Once the pointers have been sorted, the values they point to are displayed in a message box. This is accomplished by using a `String` variable (`output`) and a `for` loop. The loop accesses each of the pointers stored in the pointer array `ptr` and dereferences the pointers in order. Dereferencing accesses the values in the memory cells the pointers point to, and each value is then concatenated onto `output`. When all values have been added to `output`, a message box is used to display the result—the data values from `arr` in ascending order.

The code for the `btnSort_Click()` event handler is shown in Example 11-37.

EXAMPLE 11-37: CODING btnSort_Click()

```
private: System::Void btnSort_Click(System::Object^  sender,
System::EventArgs^  e) {
    // Declare variables
    String^ output = "";
    int i, j;

    // Bubble sort the ptr array
    for (i=0;  i<7;  i++)
        for (j=0;   j<7-i;  j++)
            if  (*ptr[j] > *ptr[j+1])
                swap(&(ptr[j]),  &(ptr[j+1]));

    // Display pointers with their new address contents
    displayPtr();
    // Concatenate values in sorted order onto output String
    for (i=0;  i<8;  i++) output += (*ptr[i]).ToString() + "\r\n";
    // Draw lines connecting pointer array and data array
    drawLines();
    // Display sorted data in MessageBox
    MessageBox::Show(output,"Sorted Data");
    // Draw lines again after MessageBox is closed
    drawLines();
}
```

The **displayPtr()** method   When the values stored in the pointers need to be displayed in **textBox9** through **textBox16**, they are assigned directly. As before, conventional C++ type casting is used to change the pointer values to integers that can then be changed to text strings as shown in Example 11-38.

EXAMPLE 11-38: CODE FOR displayPtr()

```
private: void displayPtr()
{
    // Display ptr values in textBox9 - textBox16
    textBox9->Text = ((int) ptr[0]).ToString();
    textBox10->Text = ((int) ptr[1]).ToString();
    textBox11->Text = ((int) ptr[2]).ToString();
    textBox12->Text = ((int) ptr[3]).ToString();
    textBox13->Text = ((int) ptr[4]).ToString();
    textBox14->Text = ((int) ptr[5]).ToString();
    textBox15->Text = ((int) ptr[6]).ToString();
    textBox16->Text = ((int) ptr[7]).ToString();
}
```

The **drawLines()** method   The process of drawing lines was discussed in detail in the algorithm design section. The variable declarations for the **drawLines()** method are based on the data table provided in Table 11-4 and illustrated in Figures 11-33 through 11-39 using code Examples 11-28 through 11-30. Notice how the loop is used to access each element in the pointer array **ptr** and, by using pointer arithmetic, calculate the y-coordinate (**arrY**) for the end of the line. In addition, also notice how the y-coordinate for the start of the line is incremented by 32 (32 pixels) as the last statement in the body of the loop. This allows the next line to start at the next pointer array text box. The code for **drawLines()** is shown in Example 11-39.

EXAMPLE 11-39: CODE FOR drawLines()

```
private: void drawLines()
{
    // Calculate start points (ptrX, ptrY)
    int ptrX = textBox9->Location.X + textBox9->Width;
    int ptrY = textBox9->Location.Y + textBox9->Height/2;
    // Calculate end point (arrX)
    int arrX = textBox1->Location.X;
    int arrY;
    int startY = textBox1->Location.Y + textBox1->Height/2;
    // Refresh the form and draw lines
    this->Refresh();
    for (int i = 0; i < 8; i++)
    {
        arrY = startY + ((ptr[i] - &(arr[0])) * 32);
        g->DrawLine(blackPen, ptrX, ptrY, arrX, arrY);
        ptrY += 32;
    }
}
```

NOTE The vertical distance between each textbox in your program should be the same. The distance in your program may be more or less than the 32 pixels, requiring you to change all occurrences of 32 in Example 11-39. Consider making this distance a static constant instead of a literal value. Constants are preferred in this situation over "hard-coding" literal values like 32.

Testing

Run your project several times to demonstrate that it does all of the following correctly:

- When the initial interface presents itself, btnSort is disabled.
- When btnData is clicked, the following happens:
  - Random numbers are generated for the data array arr.
  - The data values stored in arr are displayed in textBox1 through textBox8.
  - The memory cell addresses of each element of arr are displayed in label1 through label8.
  - The pointer values stored in the pointer array ptr are displayed in textBox9 through textBox16.
  - The values stored in textBox9 through textBox16 match exactly those stored in label1 through label8.
  - Lines are drawn on Form1 connecting each element in the ptr array text boxes with the corresponding element in the data array text boxes.
  - btnSort is enabled.
- When btnSort is clicked the following happens:
  - The pointers are reassigned.
  - Lines between the pointer array text boxes and data array text boxes are redrawn.
  - A message box appears in which the data are displayed sorted in ascending order.
  - Following the lines from the pointer array text boxes to the data array text boxes yields the same sorted values displayed in the message box.

ON YOUR OWN

The most important concepts to grasp from this tutorial are those involving the use of pointers to access elements in other arrays. This includes the dynamic allocation of arrays, indirection, pointer dereferencing, and pointer arithmetic. The On Your Own tasks provide the opportunity to work with each of these key topics.

TASK 1. DESCENDING ORDER

Rewrite the bubble sort code so that it sorts the data in descending order.

TASK 2. REMOVING THE `swap()` METHOD

To demonstrate that you understand pointers, remove the call to the `swap()` method and replace it with a series of lines in the bubble sort that perform the swap operation.

QUICK REVIEW

1. The address-of operator (`&`) is used to access the memory cell address where storage for a variable begins.
2. Memory cell addresses can be type cast as integers for display in a text box.
3. A pointer is a memory cell address.
4. A pointer variable is a variable with a pointer as its data type.
5. Pointer variables are declared using the `*` symbol to indicate that a pointer data type is being specified (for example `int*`).
6. Pointer variables need to be initialized before they can be used.
7. A null pointer is a special value signifying an empty pointer.
8. A null pointer is assigned either 0 or the system constant `nullptr`.
9. Dynamic memory allocation refers to the allocation of memory at runtime.
10. Dynamically allocated memory comes from the heap.
11. The `new` operator is used to dynamically allocate memory.
12. The `new` operator returns a pointer to the allocated space.
13. Pointer variables can be initialized using the `new` operator.
14. A pointer to a pointer is declared using the symbols `**` (example: `int**`).
15. The address of a pointer may be assigned to a variable that is a pointer to a pointer.
16. The data stored in a memory cell can be accessed indirectly through a pointer.
17. The indirection operator is used to access the value a pointer points to.

18. Dereferencing a pointer refers to the use of indirection.

19. The use of two indirection operators (**) is called double indirection.

20. A pointer to a pointer can be dereferenced using double indirection.

21. Pass-by-reference can be accomplished using pointer variables.

22. Pointers can be returned by methods.

23. Pointers can be passed into methods as actual arguments.

24. Dynamic allocation can be used to allocate arrays.

25. Pointer arithmetic refers to the addition or subtraction of integer values from a pointer.

26. Pointer arithmetic may be used to traverse an array instead of using a loop with array element indexing.

27. Pointer arithmetic is dangerous if a pointer is increased or decreased to store an address outside the bounds of an array.

28. Pointer arithmetic can be used to implement a binary search.

29. Dynamically allocated memory can be deallocated with the `delete` operator.

30. An array of pointers can be allocated using `new`.

31. Values can be assigned when `new` is used to construct a variable.

32. Pointer arrays may be initialized with the addresses of elements in a parallel array.

33. A pointer array can be used to sort values in another array.

34. Records contain collections of data of varying types.

35. Pointers can be used to sort arrays of records without having to move the records around in memory.

36. Swapping pointer variables requires actual arguments that are pointers to pointers.

TERMS TO KNOW

delete
dereferencing
double indirection
dynamic allocation
heap
indirection
indirection operator (*)
new
null pointer
pointer

pointer arithmetic
pointer data type symbol
pointer variable
record

EXERCISES

1. Which of the following declares a pointer variable?

   a. `int * a;`

   b. `int &a;`

   c. `int a;`

   d. `(int) a;`

   e. `a = new int;`

2. Assuming that `num` is an integer variable and `numPtr` is a pointer variable (a pointer to an integer), which of the following properly assigns a value to `numPtr`?

   a. `numPtr = num;`

   b. `numPtr = * num;`

   c. `numPtr = &num;`

   d. `num = * numPtr;`

   e. `num = &numPtr;`

3. Assuming that `num` is an integer variable and `numPtr` is an initialized pointer variable (a pointer to an integer), which of the following properly assigns a value to `num`?

   a. `numPtr = num;`

   b. `numPtr = * num;`

   c. `numPtr = &num;`

   d. `num = * numPtr;`

   e. `num = &numPtr;`

4. Assuming that `num` is an integer variable and that `numPtr` is a pointer variable (a pointer to an integer), which of the following Visual C++ assignment statements causes a compiler error?

   a. `numPtr = 0;`

   b. `numPtr = nullptr;`

   c. `numPtr = &num;`

   d. `numPtr = numPtr;`

   e. `numPtr = num;`

5. Assume that `dblPtr` has been declared to be a pointer to a `double` and properly initialized. Which of the following dereferences `dblPtr`?

   a. `double *dblPtr`

   b. `dblPtr`

   c. `*dblPtr`

   d. `&dblPtr`

   e. `**dblPtr`

6. The **new** operator returns a(n)_____.

   a. integer

   b. pointer

   c. array

   d. array element

   e. primitive type

7. Assuming that `num` is an integer variable and that `numPtr` is a pointer variable (a pointer to an integer), which of the following passes a pointer into the method `method1()`?

   a. `method1(&num);`

   b. `method1(&numPtr);`

   c. `method1(numPtr);`

   d. All of the above

   e. None of them

8. Which use of the **new** operator constructs an integer and initializes it to 5 at the same time?

   a. `int* num = new int[5];`

   b. `int* num = new int(5);`

   c. `int num = new int(5);`

   d. `int* num = new int = 5;`

   e. `int* num = 5;`

9. Which use of the **new** operator dynamically allocates an array of five integers?

   a. `int* num = new int[5];`

   b. `int* num = new int(5);`

   c. `int num = new int(5);`

   d. `int* num = new int = 5;`

   e. `int* num = 5;`

10. Which use of `delete` deallocates a dynamically allocated array assigned to pointer variable `arrPtr`?

    a. `arrPtr delete;`

    b. `delete arrPtr;`

    c. `delete arrPtr[];`

    d. `delete [] arrPtr;`

    e. `delete = arrPtr [];`

11. Which of the following is a valid use of type casting?

    a. `txtAddress->Text = ((int) numPtr).ToString();`

    b. `txtAddress->Text = (int) numPtr.ToString();`

    c. `txtAddress->Text = (int) (numPtr.ToString());`

    d. `txtAddress->Text = ((int) *numPtr).ToString();`

    e. `txtAddress->Text = ((int*) numPtr).ToString();`

12. Which of the following compares the values stored in memory cells pointed to by pointer variables `num1` and `num2`?

    a. `if (&num1 > &num2)`

    b. `if (*num1 > *num2)`

    c. `if (num1 > num2)`

    d. `if (num1 > *num2)`

    e. `if (*num1 > num2)`

13. Given the following declarations:

    ```
    int num = 99;
    int* numPtr = &num;
    int** numPtrPtr = &numPtr;
    ```

    Which of the following will *not* display the value 5 in `textBox1`?

    a. `textBox1->Text = num.ToString();`

    b. `textBox1->Text = *numPtr.ToString();`

    c. `textBox1->Text = **numPtrPtr.ToString();`

    d. `textBox1->Text = (&numPtr).ToString();`

    e. `textBox1->Text = (*(&num)).ToString();`

11
1

14. Given the following method:

```
private: void setNum(double* num1, double* num2)
{
    Double::TryParse(txtNum1->Text, *num1);
    Double::TryParse(txtNum2->Text, *num2);
}
```

How would the setNum() method be called using integer variables `first` and `last` as actual arguments?

   a.   setNum(first, last);

   b.   setNum(*first, *last);

   c.   setNum(**first, **last);

   d.   setNum(&first, &last);

   e.   setNum(num1, num2);

15. Assume that `arrPtr` is a pointer to the first element in an array of five integers. Which actual argument would pass `arrPtr` into the method `readArray()`?

   a.   readArray(arrPtr);

   b.   readArray(*arrPtr);

   c.   readArray(&arrPtr);

   d.   readArray(arrPtr[]);

   e.   readArray(arrPtr[5]);

16. Assume that the actual argument for `readArray()` is the pointer to an array of five integers. Which choice contains the correct matching formal parameter?

   a.   private: void readArray(arrPtr)

   b.   private: void readArray(int arrPtr)

   c.   private: void readArray(int* arrPtr)

   d.   private: void readArray(int arrPtr[5])

   e.   private: void readArray(int &arrPtr)

For questions 17–20, assume that you have two arrays. The array `myData` is a dynamically allocated array of 10 integers. The array `dataPtr` is a dynamically allocated array of 10 pointers to integers.

17. If `myData` has already been constructed and initialized, how would the addresses of its elements be assigned to the corresponding elements of `dataPtr`?

   a.   for (i = 0; i < 10; i++) dataPtr[i] = arrPtr[i];

   b.   for (i = 0; i < 10; i++) dataPtr[i] = &arrPtr[i];

   c.   for (i = 0; i < 10; i++) dataPtr[i] = *arrPtr[i];

   d.   for (i = 0; i < 10; i++) *dataPtr[i] = arrPtr[i];

   e.   for (i = 0; i < 10; i++) &dataPtr[i] = arrPtr[i];

18. You wish to dereference the elements of `dataPtr` and concatenate them to a `String` variable called `dataList`. Which loop will perform this task?

    a. `for (i=0;i<10;i++) dataList += (&dataPtr[i]).ToString();`

    b. `for (i=0;i<10;i++) dataList += dataPtr[i].ToString();`

    c. `for (i=0;i<10;i++) dataList += (dataPtr[i]).ToString();`

    d. `for (i=0;i<10;i++) dataList += (*dataPtr[i]).ToString();`

    e. `for (i=0;i<10;i++) dataList += (**dataPtr[i]).ToString();`

19. Given the following signature line for the `swap()` method:

    `private: void swap(int** a, int** b)`

    Which of the following calls is appropriate?

    a. `swap(dataPtr[i], dataPtr[i+1]);`

    b. `swap(*dataPtr[i], *dataPtr[i+1]);`

    c. `swap(&dataPtr[i], &dataPtr[i+1]);`

    d. `swap(**dataPtr[i], **dataPtr[i+1]);`

    e. `swap(&(dataPtr[i]), &(dataPtr[i+1]));`

20. Given the following signature line for the `swap()` method:

    `private: void swap(int** a, int** b)`

    Which of the following declarations of local variable `temp` is required to allow `temp` to store a pointer to an integer?

    a. `int temp = a;`

    b. `int* temp = *a;`

    c. `int** temp = **a;`

    d. `int* temp = &a;`

    e. `int* temp = &&a;`

PROGRAMMING EXERCISES

1. Explaining the Swap

The last line of this bubble sort differs from the code used in your tutorial. This version simply passes two pointers to integers (`ptr[j]` and `ptr[j+1]`) into the `swap()` method:

```
for (i=0; i<7; i++)
   for (j=0;  j<7-i; j++)
      if (*ptr[j] > *ptr[j+1])
         swap(ptr[j], ptr[j+1]);
```

Modify your tutorial so that the last line of the bubble sort matches the one shown.

Next, modify your `swap()` method so that the formal parameters are pointers to integers, as shown here:

```
private: void swap(int* a, int* b)
{
    int* temp;
    temp = a;
    a = b;
    b = temp;
}
```

Run the program. It will compile but fail to exchange any of the values. Explain why.

2.   Summation

Modify your tutorial so that `btnSort_Click()` also adds up the sum of the values stored in the data array (`arr`) and adds a line to the bottom of the message box output indicating what the sum is, as shown in Figure 11-40. You must use pointer indirection to access the values stored in `arr`.

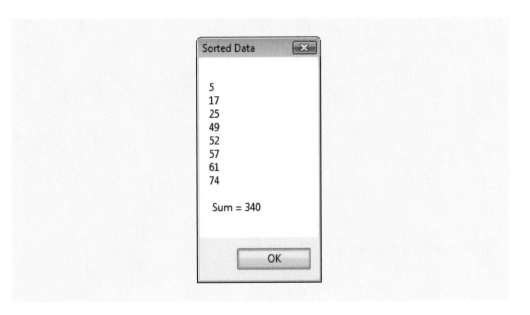

FIGURE 11-40   Message box display of sorted data with sum

3.   Selection Sort

Modify your tutorial project so that instead of a bubble sort it uses the ascending order selection sort. Your output should look the same.

4. Sequential Search

Demonstrate your knowledge of pointers and pointer arithmetic by modifying your tutorial program so that instead of a sort, it perform a search. Use the sequential search technique to search the data array (`arr`) by dereferencing pointers. Your output should look similar to that shown in Figure 11-41. If the search is successful, draw a line between the pointer array text box and the data array text box that displays the target value. Also, have a message box open indicating that the search was successful and at which address in the data array the target was found.

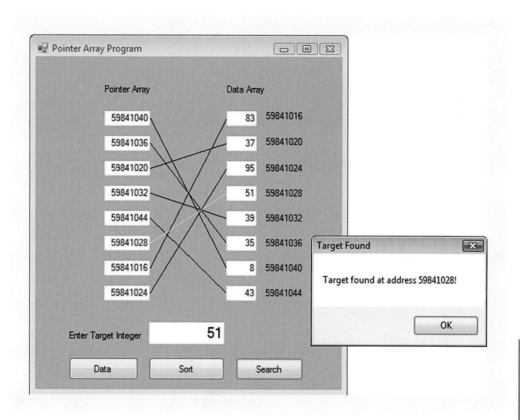

FIGURE 11-41 Sequential search output

5. Binary Search

A binary search technique was presented in Example 11-17. Create one button to do the sorting and another to perform the search, as shown in Figure 11-41. The user enters a target value, and a message box displays the result of the search. If the search is successful, draw a yellow line connecting the pointer array and data array text boxes that display the target values. Remember that the data values in `arr` are not in sorted order. This means that your binary search needs to access the data values indirectly using the pointer array `ptr`.

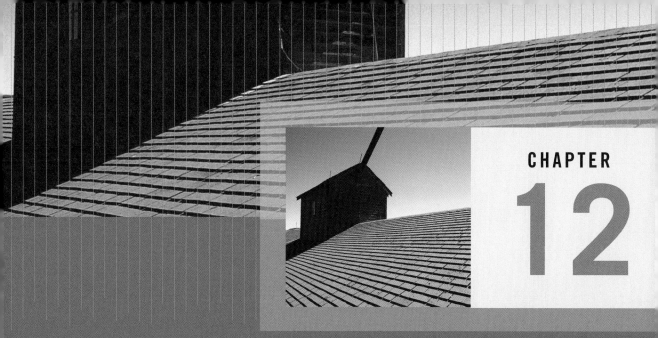

LINKED LISTS: THE Node CLASS

IN THIS CHAPTER, YOU WILL:

- Create class definitions
- Define a default constructor and a destructor
- Instantiate objects
- Add nodes to the front of a linked list
- Delete nodes from the front of a linked list
- Recursively traverse a list

Up to this point you have only examined one technique for storing multiple data items in a single structure—the array. In this chapter, you learn how to make a list of items without using an array. The list is built by linking together nodes of data with memory cell address pointers. The result is a dynamic data structure that expands or contracts to fit the number of data values the program needs to store. The first step in creating a data structure is to create a class definition for a node and then use it to make **Node** objects.

The List Data Structure

How would you define the term *list*? Your definition must be general enough to include only the essential features of all lists. For starters, you know that a list is a collection of related items. That is, a list is a way of organizing things that are alike. For example, milk, bread, and apples would be typical items contained on a grocery list, and shirts, socks, and pants would be appropriate items for a laundry list. There is a reason why the items are chosen for the list they are in (they are all grocery items or all laundry items).

In addition to the items they contain, lists also have characteristic operations. With a grocery list for example, you expect that you should be able to add new items to the list or remove ones that you no longer need. Regardless of what is in a list, the abilities to add items and delete items are fundamental operations that you would expect to be able to do with the list.

If you had a long list, such as a list of the tuition rates at colleges and universities, you might want the list to allow you to perform other, more complicated operations. You might want to be able to conveniently search the list looking for tuition rates you could afford. You might also want to sort the list in order from the most expensive to the least expensive.

In programming terminology, a general definition of an organizational structure, like a list, is called an **abstraction**. An abstraction of a list provides the essential characteristics all lists share. For example, all lists share the following traits:

- Lists are collection of related items.
- Items may be added to the list.
- Items may be deleted from the list.

The abstraction does not specify what the list must contain or how a list must be stored in memory. Although the development of the list abstraction lies beyond the scope of this book, this chapter will allow you to gain valuable experience with new forms of list implementation. Future computer science coursework will enable you to more fully appreciate the concept of list abstraction.

From your experience there is only one way to implement the concept of a list—by using an array. However, there are other alternatives that provide the same essential capabilities as arrays but go about the process of storing, retrieving, ordering, searching, and accessing data items in very different ways. As you begin to think more about lists, start by reflecting upon the list structure you know best—the array.

The Problem with Arrays

Arrays are easy to create and use because they allocate a contiguous block of memory. You have used arrays in previous chapters to implement algorithms for searching and sorting, although always with arrays of fixed size.

However, fixed-size arrays of primitive types have serious problems when it comes to both the insertion of new items as well as the deletion of items from them. Consider the difficulty of inserting and deleting items with an array of integers.

Assume that your program has declared and initialized the following array, with six elements:

```
int arr[] = {34, 48, 22, 87, 56, 17};
```

How difficult will it be for your program to add an additional, seventh, value to the array?

The answer is that with arrays of fixed size, such as this, it is not possible. The size of the array is constant. The compiler generated the code to create the array with a fixed size—six elements. No additional elements can be added.

However, you could get around this problem as shown in Algorithm 12-1.

ALGORITHM 12-1: COPYING ARRAY VALUES TO A LARGER ARRAY

1. Create a second array that is one element larger than the first.
2. Copy all of the values from the elements of the first array into their corresponding elements in the new second array.
3. Put the value you want to add in the last element of the new array.
4. Delete the original array.

This is one way out of your dilemma. However, it comes at a cost. Not only do you need to allocate a second array, but you also need to copy data values into it. Figure 12-1 illustrates the process of copying values from the original array (`arr`) into a new array (`new_arr`). The additional, seventh value (74) is assigned to the last element in `new_arr`.

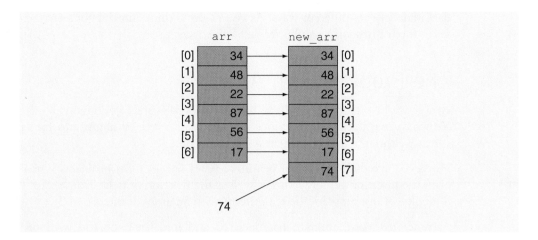

FIGURE 12-1 Insertion by copying data from `arr` into a `new_arr` and assigning the new value to the last element of `new_arr`

Although this process may seem minor for an array of six elements, it could be major for an array that started out at 6,000 elements and to which you wanted to add one more. Creating a new array and deleting the old one is inefficient both because of its use of memory and because of the need to copy data from one to the other. In fact, adding a new item is O(*n*) from the standpoint of data movements because *n* assignment statements must be made to copy the values from the elements of the original array to the new one.

Deletion is no better. The process is reversed, with a smaller array allocated and data copied over, except for the item you want to remove. This is also an O(*n*) operation because the *n* elements in **new_arr** require *n* assignment statements as the values from **arr** are copied over. Figure 12-2 illustrates the process of deleting the value 22. The point is that the deletion process, just like insertion, requires the allocation of another array of approximately the same size as the original, followed by the execution of *n* assignment statements. This is an unnecessary use of process resources and memory that can be avoided by other means—as you shall see.

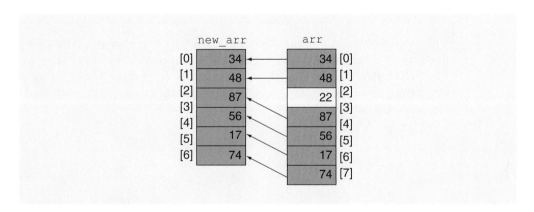

FIGURE 12-2 Deletion of the value 22 by copying data from `arr` into `new_arr`

One way to get around the insertion and deletion problems is to allocate large arrays and only utilize portions of them. For example, your initial declaration could be something like this:

```
int arr[100];
int length = 0;
```

Now you are relatively safe. You can store six values in the array (`arr`) with room left over. Later, if the program needs to store another value, you have an unused array element that can accommodate it. Figure 12-3 shows how the program could store the value 74 in an array of length 6 by assigning it to element [6]. Figure 12-3a shows the array `arr` and `length` before the insertion and Figure 12-3b shows them after insertion. You use the `length` variable to keep track of how many items are stored in the array, and you can also use it to place a new item in the structure.

```
arr[length++] = 74;
```

Because insertion of an new item involves only one operation, it is O(1).

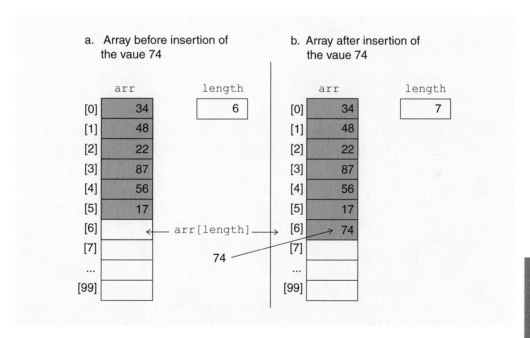

FIGURE 12-3 Insertion of an item in unused portions of the array

Deletion, however, is not as fast. Deletion does not involve a second array, but still involves repeatedly copying data into adjacent memory cells. You can see this in Figure 12-4, which illustrates the deletion of the value 22. There is no improvement in efficiency. The overall operation is still O(n).

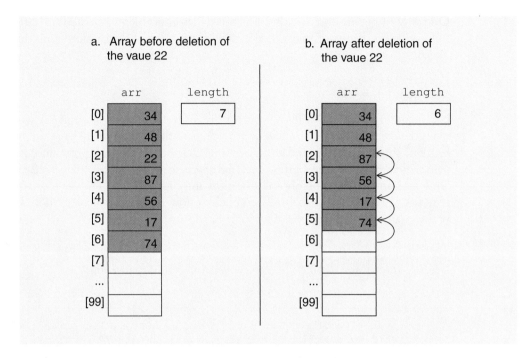

FIGURE 12-4 Deletion of the value 22 by copying data into adjacent cells

You still have the problem of size limitations. Your data structure can handle only 100 elements. It is not appropriate for situations in which more storage is needed.

Linked Lists

One way to address the problems presented by fixed-size arrays is to use another data structure that can also be used to represent a list but without constraints imposed on arrays. An example of this kind of data structure is the linked list. A **linked list** is a data structure that uses pointers to connect individual list elements. Ideally we would like the list to be defined as a class apart from Form1. However, since this will be our first experience writing class definitions we will only write a short one, the Node class definition, and allow Form1 to construct a list of nodes. In later coursework you may learn how to define a list object that more fully implements the list abstraction apart from Form1. Unlike arrays of primitive data types, an element of a linked list is a collection of several data items, called **nodes**. Each node contains at least two items. The contents of the node shown in Figure 12-5 consist of two fields of information, a data value and a pointer.

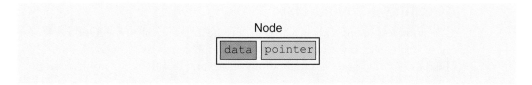

FIGURE 12-5 A linked list node

There are two types of nodes, those with pointers to other nodes and those with pointers that do not point to another node. Diagrams of these two types are shown in Figure 12-6.

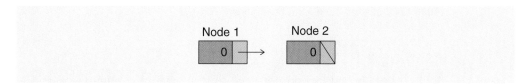

FIGURE 12-6 Node diagrams

Node 1 consists of the data value 0 and a pointer to a valid memory cell address. Node 2 consists of the data value 0 and a null pointer (indicated by the diagonal line). A **null pointer** is one that has been assigned the 0 memory cell address. This address cannot be used to store data. It is the equivalent of an empty placeholder. In Visual C++, the keyword **nullptr** is used to represent a null pointer.

The diagram of a linked list with several nodes looks like that shown in Figure 12-7. The **head** of the list is a pointer to the first node. The end of the list is the node with the null pointer. Because the head of the list is a pointer, it can be followed to the node it points to. Once there, if that node has a pointer to another node then it may be followed. The process can continue as long as each node has a pointer to another node. When the last node is reached there is nowhere to go. The null pointer signifies the end of the list.

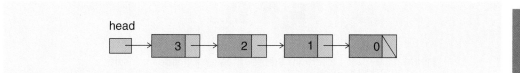

FIGURE 12-7 Linked list

Linked lists and arrays share much in common (they are both lists), but as you can see, they are implemented very differently. A fully developed treatment of the list abstraction is beyond the scope of this book. However, this chapter will allow you to create a list using Form1 to display interconnected nodes and implement a visualization of them by drawing the list on the interface.

Creating a Linked List

The most important node in a linked list is the first one, called the **head node**. A pointer to the head node is called the **head pointer** (or simply head), as shown in Figure 12-8. The pointer field in the head node is a null pointer indicating that there are no more nodes in the list.

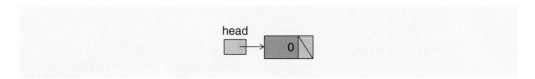

FIGURE 12-8 List creation—the head node

Inserting a Node

Unlike arrays, linked lists do not need to store data in contiguous locations. They store data wherever room is available and link the nodes together with pointers. In this example you will see how a new node is inserted at the head of a linked list. When the program needs to insert a node, it rearranges the pointers in the linked list to accommodate the new node. For example, Figure 12-9 shows three nodes (containing values 0, 1, and 2). A new node with the value 3 is to be placed into the list at the head. The first step in the insertion process is to create the new node that is to be inserted.

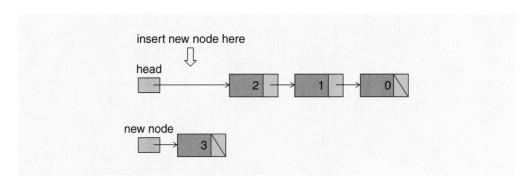

FIGURE 12-9 Node insertion, Step 1: Create new node for insertion

The second step is to assign to the new node's **next** data member a pointer to the node that will succeed it, as shown in Figure 12-10.

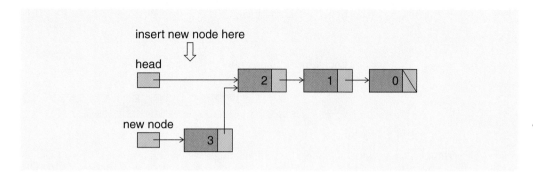

FIGURE 12-10   Node insertion, Step 2: Assigning a pointer to the succeeding node

Finally, the head is assigned a pointer to the new node, as shown in Figure 12-11.

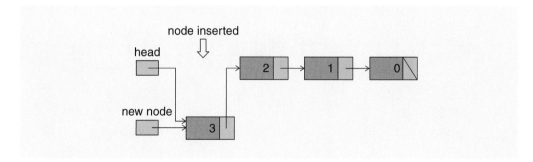

FIGURE 12-11   Node insertion, Step 3: Connecting the new node to the head.

The new node has now been incorporated into the list, as originally shown in Figure 12-7.

1
2

Deleting a Node

Deletion of a node is a four step process. You will delete the node that was inserted in the previous section to restore the list to its original state. The first step is to locate the node to be deleted (the head node), as shown in Figure 12-12.

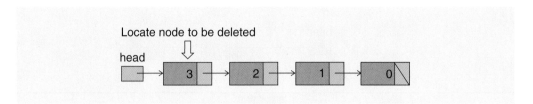

FIGURE 12-12   Node deletion, Step 1: Locating the head node

The second step is to create a temporary pointer variable and assign it to point to the node you want to delete, as shown in Figure 12-13.

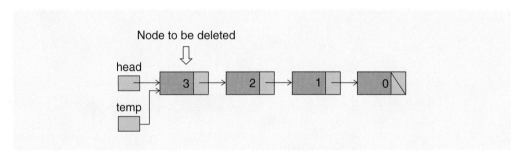

FIGURE 12-13   Node deletion, Step 2: Creating a temporary pointer

The third step is to assign the **next** pointer to the head, as shown in Figure 12-14.

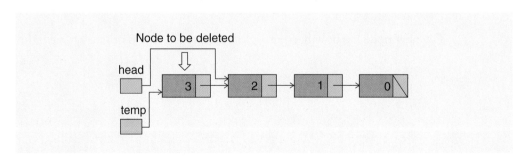

FIGURE 12-14   Node insertion, Step 3: Reassigning the head

Finally, the node you want to delete (pointed to by **temp**) can be deallocated from memory.

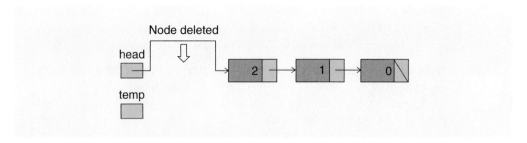

FIGURE 12-15 Node deletion, Step 4: Delete the node

Efficiency

With linked lists, insertion and deletion are handled quite economically. Once the insertion point is located, only three steps are required to insert a new node. This is O(1). Similarly, once the node to be deleted has been located, the deletion process is also only three steps and is O(1). These are large improvements over the array situation discussed earlier. The fact that a linked list can insert and delete nodes dynamically, without the need to shift data around, is a huge advantage over arrays. Also, with linked lists, you no longer need to be concerned about a data structure size limitation, except for the rare limitation of using up all available memory.

Linked lists are efficient solutions to data storage problems. However, there are disadvantages associated with linked lists. These disadvantages relate to its sequential nature. With arrays, you can access any element in the array at any time using array element subscripting. In other words, arrays allow for **random access**. For example, to access the fourth element you simply reference it (i.e., `arr[3]`). Linked lists, however, only allow for **sequential access**. Sequential access means that you cannot access any node in the list without first accessing the sequence of nodes that precedes it. For example, if you want to access the fourth data value, you must start at the head of the list and follow the pointers from one node to another in sequence until you arrive at the node you want. This is decidedly less efficient than accessing data values stored in array elements.

Class Definitions

Now that you have seen the important role that nodes play in a linked list, it is time to consider how to create a linked list. A node is an object. The linked lists you have seen consist of a collection of **Node** objects. Each **Node** object is defined to contain a data item and a pointer to the next node. Ideally we would like the list to be defined as a class apart from Form1. However, since this will be our first experience writing class definitions we will only write a short one, the Node class definition, and allow Form1 to construct a list of nodes. In later coursework you may learn how to define a list class definition that more fully implements the list abstraction apart from Form1.

Briefly review what you know about objects. Objects are created (derived) from class definitions. Objects are referred to as instances of their class. The representation of an object usually requires many memory cells. Handles (^) are used to access objects.

Unlike pointers to primitive types that are declared using the pointer symbol (*), handles are used to reference objects derived from class definitions. In previous projects you have used handles (^) to point to objects derived from system-defined classes such as `String`, `Brush`, `Pen`, `Random`, `Rectangle`, `Font`, and `Graphics`. For example, each of these following statements declares a handle to a system-defined class type:

```
System::Drawing::Pen^ blackPen;
System::Drawing::SolidBrush^ redBrush;
Random^ randomnumber;
```

Once the handle has been created, it must be initialized. In other words, a handle must be given the location of a specific object to point to. The `gcnew` operator is used to initialize handle variables. It constructs new objects and returns a handle that can be assigned to them. In the following code, `gcnew` is used to construct `SolidBrush`, `Pen`, and `Random` objects. In each case it returns a handle.

```
blackPen = gcnew Drawing::Pen(Color::Black);
redBrush = gcnew Drawing::SolidBrush(Color::Black);
randomnumber = gcnew Random(now.Millisecond);
```

In effect, the `gcnew` operator assigns an object its handle. The handle is not, strictly-speaking, a pointer but functions in a similar manner to locate an object in a special section of memory, known as the **garbage collection heap** or gc heap as shown in Figure 12-16.

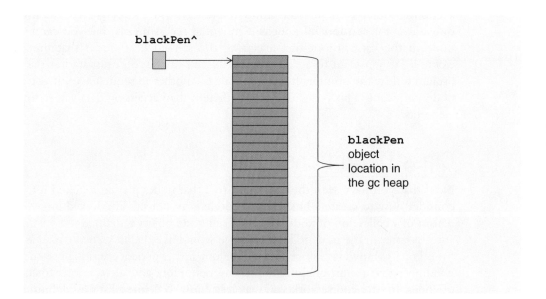

blackPen^

blackPen object location in the gc heap

FIGURE 12-16 The role of `gcnew` in allocating memory and returning a handle

The Node Class

There is no system-defined Node class definition. If you want to make a linked list consisting of a number of interconnected nodes, you need to create the definition for a Node class. Each Node object in your linked list is created from that same Node class definition.

As you will recall from earlier chapters, class definitions are like blueprints. They define a design structure that, if followed, can be used to create objects. All objects created from the same class definition are designed the same way and are called instances of that class.

In Visual C++ class definitions are called **reference classes**. You designate a reference class using the keywords **ref class**. The syntax for a ref class definition is as follows:

```
ref class Class_name
{
   class data members and methods
};
```

> **NOTE** Do not forget to include the semicolon at the end of the class definition.

All nodes in the linked list examples you have seen have the same underlying structure (they all contain a data value and a pointer). The Node ref class definition, therefore, has to include a data value and a pointer in its definition. Examine the Node ref class definition in Example 12-1. The name of the class is Node, and it contains two data members. A **data member** includes any variable with class scope. The first data member of the Node ref class is an integer (nodeData), and the second is a pointer to the next Node object (next). Both nodeData and next are also instance variables. Each instance of the Node ref class (each Node object created using this class definition) has its own unique nodeData and next instance variables.

EXAMPLE 12-1: Node CLASS DEFINITION

```
ref class Node
{
   int nodeData;
   Node^ next;
};
```

The inclusion of data values and methods within the body of a class definition is called **encapsulation**. In Example 12-1, both nodeData and next are encapsulated within the Node ref class definition.

One Node class definition could be used to instantiate many Node objects, as seen in Figure 12-17. This highlights the difference between abstraction—the definition of a concept (in this case the Node ref class definition) and **implementation**—the use of a class definition to create objects.

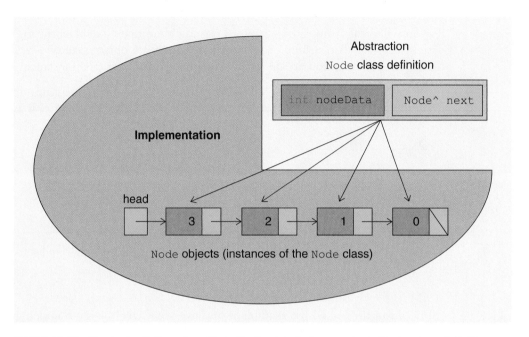

FIGURE 12-17 The instantiation of multiple Node objects from a single Node class definition

You have seen how instance variable declarations, such as nodeData and next, are encapsulated within class definitions. Every instance of the Node class has its own set of these instance variables. It is also possible to declare a variable that is shared among all objects instantiated from a class definition. This type of variable is called a **class variable**, or **static variable**. No matter how many objects are instantiated, they all share the same static variable. For example, if you wanted a program to keep track of the number of Node objects it contained, you could put a static data member declaration in the Node class definition. In Example 12-2, nodeCount is one such variable.

EXAMPLE 12-2: A STATIC INSTANCE VARIABLE (nodeCount)

```
ref class Node
{
    static int nodeCount = 0;
    int nodeData;
    Node^ next;
};
```

Each object created from this class has its own set of instance variables (nodeData and next), but there is only one class variable—nodeCount—shared among all Node objects. As you shall see, it is possible to increase nodeCount by 1 every time a node is created, thus keeping track of the number of Node objects that have been instantiated.

Constructors

Along with the instance variables that a class definition contains, most class definitions also include instance methods. Instance methods are there to provide fundamental operations that are to be built into each object instantiated from the class.

A key part of most class definitions is a public instance method, called a constructor, that tells the compiler how to construct an object from the class definition specifications. A **constructor** is a method that creates (instantiates) an object from a class definition. Constructors need to be public so that other programs have access to them. In the case of the Node class definition, a Node constructor is required in order to instantiate Node objects.

Any program that has included the file containing the Node class definition (Node.h) can run the public constructors in the Node class and make Node objects. Constructors are executed whenever an object is declared. The statement shown in Example 12-3 instantiates an object called myNode from the Node class definition using the Node class constructor.

EXAMPLE 12-3: CALLING THE Node CONSTRUCTOR THROUGH DECLARATION

```
Node myNode;
```

The general syntax for a constructor is similar to any other method; however, constructors do not have a return data type:

```
access_mode: Class_name([parameters])
{
    constructor statements;
}
```

The following features typify constructor signature lines:

- The access mode must be public if other programs are to use it to instantiate objects.
- A constructor has no return type specification.
- The constructor must have the same name as the class to which it belongs.
- The use of parameters is optional.

It is common for one class definition to have many different versions of the constructor. In that case, all versions have the same name; however, their signature lines differ according to their parameters. A constructor with no parameters is called a

default constructor. A declaration, like that shown in Example 12-3, automatically calls the default constructor. You shall encounter other types of constructors in the next chapter.

The default constructor for a Node class is shown in Example 12-4.

EXAMPLE 12-4: DEFAULT Node CONSTRUCTOR

```
Node(void)
{
    nodeData = 0;
    next = nullptr;
}
```

This default constructor creates a Node object as illustrated in Figure 12-18.

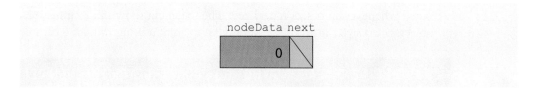

FIGURE 12-18 Newly constructed Node object.

Destructors

The deletion of a Node object can be a common occurrence. For example, if a node is declared in a method, then it has local scope and is destroyed when the method ends. Just as special methods called constructors are required to create Node objects, special methods called destructors must be used to delete them when they are no longer needed.

A **destructor** is a method that deallocates memory allocated for an object. Deallocation makes the memory available again for the program to use. Destructors have the same name as the class, preceded by the ~ (tilde) character. The general syntax for a destructor is:

```
access_mode: ~Class_name()
{
    destructor statements;
}
```

The most common access mode for a destructor is protected access. **Protected access** mode means that the destructor may only be called by methods within its class or by methods with special permission.

Destructors are most important for objects whose constructors dynamically allocate memory. This is to make sure that the deletion process explicitly deallocates any memory cells that may have been dynamically allocated.

In the case of the Node class, the constructor has not allocated memory dynamically so the destructor has an empty body, as shown in Example 12-5.

EXAMPLE 12-5: Node DESTRUCTOR

```
~Node() {}
```

Empty destructors such as this are usually omitted from class definitions entirely since the destruction process is automatic.

Class Diagrams

The complete code for the Node class you have developed is shown in Example 12-6, including its data members (nodeData and next) and constructor.

EXAMPLE 12-6: COMPLETE Node CLASS DEFINITION

```
ref class Node
{
public:
    // instance variables
    int nodeData;
    Node^ next;

    // constructor
    Node(void)
    {
        nodeData = 0;
        next = nullptr;
    }

};
```

A common tool used to assist in the development of object-oriented programs is a **Unified Modeling Language (UML)** class diagram. The Unified Modeling language is a standardized set of symbols for diagramming the structure and behavior of object-oriented programs and entities. A **UML class diagram** is a diagram that shows the members of a class and their accessibility to other classes and programs.

UML class diagrams often list the class's data members and methods in separate sections as shown in Figure 12-19.

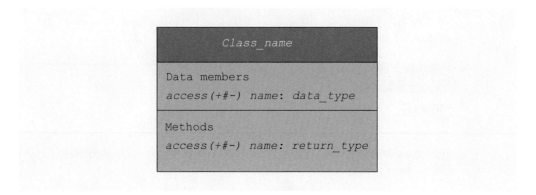

FIGURE 12-19 General UML class diagram structure

Figure 12-20 is a UML class diagram for the **Node** class definition that is shown in Example 12-6.

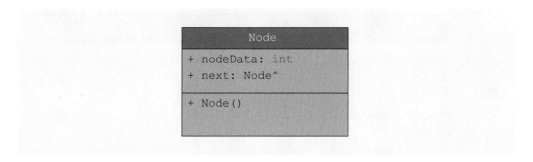

FIGURE 12-20 UML class diagram for Example 12-6

Figure 12-21 is a UML diagram for the **Node** class. The class name is listed in the top section. In the middle section of the drawing, below the class name, is a list of the data members. Each data member is identified by its mode of accessibility, name, and data type. The lower section contains similar information for class methods including accessibility, name, and return type, if applicable. The accessibility symbols are the following:

- + (**public** access)
- # (**protected** access)
- − (**private** access)

In this example, all data members and methods in the **Node** class have **public** access. In general, the **public** members of a class are defined first, then the **protected** members, and finally those whose access mode is `private`. As you shall see in the next chapter, there are important reasons why you might want to restrict data members to `private` access.

Class Definition Files

Once you have written a useful class definition you may want to use it more than once. One of the strengths of object-oriented programming is that class definitions are able to be compiled into other programs. This feature is called **code reuse**. For this reason, it is advisable to save the C++ class definition code in its own file called a **class file**. This way another program can use the class you have defined simply by including the class file in its compilation process. Programs that use class definitions from other sources like this are called **client code**.

A linked list is a common data structure, and whenever you write a program that needs one it is good to know that you will not have to rewrite the definition of a `Node` class again. Once you have your `Node` class code saved to a file, that file can be shared with any other program that needs it.

Header Files

Typically, programmers put the code for a reference class in a header file. A **header file** is a file that has the same name as the class and a .h suffix (for example, the `Node` class would be defined in a file called `Node.h`. A header file contains C++ source code that can be included in the source code of another file by the compiler. Often they are included at the top of another source code file, hence the term "header" file.

Header files are important because they allow classes that you define (such as the `Node` class) to be used by other programs to create and use objects of that class (the nodes of a linked list, for example). Header files are brought into other files, like client code, using an `#include` preprocessor directive.

For example, this `#include` statement brings the contents of `Node.h` into the current file as seen in Example 12-7. A file, like `Node.h`, that is brought into another file through an `#include` statement, is called an **include file**.

EXAMPLE 12-7: INCLUDE FILE `Node.h`

```
#include   "Node.h"
```

A **preprocessor directive** such as `#include` is not a C++ command. It is a direct instruction to the compiler on how to assemble the code from one or more files before attempting to compile it. Preprocessor directives always start with the character (`#`) and do not use semicolons at the end.

Figure 12-21 illustrates how a class file (Node.h) is included in client code, such as the program file Form1.h.

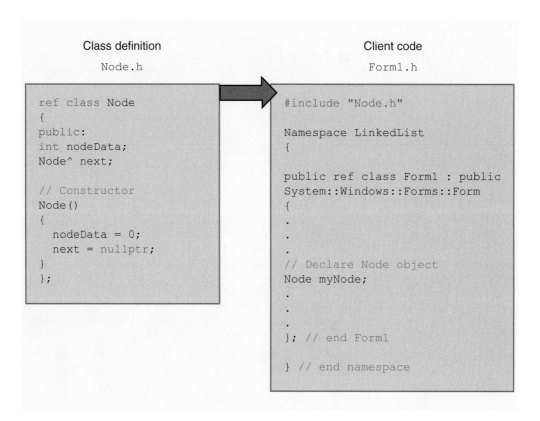

Class definition

Node.h

Client code

Form1.h

```
ref class Node
{
public:
int nodeData;
Node^ next;

// Constructor
Node()
{
  nodeData = 0;
  next = nullptr;
}
};
```

```
#include "Node.h"

Namespace LinkedList
{

public ref class Form1 : public
System::Windows::Forms::Form
{
.
.
.
// Declare Node object
Node myNode;
.
.
.
}; // end Form1

} // end namespace
```

FIGURE 12-21 Header file inclusion in client code

Implementation Files

In the tutorial, you will see exactly how to create the header file. However, there is one concern. It is possible for header files to become very large if they have many methods or if those methods are complex. To avoid files of unwieldy sizes, you can break a class definition into two files, a header file (such as Node.h) and a companion C++ code file, called an **implementation file**, using the same name but with a .cpp file extension. For example, the implementation file for Node.h would be Node.cpp. These files then work together to completely define the methods and attributes of a class as shown in Figure 12-22.

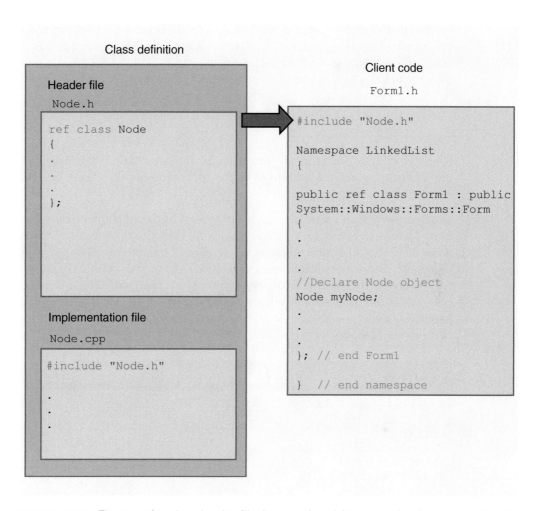

FIGURE 12-22 The use of a class header file (Node.h) and its companion implementation file (Node.cpp) to define a class for inclusion in client code

Example 12-8 shows what the implementation file **Node.cpp** would look like if the default constructor **Node()** was defined in **Node.cpp** instead of in **Node.h**.

EXAMPLE 12-8: IMPLEMENTATION FILE Node.cpp

```
#include "Node.h"
// constructor
Node::Node(void)
{
    nodeData = 0;
    next = nullptr;
}
```

Notice that the name of the method in the signature line uses the scope resolution operator (::) to identify the class to which it belongs. The general syntax for the scope resolution operator is shown here and is used to indicate which class a method or data member belongs to when read from right to left.

```
class_name::member_name
```

Scope resolution operators are necessary in implementation files because whenever a method is being defined outside of its class definition file the class it belongs to must be specified for the compiler.

Because the default constructor is now defined in the implementation file, there is no need to fully define it in the class header file. All the compiler needs to know from **Node.h** is that a default constructor is part of the **Node** class and is fully defined elsewhere. Rather than defining every statement in the default constructor, a prototype is given. A **method prototype** consists of its signature line, without a method body. Method prototypes tell the compiler how to identify the full definition. Method prototypes always end with a semicolon. The prototype for the default constructor is shown in Example 12-9.

EXAMPLE 12-9: Node DEFAULT CONSTRUCTOR PROTOTYPE

```
ref class Node
{
public:
    // instance variables
    int nodeData;
    Node^ next;

    // default constructor method prototype
    Node(void);

};
```

Notice that the prototype for the constructor contains just the original signature line followed by a semicolon. There is no body to this method, which means that the body is defined elsewhere (in the **Node.cpp** implementation file).

The relationship between the header file (`Node.h`) and the implementation file (`Node.cpp`) is shown in Figure 12-23.

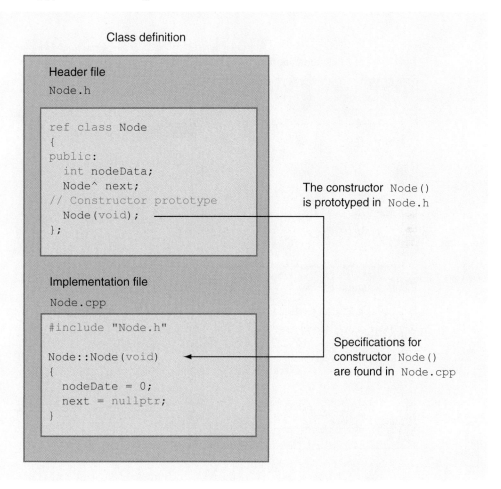

Class definition

Header file

Node.h

```
ref class Node
{
public:
    int nodeData;
    Node^ next;
// Constructor prototype
    Node(void);
};
```

The constructor `Node()` is prototyped in `Node.h`

Implementation file

Node.cpp

```
#include "Node.h"

Node::Node(void)
{
    nodeDate = 0;
    next = nullptr;
}
```

Specifications for constructor `Node()` are found in `Node.cpp`

FIGURE 12-23 Relationship between a header file and an implementation file

Class Definition Files and Client Code

So far in this chapter, you have learned about three different types of files used in an object-oriented program:

- A header file (`.h`), which is the file that establishes a class definition
- An implementation file (`.cpp`), which is the file that specifies the details of class definition methods
- Client code (`Form1.h`), which is the program that creates objects from the class definition

The relationship between the class definition files and client code is shown in Figure 12-24. Notice the use of the #include statement in the client code to bring the Node.h and Node.cpp class definition code in before compilation.

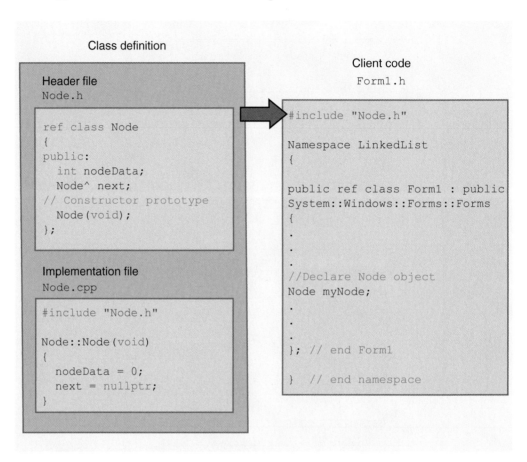

FIGURE 12-24 Class definition code and client code files

Using Node Objects

Once Node.h has been brought into a client program with an #include statement, the Node class is available to the client to construct Node objects. Node objects, once constructed, can be used in a variety of ways. They can be linked up with other nodes to form a linked list. The client code can also access the public data stored in each node.

Instantiating Node Objects

The default Node() constructor is activated by the declaration statement shown in Example 12-10. The constructor creates an instance of the Node class, the object myNode.

EXAMPLE 12-10: INSTANTIATING A Node

```
Node myNode;
```

You can also declare a variable consisting of a handle to a node and then use gcnew to allocate the node in memory and return the address for assignment to the handle, as shown in Example 12-11.

EXAMPLE 12-11: USING gcnew TO CONSTRUCT A Node OBJECT

```
Node^ temp = gcnew Node;
```

Accessing Node Attributes

Both the variable myNode (Example 12-10) and the pointer variable temp (Example 12-11) have access to the public data members (nodeData and next) of the nodes they represent.

Variables, such as myNode, access public data members, such as nodeData, using the **member access operator (.)**. For example, the default constructor assigned the value 0 to nodeData when myNode was constructed. The value in nodeData can be displayed in the manner shown in Example 12-12.

EXAMPLE 12-12: USING MEMBER ACCESS OPERATOR (.)

```
textBox1->Text = (myNode.nodeData).ToString()
```

Pointer variables on the other hand must access public data members using the **pointer member access operator (->)**. For example, the default constructor assigned the value 0 to nodeData when the memory for temp was allocated. The value in nodeData can be displayed in the manner shown in Example 12-13.

EXAMPLE 12-13: USING POINTER MEMBER ACCESS OPERATOR (->)

```
textBox1->Text = (temp->nodeData).ToString()
```

The code shown in Example 12-14 checks to see whether head->next contains an assigned address. If head->next is the null pointer, its value is 0; otherwise, its value is a positive integer representing a valid address. If next contains a valid address then head->next is assigned to temp->next.

EXAMPLE 12-14: ASSIGNING POINTERS USING THE next DATA MEMBER

```
if (head->next) temp->next = head->next;
```

Accessing static Variables

Client code can also access public static variables belonging to the Node class. Recall that static variables are shared by all objects derived from a class definition. Therefore, to access a static variable the client needs to reference the class itself, rather than to an object. In Example 12-2, you saw how to declare a public, static nodeCount variable to keep track of the number of nodes a program has created. To access the nodeCount variable the client must provide the class name it belongs to, using the scope resolution operator (::) as shown in Example 12-15.

EXAMPLE 12-15: USING THE SCOPE RESOLUTION OPERATOR (::)

```
if (Node::nodeCount >= 1) btnDelete->Enabled = true;
```

Example 12-15 checks to see if nodeCount is greater than or equal to 1. If it is, then it allows btnDelete to be enabled; otherwise, btnDelete is assumed to be disabled.

Tutorial: Linked List

This tutorial provides you with practical experience implementing the Node class definition discussed throughout previous sections. In the tutorial, you will write the Node class header file and implementation file, as well as the client code. Within the client code, you will use the Node class definition to create the nodes of a linked list data structure. The program interface draws the linked list and allows the user to insert and delete nodes, up to a maximum of seven. After the operations of insertion or deletion are carried out in memory, the resulting list is drawn on the interface.

Problem Description

This program draws a linked list on the interface using Rectangle objects to represent the Node objects. There is a direct relationship between the rectangles and connecting lines drawn on the interface and the nodes connected by pointers in memory.

The program works like this: When the program starts, the user initially sees a blank form with four buttons. Only one of the buttons (`btnHead`) is enabled. The disabled buttons appear as dimmed images, as shown in Figure 12-25.

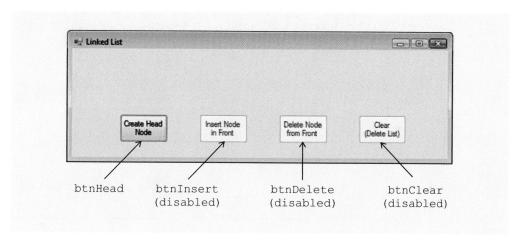

FIGURE 12-25   Initial program interface

When the user clicks `btnHead` a head node is created in memory and a representation of the entire linked list (which only has a head node in it) is drawn on the form. At that time the buttons labeled "Insert Node in Front" (`btnInsert`) and "Clear" (`btnClear`) become enabled and `btnHead` is disabled, as shown in Figure 12-26.

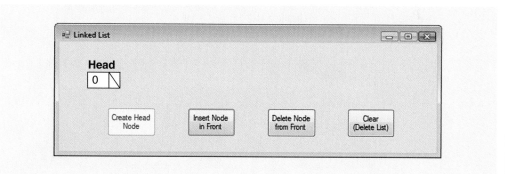

FIGURE 12-26   Interface after creation of the head node

Take a look at the representation of the head node (labeled "Head") in Figure 12-26. It consists of two `Rectangle` objects. The one on the left represents the `nodeData` data member of the node. The one on the right represents the pointer variable `next`. The head node displays the `nodeData` value 0 because it was the first node created, and the value stored in `nodeCount` was assigned to the instance variable `nodeData`. The second node created will have the value 1 stored in it. The third will have 2 in it, and so on.

The contents of the pointer variable **next** will either be drawn as a diagonal line, representing a null pointer as in Figure 12-26, or as an arrow, to represent a pointer value.

When the user clicks **btnInsert**, a new node is created in memory and assigned to the head node's pointer field (**next**), and the linked list is drawn on the interface as shown in Figure 12-27. Newly created nodes are always inserted after the head node. Once a node has been added, **btnDelete** is enabled and may be used to delete nodes, as you shall soon see.

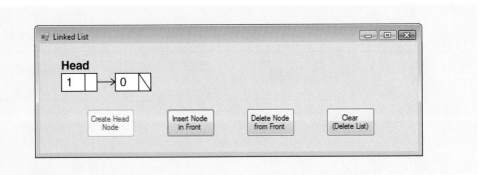

FIGURE 12-27 Interface after insertion of the first node

Clicking **btnInsert** a second time creates a new node with **nodeData** set to 2 and draws the entire linked list on the interface as shown in Figure 12-28. All new nodes are inserted into the linked list after the head node. Every new node is created using the **static** variable **nodeCount** to initialize **nodeData**. This means that the head node always displays the value 0, while the node it points to will always be the last node created and therefore display the largest value.

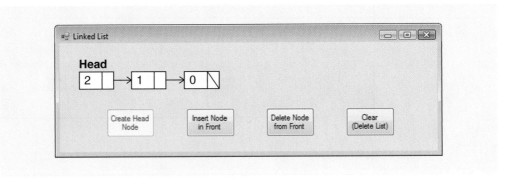

FIGURE 12-28 Interface after insertion of a second node

The role of **btnDelete** is to remove the node pointed to by the head node. Figure 12-29 shows what the interface looks like after the user clicks **btnDelete**. The most recently added node (the node displaying 2 in Figure 12-28) has been deleted.

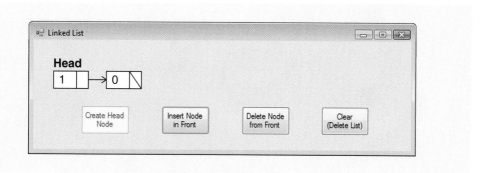

FIGURE 12-29 Interface after deletion of the node pointed to by the head node in Figure 12-28

Figure 12-30 shows the interface after the deletion of the node that displays the value 1 in Figure 12-29. The head node is the key to this linked list structure. All insertions occur at the head node and all deletions remove the node that is the head node.

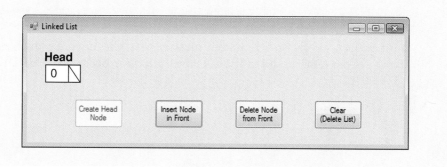

FIGURE 12-30 Interface after deletion of node 1

If the user attempts to insert more than seven nodes (which would not fit on an interface of this size), then a message box should inform her that the limit of nodes has been reached, as shown in Figure 12-31.

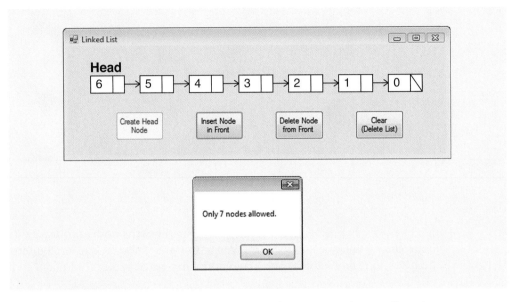

FIGURE 12-31 Message box indicating that no more than seven nodes are allowed

After the user clicks OK in the message box the interface disables btnInsert and displays the same nodes as it did before the error occurred. This situation is shown in Figure 12-32.

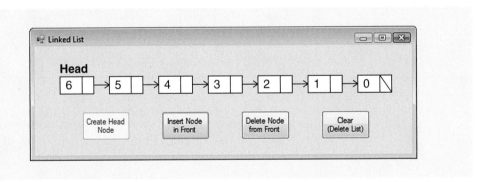

FIGURE 12-32 Interface after clicking OK on the message box in Figure 12-31

Clicking `btnClear` removes the entire list and resets the form. It removes the entire list, including the head, as shown in Figure 12-33.

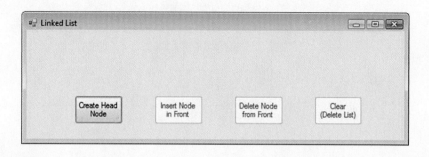

FIGURE 12-33 Interface after `btnClear` has been used to delete the entire list

Design

You need to consider numerous design issues. From the standpoint of the `Node` class definition, you must consider the kind of data structure needed to represent a node. From the standpoint of client code, you must come up with a structure for the program, including algorithms for the various buttons. The key to understanding this program is to keep in mind that the drawing of the list using rectangles on the interface is intended to portray the linked list data structure as it exists in memory. The construction of the linked list data structure through insertion and deletion of nodes happens in memory, then the drawing of the linked list is done on the interface. Maintaining the data structure and drawing its representation are two very separate tasks.

THE `Node` CLASS DEFINITION

The `Node` class definition given in Example 12-2 is perfect for this program. In it, each node is defined as having two data members (`nodeData` and `next`) similar to the `Node` class discussed previously. In addition, it has a `static` integer variable (`nodeCount`) to count the nodes as they are produced. You can also use the `nodeCount` variable to assign a value to `nodeData`. The constructor and destructor are also similar to those discussed earlier. The class definition is shown in Figure 12-34.

1
2

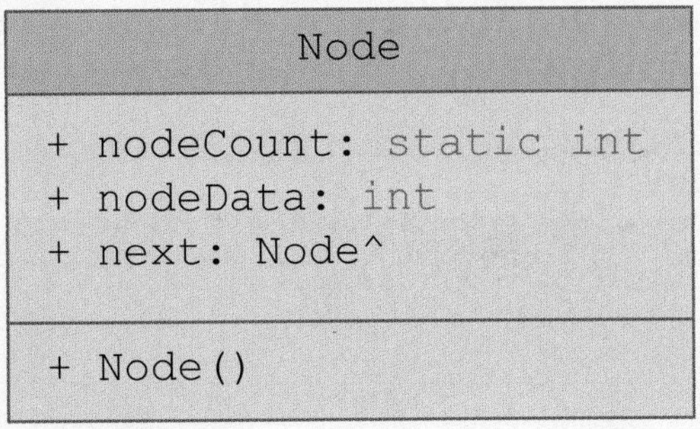

Node
+ nodeCount: static int + nodeData: int + next: Node^
+ Node()

FIGURE 12-34 Node class diagram

INTERFACE

As you saw earlier in this tutorial, the main controls consist of four buttons:

- btnHead—Creates the head node
- btnDelete—Deletes the node at the front of the list
- btnInsert—Inserts a new node at the front of the list
- btnClear—Resets the form so that the user may begin again

The interface should be large enough to accommodate the drawn representations of seven nodes using **Rectangle** objects. Figure 12-35 shows rectangles positioned using the following coordinates and dimensions:

- The upper-left corner of the rectangle representing the head node will be at the location (25, 45).
- The width of each rectangle is 50 pixels.
- The height of each rectangle is 25 pixels.
- The length of the arrow between each rectangle is 30 pixels.

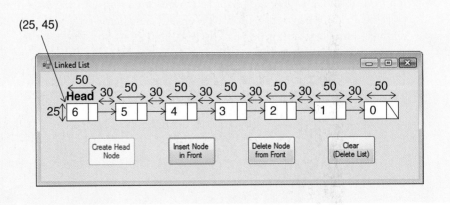

FIGURE 12-35 Interface plan to accommodate seven rectangles

DATA TABLE

The most important object in this program is the head pointer for the linked list. You should declare it as a **static** class variable as shown in Example 12-16.

EXAMPLE 12-16: HEAD POINTER DECLARATION

```
static Node^ head;
```

In addition to the head pointer, an assortment of constants and objects should be declared at the class level.

static Constants   The program requires one group of **static** constants to store the coordinates and dimensions discussed in the last section (shown in Table 12-1).

TABLE 12-1   Table of constants

Constant	Data Type	Value	Usage
headX	const int	25	x-coordinate of upper-left corner of the head node
headY	const int	45	y-coordinate of the upper-left corner of the head node
nodeLength	const int	50	Horizontal length of a node when drawn (in pixels)
nodeHeight	const int	25	Vertical height of a node when drawn (in pixels)
arrowLength	const int	30	Length of arrow representing the next pointer (in pixels)

Variables Required for Drawing   As in previous projects, you will use a **Graphics** object to draw on **Form1**. In addition, you will use a **blackPen** object to draw the lines. You will use the **blackBrush** and **whiteBrush** objects to outline and fill in the node rectangles on the interface. You will also use the **arialFont** object to draw the **nodeData** values for each node. These objects are listed in Table 12-2.

1
2

TABLE 12-2 Table of required Drawing objects

Object Name	Type	Usage
g	Graphics	Graphics object
blackPen	Pen	Used to draw lines
blackBrush	Brush	Used to draw node outlines and text
whiteBrush	Brush	Used to fill in node rectangles
arialFont	Font	Used to draw text

ALGORITHM FOR btnHead_Click()

The algorithm for btnHead_Click() is shown in Algorithm 12-2. Step 2 will call a separate method to draw the list.

ALGORITHM 12-2: HEAD NODE CREATION

1. Create a new head Node.
2. Draw the list starting at the head.
3. Disable btnHead and enable btnInsert, btnDelete and btnClear.

ALGORITHM FOR btnInsert_Click()

The algorithm for btnInsert is more involved. Items should only be inserted in the list if nodeCount is less than 7. Otherwise a message box should inform the user that additional nodes cannot be added.

If there is room for additional nodes, then btnInsert should perform the following tasks:

1. Create a new node and assign it to temp, as shown in Figure 12-36.

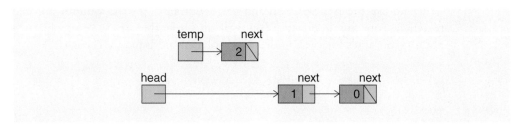

FIGURE 12-36 Creation of a new node

2. If the list has nodes in it (if `head->next` points to a node) then copy `head` into `temp->next`, as shown in Figure 12-37 to connect `temp` to the rest of the list.

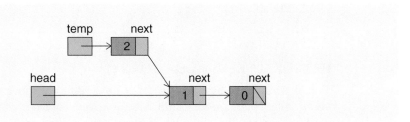

FIGURE 12-37 Assigning `temp->next`

3. Copy the address of `temp` into `head` to connect `head` to the new node as shown in Figure 12-38.

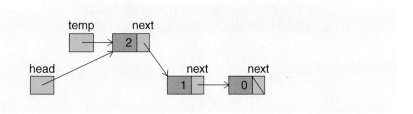

FIGURE 12-38 Connecting `head->next` to `temp`

4. Draw the list starting at the `head`.

Step 2 is the important one. If it is not done correctly, the rest of the list will be lost for good.

The full algorithm for `btnInsert_Click()` is presented in Algorithm 12-3.

Because only seven rectangles can be drawn on the interface, the linked list is not allowed to have more than seven nodes in it.

ALGORITHM 12-3: NODE INSERTION

1. Node insertion

   1.1. If `nodeCount` < 7:

      1.1.1. Create a temporary node (`temp`).

      1.1.2. Assign `head` to `temp->next`.

      1.1.3. Assign `temp` to `head`.

      1.1.4. Draw the new list.

1.2. Else `nodeCount >= 7`

    1.2.1. Display an error message.

    1.2.2. Disable `btnInsert`.

2. Enable `btnDelete`.

ALGORITHM FOR `btnDelete_Click()`

The algorithm for `btnDelete_Click()` is slightly more complicated. If `head` is not a null pointer, then a node can be deleted from the front of the list (remember to connect up the rest of the list properly). If `head` is the null pointer, then there is no node to delete.

To delete the node pointed to by `head` you use a temporary pointer variable (`temp`). Initially, `temp` is assigned the pointer in `head`. This means that now both `temp` and `head` point to the same node.

The algorithm for `btnDelete` is presented in Algorithm 12-4

ALGORITHM 12-4: NODE DELETION

1. Declare variables (`Node^ temp;`).
2. If `head` points to a node:

    2.1. Set `temp` to `head` (`temp` points to the first node, as shown in Figure 12-39).

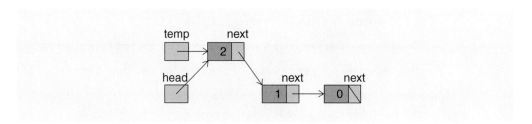

FIGURE 12-39 Assign `temp` to point to the first node

2.2. Set head to head->next (head points to the next node) as shown in Figure 12-40.

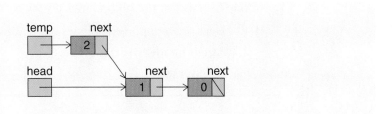

FIGURE 12-40 Assign head->next to the next node in the list (temp->next)

2.3. Delete temp, as shown in Figure 12-41.

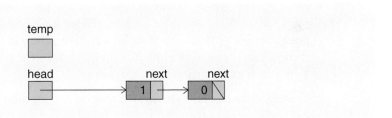

FIGURE 12-41 Deletion of temp

2.4. Subtract 1 from nodeCount.

2.5. Refresh the screen.

2.6. Draw the list.

ALGORITHM FOR btnClear_Click()

This button destroys the list by calling the method deleteList(). It then refreshes the screen and resets the buttons to their initial states (with only btnHead enabled). The tricky part—deleting the list—is explained in the next section.

ALGORITHM FOR deleteList()

Use a while loop to delete each node from head until head is the null pointer.

Algorithm 12-5 gives the while loop for the process that must be carried out to delete an entire linked list starting with the node pointed to by head.

ALGORITHM 12-5: LIST DELETION

1. While head is not the null pointer do the following

    1.1. Declare a temporary pointer assigned head.

    1.2. Assign head->next to head.

    1.3. Delete temp

ALGORITHM FOR drawNode()

You can draw the linked list recursively using a method called drawNode(). This method draws each node a set distance (nodeDistance) from the last one. drawNode() must be passed a Node handle (myNode) and a variable indicating how far from the head node rectangle the current rectangle representing a node should be drawn. The distance from the head node to the rectangle you want to draw can be calculated by multiplying nodeDistance by the number of recursive calls that have been made. The number of recursive calls this algorithm makes is its level of recursion. You can keep track of this value in an integer variable called level.

The algorithm for drawNode() is shown in Algorithm 12-6.

ALGORITHM 12-6: DRAWING NODES

1. Declare variables.

2. Calculate the x-coordinate of the upper-left corner of the rectangle by multiplying level by nodeDistance.

3. Create a rectangle to use in drawing the node.

4. Draw the node.

5. Draw the next pointer:

    5.1. If next points to a node, draw an arrow.

    5.2. Else draw a diagonal line to represent the null pointer.

6. Draw the value stored in nodeData.

7. Label the head node.

8. Increment level (to get ready for the next node).

9. If myNode->next points to a node, go there and draw it.

The recursive process draws one node, then moves on to the next node, and the next, until it has drawn the last node.

Development

This program is intended to visually represent what takes place in memory as nodes are allocated and deallocated. The development process centers on facilitating the way the visual representation is drawn.

INTERFACE

Open Visual Studio and create a new project. The interface for this project consists of a Form1 (Size = 600, 200) with four buttons (btnHead to create a head node, btnInsert to insert a node, btnDelete to delete a node, and btnClear to remove the entire list) as shown in Figure 12-25. Form1 should be wide enough to accommodate up to seven nodes.

CODING

Earlier in the chapter, the Node class definition was presented, and the process of establishing a Node.h header file and Node.cpp implementation file was discussed. In this section, you will learn how to create these files in Visual C++ and include them in the client code for your project.

The graphic representation of the linked list structure on the form, drawn using rectangles, presents no new challenges from the standpoint of producing the visual images. However, since the program must draw a representation of the linked list data structure, it will be important to make sure you understand what is going on in the linked list as nodes are inserted and deleted.

Creating the Node Class Definition Files (Node.h and Node.cpp)   To create a class definition, you add a new component to your project in the form of a Node class header file (Node.h) and implementation file (Node.cpp). From the Project menu select **Add Class** as shown in Figure 12-42.

1
2

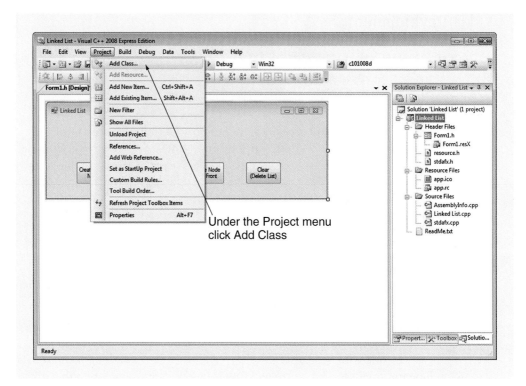

FIGURE 12-42 Adding a new class from the Project menu

In the dialog box, select **C++** under Categories and **C++ Class** under the Templates window, as shown in Figure 12-43.

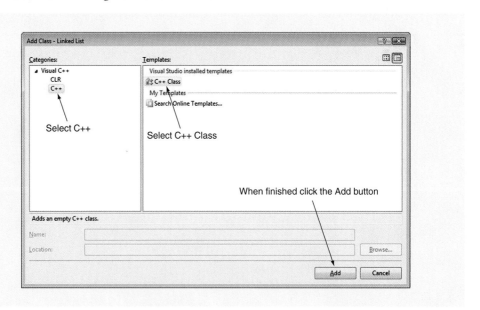

FIGURE 12-43 Selection of C++ class option

In the next dialog box, you specify a name for your class file. Make sure you enter **Node** as shown in Figure 12-44. The `.h` and `.cpp` files are named automatically to match.

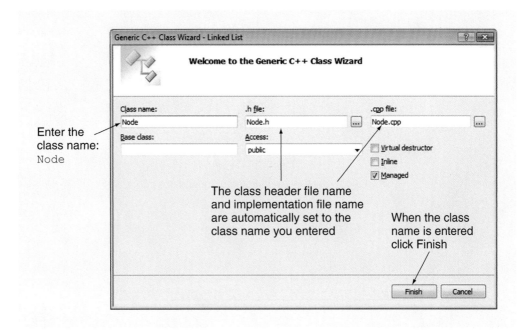

FIGURE 12-44 Naming the new class

After you click **Finish**, Visual Studio creates both a class header file named `Node.h` and an implementation file named `Node.cpp` for your project. These files show up in Solution Explorer as shown in Figure 12-45. Take a quick look at what was created for you. You can view the file under tabbed windows in the IDE by double-clicking on them in Solution Explorer.

Notice that `Node.h` contains a prototype for the `public` default constructor `Node()`.

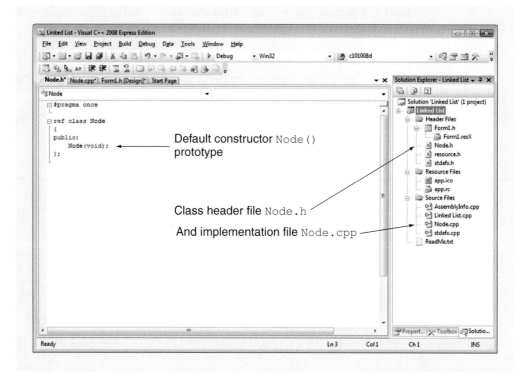

FIGURE 12-45 The class header file Node.h

The `Node.cpp` file is shown in Figure 12-46. The `Node.cpp` file contains an empty constructor, `Node::Node(void)`.

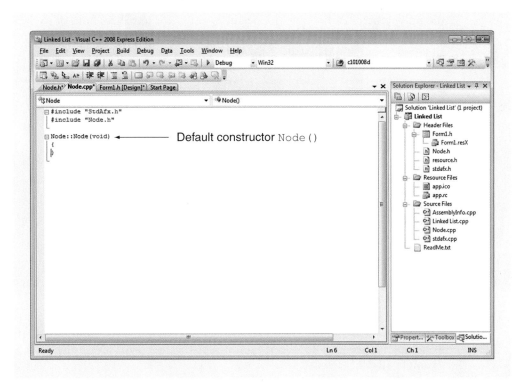

FIGURE 12-46 `Node.cpp` file window

Coding Node.h With the `Node.h` header file created, your next order of business is to write the code defining this class. Make sure you are in `Node.h` (not `Node.cpp`) and enter the code shown in Example 12-17. These lines add the `static` variable `nodeCount` and `public` instance variables `nodeData` and `next` as well the destructor `~Node()` to the `Node` class definition.

EXAMPLE 12-17: `Node.h` CLASS DEFINITION

```
#pragma once

ref class Node
{
public:
    static int nodeCount = 0;
    int nodeData;
    Node^ next;

    // constructor prototype
    Node(void);
};
```

Coding Node.cpp   Next, you need to code the constructor in Node.cpp. Add the code shown in Example 12-18 to the default constructor. These lines assign the value stored in nodeCount to the data member nodeData and set the pointer variable next to the null pointer. In this way, the default constructor initializes both of its data members as it creates a new node. Also note that the postfix incrementation operator (++) is used to add 1 to nodeCount after its value was assigned to nodeData.

EXAMPLE 12-18: THE Node.cpp IMPLEMENTATION FILE

```
#include "StdAfx.h"
#include "Node.h"

// constructor
Node::Node(void)
{
    nodeData = nodeCount++;
    next = nullptr;
}
```

At this point you should save your work. Compile your program to check for errors before moving on to coding the client code file Form1.h.

Client Code Issues   Go to Form1.h and scroll to the very top of the file. For Form1.h to be able to use the Node class definition, the first two lines must be those shown in Example 12-19.

EXAMPLE 12-19: INCLUDING Node.h IN THE CLIENT

```
#pragma once
#include "Node.h"
```

The **#pragma once** preprocessor directive is automatically provided to prevent a file from being compiled more than once in the same project. Enter the #include "Node.h" preprocessor directive as the second line in the file.

Now go to the Design window for Form1.h. Double-click on the form to open the Form1_Load() event handler in the code window.

Immediately above Form1.h you need to enter the code for static constants and instance objects (refer to Tables 12-1 and 12-2). These are shown in Example 12-20.

EXAMPLE 12-20: CLIENT CODE CONSTANTS AND INSTANCE VARIABLES

```
// location and dimension constants
static const int headX = 25;
static const int headY = 45;
static const int nodeLength = 50;
static const int nodeHeight = 25;
static const int arrowLength = 30;

// head node handle
static Node^ head = nullptr;

// Declare Graphics and Drawing objects
static Graphics^ g;
static Brush^ whiteBrush;
static Pen^ blackPen;
static SolidBrush^ blackBrush;
static Drawing::Font^ arialFont;
```

The `Drawing` objects are constructed in `Form1_Load()` as shown in Example 12-21.

EXAMPLE 12-21: CODE FOR `Form1_Load()`

```
private: System::Void Form1_Load(System::Object^
sender, System::EventArgs^  e) {
   g = this->CreateGraphics();
whiteBrush = gcnew System::Drawing::SolidBrush(Color::White);
   blackPen = gcnew System::Drawing::Pen(Color::Black);
   blackBrush = gcnew System::Drawing::SolidBrush(Color::Black);
   arialFont = gcnew System::Drawing::Font("Arial",12);
   reset();
}
```

The last line of `Form1_Load()` calls a `private` instance method `reset()` to set the various `Enabled` properties of the buttons, as shown in Example 12-22. Notice that `reset()` also sets `nodeCount` to 0. This implies that `reset()` is only called prior to the creation of a new linked list.

EXAMPLE 12-22: CODE FOR THE `reset()` METHOD

```
private: void reset()
{
   btnDelete->Enabled = false;
   btnInsert->Enabled = false;
   btnHead->Enabled = true;
   btnClear->Enabled = false;
   Node::nodeCount = 0;
}
```

Code for btnHead_Click()   The head node is instantiated (using **gcnew**) and drawn (using an instance method called **drawNode()**) in the **btnHead_Click()** click event, shown in Example 12-23. Note that the code also enables or disables other buttons as appropriate.

EXAMPLE 12-23: CODE FOR btnHead_Click()

```
private: System::Void btnHead_Click(System::Object^
sender, System::EventArgs^  e) {
   if (!head) head = gcnew Node;
   drawNode(head, 0);
   btnInsert->Enabled = true;
   btnDelete->Enabled = true;
   btnHead->Enabled = false;
   btnClear->Enabled = true;
}
```

Code for btnInsert_Click()   The algorithm for **btnInsert_Click()** was presented earlier. Because the interface can only accommodate seven rectangles, an error message is displayed when **nodeCount**, which starts at 0, reaches seven.

The insertion process creates a temporary node and attaches it to the head node through the temporary node's **next** pointer. The code for this method is shown in Example 12-24. It is helpful to sketch the insertion process on paper using diagrams similar to Figures 12-36 through 12-38 presented earlier in this chapter, to make sure you can follow the steps. Once the node is inserted, this event handler calls a programmer-defined instance method (**drawNode()**) to draw the list. **drawNode()** takes two actual parameters. The first is a pointer to the node it must draw. The second is an indicator of how far away from the first rectangle this new rectangle should be. Because the head node is the first node in the list, its second parameter is 0.

EXAMPLE 12-24: CODE FOR btnInsert_Click()

```
private: System::Void btnInsert_Click(System::Object^
sender, System::EventArgs^  e)
{
   if (Node::nodeCount < 7)
   {
      Node^ temp = gcnew Node;
      temp->next = head;
      head = temp;
      drawNode(head, 0);
   }
```

```
    else
    {
        MessageBox::Show("Only 7 nodes allowed.");
        btnInsert->Enabled = false;
        btnDelete->Enabled = true;
    }
}
```

Code for drawNode() The method signature line for drawNode() is shown in Example 12-25.

EXAMPLE 12-25: SIGNATURE LINE FOR METHOD drawNode()

```
private: void drawNode(Node^ myNode, int level)
```

drawNode() receives a handle pointing to a node (myNode) and an integer variable (level) indicating the position at which the node should be drawn on the interface.

The algorithm for drawNode() describes two main tasks: drawing the node whose pointer it has been given, and recursively moving to the next node in the list to draw it. Recursion stops when next is the null pointer, indicating that the last node in the list has been reached.

The recursive code for Steps 8 and 9 of Algorithm 12-6 are implemented as shown in Example 12-26.

EXAMPLE 12-26: RECURSIVE CALL TO METHOD drawNode()

```
level++;
if (myNode->next)
{
    drawNode(myNode->next, level);
}
```

12

The program must draw each rectangle at a different distance from the rectangle that represents the head node. The distance between the upper-left corner of the head node and that of any other node is a multiple of **nodeDistance**, as shown in Figure 12-47.

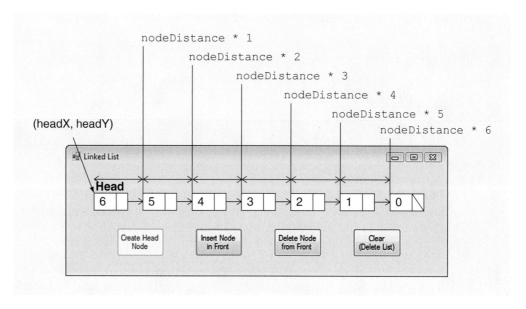

FIGURE 12-47 Locations for drawing node rectangles

The multiplier (1, 2, 3, etc.) is stored in the formal parameter **level**. The exact x-coordinate location of the upper-left corner of any node is:

```
x = headX + (nodeDistance * level);
```

The complete code for this method is shown in Example 12-27.

EXAMPLE 12-27: THE COMPLETED CODE FOR drawNode()

```
private: void drawNode(Node^ myNode, int level)
{   // Step 1: Declare variables
    int x;
    int nodeDistance = nodeLength + arrowLength;
    // Step 2: calculate  x coord of the corner
    x = headX+(nodeDistance * level);
    // Step 3: Create a rectangle
    Drawing::Rectangle nodeRect(x,headY,nodeLength,nodeHeight);
    // Step 4: Draw the Node
    g->FillRectangle(whiteBrush,nodeRect);
    g->DrawRectangle(blackPen,nodeRect);
    g->DrawLine(blackPen,x+nodeLength-15,headY,x+nodeLength-15,headY+nodeHeight);
```

```
// Step 5: Draw next
if (myNode->next) // Step 5.1 if next Node draw arrow
{
    g->DrawLine(blackPen,x+nodeLength,headY+12,x+nodeDistance,headY+12);
    g->DrawLine(blackPen,x+nodeLength+25,headY+7,x+nodeDistance,headY+12);
    g->DrawLine(blackPen,x+nodeLength+25,headY+17,x+nodeDistance,headY+12);
}
else // Step 5.2 if there is no next Node draw null pointer
    g->DrawLine(blackPen,x+nodeLength,headY,x+nodeLength-15,headY+25);
// Step 6: Draw nodeData
g->DrawString(myNode->nodeData.ToString(),arialFont,blackBrush,x+5,headY+5);

// Step 7: Label head node
g->DrawString("Head",arialFont,blackBrush,headX,headY-20);
// Step 8: Increment level
level++;
// Step 9: If next points to a Node go there and draw it
if (myNode->next)
    drawNode(myNode->next, level);
}
```

The numbered steps in the comments correspond to those in Algorithm 12-6 from the Design section. Most involve drawing tasks using the `Brush`, `Pen`, `Font`, `Graphics`, and `Rectangle` objects you have become familiar with in previous projects.

Testing

At this point you should have completed the following tasks:

- Writing the code for `Node.h` and `Node.cpp`
- Inserting the command `#include "Node.h"` in `Form1.h`
- Declaring the `static` constants and instance methods required by `Form1.h`
- Coding the client code event handlers:
  - `Form1_Load()`
  - `btnHead_Click()`
  - `btnInsert_Click()`
- Coding the programmer-defined instance method `drawNode()`

This is enough to allow your program to create a head node and insert nodes after it. Test your program, making sure it does not allow more than seven nodes in the list. You will tackle the deletion capabilities in the On Your Own section that follows.

1
2

ON YOUR OWN

You now have completed a project that creates a linked list, allows the user to insert nodes, and draws a visual representation of the linked list on the interface. The On Your Own tasks address additional capabilities you want your project to support.

TASK 1: CODING btnDelete_Click()

The program you created in the tutorial allows the user to insert nodes but not delete them. On your own, write the code for btnDelete_Click(). An algorithm for this button is provided in the Design section of the tutorial (Algorithm 12-4).

TASK 2: CODING btnClear_Click() AND deleteList()

Complete the program by writing the code for btnClear_Click(). This button deletes the list by calling the method deleteList(). The algorithm for deleteList() was presented earlier (Algorithm 12-5). The code for deleteList() is shown in Example 12-28.

EXAMPLE 12-28

```
void deleteList(Node^ node)
{
  while(head)
  {
    Node^ temp = head;
    head = head->next;
    delete temp;
    Node::nodeCount--;
  }
}
```

This code removes the entire list starting from the back instead of the front, with the head node being the last one deleted.

TASK 3: FINAL TESTING

Test your completed application and verify that it works correctly. Your project should do the following:

- Disable all buttons except btnHead on startup.
- Disable btnHead after a head node has been created.
- Enable btnInsert after the head node was created.

- Disable `btnInsert` when seven nodes have been created.
- Enable `btnDelete` after one node has been added to the list.
- Disable `btnDelete` when only the head node exists.
- Correctly insert nodes in the list.
- Correctly delete nodes from the list.
- Correctly number the nodes as they are inserted and deleted.

QUICK REVIEW

1. The essential elements of a data structure are its abstraction.
2. At the abstraction level, all lists are collections of related items.
3. At the abstraction level, all lists must allow items to be inserted and deleted.
4. Arrays and linked lists are two ways that lists can be implemented.
5. Arrays are useful because their elements can be accessed quickly.
6. A problem with arrays is that insertion and deletion is slow—O(n).
7. A node is an object containing data items and a pointer to the another node (a `next` pointer).
8. Linked lists are list data structures that use pointers to connect nodes.
9. If a node is at the end of a list, its pointer is a null pointer.
10. The first node in a list is the head node.
11. The second node in a list is accessed through the head node's `next` pointer.
12. A node in a linked list must be accessed through the pointer from the previous node.
13. You can easily expand a linked list to accommodate the amount of data you want to store.
14. To insert data into a list, you must reassign pointers at the spot of insertion.
15. Deletion of a node also involves reassigning pointers and then deleting memory allocated to the `next` pointer.
16. You can write a program that inserts data into a linked list or deletes data from a linked list in O(1) operations.
17. You create objects from class definitions through a process called instantiation.
18. Objects are instances of the classes from which they were created.
19. A Visual C++ class is called a reference class (`ref class`).
20. Classes are composed of collections of data (data members) and methods.
21. `static` variables are shared by all objects of the class.

22.   Instance variables and methods are unique to each object.

23.   You use a constructor to create an object from a class definition.

24.   Constructors are methods that have the same name as the class.

25.   Constructors without parameters are called default constructors.

26.   Destructors deallocate memory when a object is deleted.

27.   Destructors have the same name as the class preceded by a tilde ($\sim$).

28.   UML is a standardized way of diagramming object-oriented structures.

29.   A UML class diagram shows the data members and methods that belong to a class along with their accessibility and return types.

30.   You create class definitions in header files.

31.   A preprocessor directive helps govern how code files are put together. It runs before the program is compiled.

32.   The `#pragma once` preprocessor directive assures that a file will not be compiled more than once in the same project.

33.   Methods that are too long for the header file class definition may be put in another file called an implementation file.

34.   The `#include` preprocessor directive brings the source code from a class header file into another source code file.

35.   When an implementation file defines a method, the name of the class that method belongs to must precede the method name in the definition (i.e., `Node::`*Method*`()`).

36.   Methods that are defined in an implementation file must be prototyped in the class header file.

37.   A method prototype consists of the signature line followed by a semicolon, with no method body.

38.   Client code is the program that instantiates objects from class definitions. The `#include` preprocessor directive is used to bring a class definition header file into client code.

39.   The `gcnew` command constructs `ref class` objects.

TERMS TO KNOW

`#include`

`#pragma once`

abstraction

class file

class variable

client code

code reuse

constructor

data member

default constructor

destructor

encapsulation

garbage collection heap (gc heap)

head

head node

head pointer

header file

implementation

implementation file

include file

linked list

member access operator (.)

method prototype

node

null pointer

`nullptr`

pointer member access operator (->)

preprocessor directive

`protected` access

random access

`ref class`

reference class

sequential access

`static` variable

traversing a list

Unified Modeling Language (UML)

UML class diagram

1
2

EXERCISES

For Questions 1–4, assume that `arr` is a fixed size array of 100 elements, and that the first 75 elements contain data values. The variable n keeps track of the number of values stored in the array.

1. To insert a new item at the end of the list:

   a. All data in the array must slide down the array one element.

   b. The new item is stored in `arr[99]`.

   c. The new item is stored in `arr[n]`.

   d. Each item must be accessed in sequence before the insertion point is located.

   e. All of the above

2. To remove an item from the end of the list:

   a. All data in the array must slide down the array one element.

   b. The value stored in `arr[99]` must be deleted.

   c. The value stored in `arr[n]` must be deleted.

   d. n needs to be decremented `(n--)`.

   e. Data must be copied into an array of size 99.

3. To insert a new item in the middle of the list:

   a. Only one step is required.

   b. Half the items in the list need to be relocated.

   c. The new item is stored in `arr[n]`.

   d. Data needs to be copied into a new array.

   e. Up to half the array elements need to be deleted.

4. To delete an item from the middle of the list:

   a. Only one step is required.

   b. Half the items in the list need to be relocated.

   c. The deleted item is `arr[n]`.

   d. Data needs to be copied into a new array.

   e. Up to half the array elements need to be deleted.

5. Which of the following statements declares t to be a handle to an object of the `Thing` class?

   a. `Thing^ t;`

   b. `Thing t;`

   c. `Thing::Thing(t);`

   d. `~Thing() { };`

   e. `#include "Thing.h"`

6. Which of the following statements defines a destructor?

   a. `Thing^ t;`

   b. `Thing t;`

   c. `Thing::Thing(t);`

   d. `~Thing() { };`

   e. `#include "Thing.h"`

7. Which of the following statements defines a constructor?

   a. `Thing^ t;`

   b. `Thing t;`

   c. `Thing::Thing(t);`

   d. `~Thing() { };`

   e. `#include "Thing.h"`

8. Which of the following statements instantiates a `Thing` object?

   a. `Thing^ t;`

   b. `Thing t;`

   c. `Thing::Thing(t);`

   d. `~Thing() { };`

   e. `#include "Thing.h"`

9. Which of the following statements inserts the class definition file into a source code file?

   a. `Thing^ t;`

   b. `Thing t;`

   c. `Thing::Thing(t);`

   d. `~Thing() { };`

   e. `#include "Thing.h"`

10. A `static` data member of a class:

    a. Is created for every instance of a class.

    b. Is created for every object instantiated from a class.

    c. Is a constant.

    d. Is shared by all objects of that class.

    e. Must be declared outside of the class definition.

11. A UML class diagram:

    a. Lists the data members of a class.

    b. Lists the methods belonging to a class.

    c. Shows the access mode data members and methods.

    d. Shows the return type for class methods.

    e. All of the above

1
2

12. A class header file:

   a. Is called "client code".

   b. Is also called the implementation file.

   c. Is where the class definition resides.

   d. Uses and `#include` preprocessor directive.

   e. All of the above

13. A file that creates objects from the class definition

   a. Is called "client code".

   b. Is also called the implementation file.

   c. Is where the class definition resides.

   d. Does not use the class definition to instantiate objects.

   e. All of the above

14. A `.cpp` source code file that contains expanded class method definitions:

   a. Is called "client code".

   b. Is also called the implementation file.

   c. Is where the class definition resides.

   d. Does not use an `#include` preprocessor directive.

   e. All of the above

15. `#pragma once`:

   a. Is a preprocessor directive.

   b. Makes sure only one copy of a source code file is compiled into a project.

   c. Should be the first line in a class definition header file.

   d. All of the above

16. A class method prototype:

   a. Is used in implementation files.

   b. Is used in client code.

   c. Is used in class header files.

   d. Is used to define a method.

   e. Does not end with a semicolon.

17. Which of the following is a method prototype?

   a. `Node::Node(void)`

   b. `ref class Node`

   c. `Node(void)`

   d. `~Node() { delete next; }`

   e. `Node(void);`

18. Given a linked list of Node objects with a head node handle called head, what does this C++ statement do?

    `temp->next = head->next;`

    a. Assign a new head node.

    b. Reassign the head node's next pointer.

    c. Assign temp's next pointer to the same node that head points to.

    d. Assign temp's next pointer to the same node that head->next points to.

    e. None of the above

19. From client code, what is the proper way to increment the public static variable count belonging to the Item class?

    a. `count++;`

    b. `Count::Item++;`

    c. `Item::count++;`

    d. `Item->count++;`

    e. `Count->item++;`

20. The last character in a class definition must be:

    a. `;`

    b. `}`

    c. `)`

    d. `.`

    e. A space

PROGRAMMING EXERCISES

1. Reusing the Node Class with a New Client

The Node class you used in the project you created in this chapter's tutorial can be used by other projects. Create a project with an identical Node class definition (you can copy the entire project file and rename it). Modify the program by adding another button to the form (btnDisplay) and a multiline text box (txtList). Your program should display the contents of the list in the text box when btnDisplay is clicked, as shown in Figure 12-48.

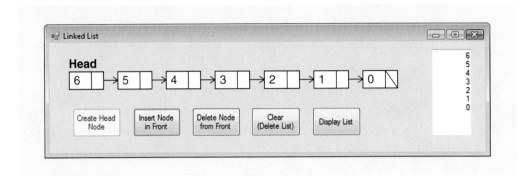

FIGURE 12-48 Programming Exercise 1

2. Adding a Sum

Modify the linked list program you created in the chapter by adding a button (**btnSum**) and a text box (**txtSum**). When the user clicks **btnSum**, the program should add up the contents of all the nodes in the list (**nodeData**) and display the value in **txtSum**, as shown in Figure 12-49.

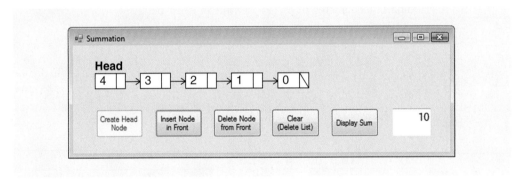

FIGURE 12-49 Adding up the sum of nodeData values in a linked list

3. Searching for a Target Value

Modify your linked list program by adding a button (**btnSearch**) and a text box (**txtTarget**). When the user clicks **btnSearch**, the program should read an integer target value from **txtTarget** and then search for the target value in the list by comparing it to each of the **nodeData** values in each node. Display a message box indicating whether the target was found, as shown in Figure 12-50.

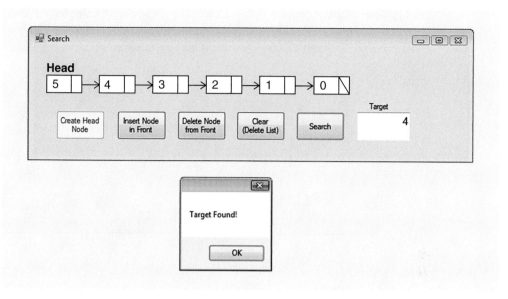

FIGURE 12-50 Searching for a target value in a linked list

4. Insertion at the End of the List

At this point, your program can insert and delete only from the front of the list (the head node). The result is that data values are stored in descending order from the head node. Data could be stored in ascending order if nodes were inserted at the end of the list instead of from the front. This necessitates a list with a pointer to the tail node as shown in Figure 12-51.

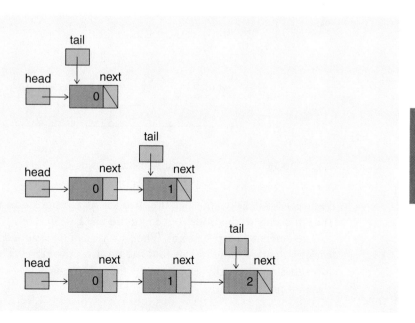

FIGURE 12-51 Adding nodes to the end of the list

Modify your tutorial project (you can make a copy and rename it) so that all insertions take place at the tail. You do not need to implement node deletion. The typical interface display should show an ordered list, as in Figure 12-52:

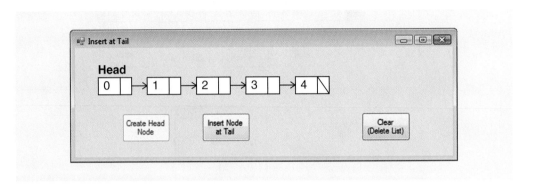

FIGURE 12-52 Ordered list resulting from insertion at tail

5. Deletion from the Tail

Add deletion capability to the project you worked on in Programming Exercise 4. For this you will need to maintain a pointer to the node that `tail` points to. The interface, after node 4 from Figure 12-52 is deleted, is shown in Figure 12-53.

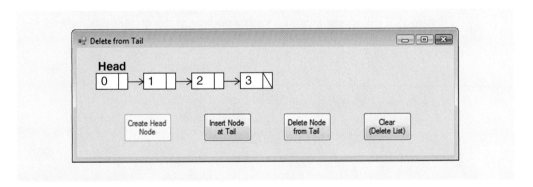

FIGURE 12-53 Linked list program—deletion using `tail`

Figure 12-54 shows the deletion process as a progression of steps. A temporary pointer (`temp`) points to the node preceding the `tail`. Using temp, the node at the end of the list can be deleted (`temp->next`). Then `tail` can be assigned the value stored in `temp`. The trick to this assignment is to find the position for `temp`. This can be done using a `while` loop that repeatededly assigns `temp` the value `temp->next` until `temp->next->next` is the null pointer.

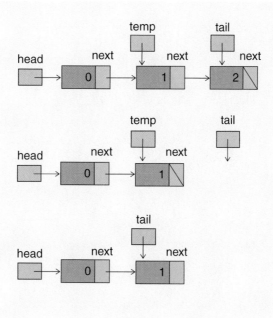

FIGURE 12-54 Deletion from the tail of the list

OBJECT-ORIENTED PROGRAMMING

IN THIS CHAPTER, YOU WILL:

- Design class definitions
- Implement data hiding and encapsulation
- Use accessor and mutator methods
- Implement an initializing constructor
- Use `public`, and `private` access modes
- Create and reference a two-dimensional array

This chapter focuses on object–oriented programming (OOP) and starts by quickly reviewing what you know about this topic. OOP revolves around abstraction. **Abstraction** is the identification of the essential elements that underlie a phenomenon. Class definitions are abstractions. You create class definitions that embody the essential elements of a concept and then instantiate objects from them. One class definition can be used to instantiate multiple objects. You have seen this in several forms. In many of your projects in this book you have used system-defined classes to create objects such as buttons, as shown in Figure 13-1.

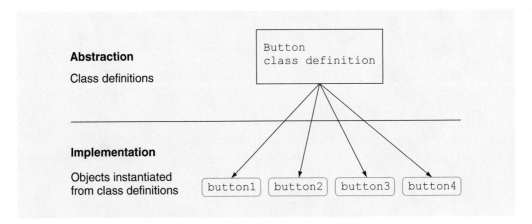

FIGURE 13-1 Multiple instances of the system-defined Button class

In Chapter 12, you discovered that you can define your own class definitions (the Node class definition) and instantiate objects from it, as shown in Figure 13-2.

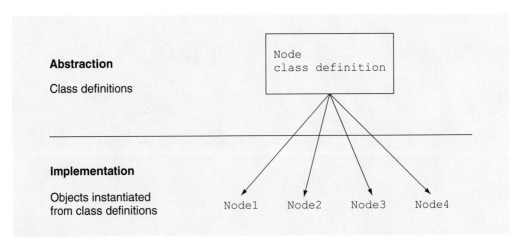

FIGURE 13-2 Multiple instances of the user-defined Node class

Class definitions typically consist of both data members (attributes) and methods. In Chapter 12, you saw that the data members of the **Node** class were **nodeData** (an integer) and **next** (a pointer to a **Node**). There were no methods, other than the constructor for the **Node** class. In this chapter, you will begin to branch out more into the world of OOP by creating class definitions that have additional methods. You will also learn how to provide other programs that create objects from your class definitions with built-in methods that guard against unintentional errors.

OOP Example

Consider the following program. The size of Form1 is 520 × 300 pixels and the size of **panel1** is 475 × 175 pixels. When the user clicks **btnStart**, four frogs appear on the left side of the interface in different positions, as shown in Figure 13-3.

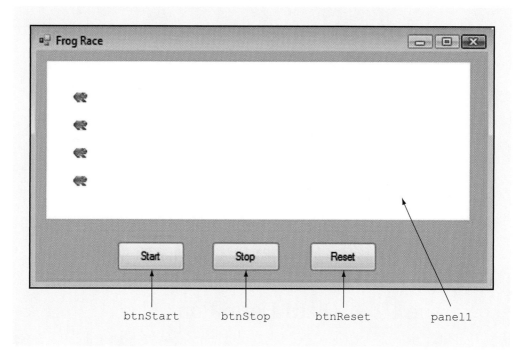

FIGURE 13-3 Starting locations for frog race

They begin to hop across the screen at random intervals until one reaches the other side of the screen, at which point it is declared the winner, as shown in Figure 13-4.

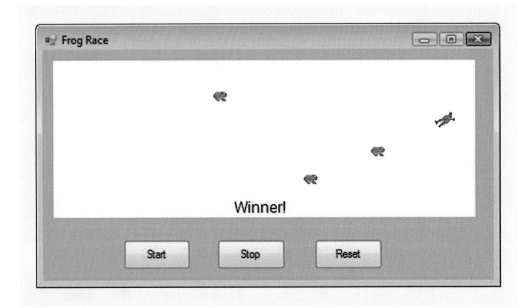

FIGURE 13-4 Frog program interface

Each frog is an instance of the **Frog** class definition. The **Frog** class definition is located in a file called **Frog.h** within the project, just as the **Node** class definition was located within the file **Node.h** in the Chapter 12 tutorial.

 NOTE All of the icon files required for programs in this chapter are contained in a Zip file named Icons which is available from this book's webpage at http://www.course.com.

After you have downloaded and extracted the Icons folder, remove the icons named frog_sitting.ico and frog_hopping.ico and drag them into your project folder (within your solution folder), as you did for the image used in Chapter 6.

The Frog Class Definition

Let us consider what you need to include in a **Frog** class definition. There will be two static variables (**sittingIcon** and **hoppingIcon**) that will be shared among all instances of the **Frog** class. These are assigned icon files in the following manner:

```
// Class variables
static Drawing::Icon^ sittingIcon = gcnew Drawing::Icon("frog_sitting.ico");
static Drawing::Icon^ hoppingIcon = gcnew Drawing::Icon("frog_hopping.ico");
```

Frogs will need to move across the interface. This means they have to have data members that store the x- and y-coordinates of the frog. In addition each frog is associated with an icon (either sitting or leaping). A public method called **showIcon()** may be used to display the appropriate frog image. If the icon data member is set to 0 then the **sittingIcon** is displayed. If the icon data member is set to 1 then the `hoppingIcon` is displayed. Code for this method is shown in the `Frog` class definition (Example 13-1):

EXAMPLE 13-1: `Frog` CLASS DEFINITION

```
using namespace System;

ref class Frog
{
public:
// Class variables
    static Drawing::Icon^ sittingIcon = gcnew Drawing::Icon("frog_sitting.ico");
    static Drawing::Icon^ hoppingIcon = gcnew Drawing::Icon("frog_hopping.ico");

// Instance variables
    int x;
    int y;
    int icon;

// Default constructor
    Frog(void);

// Instance method
    Drawing::Icon^ showIcon()
    {
        if (icon == 0) return sittingIcon;
        else return hoppingIcon;
    }
};
```

Instantiation and Use

This class definition is enough to allow us to write a simple client program.

Example 13-2 shows the construction and initialization of `frog1` from within `btnStart_Click()`.

EXAMPLE 13-2: CONSTRUCTING AND INITIALIZING A `Frog` OBJECT

```
private: System::Void btnStart_Click(System::Object^  sender, System::
EventArgs^  e) {
    // Create a frog
    Drawing::Graphics^ g = panel1->CreateGraphics();
    Frog^ frog1 = gcnew Frog();   // Default Ctor
    frog1->x = 25; // Initialize x
    frog1->y = 25; // Initialize y
```

```
    frog1->icon = 0;   // Initialize icon
    Rectangle frog1Rect = Rectangle(frog1->x,frog1->y,25,25);
    g->DrawIcon(frog1->showIcon(),frog1Rect);
}
```

The first line creates the Graphics object (g). The second line executes the Frog constructor, allocating memory for a Frog instance (frog1). The second line assigns the location 25 to the x data member of frog1. The third line assigns the location 25 to the y data member of frog1.

Making frog1 appear on the interface is a matter of creating a Rectangle object (frog1Rect) using frog1's x and y member values as coordinates and displaying frog1's icon in the Rectangle using frog1->showIcon(). The result is shown in Figure 13-5.

FIGURE 13-5 Using btnStart_Click() to create a Frog object

Initializing Constructors

However, this approach has a number of problems associated with it. Some of these are simply inconveniences while others involve unsafe programming practices.

The inconveniences are the easiest to notice and deal with. One major inconvenience for a programmer using the Frog class is that he or she has to write several statements to initialize the x, y, and icon data members of each frog. You saw in Example 13-2 that initialization requires several steps. Imagine a program in which hundreds of frogs were instantiated. All of them need to be initialized and this would take many lines of somewhat redundant code.

It would be easier if the programmer could call a constructor that did the initialization automatically, in a manner like that shown in Example 13-3 where the integer values 25 and 25 indicate the starting x and y coordinates of this frog.

EXAMPLE 13-3: CALLING AN INITIALIZING CONSTRUCTOR

```
frog1 = gcnew Frog(25,25);
```

Constructors that initialize the data members of the objects they create are called **initializing constructors**.

The default constructor (`Frog(void)`) does no initialization and has no parameters. You need to create another constructor with parameters that can be used to assign the data members **x** and **y**. In addition, since all frogs start at a sitting position, you might as well initialize `icon` as well. The code for an initializing constructor is shown in Example 13-4.

EXAMPLE 13-4: INITIALIZING CONSTRUCTOR

```
// Initializing constructor
Frog(int xcoord, int ycoord)
{
    x = xcoord;
    y = ycoord;
    icon = 0;
}
```

The initializing constructor assigns the value of the first formal parameter to data member **x**. It assigns the value of the second formal parameter to data member **y**. Finally, it initializes `icon` to 0.

This makes the instantiation of `Frog` objects much more straightforward for the client programmer. In fact, it also makes the default constructor obsolete. It is not a good idea to allow programmers using your `Frog` class definition to create `Frog` objects without **x** and **y** coordinates or the `icon` initialized. By making the initializing constructor `public` and the default constructor `private`, you can force the client to always use the initializing constructor and guarantee that every `Frog` instance has a location and an icon.

The revised `Frog` class now looks like that shown in Example 13-5. Notice that the default constructor is now listed under the `private` heading while the initializing constructor is `public`.

1
3

EXAMPLE 13-5: FROG CLASS WITH INITIALIZING CONSTRUCTOR

```
using namespace System;

ref class Frog
{
public:
    // Class variables
    static Drawing::Icon^ sittingIcon = gcnew Drawing::Icon("frog_sitting.ico");
    static Drawing::Icon^ hoppingIcon = gcnew Drawing::Icon("frog_hopping.ico");

    // Instance variables
    int x;
    int y;
    int icon;

    // Initializing constructor
    Frog(int xcoord, int ycoord)
    {
        x = xcoord;
        y = ycoord;
        icon = 0;
    }

    // Instance method
    Drawing::Icon^ showIcon()
    {
        if (icon == 0) return sittingIcon;
        else return hoppingIcon;
    }

private:
    // Default constructor
    Frog(void);   // Prototype
};
```

Data Hiding

You have just used the **private** access modifier to hide the default constructor from the client programmer. It is common practice to also hide other class members as well. For example, C++ programmers typically designate data members as **private**. This technique, which is referred to as **data hiding**, ensures that the client cannot change your program's data members indescriminately. (Recall that data members that are **public** can be changed by the client.)

Why would you want to keep the client from altering your program's data members, such as the frog's x and y coordinates?

Example 13-6 is the work of a programmer who mistakenly assumed that the x and y coordinates of a frog could be negative. When the initializing constructor is called the coordinates are set to x = –50 and y = –75. Later, x is changed to –25 and y to –25. This code will compile and execute, but the negative coordinate values position the frog off of the panel. These are mistakes that you could easily guard against.

EXAMPLE 13-6: INVALID VALUE ASSIGNMENTS

```
// Create frogs
frog1 = gcnew Frog(-50,-75);
frog1->x = -25;
frog1->y = -25;
```

Making the data members x, y, and `icon` `private` makes them no longer visible to the client and reduces the possibility of a programmer making assignment errors like this. By placing the data members into the `private` section of a class, you place them off-limits to the programmer. Data members that are `private` cannot be altered directly by the programmer. Instead, public methods must be used to interact with private data members. This is the topic of the next section.

Accessor and Mutator Methods

Data hiding is an important feature of object-oriented programming because it eliminates the possibility that a programmer creating `Frog` objects will assign invalid values to their data members. However, data hiding presents a dilemma. Consider the case of a programmer who creates `Frog` objects with the intent of making them move across the screen. The programmer needs to be allowed to change the frogs' x and y coordinates to make them move but cannot do so if x and y are hidden. Somehow, you need to design the `Frog` class so that it allows programmers to retrieve data from data members, modify data members with valid data, and still prevent invalid modifications.

The dilemma is resolved by providing accessor and mutator methods. An **accessor** (sometimes called a **get method** or **getter**) is a `public` instance method that returns the value stored in a `private` variable. A **mutator** (sometimes called a **set method** or **setter**) is a `public` instance method that is passed a value which it then assigns to a `private` data member. Unlike client code, accessors and mutators are instance methods belonging to a class; they, therefore, have access to the `public` or `private` data members of that class.

Let us first examine the concept of an accessor method. Example 13-7 shows how two such methods (`getX()` and `getY()`) are used to retrieve the values stored in the private data members x and y so that these values can be used to create a Rectangle. The accessor methods `getX()` and `getY()` are `public` members of the `Frog` class that return the value of the x and y data members of the `Frog` object from which they were called.

1
3

EXAMPLE 13-7: USING ACCESSORS TO CONSTRUCT A RECTANGLE

```
frog1Rect = Rectangle(frog1->getX(),frog1->getY(),25,25);
```

The code for these accessors, which would be located in the `public` portion of the `Frog` class definition, is shown in Example 13-8.

EXAMPLE 13-8: ACCESSOR CODE

```
// Accessors (get methods)
int getX() { return x;}
int getY() { return y;}
```

Similarly, mutator methods are used to change the value stored in **private** data members. There is a need for this whenever a frog is repositioned at the starting line. In Example 13-9 four frogs have had their **x** data members set to 25, positioning them at the start of the race (25 pixels from the left side of **panel1**) using the public method **setX()**.

EXAMPLE 13-9: USING MUTATORS TO SET X-COORDINATES

```
frog1->setX(25);
frog2->setX(25);
frog3->setX(25);
frog4->setX(25);
```

The code for the **public** mutator method **setX()** is shown in Example 13-10.

EXAMPLE 13-10: setX() MUTATOR CODE

```
void setX(int newX) { if (newX >= 0) x = newX;}
```

Notice that **setX()** has one formal parameter, the integer **newX**. Before **newX** is assigned to the **private** data member **x**, an **if** statement determines whether **newX** is a negative number. If **newX** is less than 0, then the value of **x** is not changed. This was what prompted you to put **x** and **y** into the **private** portion of the class to begin with. You did not want them to be set to erroneous values (like negative numbers). Forcing the client to use **setX()** ensures that a statement like

```
frog1->setX(-100);
```

will not endanger the program or attempt to position the frog's icon at a location that is not visible. The difference between public members (such as accessors) and private class members (such as instance variables) is shown in Figure 13-6.

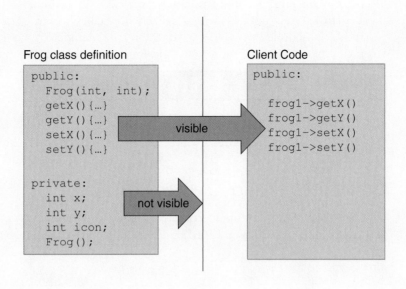

FIGURE 13-6 Visibility of public and private class members

Utility Methods

A **utility method** is an instance method that exists to serve functions other than those addressed by constructors, destructors, accessors, and mutators.

For example, consider a situation where `newX` (the formal parameter in `setX()`) must pass through a long list of verification steps before it is considered safe to assign to `x`. In this case, rather than putting all the verification code in `setX()`, it could be placed in a `private` method that `setX()` can call. Example 13-11 shows both a `public setX()` method and a `private` method called `verifyX()` that it calls. Since `verifyX()` is not intended for the client, but is a utility method used by other methods within the `Frog` class, there is no reason for it to be a `public` method.

EXAMPLE 13-11: `verifyX()` UTILITY METHOD

```
private:
    // Utility methods
    bool verifyX(int x) { return (x > 0); }
public:
    // Mutators (set methods)
    void setX(int newX) { if (verifyX(newX)) x = newX; }
```

1
3

There may be **public** utility methods as well. For example, a frog hops from one position to another on the interface. Each hop takes the frog 25 pixels to the right, which is accomplished by adding 25 to the **x** data member of the frog. This task can be taken care of by a **public** utility method (**hop()**) as shown in Example 13-10.

EXAMPLE 13-12: `hop()` **UTILITY METHOD**

```
void hop(){ x += 25; }
```

Complete `Frog` Class Definition

You can now construct a more complete definition of the **Frog** class. A UML diagram of the class and its **private** and **public** data members and methods is shown in Figure 13-7.

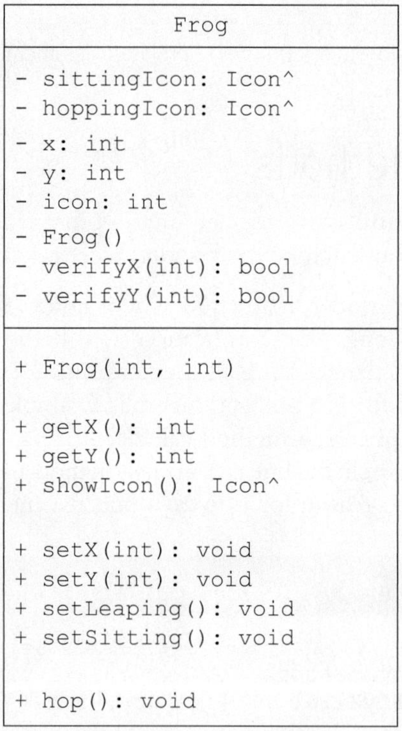

```
+-----------------------------------+
|               Frog                |
+-----------------------------------+
| - sittingIcon: Icon^              |
| - hoppingIcon: Icon^              |
| - x: int                          |
| - y: int                          |
| - icon: int                       |
|                                   |
| - Frog()                          |
| - verifyX(int): bool              |
| - verifyY(int): bool              |
+-----------------------------------+
|                                   |
| + Frog(int, int)                  |
|                                   |
| + getX(): int                     |
| + getY(): int                     |
| + showIcon(): Icon^               |
|                                   |
| + setX(int): void                 |
| + setY(int): void                 |
| + setLeaping(): void              |
| + setSitting(): void              |
|                                   |
| + hop(): void                     |
+-----------------------------------+
```

FIGURE 13-7 Frog class UML diagram

The **private** portion of the class is shown in Example 13-13. All of the items contained in this section are off-limits for the client. It contains the three data members, as well as two utility methods used to verify that **x** and **y** values are positive numbers, and the default constructor.

EXAMPLE 13-13: FROG CLASS DEFINITION (private SECTION)

```
private:
  // Class variables
  static Drawing::Icon^ sittingIcon = gcnew Drawing::Icon ("frog_sitting.ico");
  static Drawing::Icon^ hoppingIcon = gcnew Drawing::Icon("frog_hopping.ico");

  // Data members
  int x;  // x coordinate location (in pixels)
  int y;  // y coordinate location (in pixels)
  int icon;   // icon number (0 = sitting, 1 = hopping

  // Utility methods
  bool verifyX(int x) { return (x > 0); }
  bool verifyY(int y) { return (y > 0); }

  // Default constructor
  Frog(void);
```

The public portion of the class is shown in Example 13-14. All of these methods are accessible to the client. They include the initializing constructor, accessors and mutators, and the utility method hop().

EXAMPLE 13-14: FROG CLASS DEFINITION (public SECTION)

```
public:

  // Initializing constructor
  Frog(int xcoord, int ycoord)
  {
     if (verifyX(xcoord)) x = xcoord; else x = 0;
     if (verifyY(ycoord)) y = ycoord; else y = 0;
     icon = 0;
  }

  // Accessor Methods
  int getX() { return x;}
  int getY() { return y;}

  // Mutator Methods
  void setX(int newX) { if (verifyX(newX)) x = newX;}
  void setHopping() { icon = 1; }
  void setSitting() { icon = 0; }

  // Utility Methods
  Drawing::Icon^ showIcon()
  {
     if (icon == 0) return sittingIcon;
     else return hoppingIcon;
  }
  void hop(){ x += 25; }
```

1
3

Client Code

The complete client code for this example makes a great project for later (See Programming Exercise 3). However, several aspects of it are important to consider now, including how to:

- Declare constants and object handles
- Instantiate the objects
- Use object accessors
- Use object mutators
- Use object utility methods

The starting locations for the various frogs can be static constants. All frogs start at an x location of 25 pixels. The static constant STARTX will be assigned this value. Similarly, the starting y locations for the four frogs are assigned to STARTY1, STARTY2, STARTY3 and STARTY4 respectively. Declaration of four Frog objects is accomplished in a manner similar to that used for objects of the Node class in the previous chapter and System::Drawing objects in many previous chapters—by creating an instance variable that is a handle, as shown in Example 13-15.

EXAMPLE 13-15: DECLARING HANDLES

```
// Starting positions
static const int STARTX = 25;    // x coord of starting line
static const int STARTY1 = 25;   // y coord of first frog
static const int STARTY2 = 55;   // y coord of second frog
static const int STARTY3 = 85;   // y coord of third frog
static const int STARTY4 = 115;  // y coord of fourth frog

// Finish line
static const int FINISH = 400;   // x coord of finish line

// Frogs
Frog^ frog1;
Frog^ frog2;
Frog^ frog3;
Frog^ frog4;
```

Instantiation of instance objects is carried out using the initializing constructor in Form1_Load(). In Example 13-16, each Frog instance is initialized using the constants defined in Example 13-15.

EXAMPLE 13-16: CONSTRUCTING FROGS in Form1_Load()

```
// Create Frogs
frog1 = gcnew Frog(STARTX,STARTY1);
frog2 = gcnew Frog(STARTX,STARTY2);
frog3 = gcnew Frog(STARTX,STARTY3);
frog4 = gcnew Frog(STARTX,STARTY4);
```

In a method called **drawFrogs()** accessors are used to get the x- and y-coordinate of the frog for the purpose of creating a **Rectangle** object; the frog is then drawn in the rectangle. The x-coordinate accessed by **getX()** and the y-coordinate accessed by **getY()** establish the upper-left corner of the rectangle. The **Graphics** class method **DrawIcon()** is used to draw the icon (accessed using **showIcon()**) in the rectangle as shown in Example 13-17. This example draws only one frog. Additional statements could be added to draw additional frogs (see Programming Exercise 3).

EXAMPLE 13-17: THE drawFrogs() METHOD

```
private: void drawFrogs()
{
    // Refresh the panel
    panel1->Refresh();

    // Draw a frog
    frog1Rect = Rectangle(frog1->getX(),frog1->getY(),25,25);
    g->DrawIcon(frog1->showIcon(),frog1Rect);
}
```

The **setX()** mutator is used to reset the x-coordinate of frogs prior to each race. Example 13-18 shows the **reset()** method designated for this purpose. Each frog is set to the same starting point using variable **STARTX**.

EXAMPLE 13-18: THE reset() METHOD

```
private: void reset()
{
    panel1->Refresh();
    timer1->Enabled = false;
    frog1->setX(STARTX);
    frog2->setX(STARTX);
    frog3->setX(STARTX);
    frog4->setX(STARTX);
    frog1->setSitting();
    frog2->setSitting();
    frog3->setSitting();
    frog4->setSitting();

}
```

Mutators are also used to change the icon associated with a **Frog** instance. For example, the **setSitting()** method in Example 13-18 assigns 0 to the **icon** data member. The **setHopping()** method assigns the value 1 to private data member **icon**.

1
3

With each `Timer_Tick()` event the frog is initially assigned a sitting icon in the following manner:

`frog1->setSitting();`

If the frog is randomly chosen to hop, then it is assigned the hopping icon, as shown in Example 13-19. The utility method `hop()` is used to change the location of the frog. The `hop()` method alters the **private** data member (**x**), which determines the coordinate at which the frog's icon will be displayed.

EXAMPLE 13-19: RANDOMLY CHOOSING A FROG

```
randomNum = randomNumGenerator->Next(1,5);

switch (randomNum)
{
    case 1: frog1->setHopping(); frog1->hop(); break;
    case 2: frog2->setHopping(); frog2->hop(); break;
    case 3: frog3->setHopping(); frog3->hop(); break;
    case 4: frog4->setHopping(); frog4->hop(); break;
}

drawFrogs();
```

As you can see, defining classes merely establishes the foundation for the construction of objects in client code. What the client does with those objects varies depending on the problem to be solved. In this example, a race between several frogs could be simulated. However, a different client might use the **Frog** class to instantiate frogs for use in modeling an ecosystem. Yet another might use the **Frog** class to instantiate frogs for another purpose altogether. These are all examples of **code reuse**—the practice of reusing code segments, such as class definitions, in a variety of program settings. One class definition can be reused by multiple clients whenever the need for an object of that type arises.

Tutorial: Maze Program

With the **Frog** class example, you have seen how one class is instantiated in the form of multiple objects in client code. This tutorial challenges you to use more than one class in a single program. You need five icon files to complete this tutorial. You can find these icon files under the Student Downloads section of the textbook Web site at *http://www.course.com*.

The icon files are:

- cheese.ico
- mouseDown.ico
- mouseLeft.ico
- mouseRight.ico
- mouseUp.ico

Problem Analysis

The concept behind this tutorial project is to create a simulation of a two-dimensional maze in which a mouse is able to roam freely looking for hidden cheese. The maze is composed of a two-dimensional array of cells, with the cells arranged in 16 rows and 20 columns. The mouse moves from one cell in the maze to another. Before beginning this project, you may wish to review the section on two-dimensional arrays in Chapter 7.

An example of the completed program interface (through Programming Exercise 5) is shown in Figure 13-8.

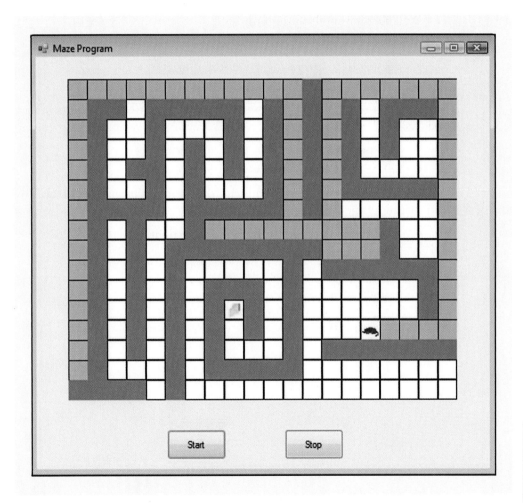

FIGURE 13-8 Completed Maze Program interface

There are two key aspects to the overall design plan: first, the class definitions for `Mouse` and `Cell` and second, the design of the client code that creates objects from these classes and uses them to simulate the maze and movement of a mouse in the maze.

Mouse **Class Definition**

A **Mouse** object must store its location (row, column) in the maze and display a mouse icon. Its methods must allow it to move from one cell to another. With this in mind, you can create the following lists of specifications.

The **Mouse** class definition has three **private** data members, similar to the Frog class definition, that will store:

- The row the mouse is in (**row**)
- The column the mouse is in (**col**)
- The **icon** indicator (**icon**)

The data members **row** and **col** need their own accessors (get methods), as follows:

- **getRow()** to return the value stored in **row**
- **getCol()** to return the value stored in **col**

In addition, the data members **row** and **col** need their own mutators (or set methods) as follows:

- **setRow()** to assign a new value to **row**
- **setCol()** to assign a new value to **col**

Finally, the **Mouse** class definition includes a set of utility methods that allow the mouse to proceed in one direction or another:

- **goRight()** to move to the cell on the right
- **goLeft()** to move to the cell on the left
- **goUp()** to move to the cell above
- **goDown()** to move to the cell below

The UML class definition for the Mouse is shown in Figure 13-9.

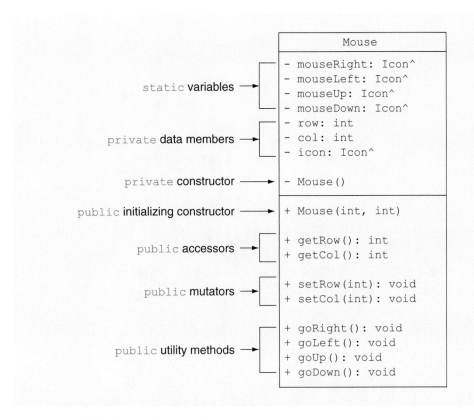

FIGURE 13-9 UML class definition of Mouse class

The UML class definition is reflected in the Visual C++ code contained in the **Mouse.h** header file, shown in Example 13-18.

EXAMPLE 13-18: THE Mouse CLASS DEFINITION

```
ref class Mouse
{

public:
    // Initializing Constructor
    Mouse(int row, int col);

    // Accessor Methods
    int getRow() { return row; }
    int getCol() { return col; }
    System::Drawing::Icon^  Mouse::getIcon();

    // Mutator Methods
    void setRow(int newRow) { row = newRow; }
    void setCol(int newCol) { col = newCol; }
```

1
3

```
   // Utility methods
   void goRight() { col++; icon = 0; }
   void goLeft() { col-; icon = 1; }
   void goUp() { row-; icon = 2; }
   void goDown() { row++; icon = 3; }

private:
   // Class variables
   static System::Drawing::Icon^ mouseRight = gcnew System::Drawing::Icon("mouseRight.ico");
   static System::Drawing::Icon^ mouseLeft = gcnew System::Drawing::Icon("mouseLeft.ico");
   static System::Drawing::Icon^ mouseUp = gcnew System::Drawing::Icon("mouseUp.ico");
   static System::Drawing::Icon^ mouseDown = gcnew System::Drawing::Icon("mouseDown.ico");

   // Private Data Members
   int row;        // row location in maze
   int col;        // column location in maze
   int icon;       // icon indicator (0=right, 1=left, 2=up, 3 =down)

   // Default constructor
   Mouse(void) { }
};
```

You will notice that the mutators—setRow() and setCol()—in Example 13-18 assign the values passed in through their parameters to row and col without checking to see if they are valid. Rewriting setRow() and setCol() so that they validate the data before assigning it is one of the On Your Own tasks at the end of this section.

The initializing constructor and utility methods are prototyped in the header file (Mouse.h) and specified in Mouse.cpp as shown in Example 13-19.

EXAMPLE 13-19: Mouse.cpp IMPLEMENTATION FILE

```
#include "Mouse.h"

Mouse::Mouse(int newRow, int newCol)
{
   // Default assignments
   row = 0;
   col = 0;
   icon = 0;

   // Verify and set to initialization parameters
   if (newRow >= 0) row = newRow;
   if (newRow >= 0) col = newCol;
}
```

```
System::Drawing::Icon^  Mouse::getIcon()
{
   if (icon == 0)
      return mouseRight;
   else if (icon == 1)
      return mouseLeft;
   else if (icon == 2)
      return mouseUp;
   else
      return mouseDown;
}
```

NOTE It is a common mistake to forget to include the class header file at the top of the .cpp implementation file. If you do not include the header file, the compiler will not know that the methods defined in the .cpp file are intended to pertain to the class definition in the header file.

The Cell Class Definition

Each `Cell` object is assigned a location (row, column) in the maze. In addition, you would like some cells to be accessible to a mouse and others (like the walls within the maze) to be inaccessible. You use a Boolean data member called `access` to indicate whether a cell can be occupied by a mouse. Also, one cell will have the cheese icon in it. You can use another Boolean data member, called `hasCheese`, to indicate whether a cell has the cheese.

The `Cell` class definition therefore consists of four `private` data members that will store:

- The row location of the cell (`row`)
- The column location of the cell (`col`)
- The accessibility setting (`access`); `true` means the mouse can occupy that cell, `false` means a mouse cannot occupy the cell
- The cheese setting (`hasCheese`); `true` means the cell has the cheese in it, `false` means the cell does not contain the cheese.

The data members `row` and `col` need their own accessor methods:

- `getRow()` to return the value stored in `row`
- `getCol()` to return the value stored in `col`
- `getAccess()` to return the Boolean value stored in `access`
- `getCheese()` to return the Boolean value stored in `hasCheese`

The only mutators methods, required are those that assign an access or cheese value:

- `setAccess()` to assign a new value to `access`
- `setCheese()` to assign a new value to `hasCheese`

1
3

The UML class definition for the cell is shown in Figure 13-10.

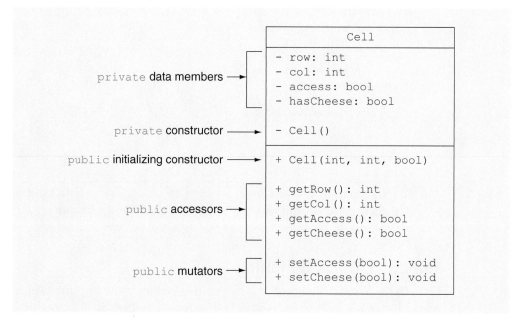

FIGURE 13-10 UML class definition of `Cell` class

The UML class diagram is reflected in the structure of the actual code in `Cell.h`, shown in Example 13-20.

EXAMPLE 13-20: THE `Cell` CLASS DEFINITION

```
ref class Cell
{
private:
// Data Members
    int row;
    int col;
    bool access;
    bool hasCheese;

// Default constructor
    Cell(void){}

public:
// Initializing constructor
    Cell(int r, int c, bool a);

// Accessors (get methods)
    bool getAccess() { return access; }
    int getRow() { return row; }
    int getCol() { return col; }
    bool getCheese() { return hasCheese; }
```

```
// Mutators (set methods)
   void setAccess(bool a) { access = a; }
   void setCheese(bool cheese) { hasCheese = true; }
};
```

Only the initializing constructor needs to be defined in the `Cell.cpp` file, as shown in Example 13-21.

EXAMPLE 13-21: THE `Cell()` INITIALIZING CONSTRUCTOR

```
#include "Cell.h"
Cell::Cell(int r, int c, bool a)
{
    if (r >= 0) row = r;
    if (c >= 0) col = c;
    access = a;
    hasCheese = false;
}
```

Design

At this point, both the `Mouse` and `Cell` classes have been defined. The design of client code must now address the real problems—how to create a program that displays a maze of cells that allows a mouse to navigate its way through it.

A maze is a two-dimensional array of cells. In your maze, the location of each cell is identified by its position in the two-dimensional array you build in your client. Each cell is identified by its row and column location. Rows are represented horizontally, as in Figure 13-11.

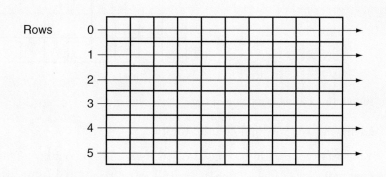

FIGURE 13-11 Rows of a maze

Columns are represented vertically as shown in Figure 13-12.

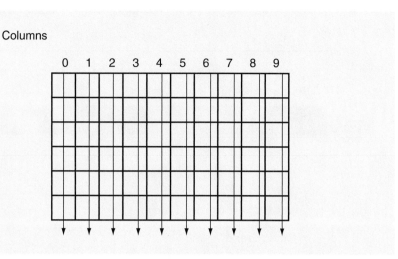

FIGURE 13-12 Columns in a maze

Individual cells are identified by their row and cell location in your client code, as shown in Figure 13-13.

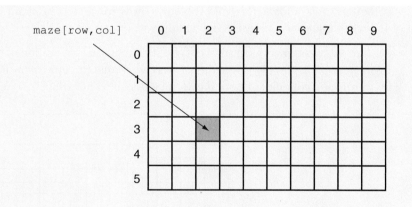

FIGURE 13-13 Cell location in a two-dimensional maze

Each cell has a row and column location.

You want your maze to consist of 16 rows and 20 columns. This means that it will be made up of 320 `Cell` objects, each of which is created from the same class definition. Among the important data members of the class are the row and the column. Because each cell must be drawn on the form, the x- and y-coordinates of the pixels in the upper-left corner should also be data members of the cells. This will facilitate the construction of the `Rectangle` objects that will graphically represent each cell.

INTERFACE

The interface for this project consists of the visual representation of the two-dimensional array of cells in a `Panel` object. Two buttons (`btnStart` and `btnStop`) are used to control the simulation of the mouse running through the maze, as shown in Figure 13-14. When the mouse finds the cheese, a message box is displayed on the form. A Timer control is used to produce the mouse animation effect.

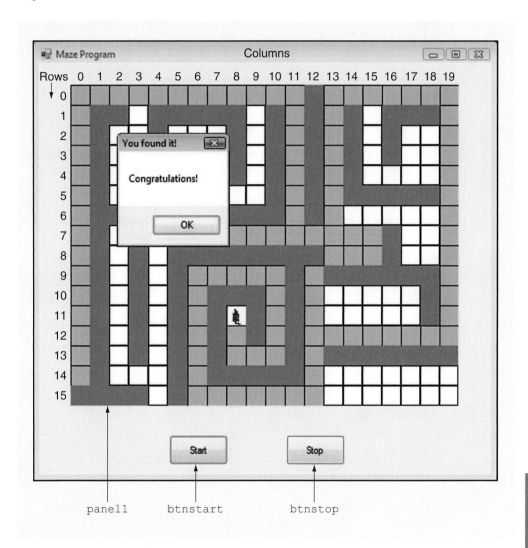

FIGURE 13-14 The Maze Program interface

DATA TABLE

This program requires constants, instance variables, and instance objects.

Static constants The program requires one group of constants to store the number of rows and columns in the maze (NUMROWS and NUMCOLS) and the number of pixels in each side of the rectangles drawn to illustrate cells (CELLSIZE). These are listed in Table 13-1.

TABLE 13-1 Table of Constants

Constant	Data Type	Value	Usage
NUMROWS	const int	16	Number of rows in the maze
NUMCOLS	const int	20	Number of columns in the maze
CELLSIZE	const int	25	Length of each side of cell (in pixels)

Objects required for drawing As in previous projects, a Graphics object is used to draw on Form1. The grayBrush and whiteBrush objects are used to fill in the rectangles that represent cells in the maze. A blackPen object is used to draw the lines around each cell. When the mouse leaves a cell, the cell is colored brown (Color::BurlyWood) by the burlyBrush object. These objects are listed in Table 13-2.

TABLE 13-2 Table of Required Drawing Objects

Object Name	Type	Usage
g	Graphics	Graphics object
blackPen	Pen	Used to draw lines around cells
grayBrush	SolidBrush	Used to fill in walls
whiteBrush	SolidBrush	Used to fill in empty cells
burlyBrush	SolidBrush	Used to fill in cells the mouse has left with the Color::BurlyWood

Instance variables The key to this program lies in using the Mouse and Cell class definitions to instantiate objects. One Mouse object is required; however, a two–dimensional array of Cell objects is needed to represent the maze. The array class is used to establish this data structure. The declaration shown in Example 13-22 creates a handle to a two–dimensional structure consisting of handles to Cell objects.

EXAMPLE 13-22: DECLARATION OF `maze`

```
array <Cell^,2>^ maze;
```

Both the maze and the cells are constructed in `Form1_Load()` as the program begins. Table 13-3 lists the instance variables required by the program.

TABLE 13-3 Table of Instance Variables

Variable	Data Type	Usage
myMouse	Mouse^	Handle to a **Mouse** object
maze	array<Cell^,2>^	Handle to a two-dimensional array of **Cell^**
direction	char	Indicates direction strategy (`'r'` = go right, `'l'` = go left, `'u'` = go up, `'d'` = go down

ALGORITHM FOR `Form1_Load()`

The `Form1_Load()` event should create the `Graphics` object and various brushes and pens required, and create the maze. Every cell in the maze requires a row and a column to be initialized. Creating the maze requires nested loops in which the outer one indicates which row of the maze a cell is assigned to and the inner loop indicates the column.

The algorithm for this portion of `Form1_Load()` is:

ALGORITHM 13-1

1. For `row = 0` to NUMROWS −1
   1.1. For `col = 0` to NUMCOLS −1
        1.1.1. Create `maze[row][col]`

ALGORITHM FOR `btnStart_Click()`

The algorithm for `btnStart_Click()` is provided in Algorithm 13-2.

1
3

ALGORITHM 13-2

1. Declare local variables.
2. Assign starting location for myMouse.
3. Assign location for the cheese.
4. Assign the initial direction ('r' = go right).
5. Create myMouse.
6. Draw the maze.
7. Draw the cheese.
8. Draw myMouse.
9. Start timer1.

Each of these instructions can be executed in one or more commands; however, the process of drawing the maze (Step 6) is complicated enough to require a separate instance method called drawMaze().

ALGORITHM FOR drawMaze()

Drawing the maze is done using nested loops. The algorithm is presented in Algorithm 13-3.

ALGORITHM 13-3

1. Declare local variables (row, col, x, y).
2. Refresh panel1.
3. For row = 0 to NUMROWS-1:

   3. 1.   For col = 0 to NUMCOLS-1:

      3.1.1.   Calculate x (col * CELLSIZE).

      3.1.2.   Calculate y (row * CELLSIZE).

      3.1.3.   Construct a rectangle using x and y.

      3.1.4.   Fill the rectangle with white.

      3.1.5.   Draw a black border around it.

ALGORITHM FOR timer1_Tick()

The timer1_Tick() event handler is crucial to the success of this program. At every timer interval, it must move the mouse to its next location. If the mouse is at the edge of the maze, then the mouse must be turned in another direction.

The algorithm for this event handler is shown in Algorithm 13-4.

ALGORITHM 13-4

1. Declare local variables (`row`, `col`, `x`, `y`).
2. Assign `row` to the row of `myMouse`.
3. Assign `col` to the col of `myMouse`.
4. Calculate `x`.
5. Calculate `y`.
6. Create a rectangle at the current mouse position.
7. Process move to next cell.

   7.1. If the mouse is not at the edge of the maze:

      7.1.1. Color the old cell.

      7.1.2. Move one cell in the chosen direction.

      7.1.3. Draw the mouse at the new cell.

      7.1.4. If that cell has the cheese in it display a message box.

   7.2. Else if the mouse is at the edge of the maze:

      7.2.1. Change the direction.

A crucial step in this algorithm is Step 7.1. Determining whether the mouse has reached the edge of the maze is a complex task that requires its own method. The algorithm for the method `edge()` describes the process.

ALGORITHM FOR `edge()`

The Boolean algorithm for `edge()` determines whether the mouse is about to move off of the boundaries of the maze. This method returns `false` if the next cell in the current direction is not an edge and `true` if it is.

The algorithm for this method is provided in Algorithm 13-5.

ALGORITHM 13-5

1. Determine if an edge has not been reached.

   1.1. If the `direction` is to the right (`'r'`):

      1.1.1. If `col` < `NUMCOLS-1` return `false`.

   1.2. Else if the `direction` is to the left (`'l'`):

      1.2.1. If `col` > 0 return `false`.

1
3

      1.3.   Else if the `direction` is to the up (`'u'`):

          1.3.1. If `row` > 0 return `false`.

      1.4.   Else if the `direction` is to the down (`'d'`):

          1.4.1. If `row` < `NUMROWS-1` return `false`.

2.   Return `true`.

Development

This project will be developed in stages. The suggested order of development is:

1. Create the `Form1` interface, but do not write code for `Form1.h`.
2. Create the `Mouse` class definition (`Mouse.h` and `Mouse.cpp`).
3. Create the `Cell` class definition (`Cell.h` and `Cell.cpp`).
4. Compile the `Mouse` and `Cell` class definitions.
5. Create the client code portion for `Form1`.

The `Mouse` and `Cell` class definition code was presented in earlier sections (Examples 13-18 through 13-21). Once you have completed the `Mouse` and `Cell` class definitions, then you need to turn your attention to `Form1`. The first stage involves creating a maze in which all of the cells are empty. The mouse is positioned at the left edge of the maze and, when the user clicks `btnStart`, the mouse proceeds to travel to the other side of the maze.

As you create the project, remember to place the required icon files into your solution folder within the project folder.

INTERFACE

The interface for this program is similar to that shown in Figure 13-14. Set the size property of `Form1` to 600, 550. The size of `panel1` should be 500, 400. Position the two buttons beneath `panel1`.

In this first version of the program, you will create a maze without walls. Position the mouse initially in row 8, column 0. Position the cheese in row 11, column 8. When the application runs, the interface should look something like that shown in Figure 13-15. The mouse will follow along the outside walls of the maze.

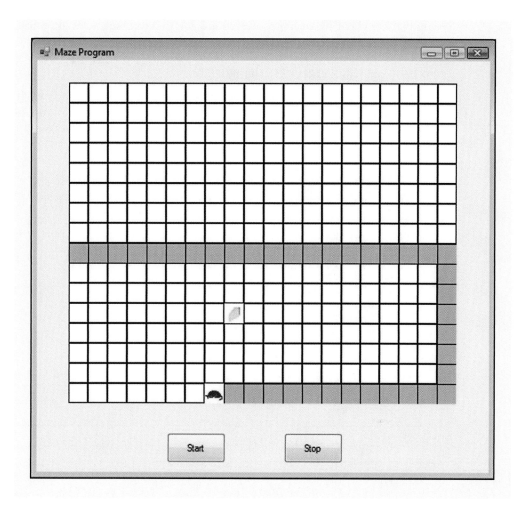

FIGURE 13-15 Interface showing maze without walls

CODING: INCLUDING `Mouse.h` AND `Cell.h`

Before `Form1` can create `Mouse` and `Cell` objects, it must have access to their class definition files. Go to the top of `Form1.h` and insert `#include` directives for each of your header files just before the namespace declaration as shown in Example 13-23 (note: your namespace name may differ from the one shown).

EXAMPLE 13-23: `#include` FILES

```
#pragma once

#include "Mouse.h"
#include "Cell.h"

namespace Maze {
```

1
3

Now that the client has access to the `Mouse` and `Cell` classes, your attention turns to the class variables, objects, and constants.

CONSTANTS, INSTANCE VARIABLES, AND OBJECTS

Example 13-24 lists the class-level instance variables, objects, and constants. In addition to the various required `Brushes`, `Pens`, and `Graphics` objects, you can now add the declarations relevant to your mouse and the maze as well as the constants identified earlier.

EXAMPLE 13-24: INSTANCE VARIABLES, OBJECTS, AND CONSTANTS

```
// Instance variables
   Mouse^ myMouse;
   array <Cell^,2>^ maze;
   char direction;
// Drawing objects
   Graphics^ g;
   Brush^ grayBrush;
   Brush^ whiteBrush;
   Brush^ burlyBrush;
   Pen^ blackPen;
// Static constants
   static const int NUMROWS = 16; // Number of rows in the maze
   static const int NUMCOLS = 20; // Number of columns in the maze
   static const int CELLSIZE = 25; // Size of a grid cell (in pixels)
```

The variable `myMouse` is a handle (a pointer to a reference object) of the `Mouse` class. The variable `maze` is a handle (a pointer to a reference object) that is a two-dimensional `array` of `Cell` handles.

CODING `Form1_Load()`

The primary task of `Form1_Load()` is to construct and initialize each cell in that structure, one by one. There are 320 of these. Fortunately, this task is easily orchestrated using nested loops. The complete code for this event handler is provided in Example 13-25.

EXAMPLE 13-25: `Form1_Load()`

```
private: System::Void Form1_Load(System::Object^
sender, System::EventArgs^ e) {
// Declare local variables
int row, col;
```

```
// Construct Drawing objects
g = panel1->CreateGraphics();
grayBrush = gcnew System::Drawing::SolidBrush(Color::Gray);
blackPen = gcnew System::Drawing::Pen(Color::Black);
whiteBrush = gcnew System::Drawing::SolidBrush(Color::White);
burlyBrush = gcnew System::Drawing::SolidBrush(Color::BurlyWood);

// Construct maze array
maze = gcnew array<Cell^, 2>(NUMROWS,NUMCOLS);
for (row = 0; row < NUMROWS; row++)
    for (col = 0; col < NUMCOLS; col++)
        maze[row,col] = gcnew Cell(row,col,true);
}
```

There are 16 rows (NUMROWS) and 20 columns (NUMCOLS) in your two-dimensional maze. The nested loops create Cell objects associated with every element. The outer loop makes 16 passes (one for each of the 16 rows). Within each pass, 20 columns of cells are created by the inner loop. The initializing constructor for a cell is called to create each cell with a different row and column value. Notice that all of your cells are constructed with their access property (the last actual argument) set to true. Because you are not including any walls in this first version of the program, the access properties will always remain set to true.

CODING btnStart_Click()

The code for this event handler follows the set of instructions laid out in your algorithm. It is shown in Example 13-26.

EXAMPLE 13-26: btnStart_Click()

```
private: System::Void btnStart_Click(System::Object^
sender, System::EventArgs^ e) {
// Local variables
    int x, y;
    Drawing::Icon^ cheese = gcnew
System::Drawing::Icon("cheese.ico");
// Starting position for mouse
    int mouseRow = 8;
    int mouseCol = 0;
// Starting location for cheese
    int cheeseRow = 11;
    int cheeseCol = 8;
// Set initial direction
    direction = 'r';
// Create myMouse
    myMouse = gcnew Mouse(mouseRow,mouseCol);
// Draw the maze
    drawMaze();
```

```
// Draw the cheese
   x = cheeseCol * CELLSIZE ;
   y = cheeseRow * CELLSIZE ;
   Rectangle cheeseRect = Rectangle(x,y,CELLSIZE,CELLSIZE);
   g->DrawIcon(cheese,cheeseRect);
   maze[cheeseRow,cheeseCol]->setCheese(true);
// Draw the mouse
   myMouse->setRow(mouseRow);
   myMouse->setCol(mouseCol);
   x = mouseCol * CELLSIZE;
   y = mouseRow * CELLSIZE;
   Rectangle mouseRect = Rectangle(x,y,CELLSIZE,CELLSIZE);
   g->DrawIcon(myMouse->getIcon(),mouseRect);
// Start the timer
   timer1->Start();
}
```

CODING THE drawMaze() METHOD

Drawing the maze requires nested for loops. Within the innermost loop, the x- and y-coordinates of each cell position are calculated and used to construct a white rectangle with a black border that represents that cell. The code for drawMaze() is shown in Example 13-27.

EXAMPLE 13-27: drawMaze()

```
private: void drawMaze()
{
// Declare local variables
int row, col;
int x, y;

// Refresh the panel
panel1->Refresh();

// Draw the empty maze
for (row = 0; row < NUMROWS; row++)
   for (col = 0; col < NUMCOLS; col++)
   {
      x = col * CELLSIZE;
      y = row * CELLSIZE;
      Rectangle gridRect = Rectangle(x,y, CELLSIZE-1,CELLSIZE-1);
      g->FillRectangle(whiteBrush,gridRect);
      g->DrawRectangle(blackPen,gridRect);
   }
}
```

CODING btnStop_Click()

The code for this event handler is trivial, as shown in Example 13-28.

EXAMPLE 13-28: btnStop_Click()

```
timer1->Stop();
```

CODING timer1_Tick()

The timer control is the most complex part of this program. The code for this method is presented in Example 13-29.

EXAMPLE 13-29: timer1_Tick()

```
private: System::Void timer1_Tick(System::Object^
sender, System::EventArgs^ e) {
// Declare local variables
    int x, y;  // x and y coordinates of myMouse
    int row, col; // row and column coordinates of myMouse
// Initialize local variables
    row = myMouse->getRow();
    col = myMouse->getCol();
    x = myMouse->getCol() * CELLSIZE;
    y = myMouse->getRow() * CELLSIZE;
// Create rectangle of current myMouse position
    Rectangle oldRect = Rectangle(x,y,CELLSIZE,CELLSIZE);

    if (!edge()) {
        // Fill old mouse position with Color::BurlyWood
        g->FillRectangle(burlyBrush,oldRect);
        g->DrawRectangle(blackPen, oldRect);
        // Move in the chosen direction
        switch (direction)
        {
        case 'r': // go to cell on the right
         myMouse->goRight(); break;
        case 'l': // go to cell on the left
         myMouse->goLeft(); break;
        case 'u': // go to cell above
         myMouse->goUp(); break;
        case 'd': // go to cell below
         myMouse->goDown(); break;
        }
        // Draw mouse at new location
        row = myMouse->getRow();
        col = myMouse->getCol();
        x = col * CELLSIZE;
        y = row * CELLSIZE;
        Rectangle mouseRect = Rectangle(x,y,CELLSIZE,CELLSIZE);
        g->DrawIcon(myMouse->getIcon(),mouseRect);
```

13

```
        if (maze[row,col]->getCheese()) {
            maze[row,col]->setCheese(false);
            timer1->Stop();
            MessageBox::Show("Congratulations!","You found it!");
        }
    }
    else // new direction
    {
        switch (direction)
        {
        case 'r': // replace right with down
         direction = 'd'; break;
        case 'l': // replace left with up
         direction = 'u'; break;
        case 'u': // replace up with right
         direction = 'r'; break;
        case 'd': // replace down with left
         direction = 'l'; break;
        }
    }
}
```

CODING THE edge() METHOD

The Boolean edge() method checks to see if the current position of the mouse is within the boundaries of the maze. It returns true if the mouse is in a cell bordering an edge of the maze and false if it is not. The code for edge() is presented in Example 13-30.

EXAMPLE 13-30: edge()

```
private: bool edge() {
    if (direction == 'r') {  // Check on the right (r)
        if (myMouse->getCol() < NUMCOLS-1) return false;
    }
    else if (direction == 'l') { // Check on the left (l)
        if (myMouse->getCol() > 0) return false;
    }
    else if (direction == 'u') { // Check up above (u)
        if (myMouse->getRow() > 0) return false;
    }
    else if (direction == 'd') { // Check down below (d)
        if (myMouse->getRow() < NUMROWS-1) return false;
    }
    return true; // Mouse is at edge
}
```

Testing

Compile and run your program. When the user clicks `btnStart`, the following should occur:

- The maze appears with 16 rows and 20 columns of white cells with black borders.

- The mouse appears in row 8, column 0.

- The cheese appears in row 11, column 8.

- The mouse appears to move from one cell to the next, from left to right across the maze.

- When the mouse reaches the edge of the maze, it turns and moves down the edge to the bottom, then across the bottom and along the edge of the maze.

ON YOUR OWN

TASK 1. STRONGER MUTATORS

In Example 13-18, the mutators for the `Mouse` class—`setRow()` and `setCol()`—are defined. Rewrite `setRow()` and `setCol()` so that they validate the data by making sure that a negative value has not been passed in before assigning it to `row` or `col`. Your specification must go in the `Mouse.cpp` file, leaving only the method prototypes in `Mouse.h`.

TASK 2. private INSTANCE METHODS

Example 13-11 shows two `private` Boolean methods—`verifyX()` and `verifyY()`—used in the `Frog` class to check and make sure that prospective x- and y-coordinate values were greater than or equal to 0. These methods were called by the mutators `setX()` and `setY()`.

Create `private` Boolean methods `verifyRow()` and `verifyCol()` for the `Mouse` class. Then rewrite `setRow()` and `setCol()`, which you defined in Task 1, so that `setRow()` calls `verifyRow()` and `setCol()` calls `verifyCol()` to perform data validation.

TASK 3. NEW UML CLASS DIAGRAM

Construct a new UML class diagram that shows the new `Mouse` class structure after you have completed Tasks 2 and 3.

1
3

QUICK REVIEW

1. An abstraction is a general definition.

2. Abstractions identify essential concepts.

3. Class definitions are abstractions.

4. Class definitions include properties and methods.

5. Objects are instances of a class.

6. Objects contain (encapsulate) all the properties and methods of their class.

7. Constructors are used to instantiate objects.

8. Initializing constructors use parameters to construct objects with specific properties.

9. Data hiding is the practice of making data members inaccessible by designating them as `private`.

10. Data members that are `private` can only be accessed by class methods.

11. Accessor and mutator methods are `public` methods that provide access to `private` data members.

12. An accessor method is a `public` method that returns the value stored in a `private` data member.

13. Accessor methods are often called get or getter methods.

14. A mutator method is a `public` method that changes the value stored in a `private` data member.

15. Mutator methods are often called set or setter methods.

16. Mutator methods can be used to screen data before it is assigned to a `private` data member.

17. Utility methods are instance methods that perform operations other than those performed by constructors, destructors, accessors, and mutators.

18. Code reuse refers to the ability to apply the same program unit to more than one application.

19. Class definitions are often reused in more than one program.

TERMS TO KNOW

abstraction
accessor method
code reuse
data hiding
get method

getter

initializing constructor

mutator method

set method

setter

utility method

EXERCISES

Use the UML class diagram shown in Figure 13-16 to answer Questions 1–5.

```
                   Song
 - title: String^
 - genre: String^
 - artist: String^

 - Song()

 + Song(String^,String^,String^ a)

 + getTitle(): String^
 + getGenre(): String^
 + getArtist(): String^

 + setTitle(String^): void
 + setGenre(String^): void
 + setArtist(String^): void
```

FIGURE 13-16 UML class diagram for Song class

1. Name the accessors, if any.
2. Name the mutators, if any.
3. Name the utility methods, if any.
4. Does this class have a **public** default constructor?
5. Does this class have a **public** initializing constructor?

6. Which of the following client code statements uses an accessor?

    a. `Student^ s = gcnew Student();`

    b. `Student^ s = gcnew Student(1234,3.24);`

    c. `s->setGPA(2.34);`

    d. `double gpa = s->getGPA();`

    e. `s->totalCredits = 102;`

7. Which of the following client code statements uses a mutator?

    a. `Student^ s = gcnew Student();`

    b. `Student^ s = gcnew Student(1234,3.24);`

    c. `s->setGPA(2.34);`

    d. `double gpa = s->getGPA();`

    e. `s->totalCredits = 102;`

8. Which of the following client code statements uses a default constructor?

    a. `Student^ s = gcnew Student();`

    b. `Student^ s = gcnew Student(1234,3.24);`

    c. `s->setGPA(2.34);`

    d. `double gpa = s->getGPA();`

    e. `s->totalCredits = 102;`

9. Which of the following client code statements uses an initializing constructor?

    a. `Student^ s = gcnew Student();`

    b. `Student^ s = gcnew Student(1234,3.24);`

    c. `s->setGPA(2.34);`

    d. `double gpa = s->getGPA();`

    e. `s->totalCredits = 102;`

10. Which of the following client code statements directly assigns a value to a class data member?

    a. `Student^ s = gcnew Student();`

    b. `Student^ s = gcnew Student(1234,3.24);`

    c. `s->setGPA(2.34);`

    d. `double gpa = s->getGPA();`

    e. `s->totalCredits = 102;`

Use the class definition shown in Figure 13-17 to answer Questions 11–15.

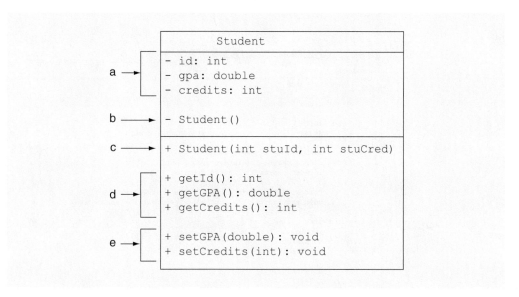

FIGURE 13-17 UML class definition for the `Student` class

11. Which section contains **public** accessors?
12. Which section contains **public** mutators?
13. Which section contains the **private** default constructor?
14. Which section contains the **private** data members?
15. Which section contains the **public** initializing constructor?

Refer to the code shown in Figure 13-18 to answer Questions 16–20. Use the line numbers at the left of the lines of code as your answers.

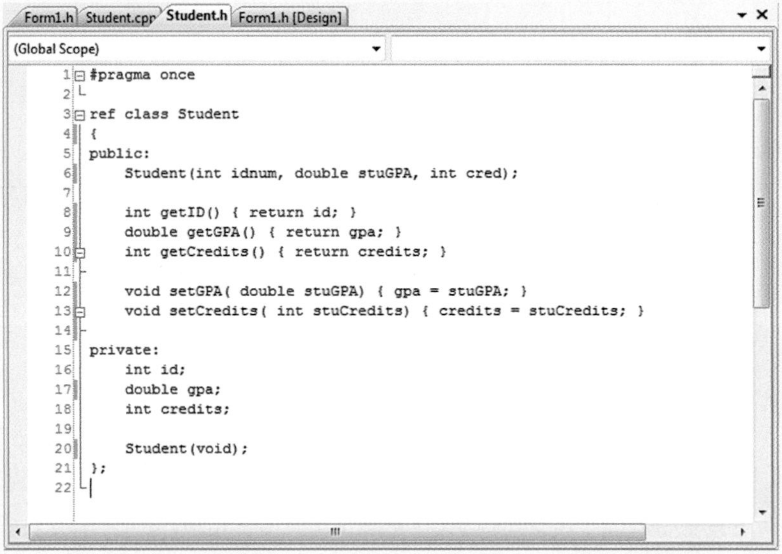

```
Form1.h  Student.cpp  Student.h  Form1.h [Design]                    ▼ ✕
(Global Scope)                              ▼                              ▼
    1 ☐ #pragma once
    2 L
    3 ☐ ref class Student
    4 ║ {
    5 ║ public:
    6 ║     Student(int idnum, double stuGPA, int cred);
    7 ║
    8 ║     int getID() { return id; }
    9 ║     double getGPA() { return gpa; }
   10 ☐   int getCredits() { return credits; }
   11 ├
   12 ║     void setGPA( double stuGPA) { gpa = stuGPA; }
   13 ☐   void setCredits( int stuCredits) { credits = stuCredits; }
   14 ├
   15 ║ private:
   16 ║     int id;
   17 ║     double gpa;
   18 ║     int credits;
   19 ║
   20 ║     Student(void);
   21 ║ };
   22 L
```

FIGURE 13-18 Student class definition

16. Which line(s) contains a method prototype?
17. Which line(s) prototypes the default constructor?
18. Which line(s) define an accessor?
19. Which line(s) define a mutator?
20. Which line(s) declare instance variables?

PROGRAMMING EXERCISES

1. Class definition

Given the UML class diagram shown in Figure 13-17 and the Student class code shown in Figure 13-18, write a complete Visual C++ definition for the Student class in which all class methods are prototyped in Student.h and defined fully in Student.cpp. Make sure that the initializing constructor and mutators only accept GPA values from 0–4.0. In addition, credits must be >= 0.

2. Implement Client Code for the Student Class

Create a program that implements the design shown in Figure 13-19. The program searches an array of Student objects looking for an ID number. If the target ID number is found, then the result is displayed. Use your Student class definition from Programming Exercise 1.

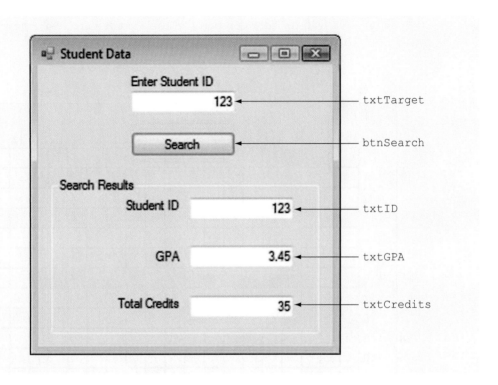

FIGURE 13-19 Student Data program interface

Construct an array of 10 students. Then use the following parallel arrays to initialize the 10 students:

```
int id[] = {123,234,345,456,567,678,789,901,159,268};
double gpa[] = {3.45, 2.76, 1.80, 3.32, 3.98, 2.31, 2.77, 2.03, 2.69,
3.03, 3.00};
int credits[] = {35, 25, 15, 12, 22, 46, 35, 76, 35, 15};
```

You may use a sequential search in this program. Loop through the Student objects looking at each ID number (student[i]->getID()) and comparing it to the target. When you find a match, display the ID, GPA, and credits for that student in the text boxes.

3. Implement the `Frog` class

In the first part of this chapter you used the `Frog` class as an example, building into it an initializing constructor, accessors, mutators, and utility methods. Using the class definition contained in Examples 13-11 and 13-12, implement a frog race program like that shown in Figures 13-3 and 13-4.

4. Add Walls to the Maze Program

A wall is a cell with the access property set to `false`. Figure 13-20 shows the maze with five walls (labeled a–e).

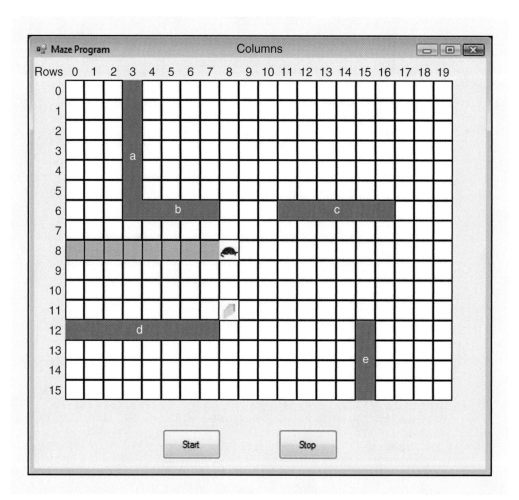

FIGURE 13-20 Maze with five walls

These walls were created in `drawMaze()` in two steps. First, the access property of the wall cells was changed to `false`, as shown here:

```
// Define walls within the maze
for (row = 0; row < 7;  row++)
   maze[row,3]->setAccess(false);    // Wall a
for (col = 3; col < 8;  col++)
   maze[6,col]->setAccess(false);    // Wall b
for (col = 11; col < 17;  col++)
   maze[6,col]->setAccess(false);    // Wall c
for (col = 0; col < 8;  col++)
   maze[12,col]->setAccess(false);   // Wall d
for (row = 12; row < numRows;  row++)
   maze[row,15]->setAccess(false);   // Wall e
```

The walls are drawn with nested loops in the exact same manner in which the original maze of white cells was drawn, except that the `grayBrush` object is used to fill the rectangles instead of the `whiteBrush` object.

Construct a maze with the exact configuration of walls as that shown in Figure 13-20.

Note, your mouse will run through the walls, even though their access property is set to `false`. This will be corrected in Programming Exercise 5.

5. Setting Walls as Barriers

You already have a Boolean method called `edge()` that returns `true` if the next cell in the current direction is out of bounds and `false` if it is not.

Create a new method called `wall()`. Your `wall()` method can check for walls by using the access property of the next cell. For example, if `direction` was set to `'r'` (right) then you would look at the `access` property of the next `Cell` to the right:

```
maze[row,col+1]->getAccess()
```

Remember that the access property returns `true` if the cell can be accessed by the mouse and `false` if that cell is a wall and cannot be accessed. Your `wall()` method should return `true` if the next cell is a wall and `false` if it is not. When you have a program in which the walls work, add additional walls until your maze looks like that in Figure 13-20. These walls will direct your mouse to the cheese. Experiment with other configurations to build your own maze.

1
3

APPENDIX A
CONCEPTS AND FEATURES
COVERED IN EACH CHAPTER

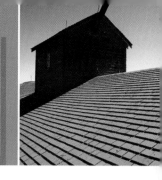

Table A-1 shows the computer science topics covered in each chapter.

TABLE A-1 Computer Science Concepts by Chapter

	Ch. 1	Ch. 2	Ch. 3	Ch. 4	Ch. 5	Ch. 6	Ch. 7	Ch. 8	Ch. 9	Ch. 10	Ch. 11	Ch. 12	Ch. 13
Fundamental components of a computer	x												
History of computer science	x												
Hardware basics	x												
Software basics	x												
Program development process	x												
Types of errors	x												
Visual Studio IDE	x												
Visual C++ programming	x												
OOP overview	x												
Objects and properties	x												

681

TABLE A-1 Computer Science Concepts by Chapter (continued)

	Ch. 1	Ch. 2	Ch. 3	Ch. 4	Ch. 5	Ch. 6	Ch. 7	Ch. 8	Ch. 9	Ch. 10	Ch. 11	Ch. 12	Ch. 13
Assignment (=)	x	x											
Pointer membership operator (->)	x	x											
Arithmetic operators		x	x										
Comments		x											
Data types		x											
Binary numbers		x	x										
Integer division		x	x										
Mod operator		x	x										
Strings		x	x										
Type casting			x										
Type conversion			x										
Algorithm		x	x	x									
Pseudocode		x	x	x									
Algorithm verification				x									
if statements				x									
if...else statements				x									
if...elseif statements				x									

TABLE A-1 Computer Science Concepts by Chapter (continued)

	Ch. 1	Ch. 2	Ch. 3	Ch. 4	Ch. 5	Ch. 6	Ch. 7	Ch. 8	Ch. 9	Ch. 10	Ch. 11	Ch. 12	Ch. 13
Logical operators				x									
Nested `if` statements				x									
Operator precedence				x									
Relational operators				x									
`switch` statement				x									
Trace table				x									
Counting					x								
`do... while` loops					x								
`for` loops					x								
Random numbers					x								
Summation					x								
`while` loops					x								
Instance methods						x							
Actual arguments						x							
Formal parameters						x							
Pass by value						x							

TABLE A-1 Computer Science Concepts by Chapter (continued)

	Ch. 1	Ch. 2	Ch. 3	Ch. 4	Ch. 5	Ch. 6	Ch. 7	Ch. 8	Ch. 9	Ch. 10	Ch. 11	Ch. 12	Ch. 13
Pass by reference						x							
Return values						x							
Static declarations						x							
Constants						x							
1-dimension arrays							x						
Passing arrays into methods							x						
Sequential search							x						
Parallel arrays							x						
Multidimen-sional arrays							x						
Binary search								x					
The Array class								x					
Big-O analysis								x					
Exchanging values									x				
Selection sort									x				
Insertion sort									x				
Bubble sort									x				
Big-O Comparison									x				

TABLE A-1 Computer Science Concepts by Chapter (continued)

	Ch. 1	Ch. 2	Ch. 3	Ch. 4	Ch. 5	Ch. 6	Ch. 7	Ch. 8	Ch. 9	Ch. 10	Ch. 11	Ch. 12	Ch. 13
Recursion										x			
Recursive backtracking										x			
Analyzing recursion										x			
Fractals										x			
Pointer syntax											x		
Indirection											x		
Dereferencing											x		
Pointer return types											x		
Pointer arrays											x		
Deleting pointers											x		
Swapping pointers											x		
Linked lists												x	
Node												x	
Insert node												x	
Delete node												x	
Head node												x	
UML class diagrams												x	x
#include												x	x

TABLE A-1 Computer Science Concepts by Chapter (continued)

	Ch. 1	Ch. 2	Ch. 3	Ch. 4	Ch. 5	Ch. 6	Ch. 7	Ch. 8	Ch. 9	Ch. 10	Ch. 11	Ch. 12	Ch. 13
Class												x	x
Constructor												x	x
Destructor												x	
`public, private`												x	x
Instantiation												x	x
Methods												x	x
header files (.h)												x	x
implementation file (.cpp)												x	x
Client code												x	x
Accessor (get)													x
Mutator (set)													x
2-d array													x
Data hiding													x
Encapsulation													x
Multiple instantiation													x

Table A-2 shows the Microsoft Visual C++ features covered in each chapter.

TABLE A-2 Microsoft Visual C++ Features by Chapter

	Ch. 1	Ch. 2	Ch. 3	Ch. 4	Ch. 5	Ch. 6	Ch. 7	Ch. 8	Ch. 9	Ch. 10	Ch. 11	Ch. 12	Ch. 13
`button1_Click()`	X												
`Button` control	X												
`Color` codes	X												
Color properties	X												
Font dialog box	X												
`TextBox` control	X												
The `this` pointer	X												
Data types		X											
Label control		X											
`Math::Pow()`		X											
`Math::Sqrt()`		X											
Scope resolution operator (`::`)		X											
`ToString()` method		X											
`TryParse()` method		X											
`Border Style` property			X										
`Convert()` methods			X										
Decrease Horizontal Spacing button			X										
`Form1_Load()`			X										

TABLE A-2 Microsoft Visual C++ Features by Chapter (continued)

	Ch. 1	Ch. 2	Ch. 3	Ch. 4	Ch. 5	Ch. 6	Ch. 7	Ch. 8	Ch. 9	Ch. 10	Ch. 11	Ch. 12	Ch. 13
Locked property			x										
MaxLength() property			x										
Multiline property			x										
Name property			x										
Naming conventions			x										
ReadOnly property			x										
Size property			x										
TextAlign property			x										
TextChanged() event			x										
ComboBox control				x									
GroupBox control				x									
Items property				x									
MessageBox:: Show()				x									
MonthCalendar control				x									
RadioButton control				x									
SelectedIndex property				x									
SelectionStart property				x									
Date::Time				x	x								
concatenation operator (+)					x								

TABLE A-2 Microsoft Visual C++ Features by Chapter (continued)

	Ch. 1	Ch. 2	Ch. 3	Ch. 4	Ch. 5	Ch. 6	Ch. 7	Ch. 8	Ch. 9	Ch. 10	Ch. 11	Ch. 12	Ch. 13
`DateTime::Now`					X								
Escape characters					X								
`gcnew`					X	X							
handle operator (^)					X								
`now.Millisecond`					X								
`Random` object					X								
`String` object					X								
`Brush` object						X							
Coordinate system						X							
`FillEllipse()` method						X							
`Graphics` object						X							
`Image::FromFile`						X							
`Math::Sin()`						X							
`Math::Cos()`						X							
`Math::PI`						X							
`Picture Box` control						X							
`Rectangle` object						X							
`System::Void`						X							
`Timer` control						X							
`Timer_Tick()` event						X							

TABLE A-2 Microsoft Visual C++ Features by Chapter (continued)

	Ch. 1	Ch. 2	Ch. 3	Ch. 4	Ch. 5	Ch. 6	Ch. 7	Ch. 8	Ch. 9	Ch. 10	Ch. 11	Ch. 12	Ch. 13
DrawRectangle() method							x						
FillRectangle() method							x						
Panel control							x						
Pen object							x						
Add() method								x					
Array class								x					
Array::SetValue()								x					
Array::Sort()								x					
ListView control								x					
String::Compare()								x					
String::ToUpper()								x					
DrawString() method									x				
Font object									x				
Close()										x			
Events button										x			
MenuStrip control										x			
toolStrip MenuItem										x			
DrawLine() method											x		
nullptr											x		

TABLE A-2 Microsoft Visual C++ Features by Chapter (continued)

	Ch. 1	Ch. 2	Ch. 3	Ch. 4	Ch. 5	Ch. 6	Ch. 7	Ch. 8	Ch. 9	Ch. 10	Ch. 11	Ch. 12	Ch. 13
TextBox.Height											x		
TextBox.Location											x		
TextBox.Location.X											x		
TextBox.Location.Y											x		
TextBox.Width											x		
ref class												x	x
two-dimensional array													x

DOCUMENTATION AND REFERENCE MATERIALS

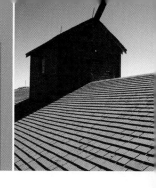

Microsoft maintains a comprehensive source of reference material on their products, especially Visual Studio and the Visual C++ compiler. For complete reference material, and in-depth discussions on Microsoft Visual C++, visit the Microsoft Developer Network (MSDN). You can search the MSDN library for information related to almost any aspect of the Visual C++ language. Here are the Web links to the major MSDN pages:

- MSDN homepage:
  - *http://msdn2.microsoft.com/en-us/library/default.aspx*
- MSDN Visual C++ Library:
  - *http://msdn2.microsoft.com/EN-US/library/60k1461a(VS.80).aspx*
- Visual C++ Reference Page:
  - *http://msdn2.microsoft.com/en-us/library/ty9hx077(VS.80).aspx*

The following Web links take you to locations on the MSDN that pertain to specific topics covered in this book. These links were current at the time this appendix was written:

- Array Class Members:
  - *http://msdn2.microsoft.com/en-us/library/system.array_members.aspx*
- Color Codes:
  - *http://msdn2.microsoft.com/en-us/library/ms531197.aspx*
- Convert Methods:
  - *http://msdn2.microsoft.com/en-us/library/system.convert_methods.aspx*
- Date::Time Class Members:
  - *http://msdn2.microsoft.com/en-us/library/system.datetime_members.aspx*
- Data Types:
  - *http://msdn2.microsoft.com/en-us/library/z8336xfc(VS.71).aspx*
- Escape Character Codes:
  - *http://msdn2.microsoft.com/en-us/library/ms857307.aspx*

- Graphics Class Methods:
  - *http://msdn2.microsoft.com/en-us/library/system.drawing.graphics_methods.aspx*
- Math Class Members:
  - *http://msdn2.microsoft.com/en-us/library/system.math_members.aspx*
- Operator Precedence:
  - *http://msdn2.microsoft.com/en-us/library/126fe14k(VS.71).aspx*
- String Class Members:
  - *http://msdn2.microsoft.com/en-us/library/system.string_members.aspx*
- System::Drawing Namespace:
  - *http://msdn2.microsoft.com/en-us/library/system.drawing.aspx*
- System Namespace:
  - *http://msdn2.microsoft.com/en-us/library/system.aspx*
- Visual C++ Keywords:
  - *http://msdn2.microsoft.com/en-us/library/2e6a4at9(VS.71).aspx*
- Windows Forms (including Common Dialogs):
  - *http://msdn2.microsoft.com/en-us/library/system.windows.forms.aspx*

ASCII Table

Table B-1 describes the ASCII characters, and provides their decimal and binary equivalents.

TABLE B-1 ASCII Table

Decimal	Binary	Character	Description
0	00000000	NUL	NULL character
1	00000001	SOH	Start of heading
2	00000010	STX	Start of text
3	00000011	ETX	End of text
4	00000100	EOT	End of transmission
5	00000101	ENQ	Enquiry

TABLE B-1 ASCII Table (continued)

Decimal	Binary	Character	Description
6	00000110	ACK	Acknowledgement
7	00000111	BEL	Bell (\a)
8	00001000	BS	Backspace (\b)
9	00001001	HT	Horizontal tab (\t)
10	00001010	LF	Line feed (\n)
11	00001011	VT	Vertical tab
12	00001100	FF	Form feed (\f)
13	00001101	CR	Carriage return (\r)
14	00001110	SO	Shift out
15	00001111	SI	Shift in
16	00010000	DLE	Data link escape
17	00010001	DC1	Device control 1
18	00010010	DC2	Device control 2
19	00010011	DC3	Device control 3
20	00010100	DC4	Device control 4
21	00010101	NAK	Negative acknowledgement
22	00010110	SYN	Synchronous idle
23	00010111	ETB	End of transmission block
24	00011000	CAN	Cancel
25	00011001	EM	End of medium
26	00011010	SUB	Substitute
27	00011011	ESC	Escape (\e)

TABLE B-1   ASCII Table (continued)

Decimal	Binary	Character	Description
28	00011100	FS	File separator
29	00011101	GS	Group separator
30	00011110	RS	Record separator
31	00011111	US	Unit separator
32	00100000	SP	Space
33	00100001	!	Exclamation mark
34	00100010	"	Double quotation mark
35	00100011	#	Number sign
36	00100100	$	Dollar sign
37	00100101	%	Percent sign
38	00100110	&	Ampersand
39	00100111	'	Apostrophe
40	00101000	(	Open parenthesis
41	00101001	)	Close parenthesis
42	00101010	*	Asterisk
43	00101011	+	Plus
44	00101100	,	Comma
45	00101101	–	Minus
46	00101110	.	Hyphen
47	00101111	/	Forward slash
48	00110000	0	
49	00110001	1	

TABLE B-1 ASCII Table (continued)

Decimal	Binary	Character	Description
50	00110010	2	
51	00110011	3	
52	00110100	4	
53	00110101	5	
54	00110110	6	
55	00110111	7	
56	00111000	8	
57	00111001	9	
58	00111010	:	Colon
59	00111011	;	Semicolon
60	00111100	<	Less than
61	00111101	=	Equal
62	00111110	>	Greater than
63	00111111	?	Question mark
64	01000000	@	At sign
65	01000001	A	
66	01000010	B	
67	01000011	C	
68	01000100	D	
69	01000101	E	
70	01000110	F	
71	01000111	G	

TABLE B-1 ASCII Table (continued)

Decimal	Binary	Character	Description
72	01001000	H	
73	01001001	I	
74	01001010	J	
75	01001011	K	
76	01001100	L	
77	01001101	M	
78	01001110	N	
79	01001111	O	
80	01010000	P	
81	01010001	Q	
82	01010010	R	
83	01010011	S	
84	01010100	T	
85	01010101	U	
86	01010110	V	
87	01010111	W	
88	01011000	X	
89	01011001	Y	
90	01011010	Z	
91	01011011	[	Open bracket
92	01011100	\	Backslash (\)
93	01011101	]	Close bracket

TABLE B-1 ASCII Table (continued)

Decimal	Binary	Character	Description
94	01011110	^	Caret
95	01011111	_	Underscore
96	01100000	`	Grave accent mark
97	01100001	a	
98	01100010	b	
99	01100011	c	
100	01100100	d	
101	01100101	e	
102	01100110	f	
103	01100111	g	
104	01101000	h	
105	01101001	i	
106	01101010	j	
107	01101011	k	
108	01101100	l	
109	01101101	m	
110	01101110	n	
111	01101111	o	
112	01110000	p	
113	01110001	q	
114	01110010	r	
115	01110011	s	

TABLE B-1 ASCII Table (continued)

Decimal	Binary	Character	Description
116	01110100	t	
117	01110101	u	
118	01110110	v	
119	01110111	w	
120	01111000	x	
121	01111001	y	
122	01111010	z	
123	01111011	{	Open brace
124	01111100	|	Bar
125	01111101	}	Close brace
126	01111110	~	Tilde
127	01111111	DEL	Delete

C++ Keywords

Keywords, sometimes called reserved words, are identifiers that have already been assigned a meaning by the programming language. They cannot be used by the programmer for any other purpose than their original, intended use. There are two types of keywords: standard C++ keywords (common to all ISO standard C++ programs) and Microsoft Visual C++ keywords. Table B-2 lists the standard keywords. The MSDN link for Visual C++ keywords was included in the list of MSDN websites at the beginning of this appendix.

TABLE B-2 Standard C/C++ Keywords

abstract	friend	try
array	goto	typedef
bool	if	union
break	int	unsigned
case	long	using
catch	namespace	void
char	new	while
class	operator	
const	private	
const_cast	protected	
continue	public	
default	reinterpret_cast	
delegate	return	
delete	safecast	
deprecated	short	
do	signed	
double	sizeof	
dynamic_cast	static	
else	struct	
enum	switch	
false	this	
float	throw	
for	true	

COMMON ERRORS

Although it is impossible to predict every error that might occur in a program, you can expect to see some errors relatively often. A number of these common errors and suggestions for their solutions are provided in this appendix. The program shown in Figure C-1 will be used to illustrate some error conditions and how to fix them.

This program has a text box (**textBox1**), button (**button1**), label (**label1**), and another text box (**textBox2**). When the user clicks the button, the program displays a random number between 0 and 99 in **textBox2**. This is the user's lucky number.

FIGURE C-1 Lucky number program

Error C2143: Missing ; Before `using`

Sometimes you will find that the compiler cannot determine where the end of your program is. As a result, it flags the first line in the program segment it cannot figure out, as shown in Figure C-2.

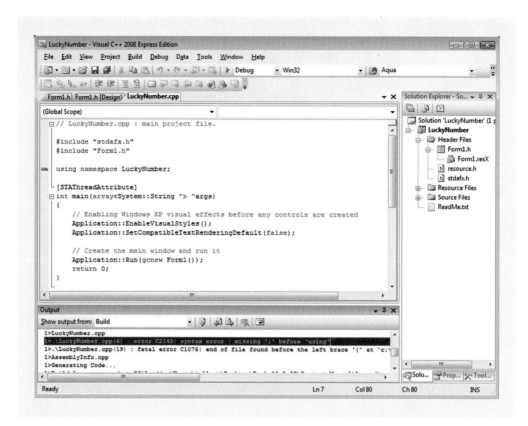

FIGURE C-2 Error in `LuckyNumber.cpp`

What You Probably Did Wrong: Deleting a } by Mistake

This is an interesting error message because it says that the problem lies in a C++ program file you have never had anything to do with (`LuckyNumber.cpp`). You probably did not know it even existed. In the Solution Explorer, you can see the location of the file in the Source Code folder, as shown in Figure C-3.

Your project consists of many files. The one shown in Figure C-3 is the starting point for your application. It is called the `main()` method. Notice that it brings in `Form1.h` through an include statement: `#include "Form1.h"`. As you know, `Form1.h` contains all the code for your interface. It is usually the only file you ever work in.

If an error occurs before the `using namespace LuckyNumber;` line, it can only be because the file just included (`Form1.h`) did not end properly.

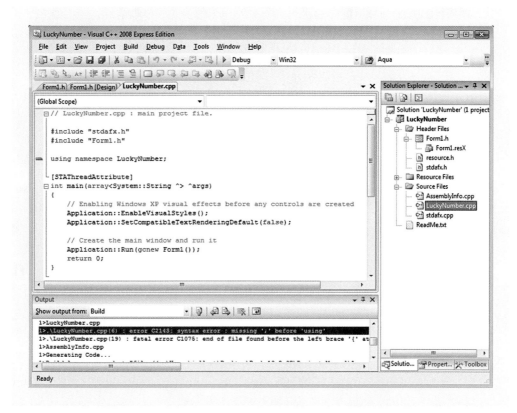

FIGURE C-3 Locating `LuckyNumber.cpp` in the Solution Explorer window

If you look at `Form1.h` the problem is easy to spot. It probably has nothing to do with a `;`. Instead, it has everything to do with making sure that all of the event handlers have matching curly brackets `{ }`, which define their extent.

Here are the contents of `Form1.h` in the region of code you are writing. The last two lines (`};`) and (`}`) mark the end of your Form1 class definition and your project namespace.

```
private: System::Void btnLucky_Click(System::Object^
sender, System::EventArgs^  e) {
                textBox2->Text = "7";
};
}
```

All event handlers must have been fully defined before these last two lines with closing brackets are encountered. However, it seems that you have somehow deleted the closing bracket `}` that is supposed to match the opening bracket `{` that began `btnLucky`'s event handler.

```
private: System::Void btnLucky_Click(System::Object^
sender, System::EventArgs^  e) {
                textBox2->Text = "7";
//      } is missing here
};
}
```

How to Fix It

Once you have identified where the missing } goes, you just need to insert it into the code.

```
private: System::Void btnLucky_Click(System::Object^
sender, System::EventArgs^  e) {
                textBox2->Text = "7";
    }
};
}
```

Be very careful whenever you use pairs of curly brackets { }. Forgetting the closing bracket will send the compiler on a wild goose chase looking for the missing } in files other than Form1.h.

Error C2039: Event Handler Is Not a Member of **Form1** (Version 1)

There are several different ways to get this error message. This section deals with one of them, which we'll call Version 1. The next section explains the second way, which we'll call Version 2. The error message reads as follows:

```
error C2039: 'button1_Click()': is not a member of 'LuckyNumber::Form1'
```

This is often followed by another error message:

```
error C2065: 'button1_Click': undeclared identifier
```

What You Probably Did Wrong: Changing an Event Handler Name Manually

There are two easy ways to do something that produces these error messages. First, you might have manually changed the name of an event handler. Second, you might have deleted an event handler. Either way, the compiler will be confused because the contents of your event handler section are not what it was led to believe it would encounter.

For example, assume that your program has a button called button1 as shown in Figure C-4.

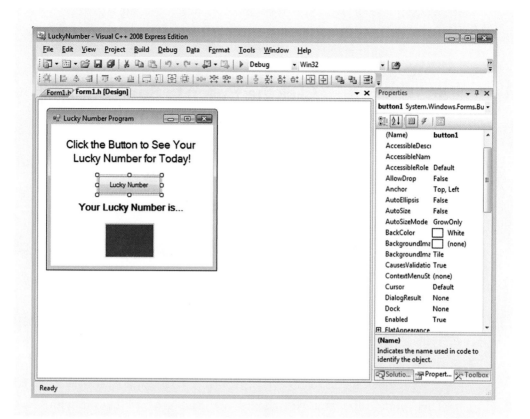

FIGURE C-4 `button1`

Also, suppose that you have already created the event handler (`button1_Click`) as follows:

```
private: System::Void button1_Click(System::Object^
sender, System::EventArgs^  e) {
            textBox2->Text = "7";
        }
```

Your program looks like Figure C-5 when it runs. This is what you want.

FIGURE C-5 The program runs correctly

Then you realize that you should not have left the button with its default name (button1). In keeping with your program design specifications you want to change it to btnLucky. So you go to the Properties window and make the change as shown in Figure C-6.

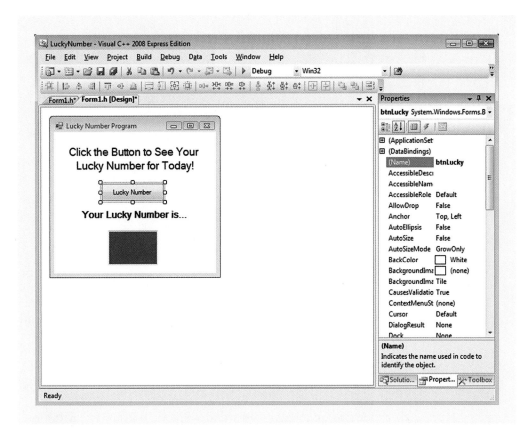

FIGURE C-6   Changing the name of `button1` to `btnLucky`

The good news is that your program will still work. However, your button is named `btnLucky`, while the event handler is still called `button1_Click()`. This is OK, unless you decide to change the name of the event handler to `btnLucky_Click()` manually.

```
private: System::Void btnLucky_Click(System::Object^
sender, System::EventArgs^  e) {
            textBox2->Text = "7";
        }
```

Now your program will not compile and gives you the error messages shown in Figure C-7.

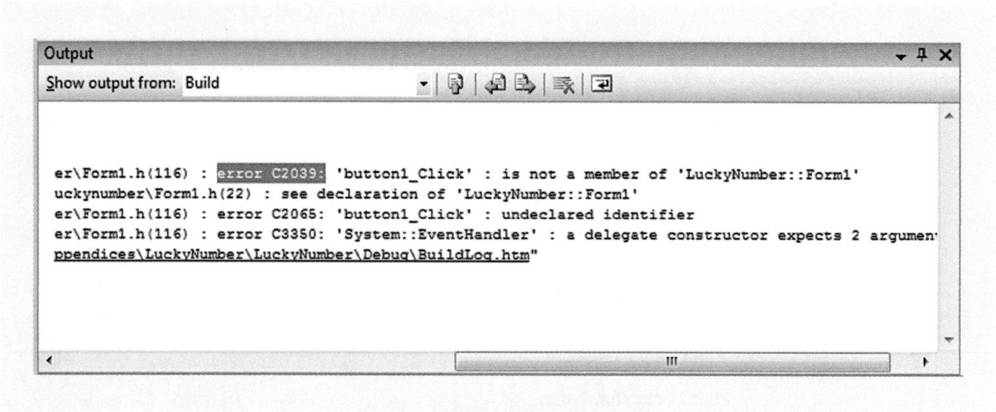

FIGURE C-7 `button1_Click` is not a member of `LuckyNumber::Form1`

All three error messages shown in Figure C-7 relate to the same problem. The compiler still expects to find the `button1_Click` event handler.

If you are not interested in further explanation, skip ahead to the section titled "How to Fix It" and use the first of the two methods described to correct the problem. If you would like further explanation, the remainder of this section explains what happened. (Note that you'll need this explanation to use the second method described in the "How to Fix It" section.) When you originally created `button1` a block of code was automatically generated to define the object in relation to `Form1`. When you changed the name of `button1` to `btnLucky`, this section of code updated itself. It looks like this:

```
// btnLucky
//
this->btnLucky->Location = System::Drawing::Point(85, 90);
this->btnLucky->Name = L"btnLucky";
this->btnLucky->Size = System::Drawing::Size(113, 32);
this->btnLucky->TabIndex = 4;
this->btnLucky->Text = L"Lucky Number";
this->btnLucky->UseVisualStyleBackColor = true;
this->btnLucky->Click += gcnew System::EventHandler(this,
&Form1::button1_Click);
```

Notice that the last command (which wraps across two lines) contains the code that establishes the click event for `btnLucky`. This event was already created when `button1` was the correct name. The click event code still existed and was called `button1_Click`. The last line in the code above attaches `button1_Click` as the proper click event code for `btnLucky`.

When you changed the name of `button1_Click` to `btnLucky_Click()`, this line did not automatically change. It instructs the compiler to look for a routine called `button1_Click` and finding none, the compiler produces the error messages.

How to Fix It

The first way to fix this problem to go to the form and delete the button from the interface. (Note, this will not delete its `Click()` event handler from the code.) Now create another button and name it as you originally wanted (`btnLucky`). When you are finished setting its properties you can double-click it to generate its event handler. Copy and paste the code from the previous event handler into the new one. You can now safely delete the old `Click()` event handler and use the new one.

A second way to fix this problem involves changing the name `button1` to `btnLucky` in the Windows Form Designer code line causing the error. This requires that you locate and edit a line of code in the Windows Form Designer code section of your program, which this book does not encourage. Unless you are sure that you understand how to edit the Windows Form Designer code section, you should fix the bug using the method described above.

```
this->btnLucky->Click += gcnew System::Eventhandler
(this, &Form1::btnLucky_Click);
```

Error C2039: Event Handler Is Not a Member of **Form1** (Version 2)

The second cause of this error message is also easy to inadvertently create. If the first solution did not apply to your situation then this one may.

What You Probably Did Wrong: Deleting an Unused Event Handler

The second way this error message could be produced is if you accidentally double-click on a control in design view producing an empty event handler you do not want. For example, it is easy to accidentally double-clicked `textBox1` when selecting it, as in Figure C-8.

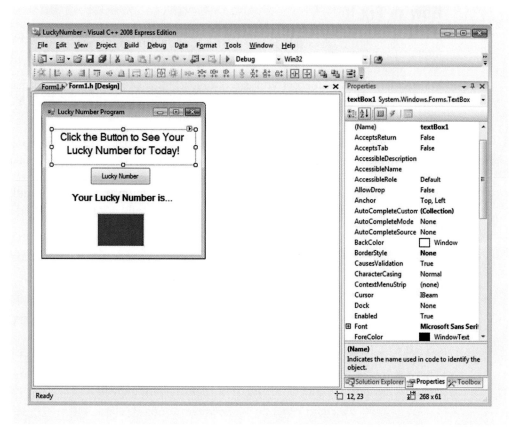

FIGURE C-8 The selected object (`textBox1`) could be double-clicked by accident

If you did accidentally double-click, then the following event handler is automatically created:

```
#pragma endregion
private: System::Void textBox1_TextChanged(
System::Object^  sender, System::EventArgs^  e) {
}
```

When the code editor starts, displaying an event handler that you do not want, the natural reaction is to delete this event handler since you do not need it and it was produced by mistake. Once you delete it however, the same errors (C2039 and C2065) occur as in the previous example. The compiler still expects to find the event handler you deleted.

How to Fix It

The easiest way to fix this problem is to go to the form and delete the text box. Then, create a new one in its place.

Rebuilding your Program

In general, if you encounter a strange error that provides no meaningful error message, you should try to rebuild your program from scratch. The rebuilding process forces the program to do a complete recompile and occasionally this can alleviate some errors. To rebuild the project, go to the Build menu and select Rebuild Solution as shown in Figure C-9.

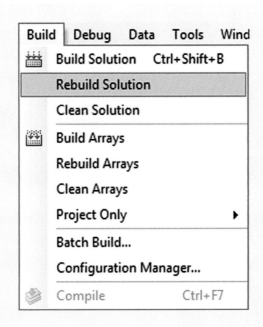

FIGURE C-9 Rebuilding a solution

When the rebuilding process is complete you can run the program as before. Rebuilding the program generates the code to link your compiled program with the current resource files it needs to execute properly. The rebuilding process also removes previous references to older resource files.

INDEX

Note:
- Bold page numbers indicate definitions.
- Italic page numbers indicate illustrations.
- Page numbers followed by *(2)* indicate two separate references.
- Page numbers followed by *n* indicate notes.
- Page numbers followed by *qr* indicate quick reviews.
- Page numbers followed by *sk* indicate sketches.
- Page numbers followed by *t* indicate tables.
- Page numbers enclosed in parentheses, as in "traversing arrays, (331), (338-339), **347**-348" indicate passages in which the topics indexed are not identified by the term under which they are indexed.
- In general cross-references, a target term that includes ellipsis points, as in "*See also specific* btn..._Click() *event handlers*", points to all the headings made up of this term with unique names in place of the ellipsis points.

Symbols

& (ampersand): address-of operator, 285, 514, 523

&& (ampersands). *See* and operator (&&)

' (apostrophe). *See* ' ' (single quotes)

-> (arrow): pointer member access operator, 45, **47**, 392, **597**

* (asterisk):
  indirection operator, **519**, 521, 522*n*
  pointer declaration (data type) symbol, **515**, 522*n*
  See also multiplication operator

** (asterisks):
  double indirection operator, **521**
  double pointer declaration symbol, 518, 539, 558

*= (asterisk-equal sign): multiplication assignment operator, 92, 244–245

*/ (asterisk-slash): block comment delimiter, 102

\ (backslash): escape character, **253**

^ (caret): handle operator/designator, 245, 388

, (comma): parameter delimiter, 85, 276

{ } (curly brackets):
  array value list delimiters, 330
  code delimiters, 44, 169, 185, 186
  missing '}' error, 702–704

. (dot): member access operator, 597

:: (double colon): scope resolution operator, **85**, 271, 594, 598

"" (double quotes): string delimiters, 48, 245

= (equal sign). *See* assignment operator

== (equal signs). *See* equal to operator

! (exclamation mark):
  factorial symbol, 243, 460
  not operator, 173–174, 174*t*, 333*n*

!= (exclamation-equal sign): not equal to operator, 167, 168*t*

> (greater than sign): greater than operator, 168*t*

>= (greater than or equal to sign): greater than or equal to operator, 168*t*

< (less than sign): less than operator, 168*t*

<= (less than or equal to sign): less than or equal to operator, 168*t*

– (minus sign): private access mode symbol, 590
  See also subtraction operator

-= (minus-equal sign): subtraction assignment operator, 92

(number sign): protected access mode symbol, 590

#include directive, 591–592

#pragma endregion statement, 226–227

#pragma once directive, 616

() (parentheses). *See* parentheses

% (percent sign). *See* mod operator

%= (percent-equal sign): mod assignment operator, 92

π (PI): constant, 273

+ (plus sign): `public` access mode symbol, 590
  See also addition operator; concatenation operator
+= (plus-equal sign):
  addition assignment operator, 92
  concatenation assignment operator, 246
? (question mark): undefined variable symbol, 197
; (semicolon): statement terminator, 49, 585
' ' (single quotes): character delimiters, 78
/ (slash). *See* division operator
/* (slash-asterisk): block comment delimiter, 102
/= (slash-equal sign): division assignment operator, 92
// (slashes): line comment indicator, 102
[ ] (square brackets):
  array identification symbol/delimiters, 329, 330
  array subscript delimiters, *328*
  optional feature delimiters, 185
|| (vertical bars). *See* or operator (||)

A

ABC computer, 8, 9
abstraction, **574**, 623*qr*, 672*qr*
  of class definitions, 586, *586*, 636–637, *636*
  of lists, 574, 579, 623*qr*
access mode symbols, 590–591
access modes (of methods), **275**, *276*
  class member definition order, 590–591
  `protected` mode, **588**
accessing array elements, 329*n*, 330–331, 338–339, 583
accessing data members, 597
accessing data through pointers, 519–522
accessing nodes, 583, 597
accessing `static` variables, 598

accessor methods, **643**–644, 672*qr*
accumulating products, 243–245
accumulating sums. *See* summation
actual argument lists, 281
actual arguments (of methods), **281**
`Add()` method (`Items` collections), 398
addition assignment operator (+=), 92
addition assignment process, 87–88, *88*
addition operator (+), 87*t*
  precedence in arithmetic expressions, 88–90
addition program tutorial, 95–104
address-of operator (&), 285, 514, 523
addresses. *See* memory cell addresses
algorithms, 74–**75**, 106*qr*
  addition algorithm, 97
  binary conversion algorithm, 133–134
  binary search algorithm, 371–378
  bubble sort algorithm, 429
  for Calculate buttons, 191–195, 221
  for click event handlers. *See under* `button1_Click()` event handler; *and specific* `btn..._Click()` *event handlers*
  `deleteList()` method algorithm, 609–610
  `DrawArray()` method algorithm, 445
  `DrawBranch()` method algorithm, 475–476, 483
  `DrawFractal()` method algorithm, 483
  `drawLines()` method algorithm, 552–557
  `drawNode()` method algorithm, 610
  efficiency, 441

finding the largest value in arrays, 331
finding the smallest value in arrays, 428
`Form1_Load()` event handler algorithms, 190, 257, 661
high-level algorithms, **75**, **133**, 133
insertion sort algorithm, 432–438
low-level algorithms, **75**, **133**, 133–134
menu item algorithms, 482
planetary motion algorithm, 301–302
recursive factorial algorithm, 463–465
selection sort algorithm, 425
sorting methods (strategies), 422–440, 450–451*qr*; big-O value, 440; comparative efficiency, 441; nested loops as used in, 423.
  See also bubble sort; insertion sort; selection sort
stepwise refinement/development of, **133**, 154*qr*
`Swap()` method algorithm, 419
verifying, 196–200
aligning text: in textboxes, 99, 146
ALU (arithmetic logic unit), **6**
American Standard Code for Information Interchange. *See* ASCII
ampersand (&): address-of operator, 285, 514, 523
ampersands (&&). *See* and operator (&&)
and operator (&&), 174–176, 176*t*
  vs. or operator (||), 176–178, 179
angles:
  converting degrees to radians, 272–274, 289–290
  drawing fractal images at, 497–499

apostrophe. *See* single quotes
application methods, **270**–271, 274–276, *277,* 311–312*qr*
  See also event handlers; programmer-defined methods
application software, **11**, *11,* 16
architecture (hardware), **17**
argument lists (actual argument lists), 281
arguments (actual arguments), **281**
arithmetic expressions, **86**
  operator precedence in, **88**–90
arithmetic logic unit (ALU), **6**
arithmetic operators, **86**–88, 86–87*t,* 108*qr*
  associativity, 87
  precedence in arithmetic expressions, **88**–90
array class, 387–391
  methods, 389–391; MSDN website resource, 691
  objects. *See* object arrays (**array** class objects); **String** arrays
array elements, **328**
  accessing, 329*n,* 330–331, 338–339, 583
  adding, 575–576, 577
  assigning data to, 329–330
  copying into new arrays, 575–576
  corresponding elements in parallel arrays, **342**
  deleting, 576, 577
  finding target values. *See* searching arrays
  index values, **328**
  of object/**String** arrays. *See* object array elements; **String** array elements
  passing into methods, 332–333, 362*qr*
  in pointer arrays. *See* pointer array elements
  sorting. *See* sorting arrays
  summation of, 331
  swapping values, 418–422
Array namespace, 405*qr*

arrays, **328**–361, 362–363*qr*
  big-O (order of complexity), 576, 577
  data types, 329
  declaring, 329–330
  dynamic. *See* dynamic arrays
  elements in. *See* array elements
  fixed-size problems, 575–578
  identification symbol/ delimiters ([ ]), 329, 330
  multidimensional arrays, **345**. *See also* two-dimensional arrays
  one-dimensional. *See* arrays (one-dimensional)
  of pointers. *See* pointer arrays
  sizing, 329
  two-dimensional. *See* two-dimensional arrays
arrays (one-dimensional), **328**–345, *328,* 362*qr,* 623*qr*
  adding elements to, 575–576, 577
  big-O (order of complexity), 576, 577
  declaring, 329–330
  deleting elements from, 576, 577
  dynamic. *See* dynamic arrays
  elements. *See* array elements
  exchanging values in, 418–422
  fixed-size problems, 575–578
  initializing, 329–330
  initializing pointer arrays from, 533–534
  vs. linked lists, 583
  of objects. *See* object arrays (**array** class objects); **String** arrays
  parallel arrays, 342–345
  passing into methods, 333–337, 362*qr*
  of pointers. *See* pointer arrays
  as pointers, 526–528
  searching. *See* searching arrays
  sorting. *See* sorting arrays
  of strings. *See* **String** arrays
  subscripts, **328**

  traversing, (331), (338–339), **347**–348
  tutorial, 348–361
  utilizing portions of, 577–578
  value lists, 330
arrow (–>): pointer member access operator, 45, **47**, 392, **597**
ascending order, **370**, **418**
ASCII (American Standard Code for Information Interchange) characters, **77**
  byte size, 119
  numerical equivalents and descriptions, 692–698*t*
assembly language, **17**
assigning characters to **int** variables, 120, 149–150
assigning **Graphics** objects to panels, 448
assigning pointers to nodes, 598
assigning strings:
  to **String** array elements, 389–390
  to textboxes, 48–49
assigning values:
  to array elements, 329–330
  to pointers, 516–517
  to variables, 82–83
assignment operator (=), 48–49, 82–83
  addition assignment process, 87–88, *88*
  vs. equal to operator (==), 168*n*
  shorthand operators, **92**–93, 153, 244–245, 246
associativity:
  of arithmetic operators, 87
  of relational operators, 168
asterisk (*):
  indirection operator, **519**, 521, 522*n*
  pointer declaration (data type) symbol, **515**, 522*n*
  See also multiplication operator
asterisk-equal sign (*=):
  multiplication assignment operator, 92, 244–245

asterisk-slash (* /): block
  comment delimiter, 102
asterisks (**):
  double indirection operator, **521**
  double pointer declaration
    symbol, 518, 539, 558
Atanasoff, John Vincent, 8
attributes (of classes). *See* data
  members (of classes)
attributes (of objects), **2**, *3, 5*
Auto-Hide button, 30
automated loom, 8
automatic code (C++):
  end region statement,
    226–227
  generation of, 5
averaging programs: general vs.
  single-purpose solutions,
  220–225

B

Babbage, Charles, 8
BackColor property, **146**
  specifying, 47–48, 56
background colors, changing:
  form colors, 56–57
  textbox colors, 55–56, 146
background images: adding to
  picture boxes, 303–306
backslash (\): escape character,
  253
Backus, John, 17
bar charts:
  drawing, 442, 443–445,
    447–449
  vertical bar chart project
    tutorial, 441–449
base 2 number system, **118**–119,
  153*qr*
base 10 number system, **118**,
  153*qr*
base case (of recursive method
  calls), **465**
base-10 integers: displaying
  numbers as, 150
BASIC (programming language), 18
Berry, Clifford, 8
big-O (order of complexity):
  of arrays, 576, 577
  of linked lists, 583

notation, 387, 405*qr*
of recursion, 496
of search methods, 387, 387*t*,
  405*qr*
of sort methods, 440
See also efficiency
binary arithmetic, **8**
binary computing devices, 8
binary conversion program
  tutorial, 127–152
binary number system, **118**–119,
  153*qr*
binary operators, **87**, **168**
binary searches (of arrays),
  370–380, 404–405*qr*
  algorithm, 371–378
  best-case scenario, 384
  big-O value, 387, 387*t*
  complexity function, 386, 387*t*
  example program, 378–380
  flow diagram, 377–378, *377*
  pointers in, 529–530
  results display, *394*
  variables required, 372, 404*qr,*
    529, 530
  worst-case scenario, 384–386
BinSearch() method, 378
  algorithm, 371–378
  code, 379–380
bits, **76**
  eight-bit bytes, 119
bitwise copying, **120**–121
black color coding, 47
block comment delimiters (/* * /),
  102
block comments, **102**, *103*
blue color coding, 47
bool data type, 77, 78*t*
  byte size, 119
  value range, *123*
Boolean expressions (conditional
  expressions), **166**, 168
  See also loop condition
Boolean values (Boolean data), **77**
  byte size, 119
  data type. *See* bool data type
borders (of textboxes): setting,
  146
BorderStyle property, **146**

boundaries (of textboxes): setting,
  146
break statements, 185–186,
  338
Brush objects, 291–292, 293
btnAdd_Click() event handler:
  algorithm and code, 227–228
btnBinSearch_Click() event
  handler: code, 402–403
btnCalc_Click() event
  handlers:
  algorithm, 191–195
  code, 205–207, 273–274,
    281–282, 285–286
btnClear_Click() event
  handlers:
  algorithm, 609
  code, 278
  code task, 622
btnConcat_Click() event
  handler: code, 247
btnConvert_Click() event
  handlers:
  algorithm, 133–134
  code, 149–151, 278
btnCreate_Click() event
  handler: algorithm, 257
btnData_Click() event
  handlers, 550
  algorithm, 551
  code, 258–259, 558–560
btnDelete_Click() event
  handler:
  algorithm, 608–609
  code task, 622
btnDisplay_Click() event
  handler: code, 517–518,
    520, 521–522
btnDraw_Click() event
  handler: code, 294
btnGroup_Click() event
  handler:
  algorithm, 352–353; trace
    table, 353–355
  code, 359–361
btnHead_Click() event
  handler:
  algorithm, 606
  code, 618

`btnInsert_Click()` event handler:
  algorithm, 606–608
  code, 618–619
`btnLarge_Click()` event handler: code, 525–526
`btnMean_Click()` event handler: code, 334
`btnRead_Click()` event handlers: code, 523, 524
`btnSearch_Click()` event handlers: code, 338, 343–344, 378–779, 381
`btnSeqSearch_Click()` event handler:
  algorithm, 397–398
  code, 401–402
`btnShow_Click()` event handler:
  algorithm, 351–352
  code, 357–359
`btnSort_Click()` event handlers, 442, 550
  algorithm, 551–552
  code, 446–447, 560
  variables required, 443*t*
`btnStart_Click()` event handler:
  algorithm, 661–662
  code, 639–640, 667–668
`btnStop_Click()` event handler: code, 669
bubble sort, 422, 428–431, 450*qr*, 451*qr*
  algorithm, 429
  big-O value, 440
  efficiency, 441
  inner loop, 429–431
  nested loops as used in, 423
  swapping pointers in pointer arrays, 541
bugs. *See* errors (programming errors)
`button1_Click()` event handler: algorithm and code, 100–102
buttons, 26, *26,* 57*qr*
  adding, 35, 36, 54
  click event handlers, 42–46, 54–55, 59–60*qr*.

See also `button1_Click()` event handler; *and specific* `btn..._Click()` *event handlers*
  double-clicking, 42
  naming conventions for, 130–131
bytes, **76**
  eight-bit bytes, 119

C

C (programming language), 18
C++ (programming language). *See* code; standard C++; Visual C++
`CalcMean()` method, 360, 361
Calculate buttons: algorithms, 191–195, 221
  See also `btnCalc_Click()` event handlers
calls. *See* method calls
camel notation, 82*t*
caret (^): handle operator/designator, 245, 388
case sensitivity: undoing, 404
case statements, 185–186
`Cell` class definition, 655–657
central processing unit (CPU), **6**, *7*
`char` data type, 77–78, 78*t*
  byte sizes, 119
  value range, *123*
`char` variables:
  assigning the first character in strings to, 149
  integers as assigned to, 120–121
character delimiters (' '), 78
characters (character data), **77**
  assigning the first character in strings to `char` variables, 149
  assigning to `int` variables, 120, 149–150
  as binary numbers, 119
  byte sizes, 119
  converting to numbers, 127–152
  data type. *See* `char` data type

delimiters (' '), 78
  See also `char` variables; strings
chips, 10
circles: drawing, 290–293
class definition files, 591–595, 624*qr*
  and client code, 595–596
  header. *See* header files
  implementation. *See* implementation files
  include files, 591–592
  `Node` class files. *See* `Node.cpp` file; `Node.h` file
class definitions, **2**, 18, 57*qr*, 583–584, 585–586, 672*qr*
  abstraction of, 586, *586,* 636–637, *636*
  `Cell` class definition, 655–657
  files. *See* class definition files
  form header files with, 34–35; opening, 39*n*
  `Frog` class definition, 638–639
  `Mouse` class definition, 652–654
  `Node` class definitions, 585–586, 589, 591, 603–604; files (*See* `Node.cpp` file; `Node.h` file)
  `ref` class definitions, **585**
class diagrams (UML), 589–591
class files. *See* class definition files
class members:
  data members, **585**
  definition order, 590–591
  encapsulation of, **585**
  See also methods
class methods, **270**
  system-defined. *See* `System` class (library) methods
class scope, **226**
class variables. *See* `static` variables
classes, 623*qr*
  data members, **585**

classes (*continued*):
  definition files. *See* class
    definition files
  definitions of. *See* class
    definitions
  instances, 585, *636.*
    See also objects
  methods belonging to. *See* class
    methods
  reference classes, **585**
    See also array class;
      Drawing class; Form1
      class; Node class
classroom seating chart program
  tutorial, 348–361
clearing textboxes, 278
click event handlers:
  for buttons, 42–46, 54–55,
    59–60*qr.*
    See also button1_Click()
      event handler; *and specific*
      btn..._Click() *event*
      handlers
  for menu items, 491–493
click events:
  for buttons, **26**
  for menu items, 478
    See also click event handlers
client code, **591**, 595, 624*qr,*
  648–650, 657
  and class definition files,
    595–596
  constants and instance
    variables, 617
  including header files in, 591,
    592, 593, 616, 655*n,*
    665, 702
  See also Form1.h file
Close() command, 491
closing curly bracket (}): missing
  '}' error, 702–704
closing programs, 42
closing windows, 29
CLR projects: creating, 27–28
COBOL (programming language),
  17
code (Visual C++ code), **5,** 46–49
  automatic. *See* automatic code
  for button click event
    handlers. *See under*

button1_Click() event
  handler; *and specific*
  btn..._Click() *event*
  handlers
client. *See* client code
color coding, 47
delimiters (( )), 44, 169, 185,
  186
for Form1_Load() event
  handlers. *See under*
  Form1_Load() event
  handlers
keywords (reserved words), 19,
  47; MSDN website
  resource, 692
for menu item click event
  handlers, 491–493
object code, **20**
redundancy. *See* code
  redundancy
source code, **20**
for specifying properties,
  45–46, 47–48
Windows Forms Designer code,
  47
code delimiters (( )), 44, 169,
  185, 186
code redundancy, **276,** 278–279
  reducing, 279, *280*
code reuse, 591, 650, 672*qr*
Code window (Code Editor
  window), **42–46**+*figs*
  Statement Completion
    Dropdown Box, 45, *45*
  switching to, 42, 135*n*
  tab label, 42, *43*
coding. *See* programming
colons. *See* double colon
color coding (in C++ statements),
  47
  MSDN website resource, 691
colors, changing:
  form colors, 56–57
  textbox colors, 55–56, 146
columns of two-dimensional
  arrays, **345**
ComboBoxes (drop-down lists),
  177–178, 203–204
  index values, **182,** 204

comma (,): parameter delimiter,
  85, 276
comments, **102,** *103,* 109*qr*
Compare() method, 391–392,
  405*qr*
comparing strings, 391–392
comparisons (in sequential
  searches): counting and
  logging, 340–341
compilation process, 20, *21*
compiler warnings, 121
compilers (language compilers),
  12
  Visual C++ compiler, 20
complexity. *See* big-O (order of
  complexity)
complexity functions: for array
  search methods, 386–387
component tray, **303**
components (of computers), 6–7,
  7, 57–58*qr*
components (of objects), **2**
ComputeMean() method,
  334–335, 336–337
computers:
  components, 6–7, *7,* 57–58*qr*
  concept coverage in this book,
    by chapter, 679–684*t*
  early developments, 8–9
  father of the computer, 8
  generations, 9–11, 58*qr*
    See also hardware; software
concatenating strings, 90–91
  integer concatenation program,
    245–246
concatenation assignment
  operator (+=), 246
concatenation operator (+),
  90–**91,** 246
conditional expressions (Boolean
  expressions), **166,** 168
  See also loop condition
const keyword, 295
constants, 294–296, **295**
  client code constants, 617
  declaring, 295
  PI (π), 273
  static. *See* static
    constants

constructors, 587–588, 624*qr*, 672*qr*
  declaring and execution of, 587
  default. *See* default constructor
  initializing constructors, 640–642, **641**
control key. *See* Ctrl key
Control Panel: Windows Vista interface, *15, 16*
control structures (of statements), **164**, 208–209*qr*
  sequential, *164,* **164**–166
  See also loops (repetition control structures); selection control structures
control tables, 108*qr,* **131**
  addition program, 96
  binary conversion program, 132
  fractal image generation program, 480
  planetary motion program, 299
  pointer array sorting program, 549
  quality control production log, 255
  vacation planner project, 189
controller (in computers), **6**
controls (on forms), **5**
  adding, 35–36
  changing properties, 37–38, 39
  double-clicking, 135*n*
  naming conventions for, 130–131
  tables. *See* control tables *See also* buttons; ComboBoxes; GroupBoxes; labels; `ListView` controls; `MenuStrip` controls; MessageBoxes; monthCalendar controls; panels; picture boxes; RadioButtons; textboxes
`Convert` class (library) methods, **122**
  MSDN website resource, 691
  `ToDouble()` method, 272
  See also `ToString()` method

converting:
  characters to numbers, 127–152
  data types. *See* data type conversion
  degrees to radians, 272–274, 289–290
  miles to kilometers, 277–278
  numbers to strings, 94
  strings to numbers, 85–86
`ConvertToRadians()` method, 289–290
copying: bitwise copying, **120**–121
`Cos()` method, 272, 274
counters, 225
  `for` loop counters, 235, *236*
counting, **225**–226
counting specific values programs, 250–251
`.cpp` file extension, 592
CPU (central processing unit), **6**, *7*
`CreateGraphics()` method, 292
Ctrl key (control key): selecting multiple objects, 99
curly brackets ({ }):
  array value list delimiters, 330
  code delimiters, 44, 169, 185, 186
  missing '}' error, 702–704
customizing the IDE, 28–**34**

D

data, 75, 76, 106*qr*
  accessing through pointers, 519–522
  converting. *See* data type conversion
  read, process, and display data basics, 75–95; tutorial, 95–104
  types. *See* data types
  values. *See* data values
  See also inputting data; outputting data; processing data

data averaging programs: general vs. single-purpose solutions, 220–225
data hiding, **642**–643
data members (of classes), **585**
  accessing, 597
  hiding, 642–643
  `public` vs. `private`, 644, *645*
  See also `private` data members
data processing. *See* processing data
data structures, **328**
  abstraction of. *See* abstraction *See also* arrays; linked lists; object arrays (`array` class objects); `String` arrays
data tables, **97**, 97*t,* 108*qr*
  addition program, 97
  binary conversion program, 132
  classroom seating chart program, 350–351
  creating, 252–253
  fractal image generation program, 480–481
  linked list program, 605–606
  maze program, 659–661
  planetary motion program, 299–301
  pointer array sorting program, 549–550
  quality control production log, 255–256
  vacation planner project, 189–190
  vertical bar chart project, 442–444
  video inventory search program, 396–397
data type conversion, 121–124, 154*qr*
  explicit, **122**, 125
  implicit, 122–124, **123**; in concatenation operations, 246
  type casting, **122**, 125, 514–515
  as useful, 125–126

data type hierarchy, **123**–124, *123*

data types, **77**–79, 106–107*qr*
of arrays, 329
converting. *See* data type conversion
DateTime type, 189–**190**; now variable, 247
demotion of, *123,* **124**
derived. *See* derived data types
hierarchy, **123**–124, *123*
integral. *See* integral data types
MSDN website resource, 691
of parameters, 272
pointer types, 515; return types, 525–526
primitive types, 77–**78**, 78–79*t*.
See also integral data types
promotion of, **123**, *123*
return types, **275**, *276;* pointer types, 525–526
`String` type, **79**

data values:
assigning to array elements, 329–330
assigning to variables, 82–83
counting specific values programs, 250–251
displaying array element values, 330, 559
finding the largest value, 249–250, 525–526; in arrays, 331–332
finding the smallest value in arrays, 426–428
literal values vs. instance variables, 294–295
searching for array element values. *See* searching arrays
swapping array element values, 418–422

DateTime class: MSDN website resource, 691

DateTime data type, 189–**190**
now variable, 247

"Debug" button, 20, 40

debugging programs, 20, *20,* 50–52

structured walk-throughs, **196**–200

decimal number system, **118**, 153*qr*

declaring arrays, 329–330
dynamic arrays, 526–527; pointer arrays, 532–533, 539
object arrays (`array` class objects), 388, 399–400
pointer arrays, 532–533, 539
two-dimensional arrays, 329, 346, 660–661

declaring constants, 295

declaring constructors, 587

declaring derived data types, 245, 388, 399–400

declaring handles, 648

declaring pointers, 515–516, *517, 519*
to pointers, 518, *519,* 539, 558

declaring variables, **80**
assignments made while, 513
instance variables, 226
`static` variables, 586
`String` variables, 245
See also declaring handles; declaring pointers

Decrease Horizontal Spacing button, **141**

decrementation operator(s), **233**

dedicated-purpose software, **11**

default constructor, 587–**588**
header file prototype, 594
implementation file definition, 593–594

degrees (of angles): converting to radians, 272–274, 289–290

`delete` operator, 531

`deleteList()` method:
algorithm, 609–610
code task, 622

deleting dynamic arrays, 531

deleting linked lists, 609–610

deleting memory allocated to pointers, 531

deleting nodes, 582–583, 608–609

demotion of data types, *123,* **124**

dereferencing, **519**–522
summation of pointer array elements by, 533

derived data types, **79**
declaring, 245, 388, 399–400
See also handles

descending order, **418**

design stage (of programming), 22, *23,* 59*qr*
addition program, 95–97
binary conversion program, 130–134
classroom seating chart program, 349–355
fractal image generation program, 478–487
"Hello World!" program, 25–26
linked list program, 603–610
maze program, 657–664
planetary motion program, 298–302
pointer array sorting program, 548–557
quality control production log, 255–257
vacation planner project, 188–200
vertical bar chart project, 442–445
video inventory search program, 394–398

Design window (Design view), 24, *24*
returning to, 39*n,* 135*n*
tab label, 42, *43*

destructors, 588–589, 624*qr*

development stage (of programming), 22, *23,* 59*qr*
addition program, 97–103
binary conversion program, 134–151
classroom seating chart program, 355–361
fractal image generation program, 487–495

"Hello World!" program, 26–46
linked list program, 611–621
maze program, 664–670
planetary motion program, 302–309
pointer array sorting program, 557–562
quality control production log, 257–259
vacation planner project, 200–207
vertical bar chart project, 445–449
video inventory search program, 398–403
device drivers, 12
direct lookup (of array element values), 380–383, 405*qr*
big-O value, 387, 387*t*
complexity function, 386, 387*t*
sequential search vs., 384
displaying data. *See* outputting data
`displayPtr()` method, 561
division:
integer division, **124**–127, 154*qr*
by zero, 21
division assignment operator (/=), 92
division operator (/), 86*t,* **106**, **124**
precedence in arithmetic expressions, 88–90
`do...while` loops, 233–235, 251, 260*qr*
docking windows, 33
documenting programs, 102
dot (.): member access operator, 597
double alternative selection control structures, **166**, *167,* 171–172
nested structures, 180–182, 182–185, 208
See also `if...else` statements

double colon (::): scope resolution operator, **85**, 271, 594, 598
`double` data type, 78, 79*t*
byte size, 119
value range, *123*
double indirection, **521**–522
double indirection operator (**), **521**
double pointer declaration symbol (**), 518, 539, 558
double quotes (""): string delimiters, 48, 245
double-clicking controls, 135*n*
buttons, 42
forms, 39*n*
double-precision numbers, **78**
data type, 78, 79*t*
`DrawArray()` method, 442, 443–445, 446
algorithm, 445
code, 447
signature, 444
variables required, 444*t*
`DrawBranch()` method, 474–476, 482, 483, 493
algorithm, 475–476, 483; trace tables, 483–487
arguments, 493–494
calls to, 484–487, 494, 497; multiple calls, 497
code, 494–495
lines drawn per level, 496
variables required, 477*t,* 481–482
`DrawFractal()` method, 482, 483
algorithm, 483
code, 493
`drawFrogs()` method, 649
`drawIcon()` method, 649
drawing:
bar charts, 442, 443–445, 447–449
fractal images, 474–476; at angles, 497–499; by hand, 470–473; tutorial, 477–499
icons, 649

lines, 473–474, 493–494; between textboxes (*See* `drawLines()` method); branching lines (*See* fractal images, *above*)
nodes, 597, 610
shapes: circles, 290–293; ellipses, 293–294, 296–298
variables required for, 442–443, 481
`Drawing` class, 290
objects, 291–293, 294, 313*qr,* 442, 443*t,* 444*t,* 660.
See also `Graphics` objects
`Drawing` namespace. *See* `System::Drawing` namespace
`DrawLine()` method, 473–474, 494
`drawLines()` method, 550
algorithm, 552–557
code, 561
variables required, 550
`drawMaze()` method:
algorithm, 662
code, 668
`drawNode()` method:
algorithm, 610
code, 619–621
`DrawRectangle()` method, 442
`DrawString()` method, 442, 444, 449
drop-down lists. *See* ComboBoxes
dynamic allocation of memory:
for arrays, 329, 527–528
for pointer arrays, 532–533, 539
for pointers, 516
dynamic arrays:
allocation of memory for, 329, 527–528; pointer arrays, 532–533, 539
declaring, 526–527; pointer arrays, 532–533, 539
deleting, 531
initializing, 528; pointer arrays, 532–534

E

edge() method:
  algorithm, 663–664
  code, 670
efficiency:
  of algorithms, 441
  of linked lists, 583
  See also big-O (order of
    complexity)
ellipses: drawing, 293–294,
  296–298
empty string, 245
encapsulation, **585**, 672*qr*
ENIAC (computer), 9, *10*
equal sign (=). *See* assignment
    operator
equal signs (==). *See* equal to
    operator
equal to operator (==), 167, 168*t*
  vs. assignment operator (=),
    168*n*
error bar, 52, *52*
error messages:
  '<event handler>': is not a
    member of
    '<program>::Form1',
    704–710
  '<event handler>':
    undeclared
    identifier, 704, 708
  Invalid Input, 333
  meaningless messages, 711
  missing ';' before '}',
    51–52
  missing ';' before
    'using', 701–704
errors (programming errors)
    (bugs), **20**, 50–51, 58–59*qr*
  changed event handler name
    error, 704–709
  common errors, 50, 701–710
  deleted event handler error,
    704, 709–710
  locating, 51–52
  without meaningful error
    messages, 711
  missing '}' error, 702–704
  types, 21
  See also error messages
escape character (\), **253**

escape character codes, **253**
  MSDN website resource, 691
'<event handler>': is not a
    member of
    '<program>::Form1' error
    message, 704–710
'<event handler>':
    undeclared identifier
    error message, 704, 708
event handlers, **5**, 270
  algorithms for: high-level and
    low-level, 75, 133–134.
  See also algorithms
  changed name error, 704–709
  creating, 490, 492
  deleted event handler error,
    704, 709–710
  parameters for, 276
  See also click event handlers;
    Form1_Load() event
    handlers; Tick event
    handlers
events: Tick() events, 299, 306;
    Timer_Tick() events, 650
  See also click events; event
    handlers
Events button (Properties
    window), 490, 492
exchanging values in arrays,
    418–422
exclamation mark (!):
  factorial symbol, 243, 460
  not operator, 173–174, 174*t*,
    333*n*
exclamation–equal sign (!=): not
    equal to operator, 167, 168*t*
explicit type conversion, **122**,
    125

F

factorial numbers, **243**
  calculating: with for loops,
    244–245, 460–461;
    recursive approach,
    461–462
  recursive algorithm, 463–465
  recursive method, 466–468
factorial symbol (!), 243, 460
Factorial() method, 466–468
fatal errors, 21, **51**

files:
  class. *See* class definition files
  header. *See* header files
  icon files, 638*n*, 650
  implementation. *See*
    implementation files
  include files, **591–592**
  source files, 35
FillEllipse() method,
    293–294
film inventory search program.
  See video inventory search
    program
finding target values in arrays.
  See searching arrays
finding the largest value,
    249–250, 525–526
  in arrays, 331–332
findLarge() method, 525–526
first generation of computers,
    9–10
flash memory, 7*n*
float data type, 78, 79*t*
  byte size, 119
Focus() method, 274
Font property: changing, 53–54,
    100
fonts, changing: textbox fonts,
    53–54, 100
for loops, 235–241, 260–261*qr*
  accessing array elements with,
    331, 338–339
  calculating factorial numbers,
    244–245, 460–461
  common tasks, 243–253
  counting comparisons in,
    340–341
  nested loops: creating data
    tables with, 252–253;
    sorting arrays with, 423;
    traversing two-dimensional
    arrays with, 347–348
  sequential search with,
    338–340
  summation formula as mapped
    into, 241–242
  termination of, 338–339
  traversing arrays with, (331),
    (338–339), **347**–348

ForeColor property: specifying, 56

foreground colors, changing: textbox colors, 55–56

Form1 class, 274–275
linked lists and, 578, 583

Form1 objects, 226n

Form1.h file, 34, *592, 593, 595*
including, 702
opening, 39n
See also client code

Form1_Load() event handlers, **147**–148, 155qr
algorithms: maze program, 661; quality control production log, 257; vacation planner project, 190
code: binary conversion program, 147–149; circle program, 294; classroom seating chart program, 357; fractal image generation program, 491; linked list program, 617; maze program, 666–667; mileage conversion program, 278; planetary motion program, 308; pointer array sorting program, 557–558; quality control production log, 258; vacation planner project, 205; vertical bar chart project, 446; video inventory search program, 400–401

Form Layout window, 24, *24*

form load event handlers. *See* Form1_Load() event handlers

formal parameter lists. *See* parameter lists (formal)

formal parameters, **281**
See also reference parameters; value parameters

forms (windows forms), **2**, *26*
changing colors, 56–57
changing properties, 38

creating windows forms applications, *28,* 34
double-clicking, 39n
header files for, 34–35; opening, 39n
sizing/resizing, 135
See also Windows Forms Designer

formula translation: summation formula as mapped into loops, 241–243

FORTRAN (programming language), 17

fourth generation of computers, 10–11

fractal image generation program tutorial, 477–499

fractal images, **469**, *469,* 500qr
drawing, 474–476; at angles, 497–499; by hand, 470–473; tutorial, 477–499

Frog class definition, 638–639, 646–647

frog race program, 637–650

G

gc heap (garbage collection heap): locating objects in, 584

gcnew operator (command), 247, 584

general forms of statements. *See* syntax

general solutions vs. single-purpose solutions, **223**
for data averaging programs, 220–225

general-purpose software, **11**

GenerateData() method, 334–335, 335–336

generating fractal images, 474–476
tutorial, 477–496

generating random numbers, 246–248, 558

get methods (getters) (accessors), **643**–644, 672qr

GetNum() method, 333

getX method, 643

grading program:
with selection control structures: double alternative, 171–172; single alternative, 169–170
with sequential control structures only, 165–166

graphical user interfaces (GUIs), **2**
program interfaces. *See* interfaces (program interfaces)
Windows Vista interface, 12–16

Graphics objects, 291–294, 313qr, 442
assigning to panels, 448
displaying, 640
drawing. *See under* drawing
initializing, 639–640; with constructors, 640–642
instance methods for, 292–294, 442, 443–445; MSDN website resource, 692
instantiating, 639–640

greater than operator (>), 168t

greater than or equal to operator (>=), 168t

GroupBoxes, 201–202

guide diamonds, *33*

GUIs. *See* graphical user interfaces; interfaces (program interfaces)

H

.h suffix, 34, 591

handle operator/designator (^), 245, 388

handlers. *See* event handlers

handles (handle variables), 245, 388, 399–400, 584
declaring, 648
initializing, 584

hardware, 6–7
architecture, **17**
development history, 8–11
hardware/software/user relationship, *17*
Windows Vista Control Panel information on, *16*

hardware/software/user relationship, *17*

head (head pointer), **579**, **580**

head node, **580**
  creating, 606

header files, **34**, 591–592
  creating, 611–613, *615*
  for forms, 34–35; opening, 39*n*
  and implementation files, *592, 592, 593, 595,* 655*n*
  including, 591, *592, 593,* 616, 655*n*, 665, 702
  method prototypes in, **594**
  See also Form1.h file; Node.h file

header lines. *See* signatures (header lines) (of methods)

heap (memory resource), 516
  returning memory to, 531
  See also gc heap

Height property, 553

"Hello World!" program tutorial, 25–49

hiding data members, 642–643

high-level algorithms, **75**, **133**, 133

high-level programming languages, **17**–19, *19*

hop() method, 646, 650

Hopper, Grace, 17

I

icon files (for object-oriented programs), 638*n,* 650

icons:
  changing, 649–650
  drawing, 649
  Stick pin icon, 30, *30*

ICs (integrated circuits), **10**

IDE (Visual Studio), 19, 23–25, *24, 29,* 59*qr*
  customizing, 28–34
  tutorial, 25–49

IDEs (integrated development environments), **19**
  See also IDE (Visual Studio)

if statements, 168–170, **169**
  multiple action statements in, 169–170

if...else if...else statements, 184–185
  vs. switch statements, 185

if...else statements, **169**, 171–172
  multiple alternative statements, 184–185
  nested structures, 181–182, 183–185, 208, 344

Image property, 304

implementation, **586**
  of class definitions, *586, 636*

implementation files, 592–595
  header files and, *592, 592, 593, 595,* 655*n*
  Mouse class file, 654–655
  See also Node.cpp file

implicit type conversion, 122–124, **123**
  in concatenation operations, 246

#include directive, 591–592

include files, **591–592**

including header files, 591, *592, 593,* 616, 655*n*, 665, 702

incrementation operator(s), **233**

incrementing pointers, 529

index value delimiters ([ ]) (array elements), *328*

index values (of array elements), **328**

index values (of ComboBoxes), **182**, 204

indirection, **519**–522, 564–565*qr*
  double indirection, **521**–522

indirection operator (*), **519**, 521, 522*n*

inductive definitions, **469**

initialization clause (in for loops), **236**, *236*

initializing arrays, 329–330
  dynamic arrays, 528; pointer arrays, 532–534, 559
  pointer arrays, 532–534, 559

initializing constructors, 640–642, **641**, 657

initializing Graphics objects, 639–640
  with constructors, 640–642

initializing handles, 584

initializing pointers, 516–517, 553, 556

initializing variables, 82–83
  See also initializing handles; initializing pointers

input devices, **6**, *7*

inputting data (reading data): basics, 84–86
  See also specific algorithms, programs, and tutorials

inserting nodes, 580–581, 606–608

insertion sort, 422, 432–440, 451*qr*
  algorithm, 432–438
  big-O value, 440
  efficiency, 441
  inner loop, 438–440
  nested loops as used in, 423
  variables required, 438

instance methods, **270**, 311*qr*, 312*qr*
  accessor methods, **643**–644, 672*qr*
  application methods, **270**–271, 274–276, *277.*
  See also event handlers; programmer-defined methods
  constructors, 587–588
  destructors, 588–589
  for Graphics objects, 292–294, 442, 443–445; MSDN website resource, 692
  mutator methods, **643**, 644, 645, 654, 672*qr*
  with parameters, 281–288; reference parameters, 285–288, 311, 522–523; value parameters, 281–285, 311
  without parameters, 277–280
  passing array elements into, 362*qr;* by reference, 333; by value, 332–333
  passing arrays into, 333–337, 362*qr*

with return values, 288–290,
310, 313*qr;* seqSearch()
method, 343
without return values. *See* void
methods
system-defined methods, 274
utility methods, 645–646, 650
See also event handlers;
programmer-defined
methods; *and specific
instance methods*
instance variables, **226**–228,
260*qr*
client code variables, 617
declaring, 226
as handles, 400
vs. literal values, 294–295
vs. local variables, 226
static. *See* static variables
instances of classes, 585, *636*
See also objects
instantiating objects, 587
Graphics objects, 639–640
Node objects, 597
instruction lists. *See* algorithms
instruction position indicators (in
computers), **6**
int data type, 78, 79*t*
byte size, 119
int variables: assigning
characters to, 120, 149–150
Int32 class (library) methods,
271, 272
See also TryParse() method
integer concatenation program,
245–246
integer division, **124**–127, 154*qr*
integer division operator (/), **106**,
124
precedence in arithmetic
expressions, 88–90
integer quotient, **125**
integer remainders, **126**–127
displaying, 150–151
integers (integer/integral data),
78, 118–153, 153–155*qr*
as assigned to char variables,
120–121
byte sizes, 119

concatenation program,
245–246
converting strings to, 85–86
converting to strings, 94
data types. *See* integral data
types
displaying, 150
tutorial, 127–152
See also int variables
integral data types, **119**–121
value ranges, *123*
See also bool data type; char
data type; int data type;
long data type; short
data type
integrated circuits (ICs), **10**
integrated development
environments. *See* IDEs
IntelliSense feature, 45
interfaces (program interfaces), **2**
addition program, 96*sk,*
98–102
binary conversion program,
130–131*sk,* 134–147
classroom seating chart
program, 349–350*sk,* 356
component tray beneath, **303**
fractal image generation
program, 477*sk,* 478–480,
487–490
frog race program, 637–638
"Hello World!" program,
26–34
inventory program, 342, *343*
linked list program, 598–603,
604, 611
maze program, 651, 659,
664–665
modifying, 104–105
objects: making active, 36.
See also controls; forms
(windows forms)
planetary motion program,
298–299*sk,* 302–307
pointer array sorting program,
545–547, 548–549, 557
quality control production log,
255, 258
vacation planner project,
188*sk,* 200–207

vertical bar chart project,
441–442*sk*
video inventory search program,
394–395*sk,* 399
See also graphical user
interfaces (GUIs)
Interval property: setting,
306–307
Invalid Input error message,
333
inventory program, 342–343
interface, 342, *343*
See also video inventory search
program
Items collections, 398–399
Items property, 203, 398
iteration, **229**
recursion vs., 468–469
See also repetition

J

Jacquard, Joseph Marie, 8
Java (programming language), **19**
Java Virtual Machine, **19**

K

Kay, Alan, 18
Kemeny, John, 18
keywords (reserved words), 19,
47, 698
standard C++ keywords, 699*t*
Visual C++ keywords: MSDN
website resource, 692
kilometers: converting miles to,
277–278
Kurtz, Thomas, 18

L

labels (Label controls): adding,
98, 143
language compilers. *See*
compilers
language independence (of
algorithms), **75**
languages. *See* programming
languages
largest value, finding, 249–250,
525–526
in arrays, 331–332

less than operator (<), 168*t*

less than or equal to operator (<=), 168*t*

libraries: programming libraries, **19**

line comment indicator (//), 102

line comments, **102**, *103*

lines, drawing, 473–474, 493–494

between textboxes.*See* drawLines() method

branching lines.*See* fractal images

linked list program tutorial, 598–623

linked lists, 574, **578**–623, 623–624*qr*

vs. arrays, 583

big-O values, 583

creating, 580–581, 583–584

deleting, 609–610

efficiency, 583

and Form1 class, 578, 583

nodes.*See* nodes (Node objects)

tutorial, 598–623

LINUX operating system, 12

LISP (programming language), 17

lists, **574**

abstraction of, 574, 579, 623*qr*

linked.*See* linked lists

sorted lists: searching, 370–371

See also actual argument lists; ComboBoxes (drop-down lists); ListView controls; parameter lists (formal); value lists (for arrays)

ListView controls, **394**, 398–399

populating, **394**, 401

literal values: vs. instance variables, 294–295

load event handlers. *See* Form1_Load() event handlers

local variables, 226, 300

locating objects in the gc heap, 584

Location property, 552, 553

locking windows in place, 30

logic errors, **21**

logical operators, 172–180, **173**, 209*qr*

See also and operator (&&); not operator (!); or operator (||)

long data type:

byte size, 119

value range, *123*

loom, automated, 8

loop body, **229**

loop condition, **229**

in for loops, **236**, *236*

pointer arithmetic in, 529

loop control variable, **229**

in for loops, 235, *236*

incrementation/decrementation of, 232–233, 235

loops (repetition control structures), 229–241

body, **229**

common tasks, 241–253

control variable, **229**; incrementation/decrementation of, 232–233

do...while loops, 233–235, 251, 260*qr*

for.*See* for loops

iteration of, **229**; recursion vs., 468–469.

See also repetition

pre-test vs. post-test loops, **229**, *230*

summation formula as mapped into, 241–243

tutorial, 254–259

while loops, 230–233, 251, 260*qr*; summation formula as mapped into, 243

Lovelace, Ada, 8

low-level algorithms, **75**, **133**, 133–134

M

machine language, **17**

maroon color coding, 47

Math class (library) methods, 93–94, 272–274

MSDN website resource, 692

parameters, 94, 272

MaxLength property: changing, 138

maze program tutorial, 650–671

McCarthy, John, 17

mean calculation program, 334

member access operator (.), 597

memory (primary storage), **6**, *7*

allocation (static allocation) of, 77, 80–81, 513–514; for arrays, 329; for two-dimensional arrays, 346

deleting memory allocated to pointers, 531

dynamic allocation of: for arrays, 329, 527–528; for pointer arrays, 532–533; for pointers, 516

flash memory, *7n*

heap resource.*See* heap

managing, 512

memory cell addresses, **80**

assigning to pointers, 516–517

displaying, 514–515, 517–518, 559

memory cells, 79

menu headings, **478**, *478, 479*

creating, 478, 487–488, 489, 497–498

menu items, **478**, *478, 479*

algorithms, 482

click event handlers, 491–493

inserting, 478, 487–490, 497–498

MenuStrip controls, **478**–479, 480*t*, 487

MessageBoxes, 174–176

method body, 275, *276*

method calls, 281, 285, 312*qr*

actual arguments, **281**

DrawBranch() method calls, 484–487, 494, 497; multiple calls, 497

drawNode() method call, 619–620

for passing array elements into methods, 332

for passing arrays into methods, 334

recursive calls, 460, **465**;
DrawBranch() method
calls, 484–487, 494, 497;
drawNode() method call,
619–620
Swap() method call, 420
to void methods, 280,
282–284
method definitions, **275**–276,
276, 312qr
method names, **275**, *276*
method prototypes, **594**
method signature lines. *See*
signatures (header lines) (of
methods)
methods, **2**, *3, 5*, **270**–311,
311–313*qr*
access modes, **275**, *276*
actual argument lists, 281
actual arguments, **281**
application. *See* application
methods
body, 275, *276*
calls to. *See* method calls
class. *See* class methods
components, 275–276, *276*
Convert class. *See* Convert
class (library) methods
definitions, **275**–276, *276,*
312qr
Drawing class methods,
292–294
Graphics object methods,
292–294
instance. *See* instance methods
Int32 class methods, 271,
272.
See also TryParse()
method
Math class. *See* Math class
(library) methods
names, **275**, *276*
parameter lists (formal), **85**,
275, *276*, **281**
parameters. *See* parameters (of
methods)
with parameters, 281–288;
reference parameters,
285–288, 311, 522–523;

value parameters,
281–285, 311
without parameters, 277–280
programmer-defined. *See*
programmer-defined
methods
prototypes, **594**
recursive. *See* recursion
return types, **275**, *276;* pointer
types, 525–526
with return values, 288–290,
310, 313*qr;* seqSearch()
method, 343
without return values. *See* void
methods
signature lines. *See* signatures
(header lines) (of methods)
String operations, 391–392;
MSDN website resource,
692
System class. *See* System
class (library) methods
system-defined. *See* system-
defined methods
tutorial, 296–310
types, 270–271, *270, 271,*
277
value-returning methods,
288–290, 310
void. *See* void methods *See*
also instance methods; *and*
specific methods
microprocessors, 10–11
miles: converting to kilometers,
277–278
minus sign (–): private access
mode symbol, 590
See also subtraction operator
minus–equal sign (–=):
subtraction assignment
operator, 92
missing '}' error, 702–704
missing ';' before '}' error
message, 51–52
missing ';' before 'using'
error message, 701–704
mod assignment operator (%=),
92
mod operator (modulus operator)
(%), 87*t,* **126**–127

precedence in arithmetic
expressions, 88
monthCalendar controls,
189–190
Mouse class:
definition, 652–654
implementation file, 654–655
moving projects, 40
Multiline property, **146**
multiple alternative if
statements, 184–185
vs. switch statements, 185
multiple alternative selection
control structures, 182–185
multiplication assignment
operator (*=), 92, 244–245
multiplication operator (*), 86*t,*
precedence in arithmetic
expressions, 88–90
mutator methods, **643**, 644, 645,
654, 672*qr*

N

\n escape character code, 253
Name property, 37
names: for methods, **275**, *276*
namespaces:
Array namespace, 405*qr*
System namespace, 270;
MSDN website resource,
692
System::Drawing
namespace, 313; MSDN
website resource, 692
naming conventions: for controls,
130–131
naming rules: for variables,
81–82
nested double alternative
selection control structures,
180–182, 182–185, 208,
344
nested for loops:
creating data tables with,
252–253
sorting arrays with, 423
traversing two-dimensional
arrays with, 347–348

nested if...else statements, 181–182, 183–185, 208, 344

nested parentheses: in arithmetic expressions, 90

new operator, 516, 563*qr,* 564*qr*
  declaring dynamic arrays, 526–527; pointer arrays, 532–533
  declaring pointer arrays, 532–533

gcnew operator, 247, 584

Next() method, 247, 274

Node class, 585–589
  constructors, 587; default constructor, 588
  definition files. *See* Node.cpp file; Node.h file
  definitions, 585–586, 589, 591, 603–604
  UML class diagram, *604*

Node.cpp file, 592
  code, 593–594, 616
  creating, 611–613, *615*
  Node.h and, *592,* 592, *593, 595*

Node.h file, 591
  code, 615
  creating, 611–613, *614*
  including, 591, *592, 593,* 616
  and Node.cpp, *592,* 592, *593, 595*

nodes (Node objects), **578**–583, 583, 596–598, 623*qr*
  accessing, 583, 597
  assigning pointers to, 598
  constructing (drawing), 597, 610
  deleting, 582–583, 608–609
  head node, **580**; creating, 606
  inserting, 580–581, 606–608
  instantiating, 597

not equal to operator (!=), 167, 168*t*

not operator (!), 173–174, 174*t,* 333*n*

now variable, 247

null pointer, **516, 579**

nullptr keyword, 516, 579

number sign (#): protected access mode symbol, 590

numbers:
  aligning (in textboxes), 146
  binary system, **118**–119, 153*qr*
  as constants. *See* constants
  converting characters to: binary conversion program, 127–152
  converting strings to, 85–86
  converting to strings, 94
  counting specific values programs, 250–251
  data types, 77–79, 78–79*t*
  decimal system, **118,** 153*qr*
  displaying as base-10 integers, 150
  factorials. *See* factorial numbers
  finding target values in arrays. *See* searching arrays
  finding the largest value, 249–250, 525–526; in arrays, 331–332
  as instance variables vs. literal values, 294–295
  random. *See* random numbers
  as strings, 84

O

object array elements: setting the value of, 389–390
object arrays (array class objects), 387
  constructing, 388–389
  declaring, 388
  sorting, 391
  See also String arrays
object code, **20**
object event tables:
  classroom seating chart program, 350
  video inventory search program, 395
object-oriented programming (OOP), 636–671, 672*qr*
  basic concepts, 2–6.
  See also classes; methods; objects

encapsulation, **585,** 672*qr*
  languages, **2,** 18–19, 387
  tutorial, 650–671
  See also object-oriented programs
object-oriented programming languages, **2,** 18–19, 387
object-oriented programs:
  creating, 4–6
  frog race program, 637–650
  icon files for, 638*n*
  maze program, 650–671
objects, **2,** 57*qr,* 584, 585, 623*qr,* 636, 672*qr*
  arrays of. *See* object arrays (array class objects)
  design specifications, 2, 3–4
  Drawing class objects, 291–294, 313*qr*
  instantiating, 587; Graphics objects, 639–640; Node objects, 597
  interface objects: making active, 36.
  See also controls; forms (windows forms)
  locating in the gc heap, 584
  methods belonging to. *See* instance methods
  referencing, 245, 388, 584
  selected object indicators, 35
  selecting multiple objects, 99, 140
  vs. variables, 84
one-dimensional arrays. *See* arrays (one-dimensional)
OOP. *See* object-oriented programming
Open Source Movement, **12**
opening:
  form header files, 39*n*
  the Properties window, 31
  the Toolbox, 30
  windows, 53
operands, **86**
operating systems, 11, 12
  Windows Vista interface, 12–16
operator overloading, **90**

operator precedence rules, **88**–90, 180
  MSDN website resource, 692
operators:
  address-of operator (`&`), 285, 514, 523
  arithmetic. *See* arithmetic operators
  binary operators, **87**, **168**
  `delete` operator, 531
  handle operator/designator (`^`), 245, 388
  logical. *See* logical operators
  overloading of, **90**
  precedence rules, **88**–90, 180; MSDN website resource, 692
  relational operators, **167**–168
optional feature delimiters ([ ]), 185
or operator (| |), 178–180, 179*t*
  vs. and operator (`&&`), 176–178, 179
order of complexity. *See* big-O (order of complexity)
output devices, **6**, *7*
Output window, 51, *51*
outputting data (displaying data): basics, 94–95
  See also specific algorithms, programs, and tutorials

P

panels (`panel` controls), 349, 356
  assigning `Graphics` objects to, 448
parallel arrays, 342–345
parameter delimiter (`,`), 85
parameter lists (formal), **85**, **275**, *276*, **281**
  See also actual argument lists
parameters (of methods), **85**, **272**, 321*qr*
  actual. *See* actual arguments
  data types, 272
  delimiter for, 85, 276
  for event handlers, 276

formal parameters, **281**.
  See also reference parameters; value parameters
  lists. *See* parameter lists (formal)
  `Math` class method parameters, 94, 272
  methods with, 281–288; reference parameters, 285–288, 311, 522–523; value parameters, 281–285, 311
  methods without, 277–280
parentheses (()):
  in arithmetic expressions, 89–90, 108*qr*
  in type casting, 122, 125, 514–515
parsing strings, **85**–86, 107*qr*
  importance, 92
Pascal (programming language), 18
Pascal notation, 82*t*
pass-by-reference method:
  using pointers, 523–524, 564*qr*
  using reference parameters, **285**–288, 311, 312*qr*, 522–523; for passing arrays/array elements, 333–337, **335**
pass-by-value method:
  using value parameters, 281–285, **284**, 312*qr*; passing arrays/array elements, 332–333, **335**
passing array elements into methods, 332–333, 362*qr*
passing arrays into methods, 333–337, 362*qr*
percent sign (%). *See* mod operator
percent–equal sign (%=): mod assignment operator, 92
PI (π): constant, 273
picture boxes (PictureBox controls), **299**, 313*qr*
  adding background images to, 303–306
pipes. *See* or operator (| |)

planetary motion program tutorial, 296–310
plus sign (+): `public` access mode symbol, 590
  See also addition operator; concatenation operator
plus–equal sign (+=):
  addition assignment operator, 92
  concatenation assignment operator, 246
pointer arithmetic, **528**–530, 556, 564*qr*
pointer array elements: summation of, 533
pointer array sorting program tutorial, 545–563
pointer arrays, 532–534, 564*qr*
  declaring, 532–533, 539
  dynamic allocation of memory for, 532–533, 539
  initializing, 532–534, 559
  sorting arrays with, 536–544; tutorial, 545–563
  summation of elements in, 533
  swapping pointers in, 537–538, 540, 541, 564*qr*; `swap()` method, 541–544
pointer data types, 515
  return types, 525–526
pointer declaration (data type) symbol (`*`), **515**, 522*n*
pointer member access operator (–>), 45, **47**, 392, **597**
pointers (pointer variables), 512–563, **515**, 563–564*qr*
  accessing data through, 519–522
  arrays as, 526–528
  arrays of. *See* pointer arrays
  assigning addresses to, 516–517
  assigning to nodes, 598
  basic concepts, 513–522
  in binary searches, 529–530
  calculating. *See* pointer arithmetic
  declaration (data type) symbol (`*`), **515**, 522*n*

pointers (pointer variables),
(*continued*):
declaring, 515–516, *517, 519*
deleting memory allocated to,
531
displaying, 517–518
double declaration symbol
(`**`), 518, 539, 558
incrementing, 529
initializing, 516–517, 553,
556
in nodes of linked lists,
578–583
null pointer, **516**, **579**
pass-by-reference using,
523–524, 564*qr*
pointers to. *See* pointers to
pointers
swapping in pointer arrays,
537–538, 540, 541,
564*qr;* `swap()` method,
541–544
See also handles
pointers to pointers:
declaring, 518, *519,* 539, 558
displaying, 518
populating `ListView` controls,
394, 401
post-test loops, **229**, *230*
See also `do...while` loops
postfix incrementation/
decrementation operators,
233
pound sign (#): `protected`
access mode symbol, 590
`Pow()` method, 93–94
`#pragma endregion` statement,
226–227
`#pragma once` directive, 616
pre-test loops, **229**, *230*
See also `for` loops; `while`
loops
precedence. *See* operator
precedence rules
prefix incrementation/
decrementation operators,
233
preprocessor directives, 624*qr*
`#include` directive,
591–592

`#pragma endregion`
statement, 226–227
`#pragma once` directive, 616
primary storage. *See* memory
primitive data types, 77–**78**,
78–79*t*
See also integral data types
`private` access mode
(modifier), 590–**591**, 642
`private` access mode symbol
(-), 590
`private` data members:
in the `Frog` class definition,
646–647
getting data from, 643
`public` data members vs.,
644, 645
setting data in, 644, 645
`private` methods, 275
problem solving, 74–76
See also debugging programs
problem-analysis/description
stage (of programming), 22,
23, 59qr
addition program, 95
binary conversion program,
127–130
classroom seating chart
program, 348
fractal image generation
program, 477
"Hello World!" program, 25
linked list program, 598–603
maze program, 651
planetary motion program,
296–298
pointer array sorting program,
545–547
quality control production log,
254–255
vacation planner project,
186–187
vertical bar chart project,
441–442
video inventory search program,
392–394
procedural languages, 18
`ProcessAndDisplay()`
method, 282–285
processing data:

conversion requirements, 79
read, process, and display data
basics, 75–95; tutorial,
95–104
See also arrays; loops
(repetition control
structures); selection
control structures; *and
specific algorithms,
programs, and tutorials*
product accumulation, 243–245
programmer-defined methods,
270–271, **276**–290,
312–313*qr*
with parameters, 281–288;
reference parameters,
285–288, 311, 522–523;
value parameters,
281–285, 311
without parameters, 277–280
reasons for writing, 276–277
with return values, 288–290,
310, 313*qr;* `seqSearch()`
method, 343
without return values. *See* `void`
methods
types, *277*
See also instance methods;
*and specific programmer-
defined methods*
programmers: the first
programmer, 8
programming (coding):
errors in. *See* errors
(programming errors)
event handlers. *See* click event
handlers; `Form1_Load()`
event handlers; `Tick` event
handlers
process, 19–20
stages, 22, *23, 59qr*
tutorial, 25–49
See also code; debugging
programs
programming errors. *See* errors
programming languages, 58*qr*
assembly language, **17**
high-level languages, **17**–19,
19
machine language, **17**

object-oriented languages, **2**, 18–19, 387.
See also Visual C++
programming libraries, **19**
programs:
  as class definitions, 2
  closing, 42
  compilation process, 20, *21*
  debugging, 20, *20*, 50–52;
    structured walk-throughs, **196**–200
  documenting, 102
  rebuilding, 711
  running, 40–42
  testing, 49
  See also programming;
    projects; *and specific programs*
project development cycle, 22, *23*, 59*qr*
projects:
  creating, 26–28
  development cycle, 22, *23*, 59*qr*
  moving, 40
  saving, 27, 39–40
promotion of data types, **123**, *123*
properties:
  changing, 37–39
  specifying, 45–46, 47–48
  textbox property settings, 147*t*
  See also under Properties
    window; *and specific properties*
Properties window, *24*, 25, *32*, 37–39
  displaying, 31–33, 34, 37
  Events button, 490, 492
  opening, 31
  properties displayed in, 36, 37;
    for multiple selected objects, 99
property specifier (–>) (pointer membership operator), 45, 47, 392
`protected` access mode, **588**
`protected` access mode symbol (#), 590
pseudocode, **75**

`public` access mode (modifier), **590**–591
`public` access mode symbol (+), 590
`public` data members, 647
  in the `Frog` class definition, 647
  vs. `private` data members, 644, 645
punched card technology, 8

Q

quality control production log tutorial, 254–259
question mark (?): undefined variable symbol, 197
quotients:
  integer quotient, **125**
  truncation of, **124**–125

R

\r escape character code, 253
radians: converting degrees to, 272–274, 289–290
RadioButtons, 201–202, 205
  placing, 201*n*
RAM (random access memory), **6**
random access, **583**
random access memory (RAM), **6**
random number generator program, 247–248
  counting specific values programs use of, 250–251
  finding the largest value program use of, 249–250
random number generators, **246**, 558
  seeding, 247
`Random` number objects:
  constructing, 247
random numbers, **246**
  generating, 246–248, 558
read, process, and display data
  basics, 75–95
  tutorial, 95–104
`read()` method, 523
read-only memory (ROM), **6**
`ReadData()` method, 285–288
reading data. *See* inputting data
`ReadOnly` property, **144**

real numbers, **78**
  byte sizes, 119
  data types, 78, 79*t*
rebuilding programs, 711
record arrays, 534–536
  sorting, 536–544
records, **534**
`Rectangle` objects, 291, 292
  constructing, 293, 357–359, 442, 444, *447–448*F, 643
recursion, **462**–468, 499–500*qr*
  additional levels and processing time, 496
  analysis of, 496
  big-O values, 496
  calculating factorial numbers, 461–462
  in drawing fractal images, 474–476; at angles, 497–499; by hand, 470–473; tutorial, 477–499
  `drawNode()` method algorithm, 610
  factorial algorithm, 463–465
  `Factorial()` method, 466–468
  inductive definitions, **469**
  vs. iteration, 468–469
  method calls, 460, **465**;
    `DrawBranch()` method calls, 484–487, 494, 497
  tutorial, 477–499
  See also `DrawBranch()` method
recursive backtracking, **465**, *468*
recursive cases (of recursive method calls), **465**
redundancy. *See* code redundancy
`ref` class definitions, **585**
reference classes, **585**
reference method. *See* pass-by-reference method
reference parameters, **285**, 312*qr*
  declaration symbol (&), 285, 514

reference parameters (*continued*):
  pass-by-reference using, **285**–288, 311, 312*qr*, 522–523; for passing arrays/array elements, 333–337, **335**
referencing objects, 245, 388, 584
registers (in computers), **6**
relational operators, **167**–168
  associativity, 168
remainders. *See* integer remainders
renaming textboxes, 144
repetition, 220–259, 260–261*qr*
  control structures.*See* loops
  general vs. single-purpose solutions, **223**; for data averaging programs, 220–225
  recursion vs. iteration, 468–469
  user-controlled repetition, **220**–228
repositioning windows, 33
reserved words. *See* keywords
Reset() method, 279, *280,* 280
reset() method, 617, 649
resizing forms, 135
resizing handles (white squares), 35, *35*
return statements, **289**
return types (of methods), **275,** *276*
  pointer types, 525–526
return values:
  data types.*See* return types (of methods)
  methods with, 288–290, 310, 313*qr*; seqSearch() method, 343
  methods without.*See* void methods
Ritchie, Dennis, 18
\r\n escape character code, 253
ROM (read-only memory), **6**
row-major order (in two-dimensional arrays), **345**

rows of two-dimensional arrays, **345**
running programs, 40–42
runtime errors, **21**

S

Save All command, 39–40
Save As command, 39
saving projects (programs), 27, 39–40
scope (visibility):
  class scope, **226**
  of public vs. private data members, 644, *645*
scope resolution operator (::), **85,** 271, 594, 598
search domain, **370**
search logs, 341, 404
searching arrays (for target element values):
  binary search method.*See* binary searches
  complexity functions, 386, 387*t*
  direct lookup method.*See* direct lookup (of array element values)
  for the largest value, 331–332
  methods (techniques), 380–386, 405*qr*; determining the best, 386–387
  sequential search method.*See* sequential searches
  for the smallest value, 426–428
  tutorial, 392–403
searching for strings, 387–392
searching sorted lists, 370–371
  See also binary searches
seating chart program tutorial, 348–361
second generation of computers, 10
secondary storage (storage), **7,** *7*
seeding random number generators, 247
selected object indicators, 35

SelectedIndex property, 182, 205
selecting objects: multiple objects, 99, 140
selection control structures, *164,* **166**–167, 208–209*qr*
  double alternative structures, **166,** *167,* 171–172. *See also* if...else statements
  multiple alternative structures, 182–185. *See also* switch statements
  nested structures, 180–182, 182–185, 208, 344
  single alternative structures, **166,** *167,* 168–170. *See also* if statements
  tutorial, 186–207
selection sort, 422, 424–428, 450*qr,* 451*qr*
  algorithm, 425
  big-O value, 440
  efficiency, 441
  inner loop, 426–428
  nested loops as used in, 423
  variables required, 426
SelectionStart property, 205–206
semicolon (;): statement terminator, 49, 585
seqSearch() method, 338
  code, 341
  with return value, 343
sequential access, **583**
sequential control structures, *164,* **164**–166
sequential searches (of arrays), 337–341, 370
  big-O value, 387, 387*t*
  complexity function, 386, 387*t*
  counting comparisons in, 340–341
  vs. direct lookup method, 384
  logging comparisons in, 341
  in parallel arrays, 343–344
  results display, *393*
  scenarios, best-case to worst, 383–384

set methods (setters) (mutators), **643**, 644, 645, 654, 672*qr*

SetValue() method, 389–390, 400

setX() method, 644, 645, 649

shapes, drawing:
circles, 290–293
ellipses, 293–294, 296–298

short data type:
byte size, 119
value range, *123*

shorthand assignment operators, **92**–93, 153, 244–245, 246

Show() method, 175

showIcon() method, 638–639, 649

ShowNum() method, 332–333

signatures (header lines) (of methods), **275**, *276*
with an array as a formal parameter, 335
constructor signatures, 587
DrawArray() method signature, 444
drawNode() method signature, 619

Simula (programming language), 18

Sin() method, 272, 274

single alternative selection control structures, **166**, *167*, 168–170
See also if statements

single quotes (' '): character delimiters, 78

single-precision numbers, **78**
data type, 78, 79*t*

single-purpose solutions vs. general solutions, **223**
for data averaging programs, 220–225

Size property, 135, 136

SizeMode property, 305

sizing arrays, 329

sizing forms, 135

sizing textboxes, 136–137

slash (/). *See* division operator

slash-asterisk (/*): block comment delimiter, 102

slash–equal sign (/=): division assignment operator, 92

slashes (//): line comment indicator, 102

smallest value, finding: in arrays, 426–428

Smalltalk (programming language), 18

software, 11–16
development history, 17–19
hardware/software/user relationship, *17*
types, 11, *11*

Solution Explorer window, 34
displaying, 33–34, 34

solving problems, 74–76
See also debugging programs; single-purpose solutions vs. general solutions

Sort() method, 391, 401

sorted lists, searching, 370–371
See also binary searches

sorting arrays, 418–449, 450*qr*
methods (strategies/ algorithms), 422–440, 450–451*qr*; big-O value, 440; comparative efficiency, 441; nested loops as used in, 423.
See also bubble sort; insertion sort; selection sort
object/String arrays, 391
with pointer arrays, 536–544; tutorial, 545–563
record arrays, 536–544
swapping values, 418–422

sorting lists, **371**, 450*qr*

source code, **20**

source files, 35

spacing textboxes, 141–142

special characters, 77
escape character codes, **253**; MSDN website resource, 691
factorial symbol (!), 243, 460
undefined variable symbol (?), 197
See also specific symbols

split window format, *32*

Sqrt() method, 93–94, 272

square brackets ([ ]):
array identification symbol/ delimiters, 329, 330
array subscript delimiters, 328
optional feature delimiters, 185

standard C++, **2**, 19
keywords, 699*t*

Start button (Visual C++ interface), 308

Start button (Windows Vista interface), 13

Start Debugging button, 20, 40, 49

Start menu (Windows Vista interface), *14*

Statement Completion Dropdown Box, 45, *45*

statement terminator (;), 49, 585

statements:
break statements, 185–186, 338
case statements, 185–186
color coding in, 47; MSDN website resource, 691
general forms. *See* syntax (general forms)
return statements, **289**
terminator (;), 49, 585
See also if statements; if...else statements; loops; preprocessor directives; switch statements

static allocation of memory, 77, 80–81, 513–514
for arrays, 329
for two-dimensional arrays, 346

static constants, 295, 313*qr*, 605*t*
initialization of, 307

static variables (class variables), 586–587
accessing, 598
declaring, 586

stepwise refinement/development (of algorithms), **133**, 154*qr*
Stick pin icon, 30, *30*
Stop button, 308
storage (primary storage). *See* memory
storage (secondary storage), **7**, *7*
`String` array elements: assigning strings to, 389–390
`String` arrays, 387
  constructing, 388–389
  declaring, 388, 399–400
  sorting, 391
  See also `ListView` controls
`String` data type, **79**
string delimiters (`""`), 48, 245
`String` operations, 391–392
  MSDN website resource, 692
`String` variables: declaring, 245
strings (text strings), **47**, 48
  assigning the first character to `char` variables, 149
  assigning to `String` array elements, 389–390
  assigning to textboxes, 48–49
  comparing, 391–392
  concatenating, 90–91
  converting numbers to, 94
  converting to numbers, 85–86
  delimiters, 48, 245
  empty string, 245
  numbers as, 84
  parsing, **85**–86, 107*qr;* importance, 92
  searching for, 387–392
  See also `String` variables; text (in textboxes)
Stroustrup, Bjarne, 19
structured walk-throughs, **196**–200
subscript delimiters (`[ ]`) (arrays), *328*
subscripts (of arrays), **328**
subtraction assignment operator (`-=`), 92
subtraction operator (`-`), 87*t*

precedence in arithmetic expressions, 88–90
summation, **225**–226
  of array elements, 331; in pointer arrays, 533
  with `do...while` loops, 235
  with `for` loops, 237–241
  with `while` loops, 232
summation formula as mapped into loops, 241–243
`swap()` method, 541–544
`Swap()` method, 419–422, 450*qr*
  algorithm, 419
  calling, 420
  code, 419–422
swapping array element values, 418–422
  pointers in pointer arrays, 537–538, 540, 541; `swap()` method, 541–544
`switch` statements, 185–186, 209*qr*
  vs. multiple alternative `if` statements (`if...else if...else` statements), 185
switching to the Code window, 42, 135*n*
symbols. *See* special characters
syntax (general forms):
  actual argument lists, 281
  constructors, 587
  declaring arrays, 329; dynamic arrays, 527; object arrays (`array` class objects), 388
  declaring constants, 295
  declaring pointers, 515
  `delete` operator, 531
  destructors, 588
  `do...while` loops, 234–235
  `for` loops, 236
  `if` statements, 169
  `if...else` statements, 171
  MessageBoxes, 175
  method body, 275
  method calls: for passing array elements into methods,

332; for passing arrays into methods, 334; to `void` methods, 280
  method signature line with an array as a formal parameter, 335
  `new` operator, 516; declaring dynamic arrays, 527
  parameter lists (formal), 281
  `ref` class definitions, **585**
  `return` statements, 289
  scope resolution operator, 594
  `switch` statements, 185
  `while` loops, 231
syntax errors, **21**, (50–51)
  locating, 51–52
  See also error messages
`System` class (library) methods, 271–272, 288–289
  `Drawing` class methods, 292–294
  scope resolution operator (`::`), 85, 271
  See also `Convert` class (library) methods; `Int32` class (library) methods; `Math` class (library) methods
`System` identifier, 271
`System` namespace, 270
  MSDN website resource, 692
system software, **11**, *11*
  Windows Vista, 12–16
`System::Drawing` namespace, 313
  MSDN website resource, 692
`System::Void` return type, 275
system-defined methods, **270**, 311*qr,* 312*qr*
  class. *See* `System` class (library) methods
  instance methods, 274

T

`\t` escape character code, 253
table creation program, 252–253
tables. *See* data tables

Tan() method, 272, 274
target values in arrays: finding.
    See searching arrays
test scenarios, **196**
testing programs, 49
testing stage (of programming),
    22, *23,* 59*qr*
    addition program, 103
    binary conversion program,
        151–152
    classroom seating chart
        program, 353, 361
    fractal image generation
        program, 483, 495
    "Hello World!" program,
        40–42, 49
    linked list program, 621,
        622–623
    maze program, 671
    planetary motion program,
        309
    pointer array sorting program,
        562
    quality control production log,
        259
    vacation planner project,
        195–196
    vertical bar chart project, 449
    video inventory search program,
        403
text (in textboxes):
    aligning, 99, 146
    string assignment, 48–49
    string length maximum, 137;
        changing, 138
Text property, 37, 392
    changing, 38–39, 55
    data type requirement, 121
    specifying, 45–46, 47–48
    See also textboxes
text strings. *See* strings; text (in
    textboxes)
TextAlign property: changing,
    99, 146
textboxes, 26, *26*
    adding, 35
    assigning strings to, 48–49
    boundaries (borders), 146
    clearing, 278

colors, 55–56, 146
displaying array element values
    in, 330, 559
drawing lines between.*See*
    drawLines() method
fonts, 53–54, 100
multiple line option, 146
naming conventions for,
    130–131
properties, 552–553
property settings, 147*t*
ReadOnly textboxes, **144**
renaming, 144
selecting multiple, 99, 140
sizing, 136–137
spacing, 141–142
text in.*See* text (in textboxes)
vertical distance between,
    562*n*
See also Text property
third generation of computers,
    10
this keyword, 47, 48
"This project is out of date:"
    dialog box, 40, *41*
Tick event handlers, **299**, 306,
    307
    local variables in, 300–301
    See also Timer1_Tick()
        event handlers
Tick() events, 299, 306
    Timer_Tick() events, 650
    See also Tick event handlers
Timer controls, **299**, 303,
    313*qr*
    setting, 306–307, 309
Timer_Tick() events, 650
Timer1_Tick() event handlers:
    algorithms, 301–302,
        662–663
    code, 309, 669–670
ToDouble() method, 272
Toolbox, 24–25, *24, 32*
    opening, 30
toolStripMenuItems. *See*
    menu items
ToString() method, 94, 122
    displaying, 30, 34
ToUpper() method, 391–392

trace tables, **196**–200, 348
    btnGroup_Click() algorithm
        table, 353–355
    DrawBranch() algorithm
        tables, 483–487
transistors, **10**
traversing arrays, (331),
    (338–339), **347**–348
truncation (of quotients),
    124–125
TryParse() method, 85–86, *86,*
    107*qr,* 271, 288–289
    importance, 92
Turing, Alan: on computing
    (paper), 9
Turing machine, 9
tutorials:
    addition program, 95–104
    on arrays, 348–361
    binary conversion program,
        127–152
    classroom seating chart
        program, 348–361
    fractal image generation
        program, 477–499
    "Hello World!" program,
        25–49
    on the IDE, 25–49
    on integral data, 127–152
    linked list program,
        598–623
    on linked lists, 598–623
    on loops (repetition control
        structures), 254–259
    maze program, 650–671
    on methods, 296–310
    on object-oriented
        programming, 650–671
    planetary motion program,
        296–310
    pointer array sorting program,
        545–563
    quality control production log,
        254–259
    on reading, processing, and
        displaying data, 95–104
    on recursion, 477–499
    on searching arrays,
        392–403

tutorials: (*continued*):
  on selection control structures, 186–207
  on sorting arrays with pointer arrays, 545–563
  vacation planner project, 186–207
  vertical bar chart project, 441–449
  video inventory search program, 392–403
two-dimensional arrays, **345**–348, 362–363*qr*
  declaring, 329, 346, 660–661
  maze program array, 657–658
  structure, 345
  traversing, 347–348
type casting, **122**, 125, 514–515
type conversion. *See* data type conversion

U

UML class diagrams, 589–591
  Node class diagrams, *604*
unassigned variables, 448
undeclared identifier error message, 704, 708
undefined variable symbol (?), 197
undefined variables, **197**
Unicode characters, **77**
  byte size, 119
United Modeling Language class diagrams. *See* UML class diagrams
UNIX operating system, 12, 18
update clause (in for loops), **236**, *236*
user-controlled repetition, **220**–228
users: hardware/software/user relationship, *17*
utility methods, 645–646, 650
utility programs, 12

V

vacation planner project tutorial, 186–207
vacuum tubes, **9**
value lists (for arrays), 330
value method. *See* pass-by-value method
value parameters, **284**
  pass-by-value using, 281–285, **284**, 311, 312*qr;* passing arrays/array elements, 332–333, **335**
value-returning methods, 288–290, 310
values. *See* data values; index values; memory cell addresses; return values
variables, **79**–82, 107*qr*
  assigning values to, 82–83
  char.*See* char variables
  declaring.*See* declaring variables
  for DrawArray() method, 444*t*
  for DrawBranch() method, 477*t,* 481–482
  for drawing, 442–443, 481
  handle.*See* handles (handle variables)
  initializing, 82–83
  instance.*See* instance variables
  int.*See* int variables
  local variables, 226, 300
  loop control variable, **229**; incrementation/decrementation of, 232–233
  naming rules for, 81–82
  now variable, 247
  vs. objects, 84
  pointer.*See* pointers (pointer variables)
  static.*See* static variables
  unassigned variables, 448
  undefined variables, **197**
verifying algorithms, 196–200
verifyX() method, 645
vertical bar chart project tutorial, 441–449

vertical bars (| |). *See* or operator (| |)
very large-scale integration (VLSI), 10
video inventory search program tutorial, 392–403
visibility. *See* scope
Visual C++, **2**, 19*(2)*, 57*qr*
  compiler, 20
  feature coverage in this book, by chapter, 685–689*t*
  keywords: MSDN website resource, 692
  MSDN website resources, 691
Visual Studio (Microsoft), **19**
  IDE.*See* IDE (Visual Studio)
VLSI (very large-scale integration), 10
void methods (without return values), 275, 312*qr*
  calls to, 280, 282–284
  with parameters, 281–288; reference parameters, 285–288, 311, 522–523; value parameters, 281–285, 311
  without parameters, 277–280
  See also specific methods
void return type, 275
von Neumann, John: computer model, 9
von Neumann architecture, **9**

W

walk-throughs, structured, **196**–200
warnings: compiler warnings, 121
while loops, 230–233, 251, 260*qr*
  summation formula as mapped into, 243
white squares (resizing handles), 35, *35*
Width property, 553
windows:
  Code Editor.*See* Code window
  Design.*See* Design window

docking, 33
Form Layout window, 24, *24*
in the IDE, 24–25, *24*
locking in place, 30
opening, 53
Properties. *See* Properties
    window
removing (closing), 29
repositioning, 33

Solution Explorer window,
    33–34
split window format, *32*
See also Toolbox
windows forms. *See* forms
windows forms applications:
    creating, *28,* 34
Windows Forms Designer, **5**
    code written by, 47

Windows Vista, **12**
    interface, 12–16
Windows XP, **12**
Wirth, Niklaus, 18

Z

Z3 computer, 8, 9
zero, division by, 21
Zuse, Konrad, 8